AMERICAN SOCIAL INSTITUTIONS

A SOCIOLOGICAL ANALYSIS

AMERICAN SOCIAL INSTITUTIONS

A SOCIOLOGICAL ANALYSIS

J. O. Hertzler

University of Nebraska

Boston

ALLYN AND BACON, INC.

1961

Contents

Contents

THE ACQUISITION, ORGANIZATION, AND UTILIZATION OF KNOWLEDGE

MAINTENANCE

Contents

Contents

TO MY FLO

Devoted and skillful helpmeet in these many
fruitful tasks during these
many precious years

PART 1

The Systemic Organization of Human Society

The objective of this study is the sociological analysis of the major blocks of institutions of American society. These institutions are the major operative mechanisms. A competent understanding of them requires some minimal knowledge of the total organizational system of which they are a part. Human society is a systemic complex, made up of an infinite array of subsystems. It operates among and with other types of systems. Therefore the first objective of Part I is to familiarize the reader with the basic analytical concept of system *as it applies to all operating entities and then to examine briefly the nature of human social systems by designating their unique features in contrast to those of physical and biological systems. The second objective is to indicate the significance of* organization *in systems and then to examine briefly the general nature of human social organization in relation to human social systems, the essential features of social organization, its fundamental necessity, and, finally, social disorganization as a continual threat. The third objective will be to call attention to the systems peripheral, underlying, and contributory to the operation of societal systems and the major concrete structural-functional entities, so important as factors in the milieu in which institutions operate and also as contributors of institutional components. The final objective—to be conducted somewhat more extensively—will be to identify and analyze the imperative* alphabet *systems instrumental in the organization of societal behavior, all of which affect or enter into the operation of institutions.*

Fundamental Concepts,
Background Systems,
and Concrete
Components

Our purpose in this study is to gain a comprehensive and clear conception, first, of social institutions as the fundamental, operative instrumentalities of any society, the channels and models of social action, and,
second, of the characteristic structural and functional features of the
major American institutional systems. In order to understand and assess
adequately the social institutions, however, it is essential to have a working conception of human society as the great over-all operating entity
in which the institutions perform their strategic services. Such a conception involves some understanding of certain analytical concepts regarding the nature of human society as a system and as an organized
combination of subsystems; of the factorial systems underlying and
contributory to the societal systems; of the concrete structurings involved; and of the basic, imperative, instrumental systems required in
the organization of the societal behavior of individuals and groups, and
thus of the general categories of materials of which institutions are
composed.

I: System and Organization

The universe and all of its functioning entities are organized into *systems*. Human society may be thought of as a system of interdependent,

organized, structural-functional, constitutive subsystems. The analytical concepts of *system* and *organization* require brief examination.

SYSTEM AND SYSTEMS

The concept of system as a logical method or schema of describing reality has come to have a key significance and use. It is a means of analyzing fields of phenomena ranging from those of astronomy, through physico-chemical organisms and assemblies, to the interpretation of the infinitely complex human societies of modern times. It is now realized that the idea of a system of elements and events in any field of phenomena is essential to the development of the basic theory regarding that field.

System refers to some orderly combination or arrangement of parts into a whole which, in turn, is more than a conjunction, aggregate, chance assembly, of parts, and more than a mere sum of the parts. Although the parts are identifiable and although they may be semi-autonomous, they are coexistent, interdependent or complementary, interacting, consistent with each other, and mutually or reciprocally variable; they constitute a whole, and they produce an over-all unity of function and effort. The associated elements form a pattern that is relatively complete, and, in considerable degree, independent of other similar aggregations. Order, stability, and lawfulness govern within and between them and make them more or less self-sustaining.

Because of our over-all, analytical objective, our primary interest at this point is in concrete, *natural,* physico-chemical systems, especially those of living things and in human societal systems, in contrast to abstract systems, such as scientific theoretical systems, theological systems, philosophical systems, mathematical systems, or the culture of any particular people as a system. A sizable descriptive and analytical literature on physico-chemical and human societal systems exists. It is sufficient for our purpose to synthesize and summarize skeletally the conclusions of many authoritative observers and analysts regarding, first, the essential nature of natural systems in general and, second, the additional distinctive aspects of human social systems. This approach will provide us with a sort of alphabet knowledge of the basic features of the respective categories of systems.

The more readily and commonly observable features of these systems are as follows: (1) There is a plurality of parts or elements, usually more or less differentiated and heterogeneous. (2) There is a structuring; that is, a configuration or patterned relationship of the functionally interacting components. (3) The parts are integrated into a functional whole. When there is a low level of integration, there is inaction and usually dissolution of the system. (4) The parts are energized. Forces of various kinds play through them. These energies express themselves in the processes of all kinds that constitute the systems as operating entities. When the energies in any of the crucial parts or the whole cease to exert themselves, then the system dies. (5) Systems exist in time; they have a life and go on, in some instances for a very long time. (6) Every system is ever changing; it is, in fact, a multifaceted process rather than a unitary and fixed entity. (7) As long as the system exists there is a relative—never a perfect, final, or permanent—equilibrium of elements and energies, internally, and externally with other systems. (8) Systems have relative constancy, identity, and stability of existence. The parts may disappear or die, but the whole goes on—for a time. (9) Systems have boundaries—limits within which each retains its structural and functional entity. (10) They have an array of external relations, particularly ecological relations, and location in space, and adjust themselves to their various environments. (11) Systems exhibit a life-cycle, usually consisting of development, level maintenance, senescence, and disintegration. (12) Almost all systems are congeries of continually changing but coexisting and interdependent subsystems.

A human social system, like any system, is a patterned collection with relations of interconnection and interdependence, and mutual and reciprocal functioning of the parts. It has all of the common characteristics of natural systems just noted. Many of these features, however, take peculiar form in human social systems by virtue of the fact that they consist of interacting *human beings*. In addition, they have a number of distinctive features that have *no* counterparts whatsoever among other systems. In as much as most of these features will be discussed in appropriate places and contexts in this study, they are merely named at this point.

(1) Symbolic communication.

(2) A background of culture relatively meaningful to all or most of the members.

(3) Complexity and heterogeneity of population, functions, collectivities, and subsystems.

(4) Mental and spiritual life of the members.

(5) Value orientation.

(6) Goal attainment.

(7) Ideological agreement and psychic and moral unity.

(8) Culturally established patterns of action.

(9) Sociocultural regulation and maintenance.

(10) Institutional setting and ordering.

(11) Deliberate boundary maintenance.

(12) Social reorganization and reconstruction.

(13) A constructed—not a "nature-given"—mechanism.

ORGANIZATION AND SOCIAL ORGANIZATION

The concepts of system and organization as used in the analysis of operating entities are entwined; sometimes, though mistakenly, they are used synonymously. Here they will be used as distinct, though related, concepts. By system in the concrete sense is meant the assembly and interrelationship, in some phenomenal field, of regularly interacting or interdependent parts into a distinctive, integrated, operative whole. Organization refers to a major characteristic of systems. It is concerned with various postulated, crucial, high level aspects that must be understood if there is to be any prediction and manipulation. In general, organization means the orderly functional correlation and coordination of differentiated but interdependent parts or entities according to certain principles, rules, and limits, and by means of certain specialized agents and sequential processes, so that they function together as a whole and in a synchronized manner, and produce a collective result not obtainable otherwise.

Organization is not rare, and it is not mysterious. All nature is organized, not only in breadth but also in depth, and its organization ascends progressively from the smallest and simplest aggregates into the more complex, heterogeneous, widely inclusive orders. Organization is a universal tendency and an essential aspect of every system, whether a solar system, a biological organism, a mechanism such as a typewriter, an animal or human community or society, or any of the effective subsystems of these. It is the way chaos is converted into order, and mysfunction and dysfunction are converted into effective functioning. Every system has an organization; any set of related elements in order to act together effectively over some period of time must be organized.

Human society is no exception as far as either the facts or principles of organization are concerned. Social organization of some degree and kind is as old as mankind. All human experience has demonstrated the practical necessity of some organization for the attainment of any of the purposes requiring the joint action of two or more persons. As soon as an aggregation *does* something, or even attempts to do something, it undergoes some degree of organization, spontaneous or deliberate, informal or formal. The very interdependency of men requires them, in most of their actions, to develop the essential features of a team.

No assemblage of human beings living a life in common has ever been discovered that did not possess some form of social organization; nowhere do we find a horde in which the relations between its individuals and groups are completely anarchic. A society's functional effectiveness and its durability depend on the ordering of its constituent elements by organization. A society is *a field of action, formed in action, existing for action,* and *it must be organized for action.*

Whenever and wherever there is social organization, it shows five fundamental features.

An established structuring—a schema or network—of relationships among the interacting persons. The patterns of relationship are of many different kinds—all manner of groups and organizations, areal combinations, hierarchical relations, and so on—and of different degrees of extent and intensity, of proximity, and of impersonality and indirectness.

A system of coordinated functional activities. The interrelated persons and groups engage in standardized actions in the different common and recurrent relationships. The actions of the members are ordered, programmed, chartered, and coordinated; to use a term to be examined comprehensively below, they are *institutionalized.*

The ends—the results. The joint chartered actions have meaning for the participants and are pursued to achieve some purpose or objective, to produce some identifiable result, though the actors are not always conscious of the fact.

The agents of ordering. The organization is not automatic; there are always *agents.* These fall into two interrelated and interfunctioning categories: (a) the human agents—leaders, officers, administrators, or other functionaries; (b) the sociocultural agents—the folkways, mores, customs, and specific sets of rules and regulations, but above all the complex systems of charters, purposive associations, especially in the form of bureaucratic machinery, and the bodies of sanctions governing all of the major departments of social action of every community or society—known as social institutions.

Processes. Finally, social organization is always a combination of processes and procedures. The very activities of the component individuals and groups take the form of processes that produce the sufficient degree of arrangement, order, maintenance, and regulation among the components to assure the existence of the whole.

Certain fundamental considerations relating to the existence and operation of any social system or subsystem are involved, as follows.

The relations of diverse people, categories, and groups must be established, patterned, and coordinated. The people constituting social systems are different as to innate ability, personality, learning, and skill. They have diverse demographic composition. There are many sociocultural differences among and between them, including different kinds of social spacing and distances based on various social differentiations and stratifications; in this same connection, in the larger systems there may be serious racial and ethnic differences. There are many degrees and varieties of functional specialization among them as they carry on the many complementary functions essential to joint living that require reciprocity. They differ in social interests and in social motivation; there are always parasites, predators, cheaters, and recalcitrants among them.

But if either the diverse and specialized individual components, or the system as a whole, is to function and survive, there must be effective cooperation; to assure this, there must be a systematic patterning and coordination of the activities of the persons and groups involved. A great number of possible actions must be prohibited and prevented, and an even greater number must be obligatory because they are so crucial to the maintenance of the system.

The provision of all levels of needs and wants of the people depends upon organization. Without organization there can be no provision for the physical needs (food, clothing, shelter, and accessibility); no protection against internal hazards (disease, accident, injury, neglect, physical catastrophe); no protection against external hazards (invasion, war); no provision of communication; no satisfaction of higher needs (knowledge, intellectual cooperation and exploration, explaining natural phenomena, giving expression to aesthetic urges, explaining man's role in the universe, adjusting to the supernatural).

The creation and maintenance of social order, operation, and stability rest upon social organization. Every sort of human achievement, from the simplest economic production to artistic creation or to the formation of political, theoretical, or religious systems, is precarious and ephemeral if not protected by forms of social control against anarchy, disorder, confusion, crime, and so on. From earliest times, among the main functions of social organization have been the controlling of disruptive behavior, the defending of social systems against constant threats, and the insuring to each individual and group the pursuit of its legitimate interests and the more or less permanent possession of the products of its efforts. It is the only way of insuring the continuity of the systems themselves.

A considerable degree of predictability in interpersonal and intergroup relations is essential. The behavior of human beings among and with their fellows cannot be haphazard and chaotic. Most of the action of associated people must be established and programmed. Consider what life would be like if, each morning upon rising, we had no assurance of any accepted, regularized, and guaranteed behavior on the part of our fellows. But with the patterned and established obligation-relations that are such an important aspect of social organization, we know what is expected of us in every typical relationship in any of the social systems in which we participate, and we can predict in large measure what every person, every group, every category of human beings, every purposive organization will do in each type and condition of social situation and context. In fact, predictability can be posited as the practical test and measure of social organization.

SOCIAL DISORGANIZATION

One cannot discuss social organization adequately without calling attention to the continual threat to it—social *dis*organization; that is, the conditions, forces, and processes resulting from inevitable change that make for the impairment of social organization. Social disorganization is by no means an exceptional phenomenon. In some measure, it exists in all social systems at all times.

Disorganization implies a standard of some sort. In social organization, there is a conception of how a social system of healthy parts, adequate interrelations, and functional effectiveness would work. Disorganization is a departure from such a norm.

In *social* disorganization there is, first, *destructuralization,* which consists of the destruction of groups, organizations, and institutions, and the impairment of relationships between individuals, categories, institutions, and strata. There is, second, *defunctionalization,* which involves the reduction of operative efficiency.

Institutionally organized social action is the main means of forestalling and correcting social disorganization in modern society. We should, therefore, be aware of the more outstanding aspects of social disorganization—of the characteristics that identify a social system as suffering some degree of social disorganization. The following are important and more or less interdependent.

There is a lack of sufficient number, strength, clarity, and internalization of common meanings and values among enough members of the system.

There is confusion or inconsistency of norms or codes governing the different departments of life, and the resultant loss of means of consensus among the people; the inconsistent and non-conforming behavior among individuals and groups; and the inability of people to make accurate predictions regarding each other's social actions.

Because of the confusion of norms, there is also usually confusion, conflict, and inconsistency of roles; that is, the patterns of individual action in the different types of daily relationships.

There is often a serious social-psychological, social, and cultural separation, spacing, and distance among individuals, groups, and categories that interfere with communication, consensus, and common participation.

Invariably there is limited participation in the necessary social activities, because of social ignorance, lethargy, or some sort of ethical perversion.

Serious conflict situations exist; for example, conflicts of beliefs and creeds along ethical, political, and religious lines, conflicts among racial, national, occupational, class, religious, or regional groups.

Social unrest and demoralization is likely. The unrest is an expression and focalization of the insecurity, confusion, dissatisfaction, and discontent of many people. The demoralization shows itself in the inability of members to maintain steadfastness of purpose, to meet individual and group crises effectively, and, in their lack of motivation, to participate effectively in necessary activities.

There is invariably noticeable personal and personality disorganization. Because of the other conditions of disorganization, people suffer "shocks." The personality disorganization expresses itself in many ways, depending upon personal and social conditions, such as apathy, frustration, tension, resentment, or hostility, in various forms of sabotage and opposition activities, in such extreme manifestations as crime, desertion, alcoholism, drug addiction, suicide, neurotic and psychopathic tendencies, and other bizarre and eccentric compensatory, escapist, underconforming, or otherwise deviant forms of behavior.

A *society* is the most inclusive social organization. It incorporates all of the individuals and all of the societal subsystems, with their various instruments and processes, and combines them in their various interactions, interdependencies, and reciprocities. It is the largest relatively permanent grouping whose members share a common physical setting, common interests and goals, a common mode of life, and a common destiny. It carries on, as an over-all operating mechanism, all of the functions necessary to meet the individual and collective needs for survival, continuity, and prosperity. It is, in brief, a living fabric or web of interacting people and functioning social structures, and a complex, differentiated, but coherent, unified, continuing, self-perpetuating, relatively self-contained, widely inclusive social entity.

The sequence of analysis for the remainder of this book will consist of the examination of three inseparable aspects of human society: first, the underlying and contributory systems and the concrete societal structurings; second, the instrumental systems in the organization of societal behavior; and, third—the major analytical enterprise—the nature and crucial place of social institutions in general and, particularly, the great institutional systems as the major operative subdivisions of any modern society.

An understanding of the first two general categories of systems is essential in order to understand the general sociocultural orientation and, specifically, the relations, components, and operation of the institutional systems.

II: The Systems Underlying and Contributory to the Societal Systems

Social systems do not stand alone, nor are they self-sufficient. There exist related systems of phenomena. Although external to social systems, some of them set up particular conditions that must be met if the social systems are to survive. In most instances, these other systems have reciprocal relations with social systems. But what happens to and what happens in a social system are always influenced by these other systems. All of them are man-modified, and some are man-made. They are not constant as factors, however; they vary in effect, in some instances as a consequence of forces beyond control of men, and in others as a consequence of the actions of men. These, along with social systems, may be looked upon as the total complex of factors affecting the life of man on earth.

These other systems, upon which social organization rests, consist of (1) the basic external natural environment, in both its physical and biological aspects, from which man cannot escape; (2) the demographic organization, in terms of the numbers, composition, distribution, and movement of the people involved in a social system; and (3) the cultural system.

THE NATURAL ENVIRONMENT

All social systems, however simple or complex, must work out their destiny within the elemental arena of the natural physical and natural biological environments. The major elements of this natural environment are the cosmic factors inherent in the universe, such as the sun and moon and other planetary systems; the physical forces and conditions, such as altitude, gravity, the sun's heat, and so on; the physiographic or land-form features, such as plains, deserts, mountains, river valleys; climatic factors—the seasons and the weather; the inorganic physical resources, including the minerals and metals and the other physico-chemical elements, and the organic resources consisting of all forms of plant and animal life; the all-important soil itself—a combination of physiographic, inorganic, and organic elements; and—as important as any other feature—space itself.

The natural environment provides man's living space and the factors affecting the location of his settlements, the size, density, distribution, and physical movement of his populations. Here are the physical forces, conditions, and rhythms which, in part at least, determine the major organizations and routines of life, and which require adjustment, individually and collectively, on the part of men. Here are all the resources of sustenance, clothing, housing, and all of the other physical and biological essentials of existence. Here are the elements that produce the energies in man and provide the external energies utilized by man. Here is the material upon which all individual and collective human life rests; and these influences are never stilled.

Men live and survive, and their societies function, only when they adequately meet the exigencies of this physical situation. Any society that has endured for more than a generation has developed patterns of organization and functioning that guarantee survival and comfort to its individuals.

These physical environmental factors are modified by man's technologies. His technologies are mainly devoted to protecting himself against, and utilizing, the physical environment. Yet however highly developed man's technologies may become, the physical environmental factors will set the ultimate limits beyond which his individual and social life cannot go.

The Demographic Structure

A human society is composed elementally of the total number of people occupying its determined territory at any given time; it consists of a *population*.

The human beings are the elemental units of every social structure; all of the activities or behavioral events are properties of aggregates of people; all relations between them are *social* relations. Not only are they the unit elements of every structure and the participants in every process, but they are also the dynamic elements in all action. All else is neutral nature operating according to natural laws. Their well-being, as they interpret it, is the motivating force of society.

If a social system is to continue, there must be replacement of members through births that at least equal the deaths or through receiving newcomers from the outside.

The population of any given social system differs from that of others, which accounts in some part for the differences between systems. The population of a given society provides the possibilities for, and also sets the limits of, organized group life, and at the same time, the social organization affects the population.

Size, or the total number of the population, determines many features of the collective life, and as the size of the social aggregate increases, the behavior of the members of the group also changes. Population size, for example, imposes limits on the extent of specialization in that it determines the number of human beings available for various functions, the number of activities to be carried on simultaneously, and the number of users of given specialized products and services. In a small population, a tiny village or shop, for example, the degree of specialization is necessarily slight, while, on the other hand, every increase in size increases the extent to which specialization may be developed. Larger populations are usually more heterogeneous; hence, they may be expected to have a greater range and diversity of individual abilities and thus contain a greater assortment of potential specialists and offer greater opportunity for intensive specialization, as well as a greater variety of demands. Various other organizational aspects are affected by population—resources, technological and economic organization, political organization, crowding, traffic regulations, sanitation and health, delinquency and crime, and recreation. Also, the size and density of a population may be related to certain other population characteristics; for example, in the United States it seems to be a fact that the larger the city, the lower the birth rate.

Population numbers and growth in relation to the resources of the people and the technologies by which the resources are made accessible and usable is an important consideration in the wealth, income, leisure, feeling of security, and the general welfare.

The members of a given society are unequally distributed within their area. There is greater density, or a larger number of persons per square mile, for example, in fertile and metropolitan areas. The distribution roughly affects the volume, frequency, and variety of social contacts and the kinds of collective activities that are possible in various localities, and it involves the potential complexity of group organization. Societies differ with respect to the urban-rural nature and the size of both local and regional component communities within the larger society.

The peculiar composition of each society gives it many of its distinctive characteristics. The age and sex structure of a people provides a basic bio-social structure that is known as its *population pyramid*. Its symmetry or asymmetry is a matter of balance or unbalance in its sex and age group ratios, and this, in turn, is related to a great number of historical social conditions.

Modern societies are also characterized by broad, socially derived differences in the composition of the population; for example, marital status (according to the categories of the single, the married, the widowed, and the divorced), urban-rural residence, occupation and other labor force characteristics, socio-economic (especially wealth and income), status, nativity and race, educational level, religious affiliation; in fact, all manner of cultural differences. These compositional factors relate to the kind and composition of groups in the society, its fertility, mortality, and morbidity rates, its marital performance, its labor force, its economic and technical organization and proficiency, its settlement patterns, its status structure, its social control system, its social psyche and ethos, most of its institutions, and a host of other social organizational features.

The social institutions of a people must adjust to, or correlate with, population conditions and changes. Thus, for example, there is some evidence that people are more likely to have polygyny where there has been a plentiful supply of women, and polyandry (among Todas, for instance) where there has been a preponderance of males; educational institutions have to add equipment, staff, and functions when there is an increase in the proportion of children and youths in the population; political and economic institutions have to modify both their internal and external functioning with almost every kind and degree of population change; health, recreation, and other welfare institutions must meet changes in age groups, changes in racial makeup, changes in class and occupational makeup, changes in density (crowding); scientific-technological institutions are involved in every population situation and change.

The increase or decrease of numbers means a new adjustment to the physical environment, altered potentialities of social organization, in that there are opened up new possibilities or are imposed new limitations, and changing relationships with other societies; all of the institutions involved must in turn adjust themselves to the new conditions and functional demands made upon them. Similarly, such a population factor as migration has tremendous social effects both in the communities of departure and reception. For example, the migration from the country to the city in the United States has produced effects on the general social, economic, and political structure and institutions of both the rural and urban communities.

In general, population can be conceived of as one of the principal causes of social phenomena. At the same time, social customs and institutions, the social control system, and the technical system, to mention only the most obvious social organizational features, have a profound effect upon all aspects and processes of demographic organization.

THE CULTURAL SYSTEM

Every human society has a culture; in fact, culture, above all else, explains man's uniqueness. Unlike any other species, man has always been distinguished by the fact that he is the culture-producing, culture-maintaining, culture-transmitting, and culture-perpetuating animal. He is never merely a passive product of automatic processes, but is always aggressive and creative in some measure. Individually and collectively, men do not act merely on the basis of biologically inherited behavior patterns. They germinate ideas and come to conclusions; they remember what has been successful; in brief, men learn by experience.

Even more important than this ability to profit by experience is the fact that men have powers of construction and can intervene in their world to modify its materials and make them serviceable.

By culture we mean what man has himself created, unconsciously and consciously, in adapting to his world: the modifications of nature that he has brought about in the way of manipulation and utilization of nature's processes; the modifiers of nature that he has devised in the form of all sorts of tools, appliances, and other paraphernalia; the behavior patterns (habits, skills, techniques, essential social routines, usages) that he has developed; his knowledge, ideas, beliefs, rules, values, expectations, the vehicles and systems of meanings and purposes.[1]

These elements embody the long experience of man in living in his physical, social, and mental-spiritual world. Man transmits them to posterity so that they bind human experience into a continuous adjustive and creative process.

Men often borrow these elements from their fellows both near and remote in time and space, modify them, and apply them in their own scheme of living.

Culture has the special structural and functional forms that constitute a system. A particular culture consists of something more than the sum of its parts. It has some underlying unity. There is "a specific interrelation of the component parts, a nexus that holds them together strongly, and tends to preserve the basic plan."[2]

White, in his definitive study, points out that we can consider culture apart from its human contrivers and carriers. With the advance of scientific examination of culture, there has come the recognition of it "as a distinct class of events, as a distinct order of phenomena." It "is a continuum, a stream of events, that flows freely down through time from one generation to another and laterally from one race or habitat to another." It is "a thing *sui generis*," "a class of events and processes [and, one might add, of material and non-material instrumentalities], that behaves in terms of its own principles and laws and which consequently can be explained only in terms of its own elements and proc-

---

[1] I. T. Sanders, *et al.,* and H. Becker (ed. of the 1-vol. ed.), *Societies around the World*. New York: Dryden, 1956, pp. 14–15. These authors present culture—all that is man-made—under the three categories of (1) artifacts: physical objects made by man; (2) sociofacts: social arrangements, patterns of social relations among the people of a society; and (3) mentifacts: rules of behavior, and values, which relate chiefly to the mental life of the people.

[2] A. L. Kroeber, *Anthropology*. New York: Harcourt, Brace, 1948, pp. 312–316, esp. p. 313.

esses." It is a self-contained, self-determined affair, but always creates new combinations and syntheses.[3]

Although culture is a distinct and separate system, it bears a peculiar relationship to each of the other systems because of its specific nature, function, and effect. By means of knowledge and techniques that enable him to maintain himself, his land, and other life resources, man has been able to exercise preference and to control his fertility, morbidity, mortality, location, and migration.

With respect to areal grouping and ecological organization, man reacts as a cultural creature rather than as a biological species. Competition-cooperation is always culturally determined; sites are often chosen for reasons other than natural suitability; habitats are chosen and modified in many ways; barriers to accessibility may be removed or surmounted; spatial and time factors are diminished in significance by advances in communication and transportation. Man's communities, as functionally inclusive territorial groupings, reflect their cultural history, especially cultural experiences and values; their structural-functional organization is culturally determined; they, too, are important culture-perpetuating agencies.

Two subsystems of every culture are basic. One of these is the communication system whereby men transmit to each other and record their meaningful experiences and directives by means of various signs, symbolic devices, and procedures. Communication is so basic that it has long been institutionalized in some measure and will be discussed as such in Chapter Eight.

Every society must also have another basic cultural feature—a technological system; that is, the system of instruments and procedures whereby man has modified the physical and biological environments. This system also includes the manipulation and utilization of all of man's discovered and invented sociocultural devices and techniques. These technologies he employs in the interest not only of his survival but also of his physical, psychological, and social prosperity. The technological system too has been institutionalized, and is treated at length in Chapter Nine. All of the other institutions rest upon physical, biological, or societal technologies; technology is the basis of all institutional construction and of all societal reorganization.

Society refers to the existent, interrelated aggregate of individuals and groups of people that have learned to work and live together as an organized whole. The *culture system* furnishes the design and the ways of life of that society.

The social system and the culture system are so much intertwined

[3] L. A. White, *The Science of Culture*. New York: Farrar, Straus, 1949, pp. xviii, 115, 141, 339, 363–364.

that we frequently use the term *sociocultural* when referring to a structural condition or form of action.

III: The Concrete Structurings

The human beings of a society are combined and arranged in *structurings.* The basic structuring consists of *groups,* including the large-scale formal organizations and the areal or territorial groups known as communities. Individuals, groups, and institutionalized organizations of individuals and groups also have competitive, complementary, and reciprocal functional relations and consequent determinable location, arrangement, and configuration in space on the surface of the earth, in the form of an *ecological system.* Every society has a *stratification system;* that is, a societal ecology consisting of hierarchically arranged and socially spaced horizontal layers or strata of individuals, groups, and categories.

GROUPS

A group is any number of persons interacting with each other with some continuity and in some patterned manner, who share some one or more common interests and carry on some social activity, who recognize themselves as a distinct social entity, and are usually so recognized by others because of their particular meaningful reciprocal behavior. Almost every phase of the individual's existence as a human being involves acting in groups, and nearly everything he does is group-determined and -influenced. The immediate social groups to which individuals belong are the link between them and their larger society. In fact, the larger society is represented to every individual by the groups of which he is a member.

Groups have major structural significance in a society. Since they are all combinations of two or more communicating, reacting, and functionally interacting human beings, they are the fundamental concrete units or elements or associational forms of which a society is composed. Their significance and place in societal organization is somewhat analogous, in the biological realm, to the different combinations of cells that constitute all of the varied morphological features of living things. They form the stable framework of society. They perform as operative or functional *units,* connected, interdependent, and reciprocal.

Although groups are the framework and the operative agents of a society, it should also be noted that just as individuals function only through groups so groups function through the larger society. The underlying and contributory systems just examined have their major societal significance through their effects on groups.

The essential nature of groups and, at the same time, the diversity of groups and the criteria of group differentiation can be brought out by noting the following.

Groups may vary in size from as few as two members to millions.

The communication among the members may be direct or indirect, depending upon the number, complexity, and area of the group.

There is always stimulus-response or give-and-take among the members; this is the distinctive difference between groups and mere aggregations or categories.

Groups vary in intimacy from those where relations are face to face, sympathetic, and often amount to close personal friendship, to those in which the relations are long range, impersonal, anonymous, and more or less mechanical.

The interaction is over some period of time, but that period may be ten minutes, or (in the case of nations) ten centuries.

The behavior within the group is always patterned to some extent on statuses and roles, rights and duties, and on dominance-submission and leader-follower principles. There are also norms governing conduct toward members of other groups.

The network of reciprocal relations may be very simple or very complex.

The members are associated, consciously or unconsciously, for the pursuit of some common interests or the achievement of some purpose, but the intensity and societal importance of such interests or purposes will vary greatly, ranging from those about which the members are almost unconscious to those whose accomplishment is the *raison d'être* of the organization and determines the form of the organization.

Groups vary greatly as to the functions they perform. Some carry on a single function (a friendship or a play group); some are multifunctional (a family or a huge corporation).

The members possess an awareness of common membership; they recognize each other as members, though perhaps at a distance and without personal contact. The members possess a sense of corporate identity that sets them apart from other aggregations. The unity in some cases may rest upon fundamental *similarities,* such as sex and age, or racial, ethnic, and cultural; in others upon basic *differences* with the recognition of an interdependence and complementary nature of parts that demand integration (for example, a particular family or the personnel of a huge, industrial organization).

The bonds that bind the members together may vary greatly in kind and strength, depending upon the kind of group and the conditions and relations of the group at the time. Examples of bonds are friendship, local, genetic, vocational, professional, racial, national, cultural, status, economic, political, juristic, religious, and educational.

Groups vary in voluntariness of membership. In some, membership is largely involuntary, being acquired by birth (for example, in a family or a state), automatically by residence in an area, or because of presumed institutional necessity (for example, a child under a given age in a school group). In most other groups, membership is in some measure voluntary; that is, individuals are more or less free to enter into the group type of relationship and join or not as they choose.

All groups involve relations and placement of members in both physical and social space. The physical spacing is mainly on a horizontal plane, and groups will vary from those small ones in which the individuals occupy a small space and are within eyeshot and earshot of each other to those vast derivative groups in which the members are widely dispersed in space. The social spacing in every group, large and small, is both horizontal—differentiated roles and functions—and vertical—gradation of prestige, power, and responsibility. Both the physical and social spacing in groups can be represented in diagrammatical form.

All groups have organization, but it will vary—depending upon size, heterogeneity of members, gravity of purposes, and complexity of functions—from groups in which it is spontaneous, simple, and informal, to those massive, modern groupings, operative in crucial areas of societal life, in which the organization is carefully and continuously planned, formally defined and standardized, and conducted as a bureaucracy.

SMALL AND LARGE GROUPS. The term *small group* is used with various meanings. It implies a small number of individuals together in a situation; but *how* small or large a number?[4] Although an arbitrary figure cannot be set, under most physical conditions, indoors or outdoors, thirty people would probably be the greatest number capable of meeting the conditions of a small group, and in most instances the number would be considerably less.[5] If small groups exceed a certain number, the interaction becomes more and more impersonal and diffused, and the collectivity takes on the nature of a crowd.

Small groups are by no means all of a piece structurally and functionally. We may distinguish particularly between (1) the natural and (2) the formal and contrived small groups.

The small, natural groups occur in the human social world without any forcing or artifice. They are of a genetic nature, or—and this identifies the great bulk of them—they are spontaneous expressions of the

[4] Cf. Muzafer Sherif, "Integrating Field Work and Laboratory in Small Group Research," *Am. Soc. Rev.*, 19 (Dec., 1954): 259–711, esp. 762.

[5] Cf. W. L. Warner and P. S. Lunt, *The Social Life of the Modern Community*. New Haven: Yale Univ. Press, 1941, pp. 110–111.

social nature of human beings. They function to satisfy such primary needs as love (the married pair), family, fellowship, congeniality, being happy together, or consoling and sorrowing together (friendship groups, neighborhood circles), thinking and arguing together, satisfying a sense of more or less exclusive belonging (the clique and the "mutual admiration circle," possibly boys' gangs), and as a spontaneously developing operative means of carrying on simple utilitarian tasks (mutual aid groups). The contact and communication are direct and face to face; the relationships are primary, personal; the members usually have strong feelings of identification with the group, and usually participate freely, though not necessarily equally, in its activities. The division of labor and the hierarchical arrangement are very limited, and the leadership is of a purely personal nature. The roles, both as prescriptions and proscriptions of behavior, are usually rather loose. Survival involves, in considerable part, the presence and persistence of feelings of liking among the group members as distinct from the formally organized groups, small and large, where the conduct of the established task is the *raison d'être* and where the characteristic relationships are largely formal and contractual.

Over against these are the contrived and formally organized small groups, sometimes referred to as problem-solving small groups. Notable forms of these are the board meeting, the seminar, the smaller classroom group, panels, small organized work groups (such as a crew of telephone linemen, a bomber crew, the men manning a fire truck, and athletic teams), and decision-making committees. Such small groups, of course, have face-to-face relations, direct communication, an awareness of common membership, and other features of the natural small group. Their distinctiveness, however, is based on the fact that they have a specific, previously known purpose, rules and organized procedures for their functioning, and usually more or less fixed power relations.

These small groups are the smallest types of interacting, joint-participation units in a community or society. They are the elemental group material out of which all larger units are formed.

The *large* group may range in size from a number just exceeding that of a small group to a collectivity of millions upon millions, such as a nation. Many features of large groups have already been brought out in our analysis of the nature of a society; certain other features, specifically significant from the point of view of large groups as instruments of societal organization, will be noted in the next section in which the large-scale formal organization will be examined, and in the ensuing section on the community.

Certain characteristics inevitably come about as the result of size. Although a few of the members may have direct contacts with each other and hence enjoy a certain amount of direct communication, because of the very size and the physical area of the group, the bulk of the contacts are of a secondary nature, and thus most of the inter-member communication is indirect and long range. Although there may be as frequent interaction between *some* members as between members of small groups, even that interaction is usually less intimate, less intense, more casual, more impersonal. Most of the contacts are entirely indirect, handled through long-distance communication; the two or more persons involved may never see each other.

As the size of the group increases, the members become less known to each other. They may be able to identify each other as members only on the basis of very general criteria; for example, as members of a given socio-economic class, or as employees in a particular industrial plant, or as members of ethnic or local groups.

As size increases, there is increase in the division of labor and specialization. The members are differentiated as to functions, and the activities become highly specialized.

As groups increase in size, there is the need for more deliberate organization.

A need then arises for fixed norms for all of the standard relationships, and for organizational, institutional means of achieving and maintaining conformity to the norms.

Because of their secondary nature, the relations become more and more formal and contractual.

Since a considerable number of unequal persons are being societally organized, the structure becomes notably hierarchical.

As the size increases, there is greater likelihood of subgroups appearing; that is, the large group becomes a more and more complex combination of interdependent and reciprocal subgroups. These subgroups appear on both the horizontal and vertical planes of interaction. In other words, size is roughly correlated with structural complexity.[6]

NON-FORMALLY AND FORMALLY ORGANIZED GROUPS. The outstanding feature of *non-formally* organized groups from the point of view of societal organization is the fact that they are not specially established and organized to carry out specific, consciously planned group or societal objectives. They range from the spontaneous or natural small groups examined above to the larger, diffused combinations of similarly constituted and minded, but loosely knit, individuals and groups. Although every combination of human beings has, or develops, some

---

[6] On the size of groups as a factor in the nature and quality of interaction as examined in a large number of experiments and studies, see E. F. Borgatta and L. S. Cottrell, Jr., "Directions for Research in Group Behavior," *Am. Jour. Soc.,* 63 (July, 1957): 42–48.

organization, in the case of these non-formal or informal groups, the organization that exists or that does appear is of a spontaneous and rudimentary nature among the small, natural groups, and of a vague, almost herd-like nature among the larger diffused, secondary entities. However, all of these non-formal groups can be converted into, or combined into, highly purposive and formally organized groups, or such groups can develop from within; for example, an array of neighbors can become a local reform organization; a fighting or other specifically functioning organization may develop among persons of common ethnicity; or a union may develop among the practitioners of a particular vocation.

From the point of view of total operation in society, the groups of central importance are those that are *formally* organized and that are ordinarily designated as associations or organizations. They usually consist of persons who are (1) acting deliberately, collectively, and more or less permanently, (2) in a formally and systematically organized manner, (3) in accordance with planned and established principles of operation, (4) with an administrative personnel, (5) in order to achieve certain more or less specifically formulated common or complementary interests and purposes by means of their specialized but coordinated cooperative activities. It will be recalled that one variety of the small group—the problem-solving group—is contrived and formally organized. In the main, however, although purposive, the tasks of such groups are usually relatively simple, their objectives are limited, the participant personnel is small, and their organization is seldom very complex. Wherever and whenever tasks involve more than small-group numbers and complexities of activities, they must be conducted by means of larger, formal organizations. These are the means, growing out of long experience, and, more recently, out of much invention, whereby all complex, multiplex, long-range, purposive activities, which involve many people as participants or beneficiaries, and which require coordination of elements, must be conducted.

Specifically, the situation might be that of combining efficiently the efforts of 100,000 or 500,000 heterogeneous people (for example, the personnel of General Motors) to carry out an infinite number, and various levels, of specialized activities in order to fulfill the purposes of an organization.

Almost all of our public, semi-public, and private social agencies conducting far-reaching sociocultural regulatory and maintenance operations take this form, although there will be considerable variation in degree and structuring of organization.

These large-scale, formal organizations are known as *bureaucracies* by the social scientists and most societal managers. Their universality implies a stage of development in the conduct of a community's affairs in which division of labor, specialization, purposive planning, and hierarchic regimentation has become necessary if the tasks are to be done efficiently.

Bureaucratic organization, however, is not entirely a phenomenon of modern times. Simple societies had them to a degree, and the great ancient civilizations depended upon them for conducting certain of their more complex functions. They seem to have appeared as soon as social tasks developed of such magnitude that they could not be performed by means of primary groups or even by small-scale formal associations.

Never before, however, has there been such a proliferation of bureaucracies as during the present century. Never before has the bureaucracy been the outstanding and characteristic form of organizing the operations in almost every department of social life. Bureaucratic organization has penetrated almost every area of social life; it is more extensive in scope than ever before; because of recent developments in both physical and societal technologies, it has developed new characteristics; and most of the normal life of the great majority of people today takes place within an extended series of interlocking bureaucracies. As these large-scale operative agencies become larger and more essential in our society, a knowledge of bureaucratic morphology and physiology will become one of the most important fields of social study.

Among the factors responsible for the ubiquity of bureaucratic organization in our society are the vast number of persons involved in tasks, the multiplication of needs and wants, the extending division of labor, the increase in complexity of functions performed, and finally increasing need of predictable provision of products and services.

The major structural-functional characteristics of bureaucracies follow.

The bureaucracy takes the structural form of a pyramid, consisting of horizontal layers of administrative, technical, and other operative personnel, with the policy-makers and major decision-makers at the apex, the intermediate executives, technical experts, and managers next, and at the base the mass of members, or workers, at various skill levels. There is within each layer of organization an established assignment of tasks, rights, privileges, and responsibilities.

The administrative necessities, especially involving the exercise of authority in decision-making, commanding, and instructing, and specifying and assigning tasks, are carried out by means of what is sometimes called "line organization," which consists of a hierarchy of positions by means of which authority that is specialized for each rank is delegated downward, and which, likewise, defines who will give and who will receive what orders, commands, requests, and suggestions. The existence of this chain of command requires channels of communication for both the lateral and vertical flow or transmission of information to all elements of the organization.

Every bureaucracy, to obviate the whims and weaknesses of personalities among its personnel and avoid confusion as to how and when and by whom to conduct the multiplicity of tasks, must have an adequately established and rigorously adhered-to body of rules and regulations for each operation and every category of personnel involved. These define the procedures to be followed in each type of job, and the obligations, rights, and duties attached to each; they set up standards of proficiency and state rewards and penalties.

To perform effectively, a bureaucracy especially in its political and industrial forms, depersonalizes itself, both with respect to its internal and external relations. This appears to be due mainly to the fact that purely technical and administrative considerations should prevail if the organization is to carry on its functions; the tasks should be conducted for the most part without regard to person and in accordance with the established and calculable rules.

Division of labor and specialization, as already noted, is one of the primary reasons for the existence of large-scale organization. The whole undertaking is separated into manageable parts, and each of the units and subunits has its special but interrelated functions in the whole operation. The division of labor is usually both vertical and horizontal. Specialization consists not only in the development and utilization of administrative and technical expertness (*expertise*) at various levels of the organization, but also in that proficiency that comes even in production line tasks from concentration on one or a few separate operations.

Policy-making, planning and programming, and decision-making must be continually conducted. Policy-making is concerned with determining new or additional goals or objectives, and the dropping or modifying of existing ones. Planning and programming consists of the inventorying and specifying of the personnel, social and material instrumentalities, the types of procedure, and the sequences of action necessary to put the policies into effect. All of these rest upon decision-making; that is, coming to conclusions at the right time regarding the things to be done at the right time, place, and situation.

The multiple parts, processes, and personnel must be fitted together into an orderly, integrated, operative whole if the over-all goals are to be attained. In order to achieve this, it is necessary that there be not only centralization of authority, but also proper decentralization and relaying of authority to the various levels and departments.

Also involved is standardization of instruments and procedures, and *routinization* or getting into ordered functional and time sequences all particular operations in order to reduce or eliminate friction, prevent eccentric action, prevent overlapping of action, and obviate gaps in the necessary sequence of action.

Although bureaucracies are not immortal by any means, they do have the structure and facilities to maintain themselves through change and time. They have their corpus of rules and regulations, their established principles of operation, their planning and review procedures, their allocation of responsibility for every phase of operation, and especially their substantial mechanized and institutionalized structural forms. All levels and varieties of personnel are replaceable; they come and go. The bureaucracy maintains its organic structure, its functioning, its identity, and its direction. It may last for generations and even centuries.

THE AREAL GROUPINGS: COMMUNITIES. The analysis of the nature and place of groups in the systemic organization of society becomes complete in the treatment of the community, for the community is essentially a structural-functional integration of groups. Especially in its modern form, it is an organization, within a more or less limited and jointly inhabited area of the earth's surface, of almost all of the different kinds of groups, from the simplest and most casual, from the genetic, to the durable, bureaucratically and institutionally organized ones. It is thus a special kind of grouping of groups based upon territory. Furthermore, as a matter of wider orientation, over-all society is a sort of a community of communities; it is made up of separate but intersecting communities that share a more or less common social life. The community is not merely the sum of all these interactional parts, but is an integration of them into an area-wide operational entity.

The societal significance of the community inheres in several of its special and inimitable aspects.

Individuals and groups always cluster together and exist together in space; all of their associated life is conducted with some degree of continuity and cooperation within more or less determinate areas or localities of the earth's surface; they occupy and share a common habitat, and carry on there a common way of life. The very territory of the community with the uniqueness it imposes often becomes one of the community's chief values and a basis for the unification of its members, and for proudly identifying them in distinction to those of other communities. Each community is, thus, a spatially localized and more or less bounded combination of individuals and all kinds of groups, quasi-independent, and in some measure, distinguishable from all other communities.

All of the individual and group components within the locality are enmeshed in one way or another in a symbiotic fabric; that is, they do not only occupy land surface together in rather close proximity, but are bound together in functional specialization and interdependence—a bonding, along (1) physical, (2) territorial and ecological, (3) ideological and social-psychological, and (4) societal lines. In the community, all of these determinants of human life are unavoidable and continually noticeable and effective.

The community is the smallest territorial grouping, or for that matter, the smallest combination of individuals and groups of any sort, in which practically *all* of the different aspects of social life are covered and carried out. In its structural and functional aspects, it is almost a complete arena of social life. This is not true of any of the lesser areal aggregates; and, of course, all of the other groups, however complex and massive they may be, represent special interests and conduct only segmental or specially related complementary activities. In the community the residents find it possible to meet most of their needs—physical, psychic, social, spiritual. In the community there is all of the necessary functional diversity and, at the same time, the cooperative fullness of action to live the complete individual and social life. The community is thus a complete, corporate, societal entity; by means of it the multiple functions of men are carried on as a systematized whole.

The community is the arena of whole life for the individuals. This is a corollary of the immediately preceding aspect. By virtue of this relatively complete societal equipment in the community, we, as individuals, have almost all of our social relationships within the community and live almost all of our most characteristic, representative, and normal day-to-day life as well as our entire cycle in our community. It is in the community that we have almost all of our institutional involvements. The community is thus our immediate, pervasive, and continuous arena of participation and fulfillment. It is also our frame of reference in interpreting characters and events both within and outside of the community.

There exists also in our country what might be called the *extended community*. The small community, with its mainly primary group relationships among its members, its demographic normality and its cultural homogeneity, its strong sense of belonging and its solidarity, its relatively simple social structure, its self-containment, and its "sacred" ways, has been the predominant form in our country during the greater part of its history, when the population was mostly rural and agricultural. But with the industrialization and urbanization of the country, with the great advances in communication and in rapid and cheap transportation, with the vast increase in population, the changes in agriculture, especially its mechanization and the consequent reduction in required labor force, and the marked elevation in standards of living, and hence the extension of needs, with the vast increase in both the amount and the areal extent of functional interdependence and organization in every department of social life, the traditional small community is less and less the characteristic form as far as the daily and total living is concerned for the greater and ever greater proportion of our population. Although small communities have not disappeared by any means, fewer and fewer in the United States take on the older, ideal-typical form, and both an ever smaller actual number and smaller proportion of the people live in them. The smaller local community, it seems, is a social unit of inevitably decreasing importance in modern society, especially in urban areas.

Unavoidably, the smaller communities and their residents have become part of a much wider and more complex community network. This extended community consists of the central city, its urban fringe and satellite smaller cities, its related hinterland with the towns, villages, and agricultural or other primary-industrial areas, and their people that are under the immediate influence of the central city. The community unit thus is more than the city proper; it is a combination of the city and the adjacent subcommunities knit together by their close and inescapable daily interdependencies. This urban-rural or extended community is the kind of community in which the great bulk of the American people live.

THE ECOLOGICAL SYSTEM

Living things of all kinds and levels relate and distribute themselves with respect to each other within their given habitat or area for the fulfillment of their survival needs, and, at the same time, have a position or location for operation and a general pattern of spatial distribution. In fact, it is possible to *map* many interdependent forms of biological life. This *symbiotic* relating in a spatial patterning of living things on some portion of the earth's surface is referred to as an ecological system.

There is also a specifically *human* ecological system. Space is for men a limiting and organizing factor of great significance, for it greatly affects the relationships of men to each other as they compete, cooperate, and adjust themselves to each other. Especially important is the fact that, as the result of the symbiotic relations and the selective and adjustive procedures, the individuals, and particularly the important kinds of social structures, such as the different types of groups of men, of aggregations, of purposive organizations, and of institutions have characteristic spatial location, arrangement, and distribution with respect to each other in the territory of their communities. The competitive-cooperative processes tend to produce continually an equilibrium of the elements in space. Each type of element tends to have its own best location with respect to the other elements in order to conduct its own special functions vis-à-vis the others and as part of the total multiple operation. Thus the elements in each area at any given time are not only systematically interrelated, but also have a characteristic spatial distributional pattern.

There are continual changes in equilibrium due to migration, the changing makeup and functions of given subareas, and hence locational readjustments. These may produce the process of succession in a given area; that is, obsolescence or displacement and evacuation of old elements, and the invasion and establishment, for the time being, of new or more appropriate elements.

THE STRATIFICATION SYSTEM

Another system of cardinal importance is the stratification system. It exists because there are great differences among individuals, and because societies, especially complex ones, of necessity have an extensive division of labor and specialization of function, which utilize, in fact societally organize, for general advantage, the vast differences among individuals.

Stratification means that the population of any community or society, with its differentiated abilities, functions, positions, and roles, falls roughly into graded, horizontal layers or ranks or strata; the total strata constitute a hierarchy. The essence of a stratification system *is* this hierarchic division of society. The strata, however, are mainly generalized, loosely articulated aggregates, even categories, rather than crystallized social groups. What we have is a societal, vertical distribution of individuals and groups among the horizontal layers or strata of a society in contrast to the horizontal, physical arrangement and spacing of the ecological system. The strata may also be said to be clusters of somewhat similarly evaluated statuses. The ranks are differently evaluated and hierarchically scaled; and social prestige, esteem, deference, privileges, and rights are assigned to members on the basis of their stratum location.

In addition to its structural aspects, the stratification system also performs functions in that it locates differentiated individuals and groups in the social system, provides social integration and solidarity among unequals of a society, cooperatively distributes unlike and unequal social tasks, and provides a hierarchy and a channeling of authority and control.

The stratification system is so fundamental in the structuring of social systems and in performing certain important functions that it has come to have at least quasi-institutional features. It will be examined in some detail as to its nature and functions, its institutional aspects, and some of its special American forms in Chapter Fifteen.

B I B L I O G R A P H Y

SYSTEMS

Allport, F. H., *Theories of Perception and the Concept of Structure*. New York: Wiley, 1955, pp. 469–477.

Angyl, A., "The Structure of Wholes," *Phil. of Science,* 6 (Jan., 1939): 25–37.

Benjamin, A. C., *The Logical Structure of Science*. London: Kegan Paul, Trench, Trubner & Co., 1936, Chaps. III, IV, VII, XI.

Blum, H. F., *Time's Arrow and Evolution*. Princeton: Princeton Univ. Press, 1951.

Bornemisza, S. T., *The Unified System Concept in Nature*. New York: Vantage Press, 1939.

Bronowski, J., *The Common Sense of Science*. Cambridge: Harvard Univ. Press, 1953, pp. 28–39.

Kantor, J. R., *Psychology and Logic*. Bloomington, Ind.: Principia Press, 1950, Vol. II, Chaps. XV, XVI.

Meadows, P., "Systems, Models, and Science," *Am. Soc. Rev.,* 22 (Feb., 1957): 3–9.

Needham, J., *Order and Life*. New Haven: Yale Univ. Press, 1946.

Radcliffe-Brown, A. R., *A Natural Science of Society*. Glencoe, Ill.: Free Press, 1957, pp. 12–65, 80–90, 124–128.

Toulmin, S. E., *The Philosophy of Science*. London: Hutchinson, 1953, pp. 31–43, 105–114.

Tustin, A., *The Mechanics of Economic Systems*. Cambridge: Harvard Univ. Press, 1953.

Vaihinger, H., *The Philosophy of "As If"* (C. K. Ogden, transl.). New York: Harcourt, Brace, 1925, Chaps. I–V, VIII, IX.

SOCIAL SYSTEMS

Evans-Pritchard, E. E., *Social Anthropology*. Glencoe, Ill.: Free Press, 1952, pp. 19–20, 49–57.

Feibleman, J. K., and Friend, J. W., "The Structure and Function of Organization," *Phil. Rev.,* 54 (Jan., 1945): 19–44.

Firey, W., "Informal Organization and the Theory of Schism," *Am. Soc. Rev.,* 13 (Feb., 1948): 15–24.

Linton, R., *The Study of Man*. New York: Appleton, 1936, pp. 105–108, 253–270.

Loomis, C. P., *Social Systems*. Princeton, N.J.: Van Nostrand, 1960.

Loomis, C. P., and Beegle, J. A., *Rural Sociology: The Strategy of Change*. Englewood Cliffs, N.J.: Prentice-Hall, 1957, pp. 1–21.

Parsons, T., *The Structure of Social Action*. New York: McGraw-Hill, 1937; on Tönnies, pp. 686–694; on Pareto, pp. 178–300, 704–708.

Parsons, T., *The Social System*. Glencoe, Ill.: Free Press, 1951.

Parsons, T., and Shils, E. A., *Toward a General Theory of Action*. Cambridge: Harvard Univ. Press, 1951, pp. 23–26, 107–109, 190–233.

SOCIAL ORGANIZATION

Boulding, K. E., *The Image: Knowledge in Life and Society*. Ann Arbor: Univ. of Michigan Press, 1956, pp. 19–31.

Broom, L., and Selznick, P., *Sociology*. Evanston, Ill.: Row, Peterson, 1955, pp. 11–44.
Brown, G. G., and Barnett, J. H., "Social Organization and Social Structure," *Am. Anth.*, 44 (Jan., 1942): 31–36.
Faris, R. E. L., *Social Disorganization*. New York: Ronald, 1955, pp. 3–33.
Firth, Raymond, *Elements of Social Organization*. New York: Phil. Lib., 1951, pp. 27–43, 75–79.
Greer, S. A., *Social Organization*. New York: Random House, 1955.
Herskovits, M. J., *Cultural Anthropology*. New York: Knopf, 1955, pp. 166–190.
Homans, G. C., "A Conceptual Scheme for the Study of Social Organization," *Am. Soc. Rev.*, 12 (Feb., 1947): 13–26.
Lenn, T. I., "Social Organization and Disorganization," in Roucek, J. S. (ed.), *Contemporary Sociology*. New York: Phil. Lib., 1958, pp. 132–150.
Rose, A. M., "A Theory of Social Organization and Disorganization," in Rose, A. M. (ed.), *Theory and Method in the Social Sciences*. Minneapolis: Univ. of Minnesota Press, 1954, pp. 3–24.
White, L. A., *The Evolution of Culture*. New York: McGraw-Hill, 1959, pp. 58–100.

SOCIAL DISORGANIZATION

Faris, R. E. L., *Social Disorganization*. New York: Ronald, 1955, pp. 34–83.
Martindale, D., "Social Disorganization: The Conflict of Normative and Empirical Approaches," in Becker, H., and Boskoff, A., *Modern Sociological Theory*. New York: Dryden, 1957, pp. 340–367. See references in footnotes.
Rose, A. M., "A Theory of Social Organization and Disorganization," in Rose, A. M. (ed.), *Theory and Method in the Social Sciences*. Minneapolis: Univ. of Minnesota Press, 1954, pp. 3–24.
Wirth, L., "Ideological Aspects of Social Disorganization," *Am. Soc. Rev.*, 5 (Aug., 1940): 472–482.

THE NATURAL ENVIRONMENT

Biersted, R., *The Social Order*. New York: McGraw-Hill, 1957, pp. 29–100.
Chapple, E. D., and Coon, C. S., *Principles of Anthropology*. New York: Holt, 1942, pp. 73–94.
Hertzler, J. O., *Society in Action*. New York: Dryden, 1954, pp. 101–107 (bibliography, pp. 410–412).
Mukerjee, R., *Man and His Habitat*. New York: Longmans, Green, 1940.
White, C. L., *Human Geography: An Ecological Study of Society*. New York: Appleton, 1948.

THE DEMOGRAPHIC STRUCTURE

Bogue, D. J., *The Population of the United States*. Glencoe, Ill.: Free Press, 1960.
Davis, K., "Population and Power in the Free World," in Spengler, J. J., and Duncan, O. D. (eds.), *Population Theory and Policy*. Glencoe, Ill.: Free Press, 1956, pp. 342–356.

Hauser, P. M., and Duncan, O. D. (eds.), *The Study of Population: An Inventory and Appraisal.* Chicago: Univ. of Chicago Press, 1959.

Hawley, A. H., *Human Ecology: A Theory of Community Organization.* Englewood Cliffs, N.J.: Prentice-Hall, 1950, pp. 77–148.

Hertzler, J. O., *Society in Action.* New York: Dryden, 1954, pp. 108–126 (bibliography, pp. 402–405).

Landis, P. H., *Population Problems* (P. K. Hatt, rev.). Philadelphia: Lippincott, 1954.

Phelps, H. A., and Henderson, D., *Population in Its Human Aspects.* New York: Appleton, 1958.

Smith, T. L., *Fundamentals of Population Study.* Philadelphia: Lippincott, 1960.

Taeuber, C., and I. B., *The Changing Population of the United States.* New York: Wiley, 1958.

United Nations, Population Division, *The Determinants and Consequences of Population Trends: A Summary of the Findings and Studies on the Relationships between Population Changes and Economic and Social Conditions.* New York, 1953.

Wrong, D. H., *Population.* New York: Random House, 1956.

THE CULTURE SYSTEM

Beals, R. L., and Hoijer, H., *An Introduction to Anthropology,* New York: Macmillan, 1953, pp. 204–228.

Hertzler, J. O., *Society in Action.* New York: Dryden, 1954, pp. 73–98 (bibliography, p. 399).

Parsons, T., and Shils, E. A., *Toward a General Theory of Action.* Cambridge: Harvard Univ. Press, 1951, pp. 21–22, 55, 162–167.

Rose, A. M., *Sociology: The Study of Human Relations.* New York: Knopf, 1956, pp. 32–43.

White, L. A., *The Science of Culture.* New York: Farrar, Straus, 1949.

GROUPS

Bates, F. L., "A Conceptual Analysis of Group Structure," *Soc. Forces,* 36 (Dec., 1957): 103–111.

Borgatta, E. F., and Cottrell, J. S., Jr., "On the Classification of Groups," *Sociometry,* 18 (Nov., 1955): 665–678.

Cartwright, D., and Zander, A., *Group Dynamics: Research and Theory,* Evanston, Ill.: Row, Peterson, 1953.

Coon, C. S., "The Universality of Natural Groupings in Human Society," *Jour. Educ. Soc.,* 20 (Nov., 1946): 163–168.

De Gré, G. L., "Outlines for a Systematic Classification of Social Groups," *Am. Soc. Rev.,* 14 (Feb., 1949): 145–148.

Hiller, E. T., *Social Relations and Structures.* New York: Harper, 1947, pp. 246–290.

Homans, G. C., *The Human Group.* New York: Harcourt, Brace, 1950.

Pellegrin, A. J., "The Achievement of High Statuses and Leadership in the Small Group," *Soc. Forces,* 32 (Oct., 1953): 10–16.

Znaniecki, F., "Social Groups as Products of Participating Individuals," *Am. Jour. Soc.,* 44 (May, 1939): 799–811.

Znaniecki, F., "Social Groups in the Modern World," in Berger, M., Abel,

T., and Page, C. H. (eds.), *Freedom and Control in Modern Society.* Princeton, N.J.: Van Nostrand, 1954, pp. 125–140.

SMALL GROUPS

Gross, E., "Primary Functions of the Small Group," *Am. Jour. Soc.,* 60 (July, 1954): 24–29.

Hare, A. P., Borgatta, E. F., and Bales, R. F., *Small Groups: Studies in Social Interaction.* New York: Knopf, 1955 (includes an annotated bibliography of 584 items, pp. 579–661).

Loomis, C. P., and Beegle, J. A., *Rural Sociology: The Strategy of Change.* Englewood Cliffs, N.J.: Prentice-Hall, 1957, pp. 103–136.

Olmstead, M. S., *The Small Group.* New York: Random House, 1959.

Special Issue on Small Group Research, *Am. Soc. Rev.,* 19 (Dec., 1954): entire issue.

LARGE-SCALE FORMAL ORGANIZATIONS

Barnard, C. I., *Organization and Management.* Cambridge: Harvard Univ. Press, 1948.

Blau, P. M., *The Dynamics of Bureaucracy.* Chicago: Univ. of Chicago Press, 1955.

Blau, P. M., *Bureaucracy in Modern Society.* New York: Random House, 1956.

Brecht, A., "How Bureaucracies Develop and Function," *Annals Am. Acad. Pol. & Soc. Science,* (Mar., 1954): 1–10.

Caplow, T., "The Criteria of Organizational Success," *Soc. Forces,* 32 (Oct., 1953): 1–9.

Dimock, M. E., "Bureaucracy Self-Examined," *Pub. Adm. Rev.,* 4 (No. 3, 1944): 197–207.

Dubin, R., *Human Relations in Administration.* Englewood Cliffs, N.J.: Prentice-Hall, 1951, pp. 154–171.

Dubin, R., *The World of Work: Industrial Society and Human Relations.* Englewood Cliffs, N.J.: Prentice-Hall, 1958, pp. 27–60, 363–384.

Hertzler, J. O., *Society in Action.* New York: Dryden, 1954, pp. 179–188 (bibliography, pp. 414–415).

LaPiere, R. T., *A Theory of Social Control.* New York: McGraw-Hill, 1954, pp. 290–316.

Merton, R. K., *et al., Reader in Bureaucracy.* Glencoe, Ill.: Free Press, 1949.

Parsons, T., *Structure and Process in Modern Societies.* Glencoe, Ill.: Free Press, 1959.

Presthus, R. V., "The Social Bases of Bureaucratic Organization," *Soc. Forces,* 38 (Dec., 1959): 103–109.

Presthus, R. V., "Behavior and Bureaucracy in Many Cultures," *Pub. Adm. Rev.,* 19 (Winter, 1959): 25–35.

Selznick, P., "An Approach to a Theory of Bureaucracy," *Am. Soc. Rev.,* 8 (Feb., 1943): 47–54.

Selznick, P., "Foundation of the Theory of Organization," *Am. Soc. Rev.,* 13 (Feb., 1948): 25–35.

Tannenbaum, A. S., "The Concept of Organizational Control," *Jour. Social Issues,* 12 (No. 2, 1956): 50–60.

Tannenbaum, A. S., and Georgopoulos, B. S., "The Distribution of Control in Formal Organizations," *Soc. Forces,* 36 (Oct., 1957): 44–50.

Warner, W. L., "Associations in America," in his *American Life: Dream and Reality*. Chicago: Univ. of Chicago Press, 1953, pp. 191–209.

Weber, Max, *The Theory of Social and Economic Organization* (Henderson, A. M., and Parsons, T., transl.). New York: Oxford Univ. Press, 1947, pp. 56–64, 136–157, 324–423.

Weiss, R. S., and Jacobson, E., "A Method for the Analysis of the Structure of Complex Organizations," *Am. Soc. Rev.*, 20 (Dec., 1955): 661–668.

THE EXTENDED COMMUNITY

Anderson, N., "Urbanism and Urbanization," *Am. Jour. Soc.*, 65 (July, 1959): 68–73.

Anderson, N., *The Urban Community: A World Perspective*. New York: Holt, 1959.

Anderson, T. R., and Collier, Jane, "Metropolitan Dominance and the Rural Hinterland," *Rural Soc.*, 21 (June, 1956): 152–157.

Beers, H. W., "The Rural Community," in Gittler, J.B. (ed.), *Review of Sociology*. New York: Wiley, 1957, pp. 186–220.

Bertrand, A. L., "Rural Locality Groups: Changing Patterns, Change Factors, and Implications," *Rural Soc.*, 19 (June, 1954): 174–179.

Bogue, D. J., *The Structure of the Metropolitan Community: A Study of Dominance and Subdominance*. Social Science Research Project, Institute for Human Adjustment. Ann Arbor, Mich.: Univ. of Michigan Press, 1949.

Davis, K., et al., *The World's Metropolitan Areas*. Berkeley: Univ. of California Press, 1959.

Duncan, O. D., and Reiss, A. J., Jr., *Social Characteristics of Urban and Rural Communities, 1950*. New York: Wiley, 1956.

Fisher, R. M. (ed.), *The Metropolis in Modern Life*. Garden City, N.Y.: Doubleday, 1955.

Fordham, J. B., *A Larger Concept of Community*. Baton Rouge, La.: Louisiana State Univ. Press, 1958.

Hawley, A. H., *The Changing Shape of Metropolitan America*. Glencoe, Ill.: Free Press, 1956.

Martin, W. T., "Ecological Change in Satellite Rural Areas," *Am. Soc. Rev.*, 22 (Apr., 1957): 173–183.

Schneider, E. V., *Industrial Sociology*. New York: McGraw-Hill, 1957, pp. 364–372.

Schnore, L. F., "The Functions of Metropolitan Suburbs," *Am. Jour. Soc.*, 61 (Mar., 1956): 453–458.

Schnore, L. F., "The Growth of Metropolitan Suburbs," *Am. Soc. Rev.*, 22 (Apr., 1957): 165–173.

Schnore, L. F., "Metropolitan Growth and Decentralization," *Am. Jour. Soc.*, 63 (Sept., 1957): 171–180.

Schnore, L. F., "Satellites and Suburbs," *Soc. Forces*, 36 (Dec., 1957): 121–127.

Thompson, W. S., *The Growth of Metropolitan Districts in the United States, 1900–1940*. Washington, D.C.: U.S. Govt. Printing Office, 1947.

Vidick, A. J., and Bensman, J., *Small Town in Mass Society*. Princeton: Princeton Univ. Press, 1958.

Whyte, W. H., et al., *The Exploding Metropolis*. Garden City, N.Y.: Doubleday, 1958.

Woodward, J. L., "Is the Community Emphasis Overdone in the Social Program?" *Harvard Educ. Rev.*, 11 (Oct., 1941): 473–480.

THE ECOLOGICAL SYSTEM

Clarke, G. L., *Elements of Ecology.* New York: Wiley, 1954, pp. 1–22, 364, 401–424, 425–448, 465–503.

Dice, L. R., *Man's Nature and Nature's Man: Ecology of Human Communities.* Ann Arbor: Univ. of Michigan Press, 1955.

Hawley, A. H., *Human Ecology: A Theory of Community Structure.* New York: Ronald, 1950, pp. 3–74, 80–103, 177–267, 371–432.

Hollingshead, A. B., "Human Ecology and Human Society," *Ecological Monographs,* 10 (1940): 354–366.

McKenzie, R. D., "The Ecological Approach to the Study of the Human Community," in Park, R. E. (ed.), *The City.* Chicago: Univ. of Chicago Press, 1925, pp. 63–79.

Quinn, J. A., "Ecological versus Social Interaction," *Soc. and Soc. Res.,* 18 (July–Aug., 1934): 565–570.

Quinn, J. A., *Human Ecology.* Englewood Cliffs, N.J.: Prentice-Hall, 1950.

Rose, A. M., *Sociology: The Study of Human Relations.* New York: Knopf, 1956, pp. 402–431.

Wirth, L., "Human Ecology," *Am. Jour. Soc.,* 50 (May, 1945): 438–488.

The Imperative Instrumental Systems in the Organization of Societal Behavior

In order to understand the nature of society, in general, as an organized operative entity, and the purpose and functions of social institutions in it, in particular, it is essential that we have some knowledge, not only of the underlying and contributory systems and the major forms of societal structuring, but also of the universal and imperative instrumental contituent elements which organize the behavior of individuals, groups, and categories for effective social action. We should be aware of their nature, the types of social conditions and situations to which they relate, and the functions they perform. They enter, in some measure, into every institutional system.

Integration of members is essential to a society if it is to exist. Therefore solidarity and harmony must prevail among the members. They must identify themselves as parts of a common societal system. The members must participate in the essential activities. They must cooperate; that is, they must act jointly. They must continually adjust to each other as changing parts of a system. Thus, an integrated society is the antithesis of one in dysfunctional fragments—one in a state of *dis*integration.

There are stern structural and situational realities that complicate integration and operation which must be faced. A society is made up of numerous heterogeneous persons, each unique in genetic endowment, in temperament, in ability, in training, and in attitudes. A society consists of numerous dissimilar categories and groupings. There are many different kinds of things that need to be done, and individuals, groups, and categories of persons are variously equipped to do them. Hence, there is division of labor and differentiation of action. Since individuals and tasks differ, there is specialization of function. Although these structural and functional subdivisions are complementary, they are often threatened by lack of coordination. Social power is distributed among the elements of society, stratified in hierarchies. At least portions of the membership of the society are segmented by lines of insulation as the result of various (and sometimes cherished) differences, such as those of race and ethnic divisions, occupation, educational level, and religious belief and practice. Such cleavages may breed, under different conditions, among some elements, apathy or a tendency to withdraw; they may make for tension, dissension, segregation, and degrees of opposition among the segments.

Integration, however, does not imply homogeneity of elements in all respects throughout a society; in fact, such an undifferentiated society would be unstructured. It does mean that there is unity in diversity, a relative equilibrium among unequals, and a relative order and stability among the potentially disorganized and antagonistic elements. But this, in turn, means organization; that is, a set of essential, elemental, and universal systems of elements, cultural and societal.

These systems provide the unifying values and ideologies, the goals and purposes, the directives and motivators for the people; they furnish the agencies for selecting and assigning individuals and categories of people to social position in the differentiated and hierarchical social structure; they contribute the procedures and agencies for regulating, maintaining, and reorganizing all elements of the society. It is these operative systems, acting together and simultaneously, that give a society its fundamental characteristics of organization, and enable it to conduct its essential functions.[1]

I: The Value System

Every society has a system of values. It is never simple and never entirely consistent, but it conditions most of the society's structural and functional features.

Men are always examining their world, thinking about it, judging it with respect to its ability to produce satisfactions. According to a widely held point of view, these judgments rest on choices between alternatives of good and bad, right and wrong, desirable and undesir-

---

[1] For general discussions of instrumental systems, see: W. R. Goldschmidt, *Man's Way: A Preface to the Understanding of Society*. Cleveland: World Pub. Co., 1959, pp. 61–105. L. A. White, *The Evolution of Culture*. New York: McGraw-Hill, 1959, pp. 142–236.

able, pleasant and unpleasant, worthwhile and worthless, efficacious and non-efficacious, allowable or non-allowable, beautiful or non-beautiful, adequate or inadequate, promising or non-promising. We refer to these many kinds of shared judgments as values. Some are common to all societies; some are unique in a given society; and some apply only in certain groupings. But, whether universal or particular, borrowed or indigenously developed, values are created; they are human discoveries and constructs that emerge from the collective experience of many people. They have grown out of problem situations of all degrees of gravity. In these situations people have concluded that certain things, conditions, occurrences, arrangements, actions, relationships, expressions and beliefs are, in the longer run, to their advantage, and that others are disadvantageous in one way or another. Thus, every aspect of man's universe of which he is aware—material, social, even what he conceives of as supernatural—is placed on an evaluational scale and has its own related set of values.

Once formed, these value judgments become a crucial and dominating part of the culture. They surround every person and every group like an all-pervading atmosphere. Since everything is valuable in some degree, we cannot escape from our value system's influence; when we know its nature and functions, we do not wish to escape from it; in fact, we look upon it as one of our most cherished possessions.[2]

Our concern with values in the present study is not to present a general sociological analysis of values, but simply to indicate the functions performed by the value system of a society, or of its major subdivisions, in its structuring and effective operation. Specifically significant is the fact that every institutional system has a distinctive body of values at its very core.

The value system of a society provides the basic elements for consensus among its members. Every society, in order to exist, by definition, has to have an ideational basis—a body of commonly held ideas about what is necessary, worthwhile, and desirable, or, put another way, common definitions and working interpretations of the standard situations.

The value system provides the society with established and commonly used criteria for acceptance or rejection. The value system also provides the society with its operating preferences in every department life, and with its established orders and gradients of preference.

The value system supplies much of a society's dynamism. Many of

   [2] Cf. Raymond Firth, *Elements of Social Organization.* New York: Phil. Lib., 1951, pp. 42–43. For the varying interpretation of values, see Franz Adler, "The Value Concept in Sociology," *Am. Jour. Soc.,* 62 (Nov., 1956): 272–279.

the values have the effect of functioning as pressures, as driving forces or imperatives spurring on to all kinds of social action. Malinowski points out that values are the prime movers of human existence. Men work to obtain the things they value, whether these be objects, ways of life, or beliefs.[3] In general, values determine what men want, and what they want is both an organizing and motivating influence in their living as individuals and as members of collectivities.

The value system provides the society with it goals and ideals. When we value anything, we often move forward, beyond, or rise above the *is* and its consequences and toward something better or that ought to be. Ideals are the imaginative representations of the most desirable, the most hoped for, the superior. Since they are more or less consistent presentations of the organization and operation of a better state of things, social or otherwise, they serve as specifications and blueprints of social action.

Thus values in the form of goals and ideals have a directional function, and they greatly influence the kind and quality of social organization ahead; for example, with respect to the amount, quality, and consistency of democracy in our relations with each other.

The value system provides the basis for the important concrete forms of social life. Values define groups and organized associations on the basis of the values held by the members; one group, for example, is a particular kind of religious-value-promoting group; another a political group, and so on. Values make groups as people assemble around common values that they cherish; for groups and organizations, values function as rallying points, as organizing centers. Values sustain groups through the cohesion and stability that they provide for the members. Within societies, values are important determinative factors in such structural features as the majority-minority group relations, in ranking within the stratification system, and in the establishment of the criteria of social class. It may also be noted that the critical differences between societies are the differences in their values, since their structure, functions, and processes are expressions of their value system. Even the most cursory comparison of American and Russian Soviet society bears this out.

Over the long run, societies are chiefly knit together by a common attachment of their members to a system of values.[4] Their societal unity lies fundamentally in their preferential interpretations and points of view, their devotion to, and effort to realize, their purposes and ends.

[3] B. Malinowski, *Freedom and Civilization.* New York: Roy, 1945, p. 137.
[4] Cf. R. C. Angell, *The Integration of American Society.* New York: McGraw-Hill, 1941, pp. 14–15.

All else—communication, systems of economic production, governmental organization, technology, education—is *instrumentality*.

II: The Normative System

Every social system, every community, every society has to have a body of standards, rules, or codes as a means of organizing the social behavior of its members toward each other and toward outsiders. These standards and rules are referred to as *norms*. They are embodiments and expressions of the basic values regarding social relations and functions. These norms indicate how the individuals and groups should think, feel, believe, and especially, how to act in almost every common or recurrent relationship and situation. Their purpose is to standardize and channel behavior in the interactional situations in the life of a society. Thus, there are political and legal norms, moral and religious norms, scientific and technological norms, familial, aesthetic, health, associational, and many other norms, even such commonplace and practical ones as prescriptions, sets of directions, and recipes. To put it concretely, these are rules that we are expected to follow; for example, in student-instructor contacts, in conducting a given office in an organization, in meeting and passing each other on the street, in husband and wife and parent-child relations, in person-property relations. The normative system provides a pattern of mutual expectations for the interacting parties.

Some norms are expressed in the form of insistent requirements or prescriptions of actions (wearing clothes, paying taxes, caring for immature offspring, staying on the right side of the highway); some as positive prohibition or proscription of behavior (nakedness, rape, murder, treason); and others in permissive or optional action (marrying, following a particular occupation, joining a particular denomination). Less definite are recommendations and disapprovals. Furthermore, not all societal norms bind all members of the community or society. There are, for example, universals, or those norms binding upon everyone; specialties, or those applying only to certain categories of persons (for example, men only) or types of groups; and alternatives, or norms permitting this or that within a given area of action (for example, having either a civil or religious marriage ceremony).

The normative system embodies all kinds of rules; the rules are not necessarily codified or even expressly formulated; some are tight and formal, others flexible and informal. But most of them impinge upon us practically every moment of our lives.

The actual sociocultural vehicles or carriers of the norms range in explicitness and imperativeness from the optional folkways, through the customs, traditions, conventions, and mores, to the highly formalized and collectively enforced laws, by-laws, and constitutions of the great organized, regulatory, institutional associations, such as those governing the operations of industrial or business corporations, religious denominations, or political units. Less emphasized in the sociological treatments, though also clearly, if not entirely, a part of the normative system, are creeds, ceremonials and rituals, etiquette forms, good manners and canons of taste; even beliefs, fads, and fashions embody normative elements.

If the members of the groups do not share the appropriate norms and abide by them, there is disorder, anarchy, chaos, actually *ab*-normality. The efficiency, stability, and continuity of a society depend upon its normative order. With an adequate set of norms, the members of a society know what to do and how to do it, and they know with fair certainty how others will perform their duties, within rather wide margins to be sure, in almost every standard situation. They also know that their conduct is judged by the manner in which they comply with these rules; in fact, conformity or non-conformity to the codal requirements makes or breaks a person among his associates.

The informal folkways, the rules relating to the relationships of persons in face-to-face groups, and those coming down from the folk past where many societal conditions were very different, although by no means abrogated or inoperative, are being vastly supplemented and replaced by objectively and deliberatively derived and formally established rules and regulations to meet the conditions characteristic of a mass society. We are a people with heterogeneous backgrounds, with differing viewpoints and interests, with considerable physical and social mobility, and hence some lack of community and stratum rootedness, engaged more and more in relationships that are anonymous and contractual, and involved in social situations that are ever changing. Social order, social integration, and joint social action cannot be based in our present-day society to any great extent on the kinds of norms that served mankind throughout most of its long social career. An increasingly large proportion of the standard or routine relationships of a modern, complex society are, and must be, based upon formally developed and written regulations, rules, ordinances, directives and laws. These grow out of specific factual situations requiring regulation; they define the situations explicitly and prescribe fairly specific obligations in the fairly specific relationships; increasingly, they are calculated and legislated by assigned, authorized, and institutionally responsible bodies in the different departments of social life—governmental, ecclesiastical, scientific, commercial, industrial, occupational, recreational.

III: The Ideological System

Every society has an ideological system over and above the particular ideologies of its many kinds of interest groups, institutionalized groups, groups promoting social movements, racial, religious and other ethnic groups, or social classes. The ideological system includes much of the value system and the normative system, but it goes beyond these and provides a sort of general or foundational philosophy of existence for the people.

The ideological system can be conceived of as the ideational organization of people, what they have in their heads about their universe, physical and social, on the basis of their experience with it. It consists of the whole complex of intellectual schemes whereby men interpret their world to themselves, render it intelligible, and adjust themselves mentally and emotionally to it.[5] The elements are expressed in articulate speech, in writing, or other symbolic form. It consists of the attitudes, ideas, the knowledges, and the theories (common sense and scientific), the beliefs, the traditions, the myths, the mythologies and theologies, the legends, superstitions, proverbs, and other folk wisdom; the values and norms, the ideals, the conceptions of purpose, goals, and ends that have accumulated through the generations. Thus, the ideological system is a society's intricately interwoven fabric of its facts, its interpretations, assumptions, and axioms, its sentiments and attitudes, its articles of faith and its creeds, its dogmas and doctrines, its conceptions of good and bad, and of useful and not useful, its standards and models, its bodies of judgments, its directives, compulsives, and taboos, its conceptions of responsibility and obligation, its convictions regarding the consequences of action, its bodies of rules, its justifications for existence, its rationalized hopes, its doctrines of ends, and its bodies of plans, policies, and programs.

The people regard these as having great—even crucial—significance for the continuity of their individual and collective life. These elements function as psychological and cultural fixations. They determine in considerable measure a society's *psyche;* that is, its mental, emotional, and impulsive predispositions; and they provide it with its *ethos;* that is, its complement of shared values, objectives, and purposes.

These ideological elements are foundation materials for all consensus among a society's members and are the elemental factors in its

[5] Cf. G. C. Homans, "A Conceptual Scheme for the Study of Social Organization," *Am. Soc. Rev.,* 12 (Feb., 1947): 17. L. A. White, *The Science of Culture.* New York: Farrar, Straus, 1949, p. 398.

unity.[6] The thoughts and actions of men center about these elements; by means of them they establish determinate relations with the objects and forces of the material universe, with the supernatural, and with their fellow men. In many ways these ideological features govern what men do technologically and societally. Finally, they enable men to face the future, as well as to interpret the past and present, and, in some measure, to predict what will happen, and to prescribe what ought to happen.

Students of society, however, cannot ignore the ideologies of its component functional groups. Their ideologies, often conflicting with each other, not only function as unifiers, as bases for consensus, as guides and directives among them, but also constitute bodies of defensive arguments as they seek legitimation for their aspirations and their actions. Although these many particularistic ideologies create a certain degree of confusion, inconsistency, and eccentricity of action, there is, nevertheless, considerable uniformity and compatibility among the elements, and a rather widespread conformity of them to the overall ideology.

If it were not for the general uniformity and consistency of a society's ideological elements just mentioned, that society would have no reason for existence and no consistent program for existence. The words of de Tocqueville are of signal pertinence here:

"A society can exist only when a great number of men consider a great number of things from the same point of view; when they hold the same opinions upon many subjects, and when the same occurrences suggest the same thoughts and impressions to their minds."[7]

Without a common body of ideas, intellectual dogmas, unconscious understandings, values, meanings, and ideals, a society's heterogeneous and differentiated population would lack the essential mental and spiritual integration, and its individuals and groups would fly off in all directions. It would be without a body of values to serve as a basis for choices; it would lack principles, expectations, motivations, and directives for necessary social action; it would be without criteria for judging and selecting its action; it would lack explanations and justifications of its various structural and functional features (its differentiated groups and categories, its inimitable patterns of relationship, such as its stratification system, its controls); it would be without guides and goals in meeting the vicissitudes of the changing world. There is a reciprocal

---

6 However, the ideological system of a people is not devoid of inconsistencies and contradictions. The diversity of cultural backgrounds of its population elements, of its interest groups, of its regions, and so on, are factors accounting for the inconsistencies and contradictions.

7 Alexis de Tocqueville, *Democracy in America* (Henry Reeve, transl.). New York: Century, 1899, Vol. I, p. 398.

relationship between the institutions of a people and its relevant ideological elements. The actional tendencies of the individuals and groups living under the institutions are organized in the patterns of the ideology, especially its values, beliefs, and rules; and, reciprocally, these patterns as they appear in the thought and behavior of the persons support the institutions.[8]

IV: The Organization of the Division of Labor and the Specialization of Function

In every society, and especially in large and complex societies, there are many kinds of tasks that need to be performed. At the same time the population consists of persons diverse in natural endowment, training, and opportunity, differentiated as groups and categories. Organizing the multiplicity of activities and the heterogeneous population that performs the tasks requires one of the most crucial systematizations of human behavior.

None of the cooperating individuals and groups constituting a society can carry on *all* of the functions necessary in a society or the *whole* of any particular social task. Furthermore, even if all individuals or groups were capable at all times, it still would be impossible without systematization to carry on simultaneously all the activities that are required.

The essential social tasks or activities of any social system are divided and subdivided among the interdependent population elements according to specific task criteria, personnel requirements, and organizational principles. The extensive and varied activities are broken down and allocated to capable individuals. In general, the division of labor is characteristic of all organization; in fact, each implies the other.

The division of tasks and specialization of function, wherever conducted in any department of activity, enables each such societal division of the whole to make its maximum contribution to the total agency or operation. Moreover the system of divided and specialized function provides the possibility for every type of person to find a place best fitted to his abilities.

Fairly effective coordination of the division of labor and specialization of function with the differentiated population is one of the basic essentials in societal integration. In general, if the organizational system is operating fairly well, the innumerable divided and specialized

[8] Cf. Ralph Turner, "Culture, Change and Confusion," *Pub. Opin. Quart.*, 4 (Dec., 1940): 579–600.

tasks are apportioned among the members according to their particular proficiencies. Dissimilar persons and categories are enabled to function within the range of their capacities, interests, cultural backgrounds, and opportunities.

Thus by interlocking diverse parts into a whole, division of labor creates social solidarity.

V: The Status-Role System

Interwoven with the system of participation just discussed is the status-role system; that is, the societal behavior system concerned with (1) the types of positions or statuses occupied by the participants in the system with respect to each other, including the factors, instrumentalities, and processes involved in their location and alignment in those positions, and (2) the roles, or the patterned parts, or regularly performed activities, in these positions. Each function in the division of labor has two aspects: the status or structural aspect, and the role or behavioral aspect. Both functions are involved in the total structural and functional pattern of a society, and are the constituent elements in all the standard patterns of relationship and reciprocity among the human beings in the society, and in all of the essential or common or recurrent activities of these individuals in their numerous relationships with each other. In effect, most of the structural and functional analyses of society are simply concerned with more detailed classifications of statuses and roles, with the analysis of different bundles of them in the departments or blocks of social life, with their significance in the stratification system, with their institutionalization, with their change, and with their maintenance.

STATUSES IN SOCIAL ORGANIZATION

Every individual and every category of individuals has a standard social position or identifiable point of location in the organizational pattern or scheme of social relations. There are, of course, an infinite number of possible patterns of relationship, and hence, of possible statuses. All of the statuses are rather definitely typed and defined, and have a structural-functional significance quite apart from any particular individuals who may occupy them at any given time. In fact, the people in the statuses come and go, but the social statuses persist as a fixed phase of the total social organization.

An almost universal way of obtaining organization is through the establishment of the statuses, each of which is related to a societal function or set of related functions. These functions are mainly in the economic, familial, political, religious, military, and educational departments of life, and every function as performed has its related status for the performer. In considerable part, most statuses exist in order to guarantee the performance of certain duties and tasks so that certain purposes and goals may be realized. The functions are performed by standard categories of persons known by such designations as father, employer, teacher, engineer, and so on. Functionally, each status has a relationship to the total operation of the society and some degree of significance in it. All of them are expressions of the interdependent structuring of a society at a given time and stage of development.

Each holder of a standard status has certain characteristic duties and obligations that relate to his function. Thus a father should provide for and protect his family; a carpenter should do proficient carpentry; and a governor should govern. But the given status also embodies and defines certain rights, privileges, opportunities, and immunities that go with the status as well as certain restrictions, limitations, and prohibitions. All of these content elements give it its distinctive and specific definition.

Each status is relative to, and usually interdependent with, the statuses of all other individual and group units. There is no such thing as solitary status; status is always social. The functions are conducted in reciprocal, complementary, or polar relationship with other persons.

The different statuses carry varying degrees of esteem or disesteem. The value placed upon the different positions seems to depend upon the group's or society's estimation or interpretation of the need for the function, of the type of social demands made upon the holder, and, in some instances, upon the moral effect of the position upon the community. The statuses involve different societal functions, which differ greatly in difficulty and importance, and require different types and combinations of characteristics, different degrees and qualities of ability, skill, will, achievement, and ethical consciousness on the part of the performers. The more highly evaluated statuses are in many instances, though not all, those that are functionally important; and for them to be functionally important means that the adequate performance of the typical functions contributes in a fundamental way to the maintenance of the community or society. Usually, the functionally most important statuses or the socially most strategic require abilities, training, and other qualities that are fairly limited in the population.

A status system is not only a means of allocation of social function; it also invokes a set of value judgments according to which individuals, categories of individuals, and groups are ranked along scales, such as superior or inferior, high or low, even social or anti-social, in relation to one another. Thus, for example, on functional grounds, we have the low status of unskilled or casual laborer, and the high status of lawyer, or physician, or corporation official; and on moral grounds, the low rank accorded the racketeer or narcotic vender. Since the status system includes every member of a group or society, every individual has some rank in every interactional situation. Each rank, in turn, carries with it some degree of esteem, privilege, deference, or ascendance, as compared with those of different rank.

With respect to the wider structural-functional significance, Newcomb has referred to the social statuses as the "construction blocks" of societies and social groups.[9] It can be said that groups or societies, as functional entities with arranged and reciprocal elements, are structures composed as statuses. All the statuses in a group or society are more or less integrated into a total system of division of function, interlocking obligations and rights, and a value-scaled hierarchy of ranks. The status interrelations are a kind of cement that binds a social system together.

ROLES IN SOCIAL ORGANIZATION

Social roles are the other major set of items in the status-role bundle. Role particularly refers to the actual behavioral aspect of societal organization; a role consists concretely of the standardized, patterned, and expected action of all actors in a given social status or position. It is the way in which a person carries into action the configuration of rights and obligations of a status position he occupies within a group. It is a status translated into action. Status has mainly a structural connotation; it is concerned with position or location of individuals, vis-à-vis others, in a social system; people occupy the different statuses. Role, on the other hand, has an operational connotation; it is the dynamic, processual, actional part of the bundle—what the actor does in his relations with others as seen in the context of its functional significance for the system; people enact or perform roles. Role behavior thus is the observable form that social participation takes as persons interact in the common or recurrent types of social situations.

Sooner or later the analyst of social organization (or disorganization, too, for that matter) must get down to the atoms of a community or society; namely, the individuals. All that is done is done by them in combinations, in types of relationships, under various conditions. *What* they do and *how* they do it is mainly a matter of the system's system of roles. Conversely, a group or society as a functioning system consists elementally of its constituent individuals performing roles. Roles have both societal and individual organizational aspects. Societally, roles are the network of concrete ways in which the multitude of tasks are carried out; they are the means of patterning, controlling, and directing behavior

[9] T. M. Newcomb, *Social Psychology*. New York: Dryden, 1950, pp. 275–280.

of all the people toward the fulfillment of these tasks; similarly, they are the means whereby the many essential functions are allocated among the members of a system. The relationships between individuals, categories, and groups are peaceful and orderly, and the functions of the group or community or society are carried out adequately *if* the roles in the many typical interactional situations are played with reasonable persistence, consistency, and accuracy.

Another societal gain occurs because by means of the role system the group or society can be quite certain that it gets its necessary action in the right way and at the right time in every particular situation. Once roles have been acquired and practiced, they function as stimulus patterns, as tendencies to respond that are set off by occasion or relationship.

The role system also provides a high degree of predictability in social relations. All social behavior is reciprocal. The role system establishes the complementary duties and expectations in all typical situations. Thus, each individual and each group of a community or society know what to expect in the way of behavior from others.

Society must be certain that most of the standard roles are adequately learned by the individuals who will have to play them. As the basic components of the total actional scheme of things, their performance in their respective positions and in quality of performance cannot be left to chance. Inculcation of roles and motivation for their performance are very important aspects of the sociocultural process.

Many of the roles are ascribed; that is, they accompany positions that are fixed by such unavoidable conditions as sex, age, family relationships, order of birth in family, race, nativity, social class, or locality. But a large portion—and a growing portion in modern society—of the roles that individuals have to play daily and throughout their lives are achieved; for example, most occupational, political, religious roles. The successful performance of these vastly differentiated roles depends upon greatly varying innate capacities, interests, knowledge and skills, and other acquirable proficiencies. Thus every group and organization must have means, ranging from the informal to the highly organized, of selecting or sorting out individuals and categories of persons on the basis of the functional and normative criteria of eligibility for the innumerable roles, and of assigning them effectively and fairly to the specialized roles on the basis of potential or tested fitness.

The discussion of the stratification system as the means of selecting and assigning people and making them operative in the differentiated and hierarchized social structure of statuses and roles should logically occur at this point in the analysis of imperative instrumentalities. It has been alluded to as a background structural system in the preceding chapter and will be treated in its institutionalized aspects in Chapter Fifteen.

VI: The Regulative Systems

An adequately organized society is a well-regulated society; and a well-regulated society is one in which social order obtains. To be sure, there exists in any society a degree of toleration and permissibility of variation, schism, opposition, individualism, anti-sociality, lack of participation and responsibility, and relative inefficiency. Nevertheless, no society can go beyond certain limits of stalemate, friction, maladjustment, or disorder if the society is to be maintained and perpetuated.[10]

It will be helpful at the outset to have some sort of over-all conception of the specific objectives of social regulation:

(1) Bring about and preserve conformity to the life-values, the norms, and the accepted and required usages of the group or society by instruction, persuasion, discipline, and compulsion.

(2) Create and preserve the cohesion of the members.

(3) Aid and preserve functional efficacy. These latter two objectives involve (among other things) placing people most effectively in the division of labor, so that they can carry out their societally-defined roles and fill adequately both their ascribed and achieved statuses.

(4) Promote the continuity of the community or society through regular biological, physical, and sociocultural maintenance, and through continuous, constructive reorganization directed toward change believed to be societally beneficial.

(5) Protect against inordinate individualization of conduct, which would undermine the positive conditions and result in anarchy. Meeting this objective requires particularly the restraint of the aggressive and selfish members.

(6) Curb individual and group deviant (variant and wayward) tendencies that lead to such anti-social conduct as conflict, criminality, immorality, exploitation of others, deliberate refusal to participate adequately, deliberate dissension, perversion, subversiveness (political and otherwise). Not only must the deviant tendencies be prevented or counteracted, but in advanced societies, efforts should be made to reform and reclaim deviant individuals and groups.

Social order does not come about automatically; and a well-regulated society, especially a huge modern one, is not self-regulatory. It is

---

[10] On social order, see: L. K. Frank, "What Is Social Order?" *Am. Jour. Soc.*, 49 (Mar., 1944): 470–477. F. Znaniecki, *Cultural Sciences: Their Origin and Development*. Urbana: Univ. of Illinois Press, 1952, pp. 1–92.

governed by a complex and extensive system of rules and usages, of socializing, enforcing, and managing ways and means.

The normative system, discussed previously, with its extensive body of rules for all types of interactions and occasions, is the basic factor in societal regulation; all regulation must be founded upon the *regula,* the rules. The major blocks of social institutions, especially the technological, familial, economic, educational, political, religious, and aesthetic institutions, are the massive instrumentalities whereby regulation in most areas of societal life is conducted.

At this point we will briefly discuss three general functional systems that are involved in all of the regulative systems.

THE SOCIALIZATION SYSTEM

The socialization system or regimen is in operation in every durable community or society. Broadly conceived, it consists of the whole set of agencies and processes whereby the entire cultural system of a society is transmitted from generation to generation and to incoming new members, and also whereby it is made operative to some extent. All of the members of a community or society have to achieve a sufficient degree of integration with their fellows and a sufficient degree of quality of participation in its functions; they need to be behaviorally proficient in *all* of the different, standard, interactional situations that they are likely to find themselves in from infancy to death.

The objective of the socialization system, therefore, is to get into the consciousness and the behavior makeup of every individual *all* of the socially defined and required ways of thinking, believing, feeling, and acting so that they will be part of his personality and be carried into effect in his every activity. What this amounts to is the internalization and canalization of all the other behavior-organizing systems here discussed. Each actor—each participant—must communicate with others; hence, he must be minimally proficient in the use of the formalized symbol system, especially the community's language, writing, and other standard signals. He must have a certain minimal amount of the extant knowledge and understand the common definitions and meanings. He must have adequate value-orientation, especially with respect to the major ideologies, goals, and the extremely important norms or rules whereby behavior is judged in almost every department of life. He will have to have the skills essential to the performance of his specialties in the general division of labor. He must acquire the behavioral patterns necessary for occupying the particular combination of statuses that his societal life requires or permits him to assume. He will have to learn the roles and role complexes, and be minimally competent in their performance. He will have to be able to live in the rank (or ranks, depending upon his social mobility) allotted him in the stratification system, and be able to get along with the occupants of other strata. And as we will note, he will have to have knowledge of the principles, requirements, and sanctions of the regulative system, and some training for conformity with these. He will have to meet the minimal requirements in all of the major functional departments of the maintenance system. He will have to be inducted into the whole complex of institutionalized patterns of the society and meet the expectations of all of the systems.[11]

Concretely, socialization means such things as speaking the group language, knowing the traditions and mores, the relevant technologies and the essential related skills, behaving in a sufficiently conformable and effective manner when working, acting in sex and generation relations, playing, moving in traffic, or acting in political and religious relations. The social element in individuals is the result of socialization. The socialized person has the "situational learnings" and the "situational leanings" for the essential positive activities of normal social life. He is "society broken."

If the socialization system is not adequately operative, it is likely that none of the behavior-organizing systems will be effective; nor will they be jointly effective in organizing the total behavior of the individuals.[12] If the socialization system does not provide the members of the society with these basic orientations, a disequilibration will very likely occur. In fact, the reverse of socialization is *desocialization,* which is a form of disorganization.

Socialization is an economical way of getting many important things done in a society. For example, the arbitrary application of physical, psychological, and social force is arduous, requires great expenditure of a society's energy, and involves the devotion of much attention and means to mere ordering of life instead of to the satisfaction of many higher wants. But if the basic behavior requirements are interiorized or built into the individuals, then individual and even group action is self-starting in most standard situations, and the use of compulsion and coercion through external social agencies is largely avoided.

We, of course, are primarily concerned with the fact that it is by means of the socialization system that standard patterns of action are continuously transmitted and instilled in most of its members. The particular regulative objective is, as far as possible, to produce persons who are so innerly conditioned and developed that they act almost automati-

[11] Cf.: T. Parsons and E. A. Shils, *Toward a General Theory of Action.* Cambridge: Harvard Univ. Press, 1951, pp. 227–228. M. J. Herskovits, *Cultural Anthropology.* New York: Knopf, 1955, p. 326.

[12] There is point to the use of the phrase "the super-ordinate socialization system." T. Parsons and R. F. Bales, *Family, Socialization and Interaction Process.* Glencoe, Ill.: Free Press, 1955, p. 212.

cally in regularized fashion—not only unconsciously and automatically, but willingly and from conviction.

From birth on, socialization is a matter of conditioning. The societally safe and essential attitudes, values, ideas, emotional sets, norms, and habits are continuously being formed and fixed. Although much of this conditioning is unobtrusive, effected by simply living in the atmosphere of social examples and pressures, organization of behavior is too important in societal organization to be left to chance. Hence, there is much deliberate and continuous informal as well as institutionally organized, inculcation, instruction, indoctrination, training, and disciplining. Especially important as socializing agencies are family groups and all levels of schools.

THE ENFORCING SYSTEM

Although every society depends on its socialization system as its primary and basic regulative agency, this system does not and cannot produce in all persons sufficiently conformable behavior in all departments of social life. Any society would prefer to have all of its essential social behavior completely inner-directed, but the socialization processes for a number of reasons are not completely effective.

First, there are weaknesses and errors in the socialization system itself. There is still confusion as to the values lying behind the very norms that should be inculcated. There is uncertainty as to the content of socialization—what is absolutely necessary to impart and at the same time possible to impart. The socializers are still to some degree groping for knowledge and principles regarding the organizing and conducting of the procedures of learning and disciplining, especially in a society such as our own in which the ancient primary group and folk processes of learning and disciplining are entirely inadequate.

Second, few people are completely free of individual weaknesses at all times, and many for one reason or other have been insufficiently trained by the socialization system. There are those with individual weaknesses or pathologies of a physical, mental, emotional, or moral nature expressed by behavior which is incompetent. Some have behavior which is deviant because of bad conditioning and other reasons. There are those who deliberately engage in anti-social behavior for selfish purposes. Others are socially defiant, escapist, and jump the fences of regulation. Many are sufficiently competent to engage in minimally adequate social activity but lack social maturity. They lack social consciousness and the ability or willingness to recognize the social effects of their own action; hence, they frequently act foolishly, irresponsibly, even anti-socially. They are careless with guns, lighted cigarettes, and empty bottles; they drive cars hazardously; they litter parks and other public places. Some of us, perhaps most of us, would do one or more of these things were it not for the threat imposed by the enforcing system. In general, it can be said that for one reason or another, very few individuals in any society are socialized enough to act completely socially in every situation at all times.

A society, however, *has* to have a certain amount of conformable overt action from everyone if it is to operate in a sufficiently orderly and functionally efficient manner. The enforcing system exists in all societies to correct the weaknesses and failures of the socialization system and to supplement it with externalized modes of regulation. People must act overtly according to the society's experiential norms with their "public selves," even if their "private selves" are at fault.[13]

There must always be some curtailment of liberty, even in the most socially efficient and democratic societies. The enforcement system is concerned with constraining, preventing, and prohibiting immoral, illegal, or otherwise socially inept or harmful action. Without some constraint upon the deviant action tendencies of individuals and groups, the coordination of action and regularity of conduct necessary to a society could not materialize. Many individuals have to be forced, or at least threatened with force, in order to conform outwardly with the norms, even if the norms are not understood or respected by them.

There is the positive regulative action that encourages desirable social behavior by prodding lazy individuals, holding out rewards of some kind for conformity. Also, the regulative system has certain corrective, reformative aspects in most societies, since it is socially economical to attempt to re-educate the social deviant by developing respect in him for the norms.

Society enforces its regulations by a *system of sanctions* whereby individuals and groups are confronted with the social consequences of their conforming and non-conforming behavior. Some actions are approved, others disapproved. The approved actions are positively sanctioned or rewarded; the disapproved actions are negatively sanctioned or penalized.

Rewarding utilizes the positive influences of promises, social approvals, and the precious social securities. Individuals, groups, communities, whole societies do much rewarding, for they have found that it is an effectual regulatory procedure. In general, it is a way of sinking the social will deep into the source-springs of human conduct.

Penalties are coercive, and their application involves degrees of prohibition, with the threat of punishment. The underlying principle seems to be that no rule is secure if it can be transgressed with impunity;

[13] Terms used by R. T. LaPiere, *The Theory of Social Control*. New York: McGraw-Hill, 1954, p. 56.

therefore, disobedience or divergence must be prevented if possible; but if it does occur, the transgressor must be penalized, both as a lesson to him and as an example to others. It might be pointed out that most societies have paid much more attention to, and have made much more use of, penalties and punishments in their regulative activities than they have of rewarding.

In a modern, complex society there is more and more resort to formal regulation, in part because so many more, or at least so many more societally significant, actions are of an impersonal, contractual, and public nature. This means that regulation too must be more and more public, and hence conducted by the state. The societally significant norms and sanctions are more and more embodied in codes, regulations, ordinances, administrative rules, and laws, planned and devised under some sort of constitutional grant by legislative and administrative bodies. These bodies of rules are interpreted by, and their presumed violators judged by, formal courts. The efforts at prevention of violation, investigation of presumed violations, and the apprehension of suspected violators is conducted by public officials—police, constabulary, militia. The correction and punishment (and efforts at reformation) are carried on in institutionalized state agencies.

THE POWER-AUTHORITY SYSTEM

This system is absolutely essential in making the regulating activities effective. Social power and social authority, like statuses and roles, are a bundle of functionally interrelated elements. Power is mainly exercised as authority; the two combine as an elemental structural-functional aspect of most social systems. This system can be said to be the means whereby social energy is exercised and directed.

Social power is a universal phenomenon in all social relationships; it is by no means confined to economic, political, and military situations. It appears in most interstatus relationships and wherever some degree of dominance of one component over another is or must be exercised. Social power usually means the ability of some person, group, or organization to introduce and employ some kind of force—not necessarily physical—in social situations, and thus, directly or indirectly, control other persons, categories, groups, or organizations. It is necessary for every social entity to present and employ force of some kind and degree in most of its relationships. Social action is not necessarily self-energizing. Furthermore, there are always social ignorances and resistances to be overcome. Thus, of necessity, the father exercises power over the child, the policeman (when necessary) over the presumed violator of the law, the boss over the workman, the teacher over the pupil, the employer over the employee, the captain over his crew, or almost any formal organization over its members. The essence of social power is coercion; that is, the capacity to require submission to the power holder's commands or demands. Coercion involves requiring, commanding, even physically forcing others to act, or to refrain from acting, in a manner chosen, not by the actor, but by the power-full. Inherent in it also, as noted above, is the ability to apply sanctions; that is, penalizing for failure to comply and rewarding for satisfactory compliance.

It is necessary to utilize social force to restrain all anti-social manifestations. The greedy, the vicious, and the lawless must be prevented from acting, and the lazy and the shirkers must be required to act; disputes must be settled and conflict prevented as far as possible; the norms must be enforced; the statuses and social strata must be ordered with respect to each other. It is necessary to curb the encroachments of stronger organizations over weaker ones, and to coordinate all maintenance and regulative procedures and agencies.

Every community and society, of necessity, has a power system; that is, a scheme of established and more or less accepted superordination and subordination. It consists of power-full elements which, however, do not always function in a uniform manner, or with mutually consistent objectives, or in a socially safe and acceptable manner. A power system may, as a matter of fact, be used in an unsocial or anti-social fashion (bossing, buccaneering, racketeering, or unauthorized physical violence). Furthermore, those who wield power usually produce change; and the change produced may not always redound to the well-being of the community.

Power of any kind, whether physical, mental, or social, implies energy that leads to effect; it is a quantity of force that bears on elements and actually or potentially causes action. It may produce results that, according to the value system of the group involved, may be good or bad, constructive or destructive. To prevent the misuse of social power, in order to channel it, and use it most effectively and with the least wear and tear on the dominated, much of it, as it applies to common and recurrent social relationships and situations, is converted into authority.

Authority is the socially acceptable, institutionalized exercise of social force in the ordering of social relationships and the conducting of social functions. It not only legitimizes power but channels and focuses it in the interests of specific and supposedly desirable action. Authority vests power in the socially right agencies. It is made effective through authorities which, with their delegated, established, and vested social power, have the form of certain persons, groups, specialized categories of persons, organized groups and associations, and institutions. These authorized agents are informally and formally granted the right to wield the power; in many types of situations, because of the specific, strategic functions of the agents in the particular social system, they are socially obligated to wield power.

Most of the authority of a society like our own is exercised through formal organizations. Here it is clearly specified and formally articulated by the norms—the rules, statutes, laws—of the association. The right to use the power is attached to or invested in certain depersonalized organizational statuses referred to as *offices*—bishops and priests, generals, presidents, foremen, managers. These have the power, the responsibility, legitimatized by the appropriate and accepted organizations and institutions of the society, to exercise dominance in the different departments of life in the interests of order and efficacy: parents advise, discipline, and correct; priests and clergy admonish and excommunicate; political officers administer public organizations and procedures, correct, arrest, judge, and punish; industrial and business managers arrange and organize operations; teachers instruct and train. In general, the status-holders and organizations exercising legitimatized social power set values, pronounce judgments, make decisions, determine policies, command the services and compliance of others, and assign, organize, and execute tasks in the different departments of social life.

The authorized person is distinguishable from a leader. The leader may inspire and direct; he may have charisma and competencies; but his leadership depends upon personal qualities; the fiat or the power of the leader lacks legitimacy. The authorized person or the official, on the other hand, does not act as a person, but as the agent of an established functional association; he *requires* action. The person subjected to an order by a competent authority has no alternative but to obey, even when he is unacquainted with the person issuing it. As Biersted puts it, "Leadership is a species of influence; authority is a function of power."

Each association, no matter how small or temporary (a promotional or review committee, or one to put on a special dinner meeting), or how large and permanent (a military establishment, a governmental department or bureau, an industrial or commercial corporation, an educational organization), has its own structure of authority. As Bierstedt points out, authority is always a property of social organization. It appears only in organized groups, never in unorganized groups or in the unorganized community; the organized group or community is organized by means of the authority. At the same time, the authority exercised is supported and sanctioned by the association or community itself. In most instances, especially in American organizations, it is the majority of the members of an association who support the authority structure and sustain it in its operation. The power behind the authority resides in the majority of its members; they delegate it to the authorized agents. The exercise of authority never extends beyond the functional boundaries of the association in which it is institutionalized.

VII: The Maintenance Systems

If a society is to endure as a functional system beyond the life of the founders or of any one generation, there are certain more or less patterned maintenance activities, based on the experience of the particular people concerned, that are essential. They are conducted according to norms, ranging from mere folkways to the most highly institutionalized rules and regulations of an ethical, scientific-technological, and political nature. The more insistent or grave become certain aspects of maintenance because of changes in societal needs, the more certain it is that the procedures and agencies involved will be more and more systematically organized; and to be organized, as we have noted, is to be regulated.

The other previously discussed regulatory systems, and for that matter all of the systems for organizing societal behavior, can be viewed as aspects of the maintenance system if the system is conceived in all of its vast dimensions and manifold functions. We are here concerned, however, with four specific subsystems that have direct and fundamental maintenance functions; namely, those concerned with (1) population, (2) physical-economic, (3) cultural, and (4) societal maintenance.

POPULATION MAINTENANCE

In order to exist, every society must maintain the number of its population. Basically, there are three sets of demographic processes involved in the number of any given population: reproduction, mortality, and migration (in and out). There must be recruitment of members in sufficient number to replace those lost by death or emigration. Although migration has probably been a recurrent factor in the number of a given population, the first two are the predominant ones for any given area, and the sole factors in the number of world population.

Elementally, population maintenance among mankind as among other species is a biological matter. But nowhere and at no time, as far as we know, has population performance among men been purely biological or natural. Sociocultural, including especially the technological and regulative, systems enter into every aspect of it to such an extent that it is, in effect, manipulated and regulated behavior as much as any other behavior. Marriage, fertility, morbidity and mortality, location, and movement and migration have been greatly influenced by values, norms, and principles, and by techniques and agencies, and have been subjected to regulative efforts both of a promotive and restrictive nature. Modern societies have not only their folkways, customs, and mores relating to all aspects of population maintenance, but an ever expanding body of policies and programs, often established in legislation, and administered by appropriate public agencies. Certain important aspects of population maintenance will be examined specifically in the treatments of the familial and the health and welfare institutions in Part 3.

PHYSICAL-ECONOMIC MAINTENANCE

A society must provide the mechanisms, physical and social, and the techniques to assure the satisfaction of the physical needs, and hence assure the physical survival of its members. There must be provision for food, clothing, shelter, and the other bodily comforts. These essentials must be adequately produced, distributed, and utilized by the population. There must be accessibility by transportation to enable them to cooperate and exchange products and services with each other, and the resources must be available to the population. There must be protection against harmful physical forces and catastrophies, harmful unhygienic environmental conditions, harmful organisms and animals, disease, injury and accident. There must be protection against humans, within and without, bent on the destruction of the members. There must be provision against societal neglect or mismanagement, and adequate administration of any of these activities. The provision of these essentials to physical existence is basic to the conduct of all other features of social and societal life; men must exist adequately in a physical sense in order to perform any of the functions of life.

To meet these needs the physical environment must be manipulated, even reconstructed; there must be continuous renewal of the material apparatus employed; there must be ever newer mechanisms and procedures for continually adjusting the population to the changing physical and biological environment.

All this maintenance involves some observance of natural laws and various kinds of social organizational regulations. Man can live economically only in areas where the physical circumstances, such as climate, topography, altitude, and resources are conducive to, or permissive of, human physical existence. Thus, he has to live and maintain himself within the limits set by nature. Thus his manipulation of the physico-chemical and biological phenomena must be based on established scientific principles (laws) and demonstrated technological procedures, consisting of rules and regulations that standardize almost all of the individual and collective work behavior and govern the use of tools and machines, as well as the innumerable and complex regular and sequential technical procedures. In other words, man, although increasingly the selector, planner, adapter, manipulator, conserver, and constructer of his physical and biological world, nevertheless, has to do these things according to scientific laws, which in turn are based on natural laws, and according to principles of action that have grown out of technological experience.

Many of the processes of physical maintenance are also complicated by the fact that they consist of satisfying unlimited wants in a world of limited extent, out of a stock of goods that is limited at any given time, and by human beings with limited energies and time for given tasks. Hence, there must be a vast array of regulations governing the men-to-men, men-to-resources, and men-to-organization situations and relations. As examples there might be mentioned the rules regarding the possession, use, exchange, and disposal of property; the rules regarding contractual relations; the rules with respect to distribution, that is, how much and to whom under varying conditions; the rules affecting value and price; the rules affecting employer-employee relations—wages, work load and so on. Communication and transportation facilities cannot be operated without rules and standardized and synchronized procedures.

Even the final consumption of economic goods and services by the members of the society is affected by a great array of folkways, customs, and regulations and laws, many of the latter government-originated. Notable are all of those influences—even pressures—involved in the standard of living: class values and norms; etiquette forms; dietary notions and rules based on religious or ethnic group taboos and sometimes prompted by scientific findings; the dictates of fads and fashions; and ordinances and laws governing prohibited items (for example, harmful drugs, weapons).[14]

CULTURE MAINTENANCE

Not only must a society concern itself continually with its physical maintenance, but its whole cultural stock in trade, its whole contrived set of behavioral tools must be kept continually abreast of its needs. This means maintaining not only its technological-mechanical procedures and agencies but also the knowledge and ideas about nature, the social behavior, aesthetic and artistic behavior, moral standards, religious beliefs and practices, and so on; it means maintaining also the society's institutional features since these affect every major depart-

[14] Economic maintenance will be examined in an institutionalized system in Chapter Eleven. See end of this chapter for a list of references.

ment of social life. Its whole distinctive, complex, man-made pattern or design of ways and means of thinking and doing things must be kept efficient. The reason for this need of continuous maintenance in every society is that its culture tends to fall behind to some degree, especially along certain lines relative to other lines; that is, the society functions less well than it could or needs to in order to continue to achieve its over-all objectives.

It is obvious that maintaining a culture is something quite different from keeping it intact. Today an intact culture would mean a static culture, and hence an ever more archaic, inept, inadequate culture and a stagnant, functionally deteriorating society. The only adequate culture is a continually developing one. This development involves several essential processes.

There must be a constant inventorying of the various culture elements in the different major departments of social life; a checking of their functional adequacy within themselves for meeting the corresponding social needs; and a checking of their reciprocal adequacy with respect to the other related aspects of culture.

The society's knowledge about all the areas of phenomena with which it is concerned, which is the basis of the major culture maintenance processes discussed next, must be continually added to and corrected by observation, experimentation, recording, and testing.

Above all, though, cultural development depends upon the innovation processes, whereby new ideas, new culture objects, new usages and mechanisms are developed independently within the framework of the given culture by utilizing its applicable knowledge and by manipulating and combining existing and available cultural components and producing new items. The actual processes of innovation, which provide means of adjusting to ever changing conditions, are discovery and invention, both closely related. It is obvious that new culture elements anywhere can be derived only from discovery and invention sometime and somewhere. These are the master processes. It should also be pointed out that deliberate discovery and invention involve important regulatory principles. They have to be conducted on the basis of established scientific facts, principles, and technological procedures.

The culture of every society is also maintained by borrowing and adapting what are deemed to be compatible, desirable, or essential elements from all other societies with which they have contact or with which contact can be made. In most modern societies this borrowing is increasingly conscious, studied, even aggressive.

Finally, the culture of any society, if it is to serve its essential functions, must be continually checked for outmoded elements, for lags, gaps, and inconsistencies.

In general, a culture must be, as far as possible, at any given time, a unified, integrated, balanced, synchronized, functioning entity. At the same time it cannot be static; it must be continually emergent and flowing; it must be discarding, merging, assimilating, and equilibrating its elements.

SOCIETAL MAINTENANCE

All of the systems organizing human behavior for efficacious societal operation that have been examined, especially the regulative subsystems, are essential to societal maintenance. The great institutional-organizational systems with their regulative maintenance functions, to be examined in Part 3, and which cover the major areas of societal operation, such as the economic, the marriage and family, the political, legal, military, the educational, the scientific-technological, the expressional, and the recreational-health-welfare systems, are the major sets of instrumentalities whereby societal maintenance is assured. Here we briefly note certain specific conditions that must prevail and certain specific processes and procedures that must be conducted if a society is to be continuously and effectively maintained. The items here discussed grow from the fact (1) that there must be a continuous bolstering and stimulating of essential socialized conduct quite apart from any system of rewards and penalties; (2) that the diverse, unequal, variously ordered and ranked, separated, dissenting, and conflicting individuals, categories, and groups must be continually adjusted to each other; (3) that a distinctly human level of living must be maintained, if the society is to carry on; and finally (4) that structural-functional reorganization must be continually carried on.

BASIC BEHAVIOR REQUIREMENTS. Among other things, if any society is to be continuously and prosperously maintained, the persons and groups must first be motivated to act along all desirable and essential lines, and second they must have morale, that is, a tone of cooperative life and social cohesiveness and loyalty.

Motivation and inducement. Social motivation is concerned with all those energizing factors, processes, and procedures that produce, or can be marshalled to produce, positive, societally contributory individual and group action. By means of it, the members of the social system are so impelled from without and within that they perform to the best of their ability their share of the activities essential to meeting the functional needs of the system. Under its stimulus, the members try to understand the norms in the different departments of social life and meet the expectations relating to them; they make effort to cooperate with others in their respective statuses; they seek to play all their socially relevant roles in a purposive, competent, fair, non-parasitic manner. Conversely, the sufficiently motivated individual's or group's behavior is *not* characterized by lethargy, by indifference, by unsocial deviance, by lack of participation, or by anti-socialness. If adequately motivated, the members *want* to act as they *should* act, not because of outer pressure, but from a socially conscious inner compulsion.

Whatever ways and means a social system may have in motivating its members to social action, it seems that these must be bolstered and supplemented by a system of inducements to act with respect to, and in the direction of, the system's specific, valued objectives. There must be something over and above joy in work; unrewarded altruism cannot be depended upon as a sufficient means of eliciting socially adequate behavior. Hence, there usually exists some system of inducements that incites people to do things in a socially adequate manner. Our social system uses *esteem,* the kind of approval that comes with the faithful fulfillment of the duties of a position, and *prestige,* the approval that comes from *having* a position—a position that has been striven for.

Morale. A society needs more than mere motivation; it needs also to have at all times that social psychic state called morale if unity and effective operation are to be maintained. Such a state is especially necessary in a society like ours which, because of its vast diversities, its intense competitive relations, and its many cleavages, must contend continually with prevailing as well as occasional crisic threats to its unity and its essential functioning.

Morale is a dynamic, unifying factor in human social action which is fundamentally essential to the stability and functional efficacy of any social system. It consists of a unified state of attitude, emotion, and thinking among the members which makes for a dominating, over-all loyalty to, and oneness of, the group, and an effective devotion and commitment to its essential objectives. When there is adequate morale, there are among the members substantial convictions as to the worthiness of group ends, beliefs, and ideals; a high level of mutual and reciprocal good will; a unity of resolution and purpose; a cohesion of members and focusing of action in the form of intelligent and organized teamwork; a willingness and readiness to make sacrifices in behalf of the causes of the group or society; and finally, an abiding belief that the group's causes can and will be realized. When morale is poor, a state of demoralization exists.

Beyond motivation and morale as essentials in societal maintenance, there is an array of adjustive processes and procedures, the more important of which will be noted.

Equalization of opportunity. In a society such as ours, with its requirements of much standardization, even regimentation, its differentiation and stratification, on the one hand, and its need for a great diversity of well-selected and well-developed abilities and skills, on the other, equalization processes, which consist of granting and maintaining certain freedoms and rights, are an essential aspect of societal maintenance. The societally essential task in this respect is *not* that of bringing the actors to a dead-level or even an average of performance, position, or social reward, but in equalizing the opportunities—educational, economic, political, cultural—for social achievement. The society needs the maximum use of its existing talents, and it is pretty generally agreed that this, in turn, requires equality of opportunity. Any considerable inequality of opportunity is bound to deprive the society of the full range of its potential talents.[15]

The freedoms have two aspects: first, they imply some degree of independence of, or immunity to, or exemption or liberation from, restraint, from submission to the power or control of others; second, they are privileges of self-direction in knowing, learning, believing, thinking, acting, and enjoying results. The *rights* are the specific freedoms claimed, permitted, guaranteed and enforced by the society for its members; in a phrase, the rights are the socially granted freedoms. A well-maintained society permits as many freedoms and grants as many rights as is consonant with general order, in order to enable as many as possible to have an equal chance or opportunity to develop and invest their capacities.

Our own American, long and proudly stressed set of rights, both the formally stated ones in our Constitution and those informally maintained, make possible a considerable number of gains in societal maintenance, notably the release and the effective utilization of many of our human potentialities and abilities; they permit our members to explore and experiment, to discover and invent, to plan and foresee along almost all lines of human interest; they function as safety valves and keep social abscesses from forming, since people can discuss matters, try out schemes, blow off steam; and finally, they make possible in some degree not only a fair selection and placement of members generally, but also the recruitment of leaders and elites.

Other processes must be maintained that tend toward the equalization of opportunities and the adjustment of unequal persons, categories, and groups to each other. One set of these are the *ordination processes,* which relate to the stratification system. The incumbents of the different strata of the system have graded differences of responsibility, esteem, prestige, and usually of social power. An important societal task is to make an effort to order, arrange, or place the variant individuals, categories, and groups of the society in the different functional and prestige levels of the stratification system in as fair and efficient man-

[15] Cf. M. M. Tumin, "Rewards and Task-Orientation," *Am. Soc. Rev.,* 20 (Aug., 1955): 419–423.

ner as possible. In brief, ordination, in the sociological sense, is a process of hierarchical niche-assignment. The principles governing this assignment are of both a predetermined and experimental-competitive nature.

The processes of both physical and social mobility perform functions that make for adjustment, stability, and superior maintenance. They permit what has been aptly termed a "healthy metabolism of the social structure" by avoiding clogging and festering in a given locality or stratum. *Physical mobility* gives dissatisfied and disadvantaged persons, provided they have the means, a chance to move from a place of lesser opportunity to one of greater opportunity. It adjusts the disharmonious distribution, or the dislocations of population, as environmental, especially economic, changes occur. It makes for effective utilization of physical, industrial, and human resources; and conduces to optimal conditions of life in both the emigrating and immigrating areas.[16]

By *social mobility* we mean the advantageous movement of individuals and small groups, mainly families, both within a stratum and up or down between strata. Both kinds of social movement serve as a means of locating people appropriately with respect to their interests or proficiencies. Movement within a stratum, for example, permits transfer to a more compatible occupation of given level or skill, or to another political party, or religious denomination. Selective movement up or down the social ladder connecting the strata of the social pyramid permits individuals and families to find location and to act in a stratum where in general their abilities and interests are appropriate to, and equilibrated with, the requirements of the position. Both kinds of social mobility also serve as a means of relieving discontent, relative misplacement, and tension. They too tend to function as safety valves by relieving social pressure; by means of them individuals and groups can flow to the social cubicles and levels where they can contribute their best social performance.[17]

Adjustment of social dissension, conflict, and differences. Although dissension and opposition are present in many forms and degrees in every society all of the time, given instances of them cannot continue and intensify if the society is to maintain sufficient order and functional efficacy. They exhaust essential human and social energies, waste and

[16] See: J. Isaacs, *Economics of Migration.* London: Kegan Paul, Trench & Trubner, 1947, pp. 70–112. E. M. Kulischer, *Europe on the Move.* New York: Columbia Univ. Press, 1948, pp. 11–12, 16–18. National Resources Committee, *The Problems of a Changing Population.* Washington, D.C.: U.S. Govt. Printing Office, 1938, pp. 9–11, 116–118.

[17] Cf.: S. Andrzejewski, "Vertical Mobility and Technical Progress," *Soc. Forces,* 29 (Oct., 1950): 48–51. P. A. Sorokin, *Social Mobility.* New York: Harper, 1927, pp. 508–515, 530–546.

destroy limited resources, disrupt other essential social processes, and separate interdependent elements. There must be mechanisms for avoiding overt friction if possible, and for peacefully working out disagreements. The two major processes in bringing about effective adjustments are those of accommodation and assimilation in their various forms.

The accommodation processes consist of the sequences of procedural steps and occurrences whereby conflicting individuals and groups are brought into working relations with each other, thus permitting the parties to function either separately with a degree of peace, or even in a minimally cooperative manner. It does not mean necessarily that understanding, harmony, unity, affection, or justice have been established, or that adjustment is permanent; but operational relationships have been effected for the time being.

Social assimilation is a gradual process, usually extending over generations, which does not merely effect more or less temporary arrangements among estranged or hostile elements, as in the case of accommodation, but also brings about a more permanent adjustment of the elements because they become as one in aims and ways. The elements, in time, come to be merged, coalesced, incorporated into a relative solidarity and cooperative society; they achieve more or less unified attitudes, ideas, values, objectives, loyalties, and generally essential social activities.

THE BASIC REORGANIZATIONAL PROCEDURES. The ultimate task in societal maintenance, or in social organization generally, for that matter, is continuous societal reorganization. This is an operation closely correlated with culture maintenance and one that includes all the other maintenance procedures discussed and much more. We noted previously that social disorganization, in some degree, is continually occurring in practically every department of social life. This, in turn, is owing to the fact that some amount of change, both spontaneous and induced, but at varying tempo, is going on in the social system as a whole and in all of its subsystems. Nothing is ever completely quiescent, static, stable, permanent in form and function. The very innovations, often consciously sought, and often desirable and essential, are not always effectively fitted into the system affected. At the same time, there may not be enough change in some departments of social life because of cultural inertia, institutionalism, reactionism, social isolation, and so on. Hence, many of a society's structural instrumentalities tend to become ossified, obsolete, decadent, distorted, and its operational procedures along some lines become overly routinized, perverted, and archaic. The factors in the social situations change in kind, in number, and in combination. As a result there is social disorganization which consists of phenomena of deviance both from structural soundness and functional efficiency. The areas in which the symptoms of such disorganization are pronounced are referred to as problem situations, that is, aspects of societal life that cause concern and require special attention. If the situation in problem areas becomes acute, it may endanger the survival of the individuals and groups involved; it most certainly impairs the quality of their life, and usually prevents them from making their best contributions to their group or the over-all system.

In other words, because of the factors causing change and because of the different amounts and tempos of social change, different interrelated structures and procedures get out of gear with each other, and consequently various kinds of functional lags and disproportions become accentuated. There is always in progress some disintegration, destruction, disruption, dislocation, crystallization, suspension, or outmoding of some basic elements of sociocultural life in the way of alteration of fundamental structures, functions, and interrelationships. At the same time, the members of a society, because of new knowledges, new specializations, new technological developments, new acquisitions from other societies, are continually experiencing, even creating, new wants and needs, and old wants and needs are of necessity reconstituted or embellished, both of these necessitating compliant, purposive, functional changes. Revised and new values and objectives appear continually. People realize that the social action must be cast in new time perspectives. The past and the future must be brought into manageable present.

Any social system, in order to maintain its sufficient stability and functional efficiency, must continually balance its equilibrating factors and processes with those that tend toward disequilibrium. There needs to be a continual realignment of societal patterns and a re-establishment of functional processes and procedures to meet the ever new needs and demands of societal operation. This involves ameliorating, checking, avoiding, or preventing some situations; discarding outmoded or survivalistic parts of some institutions or organizations; and restoring or constructing others; in some instances, it means exercising a conservative influence by protecting against overrapid change; in general, it means directing change in accordance with revised goals and along desired channels.

The supreme task in societal maintenance is thus to exercise effort continually to work out problems of strain, crisis, disequilibrium; to avoid social inefficiency and disorganization; to enable persons and groups, or even the whole society, to modify or reinforce useful reorganizational instrumentalities and procedures, and borrow and construct new ones. Or, to put it more specifically, social reorganization consists of those processes and procedures whereby human groups, usually belatedly, seek to establish in some degree revised or new systems of values, schemes of behavior, relationships, organizations, institutions, and operations to meet the requirements of the continual re-equilibration of the ever changing social order. Reorganization seeks to keep the social concern organized by reacting against the ever present effects of societal disorganization.[18]

Man has never been content merely to adapt to conditions. He has always sought to adjust himself; that is, to utilize processes and develop procedures in order to direct trends and manipulate structures, forces, and processes. The more important historical and contemporary examples of such reorganization will be briefly noted here.[19]

The most widely resorted to actional forms have been the various kinds of social movements; that is, collective action involving small or large numbers of human beings and intended to produce some reorganizational effects. They have ranged from those almost entirely unorganized (like booms and rushes) to those highly organized for the pursuit of specifically defined objectives.

We are here more particularly concerned with the latter. These are movements with well-defined goals and an ideology, a set of rules, a definite organization including a conscious and devoted membership, recognized and accepted leaders and administrators, a division of labor, established procedures, and also a general body of expectations as to the results for the society as a whole. The specific, organized movements directed toward the reorganization of some segment or all of society, rather than toward escape or withdrawal from it, or protest or worry activities, in turn, range along a continuum from social reform to social revolution.

Social reform movements accept most of the existent social order, but try to correct one or a few related aspects of the social system that seem to them to be pathological, such as certain labor, penal, health, or religious conditions, for example.

In general, social reform movements are partial, piecemeal, and mainly slight, surgical or patching endeavors. There often has seemed to be the assumption in many of them that if the particular evil were eliminated or corrected then all would be well with the world. Yet, social reform has been responsible for much of the positive reorganization achieved in the past.

At the other extreme are social-economic-political revolutions, which through most of the history of so-called civilized peoples, have been the means, often under the conditions of the time the only

[18] Cf. F. Znaniecki, *Cultural Sciences: Their Origin and Development*. Urbana: Univ. of Illinois Press, 1952, pp. 353–372.

[19] These will be examined more specifically in their major area of operation; namely, in the reorganization of institutions, in Chapter Six, Section II.

means, of conducting large-scale, long-due equalizing, corrective, or other reorganizing activities. Revolution is an adjustive phenomenon of societies in an advanced stage of development—societies that are populous, established, highly differentiated, and firmly stratified, complex as to culture, and that have a multiplicity of highly organized institutions.

Revolution is a complex procedure attempting to bring about a marked and usually a rather general alteration of the entire social system. It seeks to replace most of the old with something supposedly new and better. Old social values and many of the existing institutions, especially the economic and political, are to be replaced by new ones; social power is to be lodged with other social classes or population segments; the relations between the opposed social groups are to be completely rearranged.

Although some of the revolutions have ended the worst abuses and inefficiencies of the old economic-political regimes, generally speaking, revolution is vague with respect to its specific goals and chiefly negative and destructive.

Another method of societal reorganization is a rational one. It has been developing through the ages and its influence often has extended to fairly large areas at a time. It utilizes the best available knowledge of the society at the moment and is conducted in a temperate and systematic manner. It is a procedure that is not only socially ameliorative and corrective, but has frequently been constructive, even creative. In our present age, with its developing technologies, it offers vast possibilities for economical and efficient reorganization. It is that social movement, beyond all others, that has come to be known as *social planning*.

In our time, planning has come to be one of the major formulae of organizational action, whether private, semi-public, or public. In fact, it can be set up as a postulate that planning is the crucial and imperative procedure in any effort at organization or reorganization. Obviously, the question is not one of planning or not planning, but one of how to plan.

Social planning means the organized efforts on the part of some group or groups—often groups with political jurisdiction—to achieve socially valued ends. It is concerned with eliminating hazards, correcting untoward situations, overcoming lags, filling gaps, amending, revising or otherwise positively improving existing conditions and relationships, and constructing essential functional structures or parts thereof. It is also increasingly interested, upon the basis of a study of trends and active factors, not only in forestalling crises, but in anticipating future needs, preparing for them, and indicating ways and means of satisfying them.

Action is based on careful diagnosis and, where corrective, employs the most timely and expert therapeutics available. As a procedure it deals with each situation as cautiously, as consistently, and as comprehensively as possible; it uses the best knowledge and techniques, is as economical as possible of resources utilized, both physical and human, and proceeds in a step-by-step manner.

The very nature of social life in modern society necessitates a broadening of the scope of social planning and an increasing role for public agencies. Social life has become so complex and interdependent, so fundamentally important in satisfying almost every individual and group need, that it cannot be left to chance or spontaneous forces. Modern men are coming to realize that they must organize and operate the involved mechanism that they have brought into being, and that nothing less than the very best knowledge, procedures, and instruments will do.

They are also coming to realize that their planning procedures must be continuous—that no permanent, blanket solution can be found. Society must be in a continual process of adjustment and reorganization. The objectives cannot be achieved in a short time; planning is a long-range task. Hence, we cannot think of a planned group, organization, or society, but only of one in process of continual planning.[20]

B I B L I O G R A P H Y

VALUE SYSTEM

Aberle, D. F., "Shared Values in Complex Societies," *Am. Soc. Rev.*, 15 (Aug., 1950): 495–502.

Becker, H., *Through Values to Social Interpretations*. Durham, N.C.: Duke Univ. Press, 1950, pp. 3–92, 281–305.

Blau, P. M., "Structural Effects," *Am. Soc. Rev.*, 25 (Apr., 1960): 178–193.

Cooley, C. H., *Social Process*. New York: Scribner's, 1915, pp. 283–348.

Kluckhohn, C., *et al.*, "Values and Value-Orientations in the Theory of Action," in Parsons, T., and Shills, E. A., *Toward a General Theory of Action*. Cambridge: Harvard Univ. Press, 1951, pp. 388–435.

Mukerjee, R., *The Social Structure of Values*. London: Macmillan, 1949.

Parsons, T., *The Social System*. Glencoe, Ill.: Free Press, 1951, pp. 36–45.

THE NORMATIVE SYSTEM

Anderson, A. R., and Moore, O. K., "The Formal Analysis of Normative Concepts," *Am. Soc. Rev.*, 22 (Feb., 1957): 9–17.

Bierstedt, R., *The Social Order*. New York: McGraw-Hill, 1957, pp. 173–210.

[20] For a detailed discussion of social movements in general, of social reform movements, of social revolutions, and also of dictatorships as reorganizational social movements, in terms of the causal factors, the different types, the major characteristics, the typical life-cycle, and the societal effects of each, see Hertzler, *Society in Action*, pp. 360–380, and extensive bibliography, pp. 435–438.

Davis, K., *Human Society*. New York: Macmillan, 1949, pp. 52–82.
Morris, R. T., "A Typology of Norms," *Am. Soc. Rev.,* 21 (Oct., 1956): 610–613.
Znaniecki, F., *Culture Sciences: Their Origin and Development*. Urbana: Univ. of Illinois Press, 1952, pp. 261–329.

THE IDEOLOGICAL SYSTEM

Bendix, R., "Industrialization, Ideologies, and Social Structure," *Am. Soc. Rev.,* 24 (Oct., 1959): 613–623.
De Gré, G. L., *Society and Ideology*. New York: Columbia Univ. Press, 1943.
Halpin, Ben, "The Dynamic Elements of Culture," *Ethics,* 65 (July, 1955): 235–249, esp. 240–249.
Mannheim, K., *Ideology and Utopia: An Introduction to the Sociology of Knowledge*. New York: Harcourt, Brace, 1936.
Parsons, T., *The Social System*. Glencoe, Ill.: Free Press, 1951, pp. 348–359.
Roucek, J. S., "Ideologies," in Roucek, J. S. (ed.), *Social Control*. New York: Van Nostrand, 1956, pp. 185–204.
LaPiere, R. T., *A Theory of Social Control*. New York: McGraw-Hill, 1954, pp. 269–287.
Schweitzer, Arthur, "Ideological Groups," *Am. Soc. Rev.,* 9 (Aug., 1954): 415–426.
Wirth, L., "Ideological Aspects of Social Disorganization," *Am. Soc. Rev.,* 5 (Aug., 1940): 472–482.

THE DIVISION OF LABOR AND SPECIALIZATION OF FUNCTION

Durkheim, E., *Division of Labor in Society* (G. Simpson, transl.). New York: Macmillan, 1933.
Hiller, E. T., *Social Relations and Structures*. New York: Harper, 1947, pp. 148–153.
Sorokin, P. A., *Society, Culture, and Personality*. New York: Harper, 1947, pp. 276–379.

THE STATUS-ROLE SYSTEM

Barnard, C. I., "The Functions of Status Systems," in Merton, R. K., *et al.* (eds.), *Reader in Bureaucracy*. Glencoe, Ill.: Free Press, 1952, pp. 242–254.
Davis, K., *Human Society*. New York: Macmillan, 1949, pp. 83–119.
Hickman, C. A., and Kuhn, M. H., *Individuals, Groups, and Economic Behavior*. New York: Dryden, 1956, pp. 30–39.
Hiller, E. T., *Social Relations and Structures*. New York: Harper, 1949, pp. 331–543.
LaPiere, R. T., *A Theory of Social Control*. New York: McGraw-Hill, 1954, pp. 69–98.
Nadel, F. F., *The Theory of Social Structure*. Glencoe, Ill.: Free Press, 1957, pp. 20–124.
Parsons, T., *The Social System*. Glencoe, Ill.: Free Press, 1951, pp. 24–26, 38–40, 58–131.
Parsons, T., and Shils, E. A., *Toward a General Theory of Action*. Cam-

bridge: Harvard Univ. Press, 1951, pp. 23–26, 91–98, 190–218, 349–351.

THE SOCIALIZATION SYSTEM

Coulter, C. W., "Social Control and the Conditioning of Personality," in Roucek, J. S. (ed.), *Social Control*. Princeton, N.J.: Van Nostrand, 1956, pp. 31–47.

Landis, P. H., *Social Control: Social Organization and Disorganization in Process* (rev. ed.), Philadelphia: Lippincott, 1956, pp. 41–80, 336–367.

Parsons, T., and Shils, E. A., *Toward a General Theory of Action*. Cambridge: Harvard Univ. Press, 1951, pp. 17–19, 227–230.

Selznick, Gertrude J., "Socialization," in Broom, L., and Selznick, P., *Sociology*. Evanston, Ill.: Row, Peterson, 1955, pp. 81–123.

THE ENFORCING SYSTEM

Bennett, J. W., and Tumin, M. M., *Social Life: Structure and Function*. New York: Knopf, 1948, pp. 515–541.

Hentig, Hans von, "Punishment," *Ency. Soc. Science,* New York: Macmillan 1934, Vol. 12, pp. 712–716.

Landis, P. H., *Social Control: Social Organization and Disorganization in Process* (rev. ed.). Philadelphia: Lippincott, 1956, pp. 295–320.

LaPiere, R. T., *A Theory of Social Control*. New York: McGraw-Hill, 1954, pp. 218–248, 390–396.

Radcliffe-Brown, A. R., "Sanction Special," *Ency. Soc. Science,* New York: Macmillan, 1934, Vol. 13, pp. 531–534.

THE POWER-AUTHORITY SYSTEM

Bierstedt, R., "The Sociology of Majorities," *Am. Soc. Rev.,* 13 (Dec., 1948): 700–710.

Bierstedt, R., "An Analysis of Social Power," *Am. Soc. Rev.,* 15 (Dec., 1950): 730–738.

Bierstedt, R., "The Problem of Authority," in Berger, M., Abel, T., and Page, C. H. (eds.), *Freedom and Control in Modern Society*. Princeton: N.J.: Van Nostrand, 1954, pp. 67–81.

Gowldner, A. W., *Studies in Leadership: Leadership and Democratic Action*. New York: Harper, 1950.

Hunter, Floyd, *Community Power Structure: A Study of Decision Makers*. Chapel Hill: Univ. of North Carolina Press, 1953.

LaPiere, R. T., *A Theory of Social Control*. New York: McGraw-Hill, 1954, pp. 161–182, 364–366, 379–384.

MacIver, R. M., *The Modern State*. London: Oxford, 1926, pp. 221–231.

MacIver, R. M., *The Web of Government*. New York: Macmillan, 1947, pp. 73–113.

Thompson, J. D., "Authority and Power in Identical Organizations," *Am. Jour. Soc.,* 62 (Nov., 1956): 290–301.

POPULATION MAINTENANCE

Hauser, P. M., and Duncan, O. D. (eds.), *The Study of Population: An Inventory and Appraisal*. Chicago: Univ. of Chicago Press, 1959, Chaps. 16–21, 25, 26. This work contains thousands of bibliographical items.

Hawley, A. H., *Human Ecology: A Theory of Community Structure.* New York: Ronald, 1950, pp. 149–174.

Hertzler, J. O., *The Crisis in World Population.* Lincoln: Univ. of Nebraska Press, 1956, pp. 10–12, 86–106.

Spengler, J. J., and Duncan, O. D. (eds.), *Demographic Analysis.* Glencoe, Ill.: Free Press, 1956, esp. Chaps. II, III, V, VI.

United Nations, Population Division, *The Determinants and Consequences of Population Trends.* New York: 1953.

CULTURE MAINTENANCE

Barnett, H. G., "Culture Processes," *Am. Anth.,* 42 (Jan.–Mar., 1940): 21–48.

Barnett, H. G., *Innovation: The Basis of Culture Change.* New York: McGraw-Hill, 1952.

Brozen, Yale, "Invention, Innovation, and Imitation," *Am. Econ. Rev.,* 41 (May, 1951): 239–257.

Gilfillan, S. C., *The Sociology of Invention.* Chicago: Follett, 1955.

Hertzler, J. O., *Society in Action.* New York: Dryden, 1954, pp. 78–98.

Linton, R., *The Tree of Culture.* New York: Knopf, 1955.

MOTIVATION

Cantril, H., *The Psychology of Social Movements.* New York: Wiley, 1941, pp. 30–52.

Centers, R., "Motivational Aspects of Occupational Stratification," *Jour. Soc. Psych.,* 28 (Nov., 1948): 187–217.

Gerth, H., and Mills, C. W., *Character and Social Structure.* New York: Harcourt, Brace, 1953, pp. 112–129.

Hickman, C. A., and Kuhn, M. H., *Individuals, Groups, and Economic Behavior.* New York: Dryden, 1956, pp. 80–94.

MacIver, R. M., *Social Causation.* Boston: Ginn, 1942, pp. 195–223.

Newcomb, T. M., *Social Psychology.* New York: Dryden, 1950, pp. 74–146.

Olds, James, *The Growth and Structure of Motives: Psychological Studies in the Theory of Action.* Glencoe, Ill.: Free Press, 1955.

Sherif, Muzafer, *An Outline of Social Psychology.* New York: Harper, 1948, pp. 11–38, 250–273.

Young, P. T., *Motivation of Behavior.* New York: Wiley, 1936.

On morale and morale-building, see:

Frank, L. K., *Society as the Patient.* New Brunswick, N.J.: Rutgers Univ. Press, 1945, pp. 380–388.

Hocking, W. E., "The Nature of Morale," *Am. Jour. Soc.,* 47 (Nov., 1941): 302–320.

Krech, D., and Crutchfield, R. C., *Theory and Problems of Social Psychology.* New York: McGraw-Hill, 1948, pp. 404–417.

LaPiere, R. T., *The Theory of Social Control.* New York: McGraw-Hill, 1954, pp. 183–217.

Miller, D. C., and Form, W. H., *Industrial Sociology.* New York: Harpers, 1951, pp. 469–492.

Rose, A. M., *Sociology: The Study of Human Relations.* New York: Knopf, 1956, pp. 526–555.

On accommodation, see:

Bernard, Jessie, *American Community Behavior*. New York: Dryden, 1949, pp. 47–52, 84–102, 110–113, 305–319.
Chase, S., *Roads to Agreement*. New York: Harper, 1951.
Lewin, K., *Resolving Social Conflicts*. New York: Harper, 1948.
Park, R. E., and Burgess, E. W., *Introduction to the Science of Sociology*. Chicago: Univ. of Chicago Press, 1921, pp. 663–732.
Williams, R. M., Jr., *The Reduction of Intergroup Tensions*. New York: Social Science Research Council, 1947.

On social assimilation, see:

Gillin, J. L., and J. P., *Cultural Sociology*. New York: Macmillan, 1948, pp. 505–535.
Hiller, E. T., *Principles of Sociology*. New York: Harper, 1933, pp. 376–387.
Woolston, H. B., "The Process of Assimilation," *Soc. Forces,* 23 (May, 1945): 416–424.
For a more comprehensive analysis of the aspects of societal maintenance here examined, stressing essentially the multiple processual features, see Hertzler, pp. 335–359; for a bibliography of 138 items see pp. 431–435.

On freedoms and rights, see:

Anshen, Ruth N. (ed.), *Freedom, Its Meaning*. New York: Harcourt, Brace, 1940.
Berger, M., Abel, T., and Page, C. H. (eds.), *Social Contact and Individual Freedom in Modern Society*. Princeton, N.J.: Van Nostrand, 1954.
Landis, P. H., *Social Control* (rev. ed.), Philadelphia: Lippincott, 1956, pp. 136–138.
Malinowski, B., *Freedom and Civilization*. New York: Roy, 1945.

On ordination, see:

Cattell, R. B., "The Cultural Functions of Social Stratification: I. Regarding the Genetic Basis of Society," *Jour. Soc. Psych.* 21 (1945): 3–23.
Moore, B., Jr., "The Relation between Social Stratification and Social Control," *Sociometry,* 5 (Aug., 1942): 230–250.
Warner, W. L., Meeker, M., and Eells, K., *Social Classes in America*. Chicago: Science Research Associates, 1949, pp. 7–11.
Wiese, L. von, and Becker, H., *Systematic Sociology*. New York: Wiley, 1932, pp. 257, 348–367.

REORGANIZATION

Brogan, D. W., *The Price of Revolution*. New York: Harper, 1952.
Faris, R. E. L., *Social Disorganization*. New York: Ronald, 1952, pp. 566–617.
Gilbert, G. M., *The Psychology of Dictatorship*. New York: Ronald, 1951.
LaPiere, R. T., *The Theory of Social Control*. New York: McGraw-Hill, 1954, pp. 544–550.
Nordskog, John E., *Contemporary Social Reform Movements*. New York: Scribner's, 1954.

Sorokin, P. A., *S. O. S.: The Meaning of Our Crisis*. Boston: Beacon, 1951, pp. 143–169.

Taylor, C. C., *The Farmers' Movement: 1620–1920*. New York: Am. Book, 1953.

Turner, R. H., and Killian, L. M. (eds.), *Collective Behavior*. Englewood Cliffs, N.J.: Prentice-Hall, 1957, pp. 307–511.

Wallace, A. F. C., "Revitalization Movements," *Am. Anth.*, 58 (Apr., 1956): 264–281.

SOCIAL PLANNING

Doob, L. W., *The Plans of Men*. New Haven: Yale Univ. Press, 1940.

Frank, Jerome, "The Place of the Expert in Democratic Planning," *Phil. of Science*, 16 (Jan., 1949): 3–24.

Galloway, G. B., *et al.*, *Planning for America*. Garden City, N.Y.: Doubleday, 1954.

Hillman, A., *Community Organization and Planning*. New York: Macmillan, 1950, pp. 38–107.

Meadows, P., *The Culture of Industrial Man*. Lincoln: Univ. of Nebraska Press, 1950, pp. 192–206.

Merriam, C. E., "The Possibilities of Planning," *Am. Jour. Soc.*, 39 (Mar., 1944): 397–407.

Riemer, S., "Social Planing and Social Organization," *Am. Jour. Soc.*, 52 (Mar., 1947): 508–516.

Rodgers, C., *American Planning: Past, Present, Future*. New York: Harper, 1947.

Ross, M. G., *Community Organization: Theory and Principles*. New York: Harper, 1955, pp. 132–152.

Vance, R. B., "The Place of Planning in Social Dynamics," *Soc. Forces*, 23 (Mar., 1945): 331–334.

PART 2

The General
Theory of Social
Institutions

Our purpose in Part 2 is to provide a general theoretical orientation for the understanding of social institutions. The treatment will include an examination of the place of institutions in social organization; the nature and functions of social institutions; their experiential basis; their structural-functional components; the process of institutionalization of relations and actions; the functional and ecological relationships within one institution or between several; the changes in institutions, including malfunctioning and reorganization, the typical life-cycle, and the effects of culural contact; and, finally, the classifications of social institutions.

Social Institutions in Social Organization

Any society, as a fairly effective systematized scheme of social life, consists of a master network, framework, or constellation of social institutions. These are the great clusters of established, accepted, and implemented ways of behaving socially. The institutions are the basic units or working parts of a society, the basis of its maintenance, regulation, and reorganization, and the means through which the expressional impulses of its people are adequately and safely satisfied.[1]

The fundamental division of labor in a society is that among the society's major institutional systems. Each of the major structural-functional departments of social life—scientific-technological, familial, economic, political, educational, religious, aesthetic, health, recreational, welfare, etc.—is an institutionalized sector. The integration of these institutional systems, which are interdependent and interconnected though not necessarily harmonious and consistent with each other, make up the over-all social system of a society.

All modes of organization evidence some institutional attributes, and moreover there is a drift toward institutionalization in every social situation requiring some sort of organization. In other words, there is a considerable likelihood that every instance of collective behavior that becomes important for the participants or the society and endures will become increasingly institutionalized with the passage of time.[2]

The humanly constructed institutional system as it organizes human

---

[1] "The totality of institutions found in a concrete social group constitutes the *social organization* of this group." W. I. Thomas and F. Znaniecki, *The Polish Peasant in Europe and America.* New York: Knopf, 1920, Vol. I, p. 33. See also A. R. Radcliffe-Brown, *Structure and Function in Primitive Society.* London: Cohen & West, 1952, p. 9.

[2] Cf.: H. Gerth and C. W. Mills, *Character and Social Structure: The Philosophy of Social Institutions.* New York: Harcourt, Brace, 1953, p. 428. R. T. LaPiere, *Sociology.* New York: McGraw-Hill, 1946, p. 335.

behavior to cope with all of man's environments is what distinguishes life in human society from the instinctive behavior of animal societies. Without the coherence and stability established by institutions, society "would be a mere aggregate of human animals and not society as we know it."[3]

It is in the institutional systems that all of the other relevant organizational systems examined in Chapters One and Two become operative.

The physical environment constitutes the physical arena in which all individual and social activity occurs, and provides the physical and biological resources upon which all human life, including all that is institutionally organized, depends. It also confronts mankind with a great array of compulsives, permissives, and prohibitives.

The people are the stuff out of which institutions are formed and for which institutions exist. The institutions, in turn, affect almost every aspect of demographic performance.

The institutions unite all of the cultural patterns of the total social system. Almost all contrived physical objects—buildings, equipment, symbolic objects—and other kinds of physical culture traits and complexes have their meaning and utility in terms of the institutional activities of individuals.

All but the most casual or temporary groups are structural-functional parts of institutions. They consist of individuals in more or less standardized, and hence institutionalized, relationships, and, whether simple or complex, informally or bureaucratically organized, they exist because they are carrying on institutional functions.

The communities are the immediate arenas in which most of the institutions function, in so far as individuals and groups are directly involved. In the community the individuals and groups have their daily experience with institutions.

Most of the institutions as social systems in their more concrete manifestations have a spatial base; the ecological system furnishes a basic physical framework for them. Institutions also have ecological relations with each other in the over-all physical setting.

Almost all institutional relationships involve differentiation among persons as well as differentiation of function (division and specialization of labor), and almost all such differentiation, of necessity, is institutionalized. Furthermore, not only is there some sort of stratification in all institutional relationships, but the stratification system itself of a society has institutional features.

Most of the social systems instrumental in the organization of societal behavior are structural phases of institutions, function as part of

[3] R. M. Williams, Jr., *American Society: A Sociological Interpretation.* New York: Knopf, 1960, p. 34.

or by means of institutions, and are coordinated in an institutional manner.

The values of the value-system have their major expressions in the institutionalized activities of the people; the institutions themselves are a society's primary agencies for the realization of values. All of the goals of a society are pursued and achieved by institutional means. The norms are nearly all institutional norms; in fact, the very essence of institutionalized activity is the fact that it is norm-directed and norm-controlled.

The over-all ideological system, with its collection of knowledge and interpretations about all of man's experience, is the intellectual means whereby man adjusts himself to the natural systems and formulates essential features of his cultural and societal systems.

The status-role system works itself out in the various institutionalized areas; almost all statuses consist of positions in institutionalized relationships, and almost all roles are institutionally patterned behaviors. Each institution unites a plurality of roles.

All essential regulation is in the major divisions or departments of societal life, and these are institutionalized of necessity. It is in and through the particular institutional systems that the rule-enforcing and the power-authority systems function. Almost all of regulation is of, by, and for institutions. All maintenance, as it makes for individual and societal self-preservation, self-perpetuation, and self-expression, is satisfied by means of institutions. The over-all institutional system of a community or society is, in fact, its regulative-maintenance system.

All of the basic social processes—disorganizational as well as organizational—occur in and among persons, categories, and groups in institutional relations. All social change has its effect in the institutional relationships of the population; the institutions, in turn, in their operational aspects, are the major instruments for coping with change. Most social pathologies and social problems are due to some disorganization of one or more institutions in strategic areas of social life. This disorganization may involve the violation of institutional requirements by a considerable portion of its membership; the maladministration of the institution by its functionaries; the lag and inadequacy of some of the institutions in relation to the societal needs they are supposed to satisfy, and hence, the failure or tardiness in revising such institutions or developing new ones; or the functional disequilibrium between related institutions and institutional sectors. Societal reorganization usually starts in an institutional area of social life as a social movement, is conducted for the health of social institutions, and if it is to be effective, must proceed by means of institutionalized agencies and procedures.

Institutions provide a society's profile. Various cultural anthropologists have discovered that the most comprehensive, revealing, and accurate way to envisage the salient features of the social organization of any society under examination is to understand its major institutions and the relations between them.[4] The society, in fact, can practically be defined by an enumeration and description of its institutions. They give a distinguishing profile to an entire society and make possible the comparative analysis of the different societies. Each society has its own unique character, which is a matter of its physical environment, its regional ecological and intersocietal relations, its social-cultural history, its stage of scientific-technological and industrial-urban development. This character is reflected in the special peculiarities of the institutions of each society compared with those of other societies. Odum points out that institutions are synonymous with a society in cross section at a given time.[5] Also, when we look at a society at a given point of time and note which institutions are dominant we have a rather clear-cut indication of which needs, values, interests, and goals, and their accompanying charters (normative patterns), modal sets of activities (role-patterns), and formalized groups are most important; these give the distinctive features to the profile. Thus, for example, the Church was dominant in medieval Europe; military institutions were predominant in nineteenth- and early twentieth-century Prussia, and at the present time the Communist Party in the Soviet Union and business and government in our own society dominate.

Another most revealing way of analyzing a society is to examine its dominant and unifying culture theme. Opler,[6] referring to them as "dynamic affirmations," has defined a theme as "a postulate or position, declared or implied, and usually controlling or stimulating activity, which is tacitly approved or openly promoted in a society." Notable examples in our own society are practicality, mechanization, standardization, individualism, freedom from authority, competitive effort, productivity, achievement of wealth, and moralization of work and economic interests. The reminders or expressions of the many themes of a society are found, in negative form, in the prohibitions of certain activities, and, positively, in the approved, promoted, and required activities, both unformalized and formalized. But the great bulk of both the unformalized and formalized theme-expressing activity occurs in connection with the major institutionalized sectors of social life—with the

[4] See the well-known anthropological studies: Ruth Benedict, *Patterns of Culture*. Boston: Houghton Mifflin, 1934. Ruth Benedict, *The Chrysanthemum and the Sword*. Boston: Houghton Mifflin, 1946. Margaret Mead, *And Keep Your Powder Dry: An Anthropologist Looks at America*. New York: Morrow, 1943.

[5] H. W. Odum, *Understanding Society*. New York: Macmillan, 1947, p. 242.

[6] M. F. Opler, "Themes as Dynamic Factors in Culture," *Am. Jour. Soc.*, 51 (Nov., 1945): 198–206.

familial, political, business, religious, recreational, occupational, health, artistic, and other standard behavior of the people. Although many of the themes are universal among societies, since they usually relate to widespread needs or wants, the universal themes of each society have their own special flavor, or character, and each society has certain unique themes.

The themes permeate all the institutions and give them a coherence and uniformity of coloring and expressiveness which justifies the use of the term national character. This is what Sumner refers to as the ethos of a people. For example, most of the institutions of a democratic, decentralized, free enterprise society are sharply different from those of an autocratic, centralized, extensively regimented society.

The institutions provide for a society's continuity. The institutions of a society have a high degree of stability and function as the major mechanisms for social continuity. The individuals and most groups have a temporary stay, but the institutions continue as more or less permanent societal instruments. They thus have a time-binding function. By means of them the past lives into the present, and the present becomes organized intelligibly and continuously with the past and the future. The institutions are also at any given time a blend of historical deposits. Thus, a society's history is also in large part to be read in its institutions.

I: The Imperatives Requiring Social Institutions

The institutions are, in large degree, the product of the stable and fixed needs of individuals and groups. In fact, social institutions cannot be understood apart from the drives, wants, and interests that they represent and the needs that they are designed to satisfy. The multiple institutions are the major means whereby the people—or some proportion of them, depending on the type and function of institution—cooperatively and reciprocally satisfy these needs.

The needs can be attributed to geographical, biological, psychological, social-psychological, cultural and societal forces and conditions. Everywhere and at all times common physical and biological needs must be met such as those for nutrition, shelter, and other protection against the elements; for bodily comforts, sex gratification, bodily exertion and movement in the form of regular exercise of the muscular and nervous systems; rest and sleep, health and sanitation, and growth. Among the psychological and social psychological imperatives are the needs for relaxation, new experience, possessions as an extension of self, association in itself, affiliation, self-assertion, at least occasional aggression and dominance, exhibition, self-expression, self-esteem and prestige, recognition by and favorable response from others, occasional contrariety (acting differently from others), conformity, fellowship and occasional deferences.

Beyond these is the almost overwhelming array of sociocultural and societal imperatives; that is, stern and concrete needs for group, social, and societal survival and prosperity that are practically permanent and have undoubtedly existed since the first human groupings. It has always been necessary to suppress the injury or killing of fellow group members, except in certain special circumstances where such action, authoritatively conducted, was presumed to redound to the benefit of the group. It has been necessary for members of a given group to satisfy their wants for food and other basic material and service necessities without running afoul of each other or seriously impairing each other's access to these necessities. In a group of any size it has been necessary to satisfy such wants cooperatively; that is, by means of some established division and reciprocity of labor, involving the regulation of land ownership and use, the ownership and use of other instruments, the provision for, and the regulation of, the exchange and distribution of commodities and services, and the organization of occupations and other specialties.

It has been necessary for all groups to regulate, to an extent at least, the relations between the sexes, to produce, protect, and nurture the children, to ensure the reciprocal obligations of the generations, the different age groups and age statuses. It has always been necessary to communicate ideas, impulses, principles, and known facts adequately and in a comprehensible manner; this means that people have had to develop, maintain, and continually revise language in its various forms and extensions. It has always been necessary to organize and reorganize old knowledge, acquire new knowledge, and apply the knowledge technologically. It has always been necessary for the group to socialize new members acquired by birth or immigration; usually this has meant the transmission of the social heritage of the group from generation to generation, especially the knowledge and skills that had to do with individual and group maintenance.

It has always been necessary for groups to maintain internal order and to protect themselves against external aggression and disturbance. It has always been necessary not only to provide for the expression of the aesthetic and recreational impulses of individuals, but also to keep them in line with the moral, aesthetic, and often the religious standards of the groups. The physically sick, the delinquent and criminal, the mentally and emotionally disorganized, the incompetent have had to

be dealt with in some way to protect the rest. It has always been necessary, in some degree, to regulate the differentiated and stratified population, whether this was relatively simple or complex, and to provide
generally acceptable arrangements with respect to status, precedence,
and subordination. It has been necessary to regulate inequalities due to
variations in individual abilities, opportunities, property, and wealth.
It has always been necessary to have some sort of an adequate explanation of the visible universe and some means of understanding the supernatural; almost all people have provided themselves with a cosmology
and eschatology. It has even been deemed necessary to meet, often in
a vague and groping way, certain abstract needs, such as those for
justice, freedom, progress.

It is also necessary to institutionalize social behavior because of
the socially ignorant and the socially infantile who are unconscious
of, or immune to, any conception of their social obligations and responsibilities.[7]

Needs such as these have always called into existence appropriate
means of dealing with them.[8]

II: The Nature of Social Institutions

There are many definitions of institutions, each colored by the special
approach of the definer. Each tends to stress one or more pertinent
features and functions of institutions. This diversity indicates, however, that institutions are not simple phenomena, and that it is not easy
to confine a definition of them to a single short sentence, or to use a

[7] On imperatives, see: H. A. Murray, *Explorations in Personality*. New York:
Oxford Univ. Press, 1938, pp. 80–83. G. P. Murdock, "The Common Denomi-
nator of Cultures," in R. Linton (ed.), *The Science of Man in the World Crisis*.
New York: Columbia Univ. Press, 1945, pp. 123–141. B. Malinowski, "The
Group and the Individual in Functional Analysis," *Am. Jour. Soc.*, 44 (May,
1939): 938–964, esp. 963.

[8] It should be noted in all candor that *not all* institutions are beneficial for the
majority of the people of the community or society. Every society has *anti*-social
institutions—institutions related to certain presumed needs, but needs which,
as satisfied in an organized way, run counter to certain widely advertized ethical
principles. Thus in the United States we have the institutionalization of racketeering, "dope" running, prostitution, gambling, etc., as forms of effective organization of these activities by those engaged in them. The examination of the anti-
social institutions, and the impairments of the positively functional institutions
that produce anti-social effects is a very important part of the study of social *disorganization* as now treated. Although these are imporant in the operation of a
society, our primary concern is with social organization. Moreover, the vast bulk
of mankind's institutions are of positive rather than negative significance.

capsular explanation, and still do them justice.[9] Our frame of reference is the widely inclusive one of social organization; hence, we will attempt to define institutions in their various structural and functional manifestations. Our task of defining will also involve an attempt to synthesize the viewpoints and provide a conception of wider usefulness.

As a starting definition, it can be said that *a social institution* is (1) a set of chartered and sanctioned behavioral directives and expectations, both of a positive and prohibitive nature, (2) expressed by the individuals involved as patterned roles for the various social positions and situations, and (3) aided by a complex of conformity-producing social usages and procedures and implementing social organizations, symbolic materials and, in most instances, physical equipment, whereby human beings systematically satisfy some basic need or related needs. An institution, as will be noted below in greater detail, consists of a rationale, with its concrete meanings, values, objectives and ideology, a normative or codal structure, a complex positional (status) and behavioral (role) and also coordinative organizational structuring of the members or participants, and a variety of symbolic and physical implementing agencies or mechanisms. The basic element, though, and the functional essence of an institution, is the fact that it is a *system* of required, concerted, cooperative, and reciprocal practices or activities whereby the people concerned satisfy their individual and social needs. These practices are recognized as desirable or essential, and they are expected of all people in the particular situations. Especially important is the fact that they are organized, that is, established, regularized, chartered, endorsed, and enforced, and hence made predictable and effective in all of the common or recurrent relational-functional situations. All of the other features relate to this key aspect. As Durkheim put it long ago, institutions are "all the beliefs and all the modes of conduct instituted by the collectivity."[10]

This rationale and these functional practices and instruments are sustained and enforced by public opinion, or at least by the opinion of

[9] Among what is here referred to as the capsular conceptions, we note that from the "action" point of view, institutions are "crystallized ways of acting" or "established patterns." Some role theorists think of them as "patterns of roles" or "role-integrates." From the regulative point of view, they are normative patterns or systems. From the social psychological angle, they are "systems of habits," or clusters or groups of complex behavior patterns. From the organizational point of view (in the narrower sense of organization), they are "organizations of collective activity," or "groups of people organized to carry out certain purposes." This by no means exhausts the list of special viewpoints. These capsular conceptions, while convenient, and although they point to fundamental and universal features of institutions, are too neat and simple, and overlook or avoid the complex nature of institutions.

[10] E. Durkheim, *Rules of Sociological Method*. Glencoe, Ill.: Free Press, 1938, p. lvi.

the institutional groups or the population as affected in the particular need area, since the institution is identified with the interests of the larger or lesser body.

The particular institution as conceptualized by a community or society is a "model." It sets up ideal-typical goals as to what is legitimately expected, and is an ideal-typical (not utopian) means of coping with typical situations and relations. The actual performance, of course, is at some variance with the model. The institution is also a system in itself, apart from its particular members, participants, or beneficiaries at any given time. Its individual role-performers come and go, may die and be forgotten; the buildings that house the institution may be destroyed and reconstructed; the regulations and traditions may change. But the institution as a complex entity of established requirements, sociocultural features with durable social structurings and persistent and insistent functions to be performed continues.

Also, the same individuals may be—in fact, unavoidably are—members of many institutional systems.

III: The Experiental Basis for Institutions as Essential Societal Mechanisms

Institutions have grown out of human social experience, whereby men became aware of the fact that their needs could only be satisfied in systematic fashion. The formation of the institutions themselves proceeded on an experiential and consciously experimental basis.

When any set of social activities involves a considerable number of persons and has become important in the welfare and perpetuation of a society; when relationships may lead to a clash of interests or confusion of aims or any other form of antagonism or misconception; when individuals or categories have definite related functions to perform; when the behavior of all concerned must be predictable to a certain extent; if a community or society is to have any functional efficiency, permanence, and stability; *then* these relationships or activities must be structured and functionalized; that is, institutionalized.

As soon as an aggregation of persons becomes a *system* of relationships and carries on any satisfying social function, however simple it may be, it must take on the machinery of an institution. When any *new* type of relationship or interperson activity becomes recurrent and essential, it must be institutionalized. The only alternative would be to invent adequate rules and procedures for the particular relationship or function on the spot and at the moment; and this few individuals or groups are capable of doing.

Thus, there exist for each situation in a social organization recognized usages and principles of action. They are established in the social heritage and in the ways of life of a people. They surround every individual like a continuous, all-pervading climate.

In every society, the institutions are not only the main products but also the main repositories of all the social experiences involved in successfully establishing and maintaining social order and operation.

Institutions have not sprung into being fully-formed and fully-functional at the moment when some new need for adjustment arose. Most institutions appear, not immediately as the result of deliberate planning and formulation, but over a period of time, as a developmental process based on experience. They have emerged through successive stages, each of which evidences a greater awareness of actually or potentially successful requirements, actions, and agents. Historically, institutions have grown piecemeal by minor adjustments and innumerable small accretions.

The classical analysis of successive stages in the emergence of institutional essentials is that of W. G. Sumner and his disciple and collaborator, A. G. Keller.[11] According to them every institution is the product of a sequence of processes, each producing its own social form; it is, in fact, a chain of sequences, whereby institutional status of the antecedent forms is finally achieved.

On the basis of early experience with a new situation, certain ways, sometimes accidentally hit upon by the people concerned but also sometimes resulting from considerable experimentation, come about that seem to be efficacious. When frequently repeated, they become habitual folkways—useful "ways of the folk." They answer the purpose better than any other ways of doing the necessary things in the new but definitely existent situation. If these folkways work more or less well, they are likely to be continued and become more and more imperative, acquiring a momentum of their own.

When substantial convictions develop to the effect that these ways are directly conducive and essential to societal welfare, they acquire an ethical rightness; the members of the group come to believe that they are the only right ways and that departure from them invites calamity. When the ways have reached this stage, they are known as *mores,* and are compulsive whereas the folkways were considered only desirable. Less compulsive than the mores, but also a development from the folkways, are the *customs,* which are usages that have acquired rightness (or sanction) because of their persistence in time. When these more or

---

[11] See: W. G. Sumner, *Folkways.* Boston: Ginn, 1906, pp. 2–3, 30, 35, 49, 53–55, 76–77. W. G. Sumner and A. G. Keller, *The Science of Society.* New Haven: Yale Univ. Press, 1927, esp. Vol. I, pp. 3, 29, 34, 43, 88–89.

less vaguely defined and formalized mores and customs, on the basis of further experience and informal and formal experimentation, are elevated into the realm of the conscious and deliberate and are made more definite and specific in matters of rules, prescribed and proscribed acts, and the apparatus or agencies employed; when they are provided with a framework or structure, and a more rational, utilitarian and positive character is added; when they are formally sanctioned and made enforceable; when they are systematized and implemented, they become *institutions*.

This emergence of institutions probably has never been an entirely spontaneous and automatic process. Always there has been much rational intention, much invention, as well as discovery, and much deliberate, though not always informed and systematic, construction. But in our age and society, the organization of the institutional stage is speeded up and carried through with a rational deliberateness and effectiveness never known before. Increasingly, at least in some sectors of social life, the earlier stages are omitted or by-passed, and we make our institutions as the need arises. At the same time, even in our age, the most recent enacted institution will not have been created entirely *de novo;* various principles of operation and patterns of organization will have been taken over from other times and other institutional fields.

IV: The Functions of Institutions

Some of the most important societal functions of institutions have already been indicated above with some explicitness, for it is impossible to define anything without calling attention to what it does. Any discussion of the needs that call forth institutions implies, *pari passu,* the types of functional activities necessary to satisfy them. The general functions deserve further treatment, and also attention should be called to certain less frequently mentioned aspects of these major functions and to certain additional functions.

Most of the functions essential to the operation of a society are conducted by institutions. It is by means of the institutions that the relationships and functional activities are ordered, regulated, standardized, coordinated and correlated. Very few of the active institutions of a society at a given time could be withdrawn without greatly impairing the operation of that society.

The regulative or social control functions are of crucial importance. The need of regulation in *any* system, including especially social systems, was noted in Chapter One, and certain general instrumental features of the regulative systems of human societies were indicated in Chapter Two. Institutions are peculiarly effective as control agencies in that, increasingly, they substitute an external, objective, depersonalized social control of conduct for the impulsive, subjective, or individual control. Of course it is true that it is an individual and not the institution that provides the model or that forces the conduct, but the action of this individual is standardized and in many instances formally authorized. Never before have men been in a position where institutional control could be as objectified as it is now.

It is by means of most of the major categories of institutions—though some are more directly functional than others in this respect—that societies forestall behavior that is destructive of social order and operation, and also assures themselves that there will be no absence, breakdown, or intolerable impairment of positive socialized and societally necessary behavior. Hence, the institutions embody the informal and formal norms and rules, set and administer the sanctions, and exercise the physical and psychical pressures and controls. Almost all of the social control agents and devices, such as folkways, conventions, customs, traditions, beliefs, mores and moral codes, civil and religious law, ritual and ceremony, the special regulative and ordinative organizations and functionaries, operate in and through the institutions. The institutions do this controlling with the approval and in most instances with the organized force of the community behind them.

The regulative functions of institutions are related to the all-pervading ethical system. Every action—familial, economic, technological, political, educational, religious—has a moral quality, and is evaluated with respect to its propriety; that is, its rightness or wrongness, its acceptability or non-acceptability, as conceived by the group, community, or society. For example, the principles or standards of propriety can be found in the institutionalized sexual, domestic, economic, and political relationships. Institutions cannot escape this involvement in morality, for by their very nature they determine conduct and consequences of conduct. This morality not only provides the rules and standards whereby behavior is defined, but it also provides the essential quality that gives meaning and value to the activity of individuals and groups in relation to one another in society. It is a social cement between social action and social ends.

A regulative function not so widely appreciated, because of the emphasis upon traditional social control functions, is that which certain institutions exercise over conflict, both within a society and between societies, paradoxical as this may seem at first glance. Thanks to the revival of interest in Simmel's classic treatment of conflict and to several recent studies, in part at least taking their cues from Simmel, attention has been refocused upon the institutional organization and regulation of conflict.[12]

Conflict, in most of its forms, is more dysfunctional than functional. However, everywhere conflict situations and and processes are universal and unavoidable features of every society. Conflict is likely to occur as long as there is a scarcity of desired objects; a scarcity of desirable states of affairs, for example preferred social positions; a scarcity of resources in nature and culture; and variations of power among persons and groups.[13] Conflict has to be accepted as a stern necessity. A basic social function, therefore, is that of institutionalizing the major forms of conflict in a society. This particular sort of institutionalizing has many of the features of institutionalization generally. Notable are the recognition of the conflict groups and their identification as such; the establishment of more or less explicit rules governing the standard forms of conflict, especially *between* groups; the more or less systematized organization of the division of labor, of the varied responsibilities of the personnel of administration and command, of means of obtaining obedience within the conflict group, and the provision of other essential physical, social psychological, and social instrumentalities; the acceptance and establishment of regularized policies and procedures for conducting the different forms of conflict; developing the means of establishing and enforcing the sanctions as they apply both within conflict groups and between the conflicting groups. There is also the tendency to institutionalize the methods for resolving the conflict, such as settlement by arbitration, mediation, negotiation, legislation and judicial settlement.[14]

Not only is conflict institutionalized, but in its institutionalized forms it has group-maintaining functions. As a new form of conflict appears it acts as a stimulus for establishing new rules, norms, associational forms and procedures, and thus serves as an organizing, even a socializing, agent for both contending parties. Institutionalized conflict in general serves to regulate systems of relationships. It clears the air in that it eliminates the accumulation of blocked and hostile dispositions by allowing their ordered behavioral expression; it provides an outlet for the release of hostilities and drives ordinarily suppressed or at least

[12] Cf.: Georg Simmel, *Conflict* (K. H. Wolff, transl.). Glencoe, Ill.: Free Press, 1955. Lewis A. Coser, *The Functions of Social Conflict*. Glencoe, Ill.: Free Press, 1956. Raymond W. Mack and Richard C. Snyder, "The Analysis of Social Conflict—Toward an Overview and Synthesis," *Conflict Resolution,* 1 (June, 1957): 212–248.

[13] Mack and Snyder, *op. cit.,* p. 223.

[14] In contrast to institutionalized conflict, Mack and Snyder point out: "Noninstitutionalized conflict or conflict interaction having a low degree of institutionalization is marked by chronic recurrence of unsettled issues, by an absence of agreed procedures for review of relations, and by discontinuity of interaction or drastic shifts in the mode of resolution." *Op. cit.,* p. 234.

deplored by the group. In other words, institutionalized conflict provides a safety-valve function, which, obviously, is of importance in maintaining the structure of the social system as a whole.[15]

Practically all institutions function as conditioning and socializing agents, over and beyond those institutions such as the familial and the educational, which are specifically charged with the task of inducting succeeding generations into the beliefs and ways of the preceding generations. For example, in the diversified institutional atmosphere to which the growing boy is exposed, he learns about occupations, about buying and selling, about consumption standards and ways, how to play baseball, basketball and other games; he absorbs the spirit and content of husband and father roles; he learns language and the use of other communicative agents, political beliefs and ways, religious norms and activities, some of the conventions and decencies, traffic rules, and so on. The appropriate actions are cultivated and stabilized in him by the respective institutions, and any institution, once established, will have such influence upon him throughout his life. Men are the consequences of their institutions. One of the primary functions of any institution is to reproduce, preserve, and transmit to persons the uniform patterns of behavior by which they can meet the recurrent types of situations that arise from day to day; they serve as conditioners and cultivators of habits of conformity and functional proficiency.

Institutions also function as guides and directors and containers of individual (and group) behavior. The institutions tell the individual how to think and what to do. The institutions, as it has been variously put in this connection, are the "avenues" along which they can safely adjust themselves to other individuals and the groups to which they belong; the "behavioral stockades" or "fences" surrounding social behavior; the "white line" down the center of the highway that tells the motorist what is right side and wrong side; the "direction posts" that people follow. In this respect the institutions of a community or society enable the individual members to satisfy their elemental biological and psychological urges, drives, and needs in a sufficient, guaranteed, socially acceptable manner. In general, the institutional rules and procedures provide ready-made, well-tried patterns of behavior for the solution of the great bulk of individual adjustment problems. The members do not have to think through all these situations for themselves.

Institutions function as motivators to appropriate action in particular situations. The institutions embody the standard expectations as to what is imperative in the way of behavior in most of the major departments and circumstances of life. In the atmosphere of institutions we feel pressing upon us the necessity of meeting the expectations of others

---

[15] See in this connection the excellent treatment by Coser, *op. cit.,* pp. 39–48.

in our various statuses and roles, in meeting duties and responsibilities. When new institutions arise, they stimulate and motivate new forms of behavior not only among those who have contributed to the development of the new institution, but among all who become aware of it or are influenced by it; thus, new economic institutions or institutional forms stimulate new forms and habits of consumption.

Institutions function as carriers of the society's culture. In them are found most of the outstanding, constructive, cultural elements that the centuries with their inexorable testing and selective processes have permitted to endure and develop. The great recognized values in the social life of men are embodied in their institutions and through them are safeguarded and transmitted to posterity. What is not found in institutions is essentially individualistic, or eccentric, or momentary, and not comprised in the common life. Hence, a society's culture is largely a summation of its institutions, and its institutions are largely an embodiment of its culture.

Social institutions also function as preserving and conserving agencies in social life. In fact, since they express and protect the values and most of the other precious gains of human and social experience, and since they establish and preserve order, most of them, of necessity, are conservative and conservational in effect. The institutions also, in general, represent group habits that have come down from the past and which are, in many cases, the result of the work and the intelligence of men in the past, and therefore respected. This influence of habit checks the desire for premature reorganization and consequently causes changes in most institutions to take place gradually without seriously disturbing the life or structure of society.

Another aspect of the conservative tendency is the fact that as soon as an institution develops a supposedly indispensable function, a substantial clientele, and a definite set of functionaries, it becomes interested not only in maintaining itself, but also in preserving the situations that gave it its reason for existence and its standing. Also, because of their strength and certainty, they serve as buffers between people and the rapid and tremendous changes that are taking place in all departments of modern life.

BIBLIOGRAPHY

Angell, R. C., *The Integration of American Society: A Study of Groups and Institutions.* New York: McGraw-Hill, 1941, pp. 24–28.
Angell, R. C., *Free Society and Moral Crisis.* Ann Arbor: Univ. of Michigan Press, 1958, pp. 29–31, 85–104.
Bierstedt, R., *The Social Order.* New York: McGraw-Hill, 1957, pp. 298–306.

Cooley, C. H., *Social Organization*. New York: Scribner's, 1910, pp. 313–326.
Ellsworth, J. S., Jr., *Factory Folkways: A Study of Institutional Structure and Change*. New Haven: Yale Univ. Press, 1952, pp. 89–111.
Feibleman, J. K., *The Institutions of Society*. London: Allen & Unwin, 1956, pp. 3–39, 143–261.
Gerth, H., and Mills, C. W., *Character and Social Structure: The Psychology of Social Institutions*. Harcourt, Brace, 1953.
Hanson, R. C., "Institutions," in Roucek, J. S. (ed.), *Contemporary Sociology*. New York: Phil. Lib., 1958, pp. 64–86.
Hoffsomer, H., *The Sociology of American Life*. Englewood Cliffs, N.J.: Prentice-Hall, 1958, pp. 308–315.
Hughes, E. C., "Institutions and the Community," in Lee, A. M. (ed.), *Principles of Sociology*. New York: Barnes & Noble, 1951, pp. 230–231, 248–255.
Landecker, W. S., "Institutions and Social Integration," *Papers of the Michigan Academy of Sciences, Arts, and Letters*, Vol. 39, 1954, pp. 477–493.
LaPiere, R. T., *Sociology*. New York: McGraw-Hill, 1946, pp. 334–363.
MacIver, R. M., *Community: A Sociological Study*. London: Macmillan, 1917, pp. 153–165.
Malinowski, B., "The Group and the Individual in Functional Analysis," *Am. Jour. Soc.*, 44 (May, 1939): 938–964.
Malinowski, B., *A Scientific Theory of Culture*. Chapel Hill: Univ. of North Carolina Press, 1944, pp. 36–66, 120–131, 158–170.
Malinowski, B., *Freedom and Civilization*. New York: Roy, 1945, pp. 153–171.
Martindale, D., *American Society*. Princeton, N.J.: Van Nostrand, 1960, pp. 152–155, 256–267.
Parsons, T., *The Social System*. Glencoe, Ill.: Free Press, 1951, pp. 36–58.
Perry, R. B., *Realms of Value: A Critique of Civilization*. Cambridge: Harvard Univ. Press, 1954, pp. 153–167.
Radcliffe-Brown, A. R., *Structure and Function in Primitive Society*. London: Cohen & West, Ltd., 1952, pp. 3–14.
Rose, A. M., *Sociology: The Study of Social Relations*. New York: Knopf, 1956, pp. 124–148.
Rose, A. M., "The Comparative Study of Institutions," in Rose, A. M. (ed.), *The Institutions of Advanced Societies*. Minneapolis: Univ. of Minnesota Press, 1958, pp. 3–42.
Thomas, W. I., and Znaniecki, F., *The Polish Peasant in Europe and America*. New York: Knopf, 1920, Vol. I, pp. 31–35.
Williams, R. M., Jr., *American Society: A Sociological Interpretation*. New York: Knopf, 1960, pp. 30–35, 511–540.

For other treatments of American institutions as they contribute to our profile or as they reflect characteristic themes of American life, by both American and foreign observers, see:

Bernard, Jessie, "The United States (Institutions of)," in Rose, A. M. (ed.), *The Institutions of Advanced Societies*. Minneapolis: Univ. of Minnesota Press, 1958, pp. 592–776.
Brogan, D. W., *The American Character*. New York: Knopf, 1944.
Brogan, D. W., *American Themes*. New York: Harper, 1949.

Commager, H. S., *The American Mind: An Interpretation of American Thought and Character*. New Haven: Yale Univ. Press, 1950.

Freeman, L. C., and Winch, R. F., "Societal Complexity: An Empirical Test of a Typology of Societies," *Am. Jour. Soc.*, 62 (Mar., 1957): 461–466.

Gorer, Geoffrey, *The American People*. New York: Norton, 1948.

Gunther, J., *Inside U.S.A.*, New York: Harper, 1951.

Lerner, Max, *America as a Civilization: Life and Thought in the United States Today*. New York: Simon & Schuster, 1957.

Meadows, P., and Torrence, W. D., "American Culture Themes: An Analysis of Foreign Observer Literature," *Soc. & Soc. Res.*, 43 (Sept.–Oct., 1958): 3–7.

Roe, E., and Willowby, G., "Culture Profiles and Emphases," *Am. Jour. Soc.*, 63 (Mar., 1958): 476–490.

Sirjamaki, John, "A Footnote to an Anthropological Approach to the Study of American Culture," *Soc. Forces*, 25 (Mar., 1947): 253–263.

Stewart, G. R., *American Ways of Life*. Garden City, N.Y.: Doubleday, 1954.

Tocqueville, A. de, *Democracy in America*. (ed. by Phillips Bradley), New York: Knopf, 1954.

Warner, W. L., *American Life: Dream and Reality*. Chicago: Univ. of Chicago Press, 1953.

Williams, R. M., Jr., *American Society: A Sociological Interpretation*. New York: Knopf, 1960.

It might also be noted that the extensive materials in the Yale "Cross-Cultural Survey and the Human Relations Area Files" relate almost entirely to particular institutions and institutional features of the different peoples and cultures.

Institutionalization: The Organization of an Institution

In our dynamic age and society new problem situations are continually arising. Spectacular demographic changes, great technological developments such as mechanization of agriculture, utilization of atomic fission are taking place. Culture contacts are quickened, multiplied, and intensified. Patterns of thought are shifting. The number of human beings involved in new situations are increasingly complexly interrelated and interdependent. The number and complexity of new individual and social problem-need situations will increase in the very near future, requiring many new social activities of an instrumental, regulative, and integrative nature. These procedural needs can be met satisfactorily, on the basis of all of our experience to date, only by *institutionalization;* that is, by formally establishing, regularizing, coordinating, and effectively organizing the essential structural components or agencies, abstract and concrete, and by setting up and maintaining appropriate procedures.[1] As Parsons and Shils put it, "It is impossible for a functionally important sector of the social system to be organized and stabilized without some degree of institutionalization."[2] The drift of all collective behavior is toward institutionalization.

In addition to the necessity of constructing new institutions to meet new needs, it is also necessary to revise continually existing institutions. Some institutions, or at least some of their features, may need to be discarded altogether, but many institutions remain necessary in their respective sectors of social life, and therefore eventually need revising.

---

[1] *Institutionalization* should be distinguished from *institutionalism,* which is the tendency of institutions to harden, rigidify, or become archaic; this latter concept will be examined in Chapter Six.

[2] T. Parsons and E. A. Shils, *Toward a General Theory of Action.* Cambridge: Harvard Univ. Press, 1951, p. 174.

In order to revise an institution, it is absolutely necessary to know the nature and function of all of the essential, interrelated model parts. Furthermore, the use of a rapidly developing social technology in the construction and reorganization of institutions suggests that not only every social scientist but also every citizen in a democratic society should know what in the long experience of mankind has come to be fundamental as structural components and functional procedures.

I: The Structural-Functional Components

Effective institutions are not simple. They are composed of a variety of elements, abstract and concrete, the particular combination of which gives them their characteristic structure and makes possible their essential functioning. These tangible and intangible pattern-parts or submechanisms—valuational, ideological, normative-regulative, behavioral, associational, symbolic, physical—are sometimes difficult to distinguish and classify in each institution. They are not mutually exclusive, but frequently overlap. They do not have equal weight in all institutions or in the institutions of all of the different need sectors. There is much greater stress on certain components in some institutional areas than in other areas: for example, value elements loom large in religious institutions but are almost negligible in language institutions; large-scale, formal organizations are of central significance in political, industrial, and commercial institutions; ideological features are important in political and religious institutions but almost absent in communicative and scientific institutions. These components are not equally operational in a given institution at different stages of its development or in the course of its functions; hence, they are not always equally evident.

The efficacy of a particular institution is not dependent upon the number of elements it contains, but upon the degree of development and volume of elements that is most appropriate for its functions. These elements operate variably but work together as a unity.

Although a distinction is not, and cannot be, absolute, a separation can be made between the abstract and concrete natures of institutions.

THE MORE ABSTRACT COMPONENTS

THE RATIONALE COMPLEX. First of all, an institution rests upon, embodies, and synthesizes the body of concepts, meanings, values, beliefs, agreements, preferences, objectives, and justifications that have developed around an area and need; in brief, an institution is based on a rationale and an ideology.[3]

Whatever is definitely established by human beings requires a supporting and interpretive theory of reality. Institutions are no exception. Behind every institution is a metaphysics or set of beliefs about the particular area of reality involved; for example, about the reality, the actuality, of economic things and relations, of sexual and generational relations and needs, and, of course, of the elemental relationship of these to human life.

At the heart of every institution there is a concept or set of concepts or at least an implied system of ideas and principles. Thus at the heart of the family there is the concept of ordered relations of the sexes and the generations; in property, an order regarding ownership or use of things and creatures; in all educational institutions, the idea that the young and the newcomers need systematic socialization and that experience needs to be deliberately imparted to the next generation; in economic institutions, the concept of orderly and adequate satisfaction of wants by processes of production, distribution, and consumption; in religious institutions, the idea of ordered relationships with deity or deities; in scientific institutions, a conception of orderly procedure in the discovery, organization, and presentation of truth. Inherent in every institution is an implied or expressed idea of purpose and function.

The institutional metaphysics and conceptual structuring relate in turn to another abstract component; namely, the value-structure. Here the concern is with both the general value-system and value-orientations of the society or community as these affect the choices, goals, criteria, and efforts of the people, *and* with the particular values developed around and relevant to the particular types of need areas. Values are current estimates of the significance of things, of actions, of relationships, and of events. They are constructs emerging from collective human experience, especially with respect to the consequences of action, imagined or real. They take the form of preferential judgments concerned with good and bad, right and wrong, efficient and inefficient, expedient and inexpedient, desirable and undesirable, necessary and unnecessary, and useful and useless. They relate to areas of experience that have meaning and importance for the participants. This means that every institutionalized department of life is governed by social values; they are explicit in almost every human action, whether these actions be of an instrumental, expressive, or goal-achieving nature. Without the value-structure of the institution, there would be no specific motivation to much of institutional action, no purposes, no goal or goals

[3] See W. G. Sumner, *Folkways*. Boston: Ginn, 1906, pp. 53–54.

to aspire to, and no tests or determinants of the action. Here is the essence and dynamic of institutions; all else is effecting mechanism.

The very sanction and authority of the institution as a whole depend upon the degree to which the institution conforms to a value-scale, which, however, is tested, renewed, and rescaled by the experience of generations.[4] On the other hand, since the institutions are the major shaping and dynamic factors in the lives of men, they define, order, conserve, and share these bodies of values, and apply, exemplify, and otherwise make them operative among associated men.

The final abstract structural element of every operative institution is its ideology which is related to, and in some measure emerges from, the body of meanings and interpretations, the conceptualization of principles, purposes, and relevant values. Although many members could not state them explicitly, there exist socially provided explanations for the existence of every institution, which provide a belief transcending its members. The ideology is the publicly supported and generally held presentation of the institution and the basis of the emotional attachment to it.

THE NORMATIVE STRUCTURE. Institutions are looked upon by some as consisting mainly of complexes of obligatory norms for conduct. Williams speaks of the norms as "linked together into the clusters or complexes we have termed 'institutions,'" and Levy refers to an institution as "a particular type of normative pattern."[5] The particular constituent norms may be unwritten or written, of an informal or a formal nature. Many, especially those of the older and universal institutions, inhere in such media for establishing behavior requirements as folkways, admonitions and proverbs, commandments, customs, taboos, creeds, myths, and legends. In the more highly organized societies—ancient, medieval, modern—the crucial norms are specifically and formally presented in the codified legislative statutes and judicial decisions, and in the charters, code books, constitutions, and by-laws of each purposive association.

The normative structure translates the basic ideas and principles, the body of values, and the ideology of the institution into a set of more or less explicitly indicated requirements of action. The relationship of the norms to the value structure is especially significant. In this connection, William speaks of the term "institution" as referring "to a

---

[4] Cf. R. Mukerjee, *The Social Structure of Values*. London: Macmillan, 1949, pp. 296–308.

[5] R. M. Williams, Jr., *American Society: A Sociological Interpretation*. New York: Knopf, 1960, p. 379. M. J. Levy, Jr., *The Structure of Society*. Princeton: Princeton Univ. Press, 1952, pp. 101–109, 193–197. See also A. R. Radcliffe-Brown, *Structure and Function in Primitive Society*. London: Cohen & West, Ltd., 1952, p. 10.

set of institutional norms that *cohere* around a relatively distinct and socially important complex of values." [6]

The institutional norms are felt as *moral* and often as *legal* imperatives. They set up the mutual expectancies for conforming patterns of behavior and thus give calculability to the behavior.

The norms of a society are not haphazard and unsystematized; they are related to one another in definite patterns; these patterns are mainly those of major institutions—economic, political, religious, and so on. In fact, the institutions of a society embody most of the features of its general normative system. If the norms were not part of these distinguishable institutional mechanisms, they would be confused and inoperative; that is, the institutions are the means of specifically calling attention to the norms and making them functionally effective. All institutions have some kind of coherently organized codal system, though the range in fixity, explicitness, formality, and social weight attached is great. Thus, states have their constitutions, the enactments of their legislative bodies, their treaties and conventions with foreign countries, their court decisions, their common law, their administrative rules and regulations, as well as unwritten rules, principles, practices, and implications governing the informal but public relationships of the citizenry. Underlying the family relationships are not only the various legal statutes governing its formation, composition, maintenance, and perpetuation, but also a set of unwritten demands governing relations of husband and wife, and parents and children. All scientific, religious, and educational institutions have both their written and implied requirements that are related to the underlying concept of the institutional functions. Aesthetic institutions rest upon basic canons of beauty, art, and technique that are current in the relationships and obvious in the overt expressions of the artists. Cultural life and the etiquette of polite society are also at any given time a matter of rather precise principles and requirements. Of course, the highly functional adjustment agencies, such as the political, economic, domestic, or health institutions, are more likely to develop effective and binding codes than the less competitive and less vital institutions, such as the recreational, the aesthetic, or those of polite intercourse.

An especially significant operative feature of the normative structure is that it not only provides the channels of institutional action, but it also provides the sanctions; that is, it prescribes the penalties for violation of proscribed action or the failure to perform required action, and indicates the rewards for conforming action. These sanctions may be vague and mild, or they may be highly explicit and severe. The severity of the penalties is dictated mainly by the importance to the group or

[6] Williams, *op. cit.,* p. 31. Italics mine.

society of the social values involved in the particular type of situation. The best index of the institutional norms of a group or society is the degree of moral indignation aroused by their violation and the severity of the penalties decreed against the violators.

Some institutional norms may continue to be highly effective in the folkways and mores of a particular area even though the legal norms in that particular area of behavior or social relationships set up different rules and criteria of action. In some parts of the United States at the present time, for example, desegregation is a part of the laws and court decisions, but segregation still remains in the folkways and mores.

THE MORE CONCRETE COMPONENTS

THE PERSONNEL STRUCTURES. The personnel of an institution consists of those qualified persons who are involved in its relationships and directly participating in its activities as they attempt to satisfy cooperatively and reciprocally (or even competitively in some situations) certain categories of needs, and who are recognized by society as such a structural-functional entity in contrast to the members of other institutions. They are the people who express in their behavior the rationale of the institution, who conform to—in fact, are governed by—its normative structure, and who perform its various functions.

The personnel of a particular institution is determined by the nature of the needs to be satisfied and the consequent functions to be performed. For example, males and females of reproductive age set up families and form a grouping of parents and children (and, depending upon the specific type of family, of other kinsmen); an aesthetic institutional group is determined not by sex or age dependency and complementarity, but by the need for aesthetic expression. In the process of institutionalization, the particular categories and combinations of people to be served must first be determined.

Eligibility for membership varies in different institutional areas and subareas. Membership in a given family or the state, for example, cannot be avoided; all men are born into them. All men are in some degree qualified to belong to some political, legal, economic, scientific, aesthetic, educational, or religious institution. All men do belong to some variety of institutional group or category in almost every institutional area or sector. But there are specific qualifications for membership and participation in many specialized groups and organizations carrying certain types of institutional functions.[7]

The examination of the personnel structuring of an institution divides

[7] Cf. R. B. Perry, *Realms of Value: A Critique of Civilization*. Cambridge: Harvard Univ. Press, 1954, pp. 154–155.

itself into (1) the patterned role-performing in the statuses and (2) the groups, including the special associations or purposive organizations into which the personnel of many institutions are organized (the associational system or structure) in order to conduct more effectively the institution's functions.

The status-role structure. Each institution is not only a scheme for providing different satisfactions, but also a scheme of division of labor. The division of action among the membership rests upon different principles. Much of it is based on functional grounds; the different functions of the institution must be carried on by persons in different social positions. It also rests in part upon innate, that is, biogenic or psychogenic traits of the different members, and also upon socioculturally acquired qualifications for different functions. Also, in most institutions, there is some sort of ranking or hierarchization of members in terms of the institution's purposes. Some actors in the division of action scheme are more active or more directly contributory to the ends of the institution, while others are more passive.

This is another way of saying that each institution has its status-role complex. The statuses or ranked positions that the individuals of a society hold in relationship to each other are almost entirely positions in the institutionalized sectors of social life. Each status relates to a societally important type of function. Family institutions have father and mother, husband and wife, parent and child statuses; economic institutions have those of manager, clerk, and machine tender; educational institutions have those of administrators, teachers, visiting nurse, and pupils. Each status requires certain duties and responsibilities, but also provides certain rights and privileges. The statuses are always reciprocally related to each other so that the status structure is at least a two-way and usually a multi-way exchange of services and effects.

The specific activities that individuals and categories of individuals carry on are more or less defined by the group concerned or by the whole society. These standardized configurations of action are the roles. Each institution has its appropriate and peculiar role system, adequate in its number and variety of roles. Each individual not only plays roles in every institutional sector of social life, but usually also plays at least several roles in every institution of which he is a part. In fact, almost all the standard roles that individuals play are institutional roles.

The role-system of the institution, however, is independent of the individuals performing the roles. Its personnel is constantly reconstructed as individuals cease to be involved in the institutional complex of action.

The expectations of the roles flow from, and are oriented to, the general value-system of the community as it relates to the particular interest area, and the actions are defined and dictated by the rules of the normative system. The roles are concrete, dynamic expressions of the normative system, in conformity with it. If they fail in this, the aims of the institutions will not be served.

Each role involves personal characteristics, such as sex, age, special interests, certain technical or other acquired proficiencies. Each role has its own action-routines of an active or passive nature. Each role has its obligations as well as its privileges.

The institutional role itself is largely a product of historical experience—trial and error as well as deliberate devising and addition. It is partly a matter of folkways, folk values, mores, expediencies, utilities, rules, and even formal codal requirements. The expectations of the roles are continually coming into being, and frequently into conflict with each other. They become adjusted and altered, and often some elements of an institution disappear entirely over the course of an institution's life-cycle.

The role may become representative of abstract ideals if institutional groups establish not only specifications regarding concrete duties but also ideals of behavior which they seek to make effective in the area.

At any given time and place the model, or standard pattern, of actional content and expectation of most of the essential roles is formalized and fixed—even stereotyped—and usually known adequately by those who need to perform them or wish to perform them. In fact, society stresses the stable feature of the role; variations are minimized and often discouraged. Thus roles represent constancies of behavior.

Every community has its "atmosphere" of roles which is absorbed by most members. The more common and recurrent roles are widely known and understood and often can be performed without much rehearsal. Others, involving training and special techniques, require practice in their performance, but the content of such roles is well-known at least to all who are likely to be in situations where they would be expected to perform them. For example, when a young woman marries, she assumes the role of wife; the requirements of the new role are clear to her and to others in its outlines.

The members of the institution always play their roles relative to each other as part of a pattern of reciprocity and complementarity. The relationships may be dyadic (between two), triadic (between three), or of higher order. Consider, for example, the dyadic role of reciprocities and complementarities among the relatively small personnel of the nuclear family: husband-wife, brother-sister, father-son, father-daughter, mother-son, and mother-daughter. There are, of course, triadic combinations and situations involving all of the role-players of the family. Consider the infinitely greater array and complexity of reciprocities and complementarities in economic or political relations. The reciprocity may take a variety of forms. For example, it may be a matter of cooperative, or joint, or complementary action, as in the case of husband and wife; the relationship may be one of dominance and submission, as in the case of parent and child or manager and subordinate, in some phases of their role-playing; it may be a matter of succorance-dependence (father-child); it may take the form of producer and consumer. It can be said that an institution is a system of roles, "a complex of institutional role integrates"; it "is made up of a plurality of interdependent role-patterns or components of them."[8]

The group structuring. The groupings of the institutional personnel, that is, the combinations of interacting or associating role-performing personnel, (1) are made up of the persons, variously differentiated but elementally interdependent, who by joint and reciprocal action satisfy some portion of each other's needs and (2) are more or less standardized clusterings of interrelated individuals, groups, and functional categories of persons that more or less consciously and in more or less organized form carry on for the community or society the various kinds and complexes of institutional activities.

Regardless of the degree of formal organization of an institutional group, almost every one of them presents the following characteristics and essential features: (1) a particular value-orientation, for example, the religious values of a church, or the recreational values of a bowling league; (2) established tests of selection and admittance to the group, based on the ends to be pursued and the functions to be conducted; (3) a goal or combination of goals, according to which the members orient their actions; and (4) the integrated roles of the members.[9]

The institutional group is one of the most obvious aspects of institutions and is occasionally mistaken for the whole. It is true that institutions as regularized action systems manifest themselves visibly through their specific groups and through the behavior of the participants in these groups. It is the records of the behavior of groups that tell us about the nature of most of the institutions of the past.

However, the fundamental distinction between institution and group must be kept in mind. For example, *the* family in any society is a predetermined rationale with a set of procedures, whereby certain individual and societal needs are satisfied. But each individual family consists, concretely, of a combination of human beings—husband or hus-

---

[8] T. Parsons, *The Social System*. Glencoe, Ill.: Free Press, 1951, p. 39. On institutional roles and role-structure, see: J. S. Himes, "Changing Social Roles in the New South," *S-W Soc. Science Quart.*, 37 (Dec., 1956): 234–242. A. M. Rose, *Sociology: The Study of Human Relations*. New York: Knopf, 1956, pp. 130–131, 135. S. F. Nadel, *The Theory of Social Structure*. Glencoe, Ill.: Free Press, 1957, pp. 20–124.

[9] Cf. E. T. Hiller, "Institutions and Institutional Groups," *Soc. Forces*, 20 (Mar., 1942): 297–306.

bands, wife or wives, children, and collateral kinsmen—who have the needs to be satisfied and carry on some portion of the functions. There are, of course, all manner of other institutional groups—work groups, educational groups, recreational groups, political groups, military groups, religious groups, power-prestige groups, and social welfare groups. Within a given institution there usually are not only many groups but also many varieties of subgroups.

These groupings, however, all pursue their principle and auxiliary functions in ways that have become standardized in the society. They are types of groupings that are themselves institutionalized. The institutional group exists as the combination of beneficiaries of at least some of the institution's functions and as the socioculturally organized human instrument for carrying on certain aspects of the institution's functioning. But the institution as a whole has a larger existence. It has a reality prior to, and independent of, any given grouping of individuals and determines the specific combination of persons and the form of, and activities of, this combination. The particular groups, in any of their forms, may deteriorate, or break up and disappear, but the institution goes on. A particular family may be broken by divorce or greatly impaired by the death of one or more members, but the permanent monogamous family goes on. Finally, each institutional group is a separate and somewhat unique affair, existing in a limited portion of time, while the institution is ideal, universal, and more or less permanent.

Most of the groups of which we are a part and in which we participate, other than those that are casual, highly eccentric, and temporary, are institutional groups.

The membership of each institutional group, however, is composed of a selected personnel determined by the institutional function. It is a system of exclusion as well as inclusion; it keeps out as well as takes in. To get in, you have to conform to the institutional pattern: to set up a family, you marry; to join a business organization, you get hired in; to join a religious body, you subscribe to certain creedal principles; to get into Congress as a member, you must be duly elected or appointed.

The groups in almost every institutionalized need area are of both an informal and formal nature. Increasingly, however, the more formal organizations of personnel, or associations, tend to be resorted to of necessity in conducting the institution's functions. Associations are groups of people specifically and purposively organized for the pursuit of particular interests or goals. Any joint action requiring systematization is conducted by means of an association. In the association, definite duties are imposed and rights bestowed upon the constituent individuals; there are appropriate methods and agents of functioning, especially devised administrative machinery.

The state itself, and its political parties, its bureaus and departments, its legislative bodies, the courts, the police systems, and so on, are associations through which the different phases and functions of government are expressed and conducted; the denominations and sects, the organizations of laymen and clergymen, are associations through which religion functions in American life; the schools, colleges, and universities, with their teaching staffs, teachers' associations, administrative bodies, school boards, boards of trustees, and so on, are associations through which educational functions are carried on; corporations, boards of trade, boards of directors, banks, clearing houses, stock and produce exchanges, factories, and stores are associations carrying on industry, finance, and commerce; families are patterned associations expressive of ordered sexual and parent-child relations; art schools and art institutes are associations embodying certain phases of aesthetic institutions; scientific societies and research organizations are concerned with science as an institution. Even in the case of language as an institution, there are organizations of professionals, such as teachers, and organizations for the promotion and correction of language. In the area of recreation, there are the recreation boards of cities and the corporations to provide commercialized recreation. These associations are all tangible and organized combinations of at least certain portions of the total personnel, and either demonstrably or presumably essential to the adequate functioning of the institution.

Wherever we find an institution, we find at least one association; in the highly developed and highly diversified institutionalized need areas, for example the economic or political, we find many of them. Institutions and associations are concomitant and correlative phenomena. Most of the associations of a society, if they have any durability and utility whatsoever, are the visible, organized, and living aspects of institutions, and the perceptible machines through which the rationale and the purposes are carried into effective action. They promote the underlying meanings and concepts, embellish and effectuate the ideology, maintain and revise the codes, are the arena in which most of the roles are performed, and are the source of the stimuli that produce most of the conditioning to, and instruction in, institutional ways.

In the more formally organized institutional associations—those bureaucratically organized—there are special categories of personnel of great significance referred to as *functionaries*. All persons connected with institutions, even the rank and file members, are functionaries in the sense that they have functions of one sort or another to perform. But in the large-scale, formal organizations, there are certain categories of participants, consisting of special individuals and groups vested with specialized duties of an administrative or technical nature. The *administrative* functionaries, usually selected in some appropriate manner for appropriate abilities and skills, are vested with authority and administrative power, enforce decisions of the policy-making bodies, and coordinate not only all of the role-playing individuals and lesser groupings but also the machinery of the formal association itself and the system of symbols and the physical equipment. Specifically, it is the function of administrators to make decisions, to apply sanctions against those who fail to meet the expectations of their particular job in the whole undertaking, to select assistants to whom authority may be delegated, to assume responsibility for organizing the division of labor and for assigning the tasks, and, in general, to keep the whole institutionalized system moving efficiently.[10]

The *specialist* functionaries are ordinarily thought of as those with specialized knowledge and technical skills who often render professional services. In general, ministers and bishops are functionaries of the church; the officials of corporations, plant managers, and supervisors are economic functionaries; teachers, superintendents, and supervisors are functionaries of the school; government has its legislative, executive, administrative, judicial, technical, and military functionaries; doctors and nurses render special services in health organizations.

In connection with the functionaries as important elements in the process of institutionalization, attention should be called to the increasing significance of *professionalization*. It relates directly to the increase of knowledge and technical specialization, and the fact that in one institutional area after another there are a growing number of specialist functionaries who develop and utilize these special knowledges. Not only do we have the traditional professions in the fields of religion, law, teaching, and medicine, but more recently there has developed professionalization among scientists, accountants, actuaries, journalists, engineers, nurses, credit men, insurance consultants, social workers, public servants, and—increasingly—business men.

THE PHYSICAL EQUIPMENT. In order to ensure effective functioning, it is essential that every institution have some physical paraphernalia or equipment, though the amount and kind may differ greatly among the different institutions—what L. L. Bernard referred to long ago as the "physical extensions" of institutions.[11] These physical features are an external aspect, an aspect in time and space. Along with the personnel

[10] Cf.: H. Gerth and C. W. Mills, *Character and Social Structure: The Psychology of Institutions.* New York: Harcourt, Brace, 1953, pp. 416–424. H. S. Becker, "The Teacher in the Authority System of the Public School," *Jour. Educ. Soc.,* 27 (Nov., 1953): 128–141.

[11] L. L. Bernard, *An Introduction to Social Psychology.* New York: Holt, 1926, pp. 564–565.

elements, especially the organized associational aspects, these are the elements that the man in the street usually has in mind when he thinks of institutions; they are for him the whole content, probably because they are the most readily perceived as component structural entities and functional agents.

Two main kinds of physical equipment in institutions are ordinarily distinguished. First, there are those items of symbolic significance; that is, physical objects that have come to be charged with sentimental meaning in the particular culture or at any rate among the personnel of the particular institution. These are intended to convey some of the meanings of the institution. In some instances, however, the institutional symbols not only convey the meaning of the institution to its own personnel, but also to those, even in other societies and cultures, who have contact with the institution. Thus, the cross is the physical symbol of Christianity; the crescent, the symbol of Mohammedanism; the statues of Buddha, the symbol of Buddhism; the wedding ring, the symbol of marriage; the flag, crowns, and scepters, the symbols of government; the hearth, the family crest, heirlooms (and today the station wagon), symbols of family; the double-headed serpent coiled about the staff, the symbol of medical science and technology; and uniforms, robes, vestments, stripes, badges, and other insignia, symbols of a variety of institutional activities.

Even more essential is the utilitarian material and mechanical equipment, the material outfit. It is possible for some institutions to function with very little such equipment; but, in general, most institutions depend heavily upon all manner of material property. For example: land and buildings; offices and furniture; homesteads and chattels; money; apparatus for communication and transportation; factories, tools, and machines; classrooms, libraries, books, blackboards and desks, and laboratories; court houses, city halls, police and fire stations, jails and penitentiaries, weapons of various sorts; church edifices and altars; art galleries and museums.

II: Making Institutionalization Effective

The component parts must exist if the institution is to function, but the *raison d'être* of institutions is not to exist as structures, but to get specific jobs done. As Feibleman has put it, the institution is "a sort of manufacturing plant, a structure of men and material and procedures intended to turn out a certain product."[12] To this end, members must

[12] J. K. Feibleman, "Institutions, Law and Morals," *Tulane Law Rev.,* 31 (1957): 503–516.

behave in certain ways, individually, jointly, or reciprocally, in the social situations where social experience has deemed standardization and establishment of action to be desirable or essential.

We are not concerned in this section with the rationale of institutions but with some of the essential and typical techniques, procedures, and devices whereby institutions "work"; whereby they grip individuals, groups, and categories and make them behave along institutional lines; whereby the institutions maintain and perpetuate themselves as functional instruments.

Some of these procedures operate unconsciously and passively; in fact, because of a feeling, if not a reasoned conclusion, that the institutionalized ways of life are a bulwark against disorder and the failure of need-satisfaction, there seems to be a self-generation and automatic accumulation of supports. There is, for example, in the course of the establishment of most institutions, the development and use of various "re-enforcements,"[13] such as the folklore and traditions relating to the institution, the historical accounts about it, its complex of stories, precepts, myths, fictions, anecdotes, sentiments, beliefs, ideas, and doctrines. These constitute what is sometimes also referred to as the traditionalism of the institution. There must be a certain complement of these to make the institution workable and durable. They express, make vivid, and strengthen the purposes, principles, and standards of the institution.

Because of our concern, not only with the operation as such of the long-standing blocks of institutions, but also with the operation of those in the newly institutionalized areas of modern life, the more active organizational and operative procedures and techniques for making institutions work should be especially stressed.

There is, first, the necessity of integrating and coordinating the integral functional components—the rationale, the normative system, the personnel and group elements, the equipment—so that they function together. This is the institutional aspect of the eternal problem of equilibrium and adjustment of parts; of avoiding overstress or understress of certain components compared with others in the over-all operation; of avoiding dislocations and lags among the components. The relative play permitted or required of the different components will vary with the functions of the particular institutions or the institutions of a given sector of life, and with the value system of the society at the time.

Informal and formal procedures for training the personnel for institutional performance are essential. The people involved need to be

---

[13] An apt term used by J. S. Ellsworth, *Factory Folkways: A Study of Institutional Structure and Change.* New Haven: Yale Univ. Press, 1952, p. 94.

oriented to the types of social situations to which the institution applies, both mentally and with respect to their overt behavior. The institution's concepts, values, social attitudes, and norms need to be imparted to them. The goals of the institution need to be internalized so that the members acquire the spirit of the goals, and develop pertinent aspirations. The members need to be instructed regarding the variety and quality of role-performance and need to have some training for the performance of these activities. They need to be made conscious of the sanctions, both of the penalties attached to inadequate performance or violations and of the positive sanctions which produce approval, recognition, esteem, and other even more substantial rewards.[14]

Closely related to the instructional procedures is the effective manipulation of the institution's symbol system. The pertinent symbols are not merely those of habitually used and systematized language, but all sorts of visible or audible signs that represent in a convenient, expedient, clear, and simple way an institutional event or process. The power of symbols to translate the abstract elements of the institution into concrete and communicable reality can be seen in the effects upon behavior of flags and emblems, of insignia, of imaginative national figures like Uncle Sam or John Bull, of songs, hymns and anthems, of slogans and catchwords ("Equality, Liberty, and Fraternity").

The development and manipulation of symbols in the effective operation of the institution is important for several reasons. Symbolic processes are economical ways of obtaining institutionalized behavior. They function as widely comprehensible carriers of the institution's meanings—even the most abstract ones. In a quiet and non-spectacular way, they call forth emotionally toned attitudes; they appeal to the imagination, focus attention, allay doubts, emphasize ideals of behavior, and glorify practices; they can function most effectively as "cues" or "triggers" to desirable or essential action. But by no means the least of their functions is their effectiveness as a means of emotionally and functionally binding the people together. Loewenstein points out that participation in symbolic recognition of a collective value promotes solidarity and unanimity in the group; also, the symbolism creates, focuses, and externalizes allegiance to the common institutional cause, and hence increases the efficacy and unity of the institutional action.[15]

Although symbols are helpful in all institutional systems, they are not equally useful in the different institutionalized sectors of social

---

[14] So important is this procedure that all societies have a special set of institutions, the educational institutions, among whose main functions is that of making all of the other institutions effective. These will be discussed in Chapter Thirteen.

[15] See especially the keen analysis of the institutional use of symbols by Karl Loewenstein, "The Influence of Symbols of Politics," in R. V. Peel and J. S. Roucek (eds.), *Introduction to Politics*. New York: Crowell, 1946, pp. 62–84.

life; for example, symbols used in the sense discussed above are seemingly more effective in the familial, political, religious, and educational areas than they are in the economic, scientific-technological, or social welfare areas. Furthermore, specific interests of different institutions are defined in terms of specialized symbols appropriate to their respective contexts; for example, as a negative illustration, a lilting singing commercial would be ludicrous advertising a chemical fertilizer.

It is necessary to have what Max Weber referred to as routinization.[16] The actions of the personnel need to be standardized as to content and established, both in functional and time sequence, and to some extent made habitual, so that they are unconsciously performed in the different typical situations. All of the operatives must acquire facility in the routinized actions; the roles must be played in their place and time with at least minimal expertness. Even a degree of stereotyping of values and attitudes is desirable. It is also necessary that the various instruments be handled competently through proper practice and at the proper times and places. Gerth and Mills point out that the whole array of technologies involved in the operation and maintenance of the institution need to be "instituted."[17]

It is a matter of particular benefit to some institutions to enhance their routinization and to add certain additional grooving, enforcement, and value emphasis to desirable or essential institutional performance by ritualizing and ceremonializing the behavior. To ritualize is to establish a more or less formalized rhythm and sequence of action—a "prescribed set of words and acts"—used practically without variation, in carrying on the crucial activity of the institution. Thus, familial, religious, political, educational, and many economic institutions ritualize many of their important actions. Ritualization makes such action automatic or habitual, more regular, exact, and more expectable; and it enables action to be carried out with a minimum of on-the-spot contrivance and of responsibility on the part of the performer, reducing the necessity of continuous instruction and constant social pressures.

Ceremonialization applies particularly to behavior on special institutional occasions—occasions that put into sharp focus the basic values, the supreme goals, and the crucial social significance of the institution. In familial institutions, such occasions are the wedding or the baptism or consecration of the child; in religious institutions, the recital of the Apostle's Creed or the taking of communion; in educational institutions, the honors convocation and the graduation proceedings. The ceremony, as noted, recalls attention to the cherished and sanctified institutional

[16] H. Gerth and C. W. Mills, (transls. and eds.), *From Max Weber: Essays in Sociology*. New York: Oxford Univ. Press, 1946, pp. 296–297.
[17] H. Gerth and C. W. Mills, *Character and Social Structure: The Psychology of Social Institutions*. New York: Harcourt, Brace, 1953, pp. 388–392.

values involved. It also tinges the institution itself with impressiveness, solemnity, and gravity. Both ritual and ceremony recommunicate the underlying values and meanings by means of their symbolic action; both help to re-cement the institutional group and enhance its devotion to its objectives.[18]

Most modern institutions require that many—often the most important—of their functions be carried on by means of large-scale formal organizations. As instances, in the institutional sectors, we note the industrial or commercial corporations, the charitable foundation, the church, the hospital, the army, the law-enforcing agency, the public school system, the college or university. The health, effective functioning, and durability of the institution—its workability—rest upon making its formal organizations "work." This means maintaining a system of administration. There is an extensive literature on this subject developed by theorists and practitioners, especially in the areas of political, business, and school administration; and sociologists have been paying increasing analytical attention to this subject.[19] Some of the more obvious and pertinent procedural aspects of the performance of the bureaucracies of institutions will be mentioned.

There is, first, the effective manipulation, both for the institution's particular personnel and for the public at large, of the institution's ideology with its values, beliefs, myths, rationalizations, statements of general social and societal objectives. This is essential (1) for the effectiveness and consistency of operation of the organization and (2) for the acquisition and retention of the community's or the society's support, since the organization depends on these not only for its customers or clientele, but also for its directly operative personnel, its finances, and materials.

An institution must set its own goals and reinterpret them as external and internal changes occur.

This, in turn, requires the formulation of policies, the drawing up of plans, and the building of programs combining many kinds and levels of action.

Finally there is the operation of the complex over-all organization itself. This involves:

(1) Logical and technical specialization, separation, and integration of tasks.

(2) The hierarchization of structural instruments and functional procedures.

---

[18] See L. S. Cressman, "Ritual the Conserver," *Am. Jour. Soc.,* 35 (Jan., 1930): 564-.572. Also the excellent study, Orrin E. Klapp, *Ritual and Cult: A Sociological Interpretation.* Washington, D.C.: Public Affairs Press, 1956.

[19] See, for example, the bibliography in Hertzler, *Society in Action,* pp. 415–416.

(3) Assigning functions to the different administrative and technical levels of the hierarchy and among the departments on the same level; assigning personnel to their "spheres of competence," to use Weber's terminology.

(4) Developing the sequences of superior-subordinate relationships, exercising adequate authority, and maintaining the line of command.

(5) Standardizing the operations, developing them as manageable units, and maintaining calendarity; that is, a definite sequence and time schedule of activities.

(6) Coordinating for fluid and efficient functioning all of the vertical and horizontal subdivisions.

(7) Developing and maintaining the channels of communication, both lateral and vertical.

(8) Maintaining discipline.

(9) Maintaining leadership and technical and professional expertize. This means particularly (a) adequate means of recruiting and selecting the executive and administrative officials and the technical experts for the different hierarchical levels and the different departments and (b) arranging for the continued replacement of departed and retired leaders and experts.

(10) In many cases, maintaining examination and training programs, both for the administratively and technically specialized and for the rank and file personnel.

(11) Maintaining the means of avoiding internal conflict (that is, with its rank and file personnel), schism, and disorganization.

III: Institutions in Modern Society

The institutional system of modern, complex, greatly extending, and rapidly changing society becomes increasingly difficult to comprehend. The institutions increase greatly in number; they are found in greatly modified form in some sectors; many of them become increasingly specialized as to function; their functions change continually; institutionalization is extended into areas of social life heretofore non-institutionalized; there is considerable inter-institutional transfer of functions; reorganization of standards and functions occurs in them, though usually somewhat belatedly and at greatly varying rates in the different sectors. Some of these situations and changes need to be examined in their present societal content, but the factors and types of adjustment will be more sharply focused and delineated, if we briefly contrast the institutions and institutional organization of the simpler folk societies with those of modern society.

THE INSTITUTIONS OF THE SIMPLER SOCIETIES

Most of the institutions, and the general institutional system for that matter, of the simpler societies are rather simple and concrete, though occasionally some institution, like the marriage systems of some of the Australian tribesmen, turns out to be amazingly intricate and involved. The prevailing simplicity is due to several factors.

The institutions are mainly those of people living in primary groups —the extended family, the small village. The institutions do not need complicated organizational machinery and procedures. The needs to be met are quite concrete and relatively few as to number. The institutions operate directly and largely spontaneously with the certain force of the whole community behind them. Every person in the community is in some degree a participant in all of its institutions; no one can escape from the community's institutional requirements.

The institutions of the simple societies are largely subjective rather than objective in content. The institutionalized behavior of the individuals is largely of a customary and habitual nature; the cooperative execution of institutional tasks is accomplished through communication by verbal and gesture symbols; the discussion is informal; the direction takes place through personal contact; much of the behavior is imitative.

In the very simple societies, the institutions are relatively undifferentiated. This is largely because a simple division of labor prevails in such societies. In many simple societies, one generalized institution, the family, particularly in the form of the kinship group, takes care of most of the basic functions. It provides for orderly sex satisfaction and the bearing, rearing, and educating of the young. It also orders the relations of the age groups; it functions along economic lines as the basic production unit with its occupational division and organization as well as the basic consumption unit; it is the primary source of education; it provides the "social security" services; it carries on many of the religious functions; it even conducts rudimentary political functions in that it orders certain intragroup as well as intergroup and external relations (for example, some war activities). As another instance of the limited differentiation, the special institutional functionaries or professionals are often relatively undifferentiated; some of them, the medicine men, political chiefs, and priests, for example, are almost indistinguishable, so that instead of three different institutions—medicine, government and religion—there seems to be only one.

Simple societies are relatively static. They are rather isolated, having limited contact with other societies. They are homogeneous as to population. The ancient established ways suffice. Hence, there is no great need of continually adjusting institutions to new conditions or even of contriving new institutions.

THE INSTITUTIONS OF MODERN SOCIETIES

A modern society is quite different. The commercial, scientific-technological, industrial, intellectual-spiritual, demographic, political, and managerial revolutions of the last three centuries have also effected a revolution in social institutions. Aspects of this latter revolution are revealed in a society like our own.

There is, first of all, the utter necessity of institutionalizing more and more areas of social life. In a modern, mass society there is a great amount of impersonality, anonymity, individualization, physical and social mobility, social distance and strangeness among the people; their interests are varied, and their relationships are complex and diffuse; their life is secularized to a high degree; and their normative order is in a somewhat anomic state. At the same time, interdependence increases in amount and complexity, and the social relationships and situations requiring ordering and control increase in kind, number, and social gravity. Yet, there must be effective operation, and the sheer impersonality, complexity, bigness, and normative uncertainty and confusion demand a high degree of societal regulation.

The folkways, mores, and customs are not wholly inoperative in a mass society. They do function to some extent in the primary-group relationships wherever these survive. But the regulative influence of primary groups takes care of only a small portion of the important interrelationships nowadays, and individuals can easily escape from the control of their primary groups by losing themselves in the sea of strangers. It is obvious also that the primary controls do not take care of the secularistic-anomic tendencies in our society, nor do they apply to all of the *new* types of situations and relationships that require regulation and for which crescive instruments are inadequate.

The host of new situations, new types of relationships, and new needs point to the desirability—in fact, the necessity—of institutionalizing these areas as well as maintaining ever more effective institutionalization of the older, long-standard areas of social life, for the very anomic condition in some of these older areas is due to insufficient institutionalization.[20]

Because of the increased and elaborated division of labor of modern societies and the corresponding differentiation and specialization of functions, there has been a great institutional diversification and specialization, resulting in an extension of institutional forms, in the considerable modification of existing forms, and the actual contrivance of new ones. In contrast to the relatively generalized institutions of simple societies, we have, for example, such new specialized ones or modifi-

---

[20] Talcott Parsons, in fact, speaks of anomie as "the polar antithesis of full institutionalization." *The Social System.* Glencoe, Ill.: Free Press, 1951, p. 39.

cations of older institutions as work institutions, play and recreational institutions, health institutions, social assistance and social security institutions, and educational institutions for technical and professional training. Even the universal institutions, such as the economic, political, and religious, have become increasingly separated in some respects, and quite generally more differentiated and specialized; for example, church and state are less and less fused, and economic and political activities are becoming more and more differentiated.

There has, in fact, been such a specialization of institutions that in contemporary societies most of the major institutional sectors, even in some instances particular institutions, have become the specialties of different investigative and analytical disciplines in the social sciences, including a number of special sociologies, such as industrial sociology, family sociology, the sociology of the professions, the sociology of work, the sociology of religion, political and legal sociology, and the sociology of science.

At the same time and closely related to the fact of institutionalization, there has been a broadening and extension of institutional functions. The technological developments in almost every area of life, the multiplication of cultural contacts and cultural "feed-back," the greatly increasing heterogeneity of populations, the greatly increased organizational complexity of society, and the vast increase in the amount and range of knowledge and all manner of human insights—all have brought a great differentiation, elaboration, even in some instances an elevation of interests and values. We have complicated social psychological and societal needs far beyond the more organic ones supplied elementally by the domestic and economic institutions; in addition to the older needs, we have developed new expressional, spiritual, and idealistic needs. New or modified institutional forms are necessary to cope with new meanings and interpretations, to provide new organizational practices and meet new institutional expectations, and to regularize all manner of new special-interest groups. Because of new functional imperatives, some of the new institutions have come to be as important as the old ones, notably science-technology in our industrialized-urbanized-gadgetized culture. Similarly, the family, religion, and government have taken on a great variety of new functions. In general, whenever enough people feel that a function is vital to the satisfaction of a need, a new institution arises or a modification and functional extension of an existent institution occurs.

A somewhat parallel development is found in the fact that certain functions long conducted in a single, spontaneous way, such as recreation, the care of the aged, sick, and infirm, now cannot be adequately conducted according to modern standards and under modern conditions prevailing by the institutions once providing them; hence, owing to their

commanding importance, these activities must be specially institutionalized. Malinowski has noted that, as culture advances, organizational
activities, which on the primitive level were carried out as a by-product
of other institutions, become organized in their own right, notably military groups, admnistrative organizations, the political state, courts of
law, and the professions.[21]

Closely related to the extension of functions is the shifting of functions from one institution to another, even across sector lines. The
"logics" of given functions for given institutions and the capacity of
given institutions to conduct given functions in a particular new societal
context change. Thus, for example, the family's functions as an economic production agency have been taken over by industrial institutions,
and the responsibility for the aged has in some part shifted to semi-
public and public agencies. Many former educational, religious, and
recreational activities of the family have been transferred to other institutions. On the other hand, the family has taken on the satisfaction
of new cultural, health, and emotional needs. The Church has yielded
functions to government, while the churches in many instances have
assumed sociational, recreational, welfare, even psychiatric responsibilities.

A further aspect of modern institutional systems is the fact that they
are increasingly formalized; that is, they are characterized by organizational machinery. When life is simple and interpersonal relations are
direct, institutions can be quite informal. But in a complex environment, relationships are increasingly impersonal and long range. Hence,
there is less and less dependence upon primary-group interpretations of
relationships and customary procedures, and more and more development of contrived ways and bureaucratic organization. Modern institutions have to have written and codified rules of procedure, formal
organizations of personnel, efficient administrative organization, and a
sizable complement of physico-social techniques and agencies; in brief,
they must be legal, formal, and mechanical in operation.

The rules and requirements of modern institutions must be definitely,
but simply, stated and known throughout the entire area of contact; and
the penalties that attach to the violations should be specific and certain
of application; this is best assured through organizations with definitely
assigned responsibility. Although the personal touch is desirable, most
of the institutions of a modern society are effective only in so far as they
are well-constituted in the rationality and timeliness of their codal features, the impersonality of their organizational forms, and the capability
and aggressiveness of their functionaries. Enforcement must be objectively punitive, a matter of impersonal pressures by semi-public boards

---

[21] B. Malinowski, *Freedom and Civilization*. New York: Roy, 1945, p. 154.

operating under grants of power, by police or other constituted authorities. The institutions must function with mechanical impartiality, certainty, and smoothness; and such operation only comes with large-scale organization.

This essential high organization is partly due to the fact that the modern institution in its very nature and operation requires it. It is also partly owing to the fact that the people themselves, the participants and beneficiaries, simply do not know how to act institutionally in many modern situations. Their part in the complex, impersonal social machinery is difficult to determine; there is often a vagueness and impersonality of values, a confusion and ambiguity, and hence uncertainty of goals. Quite obviously the vast number of human agents cannot act randomly but only in a highly organized manner.

Thus, bureaucratic organization is increasingly essential in every need sector. There are the great commercial, financial, and industrial corporations, as well as corporations in communication and transportation. Workers are organized in massive labor unions. Religious denominations tend to become great standardized organizations rather than close-knit, spirit-satisfying congregations. Educational functions at all levels are conducted by great systems. Libraries, professional groups, charitable organizations, and the press show the same tendency toward bureaucratization. Even such areas as those of health, recreation, social work, and the familial and aesthetic institutions have formal organizations to assist with some of their functions.

Related to the fact of ever wider organization and bureaucratization is the equally obvious fact that more and more dependence must be and is placed on trained and specialized, possibly even professionalized, functionaries to administer the performance of the institutional tasks in a timely and efficient manner. Less and less can institutions depend upon even the most loyal and well-intentioned amateurs. Needs have to be determined by scientific methods; experimentation has to be carried on intelligently and on such a scale that it will not upset existing institutions; procedures have to be carefully and intelligently planned on the basis of a knowledge of the nature of the particular society and the significance of its social trends. The man in the street does not have these proficiencies.

Many modern institutions are extending—must, in fact, be operative —over ever wider geographic areas; that is, they are characterized by ever wider areal extension, brought about by the extension of almost every sort of interdependence and exchange. There may still be some local uniqueness; but these local or somewhat eccentric features do not exist at the expense of area-wide uniformities of expectancy and usage.

Institutional requirements are increasingly geared to the average man, who, although an abstraction, has come to be a veritable tyrant in modern life. This situation exists because of (1) the necessity of standardizing the behavior of ever more individuals along institutional lines and (2) because of the formalization of institutions. The unique individual must be ignored in the modern processes of institutionalization. Unavoidably, there is the uniform treatment of non-uniform persons and conditions; the innumerable and diverse individuals are treated as modal or average entities.

Finally, more and more institutions are dependent upon the state for the establishment of some of their rules, for the enforcement of their rules, for the rendering of some of their services, and for the certification of the proficiency of their service-rendering personnel. This widespread influence of the modern state on most of the institutions is noticeable in democratic as well as totalitarian societies. First of all, the regulative situation in a modern society resolves itself into the fact that its relationships are more and more of a contractual nature. Such relations require a set of fixed formulas, conformity to which is enforced by deliberately organized and specially authorized agencies.

Also, increasingly, many of the basic rules for living together have to be operative in, and enforced for, the whole society, or large parts thereof, and less-than-public organizations cannot do this. Also some of the most important rules cut across or involve the institutions of several social areas. Hence societal regulation is more and more dependent upon, and more and more conducted by, the state. In fact, the growing complexities of societies brought the modern state into being.[22]

The state is the over-all regulative, directive, and ultimate compulsive and enforcing agent of the rules of social life. It has wider coverage than almost all other institutionalized organizations in a given area, and is the only agency that fully represents the society and is authorized to use force. Hence the modern state not only conducts its traditional political regulatory activities, but also, both by what is deemed to be a necessary extension and by invitation or assignment, has assumed supplemental, and in some instances, ultimate regulatory functions in other institutional areas, as it has assumed social functions in those areas that widely affect general welfare. The modern state regulates, or aids in enforcing regulatory measures for, industry, transportation, communications, commerce, the property system, labor relations, marriage, parent-child relations, divorce, the public health agencies, and is a court of last resort for all moral safeguarding of publicational, recreational, and aesthetic activities. In the last analysis,

---

[22] The services that the modern state, particularly our own, carries on as a service-providing and constructive agency, as well as its regulatory and police functions, will be examined in the chapter on governmental institutions (Chapter Fourteen).

all other institutions and organizations depend upon the state to enforce their indispensable and irreducible social action requirements. Furthermore, all of the other regulatory agencies are held to exercise disciplinary authority, subject to the law of the state and within the bounds fixed by the law.

Significant also is the fact that the state, through the order that it creates within the society, makes it possible for other institutions to carry on their functions without interruption and delay; it is, in a sense, the necessary condition of the effective functioning of the other institutions.

The special personnel of modern institutions is coming increasingly under state supervision. The more certain occupations (for example, those of electrician, plumber, detective, drug dispenser) affect public safety and the more specialized or more critically important they become, the more the state must exercise some selective and supervisory influence. This regulation of personnel is especially important in the case of the professions, with their esoteric knowledge and highly specialized skills acquired by special advanced training, and with the highly technical nature of their services. These services (those of lawyers, doctors, teachers, public accountants, actuaries, engineers, nurses, social workers, and many levels of public servants) are so specialized that the benefiting public is not capable of judging the quality of the services rendered. The qualifications for admission to the profession, the certification of proficiency, the maintenance of standards of practice (the ethics), and when necessary, the dismissing of grossly incompetent or unethical practitioners is managed directly through the associations of the professionals. Usually, though, the state, in the case of most of the professions, has general and final regulatory responsibility and authority in these matters, since the services are indispensable to the general well-being, and a satisfactory level of quality must be assured. In general, the professional associations work with the state and often act as its deputies.

The very nature of modern society is thrusting these supervisory and regulatory, as well as a great many other institutional, functions upon the state.

BIBLIOGRAPHY

GENERAL

Bernard, Jessie, *American Family Behavior*. New York: Harper, 1942, pp. 7–24.
Broom, L., and Selznick, P., *Sociology*. Evanston, Ill.: Row, Peterson, 1955, pp. 237–249.

Chapin, F. S., *Contemporary American Institutions*. New York: Harper, 1935, pp. 13–22, 319–352.

Feibleman, J. K., *The Institutions of Society*. New York: Macmillan, 1956, pp. 143–181.

Hughes, E. C., "Institutions," in Lee, A. M. (ed.), *Principles of Sociology*. New York: Barnes & Noble, 1951, pp. 225–229, 236–247, 256–282.

Hughes, E. C., "The Ecological Aspects of Institutions," *Am. Soc. Rev.,* 1 (Apr., 1936): 180–192.

Leger, S. H., "The Concept of Institutionalization," *Soc. & Soc. Res.,* 36 (Jan., Feb., 1952): 177–182.

Panunzio, C., *Major Social Institutions*. New York: Macmillan, 1939, pp. 7–27.

Parsons, T., "The Position of Sociological Theory," *Am. Soc. Rev.,* 13 (Apr., 1948): 156–164.

Parsons, T., and Shils, E. A., *Toward a General Theory of Action*. Cambridge: Harvard Univ. Press, 1951, pp. 21–22, 40, 150–174, 191–194.

Rose, A. M., *Sociology: The Study of Human Relations*. New York: Knopf, 1956, pp. 130–135.

Selznick, P., "Foundations of the Theory of Organization," *Am. Soc. Rev.,* 13 (Feb., 1948): 25–35.

Thompson, J. D., and McEwen, W. J., "Organizational Goals and Environment: Goal-Setting as an International Process," *Am. Soc. Rev.,* 23 (Feb., 1958): 23–31.

Wiese, L., and Becker, H., *Systematic Sociology*. New York: Wiley, 1932, pp. 403–408.

SIMPLER VS. MODERN SOCIETIES

Angell, R. C., *The Integration of American Society*. New York: Harcourt, Brace, 1941.

Angell, R. C., *Free Society and Moral Crisis*. Ann Arbor: Univ. of Michigan Press, 1958.

Landis, P. H., *Social Control: Social Organization and Disorganization* (rev. ed.). Philadelphia: Lippincott, 1956, pp. 168–186.

Nisbet, R., *The Quest for Community*. New York: Oxford Univ. Press, 1953.

Redfield, R., "The Folk Society," *Am. Jour. Soc.,* 52 (Jan., 1947): 293–308.

Redfield, R., *The Primitive World and Its Transformation*. Ithaca: Cornell Univ. Press, 1953.

Redfield, R., *Peasant Society and Culture*. Chicago: Univ. of Chicago Press, 1956.

Rose, A. M., *Sociology: The Study of Human Relations*. New York: Knopf, 1956, pp. 284–301, 432–457.

Sjoberg, G., "Folk and Feudal Societies," *Am. Jour. Soc.,* 58 (Nov., 1952): 231–239.

Sjoberg, G., "The Preindustrial City," *Am. Jour. Soc.,* 60 (Mar., 1955): 438–445.

Williams, R. M., Jr., *American Society: A Sociological Interpretation*. New York: Knopf, 1960, pp. 476–510, 561–567.

The Relations of Institutions

Institutions, because of their composition, their societal functioning, and their existence in a physical spatial setting, exhibit complex inter-relationships, involving degrees of mutuality, dependency, and dominance. First, since they are structural and functional embodiments of the persons they serve, they and their constituent individuals are inextricably interrelated. Second, institutions do not exist in a societal vacuum; they are participant systems in a complex scheme of competitive-cooperative division of function, and hence are bound together in innumerable competitive, complementary, and reciprocal functional relations upon which their separate and joint existence depends. Third, they exist with each other in physical space, in the respective communities in which they operate; hence, they have spatially determined functional arrangement, location, and relationship with respect to each other.

I: The Relations of Social Institutions and Individuals

Institutions and the individuals who compose them and for whom they exist cannot be separated. All through history they have reacted upon each other in socially significant ways. Professor Small pointed out early in the present century that a very important aspect of the over-all social process is the development of persons by institutions, and institutions by persons, through time.[1]

It has already been noted that institutions serve as conditioners and socializers, as guides and directors, and as motivators of the behavior of individuals. In fact, the whole institutional environment is a strong factor in individual development and behavior; it is the dominant aspect of

[1] A. W. Small, *General Sociology*. Chicago: Univ. of Chicago Press, 1905, p. 552.

the total sociocultural environment. The institutions are in most instances the long established patterns of action and interaction that transcend the life of the individual participants in almost every common or recurrent social situation. The pressures exerted by them—their authorities and controls, their positive stimuli and prestiges, their sanctions—during the formative years of childhood and youth, when individuals have the least defense against them, create and perpetuate sentiments, attitudes, ideas and overt habits that usually endure throughout the life of the individual. Moreover this shaping and directing process continues throughout the adult years. The life of the individual becomes a series of adaptations to institutional realities. What appears so often to be intrinsic in human nature, and therefore axiomatic and apparently unchangeable, is merely an expression of institutions that are deep-seated and function efficiently in standardizing individual behavior.

A wide variety of institutional patterns can be grafted onto the human personality, or put another way, the chief source of differences in the behavior of individuals lies in the variety of institutional situations impinging upon them. Although the individual has a general personality bearing the stamp of the aggregate of institutions that make up his sociocultural complex, he also shows perceptible traces of several special institutional selves. No one person is entirely absorbed by one single institution, although a celibate priest comes close to it; each person enters into any given institution of his milieu with only a part of himself; each of his "selves" has its definite roles. Since every institution tends to build its own behavior system, every person actually consists of segments, each reflecting different institutions, but all overlapping. We might think of an adult male as consisting of a self, as a husband, an occupational self, a self as a member of the Methodist Church, a political self as a member of the Republican Party, a Masonic Lodge self, a golf club self, a discussion club self, and so on. Each of these selves might be depicted graphically as a circle. All these circles intersect. From hour to hour and day to day, the diameters of the circles and the extent to which one circle overlaps others will vary according to which institutional situation is foremost at the moment. Occasionally, these various institutional selves exist in the same individual at the same time in a state of inconsistency without influencing each other noticeably in a given situation.

Institutions also function as fields of individual activity. The individual only becomes functional when involved in an institutional relationship and activity, for institutions are the means of realizing human potentialities and urges. In participating in the institutionalized life activities, or even by merely coming into contact with them, the individual finds the opportunities for putting his interests and capacities into play in socially approved, or at least socially permissible, ways. They offer him opportunities for self-activity and personal growth, for doing satisfactory work, and for winning the approval of his fellows. It is through institutions that the individual develops his tendencies toward workmanship and creativeness, acquires facility of thought, and, in some measure at least, satisfies longings and fulfills aspirations.

Institutions not only allow the individual to develop himself, but also provide opportunities for him to make contributions to civilization, which is relatively continuous—in a sense, eternal. The institutions test those talents and abilities that are really necessary for the successful performance of a definite social function. The schools test students for ability along various lines, for competence in special functions, for powers of leadership. The scientific-technological institutions provide opportunities for demonstrating intellectual abilities in the development of knowledge, in conceptualization, in creative thinking, in discovery, invention, and all sorts of construction. The government offers tests for ability to carry responsibility, for integrity and service, for positions and qualities of leadership. Similar sorts of testing are provided by the economic, the stratification, the religious, and the aesthetic institutions. Apart from institutions the individual would be a bundle of unexpressed powers and bare possibilities. The variety of institutions in our society offers possibility of expression for all of the personality elements among the people.

On the other hand, for example in the case of the Church in Spain during the eighteenth and nineteenth centuries, if the institution is is overdeveloped and is an end in itself, the individual is overpowered; he is made a means to institutional advancement and aggrandizement, and individual ability and effort (save in the interest of the institution) are crushed. The results of institutional dominance may border on the pathological.

Finally, it should be noted that institutions and their members have symbiotic relations. Institutions survive only because they render different kinds of services to their members. The existence of each depends upon the other. Students must have facilities for schooling, and schools must have pupils and be accessible to them; families must have food, clothing, shelter, furniture, perambulators, gasoline for their automobiles, and stores and stations must have customers; people who wish to worship and receive spiritual guidance must have churches, and churches must have members.

The individual is as much cause as effect of institutions. The individuals who constitute the society are first shaped by its institutions; then the individuals, in turn, shape or even create institutions or institutional features. Just as the individual cannot be understood without a knowledge of the effects of the institutions through which he lives, so institutions cannot be studied except as results of the actions of men.

Even the rank and file individual, along with his fellows, as he participates in the wider community life with its many institutions, makes his impression upon them. In the last analysis, all institutions are the results of thousands of minds in interrelation—the results of the efforts of individual social beings to find successful rules and modes of living.

There are, however, great variations in the amount of influence different individuals have upon institutions. The exceptional, dynamic individuals have the most effect. They are the conceivers of new ideals and goals, the coordinators of thought and activity, the formers of new combinations of facts, principles, and techniques to solve new problem situations, the originators of social movements. When exceptional men are also leading men, and are strategically situated or wield some social power, they exert a great influence in shaping and directing the activities of institutions. Emerson once said that "an institution is the lengthened shadow of one man," but this may overstate the case, since exceptional men too are products of their age and are dependent upon its media of action.

However, it can be granted that many institutions, such as religious systems and denominations, educational institutions, forms of state, scientific institutions, schools of art and architecture, carry the definite impress of certain individuals. Behind the world's great religions stand such inspired geniuses as Zoroaster, Gautama, Confucius, Laotse, Jesus, and Mohammed. Among religious organizations, Presbyterianism is linked with Calvin and John Knox; Methodism, with the Wesleys; the Disciples of Christ, with Alexander Campbell; Mormonism, with Brigham Young and Joseph Smith. John Harvard, Eli Yale, Thomas Jefferson, David Starr Jordan, William Rainey Harper are names that one recalls in connection with American universities. The Red Cross means Florence Nightingale.

Change in social institutions, especially all deliberate change, is due to the action of certain individuals. All kinds of social inventions as they relate to institutions originate in individual minds.

Certain individuals have dominated institutions by force of personality or by special acquisition of social power. A mother of personal force may dominate a family in spite of the patriarchal traditions supporting the father. One man may dominate an industry as well as a corporation, at least at a certain stage, as in the case of Rockefeller, Carnegie, Hill, Ford, Sarnoff or Loew. In government, single men may dominate the institution not only by virtue of the office, but to a greater extent because of their personality; for example, Abraham Lincoln, Theodore Roosevelt, Franklin Delano Roosevelt, or Winston Churchill. Dictatorship, regardless of how it was achieved, demonstrates the same fact in even more striking form, as attested by Caesar, Cromwell, Napoleon Bonaparte, Kemal Ataturk, Stalin, Mussolini, and Hitler.

Nonetheless, while institutions may be integrated, modified, and dominated by individuals, it must not be thought that any institution that has endured is the result of the influence of one single individual, however innovative or powerful he may have been. A social institution is basically a sociocultural product and represents a totality of persons. Furthermore, the institution usually has a far longer life than the individuals who support it. The individuals come under the influence of the institution, make their mark on it, and depart; even the generations come and go; but the institution, even in a given form, often goes on indefinitely.

II: The Interrelationships of Institutions with Each Other

Institutions, in their functioning, are differentiated and specialized to a large extent, and autonomous to some extent. They need to be, for no institution can do everything, and there are many special and distinct functions to perform. However, it is only by abstraction that we can regard institutions as isolated and independent existences. The sectors and their particular institutions overlap and are functionally interrelated, interacting, competitive-cooperative, and hence interdependent in various ways and degrees. The very division of labor among them implies interrelatedness and interdependence *in* labor. They are related to each other like the parts of a clock. However, *unlike* the parts of a clock, they also compete with each other and sometimes try to weaken and destroy each other. Institutions are also influenced by factors which impinge on the community or society as a whole; for example, race, physical environment, population composition, and health conditions. The relations of institutions with each other can be resolved into those of a *positive* nature and those that are *negative*.

THE POSITIVE RELATIONS

Institutions form that master network or pattern of social relationships, societal functions, and social behavior to which the term "society" is applied.

In the first place, few institutions perform a single function; in fact, a given institution at a given time may have a variety of essential functions which tie it inextricably to other institutions. For example, although the family has always had as its signal domestic functions the maintenance of standardized sexual relations, reproduction, and the protection and preliminary socialization of the young, it has also frequently been an agency with educational, religious, recreational, health, legal, and economic functions. The state, in addition to the traditional political activities, conducts all manner of economic, educational, recreational, engineering, research, health, and other social welfare functions. The church, in addition to its worship functions, regulates morals, undertakes teaching along certain lines, and in some instances practices philanthropy and medicine, provides recreation, supports the state, and engages in politics.

Also, a single function may be served by several institutions, though any functioning along a given line by institutions in sectors other than the primary one is usually of a tangential nature. For example, the school is the main educational agency, but if we think of education as the acquisition of knowledge and proficiency necessary for a satisfactory life adjustment, it is evident that a large proportion of education is acquired in the family, the church, the playground, the fraternal order, the place of employment, by means of the press, radio, television, and motion picture.

There is, in general, an amalgamation and sharing of functions among institutions, not because of the domination or intrusion by some institutions upon the special functions of other institutions, though there is some of this, but rather because of the fact that human needs are so interrelated that in satisfying one need others are involved. Common needs tie institutions together functionally; many institutions must have the assistance of other institutions. For example, in our society practically all of the institutions make use of the agencies of mass communication in giving a public definition of their aims and policies.

Institutions in one area may exercise great influence over those in other areas. Religious institutions have recurrently dominated others and have had certain determinative effects. Max Weber gave us the classic illustration, elaborately worked out, in his analysis of the relationship between Protestantism, as it developed in the sixteenth and seventeenth centuries, and capitalism.[2] He indicated a direct connection between the religious beliefs and the practical ethics of a community, and in turn, a connection between both of these and the character of the economic system.

The institutions also support and depend upon one another. In the American community, education, for example, supports the family by reinforcing home values and extending its influence over the personal behavior of the child; a school that taught values counter to those of

[2] Max Weber, *The Protestant Ethic and the Spirit of Capitalism* (T. Parsons, transl.). London: Allen & Unwin, 1930. T. Parsons, *The Structure of Social Action*. New York: McGraw-Hill, 1937, pp. 500–578, 788.

home and family would hardly be tolerated in any community. Modern recreation depends upon institutions of business and transportation, and in its commercialized forms seeks the support of churches, schools, and the departments of government. Since education is largely a matter of public provision, it is closely related to political institutions, especially local and state governments, and more indirectly to public and private economic functions. Business and other economic organizations make use of schools, churches, newspapers, government, and other agencies in reaching their objectives; for example, the schools, which are important agencies for developing occupational proficiencies in individuals. Health and aesthetic institutions must have the assistance of a variety of other institutions.

The shifting of functions from one institution to another further underscores the fact of interrelatedness. When one institution has failed to meet a basic human need, another has frequently taken up the burden. Once, most education was conducted by the family, but when a broader cultural foundation had to be assured for larger and larger numbers of people, special teaching institutions had to be developed. Now we even have nursery schools. The imparting of so-called scientific knowledge, among the great ancient civilizations, and even up into early modern times in Europe, was largely in the hands of priests or other members of religious orders; but when it came to be a critical necessity, we developed institutionalized bodies of secular scientists to carry on the function. Family and church have given up various welfare functions which the state has taken over.

The shifting of functions among institutions may often cure one another's dysfunctions. "If the family fails to do an adequate job, school or church, or charitable organization tends to take up the function and perform it. Thus, at any particular time the tasks of any one institution are functionally related to the *responsibilities* of all the others."[3]

Particular institutions often have special significance for the development of other institutions. After language came into existence as an institutionalized form of communication, it had such importance that it not only served as the indispensable preliminary to the formation of almost all other institutions, but out of it grew writing, literature, much of education, and all the derived communicative institutions. Similarly, a considerable number of economic, educational, domestic, health, and even religious institutions cannot exist until certain political institutions appear. The stage of development of such institutions as industry, the family, science, the church, and government will modify the course of development of the educational organization.

[3] R. C. Angell, *Free Society and Moral Crisis.* Ann Arbor: Univ. of Michigan Press, 1958, p. 31.

Not only are institutions interdependent, but they are bound together in sequences of development.

Institutions frequently change with changes in other institutions. The maladjustment or the growth of function in one institution may mean a change, even a loss of function, on the part of certain other institutions. Religious beliefs, activities, and organization have varied with the state of science. Education varies with changes in science and technology, in industry, in government, in religion. Changes in any one institution are reflected in all the others. History shows many other examples. The Industrial Revolution, which was primarily a change in the economic sector, had repercussions upon family, state, church, education, and recreation. In 1929 when something else happened in the economic sphere, every other department of life felt the effects.

So close are these functional relationships of institutions that any development of defects in any of the institutional areas sets up a chain of events which produces marked effects on all the other institutions.

Finally, the relations of institutions are also revealed in their interrelatedness in individual behavior. All men in all societies in some way participate in all of the basic institutional areas and are beneficiaries of the services rendered by most of the institutions. An individual plays roles in many institutions that make overlapping demands on him, binding him together with the institutions' other beneficiaries; for the individual, everything he does in fulfilling the role attached to any one institutional status is in some way modified by role expectations attached to all his other statuses. A person's economic activities are affected by his political and legal activities; his artistic or scientific activities affect, or are affected by, his economic or religious activities. Thus each individual is an agent of societal integration through his functioning as an interconnecting medium of the institutions in society.

Some Negative Aspects

The opposition of institutions is an aspect of institutional relations every bit as important as the positive aspects. There is the milder opposition, namely competition, between institutionalized organizations of an economic, political, religious, educational, scientific, aesthetic, and recreational nature for common, established, and generally approved social ends. This competition takes several forms. It may be intrainstitutional, that is, between institutionalized groups and associations within a given institutional field, such as families, corporations in the economic field, athletic teams, political parties, rival schools of art, universities, and so on. Competition may also be interinstitutional, or between institutional organizations in different institutional fields, such as that between the family and such organizations as the Boy Scouts, the religious denominations, and various recreational agencies as they vie for the free time of the children.

The very tactics of this institutional competition underscore the relatedness of the competitive elements. There is especially the effort to withdraw from competition by excluding or avoiding relations with the competitor, as well as combining or dividing the competitive territory with him; for example, industrial, commercial, and religious denominational mergers, the dividing of foreign mission fields among American Protestant denominations, the flight of the Mormons to the Great Salt Lake Valley, the policy of colleges to get their alumni to pledge their new-born children as future students. There is also the constrained adaptation to the competitor's techniques, as when Japanese Shinto and Buddhist sects established organizations similar to American Sunday Schools to hold their children against the appeal of the American Protestant missions' Sunday Schools, or when many of the jobbers, wholesalers, and retailers of groceries formed such organizations as the Independent Grocers' Association (I.G.A.) to meet the competition of the great grocery chains. Finally, there is more intensive specialization in producing a product or rendering a service not offered by similar institutional organizations; for example, retail establishments specializing in commodity or price range.

All through history there has been much actual conflict between institutions. That is, given institutions, in the form of their organized personnel, have not merely vied with each other, but have conceived of other institutionally organized people because of their contrary ideologies and objectives, sometimes because of their very existence, as a detrimental and menacing obstacle to their functioning or to the realization of their own objectives. Consequently, they have engaged in activities of a deliberate and aggressive nature intended to weaken, coerce, dominate, eliminate from the arena of contention, or even destroy, the other institution. As examples, past and present, we have the inter-institutional conflict between the institutionally organized Old Regime and the revolutionary factions in many eras and areas, the conflict between Church and State, the conflict between the adherents of some of the great religions as they engaged in proselyting even with the sword, the conflicts between the leading families in the mediaeval city-states, the wars between nations, the conflict between workers and employers, beween rival labor unions, between socio-economic classes, and between racial and other ethic groups.

Quite apart from the oppositions among institutions, this very interrelatedness produces strains among them. The interrelation, intergearing (integration), and reciprocity of institutions in any social system is universal, but it is never complete; there are always varying degrees of inconsistency in action, lagging of some sectors and institutions, even conflict. This, of course, produces strain and some breakdown, particularly in a modern society.

In our society, many situations lead to institutional separation. There is the vast and heterogeneous population with its diversities of values, beliefs, knowledge, interests and ends, and practices. There are vast territorial extent and great regional differences in some of our major institutions, as evidenced, for example, in the diverse attitudes toward school desegregation. There is great and increasing specialization by separate, and in some cases recently or newly developed, institutions. Some of these institutions are developing and functioning more or less independently of each other, and apparently are more or less indifferent to each other. Thus, education and economic production are quite apart from the family; much recreation is either commercialized or specialized according to age, or values, or interests, and not related to family or neighborhood; religious practice is more and more separated from the family.

III: The Ecological Relations of Institutions

Institutions are also related to each other in certain ways and patterns because of the fact that they exist vis-à-vis each other in physical space. Some of the most important social institutions arise and function in a particular location in response to ecological conditions and processes; almost all institutions have ecological relationships with each other; all institutions tend to develop adaptive peculiarities and also appropriate forms in given areas; all institutions must adjust themselves spatially and functionally with ecological changes.

When we examine the functional location and distribution of institutions in space, not all of the component elements of institutions are pertinently involved. Of special importance are those identifiable overt, tangible, and concretely observable aspects which have spatial significance or location—what Chapin called "nucleated" forms.[4] This means that we are especially interested in the personnel elements—members, especially functionaries, performing the institutional functions or rendering the institution's services—and the physical extensions—the plant, meeting place, headquarters, place of business, residence, or other physical equipment involved directly in carrying on the

---

[4] F. S. Chapin, *Contemporary American Institutions: A Social Analysis.* New York: Harper, 1935, pp. 12–23. For a broader discussion of the distribution of nucleated forms in the community, see E. T. Hiller, "The Community as a Social Group," *Am. Soc. Rev.,* 6 (Apr., 1941): 189–202.

operations or recognized social offices of the institutions. From the ecological point of view, the institution consists mainly of members and functionaries conducting the institutional functions at the point of concentration or focus of its characteristic activities and services, the place and area of establishment and major operation.

The ecological order demands that a certain type of institution be in a given location—the place where it performs its best or most numerous services for the largest number of actual and potential adherents, on the basis of their location and distribution and under the conditions imposed by both the cooperation with, and the competition of, the other types of institutions. Each has its natural habitat for greatest functional proficiency. Thus a middle-class residence, a super market, a school building, a gasoline service station, an industrial plant, a mission for down-and-outers, a dancehall—each has a proper spatial position. Change of position of either institutional forms or clientele, or change of function, will affect this ecological relationship and arrangement. When institutions, for example business houses or churches, fail to change their location when their clientele move on, or when the institutions fail to change their function when the clientele change, they fail to meet the test of fitness and are eliminated.

The fundamental consideration in the location of given institutions at particular points in the community and their patterns of distribution in space is that all of the institutions are continually in a competitive-cooperative state with each other; they compete with each other for space at the same time that, because of their mutual dependence and interdependence, they cooperate in conducting their respective complementary and reciprocal functions.

As the preceding paragraph implied, the institutions of a community have symbiotic relations. In the majority of instances, institutions render specialized but essential services for others. Thus, in the financial districts of our large cities, one will find clustered together banks, stock exchanges, produce exchanges, brokers' offices, central offices of large corporations, accounting firms, insurance offices, cable offices, firms of corporation lawyers, and agencies selling domestic and foreign exchange. Or, the institutions may be in different fields but serving and dependent upon a certain type of population; thus, in areas with a large number of people with a higher standard of living will be clustered the larger and more expensive hotels, the more expensive restaurants, night clubs, theaters, and specialty shops.

These symbiotic relations between institutions sometimes result in some institutions becoming dominant while others have a subordinate position. The dominant institutions or services act as integrating centers about which others cluster because of their dependence upon them and the benefits they derive from proximity to them. A college and its campus, with its thousands of students, is the basis of restaurants, cafeterias, and various other eating and drinking places, fraternity, rooming and apartment houses, book and stationery shops. In the larger area of the extended community, the same phenomenon may be observed. The city is the center of dominance, and many of its economic, political, and cultural institutions dominate the entire surrounding area, though dependent upon the hinterland for their support. Thus, the metropolitan banks and clearing houses dominate the financial institutions of the smaller cities and towns of the area; the city wholesale houses dominate the retail trade of the countryside; the entire diocesan activities are connected with the cathedral of the city; the influence of the capital city is felt in every local courthouse, court, and law-enforcing or administrative office.

Every community has its own pattern of arrangement of the concrete institutional agents. The spatial pattern may be that of an open country community, a village, a small- or medium-sized city, or a metropolis with its metropolitan area. In each case, certain factors have determinative influence. They are: (1) the nature and size of the community; (2) the distribution over the land area of the population to be served; (3) the suitability of the land for different uses; (4) the interdependence of men who live on the land, and the fact that they must be in proximity to each other to produce and exchange their things and services; (5) the significance of space cost and time-energy cost, that is, the unavoidable costs due to distances to be traversed and the time and energy to traverse them; (6) the related factors of the form and facility of the means of communication and transportation, which are the means of coping with space and time costs; (7) the nature of the peculiar services that each type of institution renders, for example families may be widely dispersed, while banks and fire stations must meet specific conditions of location; (8) the type of division and specialization of functions among the institutions of the different fields of social life—familial, economic, educational, and so on; and, finally (9) the degree of functional monopoly that certain types of institutions have in the spatial area.

The larger metropolitan area—the extended community as we have referred to it—with its multiplicity of institutions will show a complex arrangement. The institutions of the city, or cities themselves, will be arranged according to some variation and combination of the concentric zone, the sector, and the subcenter principles. (1) There is the downtown business district with its special sectors given over to theaters, large retail establishments, the financial district, buildings housing corporation and professional offices, large and expensive hotels. At the fringe of the central business district, there will be smaller and cheaper shops, hotels, garages, railway and bus depots. (2) The wholesale, jobbing, and light manufacturing districts will be on the essential transport lines, but also readily accessible to the main business districts and to the radial arteries of transportation. (3) The heavy manufacturing districts will be on cheaper land where there is plenty of space for production-line layout, storage, and parking areas for employees, and also where the plants have rail, water, or highway transportation facilities. (4) Residential areas or sectors, ordinarily utilizing around eighty per cent of the land in American cities, will vary very widely in type, size, shape, and location, since they depend upon such factors as the wealth and income, the ethnicity, the occupational level and socio-economic class of the occupants. Usually, as one goes from the center of the city to the periphery, the residential use of land tends to become less intensive. Every city differs in the pattern of its residential areas, depending upon its topography, the locations of its industries, its special institutional services (for example, a university), the location of its transportation arteries, its subcenters, its prestige areas, and so on. (5) Throughout the city there are subcenters or lesser business districts on the main arteries at their intersection with crosstown streets and transportation lines. Here more general, continuously needed, and less specialized (neighborhood) services are rendered than at the main centers. (6) Parks and other public recreational areas are located in various places. Smaller ones may be contiguous to business and intensively used residential areas. Larger ones will utilize creek or river valleys, accessible land with special topographical and floral features, or land thus far useless for other occupance. (7) At the outer reaches of the city and just beyond will be the larger estate and country club areas, the residential suburbs, the holdings of the rural-dwelling but urban-employed families, interspersed along the trunk highways with roadhouses, outdoor theaters, motels, auto graveyards and dumps, and, increasingly, multipurpose shopping centers with their extensive parking space. (8) In the hinterland are the more distant commuter areas, the city's separated satellite "dormitory" or residential towns and cities, its satellite industrial towns and cities on the rail and highway transportation axes running out from the central city, with open country, predominantly agricultural in use, between the satellite areas and the city, surrounding each satellite area.

As the communities grow or contract, there is a change of location of the different types of related institutional agencies. In America we are confronted mainly with continually growing communities. There is increase in the number of the population and outward extension of the community limits and activities. As technological developments occur, with new developments in transportation, there are changes in land use. There are changes in institutional relations and location as the subareas within the over-all community change in function, and as the functional relations of the given community and all other inter-dependent communities change. As a result of such changes, there is relocation of institutional members and of institutional plants, head-quarters, and other concrete service agencies.

With the growth and the increasing problems of space and time cost, there is a transfer of various commercial and special service functions from the crowded and spatially limited central business district to subcenters and to the developing outlying shopping and service centers. With the cultural assimilation of diverse population elements and humanitarian and regulative developments, there will be the disappearance or transformation of certain segregated areas.

In general, there is succession or a series of stages in which the functions of the specialized portions of the total area change; that is, there is a change in type and composition of population, in dominant institutions, in characteristic social functions performed, and in land use. Skyscraper apartments replace slums; suburbs replace farms; multiple dwellings replace single dwellings.

The fundamental ecological process involved is that of invasion-evacuation; new or different population elements and institutions gradually penetrate an area already occupied, and drive out and displace the old people, groups, and institutions.

BIBLIOGRAPHY

GENERAL

Cooley, C. H., *Social Organization*. New York: Scribner's, 1915, pp. 313–341.

Feibleman, J. K., *The Institutions of Society*. London: Allen & Unwin, 1956, pp. 77–86, 316–321.

Gerth, H., and Mills, C. W., *Character and Social Structure: The Psychology of Social Institutions*. New York: Harcourt, Brace, 1953, pp. 165–191.

Hughes, E. C., "Institutional Office and the Person," *Am. Jour. Soc.,* 43 (Nov., 1937): 404–412.

Malinowski, B., "The Group and the Individual in Functional Analysis," *Am. Jour. Soc.,* 44 (May, 1939): 938–964.

INTERRELATIONS

Angell, R. C., *The Integration of American Society*. New York: McGraw-Hill, 1941, pp. 24–28.

Benedict, Ruth, *Patterns of Culture*. Boston: Houghton Mifflin, 1934, pp. 45–56.

Bennett, J. W., and Tumin, M. M., *Social Life: Structure and Function*. New York: Knopf, 1948, pp. 170–174, 187–188.

Feibleman, J. K., *The Institutions of Society*. London: Allen & Unwin, 1956, pp. 224–227, 245–261.

Hertzler, J. O., *Society in Action*. New York: Dryden, 1954, pp. 263–289.
Ogburn, W. F., and Nimkoff, M. F., *Sociology*. Boston: Houghton Mifflin, 1950, pp. 488–504.
Perry, R. B., *Realms of Value: A Critique of Civilization*. Cambridge: Harvard Univ. Press, 1954, pp. 166–167.
Williams, R. M., Jr., *American Society: A Sociological Interpretation*. New York: Knopf, 1960, pp. 515–538.

ECOLOGICAL RELATIONS

Bogue, D. J., *The Structure of the Metropolitan Community*. Ann Arbor: Univ. of Michigan. Institute for Human Adjustment, 1949.
Bogue, D. J., *Metropolitan Decentralization: A Study of Differential Growth*. Oxford, Ohio: Scripps Foundation Studies in Population Distribution, No. 2., Aug., 1950.
Chapin, F. S., Jr., *Urban Land Use Planning*. New York: Harper, 1957.
Galpin, C. J., *The Social Anatomy of an Agricultural Village*. Agricultural Experiment Station of the Univ. of Wisconsin Research Bull. 34, Madison, Wis., 1915.
Hawley, A. H., "An Ecological Study of Urban Service Institutions," *Am. Soc. Rev.*, 6 (Oct., 1941): 629–639.
Hawley, A. H., *Human Ecology: A Theory of Community Structure*. New York: Ronald, 1950, pp. 234–432.
Hertzler, J. O., *Society in Action*. New York: Dryden, 1954, pp. 131–135.
Hoyt, Homer, *The Structure and Growth of Residential Neighborhoods in American Cities*. Washington, D.C.: Federal Housing Administration, 1939.
Hughes, E. C., "The Ecological Aspect of Institutions," *Am. Soc. Rev.*, 1 (Apr., 1936): 180–188.
Park, R. E., "Succession, An Ecological Concept," *Am. Soc. Rev.*, 1 (Apr., 1936): 171–179.
Quinn, J. A., *Human Ecology*. Englewood Cliffs, N.J.: Prentice-Hall, 1950, pp. 33–162, 266–290, 299–308.

Changing Institutions and Social Change

Institutions, partly evolved and partly contrived agencies, are never perfect. When we note them in an ever changing setting, we are further impressed with the limitations of their functioning at any given time, even of their malfunctioning. They are not self-adjusting to time and circumstance. As products of the past, they are always in considerable measure geared to the past, and therefore never in full accord with the requirements of the present.

Institutional change and *social* change are inseparable. Social change affects every existing institution and institutional sector, though not in the same degree, depending upon the relative interest dominance or the functional pertinence of the institution or sector at the moment.

Among the major types of change affecting institutions are those in the physical environment, whether due to natural or technological factors; demographic changes; and especially, the multiplying and ever extending sociocultural changes. This latter category of changes results from extended communication and transportation, culture contact, discovery and invention, social psychological currents and crises, the rapidly extending industrialized-urbanized life, and the efforts of leaders, interest groups, and purposive associations.

Institutions *must* change to retain a minimal degree of functional adequacy, or they perish as subsystems—eventually. They make a sufficient degree of compliant and timely structural-functional adjustment to the altered conditions of the life of the community or society in response to the new needs of its people, or the social life which the institutions standardize, regularize, and maintain become chaotic. Moreover, the long-run adequacy of the functional effectiveness of the institution depends upon its ability to meet the new complement of needs in an *optimal* manner; that is, in the way theoretically right or best under the circumstances, as determined with modern social scientific experience and knowledge, by modifications that are neither too much nor too little, neither too slow nor too fast. Finally, in this continuous necessary adjustment of institutions to social change, it is essential that both the subinstitutions within a given system or sector and the institutions of the various sectors be coordinated continually with each other functionally and temporally.

I: The Malfunctioning of Institutions

There are many factors responsible for the malfunctioning of institutions. These factors are of a natural, sociocultural, and intrainstitutional and interinstitutional nature. The malfunctioning itself also takes many forms.

Although there is considerable variation both among the major institutional sectors and among the components of given institutional systems, there is a general tendency for most institutions to change slowly and to resist most change. This is largely because of the fact that men are so greatly dependent upon their institutions, devoted to them and accustomed to them; for institutions are the ways their lives are lived, the means whereby their fundamental needs are met, the ways disorder and danger are avoided. With their precious codes, traditions, rituals, sentiments, and memories of great past institutional events and functionaries, the institutions tend to develop a certain sanctity of their own. Consequently, men are loath to change them; they will endure suffering and loss rather than deliberately drop from their social system an institution or an institutional form to which they have become accustomed.

Thus, most institutions tend to be conservative in the extreme. They seem to have a life of their own and a justification in themselves after they have been in existence for some time. Many outlive their usefulness, at least in part. Few have in them any tendency toward, or provision for, terminating their existence when their work is done; they tend to persist indefinitely, even though the need they were originally intended to satisfy has disappeared and been forgotten, or has so changed as to require different adjustments. They tend to achieve an immortality of the form, but not of the spirit. At the same time, these outgrown and often useless institutions emphasize authority and precedent, assume a dignity and poise supposedly born of ripe experience, develop habits of casuistry, scorn innovations, and become self-satisfied and dogmatic. They develop an inertia and an imperviousness to change.

It is only realistic to point out, on the other hand, that institutions must have fixed and established ways of carrying on their business. No society whose institutions are ephemeral or flabby can prosper or endure. If the institutions are too easily modified, they are pernicious. Comparative rigidity of institutions gives the group greater stability than its members could achieve alone. It obviates disturbance, precipitous change, and interruptions of normal functioning. It gives society a degree of permanence and prevents it from being upset by each passing influence. It enables changes to come more gradually; the individuals can become accustomed to the newer conditions as the older pass away; adequate foundations can be built for the next step; the premature appearance of revisions is prevented.

Yet, institutions dare not lose their flexibility and their responsiveness to human needs, desires, and expectations. Social prosperity demands that this fixity and persistence be not carried beyond a certain point, lest there be loss in functional efficiency.

The particular diseases involved in institutional inflexibility are (1) the rigidifying or ossification of institutions, (2) the persistence of archaic forms (survivalisms), and (3) excessive formalization or bureaucratization.

Cooley has presented the classical treatment of the first phase.[1] We will only present the outlines of the problem. The inflexibility expresses itself, first, in the form of elaborate and relatively unchanging structures, including especially long-established patterned ways and relationships and proliferated administrative organization. Second, it is revealed in complicated and extensive procedures with a large amount of continuity. These procedures are often elaborately ritualized and ceremonialized, and sometimes pursued for their own sake. There is often a seeming unawareness of the need-conditions that called the institution into being, the service of which is the institution's justification. Third, the institution is supported by a body of sacred, unquestioned, and fixed beliefs, rules, traditions, rationalizations, and sanctions. These structures, procedures, and rationale elements are deeply rooted in the attitudes and habits—in fact, in the *Weltanschauung*—of most of the personnel, and are almost mechanically observed. The participants are rule-bound, ritual-bound, engrossed in motions rather than in fulfilling the spirit of the institution and in effectively performing its functions. Action is overstandardized, overroutinized. Suggested alterations are emotionally resisted. The reluctance to change, whether

[1] Cf. C. H. Cooley, *Social Organization*. New York: Scribner's, 1915, pp. 342–355. See also: R. M. MacIver, *Community: A Sociological Study*. London: Macmillan, 1924, p. 161. C. Panunzio, *Major Social Institutions*. New York: Macmillan, 1939, pp. 468–478. L. L. Bernard, *Introduction to Sociology*. New York: Crowell, 1942, pp. 891–900. R. T. LaPiere, *Sociology*. New York: McGraw-Hill, 1946, pp. 343–348, 361–363. R. E. L. Faris, *Social Disorganization*. New York: Ronald, 1955, pp. 63–66.

by dropping old elements or adding new, is more automatic than calculated, more a matter of sentimental and habitual attachment to familiar ways, than a matter of thought regarding existing conditions or an examination of them.[2]

The survivalistic tendency is the tendency of institutions, or especially parts of institutions, to survive at least in given form and functioning beyond their time of appropriateness and efficiency. There is a tendency for them to become archaisms, bearers of social fossils, crystallized depositories of outmoded attitudes, beliefs, ideas, codes, habits, and social procedure. An institution, or an important part of it, may live on as an atrophied element in society, retaining its status because of its history, but losing its potency in the society's daily life. For example, because of the marked development of the middle classes, many of the well-institutionalized attitudes, pretensions, and ways of life of the hereditary nobility of England and France and of the older American "dollarocracy" have come to be little more than museum items.

The third related defunctionalizing tendency is that of overorganization or excessive bureaucratization.[3] Bureaucratic organization, of course, is necessary and inevitable in any institutional organization, especially as the organization becomes large, complex, and impersonal. The danger lies in bureaucratization becoming an end in itself. Then the rules become numerous and rigid; the offices multiply so that they interfere with each other and become so specialized that they approach functional insignificance; the chain of command takes more time, becomes longer and cumbersome; the functioning tends to become stereotyped, inflexible, and mechanical; the bureaucrats themselves come to be interested in the maintenance of their positions—their vested interests—rather than in the ultimate purposes; the hierarchical arrangement is carefully preserved, even extended, and the ranks are dominated, sometimes in a stultifying and personality-crushing manner, by those above; departments and operations tend to become ensnarled in red tape; all are interested in self-maintenance of the organization and operation of the institution above all else.

This high organization, if carried too far, easily becomes an obstacle to the proper operation of the institution. Mechanism becomes supreme;

---

[2] LaPiere says in this connection, "Because the members of the institutional unit have been selected and socialized into the institutional pattern, they think and act in institutional terms; and the motivations, interests, values, and attitudes that are appropriate to the institutional way of life are to them inevitable and normal." *Op. cit.*, p. 345.

[3] For a more extensive treatment of the pathologies of bureaucracies, see M. E. Dimock, "Bureaucracy Self-Examined," *Pub. Admin. Rev.*, 4 (No. 3, 1944): 197–207. Also in R. K. Merton, *et al.*, *Reader in Bureaucracy*. Glencoe, Ill.: Free Press, 1952, pp. 397–406.

in fact, the institution becomes the victim of its own complex machinery. It is almost a truism that whatever is organized is powerfully concerned for its own life. Most institutions are so obsessed by the need of preserving their corporate existence at all hazards that individual variations of procedure are vigorously suppressed. There is an insistence upon punctilious adherence to formalized procedures. The regulations and ideology are transformed into absolutes. The superstructure of ceremonial, ritual, and protocol, once devised as a means of dramatizing and implementing the functioning of the institution, becomes a mass of minutiae of action with no justification. Under such conditions, the motivating idea, the spirit, and the vitality of the institution is submerged under the form.

Closely related to overorganization—in fact, usually included in it— is the tendency to overroutinization of institutionalized activity. Although routine is essential, it is also easy and "psychologically cheap," as Cooley pointed out long ago.[4] High routinization comes about in considerable part because it requires no inventiveness, little ingenuity, thought, or imagination; it calls for much less energy than a fresh approach. The "good old ways" to which everyone has been habituated are followed.

It must not be thought, however, that a long-established institution is useless because of rigidity or formalism, or that it is cluttered up with survivals. Nor are the only good institutions new ones. There may be institutions, for example the Supreme Court, that are ancient yet still efficiently serve their appropriate functions in this modern age. But this, to a full degree, is quite exceptional.

There are many causes of this inflexibility, survivance, and overorganization of institutions. Some of the more obvious and important ones will be briefly noted.

Institutions are established structures. They must be in order to endure and function. The first thing that is done in establishing an institution is to draw up a constitution and rules of procedure, form an association or organization, build up a lore and tradition, select guardians and functionaries to keep it intact, and standardize its machinery and activity. This tends to give the institution great importance and causes it to become highly organized and formalized. This high organization is both inevitable and essential, but it easily results in the effects noted as symptoms of the disease of overorganization.

Institutions are products of the past. They are products of man's experience, of his work, cogitation, and organization. They are established ways and "good things"; hence, they are cherished and respected. Usually, the older they are the more revered and inviolate they are. They

<hr/>

[4] C. H. Cooley, *Social Organization*, New York: Scribner's, 1915, p. 343.

only change as a rule when practically the entire group is firmly convinced, usually by some humiliating experience, that they work badly. This situation helps to preserve institutions that have long since lost their social utility. Also, because of their roots in the past, institutions tend to test conduct and social relations by the dictates of precedent rather than experimentation.

Institutions are control and conservation agents. They are admittedly conserving agencies in many cases; they include ideas regarding order and methods for successfully maintaining order and well-being, and hence are seen to be vital to the functioning of the community. Even new institutions must fit into the conserving pattern, and their exuberance and extremism must be toned down. Creeds, constitutions, charters, policies come to be accepted as eternal verities. Authority must be insisted upon, and authority easily degenerates into dogmatism and absolutism. All this tends to cause the survival of some institutions long after they have ceased to be useful.

Many institutions are in charge of administrators, who often become conservative, even reactionary. Leaders and administrators of institutional organizations are often prosperous and comfortable, once their position is secure. But they, like other human beings, tend to tire; and consequently, they try to avoid new and complicating situations in the interest of economy of energy; they attempt to routinize the duties of their office as far as possible. Furthermore, old men are usually in charge of institutions; and old men are invariably conservative. Even the strong-minded and highly educated among the old men tend to abide by their earlier judgments. Among them, safety, stability, and routine are sought above all else.

Some institutions have a protected position. They attempt to create for themselves protection not only against assault and change, but even against examination and criticism. Institutions in certain areas particularly attempt to safeguard their fallibility and violability against critical or other dynamic influences by invoking some sacred dogma, by manipulating the supernatural, or by stressing certain ancient sentiments, superstitions, or traditions. They hide behind some doctrine of expediency, some generally accepted fiction of inspiration, revelation, or unchallengeable wisdom of the founding fathers, some time-honored apology, some major human fear, some vested thoughtway, or even some appealing slogan or figure of speech. Protective ideologies, consisting of ancient mythologies and modern rationalizations and apologies, are studiously perpetuated and diffused. A general set of attitudes and convictions comes to prevail, which causes any questioning of the sanctified institution to be treated as sacrilegious. The skeptic may be labelled a "dangerous" person. Any suggestion of abandonment of the entrenched position is madness or treason. As examples there need be cited only such institutions as the older and established churches and most of their subinstitutions, almost any established state, especially its constitution, the institutions of a given family or stratification system, property, and many of the institutions of the economic system. They tend to survive in the social order in their particular forms not because they have great inherent value or notable efficiency, but because they have acquired a protected position.

There exists the difficulty of seeing institutions objectively. All individuals are born into, and grow up under, a given set of institutions; they are conditioned by them before they are capable of discrimination, and their attitudes, ideas, and values, as well as their overt behavior, are institutionally established. The human beings are so much a part of their institutions, so much immersed in them, and unconsciously so much in accord with them, that they do not see them objectively. The institutions are not only generally accepted as natural, but seem the only conceivable response to the various group needs. Hence, the people are usually unable to examine them critically to note whether they are functioning imperfectly or not; indeed, the institutional personnel frequently scorn as presumptuous a searching analysis of the functions and functioning of their institutions.

Efficient institutional principles are made precedents. The very success of an institution may be a factor in its increasing rigidity. As soon as it begins to be efficient, especially when it relates to matters important in the daily life of the people, the effective working principles are immediately made binding precedents. This is true among almost all people without exception. That which works, or has worked, in a world of trial and error, gives men a sense of security and comfort. Here is a tested bulwark against mischance which must be preserved. Among primitives, the origins of cherished institutions are attributed to their divinities. Some fiction of superhuman, or at any rate sanctified and uncensorable establishment, attaches itself to many of the institutions of moderns as well.

Institutions engender loyalty, pride, and sentiment which promote their persistence. People develop a pride in, and a loyalty and devotion to, their great joint projects. Institutions are no exception. Many institutions have touching sentiments and recollections attached to them and are firmly entwined in the affections of their participants. Thus, men found a college, sacrifice for it, and come to love it; they insist upon its perpetuation even if every unprejudiced observer knows that "dear old Siwash" should be permitted to die or be merged with another college. The same sort of thing may hold true for family, church, and political institution.

New institutions in large measure must be made out of old materials. As Durkheim put it, "It is . . . a very general fact that new institutions first fall into the mould of old institutions."[5] Men find it largely impossible to construct an absolutely new social device with heretofore unused materials and untried plans. Not only are institutions usually constructed out of existing materials, but old ones usually are the point of departure, the foundation, or even the models, at least to a certain extent. The new and modified institution has to depend upon the established knowledge, the effective techniques, and the existing supporting group-confidence in a given set of procedures. The result has frequently been institutions that were still dominated by the past. The early Church, for example, borrowed most of its concepts from the current religious and ethical philosophies and much of its organizational form from the political kingdoms of the world of its time.

Some of the effects of these tendencies toward inflexibility have already been implied. The more important ones will be specifically mentioned.

Antiquated mechanisms and outmoded routines persist. Men can become slaves of their ancestors' machines. Old features and functions of old institutions which are no longer of use may continue to be maintained at a cost of energy, and with a personnel which may be, in fact usually is, sadly needed elsewhere. The time and the energies of the functionaries, and sometimes the personnel as a whole, may be given to a preoccupation with non-essential machinery or superficial details. This disease is to be found in the church, in government, in education, in industry, in the so-called service agencies. The personnel drifts into a perfunctory and mechanical way of doing its work. The idea of function has faded from the minds of the functionaries. The holders of offices are more concerned with the perquisites of their offices than with the human values and social functions; the offices, in fact, come to transcend persons and issues. The standardized curriculum of the school or college becomes a convention and then a tradition; the teachers tend to fall into routine, losing their power to inspire and lead. The religious belief is crystallized into a creed and a vast organization; the clergy becomes more intent on ritual, orthodoxy, and observation of creeds and forms than on kindling religious fervor. The method of trial becomes a fixed procedure; the judge follows ancient precedents and forms, regardless of their lack of adaptability to the case in point. Because of this persistence of forms and procedures, institutions often show very little plasticity. This is sometimes demonstrated by the great

---

[5] E. Durkheim, *The Division of Labor* (G. Simpson, transl.). Glencoe, Ill.: Free Press, 1933, p. 189.

difficulty of adaptation of institutions when they are transplanted from the site of their origin and development to a new environment.[6]

Individual and group activity is fettered. The set patterns establish limits and discourage or even inhibit learning and experimentation. Checking and criticism are taboo; initiative is stifled. As individuals become fixed and grooved in the institutional structure, their energies and interests are canalized; any new or spontaneous action is discouraged. With the emphasis on conventionalities and formalities, the dynamic spirit of the group is crushed also.

Institutions may develop a sanctity and an infallibility which causes them to become ends in themselves—final values, above question. The end or ends uppermost at the start of the institution may gradually evaporate; but the routinized procedures, sanctified values, and thought-ways remain and become permanent, requiring no social justification. When this happens, schools founded for the search of truth can become obsessed with the elaboration of curricula, "methods," and administrative machinery; a church can become a system of cut-and-dried dogma and soulless ritualism. Law can become legalism, art forms can become academic. The external form is stressed rather than the vital principle.

Distortion or loss of function can occur. The very persistence of an institution may result in its conversion to uses for which it was never intended. Hamilton gave several illustrations. Equity, which started out as an informal method of doing justice, has come to possess all of the appurtenances of a system of law. Communities of ascetics develop into wealthy monastic establishments; political parties dedicated to personal freedom and human equality become the champions of vested wealth. Hamilton quotes a sentence that strikingly summarizes the proneness of an institution to go astray: "St. Francis of Assisi set out to bring people to sweetness and light, and left in his wake a plague of gray friars."[7]

If the institutions do not change sufficiently to meet the new needs, one of two results is likely to occur. First, if the institution does not occupy too strategic a position, or if in its form at the moment it is not an absolute obstacle to general development, it will become increasingly ill-adapted to the age, lose its vitality, suffer from dry rot, and in time fall into crumbling ruin. Second, if the institutional functions are highly important, for example those of certain basic political, economic, or religious institutions, there has been no alternative *in the past*

---

[6] For an excellent discussion of this situation in the American scene, see Carl F. Kraenzel, *The Great Plains in Transition*. Norman: Univ. of Oklahoma Press, 1955, pp. 165–193.

[7] W. H. Hamilton, "Institution," *Ency. Soc. Sciences*. New York: Macmillan, 1932, Vol. 8, p. 86.

for relieving the strained situation but to overthrow or wreck the institutions by revolutionary process and substitute for them others which, it was contended, more correctly expressed the new social content and context. A large proportion of the revolutions of history whether social, economic, political, or religious, or any combination of these, have been bound up closely with the rigidity and lethargy and archaism of crucial institutions. Notable are the Protestant Reformation, the Cromwellian Revolution, the American and French Revolutions, and the Chinese, Mexican, and Russian revolutions.

Revolutionary changes on a smaller scale are more frequent, as when a portion of a religious denomination becomes strong enough to overthrow a harassing and repressive doctrine or credal element, or a generation throws off ancient parental restrictions, or a particular form of administration in a city or state government becomes unbearable and is swept away *in toto*.

Another important set of factors producing social malfunctioning of institutions is the different kinds and degrees of lag or discrepancy in adjustment of institutions.[8] There is, first, the tendency of some institutions, or even entire sectors, to lag behind the changing culture of the society. This relates to the tendency, just discussed, especially of some institutions, to become antiquated, relatively unchanging, and resistant to change. In our present-day dynamic society, some of our institutions have demonstrated tardy adjustment to the intellectual, scientific, and especially the technological advances of recent times. They have changed more slowly than technological conditions required. Such lag has been exemplified especially in certain familial, religious, political, and recreational institutional forms and procedures. Second, and closely related to this type of lag, is the fact that the different, vitally interdependent institutional sectors do not change in parallel degree and in sufficiently synchronized fashion. In contemporary American society, we have very unequal rates of change in economic life, in government, in education, in science, and in religion. The scientific discoveries and inventions—the major change-producing factors in our era—instigate changes first in the economic (and also the military), organization, and in the procedures directly connected with these. Families, in many of their activities, especially those relating to making a living, and some of the regulatory governmental institutional forms will of necessity adjust rather soon; educational institutions, particularly in their curricula, may adjust later; usually compliant religious and social-ethical adjustments come quite belatedly. Third, sometimes

---

[8] For a quick review of the concept of lag, see A. Boskoff, "Social Change: Major Problems in the Emergence of Theoretical and Research Foci," in H. Becker and A. Boskoff (eds.), *Modern Sociological Theory*. New York: Dryden, 1957, pp. 260–302, esp. pp. 299–300.

there is lag within an institutional system in the change of some component parts as compared with others. For example, the institutional procedures, in fact, the very behavior of the members, under the stress of the necessity of acting in utilitarian fashion, may change much more rapidly than the rationale, especially the underlying social values and beliefs. Thus, in the family area we may have at the same time patriarchal beliefs and considerable emancipated behavior; in government we may believe, even preach, a great array of freedoms, and actually promote and practice much statism or restrict precious rights for certain segments of the population for the sake of some special-interest groups.

Thus, there may be adequate development of some institutional sectors, of some institutions, and of some institutional components, and belated development of others. This means that, frequently, various crucial parts of a community or society are operating with varying degrees of efficiency in the given societal context, and at unsynchronized tempos. There is some malintegration of some institutions with society as a whole, and malintegration of some institutions with each other. Hence, there is disequilibrium of interdependent functional elements, and functional inadequacy in the affected areas.

All institutions and institutional sectors are interdependent. There is also some shifting of functions as institutions as well as the society change, occasioned in some instances by the necessity of having a type of function carried on more efficiently. There is also a tendency for some institutions to give up or transfer functions to other institutions, and hence become overdependent on these other institutions. This points to inadequate functioning in some respects, and creates the possibility of malfunctioning in both the giving and receiving institutions. In our society, for example, most of the other institutions have come to depend on the state to assume many of their old functions as well as carry on new functions which traditionally would have been within the sphere of the other institutions. [9] Conversely, in many instances, the family has come to depend upon the schools for the instruction of the children in basic morals, basic religion, and increasingly (if the information is to be imparted decently and systematically) for sex facts.

For the institutions that are freely, even unnecessarily, giving up functions, it sometimes means a loss of the sense of responsibility regarding proper functions in the general institutional division of labor and an underassumption of responsibility, an avoidance of functioning or underfunctioning, often a weakening. Furthermore, the institutions to which functions are shifted are not always suitable as agents. The

[9] Various instances will be noted in the examination of the major sectors of institutions below.

institution assuming many new and possibly "foreign" functions may be called upon to perform beyond its responsibility and even beyond its capacity for adequate performance. Such an institution may also, through its multiple, even excessive, functioning, create a critical dependence upon, or it may assume a crippling dominance over, the other institutions. If such an institution were impaired, in time of crisis, for example, it might seriously affect the functioning of the entire society.

In contrast to overdependence is the disposition of most institutions to regard themselves as independent entities in the community or society. There is a consciousness of specific functional jurisdiction among the members of the particular institution as they think of themselves as participants and beneficiaries. Each institution has a vast self-interest; its organizations exemplify this and enhance it; it is the business of its functionaries to promote this. The uniqueness of its structures, functions, and procedures tends to be stressed; its symbols are presented, and its rituals and ceremonials are conducted, as almost sacred and unparalleled aspects. Thus, the educational world is separated from the business world; the political from the aesthetic world. In a university, the colleges and even the departments are walled off from each other.

As in many other aspects of societal life, conflict also has malfunctioning effects as it occurs within and among institutions. Short of actual conflict, the operation of various institutions, especially the older and more massive ones, in a complex society, may reveal a web of contradictions and cross-purposes not intended and sometimes not even recognized. The situation among the major departments of our federal government is a common case in point. Then there is the multiplicity of intrainstitutional struggles which not only impair the functioning of the particular institutions in which they occur, but also the entire community or society of which they are critical functional agents.

Within the family, there may be opposition between males and females, young and old, young folks and in-laws on the basis of patriarchal versus modern or emancipated conceptions of roles. Within an industrial or commercial corporation, there may be conflict between different factions, between sales force and office personnel, not to mention that between management and labor.

Educational institutions, as the result of ethnic and racial cleavages in the community, may be torn apart by the segregation-antisegregation convulsion. There is the contention between the humanities and the sciences in some universities; and among the sciences, the starvation of the social sciences for research funds as compared with the physical sciences. Within the Roman Catholic Church, there has been the antagonism between the Holy Orders and between divisions within the Orders, and between language and nationality factions both at the congregational and in the administrative levels. The contention between the right and left wings of labor organizations or the labor movement demonstrates itself recurrently. In the health field, there is the occasional antagonism between doctors connected with public health agencies and private practitioners, between the clinic or associated specialists and the separate practitioners. In so many institutions, there is the conflict as to the jurisdiction and responsibilities of the different categories of personnel, and occasionally a conflict as to the auspices under which a given institutional function is to be conducted; for example, the question of public schools versus parochial schools.

There is also the marked contradiction within institutions or institutional sectors with respect to values, ideas, ideals, and objectives; for example, that between the proponents of public recreation and those providing commercial recreation, the conflict between conservatives and progressives, modernism and fundamentalism.

When the individuals and groups within an institution are working at cross purposes or are in a state of strife, there is malfunctioning, for there is lack of consensus as to values and meanings, no recognition of or devotion to common aims, no team work.

At the level of *inter*institutional conflict, there is the occasional struggle between a single institution and the rest of the social systems, such as that which came with the ascendence and dominance of the medieval Church. Today, there is occasionally some slight evidence of such an antagonism between the ascendent educational and scientific institutions. There also are struggles between institutions of major sectors, such as that historical one between Church and State, or the more recent contentions between economic and governmental institutions.[10]

Not all institutions contribute to general well-being; for example, the institutionalized activities of predatory, criminal, and otherwise anti-social individuals and groups—racketeers, drug or dope rings, smugglers, auto-theft rings, counterfeiters, white slavers, as well as the institutions built around great misleaders, the dictators and other "cultural barbarians" of history. These satisfy the anti-social needs of the participants, but hurt society as a whole. Such anti-social activities require much compensatory, corrective, and protective activity on the part of the legitimate institutions in order to avoid being undermined and to protect society against the more pestilential effects of the vicious institutions. The benefits, questionable in themselves, accrue to the exploitive and criminal few; the vast wastes and costs are borne by the many.

The above factors are by no means all of those making for the mal-

[10] On institutional conflict, see: C. Panunzio, *Major Social Institutions.* New York: Macmillan, 1939, pp. 431–441. J. K. Feibleman, *The Institutions of Society.* London: Allen & Unwin, 1956, pp. 249–255.

functioning of institutions. There may also be the deliberate distortion or perversion of structures and procedures by elements with or without the institution, as when a special faction captures the institution and manipulates it for its own selfish ends, or when educational or governmental institutions become the tools of special-interest pressure groups, or when the church or communicative institutions fall into the hands of a political clique. There is also, obviously, the transfer of functions with poor adjustive effects, or the loss of functions to other agencies, whether voluntarily or by appropriation.

The general effect of these factors is to produce a state of disorganization in the affected institutions. The values are uncertain; the norms that are supposed to regulate the personnel are no longer effective; there is a relative lack of integration, internal equilibrium, and consistency among the constituent parts and procedures. Consequently, there is an inner confusion and deterioration; there is inefficiency in meeting the objectives; wants and needs are poorly satisfied or not satisfied at all. The institution fails to meet its obligations as a functional agency. It may lose important portions of its membership. It may decay, even disappear.

Because of the crucial organizational and functional importance of institutions in every community or society, there is a close relationship between institutional and social disorganization. Or, conversely, an orderly, smoothly functioning society consists essentially of efficiently operating institutions. Within each society there is a "strain toward consistency" on the part of all institutions. Where this strain for consistency is weak, where the economic or political or familial or educational institutions, for example, are not performing their basic functions, all other institutions suffer some impairment, and the society as a whole shows a degree of disintegration and malaise. In general, societal illness is due to illness in one or more important institutions or institutional sectors. Social problems and social failures inhere in the malfunctioning institutions. Just as we can get the sociocultural profile of a society from its institutions, so we can determine its state of health from them, and vice versa.

Readjustment must be timely in all institutional fields; there can be no great lagging of some institutions as compared with others. Every society must be in a state of continuous orientation. Cognizance of problems of functioning should be taken before malfunctioning reaches overwhelming proportions; if action comes too late, it is forced and frantic, too often injudicious and unsound. Hence, rather than wait until a crisis occurs, institutions should be examined continually to see whether they are satisfying the specific needs for which they were devised, or are doing any useful work. Some archiac or hopelessly ineffective ones should be discarded altogether; others will need to be restored, reconstructed, and added to. It has also been frequently necessary to create not only new institutions but also new institutional sectors.

II: The Reorganization of Institutions

There is some awareness of a "crisis" condition when important institutions of a society are sick; that is, an awareness that the equilibrating factors and processes are not meeting the needs and demands of societal operation, that there is threat of disintegration, disruption, destruction, dislocation, or suspension of basic elements of sociocultural life. The challenge of the crisis situation may not always be met adequately; but crisis situations are always incentive situations. The feeling of crisis, or of the possibility of crisis, is the major motivating factor in all creative and reorganizational efforts, both those more or less unconsciously or informally engaged in and those of an organized and planned nature.

Since most people of a society are in some measure aware of the fact that most of their institutions are vitally important, their deterioration and disorganization usually is counteracted and stopped short of dissolution; correction is sought for the maladjustment of the institutions to each other and to the social system as a whole. In most instances, such efforts lead to reorganization, or what might be referred to as re-institutionalization. In our day we have as examples such newly institutionalized sectors as occupations, recreation, science and research, social work, and communications.

Institutions are, of course, altered by the operation of natural and social forces through the passing of time, and some of these alterations are positive and beneficial adaptations. But, especially in modern societies, the automatic adjustments are too expensively "natural," and usually "too little and too late."

Human experience has demonstrated, however, that few social institutions are wholly incapable of modification. Institutions are not obstinate physical phenomena but rather social constructs, essentially malleable and modifiable. Men have discovered that they can, to some degree, deliberately transform and adjust their institutions by the manipulation of sociocultural agencies and procedures. They know also that by proper renovation the useful life of most institutions may be prolonged indefinitely. Utilizing a going concern, even though somewhat impaired, is more economical in most cases than starting *de novo*. Obviously, also, no society can afford to scrap institutions in a wholesale manner. Hence, disorganization is usually counteracted or stopped long before it reaches the state of dissolution.

SOCIAL MOVEMENTS

Historically, social movements have been important factors both in the reorganization of existing institutions and in the appearance of new ones. Social movements always grow out of what is viewed as a crisis situation by a portion of the people of the society. The population segments involved in the social movement may be concerned on idealistic grounds, or on humanitarian grounds, with a desire for enhancement of social well-being along specific or general lines, or they may be concerned on utilitarian or pragmatic, and even selfish grounds, because their personal or group interests are impaired by the existing situation. The crises are invariably owing in large part to the breakdown or the malfunctioning of certain key institutions or entire sectors, or owing to the lack of new covering institutions.

Most social movements, then, are largely concerned with modifying institutions. Social movements may be specialized by institutional orders or spheres, or they may include several or all orders within the societal system.[11] When the movements are effective, inadequacies or perversion of personnel, structural organization, policies, and procedures of the institution are overcome, and new ideologies and activities become accepted forms of institutional life.

Every social movement terminates in a new social institution, historically, and nearly every new institution grows out of a social movement. As Park pointed out, "Every social movement may . . . be described as a potential institution. And every institution may in turn be described as a movement that was once active and eruptive, like a volcano, but has since settled down to something like routine activity."[12]

The two major categories of social movements are social reform movements and social revolutions. Each seeks and, where effective, produces characteristic forms of institutional reorganization.

Social reform movements accept the existing social order, but seek to overcome malfunctioning in some particular institutionalized area of social life. The movement may seek to (1) eliminate some single institution or several closely related institutions or institutionalized practices (for example, slavery, child labor, labor racketeering); (2) prohibit certain practices (the sale and consumption of alcoholic liquors); (3) remedy, ameliorate, or remodel certain existing institutions or prac-

[11] Cf. H. Gerth and C. W. Mills, *Character and Social Structure*. New York: Harcourt, Brace, 1953, pp. 440–441.

[12] R. E. Park, "Symbiosis and Socialization: A Frame of Reference for the Study of Society," *Am. Jour. Soc.*, 45 (July, 1939): 1–25, esp. 6–10.

tices (reform of justice, penal reform, taxation reform, marriage-divorce reform); (4) introduce or attempt to achieve greater efficiency or wider use of certain institutional practices (the more expedient and effective use of contraception by the lower classes or by the population of overpopulated and underdeveloped countries); or (5) institutionalize some activity heretofore uninstitutionalized (establishment of public recreation, the regulation of safety and health). Social reform movements may, under given circumstances, be the only or the best way of achieving even a modicum or reorganization. Their inherent shortcomings, however, lie in the fact that they fail to see the problem in its wider relationships and interdependence; they are particularistic in objective; they pay attention only to a single or a few related aspects and measures; and if they accomplish anything, it is partial and piecemeal.

The proponents of social-economic-political revolution are not satisfied with all or most of the existent social-institutional order. For them, the defects are so grave and widespread that only large-scale, even society-wide, corrective or other reorganizational activities will suffice. Hence, they seek the alteration of the entire social system, or at least of certain related key or major sectors, such as the economic and political, and sometimes also, the religious sector. Often a re-allocation of social power is sought, which will cause the societal functioning to work to a much greater extent in behalf of large and heretofore powerless segments of the population. Historically, revolutions have accomplished much beneficial reorganization; in their context, they were the only way of bringing about a more tolerable condition. Certainly the French Revolution in the eighteenth century and the Mexican, Chinese, and Russian Revolutions of the present century have brought about profound and widespread modification of institutions with both intentional and unintended effects.

But, the goals of revolutions are often vague. Revolutions are chiefly negative (they often do not know what to do when they have unseated the "old regime"); they are wasteful and destructive of physical and cultural resources, of human and social energy, of essential and societal structures; in many instances, they are concerned, not with achieving general benefits, but with eliminating the institutions that vex the revolutionary clique, particularly its ideologists and organizers; they overlook much and often injure much that is good, even irreplaceable, "throwing the baby out with the bath."

SCIENTIFIC SOCIAL PLANNING

Because of the partial, episodic, palliative, bungling, and usually enormously expensive nature of institutional reorganization through social movements, historically men have, as soon as specific and applicable knowledge and technology were available, attempted some rational and systematic reorganization. It has only been in very recent times, however, that men have felt any great possibility of reorganizing their institutions by deliberate scientific social planning. The advancement of the social sciences, especially during the present century, has given assurances of the essential guidance and revision of institutions in a scientifically studied, planned, and executed manner. Planned reorganization merely implies that conscious, informed, and coordinated control and direction, scientifically achieved, are substituted for slow, aimless, partial, and blundering methods, and uneven, ill-considered, destructive, wholesale methods.

The advances in sociology as a science are especially significant in the study and the telic reorganization of social institutions. Sociologists have a rapidly accumulating body of reliable, tested knowledge regarding the social situations that necessitate institutional organization, the consequent structural forms this organization must take, and the functions the institutions must perform. With the use of historical as well as contemporary data, we have been able to interpret causally the defects in the institutions as constituted and the mistakes made in their administration. We can also analyze, evaluate, and anticipate trends, both in social change generally and in institutions in particular. Above all, we are increasingly able by our control of conditions and processes to correct the operation of institutions, and by means of our knowledge of the essentials of institutions and of the principles of social engineering to invent new ones which meet definite specifications and at the same time fit in with the various limitations that exist.

This process of reorganization of institutions on the basis of scientific knowledge and methods goes on slowly as yet. Furthermore, it is not equally noticeable in all institutional fields. It is most noticeable in the industrial, governmental, health, recreational, communicative, scientific, and educational sectors. In spite of occasional opposition, it is entering the fields of religion and domestic institutions. It may even in time have some effect on aesthetic and stratification institutions. But this increasing fund of scientific social knowledge, the increasingly better investigative techniques, and the great advances in social invention and social engineering are the most hopeful facts in institutional reorganization and construction, or, for that matter, in social advance in general.

Scientific reorganization involves several essential stages. First, it requires a careful audit of the institutions that seem to require corrective attention. For that matter, there should be a periodic audit of all of the institutions of a society. They should be examined to see whether they are satisfying the specific needs for which they were designed.

Every institutional group frequently needs to ask itself whether its institutions are really accomplishing well enough what they are supposed to do. But more careful social insights are needed. The physical, biological, psychological, and social forces that affect the particular social relationships and functions must be known. The social and other processes that have produced the institution, and those that have brought about its present malfunctioning should be comprehended. Also, the pertinent trends of the present should be known, and those of the near future should be anticipated as far as possible.

Second, closely related to, and involving, the preceding is the necessity of painstaking investigation and research. This includes several requisites. (1) It means not only accumulating the best data about the situation by the best available investigative procedures, but also marshalling all the established scientific principles that have a bearing on the matter. (2) Essential also is a careful inventory of past successes and failures, and the reasons for them, with respect to the treatment of the type of institutional reorganizational problem. (3) A careful and comprehensive itemization of all of the pertinent resources is needed, such as physical-economic materials and means, technological procedures and instruments, usable social organizations, and other institutional facilities.

As evidence of some measure of activity along these lines, it may be noted that today we have in progress all kinds of studies regarding marriage and family problems; in the field of political institutions, we have legislative reference bureaus; and in some cities, government "research institutes"; economic institutions use "population analysis" and "market analysis"; educational institutions are conducting investigations as to coverage, curriculum, and physical plants.

Third, scientific reorganization requires a rather precise definition of the goal or goals, especially in terms of what is acceptable and feasible, and what can reasonably be accomplished under all of the known and anticipated circumstances. This definition rests in considerable part on (1) the basic function of the institution in the division of labor and (2) upon the constructive resources, including instruments and techniques, available.

Fourth, there is the development of the specific, sequential, procedural attack, based upon all of the pertinent knowledge that has been accumulated and all of the available techniques—physical, psychological, sociological. It consists of (1) establishing the basic policies, that is, the specific formulation or statement of the corrective, preventive, or constructive actions that seem to be essential in the pursuit of the basic objectives; (2) building a program of action, that is, preparing creatively, and in line with the policy, the blueprint for the reorganization that is sought, drawing up the specifications of elements required, and setting the sequences of action to be followed; (3) selecting, establishing, and conducting the actual engineering techniques, and such other activities as manipulating pertinent attitudes, beliefs, and stereotypes, developing supporting opinion and will, using and managing the personnel, especially in organized form, and employing the great variety of energies, resources, instruments, and processes.

As institutions become increasingly larger and complex, it is only reasonable to expect that institutional reorganization itself will become increasingly complex. It is equally reasonable to assume that it will become one of the most important fields of social knowledge and social technology.

Modern communication and transportation, with the resultant physical and social mobility of persons, modern urbanism, and the many mass effects of mechanical inventions have given secondary relationships and secondary groups central significance in society. Some of the effects of this secondary group situation upon social institutions were noted in the preceding chapter. Any reorganization of institutions must also take these facts into consideration.

Most of the reconstruction or new construction will have to come about as a deliberate act of planning on the part of more or less specialized and specifically interested semi-public or public bodies. The rank and file individuals involved are today so far-flung in space, so heterogeneous in interests, culture and demographic characteristics, so distant from each other socially, that a consensus, except in the most exceptional cases, cannot be conceived of as developing within a sufficient period of time. For the same reasons also, and because of the much more complicated nature of the social situations that should be governed by the institutions, no consensus that might be arrived at could adequately set forth the numerous organizational features and functional and implementing devices to make it operative. Increasingly, public opinion in such cases must confine itself to exerting pressure that brings about action on the part of the special groups charged with institutional responsibilities, and to approving or disapproving a *fait accompli*.

More and more reorganization focuses upon the bureaucratic organizations that carry on most of the business of modern institutions. The many heterogeneous persons, socially distant and separated, and impersonal and anonymous in their relationships, cannot be expected to act except as the atoms of belief and interest from which public opinion is concocted. The functional organizations must not only plan the revisions, but carry them into effect. This implies propagandizing in their own behalf, and instructing their members in their new performances.

The great bulk of the new institutional requirements will have to be taught formally. Universal comprehension and spontaneous absorption cannot be depended upon as they can in a slow-moving, primary group society. Parents, teachers, research scientists, professionalized functionaries, public officials, press and radio have to be marshalled to carry on this task cooperatively and consistently. Even the motivations will have to be developed by deliberate processes, with full cognizance of the pitfalls that lie in the way of such effort.[13]

III: The Typical Life-Cycle of Institutions

Historically, institutions have not necessarily been continuous or eternal. A given institutional organization may live on for a long time, sometimes a *very* long time; but it also undergoes sequential changes in its structure, its procedures, and sometimes its spirit and objectives. In brief, it has a life history, which takes the form of a fairly typical life-cycle. This cycle begins with a crisis in some department of need-satisfaction and in some sort of social movement, and continues with the development of structures and functions. The institution reaches its peak of efficiency, then deteriorates in effectiveness if not in structural form, and ends by its death or by such a complete transformation that it may quite accurately be said to have ceased to exist in the formerly known form. Angell has sketched four successive stages in this typical cycle.[14] A concise and considerably modified analysis of his four stages, with the addition of a fifth by the present writer, follows.

Period of incipient organization. In this initial period, some need, usually demonstrated in a crisis, becomes strongly felt, and tentative efforts are made to meet it. The institutional organization may begin in an enthusiastic social movement, such as first-century Christianity, eighteenth-century Methodism, or the labor organizations and farmers' organizations in the last decades of the nineteenth century in the United States. Sometimes it may emerge gradually out of the folkways and mores relating to some need, like certain forms of family or educational agency, or it may begin in a cool and calculated manner as the result of broad consensus; for example, the United Nations or a housing authority.

The significant feature at this stage is that institutional forms are appearing. The sect that may have begun as a tangential movement becomes the organized denomination. The real estate salesmen and man-

---

[13] For references on social movements and scientific planning in institutional reorganization, see those presented in the bibliography for Chapter Two.

[14] In C. H. Cooley, R. C. Angell and L. J. Carr, *Introductory Sociology*. New York: Scribner's, 1933, pp. 406–414.

agers in a city become a self-conscious group aware of the necessity of controlling practices in the selling, rental, and management of properties. At this stage, leaders appear who serve as inciters and as crystallizers of sentiments and ideas; they also function as formulators of codes, policies, and discipline, and as administrative functionaries. To insure a supply of functionaries and necessary succession, the group develops criteria for their selection and elevation. The duties of the members and the special functions of the leaders and professional functionaries are determined; the necessary organization is effected, including the administrative machinery; the basic concepts are clarified; constitutions, rituals, and ceremonies are developed, and ideologies elaborated. To use Hughes's apt phrase, the upshot of the process of institutionalization at this stage has been to make the form of meeting the need "perennial" rather than "episodic."[15]

Period of efficiency. The institution in its organizational form is now in its early maturity. The various social needs are met by complementary structures, functions, and procedures. The institution is fully accepted, though not always approved, by its actual members or society as a whole. The functionaries are performing with enthusiasm and efficiency; the potential values and objectives are being realized in considerable part; the codes are accepted and enforced; and the rituals and procedures are still means rather than ends. The need-fulfilling agency is an efficient going concern, enjoying its maximum vitality.

Period of formalism. This is the period when the human purposes implicit in the institution begin to be obscured. The mechanisms become ends in themselves. The positions of the functionaries become sinecures, and the functionaries themselves function by rote; the codes and ideologies develop sanctities of their own; the rituals and procedures degenerate into often well-embroidered but empty formalities. There is much evidence of organization, but less vitality and functioning. It stultifies, misdirects, or fails to utilize the energies of its members. The standing need is poorly satisfied, if at all.

Period of disorganization. Now the arthritic organism is showing this and other diseases effecting its malfunctioning. It has become unresponsive to social and personal needs, lost the confidence of its membership, and lost most of its effectiveness as an instrumentality. Those who still embrace it nominally ignore it in practice or conform half-heartedly. Many have withdrawn entirely and are seeking their need-satisfaction elsewhere or are going unserved. Those who are professionally or emotionally attached to it will make efforts to preserve it, but few people

15 E. C. Hughes, *The Growth of an Institution: The Chicago Real Estate Board.* Chicago: Society for Social Research of the Univ. of Chicago, Series 11, No. 1, 1931, p. 107.

can be loyal to a lifeless and futile form after its major utility has been lost.

Death or reorganization. When an institution is in the state of disorganization, one of two things may happen. If it is so decayed, or if rival institutions are sapping its vitality, it will eventually die and disappear. If, however, the need still exists and important functions still must be performed, a portion of its membership may put it, in all of its significant elements, through a transforming reorganization. Then it, in its new form or forms, may appear as a new institution in the incipient stage; and the life-cycle repeats itself.

IV: Institutional Change from Cultural Contact

At first glance the discussion of the effects upon institutions when peoples and cultures meet might seem somewhat extraneous in the light of this study's concern with the social organization and social institutions of a modern, industrialized, urbanized, highly technologized and statized society, particularly our own. But no society, however massive, dominant, or self-satisfied, functions in a social vacuum, without relations with other societies and cultures.

Today, as far as we know, there are no untouched peoples anywhere, and very few compact, homogeneous, isolated groups; the jet airplane has brought the peoples of the continents within a few hours of each other. Even the nations most favored as to material resources and most developed technologically are increasingly dependent upon the economic resources of the entire world. Politically every people is involved with every other as an actual or potential subject, ally, or foe. There is every reason for assuming that these tendencies will increase and accelerate.

Yet, the many peoples and cultures are not alike. They differ greatly as to racial stock and nationality, as to physical setting and ecological relations, as to length and content of their cultural history, as to degree and level of economic and technological development, as to the general educational levels of their populations, as to language, as to background philosophies and *Weltanschauung,* as to political experience, sophistication, and capacity for self-government, as to internal stratification systems, and as to social-economic-political ideologies. Hence there can exist incomprehensibility, confusion, perplexity, and frustration as to each other's values, standards, interpretations, and procedures. At the same time peoples and cultures continually and potently influence each other. Not only is there ever increasing, almost automatic, diffusion of cultural elements, but also much formal, intentional, and deliberately organized transmission for humanistic, utilitarian and ideological-propagandist ends.

Because of the close and inescapable contacts between peoples, there is a great amount of reciprocal exchange among institutions and institutional elements. At the same time, any culture that has a considerable degree of permanence, universality, and independence is a more or less unique synthesis of institutions. In such an established culture, the institutions, as the result of long internal adjustment processes, are usually functionally coordinated and present a considerable degree of consistency with each other. However, change has always come, both internally and from outside influences, owing to migration, conquest, colonization, commercial penetration, religious and educational missionization, and especially modern global communication. But this reciprocal influence from without has never been as massive or persistent as it is now. Although serious clash and dislocation of institutions may not always occur, modification unavoidably does. No system of institutions is in a state of quietude or even approximate equilibrium; there are institutional organizational problems everywhere.

Advanced or modernized countries, constituting probably less than one-third of the world's population, consist of those with highly developed technologies and economies, with a high degree of industrialization, urbanization, political development, and sophistication. Underdeveloped peoples are all the rest of the world's people. There is considerable deliberate contact and exchange between the two because of the efforts of many of the underdeveloped peoples to modernize and the related efforts of some of the advanced people to aid them. Most of the aid involves deliberate reorganization of institutions, and all of the interrelationships have modifying influence. The influence of the institutions of the advanced peoples—at least of the scientific-technological, the economic, and the political institutions—on the underdeveloped people is infinitely greater than the reverse effect. But the institutions of the advanced people are affected, nevertheless, by their contacts with the underdeveloped peoples, particularly when some of their institutional concepts, norms, and the procedures must undergo considerable readjustment in the process of giving aid.

Our own American society is an important "giver" of institutional elements, both involuntarily, when it is imitated by others, and voluntarily, through educational and religious missions, commercial penetration, and numerous "aid" activities. At the same time, there is always something in the way of feedback.

On the basis of the rather wide experience and the widely accepted, almost commonplace, anthropological and sociological knowledge that has accumulated since students of society began noting the characteristics and effects of the contacts of peoples upon institutions, some of the more important aspects of what happens or is likely to happen can be noted and presented as a set of concise propositions.

(1) If freedom to adopt prevails, the borrowing of institutional elements will rest upon factors of utility, compatibility, and prestige. If institutional procedures promise distinct utility under given conditions, they are likely to be taken over. At the same time, although there is a broad zone of uncertainty, the traits to be borrowed must not conflict sharply with existing values, attitudes, and procedures, if incorporated. Also, the relative prestige of the donor and receiving groups is an important factor.

(2) Cultural contact, which involves both diffusion and borrowing of institutional elements, greatly accelerates the processes of change continually going on in institutions. With this contact, the occasions necessitating change increase in number, the stimuli inducing change are multiplied, and comparisons of forms and functions are inevitable. There are, for example, the very obvious changes in our economic, political, scientific-technological, and educational systems necessitated by our increasingly crucial contacts with the U.S.S.R. Such institutional changes will usually be roughly proportional to the respective amount of borrowing done.

(3) When cultures meet, there is usually considerable mixing and borrowing, as well as selection of institutional elements. In general, although each culture is a unique combination of well-guarded "precious" elements, at the same time almost all culture has great vitality, is highly contagious, and has considerable capacity for adapting itself to the changing scene. Usually the borrowing is to some extent a reciprocal process; but it is also usually relative, selective, and graded—never a wholesale affair. The borrowings may range from minutiae to entire institutions; in most instances, they are piecemeal.

(4) The reciprocity is rarely even an approximately equal exchange of elements, but varies with the respective degrees of cultural development. Higher cultures may borrow many institutional elements from each other, but are not so likely to borrow from the lower cultures, although there are notable exceptions, such as words, exotic food items, dances, and art forms. The lower cultures are more likely to borrow many items, especially of a technological, economic, and political nature.

(5) For each culture there will be, in varying degrees, the modification of some institutional elements, the addition of some, the elimination of some of their own, and the possible substitution of foreign elements, restrictions upon the use of some of their old elements, and the ignoring or overlooking of certain desirable and applicable foreign elements. Most institutional traits that are borrowed are somewhat

altered in structure, function, and ideational elements as they are incorporated in the respective receiving cultures.

(6) As the result of the culture contact, there is usually the necessity of creating some new institutional forms to enable the particular social system with its inimitable culture to compete effectively with other systems; for example, the countries on the different sides of the iron curtain.

(7) The contact of alien cultures disturbs the institutional equilibrium of both or all of the cultures involved and, temporarily at least, may create a state of social disorganization. There are conflicting currents of values; divergent norms and functional routines are competing for the allegiance and participation of the people. There is usually a sort of "interlude of confusion," which will vary in intensity in a particular country with the amount and kind of elements borrowed. Generally, also, the inferior or lesser developed culture and the numerically smaller contacting group suffer the greater disorganization. Striking historical examples of this disorganization have been found in those areas where the cultures of preliterate and of literate peoples come into contact through exploration, conquest, and commercial and religious penetration; in some cases there was the almost complete destruction of the social organization and culture of the preliterate group; in most cases there was great disorganization. The disorganization of the institutional life among American immigrants as the result of their transfer to a marked different institutional complex is well known.[16]

(8) The general tendency, in the long run, is toward some kind of equilibration among the institutional elements of the contacting cultures. Usually the fusion, like the borrowing of institutional elements, if free, rests upon factors of utility, compatibility, and prestige of the elements. But the process is seldom one of complete equality or freedom. The adjustment of elements in given cases may include very unequal quantities of elements from the respective cultures. The institutions, or many parts of the institutions of the higher cultures, or of the numerically, or politically, or militarily, or economically stronger group may be dominant. Today many of the institutional elements that are being incorporated into the cultures of the underdeveloped and transitional peoples are accepted by them by force of circumstances; they have no alternatives if their developmental objectives are to be attained. In general, there has to be an accommodation of indigenous and foreign elements if the society is to endure. Conflict between the institutional forms and procedures, especially of the major institutions, cannot continue, for the institutions are the functional mechanisms of

16 Cf., for example, W. I. Thomas and F. Znaniecki, *The Polish Peasant in Europe and America*. New York: Knopf, 1927, Vol. I, pp. 103–104; Vol. II, pp. 1119–1129, 1467–1704.

the group. The equilibration today among both the advanced and the underdeveloped and transitional peoples is increasingly a matter of deliberate, planned reorganization. A striking modern phenomenon is that of various underdeveloped peoples through their governments bringing great pressure upon themselves to adopt alien elements (for example, modern agricultural practices, certain political procedures, death and birth control practices) into their everyday ways of life.

(9) In so far as there is a dissolution of institutions or institutional elements as the result of contact, it will not usually be sudden or universal. There are positive resistances to be overcome in the form of emotional attachments, long established values, ingrained habits, group solidarities, and the very inflexibility of institutional organization.

(10) There is usually a transformation of values and at least a partial destruction of valuational and attitudinal unity among one or all of the peoples involved in the contact. Similarly, new or revised social values have to be established for one or all groups.

(11) When institutions meet, usually the superficial and overt aspects, the more comprehensible, the more readily and completely expressed, the more applicable features, such as practical techniques, physical artifacts and gadgets, and associational forms, change first, while the ideologies, the evaluational phases, and the related attitudes resist change and are more slowly modified.

(12) Historically, the institutions of predominantly urban people have changed more readily than those of predominantly rural people. Urbanization itself is a profound change. Urban life is much more prone to change because of the multiplicity of contacts, the ecological changes with growth or decline, the diversity and conflicts of interests and activities. The urban people are keyed to change. Urban populations are usually heterogeneous and divided into many groups embracing numerous cultural features and demonstrating considerable tolerance and receptivity; the social roles are almost infinitely numerous, and social participations multitudinously splintered and differentiated; social stratification is usually complex and invites continual readjustment, although this varies with the degree of vertical social mobility prevailing. Escape from established conformity pressures is easy. There are a vast number of new things, ideas, beliefs, and ways which invite imitation and eccentricity.

Thus, the institutions of the urban population change more readily than those of the rural population, though in the United States, with its universally influential mass communication agencies, its general physical and social mobility, and the notable application of technology in agriculture, the difference is less and less noticeable.

(13) Related to the preceding proposition is the one which states that the institutions bound up with primary group interests, activities,

and relations (as in the family, especially the extended family, and the village community) resist change longer than those involved in secondary group relations. Predominantly, secondary group communities have less value uniformity, fewer common precious historical ties, more diverse norms, more differentiated conformity requirements, more anomie and societal strains.

(14) In general, also, the institutions of more literate peoples, or people with a higher general level of formal education, change more readily and more widely than those of illiterate populations or those with a relatively lower educational level. The contacts, the extending awareness, the new knowledges, and the perspectives and inducements that literacy and education make possible, even unavoidable, may actually seem to force such people to change many of their institutional values, forms, and ways.

(15) The stratification system of a given people usually involves a differential rate and degree of institutional change among the respective stratum segments. Generally, the upper strata in the first place have social institutions based in large measure upon more diversified and widespread cultural interests than the lower strata. They have almost universally a readier and more frequent physical movement and contact, a greater degree of universality in their stratum as well as in their general cultural attitudes, values, interests, manners, and customs. They are less bound by habitation and have much broader cultural horizons. Except for the most advanced peoples, the upper strata are more likely to be educated at foreign universities, speak the languages of other peoples, read each other's literature, meet at the world's Grand Hotels, marry across national lines, and enjoy foreign commodities. This has unavoidably led to greater cultural catholicity, even eagerness to take over prestigeful foreign elements, and to something in the way of common institutions among them.

The lower classes, especially the rural peasantry, have less mobility and more limited communication. They are, in fact, usually isolated, both physically and socially. They are usually more bound to racial, local, provincial, and primary group attitudes and usages; and have lower and narrower cultural horizons, and, what is particularly significant in our study, a narrower set of institutions more rigidly adhered to. Institutional change, therefore, is more likely to cause the lower class person to suffer serious dislocation and often disorganization.

BIBLIOGRAPHY

MALFUNCTIONING OF INSTITUTIONS

Cooley, C. H., *Social Organization*. New York: Scribner's, 1915, pp. 342–355.

Cuber, J. F., "Some Aspects of Institutional Disorganization," *Am. Soc. Rev.,* 5 (Aug., 1940): 483–488.

Faris, R. E. L., *Social Disorganization.* New York: Ronald, 1948, pp. 19–49, 63–67, 371–407.

Feibleman, J. K., *The Institutions of Society.* New York: Macmillan, 1956, pp. 249–255.

Hamilton, W. H., "Institutions," *Encyc. Soc. Sciences.* New York: Macmillan, 1932, Vol. 8, pp. 84–89.

Herman, A. P., *An Approach to Social Problems.* Boston: Ginn, 1949, pp. 406–441, 481–485.

Hertzler, J. O., "Crises and Dictatorships," *Am. Soc. Rev.,* 5 (Apr., 1940): 157–169.

Hertzler, J. O., "The Causal and Contributory Factors of Dictatorship," *Soc. & Soc. Res.,* 24 (Sept.–Oct., 1932): 3–21.

Panunzio, C., *Major Social Institutions.* New York: Macmillan, 1939, pp. 411–457, 468–478.

Toynbee, A. J., *A Study of History* (1 vol. ed., abridged by D. C. Somervell). New York: Oxford Univ. Press, 1947, pp. 244–558.

Wiese, L. von, and Becker, H., *Systematic Sociology.* New York: Wiley, 1932, pp. 368–394.

TYPICAL LIFE-CYCLE OF INSTITUTIONS

Cooley, C. H., Angell, R. C., and Carr, L. J., *Introductory Sociology.* New York: Scribner's, 1953, pp. 406–414.

Feibleman, J. K., *The Institutions of Society.* London: Allen & Unwin, 1956, pp. 295–315.

Freeman, Ellis, *Social Psychology.* New York: Holt, 1936, pp. 378–386.

Meadows, P., "Sequence in Revolution," *Am. Soc. Rev.,* 5 (Oct., 1941): 702–709.

Hertzler, J. O., "The Typical Life-Cycle of Dictatorships," *Soc. Forces,* 17 (Mar., 1939): 303–309.

INSTITUTIONAL CHANGE

Barnett, H. G., "Culture Processes," *Am. Anth.,* 42 (Jan.–Mar., 1940): 21–48.

Hallowell, A. I., "Socio-Psychological Aspects of Acculturation," in Linton, R. (ed.), *The Science of Man in the World Crisis.* New York: Columbia Univ. Press, 1945, pp. 171–200.

Herskovits, M. J., *Acculturation: The Study of Culture Contact.* New York: J. J. Augustin, 1938.

Hertzler, J. O., *Society in Action.* New York: Dryden, 1954, pp. 83–92.

Linton, R., *The Study of Man.* New York: Appleton, 1936, pp. 324–336.

Linton, R. (ed.), *Acculturation in Seven American Indian Tribes.* New York: Appleton, 1940.

Mead, Margaret, *The Changing Culture of an Indian Tribe.* New York: Columbia Univ. Press, 1932.

Pitt-Rivers, G. H. L. F., *The Clash of Cultures and the Contest of Races.* London: Routledge & Sons, 1927.

The Classification
of Institutions

In a systemic, structural-functional treatment of institutions, it is desirable to have a working functional classification of the major blocks of institutions in American society that will be examined in Part 3.

Although institutions have functional interrelationships, each has, at the same time, distinctive makeup and functions. It is these differences that provide the basis for the classification of institutions as differentiated-cooperative agencies in the over-all social system.

I: Distinctive Functionality

Each institution has at least one primary and definitive function to perform; it has a major and strategic need-satisfying responsibility in the general division of labor of the society. The fact that given institutions at a given time carry on secondary or auxiliary functions should not obscure the primary function; for example, in spite of the multiplicity of auxiliary functions assumed by the modern state, its basic and non-transferable functions are still preservation of order within an area of political jurisdiction and protection against external hazards; the church may do some educating, and even provide recreational and occasional cafeteria and psychiatric services, but its main task is to advance spirituality, to transform conduct ethically, and to promote the Kingdom of God. When long-standing and basic institutions lose functions, we see the primary function standing out clearly; for example, in the case of the family, factories may be carrying on many of its traditional productive functions, nursery schools may be supplanting parental influence, elementary and secondary schools may be taking over ethical and occupational instruction, the church may be providing religious conditioning, but the fact that emerges from all this transference is that the primary function of the family is still to provide for the socially satisfactory and safe biological reproduction and replacement of the population, and the rearing and preliminary socialization of children.

Because of this distinctive function or set of related functions, each institutional cluster or sector tends to be distinctive in its patterns. Each has its own specialized personnel—parents, or citizens, or producers and consumers—and the different institutional statuses are differently evaluated by the society. Each has its distinct system of values, beliefs, knowledge, and symbols. Each has its special types of activities, roles, and organization of activities. In order to regulate these activities, each has to have special rules. Each has its special kinds of groupings and organizations; for example, a nuclear family is quite different from a work group or a religious congregation; a church, from a commercial or industrial corporation; a family service agency, from an army. Each must have its own kind of physical equipment.

II: Typical Classifications

There may be several different classificatory schemes for a given body or sector of phenomena, each of which may be highly revealing of certain substantive aspects. The field of social institutions is by no means an exception; there are a considerable number of classifications, which vary with the analytical objectives of the classifiers.

Some classifications are based on the presumed kind, level, or degree of development or formulation of institutions. Sumner,[1] for example, distinguished between *crescive* institutions, that is, those that have developed automatically and spontaneously, by more or less discernible processes and stages, out of subinstitutional forms, and the *enacted* institutions, which are "products of rational invention and intention," these latter, especially, belonging to high civilization. Sumner admitted, however, that pure enacted institutions that are strong and prosperous are hard to find. In general, although given institutions seem to be primarily crescive or enacted, actually they are both in varying degrees. Somewhat along this same line is Bernard's distinction between *matured* and *immature* institutions,[2] the matured institutions being those in which the beliefs, principles, or prescriptions are standardized and definitely fixed in the form of a code or creed, and which have a relatively completely developed and more or less self-formulating personnel, overt organization, procedure, and mechanical equipment, and which

---

[1] W. G. Sumner, *Folkways.* Boston: Ginn, 1906, pp. 54–55.

[2] L. L. Bernard, *An Introduction to Sociology.* New York: Crowell, 1942, pp. 878–882.

"are largely self-regulatory and self-enforcing with respect to their principles, creeds, and constitutions." The institutions regarded as vital for social control purposes are the ones most likely to have these features of maturity.

Another rather common classification is that between the *universal* and the *particular* institutions, the particular ones usually being characteristic only of more highly developed societies.[3] Evidence seems to indicate that the only separate and distinguishable *blocks* of institutions that are found in *all* societies—the simplest primitive, the ancient, the underdeveloped, and the modern complex ones—are the familial, the economic, and the religious. Even the educational and political institutions, often mentioned as "universal," when considered as specialized institutions apart from other sectors, come only when a society reaches a certain degree of specialization and complexity.

Institutions are also classified as *primary, secondary,* and *tertiary*.[4] Barnes, for example, refers to the primary or fundamental institutions as those that are elemental and spontaneous in their origin and development, and lists among them the family, property, industry, basic occupations, government, communication, education, and religion. The secondary institutions, which come as civilization develops, are of a deliberate nature, and usually are subordinate within the larger field of primary institutions; examples are science, technology, recreational institutions, art, and music. De Gré refers to the primary institutions as "those established modes of procedure without which no society would be capable of maintaining itself," notably "subsistence and familial institutions." The secondary institutions "more clearly define the established arrangements and power relationships which emerge from the formalization and stricter implementation of the primary institutions," and include particular economic systems (slavery, feudalism, capitalism, socialism), techniques of political control, and social status systems. De Gré's new category, that of tertiary institutions, is concerned with man's attempt through symbols, rituals, ideologies, and other intellectual and creative activity to achieve a greater degree of understanding, appreciation, and control of his natural, social, and private world; examples of these institutions are art, religion, language, mythology, play, magic, and science.

---

[3] Cf.: B. Malinowski, "The Group and the Individual in Functional Analysis," *Am. Jour. Soc.,* 44 (May, 1939): 938–964, esp. 949–952. B. Malinowski, *A Systematic Theory of Culture.* Chapel Hill: Univ. of North Carolina Press, 1944, pp. 55–61. B. Malinowski, *Freedom and Civilization.* New York: Roy, 1945, p. 154.

[4] Cf.: H. E. Barnes, *Social Institutions.* Englewood Cliffs, N.J.: Prentice-Hall, 1942, pp. 31–35. G. De Gré, *Science as a Social Institution.* New York: Random House, 1955, pp. 2–3. E. B. Mercer, *The American Community.* New York: Random House, 1956, p. 189.

Perry also distinguishes between major and minor institutions, though mainly on a universalistic-restrictive participation basis.[5] All men are eligible and qualified for participation in the major-universal institutions and have some unavoidable participation in them; namely, in the ethical, political, legal, economic, scientific, aesthetic, language, educational, and religious institutions. These are "rooted in the common characteristics of human nature and human life," and "are by general consent regarded as the great or major institutions." By contrast, the restricted institutions, which Perry merely mentions, are those with voluntary membership and restricted eligibility and membership, such as a society of philatelists, an anti-vivisection society, or a social club.

Chapin, who analyzes institutions particularly from the point of view of their place in the local community, distinguishes between *specific or nucleated institutions* and the *general or diffused symbolic*.[6] The nucleated institutions possess definite locus and take specified and concrete organizational form in an area; for example, local government, local political organization, local business enterprises, the families, schools, the churches, and welfare agencies. The diffused-symbolic institutions are of a more symbolic nature and are characterized by a higher order of abstraction; for example, art, mythology, language, law, ethics, and science.

Perhaps the most meaningful classifications of institutions for any society, and especially for understanding those of a modern complex society, are *those of a functional nature;* that is, the categorizing of institutions on the basis of the major functions or related sets of functions that they perform in the divided-diversified-cooperative operation of the society. Herbert Spencer[7] long ago distinguished among the sustaining (marriage and kinship), the distributing (economic), and the regulating (ceremonial, religious, and political) systems of institutions.

Dawson and Gettys,[8] in a comprehensive and systematic analysis of institutions, present four major categories based on functionings: (1) institutions concerned with transmitting the social heritage, such as the family, and educational and religious institutions; (2) the instrumental institutions, that is, those which have extremely limited goals and highly rational and impersonal techniques for reaching them, such as the hospital, the hotel, factories, department stores, banks, and public utilities; (3) regulative institutions, which carry on "the more formally

[5] R. B. Perry, *Realms of Value: A Critique of Civilization*. Cambridge: Harvard Univ. Press, 1954, pp. 154–156.
[6] F. S. Chapin, *Contemporary American Institutions: A Sociological Analysis*. New York: Harper, 1935, pp. 13–23.
[7] H. Spencer, *Principles of Sociology*. Part II, Chaps. VII–IX.
[8] C. A. Dawson and W. E. Gettys, *An Introduction to Sociology*. New York: Ronald, 1948, pp. 263–288,

organized aspects of regulated social behavior," represented mainly by government; and (4) the integrative institutions, especially characteristic of a complex society, such as the social class system, the religious and political institutions, and labor organizations.

Parsons has two different but related three-part categories of institutions. In the *Essays*,[9] institutions are differentiated on the basis of the functional needs of their members as individuals and of the social system they compose. As such, there are three general types of institutional patterns: (1) situational patterns or patterns—actually organizations of roles—in which all individuals participate as a consequence of specific sex and age characteristics and territorial location, that is, role-patterns organized around natural and biological facts; (2) instrumental patterns, that is, patterns organized primarily about the functional role element of the relevant statuses of the social system, particularly the attainment of certain specialized goals through performing occupational roles, carrying on exchange, and through property relations; and (3) integrative patterns, that is, patterns primarily oriented toward regulating the relations of individuals in order to avoid conflict or in order to promote positive cooperation, notably stratification, authority, and religion.

In *The Social System*[10] Parsons again distinguishes three types of institutionalization, but in terms of different modes of relationship to the structure of the social relationship itself: (1) relational institutions, which define the statuses and roles of the parties in the interactive process; (2) regulative institutions, which regulate or set the limits and conditions for the pursuit of (a) the instrumental (goal-oriented), (b) the expressive (gratification-satisfying), and (c) the ego-integrative (personality integrative) interests and activities of the persons in the social system; and (3) the cultural institutions, that is, institutions not directly involving "commitments to overt action" but consisting of "patterns of cultural orientation as such" as found in beliefs, particular systems of expressive symbols (for example, "canons of taste"), and patterns of moral value-orientation.

Feibleman,[11] in the most recent comprehensive analysis of social institutions, sets up two general categories of institutions, the service institutions and the higher institutions. The service institutions, in turn, are subdivided into the constitutive and the regulative institutions. "The service institutions in general are those which furnish goods and services to all other institutions" (p. 198). The constitutive service institutions

[9] T. Parsons, *Essays on Sociological Theory: Pure and Applied*. Glencoe, Ill.: Free Press, 1949, pp. 44–45.

[10] Glencoe, Ill.: Free Press, 1951, pp. 51–58.

[11] J. K. Feibleman, *The Institutions of Society*. London: Allen & Unwin, 1956, pp. 197–227, 257.

are those which furnish the substantive goods and services; they are mainly concerned with human activity that is characterized by being primarily productive. They provide and process raw materials—human and physical—and provide the essential maintenance services. Here are listed and treated the family, transportation, communication, economics, the practical technologies and decorative arts, and education. The regulative service institutions are those which provide formal, primarily managerial services; they furnish regulations, not production; they "order the relations between men in a society by means governing the use of force" (p. 208); they consist chiefly of the state or government, law, and the military. The other major category—the higher institutions—furnishes the purpose or aim to other institutions (p. 215), and consists of the sciences, the arts, philosophy, and religion.

III: The Working Classification for Part 3

Our primary concern with institutions in this study is their place in the structural-functional organization of our own complex society.

Our classification will be purely functional in nature, the major categories to consist of a minimal number of broad but distinct areas of functioning in the total operation of our society. The particular institutions and institutional sectors (or pivotal subsystems) will be located in the general classificatory scheme on the basis of their major, nontransferable functions in the total division of labor, not on the basis of certain fringe or auxiliary functions which they perform.

An incidental distinction, based on the degree of institutional development, will be woven into the main classification and analysis of institutions. Three main types of institutions will be involved. First, there are the older, and in the main firmly regularized, established, and systematized—in brief, more mature—institutions, such as language, the familial, economic, political, religious, educational, and possibly the aesthetic institutions.

Second, there are the nascent institutional subsystems of our society; that is, institutions not yet fully developed or firmly rooted in the overall social system. They arose because of revolutionary changes in our social life that occurred during the last century, especially the changes accompanying the transformation of our society from a rural to an urban basis, the mechanization of industry, the mobility of the population, the increasing strategic importance of science and technology, and the weakening of the primary group agencies. These changes have made prominent certain social needs, many of which always existed in minor form and were satisfied incidentally and intermittently as the occasion arose, usually by other institutions. Notable are (1) scientific-technological institutions; (2) occupational, that is, vocational or work institutions, including labor unions and professions and professionalization of certain types of occupations; (3) welfare and social assistance institutions, including health, especially public health, social work, and social security agencies; (4) recreational institutions, especially those of a semi-public and public nature. There are some grounds for including here also the increasingly systematized and organized activities on behalf of the conservation of natural resources such as soil, water, minerals, energies.

Third, there is at least one instance of what should be thought of as a quasi-institution; namely, the stratification system. It has organizational forms that have some institutional characteristics, but it is lacking in certain strategic ones.

The major functional categories with the institutional sectors falling mainly within each category are as follows.

COMMUNICATION

All human interaction rests on symbolic communication. Communication is intricately and vastly organized in our society, and much analytical attention is being paid to it in its highly elaborated forms. Language, the foundation of all human communication, however, has not been widely treated as sociologically significant. Hence:

The Basic Institution of Language (Chapter Eight)

THE ACQUISITION, ORGANIZATION, AND UTILIZATION OF KNOWLEDGE

Man in society operates culturally instead of purely naturally. For this he needs tested knowledge. He does not merely submit to his various environments; he adjusts himself to them and makes increasingly successful efforts at manipulating them. Hence:

The Scientific-Technological Institutions (Chapter Nine)

MAINTENANCE

Every society must meet the fundamental and pivotal needs of human perpetuation and physical and physiological maintenance. There must be societally acceptable and adequate biological perpetuation; people must be continuously produced and in sufficient numbers. People must eat regularly and in adequate amount; they must be provided with other necessities of existence, such as clothing, shelter, and rest. To do this, a sufficient number of them must work; that is, engage in economically significant activity. A modern society's health and welfare needs must be met. There exist the problems of protection against disease and accident, of promoting physical and mental health, of maintaining physical and social security in time of crisis (family disruption, unemployment, sickness, physical handicap, old age). Hence:

> The Familial Institutions (Chapter Ten)
> Economic Institutions (Chapter Eleven)
> Welfare Institutions (Chapter Twelve)

SOCIALIZATION AND CULTURAL TRANSMISSION

The knowledge of a society, its values, its essential principles and ways of life acquired through experience must be imparted to all of its newcomers; they must be purposively fitted as societal participants. The constantly accumulating cultural elements must be continuously conveyed to the entire population, young and old. The culture generally must be perpetuated in time. Hence:

> Educational Institutions (Chapter Thirteen)

OVER-ALL REGULATION AND ORDERING

Every society must have established internal order, peace, cohesion, effective operation, and be prepared to protect itself against aggression from without. Also, its hierarchically structured and differentially evaluated population elements must be ordered, or ordinated. Hence:

> Governmental Institutions (Chapter Fourteen)
> The Stratification System: A Quasi-Institution (Chapter Fifteen)

EXPRESSION

Men everywhere and at all times have conceived of a mysterious supernatural environment to which they craved adjustment, and of an awesome and supreme supernatural agency in this vast unknown with which they felt the imperative urge of communion. Preoccupation with these needs are among the most fundamental and absorbing expressions of human consciousness. Almost all men have aesthetic needs, and a desire to give some actional or expressional form to their aesthetic urges. Hence:

> Religious Institutions (Chapter Sixteen)
> Art Institutions (Chapter Seventeen)

PART 3

The Major Systems of Institutions of American Society

The examination of the major institutional systems of our own society is the ultimate objective of our study. What has preceded has been largely a laying of foundations. The major blocks of institutions were classified under the six categories indicated in Chapter Seven. A more or less uniform pattern of treatment will be followed in the case of each of the ten blocks of institutions to be examined. Attention will be paid to the place of the institutions of the particular sector in any societal system; the important reasons for institutionalization in the particular need area; the universal characteristics and functions of the institutions of the sector, and in most instances certain "fringe" functions, that is, functions shared with, or overlapping, those of other sectors; the unique features of the particular blocks of institutions as they operate in American society, including notable trends; and, finally, in the case of most of the sectors, there will be occasional reference to special attention areas or areas of concern regarding some of the existent situations from the point of view of both utilitarian and humanistic objectives and criteria.

COMMUNICATION

The Basic Institution of Language

Adequate and effective communication is the initial and fundamental requisite in the proper functioning and maintenance of a societal system. By communication we mean the transmission of intentions and meanings among interacting creatures through the use of a common system of symbols. A symbol is an easily recognized sound, gesture, object, or mark without meaning or importance in itself, which is used to represent, direct attention to, or recall ideas, actions, emotions, or things that have social significance; in brief, it is something employed by human beings, and human beings only, to convey meanings to other human beings. It functions simply, economically, and quickly as a substitute for some object, response, or situation, often some complex and abstract reality, and evokes more or less uniform response in the communicating human beings. The meaning attached to any symbol is arbitrarily established in the particular society; if the symbols are to function effectively in communication they have to have the same meaning and value for all interacting parties. For that matter, the standardized symbols, the vehicles for their transmission, the meanings that they convey, must all be made consistent with each other; in brief, communication itself must be a system.

All human interaction is communication interaction. Communication is thus the cultural technique that stands behind all other techniques employed by men; there can be no culture without it. All cultural phenomena rest on meanings, and these meanings have to be formulated and transmitted to others; otherwise they would have neither existence nor utility. Communication makes possible various features of culture. Without it, in sufficient quantity and quality, there can be no intellectual stimulation and response, no coordination of activities, no contrivance and invention, no recording, accumulation, and transmission of experience, no planning or direction of joint effort, and no instruction. Communication alone makes community possible.

It is the *modus operandi* of social life; in fact, the available techniques of communication definitely limit the kinds and level, the range and rate, of the organized life that a people can have. As the means of communication have developed, the area of intercourse has widened, rapidity of the exchange of experience has increased, and the activities—economic, political, intellectual, and so on—have increased in volume and been refined in efficacy.

Language is the basic instrument by means of which almost all meaningful and specific human communication occurs—all beyond the very general, simple, and automatic communication provided by instinctive and reflex noises and gestures. Not only face-to-face communication but all indirect communication by modern mechanical means—printing, telephone, telegraph, teletype, radio, television—consists of language in various forms.

Language probably developed concomitantly with the earliest definitely human society. At any rate, as far back as history and prehistory enable us to penetrate, we find fully developed languages. There are substantial reasons for this. The instituted language of a people is fundamental to *all* of the other institutional systems. Language is the indispensable instrument whereby institutional lore and principles are transmitted across space and time; whereby institutional rules, controls, and compulsions are conveyed to individuals and groups, and institutional procedures are carried into effect; whereby institutional successes are recorded; whereby indoctrination in institutional values and ways come about. To a considerable extent, the complexity of institutions is determined by the complexity of the language behavior of those embracing the institutions. Language is the *institution* which all members of every human community must master in sufficient degree if they are to participate in any of its cultural and social organizational activities; without it, they are mere isolated bio-physical entities and space-filling expressions.

Language is probably man's unique characteristic and most universal and important contrivance.[1] Man's tool-making and tool-using abilities have often been referred to as a characteristic that peculiarly distinguishes him from all other species. But apes can not only use tools, but even invent them, and make them. Man alone makes, establishes, institutionalizes, and uses language. It is "the heart of what is human"; where it does not exist, there abides little that is human. The creative use of it "has given man the earth and the control thereof."[2]

A language is a voluntarily produced and socially established system

---

[1] Lewis Mumford refers to language as "the greatest of all human inventions." *The Conduct of Life*. New York: Harcourt, Brace, 1951, p. 40.

[2] Irving J. Lee, *Language Habits in Human Affairs*. New York: Harper, 1941, pp. 3, 5.

of standardized and conventionalized, that is, generally accepted, utilized, and required, symbols that have a specific and arbitrarily imposed meaning in the given society, or, technically, in the given language community. The great bulk of language is based on human speech, that is, standardized vocal sounds or "words" that have been phonetically, lexically, morphologically, and syntactically organized,[3] and that carry standard meaning. In almost all languages certain conventionalized signs and gestures also have language significance; these, however, are translatable into words, or are representative of words. Thus, among us, the wave of an arm by an acquaintance means "hello," the green light at the intersection means "go," the nod and wink mean "come on." Fundamentally, the spoken *word* is the only all-inclusive medium of communication. All other symbolic devices relate to words, imply words, are translations, substitutes, or supplements of words; they simply serve as media for representing or for extending the range and potency of words in space and time.

When a people have reached the stage of literacy in their language development, they have writing or written speech; that is, words or auditory symbols are translated into the form of physical objects, pictures, or pictograms, lines, alphabet, or other standardized, conventionalized visible figures or marks that make possible the transmission and perpetuation of meanings across space and time. In societies like our own, communication by language is further facilitated and extended by the various mechanical means of transmitting either speech or writing, such as postal service, printing in its multiple uses, telegraph and telephone, radio, photography, motion pictures, and television.

Language is a sociocultural product, like other institutions the outgrowth of common experiences. Language is the organized way of registering and recording human experience itself, while other institutions are organized ways that have developed out of experience for conducting the different types of operations. Men have a registering of consciousness regarding the attributes and consequences to them of the things, the events, the forces, the processes, and the relationships of the elements of their environments. These experiences or registerings arouse interest. Men have recall, imaginings, and reflections about them. They assess their reactions to the experiences in the form of estimates and evaluations; that is, they attach meanings to their experiences, and these meanings become working realities. But all of this meaningful human experience is expressed through the medium of language. As Bertrand Russell put it, "Language is a means of externalizing and publicizing our own experiences."[4] In language we find con-

---

[3] These organizational features will be briefly examined in Section III.
[4] Bertrand Russell, *Human Knowledge: Its Scope and Limits.* New York: Simon & Schuster, 1948, p. 60.

densed and registered all of the reality of which we are aware; it embodies our public knowledge. It ". . . binds into one vast, fluid, yet plastic whole the multitude of human experience,"[5] and functions as the common denominator of human understanding.[6]

I: The General Functions of Language

Language is not an end in itself. It is the basic set of tools of human society, and the functions that can be carried on by tools are their sole reason for existence.

Language is the means whereby all knowledge acquired through human experience is formulated; it functions as the *vehicle* of human knowledge. All that man knows, all that he can be explicit about, all that he imagines or anticipates is expressed in the words and phrases and sentences of his language; all identification, definition, conceptualization, classification, and interpretation of objects, events, and conditions is first a linguistic matter. Man does not know anything unless he can put it into precise language, and conversely what is not in the general and special languages of a people is not known.

Concretely, the knowledge is couched in names, stated as facts, ideas, principles, formulae, beliefs, surmises and imaginings. Language thus serves not only to express thoughts but also to make possible thoughts which could not exist without it. As the embodiment of the knowledge, language reflects the structure and composition of the world as a people see it (their *Weltanschauung*); this in turn has a determinative effect on their experience.[7]

Language makes possible communication at the human level. It constitutes the system of symbols which provides the common context and logic of discourse. By means of language, man conveys his facts,

[5] Stanley Gerr, "Language and Science: The Rational Functional Language of Science and Technology," *Phil. of Science,* 9 (Apr., 1942): 146–161.

[6] For an analytical model of the circumstances of the emergence of language, of its nature, of the language community, and its relationship to the physical, cultural, and social situations prevailing in its language community, see J. O. Hertzler, "Toward a Sociology of Language," *Soc. Forces,* 32 (Dec., 1953): 109–119, esp. 110–112.

[7] This aspect of language will be examined in Section IV below. The relation between language and knowedge is brought out in the following incident. When Francis Huxley returned to an East Brazilian Indian village a second year and demonstrated more familiarity and facility with the language, an Indian exclaimed, "Last year when you first came, you didn't understand anything. Now you speak properly, *now you know.*" Francis Huxley, *Affable Savages: An Anthropologist among the Urubu Indians of Brazil.* New York: Viking, 1957, p. 56. Italics mine.

principles, beliefs, interpretations of experience to others, and shares them with others.

Language also makes it possible for man to be the supreme space-binding animal; that is, able to be aware of space and to conceptualize it, but especially to control, use, maintain contacts in it, and conduct all manner of enterprises across it.

Language is the basis of all storing and preservation of knowledge (experience) and, consequently, all transmission of knowledge from generation to generation. It is the basis of all human records, of all remembering and recalling of past experience. It is the collective mind and memory of a society. The very vocabulary of a people in itself inventories every aspect of their culture and social life, past and present. Linguistic facts are often more reliable than other kinds of culture facts in establishing cultural "markers," in evidencing culture migration, culture borrowing.

Language is at the same time the agency whereby each succeeding generation receives the lore of the past. Through it, human beings can learn from the experiences of other human beings, even those from a very remote past; they do not necessarily have to perform the acts from which the experience emerged. By means of it, each person, each generation can begin where the others left off.

Furthermore, it is by means of language that man is also the sole time-binding animal; that is, able not only to transmit experience in time beyond the life span of any individual, group, generation, society, or culture, but able also to inhabit simultaneously the past (through legend, traditions, and formal records), the present, and the future (by means of declared ideals, projections, anticipations, plans, and programs). In fact, by language man can in some measure even control future events.

With the advent of writing among a people, human experience can be much more precisely formulated, more permanently and more accurately transmitted. Writing also greatly enhances the space- and time-binding potentialities of language.

Language introduces order in our experience. By means of the categories of experience that man establishes by words, he is able to respond selectively toward various phases of his experience. For example, he can conceive of some experience as concerned with things or events which he can name (nouns), others as involving action or occurrence (verbs), others as implying qualities or specially identifying characteristics (adjectives and adverbs). Thus, it is a "cow" and not a "camel"; the cow is "running," "slowly," and is "black and white." By means of language, man can identify, categorize, and relate artifacts, techniques, conditions, in fact, everything in his experience. He is enabled to conceive of the world as relatively understandable, stable, predictable, and orderly. Out of the infinitely large number and variety of objects and occurrences, he can create unity out of diversity, order out of chaos, and specificity out of undifferentiated wholes.[8]

II: Language and Social Organization

An analysis of the utilitarian part language plays in human social organization involves, first of all, the distinction between and the relation between a language community and a societal system. A language community consists of a collectivity of people who speak a common language, and among whom a great amount of communication and a high degree of mutual intelligibility usually prevail. A societal system is an organized group, usually including a large number of people covering an extensive common area, operating as a distinctive, independent entity. A language community and a societal system are not necessarily identical; a language community may extend beyond the given societal system in which the common language is spoken; it may, in fact, extend over several societal systems. For example, the English language-community includes Great Britain, the United States, Canada, Australia, New Zealand, but each of these is an independent societal system. However, the English language must be widely understood in each, if each is to operate effectively. Thus, although the language community may extend beyond the immediate societal system, every societal system must be a language community; that is, it must have a single language system within its area of jurisdiction. In other words, there can be no social organization without communication. Any communication beyond that by reflexive and instinctive signs or gestures requires social organization, especially in the form of regularized contacts and relationships.

The influence of any social system can extend only as far as its members have effective channels of communication. Also, language is a fundamental factor in determining the size of social groups, and the range and character of the relations between the members. Conversely, the larger the social unit, the more essential are mutually intelligible means of communication over the entire area.

In order that men may live together—be organized into groups— there needs to be consensus; that is, men must have a body of common information regarding the essentials of individual and joint existence, but especially a certain community of interests and solidarity of beliefs, and a certain amount of understanding, agreement, and shared knowl-

[8] Cf. A. R. Lindesmith and A. L. Strauss, *Social Psychology*. New York: Dryden, 1949, p. 50.

edge as to common values and purposes. Such a pattern of group information, group understanding, and group objective is impossible without communication media which are comprehensible to, and used by, the great majority of the members.

All common and public action in a democratic society like our own must have a supporting common public opinion. This is either non-existent or indistinct unless the persons who compose the public "live in the same world and speak and think in the same universe of discourse."[9]

Language is the medium through which human cooperation and concerted action are brought about. It is the means by which the diverse contributory activities of the people involved are coordinated and correlated with each other. In any joint action there are certain essential ingredients, all of which rest upon language that is adequate for the various special subfunctions. There must be description and specification of what the things involved are and of the actions to be engaged in. The goals and plans must be clearly formulated and transmitted to the personnel. The common procedures and techniques and the ways of using all implements must be formulated, announced, and commonly understood. This involves also the transmission of procedural traditions, of knowledge of successful usages and utilizations, and information on the nature and formation of skills. The specific actions required of all of the specialized participants must be described and prescribed; rules and regulations must be formulated, announced, and their enforcement supervised; instructions and directives or commands must be given; in the more extensive and formally organized cooperative undertakings, correspondence must be conducted, reports must be made, and records kept. Not a single interact of any kind in the over-all joint undertaking can occur without language.

Although language is not a guarantee of cooperation, it *is* an essential condition. Cooperation, in the local community as well as in the world as a whole, is perpetually thwarted by limitations and diversity of language. Conversely, the richer and wider, the more complicated and intricate, the cooperation, and the more specialized the behavior of its participants, the greater is the need for diversified, quick, accurate, common language among them.

With written language and the modern mechanical extensions of speech and writing, there can be complex, enduring, and highly integrated organizations, or bodies of cooperating individuals and groups existing and extending far beyond the range of person-to-person contacts. Notable examples are not only such secondary forms of organi-

---

[9] R. E. Park and E. W. Burgess, *Introduction to the Science of Society.* Chicago: Univ. of Chicago Press, 1921, p. 765.

zation as states and nations conducting political action over wide areas, but also the extensive associations carrying on economic production and exchange, religious activity, scientific and technological activity, sports and other forms of recreation.

Language is the principal weapon in maintaining that cohesiveness and solidarity of groups upon which their durability and the free and effective cooperation of their members depends. In the first place, as Park put it, "people who speak the same language find it convenient to live together."[10]

Social solidarity is almost synonymous with *linguistic* solidarity. Language serves more effectively than any other social trait to hold individuals together in social relationships.[11] Identity of language almost automatically creates a definite bond of understanding and sympathy among people.

Language is also significant as a cohesive factor in that it reflects and records a group's common historical experiences and transmits its traditions. Everywhere, also, language functions as the badge or symbol of the group; it is the major and obvious indicator of the group identity and of its unity and union. By means of language the out-groups are marked off from the in-group.

Often when the integrity of a people is threatened, as when they are on the defensive against cultural, especially political, inroads, they become conscious of their language as one of their most distinctive traits. It comes to be a cherished thing to be preserved at great cost if necessary. Throughout history, ethnic and national groups have maintained their identity and cohesion by rigidly adhering to their common language. For example, it was largely because of the preservation of the Polish language that the Poles retained their common identity during more than a century and a half of Russian, Austrian, and German domination. On the other hand, the acquisition of the majority language has always been one of the major elements in the assimilation of minorities, or of strangers for that matter.

Conversely, diversity of tongue has always been a serious barrier to cohesion and solidarity. This is evident in the relations not only of national and ethnic groups, but also of special groups within a given society which have their special languages and dialects. For example, the language of the upper strata sometimes diverges sharply from that of the lower strata; different regions have their dialects which are at least amusing to those of other regions; occupations and professions have their special languages, which seem to be jargon to outsiders.

[10] R. E. Park, *The Immigrant Press and Its Control.* New York: Harper, 1922, p. 51.
[11] C. M. Rosenquist, "Linguistic Changes in the Acculturation of the Swedes of Texas," *Soc. & Soc. Res.,* 16 (Jan.–Feb., 1932): 221–231.

The continuous instruction, indoctrination, and training of the young and of the newcomers to a society, as well as the constant reorientation and retooling of the entire population, essential to the society, quite obviously cannot be accomplished without language. The very learning of a word is a process of socializing the individual, making him a part of the conscious world consisting of others who use the same language.

Related to the preceding social organizational functions of language, and in a sense summarizing them, is the function of language in social control; that is, its function in regulating, directing, adjusting, and organizing the social conduct of individuals and groups in the interest of effective societal operation. Social control is impossible without a linguistic system. This becomes apparent when we note some of the detailed essentials in the social control process. The right kind of language is basic (1) in understanding the prohibitions of behavior; (2) in presenting the rules and directives; (3) in articulating and conveying the public opinion behind the sanctions; and (4) in conducting the formal and informal agencies for administering and enforcing the sanctions.

There is also a broader social control aspect of language. Since language is the means whereby people think and express their emotions and sentiments, control of the language, oral and written, and its mechanical extensions, implies control in some measure of *what* and *how* the people using the language feel; it is possible to control or at least direct their interests and mental preoccupations, and suggest responsive conduct. The efforts, ranging from those engaged in ordinary everyday conversation and address, through those of special pleaders, through advertisers and propagandists, to the rulers of totalitarian countries, are cases in point.

Language is used as a vehicle for the exercise of social influence through the intensifying of traditional attitudes and prejudices, the creation of new attitudes and beliefs, the suppression of truth or the partial use of truth, the spread of false doctrine. It does this through the modification or creation and repetition of words, phrases, and meanings.

Language is not only the basis of all other institutions, but it performs special functions for them. It provides each institution with its master symbols, special terminologies, its other communicative forms. In the economic area, the management elite and the engineers, as well as all of the trades and occupations, have their particular names and forms of expression for their operations—the names for the materials, tools, and techniques which they use. Special economic areas have their highly specialized languages—the language of the oil fields and the railroads. In connection with government, there is the whole vocabulary of organization and rulership, the terms related to the particular state's special ideology, the terms for the state's enemies, the language of diplomacy, the use of language as evidence of nationality and citizenship. The law has its highly specialized terminology and linguistic formulation. The military has a complicated language of its own concerned with organization, with the highly differentiated personnel and their respective functions, with tactics and strategy. Not only does religion have its distinctive language forms, but particular religions are often identified with a particular language; and language is sometimes made a symbol of religious faith, even to the point of becoming a shibboleth. The other institutions—domestic, educational, scientific, artistic—have their special vocabularies and constructions.[12]

III: Language as an Institutionalized System

Language is the result of the experience of men living together in human groups. Consequently, language has a history during which the operation of a complex of forces and processes has given it the various functional proficiencies just discussed. The forms and organization that it takes and the processes whereby it carries on its functions have developed gradually through internal variation, addition, selection, reorganization, and the modifications that come through transmission from generation to generation and from contacts with other languages. Nevertheless language is highly regularized and systematic; it has, in fact, the systematization and establishment of institutionalization. Most languages are probably as completely institutionalized as any of the other institutions of their speakers.

Thus language must be a system of norms—norms of grammar, vocabulary, sentence structure, pronunciation, intonation, and the like—which have to be followed whenever thought is to be expressed, communicated, or understood. There can be considerable leeway as to how fast we drive our automobiles or which occupation we follow, or when and how often we marry, or which religious organization, if any, we belong to; but, the names we give to persons and groups, or to points in time and duration of time, or to points of location or distance or direction in space, or the sentences we use in describing or explaining things and events and relations, or the directives, instructions, and commands we give to each other cannot be indefinite or equivocal. Each language,

[12] On the part of language in other institutions, see: M. Pei, *The Story of Language*. Philadelphia: Lippincott, 1949, pp. 196–284. H. Gerth and C. W. Mills, *Character and Social Structure: The Psychology of Social Institutions*. New York: Harcourt, Brace, 1953, pp. 280–286. J. Bram, *Language and Society*. Garden City, N.Y.: Doubleday, 1955, pp. 35–48.

therefore, is standard—standard English, standard German; it has its essential, universal, and standardized (conventionalized) structural forms or modes of combining its elements, its rules or codes, its modes and instruments of performance, and its meanings. Keller dramatically states, "The great wonder, when one comes to realize it, is that language, built up premeditatively by millions of unthinking and casual users, shows a regularity and orderliness . . . comparable to the regularity of the solar system."[13] At any given time, as Sapir puts it, it is "a finished organization."[14] The variations and specialties of usage by families, cliques, different social classes, occupational groups, regions, educational levels within the language community cannot depart too widely from the standard, or it becomes so eccentric as to be useless.

In brief, the language institution of a people is a more or less consistent, coherent, and patterned set of elements; hence their usage is predictable. This organization is paralleled by that which institutionalization imposes on the relations of the sexes and the generations or on the citizens of the state. If it were not for this institutionalization, every language would be a mere loose, even accidental, collection of unrelated symbols. As it is, every symbol is not an isolated element, but, according to its type, has its characteristic function and established meaning as part of the whole.

The language of each society is unique compared with that of other societies. The known languages of mankind fall into great families or bodies of languages with more or less separate origins, and with similar, distinguishing characteristics, such as the Indo-European, Sinaic, and Semitic families. These families in turn have major subdivisions, such as the Germanic and Romance languages within the Indo-European family. But all languages, as linguistic systems, have certain common institutional features.

Language, like other institutions, has a high degree of stability and durability, even rigidity, and it often resists change. Not only is it regarded as a precious thing by its speakers and hence protected against loss, invasion, or serious modification, but because of its very institutionalization, it is a highly structured affair, and most of its techniques tend to preserve it and keep it from change. Its vocabulary or stock of words is perpetuated in dictionaries. Though words are dropped and added, the added ones make their way slowly into the general language. The grammatical structure and functioning resting upon the established standards and codes change even more slowly. The mere act of writing a language tends to give rigidity to its lexicon, its grammar, and the related semantic organization of the language community.

---

[13] A. G. Keller, *Social Evolution* (rev. ed.). New York: Macmillan, 1931, p. 156.
[14] E. Sapir, "Language," *Ency. Soc. Sciences,* IX, p. 159.

The institutional aspects, sociologically considered, are first its structuring, and second its personnel and associational features.

The general structurings of language are phonological, lexical, and grammatical.[15]

The phonological or phonetic system has to do with the system of sounds with which language operates in the building of words. The distinctive unit sound parts of words, known as phonemes—concretely, consonants and vowels—are finite in number for a given language; they are not combined at random but according to certain principles, including certain sequences, and with distinctive accent or stress of syllables. These principles differ from language to language. Notable examples are the predominance of consonants in Polish compared with the greater prominence of vowels in English words or the difference in the accenting of syllables of given words between "Deep South" and "Harvard" English in our country.

The lexical or lexicographical organization is concerned with the standard words, or the innumerable combinations of phonemes, each with a more or less established meaning. Given words have to have an arbitrarily established and specifically limited meaning. Otherwise, the users could achieve no agreement as to what the words represent. This is the vocabulary aspect. The systematic nature of the words of a language is evidenced in a given language community's lexicon or dictionary; that is, its alphabetically arranged book, giving the standard pronunciations, the definitions, and the etymology of its store of words. Words, however, are always somewhat ambiguous, and vary somewhat in meaning from context to context; nevertheless, they have to have some centralized meaning.

The grammatical organization refers to the fact that in every language, words are of different kinds with different functions, and they are put together in certain standard ways, in phrases, clauses, and sentences, in order to convey meanings. These two main divisions of grammar are referred to in linguistic analysis as morphology and syntax.

Morphology. Words are not all of the same kind nor do they have the same functions in the formation of concepts and the transmission of meanings. All words are formally categorized into the so-called parts of speech, each form or type or category of speech having a distinctive and indispensable function to perform in the building of a sentence. Each type of speech part complements the others in coordinated speech. Thus, in English as we speak it, the standard parts of speech

---

[15] A fourth type of structuring, namely the semantic, or the established, conventional meaning structure with its corpus of operational definitions (the development and maintenance of which is the ultimate purpose of language), is often referred to as an independent organizational feature. It will be discussed in the following section.

or elements of the sentence consist of nouns, pronouns, adjectives, adverbs, verbs, prepositions, conjunctions, and interjections. The nouns, or names, and the verbs, or indicators of action, alone represent fully and concretely the concepts we formulate and convey. The adjectives represent some quality of the objects or situations named; the adverbs are modifiers of verbs and adjectives, often indicating the manner in which action takes place or quality is conceived. All of the other sorts of words revolve about nouns and verbs; they are supplemental technical tools serving as economizers or facilitators, or to add refinement or emphasis of meaning.

Syntax. The different functional types of symbols cannot be combined in helter-skelter fashion. Every language system has a particular structuring known as syntax. This is its formal or logical or rules aspect, sometimes referred to as the "traffic rules" of language; that is, its patterned way of putting the different word forms together in order to build clauses, sentences, and even higher units, the objective being to build good solid statements.[16] Syntax involves the proper or correct order and location in the clause or sentence of the different parts of speech; for example, placement of subject (noun or pronoun) before and object after the verb; proper use of particular number (singular or plural), gender, case, tense, mood, voice, and so on; punctuation, implied in oral speech and definitely indicated in writing, consisting of standard points or marks (commas, semicolons, dashes, brackets, periods, quotation marks, underscoring) to divide speech into phrases, clauses, and sentences for clarity, amplitude, and emphasis.

In general, the institutionalized structuring and functioning of a language are based upon established principles and are governed by rules and regulations. These rules take two forms: (1) the formal system of rules regarding the formation and transformation of words and combination of words as the necessity arises to articulate the meanings of new experiences or clarify existent meanings; and, (2) the normative rules of procedure in the use of language, that is, the regulations prescribing how to use the language forms correctly, and those prohibiting or proscribing other forms and usages.

Language, like other institutionalized ways of life, also has its own personnel, and in societies like our own, its organizations and associations of special personnel. There is, of course, the whole community of speakers of the particular language, but they are mainly its passive recipients and more or less unconscious performers of its organized behavior. The special functionaries of each language are of central insti-

---

[16] "Every utterance spoken in a given speech community follows one or the other of a finite series of meaningful arrangements, peculiar to the language of that community." R. L. Beals and H. Hoijer, *An Introduction to Anthropology.* New York: Macmillan, 1953, p. 517.

tutional significance. These are the instructors and indoctrinators of the language, both the informal ones, such as parents, older siblings, playmates, and other associates, and the formal instructors, such as the teachers in the educational system. There are the guardians or preservers of language, often also teachers, trying to preserve its "correctness" or "purity." Then there are the various associations for the formation, inculcation, preservation, improvement, extension, or other implementation of language, such as those consisting of teaching and research professionals (the American Modern Language Association and its more specialized subdivisions, for example); associations of nationalists or religionists promoting a given language as a symbol of nationality or as a means of preserving a religious organization; associations developing and promoting universal languages; the organizations of men more or less unconsciously developing pragmatic special language, such as the special terminologies and formulae of the different sciences and technologies. These various functionaries and organizations, like those of other institutions, have their necessary utilitarian material and mechanical equipment and their essential institutional procedures.

IV: The Semantic-Metalinguistic System

As the result of the comparative study of the languages of different peoples, especially comparison of the languages of primitive peoples with those of modern civilizations, it has come to be recognized not only that languages have the linguistic organization briefly examined above, but that each language also has a semantic and metalinguistic structuring which is of vast importance in almost every aspect of the life of the members of the linguistic community.

Metalinguistic structuring refers to the structuring beyond or above the linguistic structuring; that is, the body of meanings, which rest upon the inimitable, more or less established, but always limited, degrees and ways of each language for perceiving, diagnosing, conceptualizing, categorizing, and interpreting the aspects of environments, ways that are a result of the language's special and peculiar structuring as they developed.[17] This structuring, in turn, rests upon a varying combination of factors in the experiences of the people, which have operated as physical and cultural determiners and conditioners in their lives. The various language communities have lived in different physical environments which have presented different problems of survival and

[17] The principal contributors to metalinguistic analysis are indicated in the bibliography at the end of the chapter.

adjustment; they have had different levels of technological development, and consequently have had varying degrees and levels of insight into, and control over, phenomena, physical and social; they have had different degrees of physical, intellectual, and sociocultural contact; hence, they have variations in acculturation and catholicity of viewpoint. Also they have had different kinds and levels of societal experience and organization.

These experiential differences are reflected in the linguistic structures and categories of the language community—what it has names for, the morphological forms it employs, and the manner in which it uses them, but especially in its syntax, particularly in indicating the relationships between, and the modifications of, things, actions, qualities, and conditions. Every society thus has its characteristic linguistic profile.

Each language thus has its own semantic system; each language is, in fact, a more or less self-contained meaning system, inextricably bound to the linguistic system and implemented by it, and yet something apart which produces its own kind of determining and ordering. This meaning system not only embodies and summates all of the meanings already arrived at, but also has its own peculiar forms of abstraction, its own conceptions, categorizations, and interpretations of kinds and qualities of things and occurrences, of motion, action, and causation, of space, of time, of relationship. The meaning system also indicates what has *much* meaning; what has *general* meaning; what has *specific, highly specialized, and highly distinctive* meaning; and to the outsider it indicates what is *without* meaning, either because there are no guides in the language for perception (no names, definitions, or categories along a particular line) or there is an ignoring of significance.

Language evolved prior to the awareness, prior to the thought, of any of the speakers. Each language is thus somewhat determinative of the way its speakers do their thinking, particularly in their logical procedures. It is the way they express the relationship and order of facts and ideas; it channels their reasoning. As someone has put it, the grammar of language produces a grammar of thought. Furthermore, each language provides its speakers with their ethos, and with their *Weltanschauung*.

In a very real sense, people speaking different languages live in different worlds of reality. This is brought out pointedly by the difficulty of translating from one language to another, especially when the languages are unrelated. Because of the diversity of the experiential worlds, the semantic worlds are sufficiently different to make it impossible exactly or even approximately to convey similar meanings. It has been well said that "every translator is in part a traitor."

Eskimo, for example, has many words for different kinds of "snow"; English has only one. Arabic has nearly 6000 words referring to "camel" and its equipment—color, bodily structure, sex, age, movement, condition, etc.—but thirty years ago Arabic had only one word, "tomobile," to cover all makes and models of cars, trucks, buses, and tractors. Many primitives had little awareness of space; they had no need to refer to objects 282 million light years away, or to be concerned about ballistic missiles sent 5000 miles. Many had little or no conception of time as a flow and unity, but conceived of it only in its individual and momentary phases. Central Australian tribes were unable to count beyond four or five and did not need to; the Chuckchee counted in fives and tens by means of hand and foot digits, while we must keep account of a national debt in terms of hundreds of billions. Primitive languages are completely lacking in indigenous terms relating to many aspects of our technologized life. No primitive language has need for such terms as "child rejection," "upper-middle class," "production line organization," or "communication network."

English and Latin verbs have divisions of time into past, present, and future; Chinese has four parts of time at successively remote periods from *the* present, *a* present, and *a* future. In Hopi language, "lightning," "wave," "flame," "meteor," "puff of smoke" are not nouns but verbs; events of necessarily brief duration for them cannot be anything but verbs. Hopi thus has a classification of events by type of duration, something strange to our modes of thought. Hopi has a generality, not a specificity, of nouns; one says not "a glass of water" but "a water." The European-American almost inevitably speaks in terms of causation; the primitive in terms of occurrence or "eventing." The word "democracy" has very different connotations in the U.S.A. and the U.S.S.R.

The significance of the metalinguistic structuring for the language users is evident, even within a given language community, by a comparison of the much more limited cognitive and expressive world of the illiterate or poorly educated persons, with their small vocabularies and elementary syntax, with the better educated circles whose linguistic abilities permit them much more extensive awarenesses and perspectives, a wider range and greater complexity of thought and action.

The result of this metalinguistic structuring is that a given language, as the tightly instituted pattern system that it is, exercises, more than any other institution, a rigid, specially determinative, inescapable moulding and channeling influence upon all who use it. The speakers are probably less aware of this than in the case, for example, of the controls exercised by the familial or political institutions. As Benjamin L. Whorf put it:

"The background linguistic system . . . of each language is not merely a reproducing system for voicing ideas but rather is itself the shaper of ideas, the program and guide for the individual's mental activity, for his synthesis of his mental stock in trade."[18]

V: Language in a Dynamic Modern Society

The close interrelationships of language with every aspect of a society are brought out in the fact that, in a modern dynamic society like our own, every change in any department of societal life brings changes in language. New societal conditions and needs and new cultural experiences and developments require language that is continually changing in parallel fashion in volume, complexity, uniformity, and range. Ours is responsive in considerable measure.

All new knowledge and all discovery and invention require the modification of old terms, and the borrowing or actual construction of much new language, as well as the modification of old meanings in the way of extension of meaning of some terms and the rendering of greater specificity of meaning to others, and, of course, the formulation of adequately symbolized new meanings.

Scientific and technological development in a society dominated by scientific thoughtways and so utterly dependent upon technological products requires a corresponding development of vocabulary, phrases, and formulae to symbolize and express them. There must be names for new products, processes, gadgets, fabrics, drugs. These names may be coined anew (nylon, carburetor),[19] or old names may be given to new products somewhat similar functionally to old ones (tire). Atomic fission has brought with it "atomic bomb," "nuclear," "reactor," "piles," "isotopes," "chain reaction," and "fissionable," to mention only a few.

Scientists, of necessity, are responsible for devising consistent terminologies and special skeleton languages in order to communicate useful and verifiable formulations suitable for purposes of organized, cooperative workmanship. As a science advances in its conquest of its phenomenal field, its statements become more purely designative, better confirmed, and better systematized. Hence it must give specific and refined meanings to the current terms of ordinary language in order to divest them of their ambiguities and inconsistencies of meaning; there are, for example, the special standard meanings in physics attached to "mass," "velocity," "force," or in sociology to "culture," "socializa-

---

[18] "Science and Linguistics," *Tech. Rev.,* 44 (Apr., 1940): 229–231; 247–248.
[19] Sometimes the word coined for the new technological age may be rather involved; for example, the Japanese word for "fountain pen" means "ten-thousand-year brush."

tion," "community," "stratification," "power." Equally important is the invention of new symbols to refer to new products of observation and experimentation, since adequate and specific symbolism is as essential an instrument as microscopes, telescopes, and cyclotrons. A science must have sharp and suitable designative and communicative tools. These are not formed by reckless proliferation of terminology. What seems "jargon," "gobbledegook," "cabalism," "esoteric symbolism" to the uninitiated is clear and precise communication to scientists.

The more intricate and elaborate the social organization becomes, the more language must have the necessary terminology and other forms to provide for the required organizing principles and behaviors over ever wider communicating areas. The division of labor and specialization of function demand not only new general concepts but also the refinement and development of special languages, such as those of occupational and special interest groups. A wide vocabulary and an extensive body of concepts are necessary to understand the rules and membership obligations of our complicated institutions. Specialized language forms have to be developed for all of the different kinds of bureaucratic organizations—political, military, economic, health, religious. For example, there are such rather recent terms relating to large-scale formal organizations as "communication net," "expertise," "information flow," "chain of command," "line-and-staff organization."

To live in a modern city, to move around in it physically, to work, consume, and play in it, and to understand its rules of order require an extensive special linguistic equipment of words and other signs, together with the ability to use them. The very extension in the range—territorial as well as societal—of modern social organization requires greatly modified forms and new forms of knowledge and understanding, of coordination and integration, and these in turn call for new techniques of communication, both of a linguistic and technological nature.[20]

At the extra-national level of organization, unavoidably a concern of the United States, it is noteworthy that the extending contacts and extension of interest beyond national borders in the way of international economic specialization and international trade, some international scientific cooperation, involvement in the activities of the United Nations, international technological competition and ideological difference, global war, and so on, require all manner of new language.

At the same time that there are these evidences of special extension and diversification of our language, there are also tendencies toward its

[20] Cf.: M. M. Lewes, *Language in Society.* London: Thos. Nelson, 1947, Pt. III, pp. 124–198. W. L. Warner, *American Life: Dream and Reality.* Chicago: Univ. of Chicago Press, 1953, pp. 35–47; 210–213.

greater uniformity in several aspects over our entire physical and communicative area. Historically, the language of most language communities, especially the extensive ones, has been characterized by differentiations and stratifications corresponding rather closely to the social differentiation and stratification of the population. The language, or more particularly the speech, of our country also has been characterized by marked differences in vocabulary, intonation, grammar, accent, and other speech forms and speech ways, amounting to differences in dialects and jargons among its different nationality and racial stocks, some religious groups, the different social classes, the different educational and cultural levels, often between the rural and urban dwellers, and especially among the typical members of the different geo-social regions. These differences have not entirely evaporated by any means, but there is a noticeable tendency toward the diminution of all of these linguistic heterogeneities and the universalization of a uniform "American" English. The American Tower of Babel is crumbling.

Several obvious factors are involved. The restriction and marked decline of immigration has greatly reduced the number of foreign-born in our population; most of those of foreign descent are thoroughly assimilated culturally, and the second and third generations of American born have largely lost all traces of foreign colloquialisms or accent. With the upgrading of education for more and more of the population so that the achievement of a high school education is the common practice, and college education more and more recognized as a common need, correct American speech is learned in school by a greater and greater number of people. With the expanding tendency toward a more widely inclusive middle class, and especially the diminution in proportion of the so-called lower class or classes, the class distinctions in speech are fading; and with the continued stress upon upward social mobility, those aspiring to upward mobility cannot afford the stigma of lower-class speech, and, therefore, they make efforts to acquire "correct" language ways. The disappearance of physical isolation and the increase in physical mobility and regional interchange of population is causing regional differences to disappear except for an occasional local interest-group affectation. Finally, and perhaps most effective of all, is the use of a common language by the mass media of communication, especially radio and television which, except in special features involving dialect or jargon, show a marked (seemingly studied) tendency toward a nation-wide common vocabulary, grammar, phraseology, and pronunciation. What we are experiencing is not so much a blending of different dialects, or a levelling up or levelling down of speech, though both of these are occurring in some measure, but rather a resort to a uniform American speech approaching that which we have thought of as "correct English."

BIBLIOGRAPHY

METALINGUISTICS

Carroll, J. B., *The Study of Language*. Cambridge: Harvard Univ. Press, 1953, pp. 43–48.

Chase, S., "How Language Shapes Our Thoughts," *Harpers,* 208 (Apr., 1954): 76–82.

Chase, S., *Powers of Words*. New York: Harcourt, Brace, 1954, pp. 100–109.

Hoijer, H., "Cultural Implications of Some Navaho Linguistic Categories," *Language,* 27 (1951): 111–120.

Hoijer, H., "The Relation of Language to Culture," in Kroeber, A. L., (ed.), *Anthropology Today: An Encyclopedic Inventory*. Chicago: Univ. of Chicago Press, 1953, pp. 554–573.

Kluckholn, C., *Mirror for Man*. New York: Whittlesey House, 1949, pp. 159–166.

Lee, Dorothy D., "Conceptual Implications of an Indian Language," *Phil. of Science,* 5 (Jan., 1938): 89–102.

Lee, Dorothy D., "A Primitive System of Values," *Phil. of Science,* 7 (July, 1940): 355–379.

Lee, Dorothy D., "Categories of the Generic and Particular in Wintu," *Am. Anth.,* 46 (July, 1944): 362–369.

Lee, Dorothy D., "Linguistic Reflection of Wintu Thought," *Int. Jour. Am. Linguistics,* 10 (1944): 181–187.

Sapir, E., "Language and Environment," *Am. Anth.,* 14 (Apr., 1912): 226–242.

Sapir, E., "The Status of Linguistics as a Science," *Language,* 5 (1929): 207–214. Also in *Selected Writings of Edward Sapir*. Berkeley: Univ. of California Press, 1949, pp. 160–166.

Whorf, Benjamin L., "Some Verbal Categories of Hopi," *Language,* 14 (Oct., 1938): 275–286.

Whorf, Benjamin L., "Science and Linguistics," *The Technology Rev.,* 42 (Apr., 1940): 229–231, 247–248.

Whorf, Benjamin L., "Linguistics as an Exact Science," *The Technology Rev.,* 43 (Dec., 1940) 61–63, 80–83.

Whorf, Benjamin L., "Languages and Logic," *The Technology Rev.,* 43 (Apr., 1941): 250–252, 266–272.

Whorf, Benjamin L., "Language, Mind, and Reality," *E. T. C.* 9 (Spring, 1952): 167–188.

Whorf, Benjamin L., "The Relation of Habitual Thought and Behavior to Language," in Hayakawa, S. I. (ed.), *Language, Meaning, and Maturity*. New York: Harper, 1954, pp. 225–251.

LANGUAGE AS AN INSTITUTION

Beals, R. L., and Hoijer, H., *An Introduction to Anthropology*. New York: Macmillan, 1953, pp. 506–537.

Bloomfield, L., *Language*. New York: Holt, 1933.

Bram, Joseph, *Language and Society*. New York: Random House, 1955.

Carroll, J. B., *The Study of Language: A Survey of Linguistics and Related Disciplines in America*. Cambridge: Harvard Univ. Press, 1953.

Gerth, H., and Mills, C. W., *Character and Social Structure: The Psychology of Social Institutions*. New York: Harcourt, Brace, 1953, pp. 274–305.

Hayakawa, S. I., *Language in Thought and Action*. New York: Harcourt, Brace, 1949.

Hertzler, J. O., "Toward a Sociology of Language," *Soc. Forces*, 32 (Dec., 1953): 109–119.

Hiller, E. T., *Principles of Sociology*. New York: Harper, 1933, pp. 111–129.

Jespersen, O., *Language: Its Nature, Development and Origin*. New York: Macmillan, 1922.

Lewes, M. M., *Language in Society*. London: Thos. Nelson & Sons, 1947.

Lindesmith, A. R., and Strauss, A. L., *Social Psychology*. New York: Dryden, 1949, pp. 23–25, 31–62, 239–261.

Martindale, D., *American Society*. Princeton, N.J.: Van Nostrand, 1960, pp. 381–403.

Miller, G. A., *Language and Communication*. New York: McGraw-Hill, 1951.

Morris, C. W., *Signs, Language and Behavior*. Englewood Cliffs, N.J.: Prentice-Hall, 1946.

Pei, M., *The Story of Language*. Philadelphia: Lippincott, 1949, esp. "The Social Functions of Language," pp. 188–195.

Sapir, E., *Language: An Introduction to the Study of Speech*. New York: Harcourt, Brace, 1921.

Vendryes, J., *Language: A Linguistic Introduction to History*. London: Kegan Paul, French, Trubner & Co., 1925.

Woolner, A. C., *Languages in History and Politics*. New York: Oxford Univ. Press, 1938.

THE ACQUISITION, ORGANIZATION, AND UTILIZATION OF KNOWLEDGE

The Scientific-Technological Institutions

Science and technology have become indispensable and integral parts of the way of life of modern societies. During recent centuries especially, science has enabled man to reduce or even eliminate many hazards in his physical environment, improve and increase his food supply, improve his housing, provide himself with other creature comforts, acquire greater security of health and life, analyze and cope with himself as a biological and psychological creature, and comprehend and in some measure control his relationships with his fellows.

Science also affects the non-material aspects of life; its findings and ideas have an influence on all other human thought and action—philosophical, political, religious, and aesthetic. Science has in the past and is now conditioning the political and social thinking of people, their tastes, their reading, some of their leisure, and much of their educational activity. It has provided new perspectives; it has dictated a new *Weltanschauung,* and for many a new *Himmelanschauung.* Furthermore, science is essential to all social action, and is intimately integrated with every aspect of societal structure and operation. Almost no highly prized aspect of our sociocultural life would have appeared without science, and the conclusion is unavoidable that it would disappear if science were to be withdrawn.

Science, moreover, as the result of its growth and penetration of new phenomenal areas, is enjoying ever greater acceptance and is granted dominion in heretofore untouched aspects and departments of human and social life. As never before, scientific explanations of phenomena are taking precedence over mystical or theological explanations.[1]

---

[1] Cf., especially in connection with the modern functions of science, J. D. Bernal, *The Social Function of Science.* New York: Macmillan, 1939, pp. 1–12, 345–407.

Science has both direct and indirect controlling effect over the behavior of every person. There is the informal direct effect in the ways its technological applications impinge upon every one of us—the use of electricity, of the automobile, of health regimens. There are the indirect constraints noted when *other* institutions—the family, the school, economic enterprise, the church, the recreation agencies—adjust to developments in science. There are also the multiple controls exercised by formal agencies engaged in transmitting scientific knowledge, in scientific research, or in technological activities—schools, universities, research foundations, corporation and government laboratories and agencies, learned societies, especially through their reporting of discoveries.[2]

The successes of science and technology in the explanation and control of phenomena in the modern world have increased their sway and importance. In fact, their achievements create conditions requiring more knowledge, more research, and more technological development. For example, especially in the case of countries enjoying the fruits of science and technology, the technological developments in medicine, hygiene, and public health have reduced death rates without corresponding declines in birth rates. The result is a tremendous increase in population, and the consequent extension and intensification of agriculture at home or abroad requires such measures as irrigation projects, the distillation of brackish or salt water, the technology essential to pushing agriculture into colder regions, and the development of more productive plants and livestock.

Nature's Insurgent Son, to use Sir E. Ray Lankester's term, has gone so far with his development of scientific knowledge and his technological manipulation and has created such an "artificed" world and life that he cannot retreat from, impair, or curtail his scientific behavior. Modern societies must have science. Furthermore, they cannot relax a moment in its development, or there is standstill, regress, and chaos.

Science, partly because of some recognition of this situation, partly because of its wide use and the demands made upon it in some of the important departments of life, such as industry and government, and partly because of its development, professionally and organizationally, especially during the last century, has become established and organized and taken on systematically patterned forms and procedures. In brief, it has been in process of institutionalization. Today it is not a random assortment of elements and activities, but a coherent and organized structural-functional affair.

[2] Cf. F. E. Hartung, "Science as an Institution," *Phil. of Science,* 18 (Jan., 1957): 35–54, esp. 44–45.

I: The Nature of Science

In order to gain a minimal understanding of its nature, science should be approached from at least three points of view. These are (1) the distinctive purposive functions of science as an organized activity among the other institutionalized activities of modern men, (2) its substantive or content aspect, and (3) its operational aspect or methodology.

From the point of view of *special purposive functions* science is man's great means for comprehending, and then mastering and utilizing, all of his universe that is perceptible through the senses and the invented extensions, refinements, and enhancements of them. In order to be effective in any degree as an agent of control, science has had to be fundamentally concerned with the nature and operation of the phenomena of the universe; hence, it has been, and is, the quest for knowledge regarding all that man experiences. All that it is in its further aspects as an accumulated body of knowledge and as an array of investigative and manipulative methods is a positive residue of man's testing, selecting, interpreting, constructing, and otherwise profiting by his experience through the ages.

Substantively, science consists of a substantial body of systematized or methodized, tentatively substantiated, generalized and integrated, codified, and continually reconsidered and corrected knowledge. It is essentially a collection of workable *facts* which man has discovered, partly by coming upon them, but mainly by noting information about phenomena when confronted by the adjustment problems growing out of them. A few bold men, however, have, as history records, deliberately sought facts. The available knowledge about these facts takes the form of generalizations of various degrees of exactitude and certainty regarding the nature, the performance, and the relationships of the phenomena, which provide the best understanding and explanation of the particular field of phenomena to date. The analytical and interpretive statements take the form of descriptions and definitions, of assumptions and conclusions, of propositions or theorems, of postulates or axioms, and scientific principles and laws. Especially important are the tentatively validated principles and laws, which are statements of recurrent uniformities of kind and relationship, of distinctions between elements, of sequences of occurrence, and of correlations between cause and effect under given conditions.

This set of facts and principles constitutes the body of theory of any science, and is its foundation and effective content. Lundberg summarizes the theoretical systems as "man-made maps or coordinates for the correlation of human experience."[3] The analogy to a map is apt, for the theoretical system at any given time indicates (1) the areas that have been explored to some extent, (2) the known points, (3) the relations (the "highways") among the knowns, and (4) it usually disregards all details that are irrelevant to its main purpose.

The body of scientific theory existent at any given time is significant not only as the basis for all technology, control, and prediction of phenomena, but also as the point of departure and the working materials for further exploration and discovery.

One of the basic assumptions of science is that the universe is a system that operates in an orderly manner. So far, this hunch as to order, modality, and regularity has been sustained by every scientific discovery, and has been the basis of every effective invention.

The third way of looking at science, probably the most important of all, is *methodology* or "scientific method" or "research." Research or scientific method consists, first, of investigation or attempting to discover new facts and principles, or new facets of them, by exploration, observation, and experimentation. Second, the facts and principles thus discovered, if they are to become established, accepted, and usable parts of a sound body of theory in any scientific field, must be verified and tested, preferably by other scientists working under similar conditions, both as a check upon the accuracy and adequacy of the procedures and the reliability of the results and as a means of eliminating the factor of the personal equation. A further part of the process is to clarify and make more precise the concepts and classifications arrived at, to elaborate the findings, to refocus them, to develop new foci of theoretic interest, to fill in the details, and to modify or abandon existing theoretic formulations made untenable by the tested discoveries.[4] Important in this connection also is the improvement of the empirical techniques themselves, the invention of new ones, and their extension to new fields of exploration and inquiry. Another aspect, not yet adequately conducted in some fields of scientific discovery, is to determine not only the scientific but also as soon as possible the immediate and remote humane and societal consequences of the newly discovered knowledges and the newly invented operations; for example, death control or atomic fission.

Third, there are the procedures for making accessible to other scientists, technologists, and increasingly the public the tested findings of the sciences. It is especially important to divest the discovered facts and principles of some at least of their abstract character and make

[3] G. A. Lundberg, *The Foundations of Sociology.* New York: Macmillan, 1939, p. 98.
[4] Cf. W. H. Sewell, "Some Observations on Theory Testing," *Rural Soc.,* 21 (Mar., 1956): 1–2.

them more comprehensible to, and usable by, the general public. The public makes the decisions ultimately and pays the bills.

A fourth aspect of science as method, which might be referred to as an "action system," is its research regarding the application of scientific knowledge both in the way of "know about," that is, the application of the discovered and tested facts, principles, and laws, and the "know how," that is, the application of the appropriate techniques and procedures to practical ends.

These different aspects of science are not mutually exclusive; they jointly and reciprocally constitute science as the strategic social enterprise that it is.[5]

II: The Institutionalization of Science

Although scientific activity of some sort and degree has existed since the dawn of civilization, its institutionalized aspects are quite recent. In the ancient empires, science in the sense of some rudimentary investigation and interpretation of phenomena was attached to the temples of religion, and was conducted by religious personnel largely as an esoteric enterprise. Among the Greeks, it was separate from religion and was carried on as a specialized activity by a somewhat specialized personnel, as in Plato's Academy, Aristotle's Lyceum, and the vast library and museum of Alexandria; but it was still "science for science's sake." In the Middle Ages, it was carried on in the schools and the nascent universities. During this time the body of theory was developed by, and was the exclusive possession of, the philosophers and other thinkers; "pure knowledge" was their goal. Some of the Greeks, though, notably Aristotle, and some of the scholastics sought proof for their conclusions derived from their observational, and especially their logical, procedures, but most philosophy was not considered to need proof.

The available body of empirical facts and techniques was the possession of the handicraftsmen, the technicians, the artists, and the engineers. Most experimentation was conducted as a practical necessity by these craftsmen and engineers, but they were lower- or at best middle-class, and their labor was therefore not respectable.

---

[5] Note the following conclusive but condensed definition of science: "Science may ... be regarded (a) as a growing body of knowledge, (b) arrived at by conventionalized methods of observation, (c) according to an accepted series of operations, (d) which intend to describe, explain, and predict events, (e) through the discovery of regular and uniform patterns of resemblance, succession, variation, and causation of events, (f) which are regarded as occurring in a perceptual world displaying apparent orderliness." P. Meadows, "Science as Experience: A Genetic and Comparative Review," *Am. Soc. Rev.,* 14 (Oct., 1949): 592.

During the sixteenth century and after, a combination of social conditions occurred which brought about a forced liaison of science as a body of knowledge and science as a set of utilitarian and technological techniques. The new territorial discoveries leading to the transoceanic extension of empires required a wide extension of the knowledge, techniques, and instruments for navigation. Expanding populations required the increase and improvement of economic production, reflected in time in both the Industrial and Agricultural Revolutions. There was also a great extension of commerce. Developing nation-states needed all sorts of machines for large-scale warfare.

The scientific method, especially as it involved controlled observation, experimentation, and exactness of analysis, tended to become standardized in its essential steps and techniques. The scientists themselves have become a specialized profession with special organizations for the promotion of investigation and exchange of knowledge. Special journals announce the results of investigation; special buildings and all sorts of apparatus increasingly are devoted to research; financial support is provided. Scientific activity has developed into an indispensable and integral societal enterprise, and, as such, is institutionalized.

VALUES, IDEOLOGY, AND NORMS

Scientific activity, like all other institutionalized activity, rests upon a body of values. Maslow speaks of it as "itself a value system."[6] People develop a love of knowledge about things and events, a love of truth, a love of certainty; they prize the satisfactions that come from the ability to order, to create adequacy, precision, and accuracy of action, and especially to control, determine, and predict in some measure. It is such basic values as these that give science its origins and goals, provide much of the motivation and direction for scientific activity, and produce the demand for, and approval of, it.

The body of values of science in any given society, of course, also reflects the society's particular interests and objectives at the given time. A particular crisis, for example, will make certain types of scientific attention and action much more important than others.

The socially developed and maintained ideology of science takes two closely related forms. First, it involves the belief that the testing of surmises, particularly by systematic investigation, yields knowledge that is of ultimate practical value to men and can be applied usefully.[7] Second, it has a rationale, at least a more or less implicit set of reasons

---

[6] A. H. Maslow, *Motivation and Personality*. New York: Harper, 1954, pp. 6–7.
[7] Cf. R. T. LaPiere, *Sociology*. New York: McGraw-Hill, 1946, pp. 305–306.

for existence, as an organized form of social activity which justifies, motivates, and explains that activity.[8]

Science has its distinctive body of norms, which, through the moral authority they exert, influence almost every form of scientific activity. They are a special necessity for, and a continuous preoccupation of, the specialized professional personnel of science. Among these norms are such as the desirability, or even the necessity, of (1) carrying on all observation and experimentation with "antiseptic" objectivity, as free as possible of any personal emotions, wishes, prejudices, preconceptions, biases, political, religious, class, ethnic group, or other beliefs; (2) meticulously testing and validating all findings before publication, and willing and capable of offering the evidence for scrutiny; (3) reporting findings in as scrupulously honest, undogmatic, and accurate fashion as possible, and in the most clear and logical manner; (4) maintaining an attitude of humility; (5) keeping scientific activity, even that of a critical and controversial nature, above personalities; (6) maintaining emotional neutrality toward one's own and others' scientific findings; (7) making available to others scientific findings without the necessity of material reward, abiding by the obligation to advance knowledge and provide equal access to scientific knowledge to all competent persons for use in the community's interest; (8) regarding the theft or appropriation of another's scientific work, or the presentation of it as one's own, or the use without proper credit as a heinous offense, and acting accordingly; (9) maintaining a critical and sceptical attitude toward one's own work and toward all existing knowledge and procedures, in the hope of improving them; and (10) insisting upon freedom to explore and to state tested conclusions.[9]

THEORETICAL SYSTEM AND RESEARCH

The essence of science, as we have noted, is its constituent body of knowledge (its theoretical system) and the research procedures whereby this knowledge is acquired, tested, revised, and increased. Both of these, of necessity, in the light of their strategic importance show something in the way of standardized and established features.

SOME INSTITUTIONAL FEATURES. In order to serve its functions, the theoretical system must have certain of its elements definitely organized, and in order to be meaningful and usable, it must meet certain sub-

---

[8] Meadows, *op. cit.*, p. 594.

[9] Cf.: Merton, *op. cit.* Barber, *op. cit.*, pp. 84–100. H. H. Fichter and W. L. Kolb, "Ethical Limitations on Sociological Reporting," *Am. Soc. Rev.*, 18 (Oct., 1953): 544–550. C. Panunzio, *Major Social Institutions.* New York: Macmillan, 1939, pp. 331–333.

stantiated criteria of efficacy and quality. The body of knowledge as a whole must be organized. As Henri Poincaré originally wrote,[10] "A heap of unorganized facts is no more a science than a heap of bricks is a house." The body of facts and theory of any science consists minimally of certain component elements that have already been noted. These elements constitute a somewhat standardized scheme or systematic framework of descriptive, analytical, and interpretative elements. The various facts are not "knowledge" unless put in some standard and mutually comprehensible form, unless distinguished from each other on the basis of some sort of classificatory scheme, and unless they fit in somewhere in relation to each other and aid in explaining the nature and significance of something.[11]

The first aspect of the theoretical system is that of *systematic conceptualization*. As noted above, the facts do not exist as knowledge items unless they are conceptualized; that is, unless what is perceived (experienced) is presented in the form of verbalizations (the great bulk take such form), notations, formulae, or other symbols. Concepts are the elemental components by means of which the basic meanings are expressed and conveyed, and in their various combinations (definitions, propositions, postulates, laws) constitute the generalized and universalized makeup of a scientific body of knowledge. They are more or less concise, accurate, and generally acceptable, imaginative, and symbolized syntheses presenting the regular and uniform traits, qualities, and special relationships associated with the named and specifically designated things and events. They are the science's set of established terms—its "vocabulary," so to speak.

A second aspect is the *system of classification* or taxonomy. The significant feature of this aspect is lost upon many people. Facts do not speak for themselves; their significance rests on their contrasts of kind and function with each other, and their relations as specialized items with each other. Classification is the arbitrary procedure of placing or grouping conceptually expressed and accurately defined phenomena with like characteristics together in categories. The classificatory arrangement may take place according to qualitative resemblances or differences, quantitative resemblances or differences, logical sequence, chronological sequence, position in space, correlation, or some other appropriate and meaningful criterion of relatedness, concurrence, or contingency. Usually, the classes within a given phenomenal field fall into hierarchies of diminishing generality and increasing specificity.

The third aspect of any scientific theoretical system is its constructed types or models. They are indispensable both in conceptualization and

---

[10] The statement is erroneously attributed to Sir James Jeans who used it later.
[11] For a more detailed discussion of the components, see J. O. Hertzler, "The Essentials of a Theoretical System," *Midwest Sociologist,* 15 (Winter, 1953): 3–8.

as a device for establishing criteria of types and subtypes in classification. Of particular importance is the fact that, fundamentally, science builds its whole substantive content on the basis of constructed types. Scientific knowledge is in a sense a systematized collection of constructed types; they are the necessary standard, economical way of conceiving of, and working with, each variety of phenomenon that man has experienced.

Their distinctive function in systematic theory grows out of the fact that no actual natural phenomenon, physical, biological, psychological, or social, is pure or unmixed. No two sunsets, or tornadoes, or wasps of a given species, or revolutions, or Negroes, or plumbers, or American families are exactly alike. Nothing, literally nothing, is identical with anything else. But science has to make its way among all these diversities; it seeks to create order out of seeming chaos, and establish uniformity amidst seeming heterogeneity and universals among particulars. Hence, the scientist in every field constructs types or models or systematic patterns of all the observed phenomena as special instruments for identification, description, comparison, classification, and most of his other analytical and technological activities.

In constructing his model, the scientist deliberately eliminates the unique and irrelevant characteristics of types of phenomena; he deliberately selects and posits, on the basis of his best findings, the most significant common and modal characteristics. Logically, the constructed type contains all of the basically *essential* and basically *distinguishing* elements or properties of a kind of phenomenon; those which must be present to set it apart, both as a general type among other general types, and as a special type of a general kind. For example, there are the basic characteristics of *dogs* as compared with *cats;* then, among dogs, those minimally essential to characterize *airedales* as compared with *beagles* or *boxers*.

The constructed type is not a mathematical average of characteristics of a thing or occurrence; it is rather the hypothetical average. It does not deal directly with *all* of the occasional facts of experience regarding the thing or occurrence. No concrete example of it is exactly like it; for example, no airedale at a dog show, "pure bred" as it is, will conform in every detail and degree with the judge's model.

Each constructed type, in addition to being a created part of the conceptual system of the science, is in itself a system on a small scale.[12] Each one is a purposive, exclusive, coherent combination of indispensable elements. These standard and established working models, which constitute the basic structure of the theoretical system of any science,

[12] John C. McKinney, "Methodology, Procedures, and Techniques in Sociology," in H. Becker and A. Boskoff (eds.), *Modern Sociological Theory in Continuity and Change.* New York: Dryden, 1957, pp. 186–235.

are the means of identifying concrete examples of phenomena, of classifying them (since each category is a constructed type), of establishing generalizations about their form and behavior, and of predicting what will occur under given conditions.

THE CRITERIA OF A SOUND AND WELL-ORGANIZED SYSTEM. The sounder the principles of a theoretical system, the more adequately it will provide a general understanding of its phenomenal field, and the greater the likelihood that its theories will be applicable and adaptable materials in solving the problems requiring investigation and solution. Scientific theorists, representing all fields, are generally agreed upon the tests or criteria of quality and soundness. These also function as a set of norms governing theoretical systems.

(1) The theoretical system should be *economical,* that is, consist of the fewest and simplest principles and hypotheses that adequately explain and integrate the findings, but economy must not be achieved at the price of neglected facts. A body of theory will always be complicated at best. (2) It should be *valid;* that is, it should be the only possible theory, the only sound and acceptable explanation in the light of all observation, experiment, and efforts at verification to date. Its facts and stated probabilities will not be explained by any other propositions. (3) Its propositions should have *logical clarity and precision;* that is, they should clearly and specifically state the facts and relationships with which the propositions are concerned; they should not be vague or elusive. The greater the precision, the greater the likelihood of eliminating contradictory or erroneous propositions. (4) It should have *consistency;* that is, the premises and principles should be logically related and in agreement; they should be adequately integrated conceptually and not be discursive and diffuse. (5) The theories should be *universal* in acceptance and applicability. They should represent the consensus of the scientists employed in the particular area of interest and investigation, though scientists as individuals will contribute to them. They should reflect and comprehend the range, variety, and direction of research in the field. (6) Its generalizations regarding given types of phenomena should be *codified;* that is, so divested of irrelevant or exceptional or extraneous features that the essentials of the concept can be depicted as a paradigm, and the type of phenomenon can be presented in the form of a constructed type or model. (7) It should be *dynamic and fruitful;* that is, persistently and consistently leading to new hunches or hypotheses, continually growing and leading to further accumulation of facts and principles, constantly in process of correction in the light of new evidence. Its guardians must not allow it to suffer from what has been aptly dubbed "hardening of the

categories." Finally, (8) it should provide an assured *basis for prediction*. If the other criteria are met, this is quite likely to follow.

THE SYSTEMATIC NATURE OF RESEARCH PROCEDURES. The methodology of science has come to be rather definitely standardized, established, and patterned. The research procedure involves a set of rules and order which has the logic of experience behind it. Scientific work, by its very nature, of course, cannot be reduced to an absolutely routinized process. Nevertheless, the essential features of scientific method are pretty much the same in all the sciences. As Karl Pearson stated, "The unity of all science consists . . . in its method, not in its material." The standard succession of steps in a typical research procedure follow. In general, if the investigators skip too many steps in the research process, or are careless about any of them, they do not get a product.

The preliminary reconnaissance. The scientist familiarizes himself with the pertinent existent theory in connection with the phenomenal area of concern by means of bibliography and widespread reading, and makes general observations regarding the particular phenomenon or apparently related phenomena. He gets his scientific bearings, finding out what has been done, where the gaps in the knowledge are, and what kind of mistakes other investigators have made.

Definition of the problem. This step consists of specifying the problem area, determining what the investigator(s) can do about it, setting the limits, and getting the problem into focus.

Determination of the crucial elements in the problem. On the basis of what *is* known, an attempt is made to set forth what seem to be the pertinent or crucial elements and determiners, and also to note the elements and factors that are irrelevant or that offer little hope of successful attack.

The formulation of a working hypothesis. The hypothesis is a stated "smartest hunch" regarding what is likely to be found out in the particular investigation, on the basis of all possible preliminary information. It is a specific but purely provisional and approximate formulation, and is not thought of as having or requiring finality as to results. The hypothesis sets the frame of reference, indicates the types of facts that are relevant or irrelevant, and gives specific focus and objective to the problem.

Drawing up the research design. This means developing the over-all operational blueprint plan and the specifications for testing the hypothesis. It involves, first, the construction of the logical structure to be used—the steps and sequence of descriptive and analytical concepts that will most likely indicate and explain the facts that are anticipated. Then the particular standard investigative (observational and experimental) techniques, instruments, and other materials that will be used in collecting the data, and the way in which they will be used, are indicated. This aspect of design varies greatly in the different scientific fields. A design for a chemical experiment will vary considerably from one in sociology, especially in terms of the types of techniques and equipment to be used.

The collection and recording of the data. This is actually carrying on the investigative operation as anticipated, defined, and designed. In the sociological field it may involve the use of historical investigation according to well-established procedures, social surveys of both the pattern and variability types, ecological surveys, case methods, including interviewing, and questionnaire, schedule, documentary, and autobiographical and psychoanalytical techniques, experimental designs, and various statistical procedures. The statistical procedures enable the investigator quantitatively to record and count, measure, sample, arrange, compare, evaluate, and correlate his findings, and also to separate and control mathematically the variables involved. It is particularly important to *record* the findings objectively, accurately, and in a form in which the investigator and others can later comprehend and use them, and to file them so that they are not disarranged or lost. Also, it is desirable to get everything into the early record that seems to have pertinence, even if only remotely so; it may turn out to be important in the light of later findings or relationships.

The classification of the facts observed. This step involves identifying the facts discovered as to types and subtypes, and locating them in the established categories of the existing theoretical system, or possibly, if they seem to constitute new types of facts, adding appropriate rubrics to the classificatory system. However, violence can be done to the final conclusions of the project if a foreign or inappropriate system of classification is forced upon the data. The classificatory procedure should be that which reveals the data in the most refined and pertinent way.

Drawing the generalizations from the classified facts of observation. This consists in stating as precisely and comprehensively, but also as soberly and cautiously, as possible what is true or found to obtain respecting the sequence and relationship of facts. This is essentially an amplification and restatement of the hypothesis in the light of all new facts and relationships of facts discovered or uncovered in the investigation. It may confirm existing scientific generalizations or laws, necessitate some restatement of existing generalizations, or require or permit the formulation of new ones, in which case there has been a substantiation of existing knowledge or an extension of it.

Verification of the facts or principles (replication). This is especially desirable if the facts are new ones. The investigation is repeated as exactly as possible, using new but similar cases and the same or other proper procedures and devices, by the original investigator and preferably by others, under as nearly identical conditions as possible. If the findings from the replication conform to the original ones, verification is assured. This procedural step is necessary as a means of protecting the facts discovered against (a) local, strictly contemporary, or fortuitous conditions; (b) possible errors in method; (c) the personal equation of the investigator and assistants; and on occasion, (d) the too fondly held assumption or "groove" of the theoretical school to which the investigator may belong or be sympathetic with.

When these well-established steps have been satisfactorily pursued, then the new facts and principles can be confidently incorporated in the theoretical system. This then makes possible the final step in the total procedure, and the ultimate objective of all scientific endeavor.

Arriving at the deductive conclusions and making the practical applications. This includes (a) the drawing of inferences as to the worth of the possible contributions (additions) made to the body of theory; particularly, using the findings as (b) the basis for prediction of the type or types of future occurrences and conditions; and (c) using the findings in carrying on new or superior manipulation of the phenomena, especially for practical technological or engineering purposes.

The Personnel, Organizations, and Equipment

Today tens and even hundreds of thousands of persons are engaged in scientific activity, most of it on a professional level. Most of the professionalization is a very recent development, the great volume of it having occurred in the twentieth century. As in the case of all professions, the requirements of the roles are established for the performers and are of such a nature as to advance the objectives of the institution. Thus, role-functions among the scientists include such tasks as exploring for, and discovering, new features of the external world, systematizing the knowledge into a coherent, logical structure, testing and elaborating the knowledge, disseminating the knowledge, and finally, of course, applying this knowledge technologically to the solution of practical human problems.[13]

Hartung has indicated the ways in which the participant man of science is constrained and directed because of the institutional nature of science. He "is controlled (1) by the current stage of knowledge in his discipline, (2) by his training which has introduced him to the traditions as well as the techniques of his science, (3) by the trends which regard certain research areas and problems as significant or worthwhile, (4) by the control of publishing opportunities exerted by other (usually older) men in the field who are themselves products of this cultural

---

[13] Cf.: F. Znaniecki, *The Social Role of the Man of Knowledge.* New York: Columbia Univ. Press, 1940, esp. pp. 1–12. De Gré, *op. cit.,* pp. 21–24.

process, and (5) by his position as an employee of a business concern, a governmental agency, a university, a foundation or as one who is financially independent."[14]

The functions of science are performed by scientists in social organizations differing in the auspices under which they are conducted, in the intensity and specialization of the functions, and in the range of inclusiveness of the diverse scientific fields involved.

As to the auspices in our society, scientific functions are carried on mainly in universities and colleges, by industrial research groups, mainly the research departments of industrial corporations, and by governmental research groups. The universities and colleges perform three main functions. They (1) carry on pure scientific investigation and develop new knowledge, (2) train new scientists, and (3) diffuse this knowledge among the citizenry and point to its significance and the corrective and constructive obligations that it imposes.

Another type of scientific association consists of those organized around particular specialties in scientific endeavor. They fall into two main categories: (1) those consisting of the "pure scientists" in the various fields of investigative specialization, such as the American Chemical Society or the American Sociological Association, and (2) the organizations of mainly professional technical practitioners, such as the American Medical Association, and the associations of the various engineering specialists (chemical, electrical, civil, etc.). These provide a medium of exchange, of cooperation, of criticism, of mutual stimulation, and through their professional journals offer opportunities of publication and review of findings.

A third type of organization cuts across the various sciences and exists to provide a wider exchange of scientific knowledge and also to engage in the general promotion of science and the protection of scientists. Notable examples are the American Association for the Advancement of Science and the British Association for the Advancement of Science.

Others have a range of scientific interests both of an investigational and informational nature, such as the American Museum of Natural History of New York City and the American and the National Geographic Societies. There are also the various semi-popular local organizations, such as "institutes of arts and sciences" and museums.

Worthy of mention also are the organizations based on giving recognition for achievement, such as some of the academies of science, Phi Beta Kappa, and Sigma Xi. Finally, though this survey by no means exhausts the types of scientific organizations now existing in the more

---

[14] "Science as an Institution," *Phil. of Science,* 18 (Jan., 1957): 44–45. Itemizing figures added.

advanced countries, of recent origin are the various foundations which exist in considerable part to raise funds for the promotion of all sorts of scientific research, both pure and applied, and in some instances for carrying on corrective and control activities. In our country we have such foundations as the Carnegie Institute, the Rockefeller Foundation, the Ford Foundation, and the Brookings Institute.

Science has its special equipment in the form of laboratories, experimental apparatus, recording and calculating machines, and all the other special aids and devices that extend the insight, increase the accuracy, improve and make more durable the memory of man, generally increase the penetrativeness of his senses, and thus extend his powers of observation and his control over the phenomena. Mention need only be made, as an example, of the printing and other equipment used in the publication and storing of scientific findings.

III: The Technological System

In modern societies science cannot be thought of apart from technology. Certain fundamental reciprocities exist between them. But before these are discussed, the place and nature of technology in the sociocultural scheme of things should be examined.

THE PLACE AND NATURE OF TECHNOLOGY

Here we are concerned with that important subsystem of culture whereby man, from earliest times, has in some measure manipulated, altered, and utilized the physical and biological environments, to the extent that he was aware of them and had knowledge about them, in the interest not only of his survival, but also of his physical and social prosperity. Man is dependent upon the materials, forces, and processes of the natural environment; he must have food, clothing, housing, and other physical necessities; he must defend himself against disease, biological predators, and human enemies; he must have means of moving himself, his goods, and his ideas from place to place. These objectives he achieves by means of a utilitarian part of every cultural system known as the *technological system*.

Technology in some form is as old as any somewhat patterned, collective, utilitarian activity, such as building a bridge with vines as cables, constructing and navigating a war canoe, carrying on team hunting or warfare, domesticating plants and animals, or organizing initiation ceremonies. Among modern peoples it has grown more and more important in every department of their lives.

A technological system can be resolved into four sets of indispensable, interdependent component elements: (1) the existing *knowledges,* symbolically presented, about the nature and operation of the different categories of phenomena as gained through human experience, taking the form, variously, of myths, ideas, generalizations, traditions, facts and principles, and usually more or less systematized as a working philosophy toward phenomena; (2) *technics,* that is, the tools, implements, instruments, machines, and appliances whereby energies and materials are combined, harnessed, and transferred for human use; (3) *techniques,* consisting of the actual operational actions, with their patterned, sequential mechanical processes and procedures carried on by means of skills, an aspect that is more and more important in complex societies, but always existent in some measure even in the technologies of the simple societies; (4) the *organization,* that is, socially institutionalized structural and functional integration, coordination, arrangement, and management of the three preceding components *and* of the human agents, especially the scientists, workmen, engineers, supervisors, and administrators as an effective over-all system for achieving results.[15]

In modern societies where technology has come to pervade almost every phase of the material and social life of the people, there has been an extension of its meaning beyond that of manipulating only the physical and biological environments. Today, man is attempting to manipulate and control phenomena in *every* field of which he is aware and with which he is concerned; and for each field there is a special type of "engineering." Thus we have, among many, the technologies involved in civil, electrical, chemical, and mechanical engineering, and an agricultural technology, industrial technology (the factory system), commercial technology (accounting, banking), transportation and communication technology, medical technology, military technology. But it is also recognized by many that there exists what might be called a psychological technology, and most certainly a massive and complex social or societal technology is developing, resting upon the basic principles and patterns concerned with the manipulation and utilization of social phenomena, specifically with the construction, maintenance, and repair of social systems. Yet social technology, in groping, hit-and-miss form, has probably been, along with the simplest organization of hunting and collection of food items, the oldest of technologies—an indispensable and unavoidable technology ever since two or more human beings tried to live and work together.

Technology also seems to be peculiarly cumulative and contagious

---

[15] J. O. Hertzler, *Society in Action.* New York: Dryden, 1954, pp. 103–104. P. Meadows, *The Culture of Industrial Man.* Lincoln: Univ. of Nebraska Press, 1950, pp. 9–10. J. Gillin, *The Ways of Men.* New York: Appleton, 1948, pp. 357–368.

in nature. Present and more complex forms are outgrowths of previous forms. Each advance provides new means of discovering and utilizing new resources and of employing older ones more economically and efficiently. The very accumulation increases the number of culture elements that can be combined in the form of new inventions. Each advance tends to provide insights which invite further exploration. Technical advance, in fact, appears as a succession of revolutionary innovations.

A matter of special significance in our study is the close relationship between the physical and biological technologies and the types of social organization. The general conclusion of studies which examine cultures ranging from those of various primitive peoples to the most complex and extensive modern ones is that the social system is functionally dependent upon the technological system, especially upon its instruments of subsistence, the amount and variety of materials that can be utilized, and its control of energy and of space. Some go so far as to insist that social systems are *determined* by systems of technology. Certainly it can be said that the kind of technology places certain limits on the kind of social organization that is possible. There is a rough correlation between the level of technology and the possible social forms, especially with respect to the extensiveness and degree of complexity of the social system. Again, every important change in technology, particularly in the way of tapping and harnessing of a new, more efficient, and more powerful form of energy, has produced a decisive change in the structures and functions of society.

Most studies detect reciprocal relationship. Whenever and wherever a new level of culture in general and social organization in particular has been achieved, it has provided a more extensive array of materials and techniques available for combination in the form of new inventions, and has also created a new and ever more diversified set of demands for new technological means of coping with the increasingly complex physico-biological and social life.[16]

Science as a body of facts and principles, and as a set of research methods and inventive procedures for discovering, checking, and combining facts and principles, old and new, provides the relevant basic knowledge and procedures which technology *applies* to the problem situations in all phenomenal areas. Science discovers and explains the forces of nature which technology harnesses and controls. As new scientific knowledge and procedures are made accessible, they are rapidly given technical application.

[16] For a concise presentation of the important technological developments during man's career on earth and the related changes in social organization (as well as the correlated demographic changes), see J. O. Hertzler, *The Crisis in World Population.* Lincoln: Univ. of Nebraska Press, 1956, pp. 12–26.

Although this relationship between science and technology has not always been so close, since science developed more slowly than the need for technology, nevertheless, all technology, early and late, has rested on whatever scientific knowledge men had, but until recently this knowledge was largely of a chance or rule-of-thumb nature; some of it, of course, still is, especially in the less strategic areas of life. But in very recent times, every technology has come to be more and more dependent upon the scientific knowledge and method in its area of concern. In fact, the requirement for technologies to be more exact, economical, efficient, necessitates their being founded on more exact, pretested knowledge. Almost all recent developments in machine technology, agricultural technology, medicine, chemical engineering, military technology, even such new technologies as public health and social work, have been built upon knowledge derived from scientific endeavor.

Conversely, science receives much stimulation from technology as the latter demands new facts and more reliable principles. Furthermore, the very development of technology with its ever more effective instruments and techniques for further discovery and invention makes possible, even invites, scientific development. Also, today, much scientific effort is made with its technological application in mind.

TECHNOLOGY AS AN INSTITUTIONAL SYSTEM

The technological system of modern advanced societies is a thoroughly established and highly organized part of their total operation. Like science, it has come to be definitely institutionalized in recent times, though some of the institutional features go back to the great civilizations of antiquity, especially Egypt, Babylonia, China and Rome.

Technology has its basic values reflecting the prevailing opinions of the society. These values are related to the needs of the people to some extent, but in an affluent society like our own, many of them are related more particularly to current interests. These interests may be fostered or at any rate embroidered by special-interest groups; for example, the influence of automobile manufacturers, especially through their advertising, in developing and maintaining interest in ever different models, in the value of the "newest thing" in spite of the utility of that which it replaces.

The key procedures of technology and much of the technologically induced behavior of the people in general is institutionalized or shows institutional tendencies.

Invention is the basic and initiating process in all technology, for it consists of the combining of facts, principles, materials, technics, and techniques in a new manner in order to produce new or considerably modified utilitarian things or want-satisfying conditions or occurrences.

Until as recently as 1925,[17] even in our country invention was mainly an activity which individual inventors carried on in single-handed fashion in their own quarters, with their own funds, and in pursuit of their own particular "gleam." Although there is still some individual inventing, particularly under university auspices, today it is increasingly a highly institutionalized procedure carried on in the laboratories of great corporations, of endowed research institutes, and by governmental departments and bureaus. Groups of men, highly trained in science and technology and specialized as to knowledge and skills, supplementing each other, operate as teams in conducting the experimental activities. They follow rather well-established procedures. These organized inventive activities are usually governed by codes involving the use of materials and procedures and the relations of the personnel to each other. They operate in appropriate quarters with the necessary equipment and supplies. The laboratories are adequately financed for their intended activities. The inventive procedure thus conducted is not pedestrian or governed by chance, and the individual inventor is not free to do as he pleases; the whole team and its equipment are committed to a particular inventive task or objective as determined by the governors of the laboratories and funds. In the main, each such procedure is conducted according to a previously planned and organized program, and the personnel are usually under some pressure to get results. These results are protected against theft or unethical use by patent rights and copyrights.

In scientifically advanced societies like our own, a set of ways transcending the folkways and mores have come to be required of the inhabitants. They are the ways of adjustment to technology. Some of these have come to be rather highly institutionalized, and even a matter of governmental prescription and enforcement. The *technicways*[18] are the machine-patterned ways of behavior required of us if we are to live and let live in our modern technologized environments. If we are to live with the continuous flow of new physical, industrial, and commercial mechanisms and procedures, and the effects of these, we must adjust to technologically modified forces and technologically produced gadgets and conditions, such as mass production lines, automobiles, airplanes, telephones, radios, television machines, electrical power, induced rainfall, or atomic fallout.

The actual operations of producing the things, services, and conditions for the consumers—the ultimate objective of technological activ-

[17] J. B. Conant, *Science and Common Sense.* New Haven: Yale Univ. Press, 1951, p. 303.

[18] The term was contrived by Odum. Cf.: H. W. Odum, "Notes on the Technicways in Contemporary Society," *Am. Soc. Rev.,* 2 (June, 1937): 336–346. H. W. Odum, *Understanding Society.* New York: Macmillan, 1947, pp. 363–374.

ity—are carried on by the large-scale formal organizations, or bureaucracies, such as great extractive industrial operations (engaged in mining or lumbering), factories for all manner of manufacturing and processing, organizations for conducting transportation on land, sea, and in the air, for carrying on all of the forms of mechanical communication, for the operation of hospitals and public health agencies, the government agencies providing conservation, meteorological, and dozens of other technical services. In these, the personnel, scientists, engineers, planners, technicians, workmen, supervisors, and administrators are all organized in order to achieve effectively the intended results. There is the patterned structural-functional makeup: the pyramidal structure and departmentalized layers; the hierarchical order of authority; the multiple codes covering all suborganizations, relationships, and operations; the division of labor and specialization; the policy-making, planning and programming, and decision-making.

AUTOMATION

The short period of time since World War II has seen scientific-technological developments never before paralleled in an equal period of time, either in the audacity and genius of their inventiveness or in their likely revolutionary effects. Notable are the developments in electronics, nucleonics, and supersonic aeronautics. Today and tomorrow may produce other equally striking developments. Not only have these already greatly changed the machinery, tactics, and even the politics of warfare, but also they are being applied to peacetime needs and operations. The actual use of the ever expanding array of electronic devices in industry and commerce is the main contributory factor in the so-called Second Industrial Revolution; the use of fissionable materials for power promises to further accentuate this revolution.

Automation, which is mainly, though by no means entirely, an application of electronics to mechanization, is a special technological development which is the main factor in producing a new technological revolution in this second half of the twentieth century at least equal in effect to the mass production of the first half; its impact may be even greater and come faster. Peter Drucker defines it "simply though superficially as the use of machines to run machines."[19] In automation, machines perform functions in the operation of other machines heretofore performed by human beings, machines which within their competence —and this competence in some respects in certain parts and kinds of operations exceeds that of human beings—think, feel, and act like men. Automation tends to displace both man's sensory organs and brain, as

---

[19] P. Drucker, *America's Next Twenty Years*. New York: Harper, 1957, p. 18.

well as his muscular efforts. It thus is much more than the mechanization of production processes of the first half of the present century. The automating machines controlling the productive machines exercise routine judgment; they also regulate and control the main machine, causing it to carry on its operations in an invariably rhythmic, patterned, and ordered manner. Consequently the automating machinery assumes many monotonous, repetitive—and in some of its industrial applications, highly dangerous—operations. At the present stage of development, its has certain significant aspects. Several machines can be linked together so that materials are passed automatically from one unit to the next, each unit performing certain specific tasks in the sequence of operations. This might be referred to as a further stage of mechanization, consisting of a much more efficient, almost completely non-laborious transfer and assembling of materials. A second aspect is that of given instructions to the main machine—the machine setting and also signalling aspect. This occurs through the feed-back control exercised by the electronic mechanisms as electrical circuits are opened or closed as the result of different influences exercised, for example, by thermometers, altimeters, sound or light meters. A third even more revolutionary aspect is computer technology, or the data processing aspect, conducted by the various electronic machines such as AUTOFAB, UNIVAC, IBM's Electronic Data Processing Machine, the Electronic Recording Machine Accounting (ERMA) and others. These in various ways function as "brains," which upon given instructions perform thousands of mathematical, classifying, recording, summating, and other operations per second which it would take highly competent, highly trained, and highly specialized human beings hours, days, and even weeks to perform.[20]

In our country we now have automation in many of our large industries; for example, steel, automobiles, oil refining, communications (telephone dial machines, teletype), the pipe line systems, banking and insurance (check clearance, automatic printing of insurance premium notices).

We are particularly concerned with the social and societal effects of automation. In the first place, it greatly increases the output per man hour in all of the areas in which it has been undertaken. It also utilizes more efficiently the materials available, and it produces a standard and uniform quality of goods of given design or form.

Another immediate and obvious set of effects is that upon the workers. Much labor is saved on the production floor as the workers are displaced by machines. This, of course, means the diminution of

[20] Suggested in part by E. S. Bogardus, "Social Aspects of Automation," *Soc. & Soc. Res.*, 42 (May–June, 1958): 358–363.

certain jobs in the industries and offices affected. Thus automation may cause at least temporary unemployment. It also, however, reduces routine work, and overcomes much monotonous repetition. Usually, it makes the work safer and more interesting for the few remaining operatives.

It requires more highly skilled workers, workers conducting operations that require the attainment of higher levels of education than those required for straight production line work. It also tends to create the need for a wide range of new skills; thus education which stresses science and technology is particularly needed. In some instances, as automation is introduced, some workers are upgraded. Although a further reduction of hours of work has not always occurred, it is a distinct possibility. Also, the higher skills required tend to improve wage rates for the operatives.

Although automation reduces or even eliminates some jobs, at the same time it requires a considerable number of workers for new jobs, such as machine builders, machine installers, repair men, controllers of the machinery and its performance, programmers to prepare and feed information into the machines. In addition, as automation proceeds, a considerable number of educated persons will be needed as designers of machinery, draftsmen, system engineers, and mathematicians. New kinds of managers will be needed to analyze and implement the new processes. Whether the new jobs can be made to balance the discarded ones, and whether the various kinds of shifting and retraining of workers take place soon enough and easily enough to avoid shock and confusion remains to be seen.

Automation either in factory or office does not use much or cheap labor. Thus automated factories or offices will not have to be located near abundant or cheap labor supply. This fact will doubtless be reflected in further de-urbanization of such business. Also, automation encourages new small companies,[21] which manufacture electronic machines, various subassemblies used in automatic machines and appliances, and servicing equipment.

Automation has infinite possibilities for improving the quality of life generally. It makes possible new, cheaper, and better physical products, new communication and transportation facilities, the systematization and extension of human knowledge, and control of phenomena heretofore unthought of. It makes possible a great increase of leisure for everyone, which can be utilized for education, entertainment, and recreation. As Bogardus points out, the new leisure time may presently exceed the working time of most people; they will

---

[21] Cf. the development of such businesses reported in "The Idea Road," *Time*, July 13, 1959, pp. 64–66.

then need to be protected against anti-social exploitation of their leisure, and trained to use it profitably. Automation can completely revolutionize our way of life; whether this will insure fuller well-being for everyone depends on how its development is managed.

The recent developments in technology suggest heretofore unimagined possibilities in the way of human well-being, but they also point to hazards and the need for great and varied societal adjustments. For example, the conquest of most of our diseases is coming within reach; the new means of controlling solar energy and of utilizing photosynthesis point to new possibilities of increasing the food supply and, by means of various new engines and processes for converting salt or brackish water into fresh water, supplementing the present short supply; population processes can be controlled as never before.

At the same time, technological developments have created powers and means of destruction and corruption; for example, the missiles of warfare, brainwashing, and mass communication for propaganda.

The three signal technical developments of very recent times—nucleonics, aeronautics, and electronics—have already had a tremendous impact upon the peoples of the world. Vast new energy resources have become available, and yet anyone will agree that we are only on the threshold of the possibilities and problems occasioned by these technological developments.

B I B L I O G R A P H Y

SCIENTIFIC INSTITUTIONS

Anshen, Ruth N. (ed.), *Science and Man*. New York: Harcourt, Brace, 1942.

Barber, Bernard, *Science and the Social Order*. Glencoe, Ill.: Free Press, 1952.

Becker, H., *Through Values to Social Interpretation*. Durham, N.C.: Duke Univ. Press, 1950, pp. 93–127.

Bensman, J., and Vidich, A., "Social Theory in Field Research," *Am. Jour. Soc.*, 65 (May, 1960): 577–584.

Bernal, J. D., *The Social Function of Science*. New York: Macmillan, 1939.

Bernal, J. D., *Science in History*. London: Watts, 1954.

Butler, J. A. V., *Science and Human Life*. New York: Basic Books, 1957.

Conant, J. B., *On Understanding Science*. New Haven: Yale Univ. Press, 1947.

Conant, J. B., *Science and Common Sense*. New Haven: Yale Univ. Press, 1951.

De Gré, G. L., *Science as a Social Institution*. New York: Random House, 1955.

Goldschmidt, W., *Man's Way: A Preface to the Understanding of Society*. Cleveland: World Pub. Co., 1959, pp. 106–144.

Hall, A. R., *The Scientific Revolution 1500–1800*. New York: Longmans, Green, 1954, Chaps. VII–VIII.

Hartung, F. E., "Sociological Foundations of Modern Science," *Phil. of Science,* 14 (Jan., 1947): 68–95.

Hartung, F. E., "Science as an Institution," *Phil. of Science,* 18 (Jan., 1951): 35–54.

Hertzler, J. O., "The Essentials of a Theoretical System," *Midwest Sociologist,* 15 (Winter, 1953): 3–8.

Lundberg, G. A., *Can Science Save Us?* New York: Longmans, Green, 1947.

McKinney, J. C., "The Role of Constructive Typology in Scientific Sociological Analysis," *Soc. Forces,* 28 (Mar., 1950): 235–240.

McKinney, J. C., "Methodology, Procedures and Techniques in Sociology," in Becker, H., and Boskoff, A. (eds.), *Modern Sociological Theory.* New York: Dryden, 1957, pp. 186–235.

Merton, R. K., "Priorities in Scientific Discovery: A Chapter in the Sociology of Science," *Am. Soc. Rev.,* 22 (Dec., 1957): 635–659.

Parsons, T., "The Institutionalization of Scientific Investigation," in Parsons, T. (ed.), *The Social System.* Glencoe, Ill.: Free Press, 1951, pp. 335–345.

Radcliffe-Brown, A. R., *A Natural Science of Society.* Glencoe, Ill.: Free Press, 1957, pp. 28–42.

Sewell, W. H., "Some Observations on Theory Testing," *Rural Soc.,* 21 (Mar., 1956): 1–12.

Webster, M. J., "How Science Modifies Institutions," in Roucek, J. S. (ed.), *Social Control.* Princeton, N.J.: Van Nostrand, 1956, pp. 167–182.

White, L. A., *The Evolution of Culture.* New York: McGraw-Hill, 1959, pp. 362–366.

TECHNOLOGICAL INSTITUTIONS

Allen, F. R., *et al.* (eds.), *Technology and Social Change.* New York: Appleton, 1957.

Bernal, J. D., *Science in History.* London: Watts, 1954, pp. 24, 38, 177, 312–317.

Bogardus, E. S., "Social Aspects of Automation," *Soc. & Soc. Res.,* 42 (May–June, 1958): 358–363.

Childe, V. Gordon, *Man Makes Himself* (2nd ed.). London: Watts, 1941.

Childe, V. Gordon, *What Happened in History.* Harmondsworth, Middlesex: Penguin Books, 1942.

Childe, V. Gordon, *Social Evolution.* New York: Abelard Press, 1951.

Cottrell, Fred, *Energy and Society: The Relation between Energy, Social Change, and Economic Development.* New York: McGraw-Hill, 1955.

Drucker, P., *America's Next Twenty Years.* New York: Harper, 1957, pp. 17–34.

Dubin, R., *The World of Work.* Englewood Cliffs, N.J.: Prentice-Hall, 1958, pp. 191–211.

Hertzler, J. O., *Society in Action.* New York: Dryden, 1954, pp. 78–83.

Jacobson, H. B., and Roucek, J. S. (eds.), *Automation and Society.* New York: Phil. Lib., 1958.

Landis, P. H., *Social Control* (rev. ed.). Philadelphia: Lippincott, 1956, pp. 276–292.

Lillie, S., *Men, Machines and History*. London: Cobbett, 1948.

Macmillan, R. H., *Automation, Friend or Foe*. Cambridge: Cambridge University Press, 1956.

Meadows, P., "The City, Technology, and History," *Soc. Forces,* 36 (Dec., 1957): 141–147.

Ogburn, W. F., "Technology and Society," *Soc. Forces,* 17 (Oct., 1938): 1–8.

Ogburn, W. F., "Sociology and the Atom," *Am. Jour. Soc.,* 51 (Jan., 1946): 267–275.

Ogburn, W. F., *The Social Effects of Aviation*. Boston: Houghton Mifflin, 1946.

Ogburn, W. F., *Technology and International Relations*. Chicago: Univ. of Chicago Press, 1949.

Ogburn, W. F., "How Technology Changes Society," *Soc. & Soc. Res.,* 36 (Nov.–Dec., 1957): 78–83.

Ogburn, W. F., "Technology as Environment," *Soc. & Soc. Res.,* 41 (Sept.–Oct., 1956): 3–9.

Pollock, F., *Automation: A Study of Its Economic and Social Consequences*. New York: Praeger, 1957.

Redfield, R., *The Primitive World and Its Transformation*. Ithaca: Cornell Univ. Press, 1953, pp. 5–23, 111–138.

Singer, C., *Technology and History*. London: Oxford Univ. Press, 1952.

Thomas, W. L. (ed.), *Man's Role in Changing the Face of the Earth*. Chicago: Univ. of Chicago Press, 1956.

White, L. A., *The Science of Culture*. New York: Farrar, Straus, 1949, pp. 363–393.

White, L. A., *The Evolution of Culture*. New York: McGraw-Hill, 1959, pp. 18–28.

MAINTENANCE

T E N

The Familial Institutions

The institutions comprising the marriage and family system have their roots in the elemental needs of the very first social groupings formed among men. They have been and are universal in some form among all known societies. Their peculiar areas of concern are, first, ordering of the relations of the adult members of the two sexes, that is, the function of sex regulation; second, providing for the societally safe and responsible reproduction and physical care and protection of the human young, that is, the function of biological perpetuation; and, third, by virtue of the consequent relation between the generations, especially of parents and offspring, the initial introduction of the young to the lore and ways of their society, that is, the function of basic cultural induction and conditioning. As will be noted, by their very nature these institutions have also served other functions, and still do in all societies of all developmental levels; but these three functions are the ones this block alone performs in the fundamental division of labor.[1]

Examination of these institutions focuses attention on the world of the sexes, of husband and wife, of parents and children, of age groups, of the kindred and the succession of the generations, and the eternal problems of every human grouping, such as relationship, reciprocal adjustment of persons, continuity, socialization, physical and psychical security, cooperation, freedom, rights, and a variety of controls.

The elemental fact accounting for the appearance, existence, and persistence of these institutions is the bi-sexuality of the human race. The sexes, except under the most artificial conditions of deliberate

[1] Note the following almost lyrical account of the intrinsic importance of the family in life and society ". . . it is an institution founded on the laws of nature; . . . it is an association supporting and supported by every civilization, sanctioned by law, esteemed by knowledge; blessed by religion and wisdom, extolled in its highest achievements, by literature and art, and endowed with the specific attributes by all forms of economy. . . . The institution of the family has withstood all the assaults made upon it and has survived as a witness to its own indispensability in determining the character and structure of society and of man." Ruth N. Anshen (ed.), *The Family: Its Function and Destiny*. New York: Harper, 1949, p. ix.

segregation, live in proximity. The individual members are drawn together by the erotic impulse, sex drive, or sex passion. This drive is continuous and urgent in most human beings, and is effective for a longer period in the life of man than in most animals. The desire for its satisfaction is so spasmodic, so tumultuous, often so casual and indiscriminate, that it can produce serious biological and social disturbances if not properly satisfied and canalized.

The sexes are physiologically distinctive and functionally complementary to each other; because of their respective reproductive functions, they must cooperate in biologically producing the young. The young offspring resulting from such a mating, apparently more than in any other species, require the attention, care, protection, cultural influencing, and discipline emanating from both the female and the male parents. The sexes are also complementary in various other ways; not only is there a specialization of maintenance functions between the parents of the reproductive unit, but in most societies there is something in the way of a general economic division of labor on a sex basis. Since the sexes must unavoidably associate with each other, and since upon their groups the very existence and persistence of the society depend, none of these relations and organizations can be haphazard, unstable, or irresponsible. In brief, they must be, as they very evidently have been from earliest human times, substantially institutionalized. To cope with these situations, two major, distinct, but complementary and sequentially and functionally related institutions—marriage and the family—exist among all peoples.

I: The Marriage Institution

Sex attraction and the sex drive, of necessity, are subjected to a variety of societal controls. The control of mating in the interests of society constitutes the essence of the institution of marriage.

Marriage is strictly a societal institution with definite organizational objectives. Although it concerns itself with a fundamental and societally essential biological drive, it is by no means a biological necessity. The gratification of sex impulse does not require it, and human sexual intercourse was indulged in long before there was marriage. Reproduction is a biological (animal) process, and requires no societal sanctions; the male spermatozoa can penetrate the female ovum and start the gestation of a new human being quite without benefit of matrimony. Conversely, formal marriage can and does occasionally occur without mating, or at any rate without fertilization. Thus marriage is a complex of humanly originated institutional devices to keep sex passion and sex relations within bounds.

Marriage consists of a set of traditions, conventions, customs, mores, and, in higher societies, formal rules and laws which make sexual intercourse legitimate under appropriate and specified conditions. In general, it defines:

(1) The socially approved and required manner of establishing the permitted or approved sex relationship, usually involving some form of ceremony to announce the changed status of the mates.

(2) The number of persons properly permitted to enter into legitimate exclusive marital relations with each other.

(3) The restrictions, conventional and legal, upon sexual relations with respect to degree of consanguinity (the incest taboo), age (especially physiological age), group membership (forbidden or required groups), ethnicity, social class or caste, virginity, state of health, religion, occupation or profession (for example, celibate religious functionaries), and other bio-social and sociocultural characteristics of the potential partners. The marriage rules of the given society indicate "those who are outlawed, reprobated, condoned, accepted, or definitely approved" as marriage partners.[2]

(4) The rights, privileges, and duties of the sexual partners with respect to each other and the community.

(5) The acceptable circumstances, conditions, and means for the termination of marital relations (divorce).[3]

Nothing is known of the origin of marriage. A study of the social organization of the most primitive people on record or available for observation shows that various stern *social* needs had already forced upon them marriage institutions that were quite elaborate and relatively fixed and binding. Everywhere there is regulation and standardization in some form of the union of males and females rather than unrestricted and irresponsible choice or acquisition. Sexual relations other than the standard form, however, are not entirely forbidden. Some primitive societies accept premarital sex experimentation among the immature without disapproval; also, some permit males to have sex intercourse with immature girls or the women of foreign groups. Other departures from the strict exclusive relations exist, such as concubinage, where

2 R. H. Lowie, *Social Organization*. New York: Rinehart, 1948, p. 87.

3 An incidental boon resulting from marriage is the fact that it reduces and controls sexual jealousies. By assigning a given male or males to a given female or females, it at least formally removes these males and females from the arena of sexual choice, competition, and availability. Those *not* married to them *should not* be interested in them as sexual partners.

the husband has one or more supplementary wives of much lower social status than the proper wife or wives; prostitution, usually frowned upon but widespread; sexual hospitality among some people, whereby the host may offer his wife to male guests as a temporary sexual partner; occasional sexual orgies at religious or other ceremonials such as those occurring on May Day in early modern Europe.

None the less, *promiscuity* is everywhere discouraged. Many societies also have the concept of *adultery;* that is, having immoral and forbidden relations outside the marriage relationship, or with others than the rightful spouses. For those married, almost all societies have rather definite restrictions upon the extramarital sex relations of spouses. These infractions constitute *infidelity*. Such rules apply more particularly to wives, however, in most instances, perhaps partly owing to the desire for the preservation of property rights in wives. Finally, among most societies, *illegitimacy,* that is, being born of institutionally unmarried parents, carries a definite stigma.

In general, human societies have held sexual intercourse and reproduction to be allowable and even desirable; they have actually used compulsion of various kinds at different times and under given circumstances. Yet, everywhere the sex relationships have been made more or less exclusive; they have been made to conform to certain rules and limits, and, in the light of progeny issuing from such relations, effort has been made to make them more permanent. Historically, therefore, marriage may be defined as the formal (contractual) and durable union of one or more men with one or more women in socially approved cohabitation.

Among many peoples marriage serves other functions in addition to the regulation of cohabitation and the initial step in the establishment of the family.

(1) Marriage is almost everywhere a means of inaugurating an advantageous economic partnership between the sexes, of establishing the most appropriate association and cooperation between the inseparable and complementary sexes in the struggle for livelihood. In this connection, it also frequently confers property and maintenance rights and duties. (2) In most societies, it establishes the various degrees of "relatives" of the partners. Both parties acquire with their partner a new group of proponents and often of persons with various social obligations of a supportive and protective nature. Each marriage tends to create a new network of intimate relations. (3) Among Western peoples particularly, marriage is also the standardized way in which the most satisfying unitary social relationship between adult human beings is established. The well-married pair are in complementary human association; in their companionship they are achieving social as well as sexual fulfillment; they are enjoying efficient and exuberant life, com-

plete and sacrificial comradeship, community of interests and satisfactions, mutual inspiration and incentive. Marriage is increasingly entered upon as a highly desirable spiritual, social, and moral relationship, as an exclusive interchange of intellectual, affective, moral, and social qualities among the partners to it. Through its enriching and stabilizing effects upon individuals, it has such effects upon the entire societal organization.

FORMS OF MARRIAGE

Marriage takes various forms, sometimes even within a given culture. The most important categories follow.

Exogamy rests on the so-called incest taboo; that is, the avoidance of close blood or affinal relationships in reproduction. Where exogamous marriage prevails, the individual is prohibited from selecting a mate from the group of which he is a member. It is out-group marriage—selecting the mate from outside one's own family, clan, tribe, or ethnic group. *Endogamy* requires a person, by mores or law, to marry within specified groups of which he is a member, and may prevent him or punish him for marrying outside such specified groups. In some societies, including our own, people are pressed to marry within their tribe, within their caste or class, within their religious faith, within their race or nationality group. Endogamous marriage is in-group marriage.

Monogamy defines one husband and one wife. It is the closest sex monopoly. *Polygamy* refers to plural mates. It takes three forms: *polygyny,* or one husband and several wives; *polyandry,* or one wife and several husbands (rare in the present world); *monogyny,* or one jural wife, but also female concubines and female slaves. *Group marriage* is several males married to several females (rare today).

Polygyny is widely approved and widely existent among the present peoples of the earth. It is due in part, doubtless, to some surplus of females in most societies, to certain economic considerations, such as the support and utilization of the surplus females, and to male vanity where multiple wives are a badge of virility and social distinction. Monogamy is the most widely prevalent form, though, since the surplus of females is rarely very great. Even in societies approving polygyny, most marital combinations are monogamous. Monogamy offers a more balanced division of labor between the sexes under most conditions, and fewer emotional and social psychic complications. It rules out the possibility of jealousy among several wives, disputes as to rank and authority of the several wives, disputes growing out of differential recognitions of the offspring of different wives, and complications in connection with the management of the household.

Preliminary to betrothal and the formal ceremony establishing wedlock, especially in those cultures where selection is a matter of choice on the part of the partners themselves, there is the subinstitution, or body of folkways, customs, and mores, known as *courtship*. Courtship is a time of adjustment during which the parties can come, through greater intimacy, to some conclusion as to their mutual suitability. It consists of procedures of selecting, testing, and persuading the prospective marriage partner. Courtship is affected by rather generally accepted tabooed and preferential areas of selection. There are always certain groups and categories and statuses from which an individual of given social status is encouraged, and others from which he is forbidden, to choose a mate. For example, the courting of a person within a certain kinship classification, of certain social classes, places, races, nationalities, or religious affiliations may be forbidden or discouraged. Sometimes also the courting of persons who are lacking in such respects as physical or mental fitness, age, general personality, knowledge and training, personal habits, manners and breeding may be frowned upon. The courtship procedures, when institutionalized, usually include acceptable forms for enticing and testing the reactions of the future mate—display of skill, strength, or cleverness, practice of certain arts, presentation of gifts to various pertinent persons, even certain forms of sexual stimulation and experimentation.

Many people have *betrothal practices;* that is, some form of formal and publicly or semi-publicly announced agreement to marry. The formal act takes on the characteristics of a contract. Betrothal among many peoples, especially among certain classes where dynastic considerations carry social weight, may be at a very young age, even before the birth of the potential partner in some instances.

Entrance upon marriage is formally regulated in most societies. This ceremony—*the wedding*—among different peoples is so multiform as to frustrate description. The marriage may be contracted with very little or very simple ceremony, or a great deal of very elaborate ceremony, even in the same society at the same time. There are very few societies, however, which dispense altogether with ceremonial and ritualistic practices. These practices constitute a public notification and contracting of marriage on the part of the partners. Henceforth, they and their offspring can be placed in their setting as husbands, wives, children, and families; and their rights and duties toward each other are fixed and expected within the system of regulations. In advanced societies, prior to the ceremony itself, there are such preliminary actions as the announcement of the banns, or notice of intention to marry, and the issuance of licenses and certificates. The wedding also involves authorities—those authorized to certify suitability for the marriage, and to give the ceremony itself formal tone and legitimacy. The ceremony may be of a political or religious character, or both. For the community as a whole, the repetition of this ceremony gives impressiveness and social rightness to the entrance upon the socially important marriage relationship.

Since human beings are the participants in the marital relationship, there is the possibility of mistakes or dissatisfaction in the choice or assignment of mates. There is also the possibility of unforeseen situations which make the continued relationship individually or socially intolerable or undesirable. Although any disruption is regarded among most peoples as a serious matter, it occurs almost universally, though in varying degrees and manners. Among most peoples there is *divorce;* that is, a well-standardized, well-safeguarded, and socially acceptable procedure for the dissolution of marriage. The dissolution may be easy or hedged about with many restraints and checkings. The grounds for dissolution may be few or many, varying greatly in different communities; but they all are specifically stated and socially approved. In most societies, divorce includes established ways, also, of dealing with such contingencies growing out of the separation as disposition of property, allocation of children, assumption of obligation of support for children or former spouse, and even compensation for injuries or damages. The whole procedure is calculated to interfere with social cohesion as little as possible.

II: The Family as Institution

Basically, the family is an institutionalized social group consisting of adults of both sexes, at least two of whom maintain a socially approved sexual relationship (that is, they are "married") and the children of the cohabiting adults.[4] There may be variations in the marital combination; the children may be adopted as well as putative in some instances; and the personnel may extend beyond the nuclear group of immediate parents and their children and include a wider array of kinsmen, consisting of relatives of the husband, the wife, or both, and thus, possibly, including grandparents, uncles, aunts, and cousins (the extended family). These mainly genetically related people usually have a name as a group, share a common habitation more or less exclusively, and carry on as a socio-economic maintenance unit, as well as a procreative unit, the economic provision having special reference to the economic needs associated with child-bearing and child-rearing.

It is generally accepted as fact that the family is the oldest, the most basic, and most universal institution. It is also the oldest of human social

[4] Cf. G. P. Murdock, *Social Structure*. New York: Macmillan, 1949, p. 1.

units, the primordial human grouping. It is both a group with its own internal multi-functional organization and the fundamental unit in the organization of society. It is also the original structural-functional unit conducting institutional functions. Almost all institutional functions were originally phases of family life. In fact, among the simple societies, the family in a functional sense has been the only institution; practically all maintenance, regulatory, and expressional activities ordinarily performed by the members of the society, except minor trading operations and warfare, have taken place within the framework of the family, or within a small group of families living and working together. In general, it exhibits on a reduced scale or in embryo most of the phenomena of the larger society of which it is a key constituent element.[5]

"It is the cumulative group whose members have been bound into one social unit by a series of the most important ties—community of blood and biological or social kinship; dependence of the newborn on the parents and of the aged parents on the children; a series of socially and legally binding sanctions; the most intimate community of co-living, co-acting, and co-believing; community of language, mores, patterns of behavior, and moral and juridical customs; collective responsibility; the most intensive community of economic interests; and many other ties. It is difficult to name any other class of social groups so strongly integrated and bound together into one bio-psycho-social organism."[6]

The family has all of the standard components of an institution in perfect exemplification. Everywhere it has its underlying values and, to the extent that people are articulate and conceptual about it, its justificatory rationalizations and interpretations. Its immediate personnel—parents, children, and close relatives—has been repeatedly referred to above; in most of the great civilizations, it has also had extra-family organizations—economic and, especially, political and religious—promoting, influencing, and sometimes exploiting it. It has always had, as perhaps its most signal feature, a body of norms based on the value system and greatly affected by the major determining conditions of the particular society that patterned the relationships between the marital partners, between parents and their offspring, among siblings, among related families, and between the family and the larger community. These patterns are related to the roles, or sets of respon-

---

[5] Although they are inseparable, the distinction between family as *institution*, and family as *group* should be kept in mind. The family as institution is the standardized, formalized, and regularized procedure for the procreation and rearing of children; the family as group is any combination of parents, children, and relatives embodying two or more generations, carrying on these activities.

[6] P. A. Sorokin, C. C. Zimmerman, and C. J. Galpin, *A Systematic Sourcebook for Rural Sociology*. Minneapolis: Univ. of Minnesota Press, 1931, Vol. II, p. 4.

sibilities, privileges, and reciprocities, that go with each of the various positions in the familial relationship. These norms have usually also laid down the qualifications for entering and leaving the family. Historically, there have been laws defining the expected size, the composition, family living arrangements, and other emoluments by social rank of the family.

The family has always had physical paraphernalia (land, dwelling or quarters, furniture, tools, and other equipment) and its symbols (rings, hearths, crests, heirlooms) and its rituals, ceremonials, and holidays.

Historically, the family has taken various forms. From the point of view of descent, there have been three major forms: (1) *patrilineal,* in which the members are affiliated with the male kinship group; (2) *matrilineal,* or affiliation with the female kinship group; and (3) *bilateral,* as in our society, where the members are related to families of both parents. From the point of view of internal organization there have been (1) the *nuclear* or conjugal unit, consisting of husband and wife, or father and mother and their own children, and (2) the *extended,* the kinship group, or consanguineous unit (the *Grossfamilie*), made up of the blood relations and their several conjugal family units. Finally, from the point of view of authority or dominant position of the parents (this overlaps somewhat with descent), there has been the (1) *patriarchal* family, in which the father (or the oldest father) is the central and final authority; (2) *matriarchal* family, in which the mother (or oldest mother) is the main authority in decisions affecting family members; and (3) the democratic family, the type becoming increasingly prevalent, even typical, in our society, in which both parents, and in some matters the children, share the authority.

III: The Universal Functions of the Family

The functions vary in significance; some are root functions; others flow from or relate to the root functions; some of the latter have been reduced or have been transferred, in part at least, to other institutions in our society. The universal functions of the family by modal consensus of its social scientific students are as follows: the first function to be examined is performed at the biological level, the next two at the physical maintenance level, and the remainder are functions of a sociocultural and social psychological character.

The root, or primary, distinctive and non-transferable function of the family is the replacement and perpetuation of the society's personnel by biologically creating new members. The reproduction of the species can, and to some extent does, occur outside the circle of the family in all societies. But no societies have felt that they could chance very much illegitimacy. Societies have everywhere and at all times insisted that their young biologically enter human life through the safe, secure, established, responsible, and functionally effective auspices of the family. The essence of this is what Malinowski and others refer to as the "principle of legitimacy"; that is, the right, even the necessity, of every child having an institutionally acceptable father, a known, responsible, full-time, societally-assigned guardian, protector, and provider. This occurs only within the family pattern. The permanent family is thus built about the sociological need for legitimate child-bearing, within a socially approved and socially controlled parental relationship. In brief, the root function of the famliy is to serve as the societally tried and approved portal whereby human beings enter human life. Neither utopians nor authoritarians have thus far been able to transfer this function to any other agency or institution.

Because of the relatively long period of human pregnancy, the rigors of childbirth, the subsequent lactation period, and the arduous and confining nature of the care of the helpless infant, the human mother is relatively dependent for fairly long periods, and in need of protection, sustenance, and freedom from other duties. The family provides this where the father is responsible for the protection and physical maintenance of the mother.

The family functions especially for the child, however; it is the functional unit for the protection, care, and custody of the immature. The human young are completely helpless at birth, and the period of infancy and childhood and immaturity is a longer proportion of the total life span than in any other known species. During the long infancy and childhood, the young human is unable to feed, protect, or otherwise support himself; he is almost completely dependent. He needs to be shielded, protected, sustained, and otherwise maintained.

This special familial attention to the protection and care of the child is underscored by the fact that in most cases human births are single births, and more and better care is necessary for physiologically economical survival; also the human young have less instinctive equipment compared with other forms of mammalian life to enable them to live naturally; finally, the increasing complexity of human society seems, in some respects, to enhance the helplessness and to prolong the dependence of the human young.

In most societies, historically, the family has also been the unit of protection and care of two other categories of dependents; namely, the aged, and the physically and mentally incompetent or incapacitated members and relatives. This is less and less the case in modern societies, however.

In most societies through most of human history, the family has been the basic economic maintenance unit, through the cooperative production, provision, and utilization or consumption of the physical necessities of life. By virtue of specialized physiological proficiencies of the two sexes and the range of capacities among the age groups represented, the family has been a "natural" as an economic unit. At the same time, the closely interrelated mature competents and the immature or incapacitated incompetents in it have necessitated its being a maintenance unit. The man and wife have been an effective team for economic cooperation. The man, not burdened by pregnancy and the close care of small children, has been free to engage in acquisitive activities outside of the immediate household. He has functioned as the provider of physical and other necessities of existence. The wife, on the other hand, has tended to the more sedentary duties and chores within the household; she has been the preparer of things for consumption and the keeper of the household. Always the adults, and in many societies the children, have definitely established economic roles, largely on the basis of their respective proficiencies. The family, even today, is quite generally a work group in the underdeveloped areas of the world.

The following are among the more important economic functions of the family: (1) the provision of physical sustenance, especially food, shelter, clothing, and other necessities and desirabilities; (2) operation of the most typical and widespread consumption unit, jointly utilizing the means of living provided by the producers or earners; (3) related to (2), operation as the domiciliar unit of the society, in that most families are households, or people who jointly occupy living quarters of some sort (house, apartment, or groups of rooms) with the necessary equipment enabling them to accomplish their domestic functions and live together physically; (4) owning, accumulating, and transmitting the wealth or property of the world. Most of the wealth, land, and capital, even under modern conditions of corporate industry and commerce, is in the last analysis owned by and for families, and the laws of inheritance provide for the transmission of very much of it in a definite and orderly way from one generation to another among the members of the family.[7]

It is also a fact that in most societies people are located in space by where they live as families, are rated socially by the wealth of their families, and are taxed as members of a family wealth-producing or income-receiving unit.

The family, functioning at the sociocultural and social-psychological level, serves as the chief agency in the socialization of the child. It is

---

[7] Cf. B. Malinowski, "The Group and the Individual in Functional Analysis," *Am. Jour. Soc.,* 44 (May, 1929): 938–964.

effective in this respect for several reasons. The family is for all its members, but especially for the child, an inescapable nuclear or miniature society. It is his first and for a while his only social-psychic and sociocultural arena. It reaches him before the more formal educational and regulative institutions and the prevailing social pressures and currents affect him. It monopolizes his daily experiences and influences him most persistently by comparison with any of his other contacts and associations; it influences more facets of his life than any other institution.

The family contacts usually occur in an atmosphere of intimacy, affection, and relaxation, which greatly facilitates communication and encourages transmission of attitudes and habits from parents to children. The continuous exposure to parents and older siblings results in much imitation of, and unconscious conditioning by, them. In fact, parents perhaps have more socializing influence upon the child through patterns of relations which they establish unwittingly than by deliberate efforts at inculcation and discipline. The family thus, almost ideally, provides the situations, the experiences, the conducive atmosphere, and the elementary agencies whereby socialization may take place.

The socialization that the child gets in the family provides him with a variety of materials essential to his later competent societal participation. In the family he learns his language, or his mother tongue, his dialect, his modes of expression, his range of vocabulary, the basic values, beliefs, and ideologies of his society, its folkways and customs, its social standards, and its rules of conduct. Here he gets his first instructions in what is allowed and forbidden in the larger social group, what is considered true, false, just, good, desirable, stupid, beautiful, proper. He learns to control his excretory functions, and acquires his concepts and habits of cleanliness, his manners and his notion of taste, his principles of honor and decency, his financial attitudes and habits, his religious set, his standard of living, his initial political concepts, his ideals and prejudices, his attitudes toward other ethnic groups. The family is the child's first school of discipline. Among many peoples still the family is the unit in which methods of obtaining a livelihood are taught. Finally, one of the family's important functions is to "develop in children the necessary strength, toughness, and resilience to surmount the hardships of life,"[8] especially to withstand its physical, psychological, and socio-economic buffetings. Throughout the child's sojourn in the family, parents and siblings shape, stimulate, and draw out the individual. Life can never entirely erase the effects of this.

Incidentally, even the modern family continues to serve as a continuous socializing and re-socializing agent for its *adult* members also;

[8] R. E. L. Faris, *Social Disorganization*. New York: Ronald, 1955, p. 392.

grandparents, for example, experience a host of new socializing experiences.

Very closely related to the preceding function, in fact, an aspect of it, is the family's effectiveness as a culture-transmitting agency. In the process of socializing the young, it transfers in similar, though somewhat modified form and content, the knowledges, the values and rules, the customs and traditions, the effective ways of living from one generation to the next. It is thus a cultural link or bridge between the generations; and in the succession of the generations, the culture is continued without break.

It is also the chief depository of culture. It is not in the museums and archives but in the members of the family that the effective culture of the group is precipitated and preserved. Here is to be found the measure of the level of culture and the source of all culture. Thus the cultural and spiritual quality of the family in any one generation is bound to have a definite and profound influence upon the life of all succeeding generations.[9]

Because of his birth in a family, the individual acquires at the very outset of his life identification within the community as a member of a particular, permanent, and inescapable known group. The family, both for the individual and the community, functions as the individual's most significant reference group; it provides him with a distinguishing name and a lineage; in some degree it informs all who know him or are interested in him what his bio-social and social roots are, and who and what he is. In most instances, he can select, achieve, and abandon membership in other possible identifying groups; but this, except through marriage, which, after all, is in this respect simply transference to another family group, is almost impossible in the case of his family connection and identity.

In all societies, even the relatively simple ones, each family has a scalar or status position in the stratification system of the community or society. The family is thus the means whereby every individual born is initially assigned a definite orienting place in the social scheme of things, especially in the hierarchical or superordination-subordination system of his society. All of the members of the family at any given time, male or female, young or old, share this particular status position. In closed-class societies, that status is permanently fixed; in open-class societies it is the rung on the social ladder to which an individual may try to hold, or move upward or downward from.

This status position of the family has several notable effects upon its members. First, the family, whether lower or upper stratum, by virtue

---

[9] Cf. P. Schrecker, "The Family: Conveyance of Tradition," in Ruth N. Anshen, *The Family: Its Function and Destiny*. New York: Harper, 1949, pp. 406–425.

of its social and correlated culture level, tends to supply the individual with values, attitudes, ideas, types of social judgments, interpersonal skills, motivations, and habits; his very forms of speech and his manners are class-determined. Second, the scalar position of the individual's family places the individual in the society and provides him with contacts with other persons, activities, groups, and group organizations. It determines in some part his neighborhood and quality of residence. Frequently certain legal and property rights, which individuals and families enjoy or are denied, are class-determined or class-influenced. In medieval societal life, rights of ownership and inheritance of property were class-bound, and sumptuary legislation, or legislation affecting consumption of different things and services, was by its very nature class legislation. Third, the individual is treated and expected to act in ways appropriate to his family's status. This status determines how others are expected to act toward the individual until he changes that status. In most societies, also, the family status position of the individual places upon the individual the duty to maintain in the given community his family's reputation and good name.

Human beings of all ages must have affectional security if they are to be emotionally healthy. The child, especially, must be loved; he must be certain that he is noticed, appreciated, and cherished as a person by other persons. Affectional response of sufficient warmth and intensity does not come from large groups, or from agencies like the school, where formal rules and regulations govern relationships. It is attained mainly in small groups where the members live together intimately. Here, the family is the environment *par excellence,* where there is recognition and cherishing of the child or parent as an important part of the whole, where there is affection, a sense of comradeship, and a sense of belonging. Here the members can expect and do get sympathy and loyalty from each other in normal times as well as in times of trouble. Even the supposedly self-sufficient male parent, contending aggressively against the impersonal and largely unsympathetic world outside, must repair to wife and children for much of this essential sustaining response.

The family has also provided a natural and unrestrained release of the emotions in contrast to the unnatural and artificial expression required in many of the out-of-home contacts.

Historically, the family has had other functions, functions that today are carried on largely by other institutions. In many societies, most of the recreation has been provided in the family and the kin-group, especially in the form of visiting and entertaining. Religious activity has been carried on mainly in the family, and family members have been important religious functionaries. In the simpler societies, educational functions loomed large. The family has also performed political and military functions.

IV: Marriage and the Family in Contemporary Society

Marriage and the family, like all the other institutions, have to accommodate themselves to the whole complex of changes occurring in their particular society, if they are to justify themselves as operative entities and survive. This means that some widespread functions of these institutions become outmoded in the given society and disappear entirely; some functions are more or less modified to meet new conditions and new needs; some may be transferred or taken over by other institutions; certain new functions and features are acquired; some long-standing and probably irreducible and non-transferable functions survive change and time and are retained. Although the family as the elemental and central institutionalized group is the most vulnerable to change and although it shows many forms in different societies, it is at the same time the most durable.

Our special concern is with the contemporary American marriage and family institutions. Both show wide variations. The family, for example, shows considerable divergence according to race, region, social class, educational level, and ethnic group. There are all sorts of subtypes. No completely standard pattern has developed. There have been, however, common factors at work, leading to environmental and societal changes that have tended to produce noticeable modal characteristics and functional changes in marriage and the family. The examination of these changes and the depicting of the family's present functions is a way of characterizing the family in our society and of distinguishing it from its counterpart in other times and places.

In the United States, the colonial and rural family, itself a descendant in many respects of the West and Central European family, was the dominant form until the turn of the century. A comparison of the modern family with this long-standing form offers the best means of delineating the special characteristics of the contemporary family and of its modified place and functions in contemporary social organization.

With respect to the traditional marriage institution, the marriage partners largely came from other families in the neighborhood or the immediate acquaintance circle, the members of which were quite homogeneous as to values and interests, occupation, religion and education, ethnicity, and social class. It could be said that the marriages were arranged to a considerable extent. The marriages, though not always necessarily happy, were durable; relatively few of them terminated in divorce, which carried a definite stigma.

The colonial-rural family was largely patriarchal; male domination was accepted, and subordination of women and children was expected. Strict and unquestioning obedience by children to parental authority and discipline was the rule. It had many of the characteristics of the extended or consanguineous family. The immediate and collateral relatives had a high degree of unity and solidarity, and were in frequent, if not always continuous, contact with each other. The responsibilities of the members of the extended family group to each other with respect to physical maintenance, social and moral support, and protection were extensive; they were explicit in the mores and enforced by community opinion. The members shared a common socio-economic life. The family was, in fact, in most instances, almost a complete economic unit. It produced its own food and engaged in canning, curing, spinning, weaving, clothing-making, clothing-repairing, soap-making, laundering, and cleaning. The family was also in considerable measure, though not exclusively, an educational, religious, recreational, personality maintenance, social welfare, social security, and protective unit. In general, there was much self-reliance, self-sufficiency, self-maintenance. The families lived mainly in small, rather homogeneous communities, and were in close primary association with the other contiguous families.

Though the family lost members by migration to the nearby cities and new frontiers, it was relatively immobile. Often some members resided on the homestead over several generations. The family had a high durability as a group, and it was difficult to escape from its social-psychological and ethnical influence; the members in their varied and differentiated relations with each other were governed by a rugged body of long-established values, traditions, customs, and mores.

The dominant pattern of the contemporary American family is quite a different matter. The students of present American marriage and the contemporary family are pretty generally agreed that the dominant characteristics and prevailing functions, as compared with those of colonial-rural times, are largely the result of the transition from an agricultural-rural-folk society to the modern technology-dominated, industrial-urban society.

About two-thirds of all American families now actually do live in cities or metropolitan areas, and practically all are under vast urban influence and respond to urban patterns of life. This shift from country to city has brought many technologically-induced changes in the physical environment, ecological-demographic changes, attitudinal and valuational changes in the family itself as well as in other institutionalized areas of societal life, which in turn have had profound effects upon the domestic institutions. This does not mean that the family is disappearing or in process of disintegration. What is disappearing is the kind of family life we have long known. The family is coming to be a more specialized institutional grouping with unique characteristics and more limited functions.

MODERN COURTSHIP AND MARRIAGE

Just as marriage is less arranged in our present society, so courtship, the preliminary procedure in mate selection, is freer.[10] The volume of contacts with possible or prospective marriage partners is relatively great for most young folks as they meet each other in high school and college, in factories and stores and offices, in conveyances, in young people's religious organizations, and in places of public recreation. The other young persons with whom they have contact are often from other regions, or diverse as to the economic, ethnic, religious, class, and educational backgrounds of their families, and as to their own values, interests, and norms. Young folks are less restricted by circumstance as well as convention as to both the spatial and associational range of the circles in which they move.

Although there may have been some aspects or counterparts of dating in other cultures and in other times, it seems to be a significant and somewhat standardized and patterned part of our procedure of courtship. As Baber has pointed out, it permits young folks to learn to be at ease with members of the opposite sex, to have close though often fleeting companionship with selected persons, and to discover qualities desirable in a possible courtship partner.[11] Dating is a sort of "get acquainted" affair, producing social intimacy, fellowship, fun, and some physical stimulation, including petting, but without any commitment to further association on the part of either party. When the dating merges into courtship, it implies that the selection of a marital partner has been tentatively made. It is a more serious procedure than dating; the partners evaluate each other as to what seem to them to be essential compatibilities, abilities, and qualities. Although modern courtship is supposedly rooted in romantic love rather than the older sacred proprieties regarding family and class, and the established eligibilities and protocols, our American society, nevertheless, has a great array of rather highly standardized conventions, even codes, which regulate this romantic love.

Marriage in general is a very popular "estate" among Americans.

---

[10] Much attention has been paid to dating and courtship, no doubt partly because of the ready access which researchers, usually connected with colleges and universities, have to subjects.

[11] R. E. Baber, *Marriage and the Family*. New York: McGraw-Hill, 1953, p. 116.

Without going into statistics, it can be pointed out that more and more people are being married, that they are marrying earlier than two decades ago, and that a greater proportion of the population is married than before. Modern American marriage has certain peculiar characteristics, some of which make it more complicated and somewhat hazardous.

Marriage is more and more a matter of individual choice of mate. It is usually regarded as an arrangement between the two individuals immediately concerned rather than between two families or even kinship groups as was to a considerable extent the case a century ago. Whom a person marries is considered to be a matter of personal concern. Parents feel that they should not interfere, and young folks zealously insist upon freedom and independence in selecting a mate. This indicates that the family control over marriage has weakened, and in many instances has almost disappeared. It also means that older considerations regarding the family status of the respected extended families, the joining of family properties through marriage, and the like are now largely non-existent. Marriage, instead of serving group ends, is aimed at immediate personal satisfactions, sexual gratification, affection, and companionship. Important also are the facts that children marry earlier, that when they marry they leave their respective homes altogether, and are almost free from parental control when they establish their own homes. Thus, their outlets and inlets for affection and sympathy and important discussion are restricted chiefly to their marriage mates.

Much is expected of modern marriage. With the changing status of women, especially their increasing economic independence, marriage has ceased to be the only acceptable calling for women. Today women are not forced to marry for support or to gratify the whims or plans of parents, nor do they feel constrained to accept humbly what a particular marriage offers them. Marriage must be worthwhile for women. Since marriage means a large number of new expenses and responsibilities for the man, it must also give some evidence of fulfilling his expectations. People are insisting upon an array of integral satisfactions in the marriage relationship, such as love that is satisfying and enduring, a fair compatibility of aims, tastes, and sentiments, mutual sexual satisfaction, a sharing of responsibilities, joys, interests, mutual respect, sympathy, loyalty, true friendship and comradeship. Modern marriage is also conducted on democratic principles. This means that it is more and more a partnership of equals, freely exercising their respective wills and that policies affecting the partnership are a matter of mutual decision.

The very increase of marriage is itself a reflection of the craving for certain fundamental satisfactions, especially in the way of emotional security. The fellowship of the members of the modern family does not extend into the generations as it once did, and all people, including the young folks, suffer psychologically to some extent from the anonymity, impersonality, and unconnectedness of our mass society. Hypothetically, it could be stated that many young people marry for the otherwise missing, utterly essential fellowship and sustaining emotional response. They want to be part of a tight primary group, even if they have to establish it themselves, a grouping that also identifies them specifically and gives them something to be loyal to and work for.

There has been a considerable secularization of marriage in our society. Many of the traditional attitudes regarding it have been modified, and some have been abandoned. The belief in its sacramental character, as maintained by the churches, has been modified, though not entirely abandoned. There is wide acceptance of marriage merely as a civil contract. A wedding conducted only by a civil official rather than a clergyman is treated with more and more tolerance. There has, of course, been considerable change in the traditional notions regarding marital responsibilities ("to suffer and endure"), marital infidelity, the sanctity and hence the indissolubility of marriage, the heinousness of divorce, and the stigma attached to divorced persons.

At the same time that so much more is being expected and required of marriage, it is becoming more difficult and hazardous to achieve than it was in simpler and more authoritative times. The selection of a mate is becoming a problematical matter. Formerly marriage was largely contracted by young folks who had grown up in the same community and came from families well known to each other; they usually came from the same social class, even from the same religious group, and had a common culture, similar nationality backgrounds, similar interests and values, even similar family occupational backgrounds. They spent their married years in a sympathetic and closely supervised environment, consisting not only of family relations on both sides but of an interested and concerned closely knit community which expected them to succeed, and which supported them in innumerable ways.

The situation has changed, however, with ever greater heterogeneity of population, urbanization, physical and social mobility, and the secularization of ways and values. People are freer from family and local community controls, and there has been an erosion of the older endogamous attitudes. Many young folks now meet more or less fortuitously away from home. They have contacts with persons of the opposite sex with varied backgrounds. The circumstances under which they meet are often temporary and deceivingly superficial as to the knowledge about their background cultures and actual personalities. Often they do not discover until after they are married that their deep-seated attitudes, interests, standards, purposes, and character traits are so diverse as to make compatibility in the intimate relationships difficult; these differences may be altogether irreconcilable.

In our society democratic rights within the marital relations are guaranteed by statutes. There is a growing volume of laws equalizing and safeguarding rights and duties of husbands and wives. Equally significant, and occasioned in part by the increasing hazards in marrying, are the considerable number of formal limitations and requirements laid upon marriage in our society. The laws of various states specify such requirements as a minimum age of marriage, ranging from 12 to 16 for girls and from 14 to 18 for boys; that both girls and boys below the age of 21 have the consent of parents; a waiting period of varying length after applying for the marriage license; a physical examination of varying degrees of rigor (sometimes including a blood test) before the issuance of a license. Many states prohibit miscegenation; that is, the marriage of whites and members of specified colored races. All states prohibit multiple marriages, marriage between certain close relations, and the marriage of those specified as insane, feeble-minded, and epileptic. Some of these restrictions and requirements make for what might be referred to as increasingly exogamous marriages.

Although divorce or the formal dissolution of marriage is being liberalized in many states by the provision of additional legal grounds for divorce,[12] by the freer interpretation of grounds by attorneys and judges, and by reductions in residence requirements in some states, at the same time because of a continued recognition of the importance of the family unit as established by marriage, divorce continues to be rigidly controlled by law and the courts. The grounds in the statutes are specified and limited in number; each case must be formally presented to, and reviewed by, the court; eligibility for divorce must be established; the terms of settlement must be specifically stated and must be adhered to under court penalty.

However, despite all the preceding factors, American marriage shows a strain toward endogamy. A growing number of studies show that young Americans, whether they realize it or not, are limiting themselves along lines of choice.

There is a tendency to marry those with whom they have residential propinquity, even in cities, within several blocks of each other, not primarily because they live close by, but rather because given neighborhoods tend to include people of similar socio-economic status, educa-

---

[12] The most commonly recurring ones in the statistics are adultery, desertion, cruelty, mental cruelty, imprisonment, alcoholism, impotence, non-support, and insanity.

tional level, ethnic backgrounds, and other similar social characteristics.

They are more likely to marry persons of similar racial and nationality background. Marrying within their own race is forced upon young
folks in twenty-six states which prohibit interracial marriage in some
way; but the great bulk of young folks in all parts of the country greatly
prefer and consistently select mates of their own race. This also is still
true to some extent with respect to the nationality of their immediate
ancestors, though there is more frequent marriage across nationality
lines.[13]

There is a tendency to marry persons within the same or closely
similar religious faiths. Many churches deliberately encourage their
members to marry within the faith. The Roman Catholic Church has
rigid requirements about whom the candidates are to be married by
and about promises regarding the faith and religious education of the
children. But many people, especially those who take their religion
seriously, feel more comfortable with a person of the same faith in the
intimate association of marriage and the family. This involves not
merely theological similarity, but also the complex of values, ideology,
and type of people embracing the particular religious faith.

There is a tendency to marry persons from approximately the same
socio-economic class. This resolves itself into similarity of the respective originating families as to income and economic plane of living,
as to standard of living, as to occupational level, as to educational level,
as to social values, goals, and tastes, and often as to political beliefs.[14]

There is even considerable evidence to the effect that persons tend
to select mates with similar physical and psychological, as well as
social, characteristics. There seems to be a more than chance positive
correlation between mates with respect to height, weight, health, physical appearance or good looks, intelligence, various personality traits,
and social participation. This is referred to as homogamous mate selection.

The evidence of these tendencies in mate selection shows that most
marrying persons, even with all of the range they enjoy and the freedom
of choice permitted them, tend to select as mates persons with similar
backgrounds, attitudes, values, interests, and traits, people with whom
they can communicate most freely, with whom they can readily establish

---

[13] J. H. S. Bossard, "Nationality and Nativity as a Factor in Marriage," *Am.
Soc. Rev.,* 4 (Dec., 1939): 792–798. L. Nelson, "Intermarriage among Nationality Groups in a Rural Area of Minnesota," *Am. Jour. Soc.,* 48 (Mar., 1943):
585–592. R. J. R. Kennedy, "Single or Triple Melting Pot? Intermarriage Trends
in New Haven, 1870–1940," *Am. Jour. Soc.,* 49 (Jan., 1944): 331–339.

[14] Cf. P. H. Landis and K. H. Day, "Education as a Factor in Mate Selection," *Am. Soc. Rev.,* 10 (Aug., 1945): 558–560. R. Centers, "Marital Selection
and Occupational Strata," *Am. Jour. Soc.,* 54 (May, 1949): 530–535.

and maintain rapport, and hence with whom they can feel congenial and comfortable.[15]

CHARACTERISTICS OF THE MODERN AMERICAN FAMILY

In spite of the diverse elements of the American family students of the family discern rather widespread modal characteristics.

The great bulk of American families live in cities, and most of the rural and small-town families are greatly, even determinatively, influenced by industrial-urban conditions and procedures. City life has its own inimitable ways of living and thinking. Practically all husbands and fathers, except those on farms (and they are a rapidly diminishing proportion of the country's labor force), work outside the home in factory, shop, office, or store. Increasingly, most of them, even the members of the professions, work for some *organization* carrying on processing, transporting, marketing, clerical, or service-rendering activities. Likewise, increasingly, these organizations carry on mass operations and are structured as impersonal bureaucracies. Modern technology, industry, and commerce are characterized by an infinite division of labor and specialization of tasks, which have created many new occupations and an increase in the range and opportunities for employment. As one result, not only young women, spinsters, and widows, but increasingly wives and mothers, are gainfully employed outside the home, even during the period of life when they have small children. Between 1890 and 1948 the proportion of married women working outside the home increased from 4.6 to 22.0 per cent. This employment of women outside the home has increased their economic freedom, provided them with non-domestic roles, which in turn, along with other factors, has raised their status. However, this separation of place of work and the home and the diversification of jobs among the family members have produced a lack of common occupational interest. Also, partly because of the rapid changes in occupations, the educational opportunities for the young, and the diversification of occupational opportunities, the father is no longer the occupational model for his son; there is a great likelihood that the son will not follow the father's occupation. People receive money wages or salaries for their efforts, not things or services, and money, as Simmel has pointed out, has an individualizing effect. The physical plant of the family, home or living quarters and yard (if any), are small in the city and are shrinking. This means that many activities once associated with the family are now conducted "off the premises." It also

---

[15] These trends and modalities do not nullify the fact that some people *do* marry for such reasons as money, social prestige, sense of obligation (the feeling that every normal person should marry, or family pressure), lack of satisfactory alternatives, and "pure" sex attraction.

means that many families, especially those in the lower income brackets, are living under crowded conditions with attendant strains.

It can also be noted, though these points will be developed in other connections later, that city life is highly competitive, that personal relations are anonymous, that success is mainly individually achieved, and that a diversity of regimental interests and segmental activities prevails which causes the social participation of persons, particularly family members, to be diverse and divided. There are less and less family interests and activities in the city.

A signal characteristic of our American society is its mobilities—physical, social, occupational, to mention the more obvious varieties. The American family, as the basic population unit, is also increasingly characterized by these mobilities. There is among our families much physical movement from community to community and change of residence within the community. This change in physical location means new contacts, new experiences, the abandonment of some prevailing attitudes, values, and life routines, and the necessity of new patterns of behavior and adjustment, even though there may be an effort to retain old ways. There is also the tendency for a family that is occasionally or frequently on the move to have weak roots and temporary associations in the community. A family of stable residence is under the oversight and control of the community to a greater extent than one of transiency of residence. "A family which has a conception of itself as belonging to a community will be more inclined to live up to community expectations of desirable behavior than a transient family."[16]

Another form of mobility is generational mobility; that is, when young people marry, they establish a residence of their own physically removed from their respective families of origin, frequently at a considerable distance, thus reducing greatly the opportunities for contact and confining communication to long-distance media. This inevitably means some growing apart even if the generations live under similar cultural conditions.

Many American families, unlike those in societies with a more rigid stratification system, are *socially* mobile; that is, they move up and down the social ladder from one social class to another. Many evidence a definite straining to achieve a higher rung. This too is inimical to continuity of life experience, occasionally producing problems of behavior and adjustment within the family, sometimes isolating it from both the class of departure and the class of arrival. There is also *generational social mobility*. For all except the upper classes, there is a possibility and frequently the actuality of a family's grown children, singly or with their

16 E. W. Burgess and H. J. Locke, *The Family: From Institution to Companionship*. New York: Am. Book, 1945, pp. 529–530.

families, moving up or down into a stratum other than that of their family origin.

Burgess mentions the possibility of *ideational mobility* on the part of an immediate family. In the present life of cultural flux, a family may acquire values, attitudes, norms and sanctions, and habits of thought quite different from those of their respective kinship group or even their immediate families of origin. Ideational changes are bound to come as families become culturally acclimated in a different region or occupational milieu, or when they go up the social ladder.

Because of the occupational change from generation to generation, the great amount of spatial mobility, the separate location of young couples, the smaller households in urban conditions, the emphasis upon improvement of status, and a number of other factors, the tightly knit consanguine kinship system or *Grossfamilie* is breaking down and disappearing as a functional unit in our society. What we do have left in the way of Great Family attitude and action is largely confined to some clans of the upper classes who stress its perpetuation in order to control wealth and retain and transmit social status. In place of the Great Family as the effective domestic unit, we find the nuclear or restricted conjugal family consisting only of parents and their children. This new nuclear family is very much a private, separate, close-knit, face-to-face group. It is itself founded by the marriage of individually selected mates and is in large measure emancipated, not only from the larger contributory kinship groups, but also from the immediate families of origin. It has been well said that it is "not imbedded in a matrix of extended kin relations." The nuclear family does not have to fit into a large, supervisory kinship group; frequently it does not want the intrusion of relatives in its affairs, nor does it want to be obligated to the larger kinship circle. It is without the direct sympathetic association of loving kin, without the social identification, the moral, physical, and status support provided by the larger group. The special responsibilities for developing and maintaining a body of standards and procedures are imposed upon the husband and wife.

The psychological and regulative influence of the father in many families seems to be waning. It may be partly because of new conditions and partly because of resignation from certain older paternal responsibilities. The father in most families works away from home, often a considerable distance away, and the commuting takes quite a bit of his day. This means that he is away from his family a greater proportion of the waking time of the children. Other extra-home interests and activities cause him to direct his energies elsewhere. The wife and mother, on the other hand, if she is not employed outside the home—and the majority are not—can make mothering a full-time job. She has to assume more and more duties in the home. She manages the household and spends most of the family income. She is more and more important in the biological-social-cultural life of the children; she not only assumes the major responsibilities for their physical development and health, but she is coming to be also the chief indoctrinator and regulator of the children. There is some point to the views that a new sort of matriarchate is developing, and that some young folks are suffering from "momism."

Not only is there a tendency for the nuclear family to be separated and emancipated from the larger kingroup, but there is also evident a scattering and decentralization of interests, a diversification of values, viewpoints, and objectives among family members that make for individuation as persons. There also seems to be a loss of family consensus and a weakening of cohesion and discipline of the family as an integral group. In a modern family, the different members may follow several different occupations; they may have a variety of political interests and viewpoints; they may have religious diversity. Many of their interests are specialized and not shared within the group. They often have many of their interests and activities outside the family. The father has his job, his sports, his politics, his lodge; the mother has her P.T.A., clubs, bridge, shopping; the children have school, Boy and Girl Scouts, hot rod clubs, athletic contests, movies. Baber, quite appropriately, refers to this as the "centrifugal" tendency; that is, the activities of the members pulling outward from the common center, compared with the former "centripetal" tendency which pulled the members *inward* toward a common center.[17] The members are searching for their own welfare and personality development; the welfare of the family is among many a diminishing aim. This individuation is demonstrated in parent-child relationships; the child is viewed not so much as a plastic learner, but as an individual with rights as a personality. It is also reflected in the changing attitude of mates toward divorce, which might be phrased, "Go it alone if you can't go it easily together." Even the aged are more and more splintered from their families.

With the secularization of marriage goes secularization of the family. There has been a marked decline of sacred or long-standing traditional and proverbial family values, attitudes, norms, and of customary correct procedures. Faris has called attention to various sanctities which are weakening if not disappearing altogether, such as the subordination of wife and children to the male head, the obligation to bear children, the obligation of children to parents, the care of aged parents, the responsibility of all of the family toward ancestors, toward collateral relatives (cousins, aunts, uncles) and posterity.[18] Many traditional

[17] *Op. cit.,* p. 637.
[18] Faris, *op. cit.,* pp. 403–405.

practices are disappearing. Such family religious rituals as family prayers, reading the Bible aloud, and saying grace before meals are now exceptional.

The democratically oriented and organized family is emerging. Egalitarian attitudes and behavior prevail. The authoritarian attitude and behavior of husband over wife, the inferior position of women in the home, the subordination of children have come to be considered as inconsistent with democratic principles. There is greater freedom of choice and spontaneity of expression among members. Children make many of their own important choices, express their own desires and feelings, even question the opinions and recommendations of parents.[19] There is increasing respect for each member, regardless of sex or age, as an individual. The family itself is increasingly looked upon as an arena of interacting personalities in which each is freely seeking his fulfillment as a self. In fact, as a result of the democratic tendencies, the family is coming to be integrated on a new basis appropriate to the new age— a more spontaneous, egalitarian, expressive organization based on the companionship of husband and wife, parents and children, and children with each other.[20]

The modern family as a social organization is more unstable in that it is more likely to be broken by divorce than was the case with the traditional family. The relationships in the traditional family may not have been happier, but the pressure of the mores and of the families on both sides was greater.

Measured in terms of frequency of divorce, the family is less stable now than in the past. The statistical data are abundant. Suffice it to note that in 1890 the divorce rate in the U.S. was 0.5 per cent per 1000 of population; in 1940, it was 2.0; in 1946, 4.3; and in 1950, 2.6. To put it differently, in 1887 there were 55 divorces per 1000 marriages, while in 1948 (when divorces were down considerably from the peak in 1946) the rate was 225 divorces per 1000 marriages.

The following are important as factors in the increase of divorce: (1) the more precarious nature of modern marriage, indicated, for example, in the greater cultural heterogeneity of the marriage partners and the consequent difficulties of "seeing eye to eye" on important issues; (2) the reduction in the functional solidarity of the family in that the husband and wife are less dependent upon each other; (3) the increasing impersonality of community influences and the fact that

---

[19] It should be noted, however, that although children enjoy more and more autonomy and independence in the family, they are more and more controlled from outside, for example by compulsory school attendance laws, factory acts, child-labor legislation, juvenile courts, and truancy and probation officers of the courts.

[20] Cf. Burgess and Locke, *op. cit.*, p. vii.

these influences are less controlling; (4) the secularization of the old attitudes and values regarding the responsibilities of family members to each other; (5) the general liberalization of the attitude toward divorce; (6) the fact that partners expect much more from marriage and their family relations; (7) the stress upon individual happiness rather than joint stability; (8) the greater likelihood of separation, even antagonism, of interests arising from the extension of extra-family distractions.

Increased divorce does not necessarily indicate a greater amount of discord within the individual partnership than in the past. It is quite likely that the great proportion of the marriages that do survive are happier and more sturdy spiritually than were many of the marriages of arrangement of a century ago. Furthermore, divorce seldom rends a happy marriage or harmonious family, nor does its denial maintain the purity of the home. Also the considerable amount of divorce does not indicate any fear of marriage, as reflected by the ready re-marriage of the divorced.[21]

Although all families are broken ultimately by death, such disruption comes increasingly later in the family career because of the rising expectation of life. As a physical unit, the family has greater stability. With substantial improvements in health, the breakup of marriage by death of one partner, especially at a young age, is less common than it used to be. In 1900, 27.4 marriages in every 1000 ended each year in the death of one spouse; by 1957, the rate was only 16.6 per 1000, a level about 40 per cent lower than at the turn of the century. Death of the husband or wife now occurs at much older ages on the average and after many more years of married life. The average parent today has a much greater chance of surviving to see his children past their dependency period. Also, partly as a result of these health trends, a much larger proportion of the population is now married or living in a family. Widowhood has been largely postponed to a period of life when responsibility for minor children is not great. Even more striking, orphanhood (loss of one or both parents by a child under 18) is fast diminishing as a social problem. Under 1956 mortality conditions, a white child born that year faced 25 chances out of 1000 of losing his mother before he reached 18 and 57 chances of losing his father. At the turn of the century, the comparable probabilities were much higher; namely 138

[21] "Among the men and women who married in 1950 at ages 25 or older, a considerable proportion had already been divorced. One quarter of all the brides at ages 25 to 29 were divorcees, and the proportion rose to a maximum of nearly one half in the age range of 35 to 44 years. Of the brides in their early 50's, divorcees represented about a third. For grooms, the proportion previously divorced increased from one eighth for those marrying at ages 25 to 29, to a maximum of one half for those marrying at 40 to 49." *Statistical Bulletin*, Metropolitan Life Insurance Co., June, 1953, p. 6.

and 170, respectively. The chances of losing *both* father and mother before 18 declined enormously over this period, from 23 to 1.4 per 1000. In fact, we seem to be approaching the time when children are more likely to be orphans because of broken homes than because of the death of one or both parents.

Children themselves have a greatly improved chance of reaching adulthood. Today even childbearing, once so dangerous, does not raise the mortality of married women above that of others through the reproductive period or beyond. In fact, in 1930 there were 70 maternal deaths per 10,000 live births; but by 1959 there were only 4.[22]

The size of the modern American family fluctuates, in part because of the particularly closely related economic and political conditions, but generally it has shrunk in size in the last century. The modern family less typically includes the aged parents of the married couple, their unmarried sisters and brothers, their aunts and uncles, unmarried or widowed. Significant, however, is the fact that the specific nuclear unit of father, mother, and children is smaller because of the smaller number of children per family.

On the basis of the U.S. Census Bureau definition of the family, we note the following:

1790	an average of 5.7 persons per family
1880	5.0
1900	4.7
1930	4.1
1950	3.5

The smaller family is caused by a combination of factors, among which the following are significant.

The urban living unit, whether house or apartment, with its limited yard area does not lend itself well to a large number of children.

The interests outside the family alternative to child-bearing and child-caring of mothers or potential mothers, such as jobs or clubs, are occasionally mentioned.

With compulsory school attendance until late adolescence, the prohibition of child-labor, the increasing desirability of completing high school and even college, the failure of children to provide for, or even contribute to, the economic security of parents in old age, children have ceased to be an economic asset. They have become, in fact, a sheer luxury, even an economic liability, and must be desired for their own sake.

---

[22] Cf. *Statistical Bulletin,* Metropolitan Life Insurance Co., November, 1948, July, 1951, and February, 1960. The major portion of the data in this section on the physical durability of the American family has been derived from "Health and the Changing American Family" in *Progress in Health Services,* Health Information Foundation, New York, Sept., 1958.

A higher standard of living and the urge for upward social mobility is another factor in the smaller family. Couples have fewer children in order to live in a better and more prestigeful residential section, have a Buick instead of a Chevrolet, and join the country club. Children are heavy baggage to carry up the social ladder.

The final factor, of an instrumental rather than motivational nature, is the wider knowledge of, and availability of, materials for contraception, in spite of restrictive legislation and militant opposition of certain groups. Parenthood is increasingly becoming voluntary, regardless of social class, religious faith, region, or ethnicity. The very fluctuation of birthrates upward when economic and political times are good and downward when they are bad and the fact that the "child-happy" couples during the present decade stop having children after the desired number are evidence of some effective control of numbers. A recent study found that couples asked before marriage about the number of children they wanted showed only 7 per cent variation of the actual fertility at the end of twenty years.[23]

THE FUNCTIONS OF THE MODERN AMERICAN FAMILY

Most of the functions which the American family conducted when it was almost self-sufficient as a basic maintenance unit and when it functioned as the almost exclusive socializing and protecting organization have undergone considerable change. In the main, the present situation with respect to family functions is that they have unavoidably been affected by the new kinds of interinstitutional division of labor and specialization and assignment of social functions that have been taking place. The family is in a state of highly cooperative relations with many of the other private and public agencies and institutions of modern society. The family can be said to have functional extensions of itself in the factory and shop, the school, the community center, the day nursery, the P.T.A., the supervised playground, the church, the family welfare association, the public assistance organization, the social security system, the clinic and hospital, the visiting nurse's organization, the police courts.[24]

The modern American family is still the basic and indispensable institution for the biological production of the next generation, and

[23] C. F. Westhoff, P. C. Sagi, and E. L. Kelly, "Fertility through Twenty Years of Marriage: A Study in Predictive Possibilities," *Am. Soc. Rev.*, 23 (Oct., 1958): 549–556.

[24] Dr. W. A. Koppl, a social psychologist at Union College, found that the family of a representative General Electric employee in Schenectady has direct dealings in a single week with over forty different tradesmen, officials, and professionals. Cf. N. N. Foote, "Community Services," *Annals Am. Acad. Pol. & Soc. Science,* 314 (Nov., 1957): 46–56.

hence of our society's demographic continuity and societal self-perpetuation. There are no known substitutes for the family in conducting this function.[25] Although there is less public control over some traditional family functions, there is still much control of the reproductive function, including, by virtue of marriage, careful checking and regulating of potential parents with respect to age, physical and mental fitness, ethnic uniformity, and also including considerable setting up and enforcing of the responsibilities of parents for the physical, and to some extent, the moral maintenance of their children.

The family has been dislodged from its paramount place as an economic producing unit. Former production functions have been taken over by various specialized producing establishments, such as mechanized corporate farms, canneries, bakeries, and other food-processing factories, frozen food establishments, restaurants, laundries and dry-cleaning establishments, textile mills, and clothing manufactories. Even many farmers raise one or more cash crops, which are sold, and they are dependent upon the market for almost all that they consume. The family is not at the center of the society's economic activity, but rather mainly a beneficiary at its periphery.

The family is, however, still the main consumption and location unit of modern society. The family still purchases as a unit and consumes food, living space, automobiles, and all manner of appliances and services. Although the family is no longer a self-sufficient productive unit, there still is a domestic division of labor. The father still works for the family, although outside the home. He earns wages which are converted into concrete things and services consumed by the family. He still has the main responsibility for providing the means of maintenance. The wife and mother, whether also employed outside the home or not, still has the task of overseeing the household and of getting the things the father provides into consumable form. Even the children of a well-managed home still have some household chores. Physical maintenance is still a primary responsibility of the family.

The responsibility of the greater proportion of the formal education of children has shifted from the home to the school, ranging from nursery school through elementary and high school, to college and professional school. Nowadays, children spend an increasing amount of time in school, start school earlier (nursery school as early as 2 years of age), remain in school longer (even to 25 or more years of age), and attend school a longer portion of the year (3 or 4 months a year for the colonial child as against 9 to 10 months now). More and more children

---

[25] Ralph Linton points out that "the ancient trinity of father, mother and child has survived more vicissitudes than any other human relationship." "The Natural History of the Family," in Ruth N. Anshen (ed.), *The Family: Its Foundation and Destiny*. New York: Harper, 1949, p. 38.

attend nursery school and kindergarten, and a larger number attend high school and college. The school teacher at all educational levels has, in fact, become a "substitute parent." The home still gives much general experience and many important insights and outlooks, but it seems to be providing less and less preparation for the adult career. Skill training for occupation or profession, once performed principally in the family, is now taken over largely by the school.[26] The child gets many of his basic social attitudes, in highly-standardized form, from the school. There is less moral education of children at home, and more by church and school; some public school systems have set up formal courses in morals and "character education." The child even gets physical education in the schools as home plants diminish in size and as there are fewer physical chores to be done at home. Schools are moving in the direction of educating the "whole" child. The child also gets more of his socialization by means of other non-family agencies, such as the neighborhood play groups, Boy and Girl Scouts, radio, television, comic books, comic strips, the motion pictures, and even at the hands of institutionalized welfare agencies, welfare departments, and juvenile courts.

But the educating influence of the family has not been entirely lost by any means. It still has the first cultural and socializing influence on the child. It is still potent in exposing the child to basic values and attitudes, and in providing him with life perspectives. It still has the most continuous and persistent influence on the child.

The religious instruction of the children and the conducting of religious practices for all members of the family is now largely under church auspices. In general, the decline of the religious functions of the family seems to be part of its general secularization. There is less attention to religion itself in most families. This does not necessarily mean a decline in church membership on the part of the families. It may reflect a hesitancy on the part of parents in a less dogmatic age to propound theological certainties and to assume religious "authority." In many instances, the church has not so much supplanted the family as a religious agency, but has simply taken over by default the religious activities once conducted within the home.

The decline of such family religious behavior as going to church together, saying grace at meals, and reading the Bible at home, and having family prayers has been frequently noted. It also seems that although most children follow the religion of their parents, there is a considerable departure from the religious viewpoints and affiliations of the preceding generation, sometimes related to the vertical mobility,

[26] The farm family in contrast to the urban family does still furnish quite a bit of what we now call manual training, physical education, domestic science instruction, and vocational guidance instruction.

for example when a couple switches to a more prestigeful religious denomination as they move up a rung on the social ladder. Along with the general individuation and individualism, there has also come the tendency for religion, or the lack of it, to become a personal and individual concern and activity.

Recreation within the family circle has greatly changed. Because of the smaller home plant, there are fewer facilities in the home for recreation involving much physical activity or more than a few participants. Home recreation is thus more of a sedentary and passive nature, such as enjoying radio or television, listening to records, or playing bridge. The family automobile has produced new types of recreation enjoyed together by the members of the nuclear family, such as pleasure trips, picnicking, fishing and camping trips. But for the most part, the recreational interests and activities of the family members are now widely dispersed. More and more of the recreation of the family members is centered outside the home, is not done as a family, and takes the members away from home. The members enjoy their recreation at semi-public agencies, such as community centers, Y.M.C.A., Y.W.C.A., C.Y.O., country clubs, municipal, state, and national parks and playgrounds. More and more of it is in the form of commercialized entertainment: motion picture theatres, bowling alleys, dance halls, skating rinks, race tracks, sports events, amusement parks, and beaches. Home-made fun has given way to purchased entertainment.

The forms of recreation itself have changed greatly. There is not so much reading aloud, visiting, going to family reunions, to church sociables, or barn dances—events in which close friends or family members associated pleasurably. The recreation of members of the modern family is engaged in individually or by couples or with non-family persons. Also, much recreation has come to be specialized by sex and age groups.

The changes in the regulative functions of the family take several forms. First, the control of a considerable number of the traditional family activities by its own members has been progressively reduced to a much narrower area. When all sorts of functions, interests, and activities formerly taken care of within and by the family have been removed from it to be assumed elsewhere, it follows that the control over these activities has been taken from the family and is now vested in other groups. For example, the control over the economic activities of a son, once exercised by the father in the home, shop, or on the farm, is now exercised by the son's employer, trade union, or professional organization. The situation is similar with respect to educational, intellectual, recreational, and protective activity.

A second aspect relates to the regulation of the behavior of the children in the family. The parents of the present nuclear family do some controlling and disciplining of their children, though in general there seems to be less of this than in the older, more authoritarian family. More and more regulative influence is exercised over the children by such outside agencies as the school, peer group members, the police, truant officers, and juvenile court.

Especially significant is the fact that the nuclear family itself as a group is less subjected to the formerly influential informal governing influences. The social control once exercised by the extended kinship group is almost non-existent now, since so many nuclear families are separated physically and spiritually as well as spatially from the kin. Even the older formal control by public opinion, which compelled considerable conformity in the small, homogeneous community, has been lost under the conditions of the family anonymity or temporary location in many an urban community. The modern family's controls consist mainly of the general folkways, customs, and mores of the community as a whole, and those of the particular class or other specially influential group to which the family belongs, such as occasionally the religious congregation, and the community-wide formal, impersonal, and generally applicable legal sanctions as these bear upon family behavior.

The older family provided its members with much of its protection against hazardous physical forces and against harmful human elements; it took care of its sick, incompetent, injured, unemployed, aged, and indigent; it undertook to provide its own security for financial contingencies related to unemployment, illness and accident, old age, and death of the breadwinner. Now semi-public and state agencies have assumed most of these protective functions. Police, from the local to the federal level, and fire departments protect the lives and property of families. Inspectors and municipal, county, state, and federal health departments give protection against disease. The sick are cared for in hospitals or with the assistance of visiting nurses in the homes. The aged are cared for in private and public nursing homes. The indigent are supported and treated by public and private charity. The mentally incompetent and ill are taken care of in private and public institutions. Insurance companies, state agencies, labor unions, and the federal Social Security program protect individuals and families from the financial hazards that follow death, accident, illness, unemployment, and old age.

The status-conferring function also has greatly changed. The old families which emphasize breeding, tradition, and ancient position are coming to be exceptional. The significance of the historical kinship group or family line in determining the status of the newly formed family units is also waning. The present-day family's status is more and more dependent upon the occupational position and the related social achievements of the husband and father. It should also be noted that family status itself has less significance in a mass society in which the anonymous families have physical and social mobility. Although family is still important for the more socially stationary upper classes, it means less and less for the volatile middle classes as they seek to pass from humbler family-class status to more prestigeful ones. However, sight should not be lost of the fact that the status of the family, however achieved, is still important in determining the child's initial cultural level and educational opportunity.

Some of the personality-shaping functions and social-psychic services to members have always been provided by the family, but these have taken on special significances in the modern family. Never have human beings had such a need for them. They have come to be among the most important functions to be performed by the family. No other organization of human beings is so favorably structured in the institutional division of labor to conduct these functions. The nature of modern society has required that they take certain forms if the needs are to be satisfied.

There is a new significance of the affectional function. No other standard groupings can provide the warmth, the tenderness, or the intense personal affection which human beings need so desperately as can the modern family. The members expect the family to provide this; in fact, many of the marriages that end in divorce are due to the failure of affectional functions.

Related to affectional function is the personality-sustaining function. Neither husbands, wives, nor children get much, or at least sufficient, personality reinforcement in the course of most of their extra-family activities, whether in other primary groups or in their secondary group relations. Yet, such reinforcement is an essential to mental and emotional health. In most of the durable families, the members do get personality sustenance in the way of sympathetic, favorable mirrorings of self from each other, as well as some kindly administered therapeutics. There the husband and father often gets recognition for his efforts and approval of his hopes and ambitions which help him to live with his doubts and anxieties. The wife and mother feels her significance as the personal hub of the family. The children enjoy there their recognition as persons. The mother teaches the child affection and influences his early anger reactions. From her he gets his elementary concepts of right and wrong, the social graces, the basic attitudes and patterns of social and moral behavior. She remains for the child the symbol of tenderness, refuge, care, and comfort. When the child becomes conscious of the life beyond the mother and the confines of the intimate home circle, the father begins to gain special significance. He is the window on the outside world; he is the symbol of the more abstract, complex, mysterious phases and wider experiences of life; he is the medium through which the child forms his judgments regarding the nature and the obligations of the world of broader relations.

In spite of nursery schools and kindergartens, the parents are still the small child's omnipotent world, and since the first years are those of greatest plasticity and malleability, even in the modern family, the stamp of the parents on the personality of their children never wears off. It is not surprising that human beings as adults reflect in their entire lives the attitudes, beliefs, values, aspirations, emotional conditions, and the general reaction patterns of their childhood homes.

B I B L I O G R A P H Y

GENERAL

Anshen, Ruth N. (ed.), *The Family: Its Function and Destiny*. New York: Harper, 1949 (rev. ed., 1959).

Baber, R. E., *Marriage and the Family*. New York: McGraw-Hill, 1953.

Bierstedt, R., *The Social Order*. New York: McGraw-Hill, 1957, pp. 341–369.

Bossard, J. H. S., and Ball, E. S., *The Large Family System*. Philadelphia: Univ. of Pennsylvania Press, 1956.

Burgess, E. W., and Locke, H. J., *The Family: From Institution to Companionship* (2nd ed.). New York: Am. Book, 1945, 1953.

Burgess, E. W., and Wallin, P., *Engagement and Marriage*. Philadelphia: Lippincott, 1953.

Calhoun, A. W., *A Social History of the American Family*. New York: Barnes & Noble, 1945.

Cavan, Ruth S., *The American Family*. New York: Crowell, 1953.

Davis, K., *Human Society*. New York: Macmillan, 1949, pp. 392–429.

Goode, W. J., "The Theoretical Importance of Love," *Am. Soc. Rev.,* 24 (Feb., 1959): 38–47.

Hogan, J. D., and Janni, F. A. J., *American Social Legislation*. New York: Harper, 1956, pp. 143–304.

Jacobson, P. H., *American Marriage and Divorce*. New York: Rinehart, 1959.

Kirkpatrick, C., *The Family: As Process and Institution*. New York: Ronald, 1955.

MacIver, R. M., and Page, C. H., *Society: An Introductory Analysis*. New York: Rinehart, 1949, pp. 238–280.

Martindale, D., *American Society*. Princeton, N.J.: Van Nostrand, 1960, pp. 268–277.

Mead, Margaret, *Male and Female: A Study of the Sexes in a Changing World*. New York: Wm. Morrow, 1949.

Murdock, G. P., *Social Structure*. New York: Macmillan, 1949, pp. 1–23.

Ogburn, W. F., *Technology and the Changing Family*. Boston: Houghton Mifflin, 1955.

Ogburn, W. F., and Tebbitts, Clark, "The Family and Its Functions," in The President's Research Committee on Social Trends, *Recent Social Trends*. New York: McGraw-Hill, 1934, Vol. I, pp. 661–708.

Parsons, T., and Bales, R. F., *Family, Socialization, and Interaction Process.* Glencoe, Ill.: Free Press, 1955.

Sumner, W. G., and Keller, A. G., *The Science of Society.* New Haven: Yale Univ. Press, 1927, Vol. III, pp. 1485–2056.

Williams, R. M., Jr., *American Society: A Sociological Interpretation.* New York: Knopf, 1960, pp. 39–86.

Winch, R. F., *The Modern Family.* New York: Holt, 1952.

Woods, Sister Francis Jerome, *The American Family System.* New York: Harper, 1959.

Yinger, J. M., "The Changing Family in a Changing Society," *Social Casework,* 40 (Oct., 1959): 419–428.

RESIDENTIAL PROPINQUITY AND MARRIAGE

Bossard, J. H. S., "Residential Propinquity as a Factor in Marriage Selection," *Am. Jour. Soc.,* 38 (Sept., 1932): 219–244.

Clarke, A. C., "An Examination of the Operation of Residential Propinquity as a Factor in Mate Selection," *Am. Soc. Rev.,* 17 (Feb., 1952): 17–22.

Davie, M. R., and Reeves, Ruby Jo, "Propinquity of Residence Before Marriage," *Am. Jour. Soc.,* 44 (Jan., 1939): 510–517.

Kennedy, Ruby Jo Reeves, "Premarital Residential Propinquity and Ethnic Endogamy," *Am. Jour. Soc.,* 48 (Jan., 1943): 580–584.

Koller, M. R., "Residential Propinquity of White Males at Marriage in Relation to Age and Occupation of Mates, Columbus, Ohio," *Am. Soc. Rev.,* 13 (Oct., 1948): 613–616.

Schnepp, G. J., and Roberts, L. A., "Residential Propinquity and Mate Selection on a Parish Basis," *Am. Jour. Soc.,* 58 (July, 1952): 45–50.

HOMOGAMOUS MATE SELECTION

Burgess, E. W., and Wallin, P., "Homogamy and Personality Characteristics," *Jour. Abn. & Soc. Psych.,* 39 (Oct., 1944): 475–481.

Burgess, E. W., and Wallin, P., "Homogamy in Social Characteristics," *Am. Jour. Soc.,* 49 (Sept., 1943): 109–124 (also see footnotes).

Heiss, J. S., "Premarital Characteristics of the Religiously Inter-Married in an Urban Area," *Am. Soc. Rev.,* 25 (Feb., 1960): 47–55.

Hollingshead, A. B., "Cultural Factors in the Selection of Mates," *Am. Soc. Rev.,* 15 (Oct., 1950): 619–627.

Kernodle, W., "Some Implications of the Homogamy-Complementary Needs Theories of Mate Selections for Sociological Research," *Soc. Forces,* 38 (Dec., 1959): 145–152.

Ktsanes, T., "Mate Selection on the Basis of Personality Type," *Am. Soc. Rev.,* 20 (Oct., 1955): 547–551.

Winch, R. F., *Mate-Selection: A Study of Complementary Needs.* New York: Harper, 1958.

Economic Institutions

Economic institutions have their roots in the elemental need of man to possess the means of physical maintenance. The physical or material necessities of the creature body must be satisfied before any of the other necessities—sexual, intellectual, aesthetic, spiritual—are even called for. As civilization advances, the physical minima increase in number and kind and become the basis of many other satisfactions. No other activities command so much time and attention or are so compulsive and omnipresent in the life of everyone. Every human being is a direct beneficiary of economic activity as a consumer; most human beings function at least to some extent as economic producers; most people, during the years of their maturity, spend more time at work—engagement in the production of economic goods or services—than in any other category of activity. In our own American society, the persons actively engaged in working for wages, who form the so-called labor force, make up more than one-third of the total population. So pervasive are economic matters in the life of mankind that several reputable non-Marxist historians, as well as those of Marxist persuasion, have interpreted all history as being primarily economically determined.

The first and basic function of economic activity is to appropriate and transform the physical environment into goods and to convert the energies and abilities of men into services, available and usable for the satisfaction of the existence needs and the contrived wants. The elemental objective is the preservation and the physical security of human life; but beyond this there are a host of other objectives which attract more and more attention as the primary one is effectively achieved. Many economists present the main function of economic activity as being the provision of utilities (the maximizing of utility); that is, providing goods and services that are useful in that they ultimately satisfy the needs and wants of the people of the society. But, in order to satisfy the wants and needs—in order to consume—it is essential that the goods and services be produced; that is, made accessible to the intermediate producers, but especially to the consumers who are the ultimate and final users.

The organization and systematization of the economic function are necessary for several reasons. First, there must be stability and the sufficiently efficient operation of the economy. This involves the organization of (1) the physical instruments and techniques (the technology) and (2) the human beings, individually and as different kinds of work groups. Second, the economy has to attend first to the basic objectives of satisfying the primary needs and wants. Third, there must be organization, including especially regulation, to assure peace and equity in economic relationships, for the economic realm is one of limited goods and unlimited wants. No other department of life presents more occasions for disorder and aggression. It is a realm in which the strong, the brutal, and the inhumane would be the "haves," and the more gentle and decent, the "have-nots." There cannot be any cooperation (even of two persons), any division of labor, any utilization of experienced principles of cause and effect or of technological procedures without organization by means of informal or formal rules and established physical and social forms and procedures. In brief, economic life must be and is institutionalized.

Almost all of the non-economic activities of a society have an economic base. Whether the activities are of an educational, health, governmental, recreational, aesthetic, even religious nature, they rest upon the economic surplus of economic goods which the economy can produce over and above the amount needed for bare existence. In general, if the economic surplus is adequate in kind and amount and properly diffused, it conduces to health, strength, and longevity; in fact, wealth, or the existing store of valued goods, and income, or the economic inflow and augmentation, are means of power easily usable to increase welfare.

At the same time, the economic order does not stand alone; it depends on and is modified by other social institutions. Furthermore, no activity of an economic nature is exclusively economic; it is always at the same time to some extent domestic, legal, ethical, political, even aesthetic, educational or religious.

I: Fundamental Facts Regarding the Operation of the Economic System

All activity, including economic activity, involves the physical-biological-psychical creatures which *in toto* constitute the stock of human beings referred to as people. One of the fundamental facts regarding people is that they have needs and wants, which rest in large part upon their value-system. Since the values of men are expansible almost without limit, the wants that the values raise are almost infinite in number and variety. Furthermore, the people determine what and how much of the physical environment and when its elements are to be economically developed and consumed.

The major aspects of the physical environment are its inorganic and organic resources, its physiographic characteristics, and its climatic features. The physical environment provides and fixes the physical and biological essentials of man's existence in the way of available and usable materials and physical and animal energies. Its climate, topography, soil, and other resources determine the size and location of human aggregations. Its space must be traversed as men move to places of greater opportunity. Its influences may be physically stimulating as well as depressing. The physical environment is more demonstrably felt among the economic institutions than in any other institutional area. Its physical conditions influence the types of industry the people can carry on, and the occupations they pursue.

Economic functions are carried on in a finite world. Scarcity is an essential, and not an accidental, feature of the economic situation. The very term "economic" carries the meaning of scarcity. The goods and services of concern in economics are not free goods, but scarce or economic goods. Moreover, the economic utilization of resources is subject to the hard economic law of diminishing returns. The situation of people with expanding and unlimited wants living in a finite world with limited and scarce resources for their satisfaction leads to the eternal necessity of choice or preference between alternative materials or services. Men register the relative importance of their different wants by the economic choices they make.

Everything economic requires some sacrifice and expenditure for it. Input is essential to output. The stark reality of costs must be faced— the destruction of physical resources, the using up of plant and instruments, expenditure of human energies, capacities, and lives, postponing or foregoing present for future satisfactions. A fundamental objective of economic activity is to keep costs below the point where they neutralize or exceed the satisfaction-gains received. None of the scarce and costly economic goods and services acquire their utilities without work. Work is the human cost, the labor cost. It is what the human beings do who are engaged in all economic activity other than the final consumption. Not all of the people of a society need to be engaged in work. The proportion that must be is determined by the interrelationship of four factors: (1) the volume of desirable and usable resources, and the degree of their availability; (2) the amount, or number of steps, of processing they require in making them consumable; (3) the state of technological development; and (4) the standard of living.[1]

All people have some technology, or non-human implements and instruments, with techniques and procedures for organizing and using the instruments. This technology rests upon experience and knowledge, discoveries and inventions. There is almost a direct and positive correlation between the efficiency of an economic system and the degree of emancipation from the dominance of the immediate environment, on the one hand, and the degree of development of the technology, on the other, as evidenced by the difference between the Eskimo and our society.

In addition, a collection of ideas, customs, mores, beliefs, and ideologies grow up about technological-economic instruments and techniques, related to their proper use, the rights and responsibilities attached to them, the status of the different types and levels of manipulators, their justification, and their place in the total social organization.

Historically, the minimal division of labor and specialization has been on the basis of age, sex, and kinship affiliation. In complex advanced societies, economic processes are infinitely divided, and there seems to be no point of maximum specialization. In such societies useful work is allocated on the basis of sex and age, intelligence, strength, skills, and dexterities. The occupations of men, the type of tasks they perform, are infinitely divided and specialized on the basis of their special functions, the education and training required, and their social consequences. There is division and specialization by the stages of production, by steps in the assembly line in mass production, by agencies in the marketing processes, by territory or region on the basis of physiographic and demographic factors.

There must be definite assignment of power over economic things and acts by the society. This is what the *property institutions* of a society do. The first forms of property are lost in the mists of antiquity, but something existed in the way of systematic property arrangements at an early time, for as soon as there are two or more human beings, interested in their own self-preservation, in an environment of scarce and costly things, there will be some more or less definite agreement regarding the control of these valued items. Property is the institutionally defined, established, and enforced right or claim to individual or group belongings; or, conversely, it is the socially approved exclusion of individuals or social units from the use or enjoyments of scarcities except under the specific conditions of control vested in the property holders.

---

[1] Suggested in large part by G. A. Lundberg, C. C. Schrag, and O. N. Larsen, *Sociology*. New York: Harper, 1954, p. 612.

The essence of property lies in the fact that most things cannot be used unless some sort of monopoly exists. Two tribes cannot be very successful if they hunt in the same territory; two farmers cannot carry on cultivation on the same land; two families cannot peacefully occupy the same dwelling; two persons cannot properly use the same tools or ornaments; two corporations cannot use the same raw materials, plant, equipment, and bank account. When this monopoly exists, the explosive tendencies of quarreling, maneuvering, and fighting for things are reduced to a minimum, and group preservation is assured in larger measure.

Property is always a social fact. It is not an entity in itself. It consists, not of the useful tangibles and intangibles owned, but of the societally instituted bundle of rights governing their utilization. The power of society makes the right; there is no absolute claim.

Theft, abuse, and misappropriation of property have always had to be prohibited and punished. For this reason the state has been involved ever since it existed. What is property is ordinarily defined in the law of the community; property rights are ultimately interpreted, granted, and restricted by government; penalties for the violations of these rights are stated in the law; and violators are punished by the government. Hence, property is an economico-political institution, strictly speaking.

There are various types and forms of property. The two main types are private and public. In the case of private property, the rights are vested in individuals and in non-political groups such as the family or kinship unit, fraternal organizations, churches, cooperatives, partnerships, and corporations, which are acting in their own interest. In the case of public property, the rights are held by public (political) bodies such as the municipality, the county, the state, or the nation, and are administered by bureaucratic functionaries and organizations acting as agents of the political community.[2]

The forms of property, like those of other institutions, are exceedingly irregular and variable. There can be no hard and fast generalizations. Personal, joint, collective, corporate, and communal (public or state) ownership in different things or the same things may exist at the same time in a given society. The ratio of the forms to each other may differ greatly at different stages of development of the society. Americans, for example, once had other human beings as property and may in the not too distant future have other parts of the solar system as property. Social adjustments, especially those coming with techno-

[2] It is obvious that there is a large amount of public property in communistic and other totalitarian communities. It is equally obvious that there is much private, especially personal, property in predominantly communistic societies, and much publicly owned and operated property in the most individualistic countries.

logical developments, bring into existence possessions unknown to previous ages, and necessitate different uses of older forms.

Another distinction of special importance in economic organization is that between productive property, or the basic materials and instruments used for productive purposes, and consumption goods, or the produced materials intended for, and available for, final use, and hence utilitarian destruction by the members of the community.

In connection with property, it should be pointed out that *wealth* refers to the existent, accumulated store of all kinds of property possessed by an individual or a social unit, and that *income* is the inflow of property and claims to property accruing during a specific period of time.[3]

Contract, like property, is one of the central institutions of a society. It rests upon the fact that a large and important number of the relationships between individuals, between social units, and between individuals and groups involve agreements as to the reciprocal behavior of the parties. *Contract* is an institution that standardizes, sanctions, and, with the assistance of politico-legal institutions, enforces agreements, while *a* contract is essentially an agreement between two or more parties to behave in a certain specific way for a specified length of time in the future. In the economic realm, contract is imperative in the disposition and use of property in all its various forms—real estate, chattels, services, and skills. As in the maintenance of property, so the state, as an expression of the people's will, through its legislation, establishes or underwrites most of the important types of contract, and through its courts and law-enforcing agents, is the final arbiter in their interpretation and enforcement.

Very little economic activity is carried on for the sheer love of it. The remuneration of the different types of contributory elements is the essence of so-called distribution in an economic system. In very simple societies which satisfy their needs and wants by hunting, fishing, or even rudimentary agriculture, the remuneration takes the form of directly acquired products available for immediate consumption. In complex societies, the suppliers of land and other more or less durable instruments of production are rewarded in the form of rent; the suppliers of physical capacities at various levels of skill receive wages; those who provide managerial, professional, and highly specialized technical and research services receive salaries and fees; those who supply the entrepreneurial or risk-taking services receive profits; and those who save and invest, and thus provide capital funds, receive in-

[3] For sociological treatments of property institutions, see: K. Davis, *Human Society*. New York: Macmillan, 1949, pp. 453–470. R. M. Williams, Jr., *American Society: A Sociological Interpretation*. New York: Knopf, 1960, pp. 187–190.

terest, dividends, and capital gains; government is remunerated in the form of taxes. The rewards, other than those to the government, have ranged from mere subsistence of forced workers to large and elaborate ones of both a physical and social nature to call forth and compensate very special and rare abilities, and have consisted of such tangibles as goods, services, and money, and of such intangibles as special privileges, social distinction, reputation, prestige, and social power. In general, as far as the people as individuals and households are concerned, economic remuneration is the means whereby they acquire their consumption goods and services; as far as the society as an economy is concerned, remuneration *in toto* during any given period of time is the income or the flow of proceeds of its processes of production.

II: The Major Economic Functions

Most economists resolve the economic functions into two general categories of production and consumption. The nature of these functions, their place in economic organization, and the processes that are involved need to be specifically and comprehensively discussed.

PRODUCTION

Production is used in a broad way to include all economic activity short of consumption itself. It is thought of as that almost all-encompassing complex of processes whereby the resources of nature are given their final form and made available at the appropriate places and times for final consumption. For purposes of more specific analysis, production can be considered from the point of view, first, of the basic factors involved in it and, second, of its major subfunctions.

THE FACTORS OF PRODUCTION. The basic factors of production, significant at all levels, are land, labor, capital, and management.

Land. Land, as the economist uses the term, refers to much more than the land surface of the earth in terms of its forms, physical characteristics, and extent. The economist means all of man's physical setting that he uses, all that exists irrespective of man himself, all of the natural resources; for example, farm land, grazing land, mineral deposits of all kinds, forests, rivers, lakes, oceans, the fish in the sea, and the wild life of the forest and plain.

Labor. Some form of labor, that is, expenditure of human energy, is involved in all economic activity. The term refers to both performance and to the people who perform. The whole body of productive workers of a society is known as the labor force. Historically, mankind has had such labor systems as slavery, forced labor, and free labor.

Capital. The term in its most general connotation refers to all that man has wrested from nature through the application of labor regardless of whether it is still in intermediate stages of transformation or in form for final consumption. More refined analysis distinguishes between production capital and consumption capital. Production capital consists of such things as factories and commercial buildings, machines, tools, and other equipment, and patented techniques that are used to produce other goods, development funds (used, for example, for research and planning), and stores of partly processed goods on hand or under contract awaiting further stages of production. Consumption capital consists of inventories of goods that are ready for consumers but still owned by final producers, such as canned goods on a grocer's shelves.

Capital is always a product of labor; it is also essentially a result of human foresight and sacrifice. Its use is always for the future. Its accumulation requires thrift and self-denial on the part of individuals, groups, or the community or society as a whole. It requires that a choice be made between present satisfactions as against those (possibly superior ones) to be expected in the future. It develops by means of saving, that is, abstaining from immediate use or consumption of goods and services, and by investment, that is, putting to work in economically productive activities the materials and funds saved so that these activities can be maintained or extended and improved. Those who furnish the capital for productive purposes are in the last analysis those who furnish the money to operate industry; namely, the stockholders, bondholders, and financiers.

Management. Management or enterprise or entrepreneurship, the fourth factor of production, is really a part of labor, but because it occupies a position of unique importance, it is treated separately. It exists in some degree in every productive enterprise in every economy because production must be organized, and management is the organizing element. It involves managing what the firm owns and rents, acquiring raw and intermediate materials, determining what is to be made, how it will be made, and where and when it will be sold (marketing the product); it involves also policy-making, supervision and administration, risk-taking, contract-making, decision-making, labor relationships; it concerns itself with devising, programming, and directing all of the activities of the productive establishment, and planning for the future.

THE FUNCTIONS OF PRODUCTION. Production as a complex of functions will be examined from the point of view of the two somewhat distinctive, though inseparable and simultaneously occurring, major subfunctions which will be referred to here as extraction-transformation and exchange-distribution.

Extractive-transformative functions. These consist of the systematic procedures and activities whereby the things that will satisfy the maximum number of human wants of the society are acquired from nature and then, since most of these are unusable in their natural state, removed from nature, combined, reformed into useful shapes and substances, quality utilities added, and made available in sufficient quantity by the appropriate humanly devised and engineered technological processes; in brief, they are the addition of quantitative form and qualitative utilities. These activities are referred to in a general way as industry, and may be further subdivided.

(1) Extractive industry consists of the activities whereby essential materials are extracted or gathered from the store of undeveloped natural resources, such as agriculture, forestry, fishing, and mining. Agriculture, the basic extractive industry, is sometimes referred to as primary industry because it is the first industrial essential upon which all other economic activity, including other extractive industry, depends.

(2) Processing or converting industry takes at least three forms: first, manufacturing, or putting the raw materials through a succession of transforming procedures which enhance their final consumption values by making them more useful in form and quality and function, for example, turning clay into bricks (goods in the various stages of processing between raw materials and final consumption form are referred to as intermediate goods); second, power development, or converting geophysical energies or power potential, such as controlled falling water; third, using materials such as wood, stone, metal in various stages of processing in construction. The processing or converting industries are sometimes referred to as secondary production.

(3) Service activity or servicing is transforming human energies, abilities, and skills into services and providing the essential quantities and qualities of services. For the most part, it includes scarce, nonmaterial satisfactions that have to be worked for and paid for; specifically, personal services such as barbering, repair services such as TV repair, commercial services such as secretarial work, professional services such as dentistry, and entertainment and amusement services. This provision of services is sometimes referred to as tertiary production.

Exchange-distribution functions. These functions have as their objective the creation, not of form and quality utilities as in extraction-transformation, but of place, time, and possession utilities. They involve much more than getting the created things or services from the producer to the consumer. They are concerned with the procedures and instruments whereby the materials in various stages of processing are made available at the place of further processing or of final consumption, at the time for the next step in processing or for consumption. These processes also involve changes of possession. For example, raw materials are sold, or transferred to, and bought by, a parts manufacturer, the parts manufacturer sells to an assembling plant, the assembling plant sells or transfers to jobbers, and jobbers to retailers. Also, manufacturers or other processing or exchanging firms transfer their income (property in-flow) to the individuals and groups that have contributed to the creation of the output, such as the suppliers of raw and partly processed materials, the owners of land and equipment used, the suppliers of labor in all its forms, and the suppliers of capital funds. The creation of these place, time, and possession utilities can be generalized as commerce.

The exchange-distribution functions are due to certain unavoidable conditions. The different regions of a country or of the world differ greatly as to their natural resources and as to the natural and demographic facilities for the processing of these resources. To further process these materials, therefore, requires that they be transferred to the places and firms where the next step in adding form and quality utilities is to take place. Exchange is also a functional counterpart of division of labor and specialization in that essential articles or services are a matter of certain proficiencies and skills among the human performers which are not universal; different steps in the sequential processing are carried out, or different parts of a product are provided, by different firms. The processed goods are often relayed to the final consumer by means of middle men. The factors or essential elements of production fall into distinctly different categories and are differently remunerated.

The term distribution is used in general to refer to the complex of processes whereby the claims of the persons and groups which have produced things and services are satisfied. It is also used more specifically at least in two senses.

First, it may mean the transfer of all finished goods and ready services which consumers want from the producers to the consumers as efficiently as possible by means of the middle men, or shippers, jobbers, wholesalers, and retailers. Second, it may mean the division and transfer of the proceeds of organized economic activity to the various categories of contributors to the productive processes in the form of the sums paid for raw or partly processed materials, the rent paid to owners of land and rented equipment used in the transformation and exchange processes, wages, salaries, and fees paid to the labor force involved, interest and dividends paid to the suppliers of capital funds, profits taken by successful risk-takers, fares and tariffs paid to transporters, the insurance premiums paid to firms and public bodies carrying fire, accident, unemployment and other risks, and taxes paid to public bodies for protective, regulative, and welfare functions performed. This latter type of distribution rests upon the fact, recognized in all societies, that part of the total product must be directly allocated to each type of participant in the over-all economic process. It is also recognized that provision must be made for the non-producers of the society: children, the aged, the sick and crippled, the mentally incompetent.

Exchange, as well as transformation, institutions have existed in some form among the simplest societies. They grew out of the fact that acquisition of goods from other peoples by wars, raids, robberies, and piracy was a tremendously expensive, hazardous, and disorganizing procedure. To avoid hostilities, presents were given; sometimes there was a mutual exchange. But most of these methods of acquisition of things from others either caused suspicion and fear and were an incitement to retaliation, as they still are, or they resulted in the receipt of things not wanted. So everywhere various methods were developed among contiguous or accessible peoples to provide opportunities for peaceful and recurrent or even continuous exchange. One form among primitives was peaceful access; that is, access of aliens to materials geographically limited as to distribution, such as natural deposits of flint, salt, or raw copper. Other early forms were silent trade, dumb barter, and deposit barter, the general principles of these being that the articles for exchange were put in a certain well-known and appointed place—a "market place"—where security from attack was assured; persons from other tribes or areas then came and took these and put other articles of approximately equal value in their stead. As societies became more complex, more highly organized exchange institutions were developed.

The market system is the basic institutionalization of exchange and distribution in all complex societies. It is somewhat different as to instruments, procedures, and regulations in the relatively free economy of a free society compared with the controlled or managed economy of a totalitarian country. We will be concerned more particularly with the market system of a free society, though some of the principles and items mentioned are of universal significance and application. The fundamental functions in market operations are to meet demands for goods and services with supplies, adequate in amount and quality, available at the right time and place at a price that the consumer can and is willing to pay. This is the principle of supply and demand in the market. Among the major marketing problems are (1) determining what the consumers want in the way of goods and services and how much, when, and where they want them; (2) determining whether total costs can be met, plus a profit, by the prices purchasers will find it possible to pay; (3) informing the consumers of what is being produced and when and where it can be obtained; (4) getting the goods to intermediate producers and final consumers.

Buying and selling, according to explicit or implicit contract, are essential exchange operations, not only with respect to the final product, but for every category of elements entering into the entire series of processing and exchange operations. There are thus actually a number of markets or buying and selling subsystems: not only the market for consumers' goods, but also the market for raw and partly processed materials, the labor market, and the capital funds or money market.

The so-called price system is an aspect of buying and selling operations. By this is meant that everything that is bought and sold is priced in monetary terms. Costs of all sorts in producing goods and services are reckoned and stated in terms of amounts of money; the sale value of goods and services is set in terms of a specific amount of money, an amount necessary to buy the commodity or service. People indicate what they want and can afford by the price they are willing to pay. In general, all production is controlled by prices as they enter into costs and as they relate to sales. A special advantage of the price system in a complex society is that it obviates the necessity of intimate social relations in the exchange process; it tends to standardize exchange relations.

After the commodity has been finally processed, its marketing career between its purchase from the manufacturer and its sale to the final consumer involves such further essential functions as transportation, storage, standardizing, packaging, advertising, displaying, and financing.

The marketing system contains a number of institutionalized mechanisms and other facilitating devices essential to its operation:

(1) Communication, or language, writing, and all of the technological means of extending the range of these in space and time.

(2) Weights and Measures. Almost every aspect of societal life requires a systematization and standardization of weights and measures: such a system is of special significance in economic production. There must be standard weight units as a means of designating quantities of things (pounds, tons, quarts, bushels). There must be units of measurements to indicate degrees of physical conditions (for example, of temperature, light, humidity, and hardness); to determine distance and extent of space (feet or miles) as these relate, for example, to transportation of things and men and to the arrangement of equipment and men; and to determine area of space (acres, square miles, cubic feet) as these relate, for example, to land, and to the capacity of buildings and other equipment. There must be established units of time measurement (seconds, minutes, hours, weeks, months, years) as a means of

synchronizing and coordinating the actions of individuals and groups, designating duration and sequence of processes,[4] and otherwise organizing operations in intervals and extent of time.

(3) Arithmetic and Accounting. There must be arithmetic—the system of numerical computation—as a means of reckoning all weights and measures; and an accounting system as a means of recording various statistical aspects of economic transactions, especially with respect to the costs, buying, and selling, and of determining debits and credits.

(4) Transportation Systems. Transportation systems, operating on water, land, and in the air, are essential in all exchange activity, since they are the means of moving goods to those who are to provide the next increments of form utility and the means of moving finished goods to the final consumers. Transportation thus facilitates exchange between country and city; the raw materials move to city industries and consumers, and city-produced consumption goods (tools, machinery, processed foods, clothing) move to the country. Transportation also is involved in market-to-market, region-to-region, and nation-to-nation exchange. It is also the means of getting persons and families to the places where they have the greatest economic usefulness.[5] Transportation has also always been a basic factor in the creation of time utility; that is, having things and persons at the most advantageous place at the most advantageous time. This aspect is ever more important in modern societies where "time is money."

(5) Produce Exchanges. There are the established and appropriately located trading places, with their codes and rules, their accepted usages, their special functionaries and organizational forms where important raw materials, but also to some extent intermediate and final consumers' goods, are most expeditiously bought and sold. These exist as local, regional, national, and even international exchange agencies. Noteworthy among those operating on a large scale are the grain exchanges (for example, at Chicago and Winnipeg), the livestock exchanges (for example, at Omaha and Kansas City), the cotton exchanges, the minerals and metals exchanges, the Furniture Mart (Chicago), and boards of trade.

(6) Monetary-Credit System. Money is anything that is generally accepted in a given trading area in payment for goods and services (beads, coins, pieces of paper). Money came into existence as a means of obviating the various difficulties incidental to barter, such as the necessity of having two parties each with goods precisely suitable to the other in kind, quality, and quantity, and the difficulty of exchanging

---

[4] Cf., J. O. Hertzler, *Society in Action: A Study of Basic Social Processes.* New York: Dryden, 1954, pp. 44–48.

[5] Cf. H. W. Gilmore, *Transportation and the Growth of Cities.* Glencoe, Ill.: Free Press, 1953.

indivisible things like livestock for small quantities of divisible goods. Its chief functions everywhere are to serve as a convenient circulating medium of exchange and as a measure of value (price), a common denominator of value (*everything* can have a monetary value), and a store of value. Thus money is generally accepted in exchange for things and services, and it is a means of measuring the value of things, of communicating in standard quantitive terms about the economic value of things, and in keeping accounting records that state the value of inventories, assets, and equipment. Money goes through various stages of development until it consists of a commodity that has reasonably stable value, ready portability, durability, and divisibility without the parts losing their proportionate value—usually the more precious and scarce metals. Token money, ordinarily paper that stands for metal, whose currency value is usually guaranteed by some political body, also made its appearance surprisingly early. Money makes exchange flexible, and ownership of many economic items, fluid and transferable. Developments of money are checks and drafts, which are highly institutionalized substitutes for the purposes of avoiding the transportation of large quantities of metallic or token money, and for expediting the exchange of values across space. Since checks and drafts are valid only between specific parties, they also discourage the theft of money. Money, in its various forms, creates greater freedom for both buyers and sellers of goods and services; it makes possible other institutions, such as credit, banks, foreign trade facilities, and stock exchanges.

Credit is the highly specialized means of deferring payment and expediting commercial transactions by accounting methods in terms of money as a standard of value but without its actual use as physical medium. When one has a commercial credit with another person or firm, one is entitled to receive from them at some future time, according to the terms of the contract, money or goods or other financial exchange power. In a credit transaction there is always the expectation of future payment of property transferred. Credit transactions take place by means of credit instruments, such as stocks and bonds, bills of exchange, time notes, and book accounts. The deferred, or future, payment aspect of credit is brought out by the facts that a bond entitles the owner to payment at some specified future time, a savings account can be converted into future purchasing power, and an annuity policy entitles the holder to payments from the insurance company when he reaches old age.

(7) The Banking System and Stock Exchanges. Banks of some sort appeared at a relatively early stage in commercial development. Banks provide facilities for entrusting things of value to others for safekeeping or for the purpose of borrowing other things upon the security of things deposited. As we know them, banks are the various institutional forms

of depository for money and credit instruments, and for carrying on financial and credit transactions for industry, commerce, and the public at large. More specifically, a banking system such as ours conducts such functions as collecting and guaranteeing the savings of the community, acting as the depository for funds to be expended by means of checks and drafts, and acting as the agent for accounts (the clearing house service); providing an economical source of capital funds (loans) for business men and others; rationing money funds among business men and other borrowers, partly on the basis of risks involved; selling stocks and bonds, both those currently on the market, and in the case of some larger banks and trust companies, new issues, thus acting as agents in providing funds for new ventures or the expansion of existing firms; regulating the amount of money in use by expanding and contracting short-term credit for industry and commerce; and providing foreign currency exchange. In regulating credit, banks play an important part in meeting the problems of economic instability (depression-inflation) in a complex economy.

Stock exchanges—in some respects the counterpart in the money market of produce exchanges in the commodity market—are highly organized market places, with their established regulations and usages, in which stocks and bonds of corporations are bought and sold.

CONSUMPTION

The whole complex of productive functions is conducted solely in order that the other major block of economic functions, the consumption functions, can be carried on. Consumption is, in fact, the final economic act as far as the utilization of all economic goods and services is concerned. Although all producers are also consumers and most consumers are also producers in some degree, not all are so at any given moment; what some consume at a given time depends on their own past productive efforts or those of others past (ancestors) or present who have been acting productively for them. In view of the fact that, of necessity, the dominant preoccupation of every society—even the least materialistic—is consumption, it is curious that so much less attention has been paid to it than to production by the social scientists.

Societally, the family is the major consumption unit. Nevertheless, although consumption is so much an individual or family affair, and although individual and group tastes, interests, and susceptibilities are reflected in every consumption act, consumption is highly organized, even institutionalized. People consume on the basis of physical determinants, of regional and group values and norms, of social class or ethnic group patterns, and as the result of pressures and influences exercised deliberately by interested organizations.

Consumption of economic goods and services and conditions cannot be, and is not, unlimited. There are several reasons for this. First, some of the want-satisfying goods, services, and conditions are in limited supply as to quantity or quality; all economic good things are scarce, as we have noted. Second, people do not have unlimited command over, or unlimited ability to acquire, available goods and services. Third, people do not have infinite ability to enjoy any particular possible satisfaction; they are subject to the principle of satiety; the needs and wants for which people seek satisfaction have different degrees of intensity at different times; there is the principle of diminishing returns of satisfaction in enjoyment along any given line, and the tendency, facilities permitting, to switch to alternatives. Finally, very few want all sorts of goods and services; there is great diversity among individuals, families, and different groups and categories of population in the types and degrees of satisfactions sought. Therefore, people as consumers are always evaluating available things, services, purchasable conditions, weighing the satisfactions to be derived from them, and making choices among them. No person, no group, no society can consume everything, and no one wants unlimited amounts of *any*thing.

Consumption is not an end in itself, but rather a means toward other ends. Nor is consumption a simple act or set of acts. The reasons for what and why people consume range from the necessity of satisfying elemental needs relating to bare biological existence to the desire to enjoy the most refined sociocultural satisfactions and to achieve, by consumption, highly valued social and cultural ends. People in complex societies spend their wealth and income for satisfactions at various levels.

There is consumption for the sustenance of life itself, requiring at least a minimum of food, clothing, and shelter. These needs, of course, are elaborated in modern societies, especially with respect to culturally established qualities of satisfaction sought. Closely related to these are health satisfactions—the preservation of physical and mental health, and the treatment and avoidance of disease, accident, and infirmity—involving the consumption of medical care provided by doctors, dentists, other practitioners, clinics and hospitals, and the use of all sorts of pharmaceuticals.

There is consumption for variety and new experience, in the form of recreation, amusement, and travel.

There is consumption for preparation for anticipated future expenditure (some by the insurance principle), such as expenditures for health emergencies (possible illness, need of surgery), for higher education of children, for old age and retirement, for special vacations or tours (a Caribbean cruise, a trip to Europe).

There is consumption as a means of status symbolization.[6] This function of consumption is less obvious than the others. It grows from the fact that all societies have some degree of stratification. It seems that all societies—ancient and modern, democratic and totalitarian, static and dynamic, folk-agrarian and industrial-urban—have used types of goods (clothing, home and residential district, equipage, ornaments and decorations) as an objective means of indicating particular social status and as a way of distinguishing people of different status from each other. In fact, the particular item of consumption could almost be considered an index of particular social status (the plumed hat, the monocle, the Rolls Royce, the castle, the house at Bar Harbor, holidays at Palm Springs as against Coney Island, the super-dry martini). Furthermore, individuals, families, and various categories of the population have often been judged by the goods and services with which they surrounded themselves. Some more or less closed-class societies of the past actually had sumptuary (consumption) laws, one effect of which was to set and fix particular consumption forms for each of the different strata of the population.

There are certain types of fundamental factors which account for the variations in consumption among different societies, and among different individuals, families, and categories within societies, and which also have the effect of setting certain bounds in consumption among the different societies and segments of societies.

The wealth of the individual, family, or segment, or total society is a factor. The poor, whether individuals or societies, are distinctly limited as to what and how much they can consume.

Current income accruing from the earnings similarly determines consumption. Fluctuations of prices of things purchased, with wealth and income remaining the same (in monetary units), set corresponding limits to consumption. For example, if prices go up, a family will have to spend more and actually acquire less for consumption, as long as income is the same. Taxes, which must be deducted from income, also affect expenditures.

The region in which the individuals and families live, as compared with other regions, determine what goods and services are available for consumption. Regions vary also as to consumption values and vogues.

Size and age of family are important. Large families spend more on food and clothing and less on other items than smaller families with the same income. Families consisting of old people consume very differently from families with young children.

The standard of living, or what is striven for within the possible, is a determinant in the case of societies and also of individuals, families,

---

[6] The term is Parsons'. Cf. Parsons and Smelser, *op. cit.*, p. 235.

and categories within different societies. In a given society the standards of consumption rest in a large part upon the level of technological-economic development. Within a society they will be, in considerable part, determined by such factors as socio-economic class, educational level and kind of education received, ethnicity, and sometimes religious group affiliation. For example, some ethnic groups have tabooed foods, Seventh Day Adventists eat no meat, and Mormons avoid coffee and tea.

There is no pure play of economic forces upon consumers and no entirely free play of personal, family, or other group desires. Most consumption occurs according to institutionalized patterns; the choices made reflect social-psychological uniformizing influences and, along some lines, are confined within a tolerated range established by governmental regulations.

There is, of course, the fundamental fact that what people *can* consume uniformly and in kind and volume is determined by their technology and economy, and that the things and services they set store by are for the most part given them by their general culture.

Among individuals there may be a high degree of routinization and uniformity along at least some consumption lines because of a combination of habit, lethargy, and apathy. People persist in certain consumption ways as long as circumstances permit them; for example, adhering to pancakes for breakfast every morning. Most uniformity, however, is owing to institutional factors and social-psychological influences.

The folkways, mores, customs, etiquette forms, and conventions function as cultural agencies in every established area of social life which produce widespread uniformity of consumption.

The psychological currents of fads and fashions function imperiously for many sections of the population producing widespread, though temporary, uniformities in some areas of consumption, notably foods, dress, automobiles, dwelling-houses, and architecture. At their height, fads and fashions become a requirement of action for many people lest they appear uncouth or unsophisticated. Few can stand apart when "everybody's doing it."

Deliberately induced uniformity and conformity by producers is the result of highly organized, adroitly manipulated, and successful efforts at consumer control by means of advertising and sales promotion. Individuals and families are ingeniously urged, cajoled, threatened, promised, and enticed to buy particular models of things.

The major portion of what is consumed in modern societies is mass-produced rather than custom-produced, and produced for a nation-wide (or even world-wide) mass market rather than a localized market. Mass-produced things, by the nature of the processes involved, must be highly standardized. Standardized consumables mean widespread uniformity of consumption, and standard brands mean standardized consumers.

Laws—local, state, national—regulate various aspects of consumption. There are laws prohibiting the adulteration of foods, drugs, cosmetics (The Pure Food and Drug acts) and regulating the marketing of foods and the sanitary conditions under which foods and personal services are dispensed. There are laws prohibiting misleading advertising; laws producing some censorship of literature, motion pictures, and theatrical performances; building ordinances governing the construction and operation of buildings. Although these types of regulation exist in order to safeguard the consumers, they have the effect of producing certain qualitative uniformities in consumption.

III: Special Characteristics of the American Economic System

Many observers of our society from other countries conclude that economic institutions are the most conspicuous feature of our social organization. We are said to be a business civilization, devoting our vast physical resources and the largest part of our human energies to production on a massive scale, having business or market conditions and commerce as our dominant preoccupation, and evidencing lavish consumption—consumption on a scale neither possible nor demonstrable among any other contemporary people.

Our economy epitomizes the changes largely due to technological developments that have been occurring in the economic life of Western peoples in recent times, especially during the present century.

The characteristics of our economy stand out sharply when noted in contrast to the simpler peasant and mediaeval economies from which it has descended, and which still prevail in greater or lesser degree in much of the world today. The chief productive activities were agriculture and handicrafts. The technology was relatively simple, with very little use of machinery, and the tools used were mostly hand tools. There was little or no allocation of resources to technology as such. The power used was that provided by human beings, domesticated animals, and simply harnessed wind and water power. The productive activity was conducted mainly in small and simply organized social units, particularly the family or kinship group, though guilds also played an important part in some cultures. The production processes lacked a high degree of division of labor and specialization, and there was very little differentiation of function; there were relatively few occupations, and these were mainly confined to the handicrafts. Entrepreneurial functions were simple and limited. The personnel was often not clearly separable as to function, the functions of entrepreneur, workman, organizing manager, and provider of capital goods being combined in one. Exchange was carried on by barter or simple monetary operations. The market system was simple, the extent of the markets limited on the whole, and the price system usually rudimentary. A system of cash rewards did not necessarily exist. The producer and consumer were often known to each other. There was only slight attention paid to the accumulation of capital goods, since most of what was produced was used for consumption; there was no constantly expanding market for capital.[7]

In addition to having the characteristics to be noted below, our economy as a whole is said to be capitalistic (particularly private capitalism), competitive, a matter of free enterprise with private management, involving a market-price system based on supply and demand, and oriented around unrestricted profit. It is all this to a considerable extent, but not exclusively. Actually, it is a highly complex mixed system, involving some elements of many different types of systems, including private capitalism and socialism, competition and monopoly, free enterprise and highly managed enterprise, flexible and controlled prices, and other odd economic bed fellows.[8]

Our economy, in fact, almost every aspect of our physical and social life, rests upon complex and highly developed technology. Especially noteworthy is the wide use of machines in every type of economic activity. We use machines and mechanical power to a greater extent than any economic system in history. Machines are a major earmark of our civilization. It can be said with considerable certitude that in an economy like ours, the major determinant in economic activity is *not* the physical environment correlated with human strength or even skill, but technology. Along with the mechanization goes the tremendous use of mechanical power to energize the machines—power derived from coal, developing steam power and electricity, hydro-electricity, petroleum, and natural gas, and soon atomic fission. The United States uses twice as much energy per citizen as any other country.

This increasing command and development of technology has several significant effects. First, it results in a great amount of capital equipment. Second, we are committed to an ever expanding and ever diversifying technology. Third, the new developments in technology bring all sorts of economic changes. For example, the technological developments that made possible machine industries such as mining

---

[7] Cf. Raymond Firth, *Elements of Social Organization*. New York: Phil. Lib., 1951, pp. 135–136.

[8] Cf. P. C. Kelley, *Consumer Economics*. Homewood, Ill.: Richard D. Irwin, Inc., 1953, p. 11.

led to the industrial as distinct from the craft unions. Technological changes usually require reorganization of production, for example with respect to division of labor, the nature and operation of the machines and processes, and employer-labor relations. They usually bring changes in the occupational structure, add to the leisure time of the working people, and bring changes in the consumption patterns of themselves and their families. Some of the technological developments may have the effect of making possible more surpluses to exchange over wider areas. As applied to media of mass communication, the technological developments can be used to influence and persuade people to change their consumption habits.

SIGNIFICANT ASPECTS OF OUR PRODUCTION

Technological development and economic conditions and social changes which have come with it have given the production systems of modern societies, including our own, certain characteristics. Ours is an economy of mass production, the essence of which is the factory system and quite the reverse of production by the use of tools and simple, low-powered machines in the home or small shop. In the factory system we have huge productive units, using highly developed technology and functioning by means of the assembly line or production line. The operations are sequential series, minutely divided and specialized. The instruments are durable, expensive, often large and complicated, driven by mechanical power, and increasingly based on automation. The labor does not work on materials with tools to any great extent, but provides skill for tending the machines and conducting other specialized processes of a technical, inventive, supervisory, coordinative, or clerical nature. For the most part, the workers in the factory are acting together, not on the basis of any understanding of the total productive process in which they are involved or on an understanding of one another's functions, but as parts of a huge mechanism deliberately organized for coordinated action. Obviously, in mass production, the instruments, the procedures, the tasks of labor, and the products are highly standardized, and, along with the personnel, must be under united control and "under one roof."

The assembly line type of operation provides several economies and other advantageous effects. It means a great saving of time and effort on the part of the human agents. It means an efficient use of the expensive machines since most of them are in continuous operation. There is minimum movement of materials from process to process and machine to machine. Hence, there is a vast increase in the volume of product per man hour, and if these principles of organization are effectively observed, a great increase of output per dollar of capital investment. In fact, there has to be a high volume of output to justify mass operation; operations have to be big and the factory or plant large (short of suffering giantism) if the huge, fixed investment in land, buildings, and machinery is to be profitable. The farther automation is carried, the greater becomes the possibility and probably the necessity of massing.

Mass production results in several other massings of significance. There must be a massing of labor near the factories. There is also the likelihood of the massing of factories in the form of parts plants producing for nearby assembly plants, and the development of chains of factories each of which conducts one or several intermediate stages of the transformation processes. Finally, there is also the tendency not only to mass by industry, but also for complementary, interdependent, and satellite industries and commercial and service activities to concentrate ecologically, notably the manufacturing belt of northeastern United States and of the Great Lakes region. There is what amounts to a fundamental symbiotic relationship of all different types and levels of productive facilities that require massing.

A second significant aspect of our system of production need only be alluded to; that is, the fact that it is infinitely complex and its multitudinous parts and processes are intricately interdependent functionally. It is a huge network of diverse subsystems and parts and processes of subsystems. The effects of changes in any one major portion or segment of the economy, for example a strike in the steel industry or the automobile industry or in transportation, may have immediate and complex repercussions in many other parts of the system. Hence, in spite of its massiveness—like many highly complex mechanisms—it is at the same time sensitive to disequilibrating influences.

A third distinctive characteristic of our production system is that it is not conducted as an end in itself, or for the fun of it, or necessarily to produce useful things and services, but for the sake of making a profit. Through most of human history, production was rather simple, and productive efforts were devoted exclusively to producing materials for direct and immediate use. But in a mainly competitive, capitalistic, and technological economy like ours, production is a matter of many, vast, complex factors, all of which incur risks. Consequently, if production is to continue, the operations must produce something over and above immediate input as an inducement for these various contributors— firms, investors, workers, organizers, speculators—to continue their contributions. Profit also has to be made at every stage of production. As far as the productive system itself is concerned, it produces the most useful or desirable things and services because they are most likely to produce a profit. The results of production operations are measured frequently, objectively, and fairly accurately through the profit and loss statements. Thus profit is looked upon, not only as a necessary reward for all of the participants, but for what is equally important; namely, the fact that a surplus is the basis of all expansion and improvement. Unless any productive system, whether democratic-capitalistic or totalitarian-socialistic, produces something over and above costs; it is unavoidably static; and if it operates at a loss continually, it will retrogress.

Another significant feature of our productive system is that it is confined more and more to secondary and tertiary production. This is evidenced, for example, in the decline of the proportion of the labor force devoting itself to extractive industry in our country compared with a century ago. The U.S. Census Bureau indicates that in 1950 less than 14 per cent—and reported to be down to 9.5 per cent in 1957—of our labor force was employed in agriculture, forestry, fishing and mining. All of the rest, except for 1.5 per cent not reported, were engaged in manufacturing (almost 26 per cent); wholesale and retail trade (almost 19 per cent); professional and related services; transportation, communication and public utilities; personal services; construction; finance, insurance, and real estate; public administration; business and repair services; and entertainment and recreation services. Whereas three out of every four workers were producing physical goods by way of extractive industry and manufacturing, especially the former, in 1870, in 1950 over half were engaged in producing services for the economy in retail and wholesale trade, in business, personal, recreational, and governmental services; in transportation, communication, and other public utilities.

A final characteristic of our production to be noted is that mass manufacturing, if it is to be a continuous and prevailing aspect of an economy, requires a parallel mass distribution of its great volume of products. Our economy has its mass-distributing agencies. The great industrial corporations have their own related distribution systems, such as the chain of stores operated by the Goodyear and the Firestone corporations to distribute their rubber and automotive and other products. Some of the great corporations have franchise retail outlets, such as the local agencies under the General Electric franchise distributing General Electric appliances, the automobile agencies selling Ford or General Motors automobiles, or the drug stores selling McKesson-Robbins or Rexall products. Especially ubiquitous are the great chain store systems distributing foods (Safeway, Kroger, A & P), drugs (Walgreen), and automobile parts (Western Auto). Notable also are the great mail order firms, such as Sears Roebuck and Montgomery Ward. Another aspect of mass distribution is mass advertising, both as a means of informing people as to what is available for consumption and as a means of motivating them to purchase.

Finally, salesmanship and merchandising have been developed as high commercial arts. The manipulators of these arts, like the advertisers, endeavor to create new wants, and then by their displays of wares, their seductive packaging, and their flattery and promises entice and persuade the public to purchase more and more. The expert on selling tells those that he is instructing in his art that Americans are not needy people; hence, they must be induced to want what they do not need. So important has salesmanship become in American lore and life, that "to sell" is applied to much more than commercial transactions, as in case of the young man who tries to "sell" himself to a potential employer or the case of a voter who proclaims he is "sold" on a candidate.

ORGANIZATIONAL DEVELOPMENT

Another aspect of our economic system—already implied—is its highly organized and organizational nature. (1) In the first place, it is and it must be both extensively and intricately organized. The continuous mass production of goods and services requires organization to secure, allocate, and combine materials, machines, and men; to coordinate all the intermediate stages of production across time and space; to provide at the right time and place the great variety of commercial (monetary, credit, accounting, clearing) facilities and services; and to get the products through the complex transportation network to the consumers in the local, regional, national and international markets. Investment in plant, material, and equipment must be protected and justified by efficient operation. Great extension in the geographic scope and accessibility of both the goods and the people involved in the economic activities have necessitated an areal extension of organization. The various types and levels of organizations that conduct, or are involved in, these activities are more or less permanent and increasingly massive and complex; their effective operation is the consequence of organization. If the firms are small-scale enterprises (and there are still many of these, though they contribute a relatively small part of the national output) their activities must be geared to the larger firms for which in many instances they serve as contributing satellites, and they must be adjusted with all firms, large and small, with which they are competing in the market. It seems clear that our ever growing technical efficiency means still larger plants, with greater investments in them, and more intricate organization. Increasingly, our economic system is dominated by units of gigantic size.

The great bulk of the firms carrying on economic activities are formally organized. This form alone is capable of coordinating the diversity of interdependent elements and operations, for it provides such essential organizational features as the pyramidal structure, the departmentalization of functions, the hierarchical order of authority, the chain of command from the top down through the successive levels of subordinates, the impersonality of discipline, the communication net, the principles of staffing, the reign of rules, and the proficiency in policy-forming, planning, programming, and decision-making.

The corporation is a form of formal organization with all of the characteristic features of such organizations, but also with special features which fit it particularly to conduct industrial and commercial enterprises in a free economy such as ours. Although we still have some sole proprietorships and partnerships, the most important form of business organization is the corporation. Corporations, in fact, now account for more than 80 per cent of the total production of goods, workers employed, and wages paid. No other form of organization could cope with contemporary conditions. It operates in the general social system as a highly institutionalized, quasi-public organization discharging a private trust in the public interest.

The corporation raises its money by borrowing as a legal entity from financial institutions, but especially through the sale of stocks and bonds. The normal, or perhaps nominal, owners of the corporation are the shareholders, whose financial liability in the operation of the corporation, however, is limited (limited liability) to the amount of common stock they hold. The rights of ownership may be divided among a very large number of stockholders; for example, the common stock of General Motors Corporation is held by over 600,000 individuals and organizations, including other corporations, and American Telephone and Telegraph Company stock, worth $15 billion, is held by more than 1.6 million shareholders, most of them small investors. This feature of the corporation thus makes possible the aggregation of capital in units far transcending the possibilities of personal credit, and, as we will shortly note, the direct personal involvement of those who provide the capital. The rights, responsibilities, and authority for conducting the corporation are delegated to, and vested in, its board of directors, but particularly in the staff of salaried, specially selected, administrators, supervisors, and engineers—its officials or managers. They control and manage its property, form its policies, make all contracts, and are responsible for the effective performance of all of its multiple and diverse operations. In most instances, the shares of stock held by management usually represent but a small fraction of the total value of the corporation. This separate management feature of the corporation makes possible the specialization, combination, and concentration of control, extends the entrepreneur's potential range of action, and tends to develop organization at a high level. It is especially significant that the inner working of the corporate enterprise is under objective testing and measurement with respect to the manner and degree in which it is meeting its sole reason for existence; that is, turning out products or services that produce a profit.

There is in most instances a rather definite separation of ownership and management of the corporation. A striking feature of this peculiar situation has been the recent emergence of management as a self-perpetuating, largely autonomous group with little effective direction or control by the stockholders. The corporation also has a continuity of existence that borders on immortality. The investors in the corporation change continually, the personnel may come and go, some of its specific functions (and types of output) may be dropped and others added, but as a total organization, it exists indefinitely. It is obvious that the corporate form of organization not only permits its operations to be carried on with a high degree of impersonality but also makes possible through the rights and responsibilities vested in management an enormous concentration of power in a relatively few hands.[9]

Another feature of the American economic system is the fact that so many of its activities involve vast organizations and organizations of organizations. There are not only the industrial and commercial corporations, small and large, but the various types of trade associations; that is, voluntary, non-profit organizations of independent firms, even though competitive, to protect and advance certain interests common to all. Thus, there are the associations of firms within a given industry, such as those among the manufacturers of steel, automobiles, furniture, rubber goods, men's and women's clothing. We also have such over-all trade associations as the National Association of Manufacturers (N.A.M.), and the American Bankers' Association (A.B.A.), and the Chambers of Commerce, representing the industrial and commercial interests of an area and ranging from local organizations, usually chapters of a larger one, to the nation-wide United States Chamber of Commerce. Although these different types do not have identical objectives, their interests in general center around the problems and tasks of industrial and commercial ownership and management. Among the functions performed (though not by all such organizations) are research, formulating and promoting industrial and commercial policy, formulating general policy and practice in management-labor relations (some are little more than employers' associations), serving as a channel of expression of viewpoints, providing technical and market information and services, influencing legislation, carrying on lobbying activities, and sometimes making efforts to control competition through restrictive

[9] On the nature and significance of the corporation, see: P. Drucker, *Concept of the Corporation*. New York: John Day, 1946. A. A. Berle and G. C. Means, *The Modern Corporation and Private Property*. New York: Macmillan, 1933.

practices and price-fixing. Recently creators and publishers of non-corporeal property, such as musical composers, writers, and publishers (A.S.C.A.P.) have organized to insure themselves the proper monetary returns and to protect their rights in other ways.

Paralleling the organizations of industrial and commercial firms and interests are the great associations of workers, the labor unions. These exist largely as a means of enabling the workers in industry and commerce to cope with the firms, mainly corporately organized, that employ them. These unions give workers as a whole something of the monopoly over labor—counter-monopoly—that corporate managers have over the tools and materials of production; they function as a corrective for the disadvantageous position of the individual worker vis-à-vis corporate industry. They equalize the power relations between management and labor. At the same time, however, the unions have become an essential mechanism in the management of production; they provide a ready way of maintaining cooperative relations between management and labor. Because of the high mobility of the workers and the nation-wide or region-wide extent of working conditions and standards, these unions must be, and are, national or international bodies, paralleling the productive organizations in extent and intensity.

The workers are organized into two different types of unions depending on the nature of their occupation. The craft (or trade) unions consist of skilled craftsmen, such as machinists and the specialized personnel operating the railways, but especially of building craftsmen, such as carpenters, masons, electricians, steamfitters, and plumbers, each having their locals but all of them combined into national organizations. Most of these national craft unions, in turn, are organized into the over-all national organization, the American Federation of Labor (A.F.L.).

The industrial unions consist mainly of the semi-skilled, machine-tending factory workers, and also some skilled workers, employed by industries, and organized by the type of industries, such as the workers in the automobile industry (U.A.W.), the mining of coal (U.M.W.), the steel workers, the workers in the paper industry, and the drivers of automotive vehicles (the Teamsters Union). Most of the industrial unions (the mining unions are an exception) are organized into the over-all national organization, the Congress of Industrial Organization (C.I.O.). The two great national associations of unions, the A.F.L. and C.I.O., were merged into a single organization in 1955. There are also local, state, and regional federations of both craft and industrial unions paralleling state and regional employers' associations and chambers of commerce.

Like the employers' trade associations, these workers' associations exist to advance the interests of the members, both as individuals and as organizations of workers. They are concerned with such matters as higher wages, improved hours and working conditions, pay for over-time work, rest periods and holidays, job tenure, fringe benefits such as vacations and medical services, and union recognition, union security, closed shop (that is, union members only to be employed in the shop), and employment rules and conditions. They also seek to establish principles of promotion and seniority, of grievance procedures, and of hiring and firing, to mention only the most important. These items are also the main points of contention and adjudication in the negotiations of official union representatives with management. The collective bargaining procedures between organized labor and organized employers are carried on from the local to the national level. Unions also carry on industrial conflict when bargaining fails by means of boycott, slowdown, and strikes; engage in propagandist and public relations activities; and participate in lobbying in the state legislatures and the national Congress.

The growth of organized labor has led to its increasing aggressiveness, organized competence, and power. Labor is now more than able to balance the employer in organization, legislative support, and social power. It is well armed with supporting legislation and court decisions. Union executives have as great a concentration of power in their hands as the captains of industry and commerce. By virtue of their numbers and organization, workers now have great political power; they influence elections and public officials; they influence legislation, not only through their public relations and lobbying activities, but also through the blocs favoring them in the legislatures.[10]

Three other types of organizations of importance in the American economy are those in agriculture consisting of farm operators, the organizations of professionals, and those consisting of consumers, each to be discussed later at the appropriate place.

It should be noted that various government departments, bureaus, and authorities, such as the Department of the Interior, the Army Engineers, the Tennessee Valley Authority (T.V.A.), carry on extensive economic activities of far-reaching import and effect in our economy.

A final aspect of our American economy is the high degree of centralization of power that prevails in it. Not only is the power of industry and commerce enhanced and centralized through the various trade associations, but also through such relationships and combinations as interlocking directorates among corporations, through certain

[10] On labor organizations, see: R. M. Williams, Jr., *American Society: A Sociological Analysis*. New York: Knopf, 1960, pp. 200–209. E. V. Schneider, *Industrial Sociology: The Social Relations of Industry and the Community*. New York: McGraw-Hill, 1957, pp. 207–349. M. Perlman, *Labor Union Theories in America: Background and Development*. Evanston, Ill.: Row, Peterson, 1958.

degrees of monopoly involving the combination of competitors under an over-all management capable of effecting some control of output and prices, through holding companies, and through a recent appearance known as oligopoly, that is, the tendency in certain industries for the establishments to be reduced to only a few massive firms or a few firms that control the great proportion of the output; for example, the automobile industry in which Ford, General Motors, and Chrysler produce more than 95 per cent of the products, the steel and the aluminum industries, and the tobacco processing companies. Organized labor, through its nation-wide industrial and craft unions, most of them now consolidated in the A.F.L.–C.I.O., exercise power over labor, for labor, and over all economic operations and conditions affecting labor far in excess of the proportion (approximately 25 per cent) of its members in the total labor force. Several sizable groups of organized farmers, such as the Grange, the Farm Bureau, and the Farmers' Union, which include especially the technologically more advanced and large-scale farmers who turn out the great bulk of the agricultural output of the country, as well as various kinds of agricultural cooperative associations, have considerable weight in influencing legislation affecting agriculture and in the marketing of agricultural products.

CHANGE IN THE LABOR FORCE

With the change from primary to secondary and tertiary production and with the increase in specialization of economic functions, there have come great changes in the kinds of work people do and in the demographic and occupational structure of the labor force.

The first fact of importance is the vast multiplication of occupations that has come with the technological development, the related increasing diversity and specialization of economic activity of the working personnel, the rising standard of living, and the multiplication of wants. The 1949 edition of the *Dictionary of Occupational Titles,* United States Bureau of Labor, which is intended to be a comprehensive listing of all distinguishable kinds of socially accepted, remunerated work, contains 40,023 titles of 22,028 distinct occupations. These, of course, fall into several categories, the schemes of categorization depending upon the analytical objectives of the students.

The changing occupational structure is reflected in the increases or decreases of the proportions of workers in the major categories. In general, between 1940 and 1956, according to the Census Bureau and the Bureau of Labor Statistics, the number of workers in the following categories, by industrial classification, increased by the number and percentages indicated: manufacturing from 10,780,000 to 16,984,000 and up, 58 per cent; construction from 1,294,000 to 2,396,000 and up,

85 per cent; transportation, communication, and public utilities from 3,013,000 to 4,141,000 and up, 37 per cent; retail and wholesale trade from 6,940,000 to 11,674,000 and up, 68 per cent; finance from 1,436,000 to 2,225,000 and up, 55 per cent; personal services, a broad category including most of the professions and all kinds of repair services, from 3,477,000 to 5,653,000 and up, 63 per cent; and governmental services from 4,202,000 to 7,343,000 and up, 75 per cent. On the other hand, farming decreased from 9,540,000 to 5,884,000, or down 38 per cent, and mining decreased from 916,000 to 753,000, or down 18 per cent. Looking at the changes from the functional point of view, the notable ones are the rather marked increase in the proportion of workers in technical services, government, management, semi-skilled and repair jobs, coming with the increase of gadgets among consumers, in white collar, mainly clerical and trade occupations, and the increase in the proportion in the professions as well as in the number of the professions themselves. On the other hand, the great decline in common or unskilled laborers and persons employed in farming, because of the progressive mechanization and electrification, is equally significant.

Another outstanding change has been that in the age-group and sex structure of the labor force. There has been a great reduction in the percentage of the age group of 10 to 15 years that is gainfully employed; for example, in 1900 18.2 per cent of the total age group were gainfully employed, 26.1 per cent of the males and 10.2 per cent of the females; by contrast, in 1950, only 5.3 per cent of the total age group, and only 7.8 per cent of the males and 2.8 per cent of the females of the age group, were in the labor force. The change in the sex structure of the labor force between 1900 and 1950 has also been notable. In 1900 87.7 per cent of all males 14 years of age and over were in the labor force, and in 1950 they amounted to 83.7 per cent. The change with respect to females was especially significant; the percentage rose from 20.4 per cent in 1900 to 32.1 per cent in 1950. There are also more married women living with their husbands in the labor force; for example, in 1940 14.7 per cent of married women were gainfully employed; in 1950 23.8 per cent, and in 1955 27.7 per cent.

A fourth characteristic is the large and growing proportion of the labor force now members of labor unions. In 1937, the first year of the C.I.O., the total membership of the A.F.L., the C.I.O., and the independent or unaffiliated unions, according to the Bureau of the Census, amounted to about 7,218,000; in 1958 the total number had risen to slightly over 18,000,000. In 1937 the union members constituted about one-seventh of the labor force; in 1958, more than one-fourth. As of 1955, just prior to the merger of A.F.L. and C.I.O., it was estimated that the A.F.L. made up of 111 national unions had a total of about 8.6 million members; the C.I.O. with 35 national unions had a total of 5.5 millions; the independent unions about 2.5 millions. In addition, about 2 million workers were in company or quasi-independent unions. The proportion organized varies among the different categories of the labor force, however. Around 70 per cent of all workers in manufacturing and more than half of those in construction, in air, truck, and railway transportation, and in mining are pretty well organized. On the other hand, only about one-sixth of white-collar workers are unionized, and the proportion organized in farming and domestic services is almost negligible.

A final change, to be briefly noted, is the fact of increasing occupational mobility. In the first place, there is much generational change. There is much less likelihood that the son will follow his father's occupation, in many instances because the father's occupation has disappeared or young folks are moving from the farm to the city or all sorts of *new* occupations are arising. There is considerable horizontal movement, that is, from one occupation to another, requiring somewhat parallel technical proficiency and paying a somewhat similar wage. The workers also may move horizontally from plant to plant. The occupational ladder, however, providing the means or chance of working up through various levels of skill to supervisory, managerial, and executive posts, does not operate as freely as it once did. The very nature of the industrial process, with its production line of semi-skilled human-machine parts, ties the worker to a given operational level. The process does not fit him, through the acquisition of higher skills and management experience, for a foremanship and above. Furthermore, the supervisory and technical jobs require formal and expensive training. Today fewer and fewer men rise from the bottom to the top places of management and ownership in industry and business. There is growing evidence that American business leaders are increasingly recruited from the upper ranks of society and are prepared by technical and engineering schools and by universities. More and more fathers at the higher technical and executive levels are educating their sons to take their places or to occupy similar places in other industries and businesses.[11] However, although the top of the occupational ladder seems to be somewhat closed to those farther down, there does seem to be considerable vertical mobility within the area of middle range occupations (for example, from semi-skilled to skilled, from lower white-collar to upper white-collar) as a greater and greater proportion of young folks

---

[11] For an extended discussion of these and related points, see J. O. Hertzler, "Some Tendencies toward a Closed Class System in the United States," *Social Forces*, 30 (Mar., 1952): 313–323, esp. 317–318.

finish high school or have other facilities for acquiring technical and other knowledge essential to higher jobs.[12]

CHANGES IN TRANSPORTATION

The harnessing of steam and the invention of railways and steamships brought stupendous changes in transportation and all aspects of the economy relating to transportation. The railways could move great quantities of goods at high speed. Steamboats could move rapidly on canals, go upstream on rivers, and cross lakes, seas, and oceans directly without the tacking of sailing ships. But the invention of the internal combustion engine and its use in the automobile, bus, truck, and airplane have had even more far-reaching effects. These automotive vehicles can go long or short distances and where railways and canal boats could not, for example along the Alcan Highway or across the Sahara and Arabian Deserts. Now a great proportion of land transportation of both persons and things in the United States is by means of automotive vehicles. The development of air transportation has made almost any spot on the face of the earth accessible and has enabled human beings and goods to be transported at great speed. Today the airways carry far more passengers than the railways, and they are carrying an increasing volume of express and freight. These recent developments in transportation, now fundamental characteristics of our life as well as of our economy, have made possible our far-flung market system, a system that expedites the transportation of fresh fruits and vegetables from the Southwest and Southeast to all other portions of the country at all seasons, that makes it possible for the people of the remotest places to have available every type of physical standard of living item.

THE DOMINANCE OF THE MARKET MECHANISM

The market mechanism is universal in all societies, since its agents and functions are basic in the operation of the economy. There must be exchange of a most extensive and elaborate sort, and to carry on this exchange there must be the monetary system with all of its subinstitutions. Every important element in this market complex—land, capital goods, labor, money—is a matter of buying and selling, and hence is priced. But the market system can come to exercise a dominance far beyond its essential economic functions. In our society it exercises a vast influence on our value system and on our whole social organiza-

[12] On the labor force and its changes, see: A. J. Jaffe and C. D. Stewart, *Manpower Resources and Utilization.* New York: Wiley, 1951. R. Dubin, *The World of Work.* Englewood Cliffs, N.J.: Prentice-Hall, 1958, esp. pp. 127–145. E. Gross, *Work and Society.* New York: Crowell, 1958, pp. 52–98. W. E. Cole, *Urban Society.* Boston: Houghton Mifflin, 1958, pp. 255–277.

tion. Dr. Karl Polyani[13] and other keen observers have pointed out that our society is almost an adjunct of the market.

A "cash nexus," that is, the assignment of monetary worth to persons, things, and services seems to prevail in some non-economic and non-contractual areas in our life as well as being supreme in the economic realm. For example, literary, artistic, and similar productions are measured by many on the basis of the financial returns from sales. Entertainment, for the most part, has been turned into a profit-making industry. Even certain kinds of religious belief and behavior are admonished by certain very popular clergymen because they are presumed to enable people observing them to function lucratively in our present order.[14] Monetary criteria are applied in evaluating people—The Rev. Dr. So-and-So is a $15,000-a-year man, or X gets $10,000 for his portraits. Persons are rewarded on the basis of materialistic values of the market place. The "egghead" whose contributions to society are often intangible, at first at least, and effectual only in the future, gets few dollars. For many, money is the touchstone of human happiness and endeavor, even of human respect.

There is a tendency to conclude that size, number, and other quantitative expressions are evidences of high value. We cheer the mounting millions and billions being added to the national and world population, the higher prices of corporate stocks, the several million more automobiles or other gadgets and appliances produced during the year, the ever greater areas of cultivable land being taken over for shopping centers and airfields, and so on. Our contemporary steatopygous motor cars of huge tonnage may be symbolic of our worship of quantity.

In our economy every productive economic activity is expected to show a profit in the form of some material or monetary gain. We tend to give production, which is the means of acquiring profit, exaggerated stress. Then there is the tendency, in turn, to make economic goods, material or non-material, which are the results of production and not the fitting means of satisfying reasonable and legitimate needs, ends in themselves. The amassing of wealth, whether in physical or pecuniary form, is a primary endeavor of life. Wealth is sought, not as an essential to "weal-fare"—its elemental reason for existence—but, according to the prevailing cash-centered values, as a means to prestige and power, and as a symbol of personal or family worth. This situation, in the opinion of some observers from abroad, has resulted in the materialization and vulgarization in some measure of our tastes and interests, in an opulent but coarse barbarism.

Other outstanding market colorings of our life are to be found in the

---

[13] *The Great Transformation.* New York: Farrar & Rinehart, 1944, pp. 57–75.
[14] Cf. L. Schneider and S. M. Dornbusch, *Popular Religious Inspirational Books in America.* Chicago: Univ. of Chicago Press, 1958.

tremendous influence of advertising upon us and in our devotion to conspicuous display.

CONSUMPTION IN OUR SOCIETY

Consumption in our society shows the influence upon it of the market mechanism and its related values; it also presents features showing its adjustment to situations presented in a complex society.

In the first place, American consumption for the great bulk of the consumers—and unlike consumption among at least two-thirds of the world's population—is far beyond elemental need in quantity, diversity, and quality. Americans consume what they want for various reasons, and some of the wants may be quite inconsistent with each other. The great proportion of the wants are not even related to physical or physiological well-being, but are a matter of social-psychological and sociocultural considerations. People consume what they deem essential to expression of personality, what they come to think of as good or prestigeful or fashionable.

Our consumption in many respects is an induced mass consumption. Mass production requires mass and massive consumption, or its output is purely redundant. Furthermore, the articles produced on the production line or assembly line for mass consumption cannot be custommade, that is, according to individual order, but must be highly standardized as to general form, if not always in quality. Thus we consume standardized, mass-produced clothing of a given season's style, household gadgets, all manner of packaged goods (breakfast foods, cake mixes, drinks, crackers, automobiles, motion pictures, television programs). Mass production, although making an almost infinite quantity of things available for consumption, also produces an increasing uniformity and conformity in consumption. Personal and stratum (class) tastes and interests in consumption are differentially evidenced in the things consumed, in their quality or price, or in the conventional manner in which they are consumed.

Mass consumption requires mass inducement and mass standardization of the tastes and wants of the purchasers of products—the potential consumers; hence, the widespread and persistent attention to advertising. Vast advertising programs costing billions of dollars each year thrust consumption incentives and cleverly devised and presented information regarding goods and services upon us. Advertising by journals and newspapers, by radio and television, by window displays and billboards, by blaring sound-trucks, by thousands upon thousands of tons of advertising matter sent through the mail and dumped on front steps bombards us almost every waking moment. The essence of the appeal of this omnipresent advertising is that one does not act intelligently and cannot be healthy, happy, secure, or socially acceptable unless he purchases the products in question. Furthermore, our culture stresses more and more consumption on the part of each person. The person is rare indeed who does not actively strive to raise the level of his living.

What Thorstein Veblen long ago referred to as conspicuous consumption is another significant aspect of our consumption. In our competitive society, two opposing factors—on the one hand, a tendency to identify wealth with prestige, power, and cleverness, and on the other hand, the increasing anonymity and leveling of individuals and families who are competing for position in the stratification system—have led to imitative display of goods and services that the socially favored and socially powerful consume, goods meant to evidence wealth and high social level and reflect competitive-acquisitive success. Such consumption attracts social attention, gives prestige on the basis of the prevailing materialistic scale of values, and implies social significance.

Another characteristic, at first glance seemingly inconsistent with the objectives of conspicuous consumption, is the fact that the gap in consumption between the socio-economic layers of our society is closing because wealth and income differentials are shrinking. Fewer and fewer people are receiving a common laborer's wage, and a growing proportion of our population is in the middle bracket categories. Large incomes and family concentrations of wealth are being whittled down by graduated income and inheritance taxes. Modern industrial society has also vitiated the age-old distinction between a leisured class with much time for consumption and a working class. In fact, industrial and clerical workers, both blue-collar and white-collar, have as much or more leisure as entrepreneurs and professionals. Furthermore, since mass-produced goods are more and more standardized, it becomes increasingly difficult to determine economic level and societal status by means of consumption. There are still vast differentials in income, since there exist markets for both Cadillacs and Chevrolets, but today only an automobile expert can tell from a block away which automobile is which. Those people are increasingly rare who cannot afford television, the latest styles in food, clothing, and housing, the services of beauticians, vacations and tours.

The wealth and income gaps are shrinking because of such devices and programs as labor organizations and their bargaining success in raising wage scales both for the union and non-union members of the labor force; graduated income, estate and inheritance taxes and their levelling-down effect; minimum wage legislation; Social Security programs; widespread ownership of stocks and bonds by the middle and, increasingly, the working classes; graduated contributions from persons, roughly in proportion to their affluence, as obtained by Community Chests and other semi-public welfare agencies; and impartial public provision of utilities and services.

A final significant aspect of consumption in our society is the group action to aid consumers. These take two main forms. First, there are the organizations that carry on investigative and protective activities on behalf of consumers. Such organizations as the Consumers' Union and Consumers' Research Bureau carry on testing of the quality and efficiency of many kinds of consumers' goods and make this information available to the fee-paying members. Organizations like the Better Business Bureaus, now found in many communities, promote city ordinances protecting citizens against poor quality products and fraudulent sales activities; and they promote fair advertising and selling practices (for example, prohibiting use by Bureau members of terms and phrases that confuse and mislead customers). Other organizations, especially trade organizations within given industries, promote uniform terminology and standardized definitions or meanings of various terms, and also standardize the number and variety of their products. Governmental agencies at the various levels enforce pure food and drug laws, and laws against adulteration of fabrics; they enforce the certification of grades and brands (for example, in meat packing), and protect the public against monopolistic prices, misleading advertising, the unsanitary dispensing of foods in stores and eating places, the sale (for example, by hucksters) of uninspected goods.

Second, there are the various consumers' cooperative organizations made up of, and managed by, the consumer beneficiaries themselves. These organizations seek to increase the real income of members and to improve their scale of living or their well-being and security as consumers by doing such things as reducing merchandising costs (for example, by eliminating profits or some marketing operations); making available the amount and quality of those things that consumers want; providing services under certain conditions of convenience to consumers; making available services of a quality, or at a price, that agencies (for example, private public utilities) operated for profit would not or could not provide. There are all sorts of such cooperative organizations in the United States providing various kinds of services for their members: those engaged in retail distribution, in providing housing, in providing medical and hospital care, burial associations, cooperative utility organizations providing electric light and power and telephone services, credit unions supplying credit facilities for their members, and various kinds of insurance (life, accident, theft, hospital, fire, hail, and other catastrophe) associations.

THE NEW AGRICULTURE

Our basic industry, agriculture, has been undergoing greater changes in the last three decades than urban industry. Traditionally, American agriculture has been a way of life for a large part of the population. Farming has been a family enterprise utilizing both sexes and all age groups of the family, often extending over two, even three, generations; children and the aged had their chores. A large part of the farmer's product was used to feed his family and his livestock. The usually very modest "cash income" was used for sparingly purchased farm supplies and equipment, taxes, interest on loans, payments on mortgage installments, occasional doctor bills, payments to the church and preacher (though these latter were often in the form of products from the farm), and a few extras (treats from the store and attendance at the county fair). The methods were also largely traditional. The farmer used horse and mule power and relatively few pieces of machinery (plow, harrow, planter, cultivator). The larger machinery (grain harvester and threshing machine) was usually hired on a custom basis; it was not uncommon for the farmers of a rural neighborhood to band together and own such machinery cooperatively. Although the farmer used skills and much traditional craft lore, his operations did not involve highly technical, mechanical, biological, and commercial knowledge. The farms were relatively small—family-size. Farmers, except in a few specialized areas, were unorganized, independent, and highly competitive.[15] But science and technology have worked their way into agriculture recently, though with a lag.

The rapid and extensive adoption of mechanization and other technological improvements both in agricultural production and in rural living have been, and are continuing to be, a dominant factor in our changing agriculture. The very increase of machinery on farms and the decrease of animals used for power is most impressive evidence of this automation. In 1910, the first year tractors were counted, there were only 1000 in the whole of the United States; in 1920 there were 246,-000; in 1950, 3,615,000, and in 1955 some 4,800,000. Between 1940 and 1955, the tractors on United States farms increased by 300 per cent. There has been a corresponding decline in work animals; in 1910, there were 24,000,000 horses and mules in the United States, mostly on farms, and in 1954, there were only 5,000,000 left. It has been computed that each tractor displaces about 3.5 work animals. There, of course, has been the great increase both in the amount and kinds of other machinery. For example, between 1940 and 1955, cornpickers increased 500 per cent to 640,000; forage harvesters increased 100

[15] C. H. Hamilton, "The Sociology of a Changing Agriculture," *Social Forces,* 37 (Oct., 1958): 1–7.

per cent to 170,000; hay balers increased 100 per cent to 393,000; milking machines increased from 212,000 to 800,000 (377 per cent).[16] Every farm now has one or more trucks and also usually a passenger automobile. These have worked great changes not only in farming methods, but also in the entire United States farm economy.

The adoption of rural electrification on American farms should also be noted. It started slowly in the '20's, picked up momentum in the '30's, and levelled off in the 1950's, with about 94 per cent of all farms electrified in 1956.

Technology has brought on decrease in the number of farms and an increase in the average size of farms over the nation, though this latter change has not been at the same rate in different regions. According to reports by the Department of Agriculture, the number of United States farms dropped from 6,500,000 in 1920 to 5,870,950 in 1947, and 4,855,800 in 1957. At the same time, the average size of American farms has increased from 148 acres in 1920, to 174 acres in 1940, and to 240 acres in 1954.

With automation has also come both a diminishing need of manpower and a great increase in output per man. It is estimated by the Department of Agriculture that at the turn of the century, it took 9 farm hands working from dawn to dusk 6 days a week to produce enough for themselves and one city dweller; in 1955 one farmer, with his machines, and working a 40-hour week, could turn out enough food for 14 people. The amount of production per man hour on American farms has risen from an index value of only 50 in 1920 to 130 in 1955; or, to put it somewhat differently, showing the great recent increase, the output per manhour in agriculture increased 37 per cent from 1919–21 to 1938–40, and increased 78 per cent from 1938–40 to 1951–53. Farm production on the whole has increased 40 per cent since 1940 on fewer acres because of automation and such other technological advances as superior plants and animals, fertilizers, and irrigation.

Quite understandingly, it takes less and less people on the farms and a shrinking agricultural labor force to produce this ever greater output on less land. There has been a marked diminution of the farm population of the United States while the total population has been increasing at a rapid rate. The population on the farms dropped from 32 million in 1920, when it was 25.8 per cent of the total population, to 25 million in 1950, when it was 16.6 per cent of the total population, to 20.4 million in 1957, when it was 12 per cent of the population. The decline from 1950 to 1957 alone was some 4.6 million. During the last quarter century, the decrease of the farm population has averaged about 500,-

[16] *Time,* July 4, 1955, pp. 48–53.

000 per year. The reduced manpower requirements are further indicated by the fact that between 1950 and 1957 the agricultural labor force, that is, the persons 14 years of age and over actually employed in agriculture, declined from 6,628,000 to 4,815,000 (out of a total national labor force of 65 million).

Hamilton points out that most of the population loss on farms occurs through migration of persons to non-farm residences. Between 1920 and 1950, the net migration from farms to urban and rural non-farm communities is estimated to have been about 20 million people. "In this 30-year period about two-thirds of the youth born on American farms were destined ultimately to become residents of urban and rural non-farm areas." It is also estimated that between 1946 and 1955 some 2,000,000 actual farm operators migrated away from the land.[17]

American agriculture is rapidly coming to be a mechanized and capitalized industry or business, requiring heavy investment, highly competent management, and increasing specialization. This fact is reflected in the kinds of knowledges, skills, and abilities needed by modern farmers if they are to conduct a productive enterprise, and also in the organizational forms that American agriculture is taking.

The successful farm operator today must be a technical and commercial expert. He has a huge investment, not only in land, but in machinery which must be efficiently operated and maintained. He has to be a marketing expert, understanding the markets in which he sells his products and following their fluctuations from day to day. Specialized education and training are becoming increasingly necessary for the American farmer. In this connection it is significant that the agricultural peasantry—tenant farmers, share-croppers, and hired laborers—are disappearing, while owners are increasing.

Agriculture is becoming increasingly commercial; that is, carrying on production almost or entirely fulltime for the market and less and less for family subsistence. There is, for example, the development of large-scale factories in the fields, producing fruit, wine, nuts, and vegetables for the market (especially in Florida, Texas, California, and the Southwest), producing livestock for meat (beef, pork, poultry, eggs), and producing milk and dairy products. Also, some 90 per cent of American farm production is accounted for by 46 per cent of the farmers, who are primarily commercial farmers. Of commercial farms, the largest ones, that is, those selling annually more than $10,000 worth of farm products per farm, although they are only 17.5 per cent of all commercial farms, account for 59.5 per cent of the total value of products sold on such farms.

[17] Cf. S. L. McDonald, "Farm Outmigration as an Integrative Adjustment to Economic Growth," *Soc. Forces,* 34 (Dec., 1955): 119–128.

Hamilton calls attention to the increase of contract farming. The given farmer produces, under contract, for a firm which collects, processes, and markets the product. This is done increasingly in all parts of the country in the production of vegetables and fruits for canning and freezing, in the production of poultry, eggs, livestock, and dairy products, and in the production of seeds.[18]

Another structural feature of American agriculture is its protective and promotive organizations. Although not recent, they are an aspect of the so-called farmers' movement—an expression of the farmers' increasing awareness of their significance in the economy, of the discrimination against them, of other problems confronting them, and of the desirability of acting in a cooperative and organized way.[19] These organizations to some extent are parallels of the trade associations of urban industrialists and commercial firms. There have been a considerable number of these since the 1890's. The following are the most important surviving ones: The American Farm Bureau Federation, as of 1957 representing some 1,587,107 member families in the 48 states and Puerto Rico; the National Grange, with a 1957 membership of over 860,000 actual members in 37 states; and the Farmers' Union, with a 1957 membership of approximately 300,000 "working" farm families. Although the objectives of these major organizations are not identical, they all are concerned with protecting and promoting agricultural interests. They are interested in such economic matters as prices, markets, subsidies, freight rates, agricultural credit, highways and communication, taxation, conservation of soil and water and other resources, and electrification. They function as powerful pressure groups, conducting publicity and legislative lobbying activities. They also conduct programs and activities of an adult educational nature for their members, and in the local chapters they provide a meeting ground for informal visiting, discussion, and entertainment.

There are also a number of organizations in the special fields of crop production, such as the American National Cattlemen's Association, the National Association of Wheat Growers, and similar organizations among cotton, tobacco, and citrus fruit growers, and among producers of most other major crops marketed nationally or internationally. Farmers also have a large number of cooperative associations for consumers, producers, and those who market the produce.

The technological and economic changes have brought a considerable change in the American farmer's consumption. In the more mechanized areas there has been a complete shift in the demand for consumer goods. The farmers increasingly want urban things—more sophisticated wear-

---

[18] For a more extended discussion, see Hamilton, *op. cit.*, p. 5.
[19] Cf. C. C. Taylor, *The Farmers' Movement*. New York: Am. Book, 1953.

ing apparel, food, and other consumption goods. Such things were once
not to be found at the "general store," and the latter itself is disappearing in the mechanized areas. The farmers more and more do their
buying in the now readily accessible larger town or city. The change in
consumption also involves enjoying town or city personal services,
amusements, and entertainments. Moreover, farm families have the
same home conveniences as city families—mechanical refrigerators,
central heating, radio, television sets, electric washing machines, running water, bathrooms.

There has been and is a shrinking of good agricultural land in the
United States. The shrinkage has been retarded by new land brought
under crops by irrigation and other reclamation procedures. There has
also been a gain in cropland because food need not be produced
for the millions of horses and mules once so essential in agriculture.
Over and against such gains are the losses of good earth because of
population increase, urban development, land waste and misuse. It is
estimated that 17 million acres of good cropland were diverted from
cultivation between 1942 and 1956. At present, every year 1.1 million
acres are permanently taken out of crops by urban and suburban development, the expansion of industry and airports, and the construction
of new military establishments and especially of new highways. Another
7,000,000 acres are lost annually through soil erosion, tree-planting,
water-logging, salt deposits, and other contaminations.[20]

CONTROLLING MECHANISMS

Our American economy shows a large number and a considerable variety of controlling mechanisms. Some of these are self-imposed by the
elements and organizations of the economy itself; some are imposed
by government. The economic system is not entirely self-correcting or
self-regulating; competition in the market is not completely free; and
laissez-faire certainly does not prevail. Almost all economic activity,
individual and organizational, is copiously regulated, and the free market, partly, if not largely, is replaced by a highly tangible web of financial and organizational—especially governmental—controls.

In the first place, every factory, every business establishment must
have its own work rules; that is, a body of rules and regulations regarding (1) personal conduct of all of the personnel in the organization
toward each other; (2) their relations with the organization (labor-
management relations); and (3) the job tasks in the organization, that
is, operating procedures and methods. Only with such rules can be-

[20] J. J. Spengler, "The Aesthetics of Population," *Pop. Bull.,* 13 (June, 1957):
61–75.

havior and operation be predicted. They have to be policed and enforced, and each organization must have a system of penalties and deprivations, on the one hand, and one of rewards, on the other. The larger and more complex the organization, the more important the work rules.[21]

Most of the trade associations mentioned above, in addition to their protective and promotive functions, also have considerable regulatory influence. Not only do they nurture the customs of the industry, but they also establish trade practices and in some instances set up business codes.

But the most massive development of controlling mechanisms in our complex economy is the development of governmental regulation at the local, state, and especially federal level. This occurs through municipal ordinances, administrative (departmental and bureau) regulations and policies, statutory laws, and court decisions and interpretations, and also through the indirect consequences of the governmental agencies as they operate. In labor-management relations, there is a great variety of laws, rulings, and other regulations controlling or affecting minimum wages, maximum hours, conditions that protect safety and health in industrial and commercial establishments, unemployment and old age insurance, compensation in case of accident while on the job or illness due to the job, employment of women and children, the right to work, sometimes conditions for striking, and the use of conciliation, mediation, and arbitration in labor conflict in certain industries. In the protection of interests and well-being of the general public, there is the legislation prohibiting the adulteration of foods, drugs, cosmetics, and fabrics; various attempts by governmental agencies to encourage conservation and prevent waste of soils, forests, water, and other resources; and legislation seeking some equalization of distribution (especially income) through compulsory graduated income, and inheritance and estate taxes. In the regulation of industry and commerce, there is such action as the activity of the Federal Reserve Board in controlling credit and thus regulating inflationary or deflationary tendencies, the efforts to prevent unfair competition (fair trade practices acts), the prevention of monopoly (for example, the Sherman Anti-Trust Act), the occasional control of some prices, and the attempts to regulate output (for example, in agriculture and sometimes in mining).

EXTENSION OF GOVERNMENTAL ACTIVITY

The extension of governmental activity in our economic affairs is due, in part at least, to the fact that the state represents the interests of all

---

[21] Cf. R. Dubin, *The World of Work.* Englewood Cliffs, N.J.: Prentice-Hall, 1958, pp. 351–363.

members of a society. In fact, there is a general tendency among the nations of the earth, including the "free" democratic nations, to extend the sphere of the state over and into ever wider economic areas. The state is taking on not only the regulation of various aspects of economic organization, but also the ownership, administration, and operation of larger and larger sections of the economy. Though not as far advanced in the United States as among other Western nations, this tendency has been perceptible for some time, and recently has been developing at an accelerated rate. At present we have hundreds of governmentally conducted economic activities carried on at the municipal, county, state, regional, and federal level.

At the local-municipal level we find the operation of municipal gasoline service stations, gas, light, and power plants, water works, garbage collection, garbage rendering and sewage disposal plants, auditoriums and convention halls, and the provision of plays, operas, and orchestras. At the state level there are, among others, the industries conducted in the reformatories and penitentiaries (food, clothing, furniture, automobile license plates, traffic signs), though these are now mainly confined by law to production for state institutions and state agencies only. Corporately organized authorities, at the municipal, state, and interstate levels, construct and operate bridges, tunnels, water supply systems, and harbor installations. Especially notable are the Tennessee Valley Authority and the great Missouri and Columbia River projects which, among other things, produce and distribute hydroelectric power. At the federal level we find all manner of economic activities. The Federal Reserve Bank functions as the over-all bank for the entire American banking system. There are the various federal or public Corporations—not all operative at the moment—such as the Federal Surplus Commodity Corporation, the Export-Import Bank, the Federal Savings and Loan Insurance Corporation, the Federal Crop Insurance Corporation, and the Federal Housing Authority. Most of these have exercised guaranteeing or supervisory rather than productive functions, however.

In general, the various governmental activities consist of the production of commodities, the construction of public works, the operation of public utilities of all kinds and the sale of their services, and the provision of marketing, financing, and credit facilities. Although most of these are, in their very nature, monopolistic enterprises, some are carried on in competition with private or quasi-public corporations.

Just as the private corporation represents a social invention developed during recent centuries to meet the needs of an expanding technology and more complex business organization, so—we must realistically grant, whether we like or not—the government economic organizations represent a new responsiveness to the needs of an ever more complex, massive, expanding economy. These governmental agencies have been set up by the people through their properly elected, properly constituted, and responsible representative agencies; they are operated for the people; their purpose is to confer a public economic benefit and to improve and maximize the consumption of services.

TAXATION

Taxation is becoming an increasingly important factor in our economy, not only because of its increasingly heavy impact upon business enterprise and upon consumers, but also because of its secondary or auxiliary uses. Ever since we have had politically organized society, taxes have been necessary to support governmental activity; and they have always, in the long run, had to come out of national income, which means that they have been paid by productive organizations and by individual income receivers. But with the vast extension of governmental activities along regulatory, and increasingly along economic, scientific-technological, and educational lines, and with the mounting burden of past and present military expenditures, and preparedness, presumably of an "insurance nature," for possible future military operations, taxes have come to take a greater slice of the national economic product. Not only do we have the ancient taxes upon physical property, but also on intangible property (stocks, bonds, savings accounts, bank deposits); we have personal and corporate income taxes, business excess profits taxes, sales taxes, manufacturer's excise taxes on luxuries such as jewelry, cosmetics, transportation, amusements, liquor, tobacco, automobiles, tariffs on imports, taxes on gambling equipment and gambling intake, to mention only the better known and more ubiquitous varieties. The greater proportion of the middle income families of the United States pay approximately one-fourth of their annual income in direct and indirect taxes. Around one-third of the national income goes into local, state, and national taxes.

Although revenue is the major objective of taxation, it often has had, and still has, secondary or auxiliary uses, such as discouraging the consumption of presumably harmful goods and services (liquor, gambling, and horse-racing), encouraging population fertility (children as basis for income, and at times property, tax exemptions and deductions), and equalizing wealth (graduated income and inheritance taxes).

Finally, there is the relation between taxation, especially federal taxation, and our national system of public finance. Although banking policy and other indirect controls have their place, the manipulation of the tax system, that is, the deliberate variation of taxes, is coming to be looked upon as the primary instrument in stabilizing the whole economy.[22]

A final aspect of our economy to be noted is the fact that our natural resources have been wasted and that they are not inexhaustible; in fact, some of our most crucial resources are near exhaustion. Peter Drucker has pointed out that we are daily becoming more dependent upon the outside world, especially for certain basic raw materials that are so essential if we are to keep our industrial machine going. He states, "Our own cupboard—once bountifully stuffed with raw materials—already has been emptied much more than most of us realize." The supply of iron ore in the Mesabi range of Minnesota was supposed to be inexhaustible. All good ore is gone; what remains requires expensive processing. We are importing iron ore in increasing quantities from Canada, South America, and Africa. Crude oil, which we once exported in floods, now is being imported in increasing amounts. We are largely dependent upon other countries for bauxite, manganese, nickel, wood pulp, chrome, and a dozen others. Furthermore, although we have less than 7 per cent of the world's population, we are using up 50 per cent of the entire world output of raw materials.[23] There is also the difficulty of recovering from our reckless exploitation of our forests, the waste involved in the overgrazing of our national forests, the tremendous wastage of the soil though the processes of erosion by wind and uncontrolled water, bad cropping, and failure to restore depleted elements, the great waste of our flowing water in flood damage, the silting of streams, and the failure to use by proper management the water for irrigation and hydroelectric power.

The distinction between fund and flow resources must be recognized. Fund resources are those that are non-reproducible or very slowly renewable, such as mineral and metal deposits. These are man's capital which nature has stored. The flow resources are those continuously produced by nature, such as rain, water power, wind, sunshine, and some animal and vegetable life. These are man's income from nature. Items having the characteristics of both fund and flow, but inclining more toward fund resources are forests, soils, grasslands, and arable land. A policy must be pursued that depends to the greatest extent possible upon flow resources, using them in place of, or as copious supplements

[22] K. E. Boulding, "Economics: The Taming of Mammon," in Lynn White, Jr., (ed.). *Frontiers of Knowledge in the Study of Man.* New York: Harper, 1956, pp. 132–149.

[23] P. Drucker, *America's Next Twenty Years.* New York: Harper, 1957, pp. 71–89.

to, fund resources wherever and whenever technology makes this possible.

The situation with respect to our diminishing and wasted resources has led to the promotion and the practices of conservation and reclamation. These are the processes whereby valuable and non-replaceable or only slowly replaceable resources are preserved from deterioration, extermination, loss, or injury; or are restored; or satisfactory substitutes found for them; and heretofore available but unused resources are made usable. For example, with respect to the soil, our most fundamental resource, conservation-reclamation efforts involve such action as the halting of soil depletion due to continuous cropping, lack of crop rotation, or mismanagement of water that results in leaching or waterlogging. They involve preventing and correcting soil erosion by stubble-mulching, terracing of cultivated slopes, contour plowing and planting, gully-filling and planting, and the construction of grassed channel ways, retention dams, and embankments, the planting of cover strips on slopes, and shelter belts. They involve the protection of semi-arid grasslands against overgrazing and against plowing up during the wet phase of the rainfall cycle. Conservation and reclamation also involve halting overgrazing in the national forests to avoid erosion and the loss of forest seedlings; they involve timber culture or tree-farming and continuous replanting in place of timber-mining. They involve water or flood control and the extension of irrigation wherever the investment can be justified.

The National Reclamation Association, with the assistance of its state affiliates, has taken a leading part in informing the public and in promoting actual programs. Some of the large corporations processing and marketing resources, such as some of the large lumber companies, have found it to be to their own interest to conduct such activities. For the most part, however, conservation and reclamation projects are not, and cannot be, purely private affairs, but usually require considerable assistance from governmental agencies. Soil and water conservation, for example, involves all of the soil users in the particular basin or watershed. Whatever one farmer does affects all the rest. There must be an over-all integrated plan. It also involves much instruction and advising, extensive investigation, experimentation, and supervision. Such things can only be done by large, usually public, organizations, and they usually require government encouragement, operation by government agency of some of the projects and facilities, a considerable measure of governmental control, and government subsidy and financing.

Economic men of foresight and good will are stressing the long view —that some at least of what we have should be considered as an annuity fund or a reserve for the future, that each generation is the steward of the natural resources, not only for the present but for conceivable future time. Hence, prodigal use must be halted, and a prudent balance between present wants and future needs and wants must be struck; for, as Lewis Mumford put it nearly two decades ago, without vision both the resources and the people dependent upon them perish.

IV: Occupational Institutions

An area of institutionalization assuming increasing importance in the organization of complex society is that of occupations.[24] Occupations serve functions in every sector of institutional activity, but the examination of them has most direct pertinence in connection with the economic order.

Occupations or vocations involve the labor elements of economic functioning. Although people do work for various reasons, the great bulk of it is human energy expended in economic activity; that is, in the production and distribution of economically valued and assessed goods and services. Moreover, most of this work is done for remuneration, though other objectives are invariably involved, and for many people the work also may be a fine form of expression and release. Fundamentally, however, it is the means whereby individuals and families provide themselves with a livelihood.

Work is the dominating preoccupation of most of the adult members of any society. It consumes more time for more people than any other life activity, with the possible exception of sleep. Hughes has referred most appropriately to work organization as looming large as a separate and specialized system of things in our society, and to work experience as a "fateful" part of every man's life.[25] Work, of course, has a distinguished heritage in the development as well as in the continuous maintenance of society. The way of survival has been the way of work. Work is a law of life. Furthermore, the kinds of work that the people of a given area and era do, the types and degrees of proficiencies implied in their work, the complexity and the technical level of their work, the kinds of products they turn out, the needs that are fulfilled, and the standards that they set for their work cause their work to serve very effectively as a reflector and even as a gauge of their cultural and societal development. In the simple folk societies, much of the work is labor-in-common in the family and the commune. As societies increase in size, and become complex technologically and demographically, and as their

[24] Sociology is also taking special cognizance of occupations in the rapidly developing specialty, the "sociology of work."

[25] E. C. Hughes, "The Sociological Study of Work: An Editorial Foreword," *Am. Jour. Soc.*, 57 (Mar., 1952): 423–426.

needs expand and diversify, division of labor and multiplication and specialization of functions occur; then work itself becomes varied and specialized and takes the form of an increasing array of occupations.

An occupation or vocation is one of these more or less specialized ways of carrying on economically significant functions. Vocations are activities that serve social functions within a system of functional specialization. Each vocation involves the production of utilities; but the utilities are by no means confined to material things or physical satisfactions; ministers, teachers, artists, and accountants provide needed utilities. The activities of the different occupations entail various types and levels of knowledge, ability, and skill. Both the occupational proficiencies and the goods or services produced are marketable; that is, people are willing to pay for the product, even though other than purely economic needs are met by the product. Remuneration is not necessarily in the form of economic reward, though it is the major form.[26] It can be said that there is a basic occupational subsystem in the general social system; and as Hiller pointed out, all of the occupations as specialized functions "are both cause and effect of the organization of a society."[27]

The fact of central importance in our present treatment is that occupations or vocations, ever since there have been any differentially distinguishable ones, have been somewhat institutionalized; they have been more or less established, normatively standardized and patterned ways of expending marketable or at least useful energy in doing the community's work. This institutionalization is required for several reasons. First, most of the work is carried on with others as a part of a common endeavor, and all those involved must know where they stand with respect to each other as they conduct their jobs. Second, the product, whether in the way of goods or services, is for others; expectations regarding its availability and quality must be met. Third, each occupation, whether simple or complex, is a specialized set of activities that need to be conducted in an invariant and patterned way both as to procedural steps and standard of performance. Work must be institutionalized, task by task, craft by craft.

Any given piece of work, in itself, has its own natural regulations and disciplines, its own requirements, and restraints, and kinds and sequences of action. But occupations also show sociocultural character-

---

[26] "In the United States today, as in most advanced industrial countries, occupation rather than property is the source of income for most of those who receive any direct income." H. Gerth and C. W. Mills, *Character and Social Structures: The Psychology of Social Institutions*. New York: Harcourt, Brace, 1953, p. 312.

[27] E. T. Hiller, *Social Relations and Structures*. New York: Harper, 1947, p. 482.

istics which are of an institutional nature. Each occupation is a more or less organized functional category of people who do a certain kind of work—carpentering, teaching, doctoring, machine-tending, and so on. Each occupation is a system of roles which its occupants play as they work at their job. Each role system has its particular standardized behavioral essentials that distinguish it from others. Each occupational role system involves particular knowledge, attitudes, and skills. Many of the role actions come to be a matter of habit. But an occupation goes beyond role-patterning. It has its own code, or work mores, or conduct standards, prescribing what the role-playing member of the occupation is supposed to do, how to do it, and what not to do in his relations with the elements he works with, with his job associates and those in other occupations, with his employers or clients, and with the public at large. These norms are partly of an implicit, traditional, and informal nature, but increasingly in many occupations of an explicit and formal nature, and specified in the rules of work organizations and in laws and court decisions. Most occupations of any duration whatsoever have a set of sacred cultural features that have direct regularizing and sustaining significance, such as mythologies, occupational secrets, customs, rituals, distinctive costumes, argot, and special titles.[28] Combining the preceding institutional features are the actual actional forms, the standard usages and practices involving the techniques with their skills and routines, that establish and regularize the activities essential in doing the particular work. The techniques of each type of occupation constitute an assemblage of acts that are repeated on the job and can be taught and learned.[29] Most occupational functions in modern societies are carried on in, or under the influence of, formal organizations which are highly regulatory in their nature. Finally, various occupations, especially those affected with considerable public interest, have an institutional feature that assures the competence and the social responsibility of the performers; namely, certification and licensing requirements. To be certified in the more complicated occupations requires that a certain specified amount and kind of vocational training be taken and that final qualifying examinations of some sort be passed. The standards and procedures for certification may be set up by various occupational organizations themselves, such as labor unions or professional organizations. For example, in the skilled crafts the trade unions have long maintained a certification system indicated by the titles of journey-

[28] T. Caplow, *The Sociology of Work*. Minneapolis: Univ. of Minnesota Press, 1954, p. 101.
[29] The effect of the machine upon work should be noted. The activity of the machine worker tends to be regulated, standardized, and synchronized by the machine; the worker becomes an adjunct of the machine, and his routines are predetermined by it.

man and master. To qualify for journeyman status a period of apprenticeship is required. The professional organizations also establish extensive standards for training, admission, and performance. Increasingly, however, the requirements for certification, both for the skilled crafts and professions, are written into municipal or state law, and the examinations are administered, and the certificate or license issued, by authorized government agents. A special trend in this respect is that various occupations below the professional level, but involving skills or services which, if inadequately or incompetently performed, could cause social damage, are now licensed. In some cases, for example garbage and refuse collectors, certain minimum requirements regarding equipment and hauling and disposal procedures must be met. In the case of certain skilled trades, for example plumbers, steam fitters, and electricians, whose mistakes could be most dangerous, competence must be demonstrated by examinations involving the general technical knowledge of the craft, the pertinent city ordinances and their requirements, and actual proficiency in operation. It is obvious, of course, that these certification and licensing criteria tend to further standardize not only vocational preparation but also the occupational performance.[30]

In general, each occupation is a unique configuration of institutional traits. Some of the old and established ones will show all of the traits mentioned plus certain additional ones; many new occupations may lack some of them. Each type of occupation will show different dimensions of these traits.[31]

Most occupational activity, in addition to the fact that it conforms to the institutionalized features just noted, is carried on as a part of an institutionalized work system in which formal work organizations, as they have come to be called, are the central features. Occupations, in the main, in our society are practiced in such work organizations as industrial or commercial organizations (in a factory, a store, an office, or on a construction job); in recreational organizations (a professional basketball team, a bowling alley, a large-car auto-racing organization); in an educational organization (a school system, a college or university); a religious organization (as priest or clergyman, or clerical worker); and in a health organization (a city health department, a dispensary or clinic, a hospital) or in a governmental or military organization. The personnel in any work organization have a high degree of organization for several reasons. The activities of the personnel must be effectively coordinated; hence, a work organization is a formal decision-making, task- and status-assigning, and authority-power sys-

---

[30] See L. G. Thomas, *Occupational Structure and Education.* Englewood Cliffs, N.J.: Prentice-Hall, 1956, pp. 366–368.

[31] For the discussion of four groups of institutions, see Caplow, *op. cit.,* p. 102.

tem. The personnel carry on specialized activities involving knowledges and skills; hence, it is also a teaching, learning, selecting, and placing system. There must be a steady flow and quality of performance; hence, it is a system of control. In addition to the codes affecting the various categories of workers, each work organization itself has its folkways, mores, formal codes, and sanction system that operate from the inside and define duties, obligations, and sanctions. From the outside, controls are imposed by clients, competitive occupations and professions, competing organizations, trade or professional organizations (National Association of Manufacturers, American Medical Association), and public opinion in general. A work organization is always a regulatory organization, though the degree and kind of control varies; a hospital or police force must have a high degree of control; an artists' league has very little.

In addition to highly institutionalized organizations in which people do their work, there is a variety of organizations of occupationals that operate in a highly institutional manner. Notable are the labor organizations ranging from unions composed of particular categories of workers to the over-all A.F.L.-C.I.O.; the organizations of professionals, such as the American Medical Association, the American Bar Association, the American Association of University Professors, and the National Educational Association; the industrial and commercial organizations, such as the National Association of Manufacturers, the National Metal Trades Association; and the agricultural organizations, such as the National Grange, the Farmers' Union, the Farm Bureau, and the various farmers' cooperatives. These organizations render their members many different kinds of services, but their regulatory, protective, and maintenance functions are of special import.

The impetus to occupational institutionalization came with the Industrial Revolution, and with the great development of technology, the division of labor, the factory system, and the multiplication of specialized crafts.[32] These brought great changes in the economic institutions and relations, including changes in work relations and occupations, which tended to make institutionalization of occupations a social necessity. The relations between worker and employer or professional and client become increasingly long-range; the principle of *caveat emptor* (let the buyer beware) could not apply between the buyers and suppliers of labor, especially skilled and professional labor. The relations between different categories of workers themselves and between work-

[32] Historically, of course, there has long been some institutionalization of occupations; the records of the great ancient civilizations (e. g., the Code of Hammurabi) show much of it; the medieval guild system carried it to a high degree.

ers and employers became increasingly impersonal, yet, because of their interdependence, the relations became increasingly crucial. Vast masses of specialized workers doing segments of jobs, working in many places scattered over wide areas and turning out uniform products, required a high degree of standardization of working conditions, industrial and commercial techniques and procedures, personnel skills and training, and hours and wages.

In general, institutionalization of occupations facilitates the accommodation of all concerned to the work situation. More particularly, though, it indicates for the worker what is expected of him, and for the employer or client, and the public generally, it tickets what they can expect in the way of kind and quality of effort. It is, thus, a way of avoiding, and possibly also of solving, discontents and grievances. For the worker entering the occupation it presents a bill of particulars regarding essential knowledge and skills to be acquired and a program of procedures for carrying on the job. It is a basis for judging workers by fellow workers, by union or professional organization, and by clients and the public. If the worker plays his occupational role as institutionalized, observes the rules, and has something in the way of tested proficiency in the techniques, he is protected against criticisms and accusations of employers or clients. Finally, if he qualifies in these respects, he protects himself against hazards—physical, psychical, and social—while on the job.

Established and standardized occupations, as they select their occupants on the basis of the essential prerequisites, as they put their attitudinal and behavioral stamps on persons, and as they are differentially valued by the society, have definite determinative and designative effects upon the incumbents as they live and function in the total social system. Since a given occupation correlates with a certain level of income and education and use of leisure, it is a major determinant in assigning the individual and his immediate family to their social position (status) in the larger society. In this connection, it is an influential factor in deciding the family's place of residence, the kind of leisure it enjoys, with whom it spends its leisure time, and its quota of social prestige. In general, occupations are the most ostensible and the most influential way into the stratification system, probably the key determinant of location in it, and one of the most important factors in understanding the stratification system in any society. Conversely, by a person's occupation a community or society is roughly able to identify him as to the educational level he has achieved, his approximate income and spending level, his class position, sometimes his majority-minority group position, his interests and aspirations, and hence the boundaries of his culture, the types of social activities he engages in, the social organizations to which he and his family belong, his position in these organizations. Occasionally his occupation affects his political affiliation. It has been well said: "Except for those persons whose way of life and future are secured by the inheritance of great wealth, occupation is the supreme determinant of human careers."[33] It is significant that occupation, especially by virtue of the correlated income, education, and status, also is an important factor in both the kind and amount of social opportunity that the individual and his family enjoy. Although this affects all members of the family, it is particularly important with respect to the future social mobility of the children, for the occupation of the parent is a weighty element in determining the occupational status of the children when they enter employment. Occupations also involve certain degrees of power for the incumbent, directly exercised through the job itself (the lawyer or corporation executive as against the floor-sweeper or refuse collector), and indirectly, by virtue of income, class, and prestige in various other social areas (government, the church).[34]

The institutionalization of occupations has reached its highest level in the professions. Professionalization has occurred and been necessary in some degree in earlier societies with respect to certain categories of specialized occupations, notably the traditional professions of religion, teaching, medicine, and law. In our society we find an array of other occupations, some of them of rather recent development, that, because of their nature, are taking on the characteristics of professions and are being accepted as such. Notably in process of professionalization are the advertisers, accountants, actuaries, social workers, nurses, credit men, the different branches of engineering, architects, pharmacologists, life insurance consultants, real estate consultants, operators, and salesmen, many brackets of public servants, and increasingly business men.

Professionalization in modern life relates directly to the great increase and specialization of knowledge and its use in societal functioning and to the desirability—even the necessity—in the interests of the general welfare to charter and load with responsibility the roles that

[33] H. D. Anderson and P. E. Davidson, *Occupational Trends in the United States.* Stanford: Stanford Univ. Press, 1940, p. 1.

[34] On occupations as determinants and on occupational determinateness, see: H. S. Becker and J. W. Carper, "The Elements of Identification with an Occupation," *Am. Soc. Rev.,* 21 (June, 1956): 341–348. J. W. Carper and H. S. Becker, "Adjustments to Conflicting Expectations in the Development of Identification with an Occupation," *Soc. Forces,* 36 (Oct., 1957): 51–56. Gerth and Mills, *op. cit.,* pp. 309–310. Alex Inkeles and P. H. Rossi, "National Comparisons of Occupational Prestige," *Am. Jour. Soc.,* 61 (Jan., 1956): 329–339. R. W. Mack, "Occupational Determinateness: A Problem and Hypothesis in Role Theory," *Soc. Forces,* 35 (Oct., 1956): 20–25. R. W. Mack, "Occupational Ideology and the Determinate Role," *Soc. Forces,* 36 (Oct., 1957): 37–44.

the members of these vital, highly specialized occupations play. A profession is an occupation involving highly specialized knowledge and skill, usually of a highly esoteric or scientific nature, and acquired by special, intensive and extensive, advanced, formal instruction and training. This knowledge and skill is so specialized and profound that the benefiting public does not have either the knowledge or proficiency to judge the services. In general, when the learning and training are complicated and extensive, the services socially strategic and necessary, then the necessity of professionalizing the technique and practice becomes more insistent.

The actual process of professionalization involves, among several key features, two in particular: (1) the establishment and maintenance of high minimum qualifications and requirements in the way of special knowledge and practical and technical proficiency; and (2) the establishment and maintenance of high ethical standards governing the practice of the profession and the relationships of the practitioners with others. Increasingly, the specialized knowledge and skills are acquired in professional schools which require a foundation of general education as a prerequisite; the training usually involves instruction, laboratory experience, and apprenticeship practice.

Each profession also has its standards, usually stated in its code or canon of ethics. These codes emphasize the obligations of the professions to the public as a whole and particularly to their clients, patients, or employers; the kind and quality of work or service expected of members; permissible forms of compensation; types of acceptable promotion and competitive activity; obligations to fellow practitioners; forbidden acts; and general educational duties in their specialties. Sometimes special rights and privileges are also indicated.

The members of the different professions are usually organized into associations of their own, not only to maintain the organizational regulations, but also to preserve and enhance their activities in society. These include ministerial associations, bar and medical associations, associations of teachers and college professors, engineering societies. These associations usually participate in setting and accrediting curricula and training requirements of schools for the professional training, in defining requirements for admission to practice the profession, in administering examinations, in determining and developing the ethical codes, and in dismissing the incompetents and the egregious violators of the codes from the profession. Usually, however, the state has general and final regulatory responsibility and authority in most of these matters, since the services of the professions are indispensable to the general well-being, and a satisfactory level of quality must be assured. In general, the professional associations work with the state in these matters.

BIBLIOGRAPHY

GENERAL

Beals, R. L., and Hoijer, H., *An Introduction to Anthropology*. New York: Macmillan, 1953, pp. 357–381.

Beers, H. W., "The Rural Community," in Gittler, J. B. (ed.), *Review of Sociology*. New York: Wiley, 1957, pp. 196–220.

Berle, A. A., and Means, G. C., *The Modern Corporation and Private Property*. New York: Macmillan, 1933.

Boulding, K. E., "Economics: The Taming of Mammon" in White, Lynn, Jr. (ed.), *Frontiers of Knowledge in the Study of Man*. New York: Harper, 1956, pp. 132–149.

Brainerd, H. G., *Economics in Action*. New York: Oxford Univ. Press, 1959.

Caplow, T., *The Sociology of Work*. Minneapolis: Univ. of Minnesota Press, 1954.

Clark, J. M., *Economic Institutions and Human Welfare*. New York: Knopf, 1957.

Conoyer, H. G., and Vaile, R. S., *Economics of Income and Consumption*. New York: Ronald, 1951.

Davis, K., *Human Society*. New York: Macmillan, 1949, pp. 451–477.

Dewhurst, J. F., *et al.*, *America's Needs and Resources*. New York: Twentieth Century Fund, 1947.

Drucker, P., *America's Next Twenty Years*. New York: Harper, 1957, pp. 71–89.

Dubin, R., *The World of Work*. Englewood Cliffs, N.J.: Prentice-Hall, 1958.

Ebersole, Luke, *American Society: An Introductory Analysis*. New York: McGraw-Hill, 1955, pp. 335–378.

Firth, Raymond, "The Social Framework of Economic Organization," in *Elements of Social Organization*. New York: Phil. Lib., 1951, pp. 122–154.

Florence, P. S., *Industry and the State*. New York: Rinehart, 1957.

Form, W. H., and Miller, D. C., *Industry, Labor, and Community: An Institutional Analysis*. New York: Harper, 1960.

Galbraith, J. K., *The Affluent Society*. Boston: Houghton Mifflin, 1958.

Graham, Saxon, *American Culture*. New York: Harper, 1957, pp. 212–290.

Grigsby, S. E., and Linden, L. L., "The Sociology of Economic Organization," in Roucek, J. S. (ed.), *Contemporary Sociology*. New York: Phil. Lib., 1958, pp. 491–506.

Gross, E., *Work and Society*. New York: Crowell, 1958.

Hamilton, C. H., "The Sociology of Changing Agriculture," *Soc. Forces*, 37 (Oct., 1958): 1–7.

Herskovits, M. J., *The Economic Life of Primitive Peoples*. New York: Knopf, 1940.

Hofsommer, H., *The Sociology of American Life*. Englewood Cliffs, N.J.: Prentice-Hall, 1958, pp. 413–447.

Lundberg, G. A., Schrag, C. C., and Larson, O. N., *Sociology*. New York: Harper, 1954, pp. 581–619.

Martindale, D., *American Society*. Princeton, N.J.: Van Nostrand, 1960, pp. 298–356.

Miller, D. C., and Form, W. H., *Industrial Sociology*. New York: Harper, 1951.

Moore, W. E., *Industrial Relations and the Social Order*. New York: Macmillan, 1951.

Moore, W. E., *Economy and Society*. Garden City, N.Y.: Doubleday, 1955.

Ogle, M. B., Jr., Schneider, L., and Wiley, J. W., *Power, Order, and Economy*. New York: Harper, 1954.

Parsons, T., and Smelser, N. J., *Economy and Society: A Study in the Interpretation of Economic and Social Theory*. Glencoe, Ill.: Free Press, 1956.

Schneider, E. V., *Industrial Sociology: The Social Relations of Industry and the Community*. New York: McGraw-Hill, 1957, pp. 1–8, 29–46, 42–48, 51–202, 207–349.

Sumner, W. G., and Keller, A. G., *The Science of Society*. New Haven: Yale Univ. Press, 1927, Vol. I, pp. 95–350.

Warner, W. L., and Martin, N. H. (eds.), *Industrial Man: Business Men and Business Organizations*. New York: Harper, 1959.

Weber, Max, *The Theory of Social and Economic Organization*. (Henderson, A. M., and Parsons, T., transl.) Glencoe, Ill.: Free Press, 1947, pp. 158–323.

White, L. A., *The Evolution of Culture*. New York: McGraw-Hill, 1959, pp. 237–260, 329–353.

Whyte, W., *Industry and Society*. New York: McGraw-Hill, 1946.

Wilensky, H. L., and Lebeaux, C. M., *Industrial Society and Social Welfare*. New York: Russell Sage Foundation, 1958.

Williams, R. M., Jr., *American Society. A Sociological Analysis*. New York: 1960, pp. 150–214.

Winston, C. M., in Queen, S. A., Chambers, W. N., and Winston, C. M. (eds.), *The American Social System*. Boston: Houghton Mifflin, 1956, pp. 156–263.

Worcester, D. A., Jr., *Fundamentals of Political Economy*. New York: Ronald, 1953.

CONSUMPTION

Conoyer, H. O., and Vaile, R. S., *Economics of Income and Consumption*. New York: Ronald, 1951.

Gordon, L. J., *Economics for Consumers*. New York: Am. Book, 1953.

Kelley, P. C., *Consumer Economics*. Homewood, Ill.: Richard D. Irwin, Inc., 1953.

Parsons, T., and Smelser, N. J., *Economy and Society*. Glencoe, Ill.: Free Press, 1956, pp. 221–232.

Winston, C. M., "Consumers and Social Control," in Queen, S. A., Chambers, W. N., and Winston, C. M., *The American Social System*. Boston: Houghton Mifflin, 1956, pp. 183–204.

OCCUPATIONAL INSTITUTIONS

Caplow, T., *The Sociology of Work*. Minneapolis: Univ. of Minnesota Press, 1954, esp. pp. 100–141.

Dubin, R., *The World of Work*. Englewood Cliffs, N.J.: Prentice-Hall, 1958.

Gross, E., *Work and Society*. New York: Crowell, 1958.

Hiller, E. T., *Social Relations and Structures*. New York: Harper, 1947, pp. 479–493, 544–577.

Hughes, E. C., "Institutional Office and the Person," *Am. Jour. Soc.,* 43 (Nov., 1937): 404–413.
Hughes, E. C., *Men and Their Work*. Glencoe, Ill.: Free Press, 1958.

PROFESSIONS AND PROFESSIONALIZATION

Annals Am. Acad. Pol. & Soc. Science, 297 (Jan., 1955): entire number.
Carr-Saunders, A. M., *The Professions: Their Organization and Place in Society*. Oxford: Clarendon Press, 1928.
Carr-Saunders, A. M., "Metropolitan Conditions and Traditional Professional Relationships," in Fisher, R. M. (ed.), *The Metropolis in Modern Life*. Garden City, N.Y.: Doubleday, 1955, pp. 279–283.
Carr-Saunders, A. M., and Wilson, P. A., *The Professions*. Oxford: Clarendon Press, 1933.
Goode, W. J., "Community within a Community: The Professions," *Am. Soc. Rev.,* 22 (Apr., 1957): 194–200.
Gross, E., *Work and Society*. New York: Crowell, 1958, pp. 77–86.
Hiller, E. T., *Social Relations and Structures*. New York: Harper, 1947, pp. 544–580.
Landis, B. Y., *Professional Codes: A Sociological Analysis*. New York: Columbia Univ. Press, 1927.
MacIver, R. M., and Page, C. H., *Society*. New York: Rinehart, 1949, pp. 478–483.
Parsons, T., "The Professions and Social Structure," in Parsons, T. (ed.), *Essays in Sociological Theory*. Glencoe, Ill.: Free Press, 1954, pp. 34–49.

PARTICULAR OCCUPATIONS

Becker, H. S., "The Career of the Chicago Public School Teachers," *Am. Jour. Soc.,* 57 (Mar., 1952): 470–477.
Cottrell, W. F., "Of Time and the Railroader," *Am. Soc. Rev.,* 4 (Apr., 1939): 190–198.
Gold, Ray, "Janitors versus Tenants: A Status-Income Dilemma," *Am. Jour. Soc.,* 57 (Mar., 1952): 486–493.
Henry, W. E., "The Business Executive: The Psycho-Dynamics of a Social Role," *Am. Jour. Soc.,* 54 (Jan., 1949): 286–291.
Habenstein, R. W., and Lamers, W. M., *The History of American Funeral Directing*. Milwaukee: Bulfin Printers, Inc., 1955.
Merriam, A. P., and Mack, R. W., "The Jazz Community," *Soc. Forces,* 38 (Mar., 1960): 211–222.
Mills, C. W., *The New Men of Power: America's Labor Leaders*. New York: Harcourt, Brace, 1948.
Smith, L. M., "The Clergy: Authority, Structure, Ideology and Migration," *Am. Soc. Rev.,* 18 (June, 1953): 242–248.
Thorner, I., "Nursing: The Functional Significance of an Institutional Pattern," *Am. Soc. Rev.,* 20 (Oct., 1955): 531–538.
Weinberg, S. K., and Arond, H., "The Occupational Culture of the Boxer," *Am. Jour. Soc.,* 57 (Mar., 1952): 460–469.
Wray, D. E., "Marginal Men of Industry: The Foreman," *Am. Jour. Soc.,* 54 (Jan., 1949): 298–301.

Welfare Institutions

A third set of maintenance institutions is found in complex societies like our own which might be referred to as welfare institutions. The concern here is not with demographic maintenance, that is, the continuous supplying of persons to replace those dying, or with economic maintenance, that is, the provision of material goods and of reciprocal services deemed useful in satisfying human needs and wants, but with the maintenance of a quality and an adequacy of life for all members of the society, and where this has been lost for individuals and groups, a restoration of adequacy and quality of life.

In the main, the welfare institutions are a means of coping systematically with individual and social deficiencies, insufficiencies, hazards, and other adverse problem-producing conditions and situations, which result in individual distress, pain, frustration, loss of ability or opportunity to act like human beings, and various kinds of group and community disorganization. A partial catalog shows such common conditions and situations as bad heredity; ill health (mental, physical, emotional); accidents and their effects; old age and infirmity; economic insufficiency (poverty); maldistribution of income and gross economic inequality; impaired family relationships (family breakdown and broken homes); household mismanagement; ignorance and illiteracy; mental incompetence; physical handicaps, such as crippled limbs or organs, deafness, blindness, speech defects and consequent helplessness; neglected, deserted, and orphaned children; unemployment, workshyness and unemployability; delinquency and criminality; underprivilege of class or regional groups; minority groups suffering prejudice, discrimination, persecution; the tensions, frustrations, boredom and spiritual deterioration resulting from the strain of work and the routines of life and from inadequate or perverted recreation; too much leisure and misuse of leisure; inadequate housing; and the hazards of physical catastrophe such as flood, tornado, explosions, and fire.

Some of these situations and conditions are caused by physical, or biological, or psychological, or sociocultural factors, or by a combination of factors. Some are inescapable, especially those resting upon physical or genetic factors. Most are a societal responsibility, and all obviously exist at the moment and must be faced.

The welfare institutions—those that function in this domain of needs and wants—are an absolute maintenance necessity in a complex society like ours where all of the elements are so interrelated and interdependent that even a small proportion of the people cannot live in a state of ill-being. They seek to ameliorate the lot of unfortunate individuals by protection and supplementary aid; for example, they provide relief in time of economic distress due to sickness, unemployment, or accident; they treat family problem situations (death of a parent, desertion, divorce); they soften the incidence of homelessness, orphanhood, infirm and impoverished old age, physical catastrophe, economic depression or inflation. They provide care for the socially deficient and incompetent—those with physical, mental, and behavioral handicaps—and seek to rehabilitate these and restore them to the greatest usefulness that their capacities and the social circumstances permit. Some try to be corrective as well as restorative; for example, they seek to correct the types of conditions that make for family breakdown, that induce mental and emotional strain and breakdown, that make for impaired earning capacity, for household mismanagement, for delinquency and crime. Some have positive objectives; they seek to provide opportunities and conditions for physical, mental, emotional, and moral well-being by way of greater economic sufficiency and security, adequate and morally safe recreational facilities, wholesome physical conditions, good housing and healthful physical environment, amicable and socially productive relations between races, ethnic groups, and social strata. All ultimately seek to detect, and, wherever the social conditions and available scientific knowledge and technology permit, to prevent individual and social weaknesses and pathological conditions before they impair individual and societal functioning.

Many of the social welfare activities, as activities, are as old as human societies; some have had a degree of institutional form and function in some of the great ancient civilizations. The practice of charity—the care for the poor, hungry, sick, aged and infirm, the orphaned, the handicapped, the strangers—has been almost universal; there has always been some sort of effort to provide for health and to protect against mischance; there have always been efforts to cope with the delinquent and criminal; there has always been some sort of recreational activity. Most of these activities in our society, however, are still more or less nascent, groping and immature, as institutions. Nevertheless, they are getting an enormous amount of attention; vast funds, private and public, are being spent upon them; most of them are developing institutional organizational form and a professional personnel; all are having a noticeable though variable impact on our social life. They are obviously developing as institutions because modern societies sternly require established and systematized social instrumentalities that maintain and promote the general welfare of the people.

Mutual aid as practiced by the family and the clan, and conducted by means of the folkways, customs, and mores, was the way in which the poor and helpless were cared for in the simpler or primitive societies. The number of people involved as grantors and recipients was small, the relationships were of a primary nature, and the procedures were informal. Among many primitives the basic property was of a communal nature; hence, there was no likelihood of poverty or economic neglect of some of the population, and very little differentiation between rich and poor. Widows and orphans were frequently absorbed into families. Tribal ethics not uncommonly permitted the abandonment of the sick, the non-productive aged, and the grossly incompetent. Because of the shortness of life, the primitives did not have much of a problem with the aged. Health activities consisted of the use of traditional remedies and practices, some of the latter being of a magical nature and conducted by the shaman and the medicine man. In fact, natural selection operated with natural freedom and proficiency, taking care of many of the problems of dependency, helplessness, and ill health. Recreation was a regular part of everyday and day-to-day life; the work itself had its daily and seasonal fluctuations and changes, and was interspersed with much leisure. Such occasions as the religious festivals and the planting and harvesting dances and other activities provided frequent community recreation.

In the great ancient civilizations some of these functions were conducted in part by other institutions; others were conducted in a semi-institutional manner. The successive revisions of the law of the ancient Hebrews show a growing awareness of responsibility for treating such situations and a progressive development of institutionalized forms of procedure. The Greeks and Romans had various methods of relieving or removing distress, such as family or neighborly mutual aid, concubinage (sometimes referred to as a form of mother's pension), slavery, elimination by death, and various public means of relief, such as free grain, oil, and wine, placement of poor on the land, and free public baths. These ancient civilizations also had their healing superstitions, arts, practitioners, and various activities, quite apart from the pauses in the daily tasks, that provided recreation, such as the festivals and holidays, the games and sports, the dances, the dramatics and pageants.

When the Roman Empire adopted Christianity, the Church came to be important—eventually supremely important—in welfare activities, and this supremacy continued in Europe into the sixteenth century. Parishes, monasteries, and also the secular guilds distributed alms, and the guilds administered almshouses; hospitals and hospices, usually run by monasteries or religious orders, provided some care for the aged, the unemployed, the handicapped, the sick, the orphans, and accommodations for travelers, though beggary and vagabondage were rife. However, in the sixteenth century, the secularization of social welfare activities began. Cities passed ordinances setting up civilly administered poor relief; begging was punished or licensed; the able-bodied were set to work; the incompetent were cared for in institutions. But the functioning personnel was ill-trained, and the services poorly administered and more or less indiscriminate. For example, the English almshouses had in them unemployed, aged, blind, and insane people, and frequently also criminal elements.

In general, among Western peoples prior to the nineteenth century, the great bulk of welfare services available were provided informally by the family and incidentally by other local groups. The services supplementing those of the family or those required to meet new types or wider ranges of needs were provided in a somewhat institutionalized manner by certain agencies in the Church and agencies set up by governmental bodies. The Industrial Revolution, however, with its redistribution and concentration of population, its growth of cities, its industrial and health hazards, its unemployment, its sharpening of class lines, its exaggerations in the distribution of wealth, its increasing insecurity of the individual and the family, in fact, its disorganizing effect upon almost all other institutions, created a complex of greatly changed and new conditions. The traditional, the ancient, the groping, and stop-gap, partially institutionalized procedures were found to be quite inadequate. A much higher degree of institutionalization of welfare activities with the corresponding regularity, adequacy, responsibility, and expertness of action came to be absolutely essential.

Large numbers of people have difficulty adequately adjusting themselves by their own efforts to the problem conditions confronting them; for example, meeting unemployment risks, managing households with a given income, getting ready for the "rainy day." Physical health protection is a problem for them, not to mention coping with neuroses, psychoses, or alcoholism. Many have difficulty arranging their own means of recreation. Millions of people who would find little or no difficulty adjusting themselves in a simpler society are unable to do so without help in a complex society. The old family, clan, and neighborhood means of taking care of welfare needs are less and less effective. The disappearance of the extended family and the physical and emotional separation from kinsmen encourage a lessened sense of responsibility for aged, or sick, or orphaned relatives. The modern urban family lacks the facilities for providing many essential welfare services. The houses, flats, and apartments are too small to enable the family to conduct any other than its standard nuclear family activities. There is no room for the aged,

for the bed-ridden sick, for the mentally ill or retarded, for the physically handicapped, for the orphans of relatives, and—under the pressures of modern needs—no family skills or technological facilities for
caring for them. There is room for only limited, mainly sedentary, recreational activity. Thus, many social welfare activities, once assumed
by the family, now are thrown on the community.

There is the realization in our society that there must be a set of
institutions not only to take over some of the welfare functions once
performed incidentally and inadequately by other institutional systems, but also to alleviate and if possible to correct the maladjustments caused by the inadequate operation of these institutions as they
affect the well being of people and the community. For example, many
of the problems of the family, such as the broken home, do not seem
to be manageable within the present family set-up; the state seems to
need a lot of help in treating delinquency and criminality, not to mention coping with the effects of these; the effects of ignorance and illiteracy, the elimination of which is the essential function of the educational system, cannot go unattended; setbacks caused by the economic
system must be alleviated. By-products of the malfunctioning of institutions require new or special kinds of technics and techniques for their
salvage and protection.

A new ethic directly affecting welfare activity is developing in our
society, adjusted to its impersonal, secondary-group nature; namely,
that every community has a responsibility for assuring the welfare of its
inhabitants. There is increasing acceptance of the interpretation that
society in large measure creates the conditions that necessitate social
welfare activity, and that, regardless of personal condition, class, race,
or any other differential conditions, every human being is entitled to
a certain minimal quantity and quality of life. In our kind of society
this means a revision of the Golden Rule: Do unto others in an institutionalized manner to be sure that it is done certainly, equitably, universally, and efficiently, what you would have others do unto you.
Hence, the community or the greater society has the responsibility of
marshalling all of the different sorts of pertinent resources to treat
the maladjusted persons and groups. Related to this is the belief that
many individual physical, psychological, and economic ills and most
socially pathological states are not necessarily inevitable and are suscep-
tible to successful treatment, that, at any rate, efforts ought to be made
to cure and even prevent them.

Realization of the survivalistic, utilitarian, and social-economic value
of good and efficient welfare institutions is evident in communities that
feel they should not carry and need not carry any more dead weight in
the way of the economic or morally impoverished, the dependent aged,
the diseased, the handicapped, and the criminal than the present knowl-

edge and technology permit. They are realizing that it is good economy to carry on restorative activities, whereby proper treatment and training allow the occupational misfits, the physically handicapped, the emotionally unstable, the feebleminded, those in poor physical health, the habitual criminals to be as productive as possible and capable as far as possible of carrying their own load. This sort of thing is sometimes referred to as a restorative investment. Provision of community agencies organized to alleviate, correct, and prevent ill-being is now considered good community business. Conversely, there is a realization today that a community or society can have about as much dependency, poverty, illness, profligacy, perverted recreation, illiteracy, delinquency and criminality as it is willing to pay for.

Finally, there is the growing realization that most welfare services in a society like ours can be performed much better by institutionalized agencies. Most welfare problems require a great deal more than do-it-yourself treatment and are far too complicated to be managed by amateurs. Institutionalized agencies have the ability to acquire and apply the scientific knowledge; they have the trained, specialized, professional personnel; they have the necessary organizational structure and equipment. Increasingly, the responsibility for rendering many of these services is vested in public, even federal, agencies.[1]

I: Social Work Institutions

The social work institutions are the instrumental means whereby most of the social welfare activities are systematically conducted in our society. In the comprehensive and definitely institutionalized form which they have assumed during the last half century, they are among the youngest of our institutional systems. Their objectives are to utilize scientifically all sorts of personal and social resources in examining, alleviating, correcting, and preventing conditions that make for pathological individual, group, and community conditions; particularly and immediately, to restore the disorganized or subnormally operating in-

---

[1] Cf., Nels Anderson, "Welfare in the Modern Community," in his *The Urban Community: A World Perspective*. New York: Holt, 1959, pp. 403–428. The magnitude of the involvement of our federal government in welfare activities is indicated in a recent anouncement. In 1953 the government spent about 6.9 billion dollars on welfare, including the various types of payments to retired and disabled persons, to people on relief (i.e., receiving public assistance), to unemployed workers, to students, colleges and school districts for grants, loans, and school lunches, and for hospitals and other health activities. The welfare budget for the fiscal year beginning July 1, 1960 totals 20.3 billion dollars. This means that 21 cents out of every dollar the federal government spends will go for welfare. Reported by *U.S. News and World Report*, Feb. 8, 1960, pp. 60–61.

dividuals and groups to more or less normal or adequate functioning; and to keep and make individuals and groups fit to function effectively in a social system. These activities are in a large measure determined by the social values of the moment. Social work is concerned, first, with helping people do things that they cannot do for themselves because of their own condition or the nature of the situation in which they find themselves. This means helping people cope with untoward conditions and states within themselves, such as physical, emotional, or mental handicaps, ill-health or incompetence, or other individual inadequacy, such as occasioned by childhood or old age and infirmity, so that they may function as fully as their inadequacies permit, and helping normal people confronted with problems beyond their control, such as those accompanying economic depression, unemployment, death of a wage-earner, accident, illness, or physical catastrophe, or the state in which orphaned or abandoned children find themselves, so that they may be restored as normal social participants. Second, it is concerned with helping people who are in a state of bad social relationships with others to extricate or rehabilitate themselves, as in the case of delinquents and criminals, or those suffering the strains and tensions of impaired family relationships, or of minority group prejudice and discrimination. Third, it is concerned with helping people do co-operatively-collectively what they cannot do singly and by themselves, such as providing recreational facilities, carrying on all kinds of group and community corrective, preventive, creative, constructive, and re-constructive activities which counter collective weaknesses and disorganization and which redound to welfare ends in that they make possible a positive, full, individual, and social life for the people.

Institutionalized social work activities vary in form, scope, and the auspices under which they are conducted. A primary distinction among institutionalized social work activities is that between private and public agencies. Private organizations are voluntary associations of people as private citizens with a common desire and common means to contribute to the solution of some welfare problem. As Nelson points out,[2] they are usually chartered by the state and incorporated as non-profit organizations; they are operated by a board of directors representing the membership and a paid staff of professional social workers; the funds come from free-will contributions of persons or groups, sometimes from other larger organizations in which the activities are conducted, sometimes from endowments and foundations, and in many instances from local Community Chests or Funds. These privately organized activities take various forms. Industries and labor unions have organized agencies to provide for the security of workers against dis-

[2] L. Nelson, *Rural Sociology*. New York: Am. Book, 1948, p. 437.

ability, unemployment, old age, and other maladjustments. Agencies affiliated with religious organizations provide many such social work services; for example, those provided in old people's homes, orphanages and hospitals, and such institutions as the Roman Catholic Houses of the Good Shepherd; the services provided by the Protestant deacons and deaconesses, and by the Catholic healing and other social service orders; and recently the rendering of psychiatric services under church auspices. The great bulk of the private agencies, and the ones providing a great variety of services, are those local organizations or local chapters of national organizations that are usually supported at least in considerable part by local Community Chests. Notable are organizations providing family relief, counseling and rehabilitation services, mental health and hygiene services, child guidance, child placing, and other child welfare services; organizations conducting youth activities and recreational activities; organizations providing services for transients (Travelers' Aid Society); and organizations providing workshops for handicapped persons (such as the Goodwill Industries). Represented locally as parts of national organizations are the Boy Scouts, Girl Scouts, Y.M.C.A., Y.W.C.A., Y.M.H.A., the Red Cross, Association for Probation and Parole, Association for the Blind, and the Salvation Army.

Public welfare institutions are those conducted by governmental bodies; they are arms of the modern service or welfare state. They provide services at three levels. Local services are those provided by townships, counties, or municipalities and conducted under the supervision of the township or county commissioners or supervisors and special municipal boards (for example, the Board of Health). In more populous counties there may be a special Welfare Department. Services include those provided by poor farms, the giving of outdoor relief to the indigent, the provision of local recreational facilities, such as parks and playgrounds, the provision of medical and nursing services through a county or city or city-county health set-up, counseling services provided for adults on probation, juvenile delinquents, and those suffering from impaired family relations. At the state level are the various forms of assistance now usually provided jointly with federal agencies and funds for the indigent aged, the blind, dependent children and mothers, and the custodial, educational, therapeutic, correctional, and rehabilitative services offered in special institutions for the blind, deaf, feebleminded, mentally ill, and convicted delinquents and criminals, usually under the general organization and supervision of a State Board (or Division) of Public Welfare, State Board of Control, or similar title.

Federal social work has experienced a marked growth and expansion, especially since 1930. The Social Security Act of 1935 permanently established a welfare system by the federal government. It comprises three main programs. The first is the Social Insurance program which provides a federal old age and survivors insurance system (O.A.S.I.) and a federal-state system of unemployment compensation, both schemes supported by joint contributions of worker and employer. The second system, Public Assistance, provides services in cooperation with the states: general family financial assistance for distress cases, assistance to the needy aged, aid to dependent children, aid to persons with impairment of sight, hearing, and mentality, and to the permanently and totally disabled. Programs providing for child welfare services and for vocational rehabilitation are also conducted in cooperation with the states. The third major program under the Social Security Act, established under the revision of 1954, provides an array of public health services, and will be briefly discussed in Section III. The federal government also has made provisions for general relief to counteract the effect of economic dislocations, epidemics, and other physical or social disasters. In the 1930's, for example, there were extensive assistance-constructive activities carried on by the Works Progress Administration (W.P.A.) and the Civilian Conservation Corps (C.C.C.). Other organizations provided welfare assistance to certain portions of the population. The Federal Security Administration, for example, provided direct relief to farm families in extreme distress, gave loans to farmers who could not get them elsewhere, and helped farmers on poor land to move elsewhere.

In the United States the welfare activities of local and state governments are increasingly being overshadowed by those of the federal government, which covers more people, spends more money, and exerts more influence than the lesser governmental agencies combined. Social work is coming to be another major national governmental function.

Another distinction frequently made is that between general and specialized agencies. The general agencies are those designed to cover more than one form of social need; for example, the aged, the blind, the needy, and children. The typical county welfare system in the United States is a good example of such an agency. Such organizations as Catholic Welfare Associations and Jewish Welfare Associations also provide a variety of services for different categories of needy persons. However, in order to provide a quality of service, the specialized agencies are coming to be more and more important. At the private level there are the specialized agencies providing family counseling and rehabilitation services, child guidance clinics, and other child welfare services, travelers' aid (under the national Travelers' Aid Society), disaster relief (under the Red Cross Disaster Unit). At the public level there are the special agencies or special divisions of agencies concerned with family services, children's services, medical and nursing services, specialized functions under the courts, such as services for those on probation and parole.

Social work activity is closely related to other agencies and professions in the community. Social work services are provided in connection with the programs of such agencies as schools, churches, counseling and guidance agencies, courts, hospitals and clinics, boards of probation and parole, and reformatories and penitentiaries. Social workers have professional collaboration with teachers, doctors, psychiatrists, psychologists, lawyers, judges, nurses, the clergy, probation and parole officers, and other professional personnel. Social workers also conduct social work services, and engage in research and consultative activities in various national, state-wide, and local public programs that involve welfare. They are also beginning to be used in connection with the welfare services of industrial and commercial establishments and of labor organizations.

THE MAJOR OPERATIONAL TYPES OF SOCIAL WORK

A further way of understanding social work in a complex modern society is to note the different major types of operation and activity, or what amounts to the same thing, the different primary methodologies employed through the entire range of social work. The major specialized areas are case work, group work, and community organization. They are related and often overlap in particular instances of treatment; the first two especially are frequently conjoined.

SOCIAL CASE WORK. In social case work the relation is between a client with some need requiring examination and treatment and a professional social worker trained in case work procedures. It is a one-to-one relationship, and the action is person-to-person and person-by-person. Each problem individual is looked upon as a case in much the same sense that a physician views a sick or an injured person. Each individual and his problems are looked upon as unique, and the whole social work activity or method is tailored to meet the specific case. In each instance the case worker also functions somewhat like a physician. He is called in or takes over when non-social behavior, accident, unemployment, illness, family crisis, financial crisis, or other adversity creates a problem too big or complex for the individual to handle by himself.

Case work is a highly developed and at the same time a flexible procedure; it represents the very core of professional social work practice. Viewed in a very general way, in each case the social case worker tries to diagnose the state of the individual and determine the more crucial factors—individual, social environmental, physical environmental—responsible for the state the individual is in; he marshals a wide variety of resources available in the community—physical, economic, medical, psychiatric, legal, educational, recreational, and religious, depending upon the requirements of the particular case—for immediate assistance and for the program of treatment and rehabilitation. He functions as counsellor, guide, and educator. The major objective is to get the individual as far as possible to help himself out of his predicament; this involves first of all getting him to assess his own situation, and then to realize his own capacities, to face his limitations, to build up his weaknesses, to develop compensations, and to avail himself of supplements and aids in the community. Thus case work is assistance in self determination.

Case work is the major methodology in almost every kind of social work involving individuals or small social units such as families. It is the basic treatment procedure in family welfare work of all kinds such as economic distress, marital discord, personality difficulty, physical or mental handicap, incompetent management, and conflict between children and parents; in the provision of children's services of all kinds; in the social services rendered by the courts, for example in those relating to juvenile delinquents, probation, and to domestic relations problems; in the activities of social workers connected with physical and mental hospitals and some public health organizations; in the work of school social workers; and in psychiatric social work.[3]

SOCIAL GROUP WORK. Social group work deals primarily with persons in their group relationships; it is the procedure involved in helping individuals enjoy and benefit from their voluntary participation in the activities of groups specially organized for welfare ends. The activities are carried on mainly during leisure time and are primarily of a recreational and informal educational nature. Social group work aims at the growth and development of individuals through group experience. Its major purpose is to provide normal and satisfying and interesting group activities not readily available in urban community life, though on occasion it is also used in rural communities. The group activities are carried on in group agencies and are conducted under the supervision and stimulus of both professional-paid and amateur-volunteer leaders. In group work, as in case work, there are certain basic principles that

---

[3] For a fuller discussion of these different kinds of social work involving case work, see: "Social Work as a Profession," by the Council on Social Work Education, 1953, pp. 19–24. Helen L. Witmer, *Social Work: Analysis of a Social Institution*. New York: Farrar & Rinehart, 1942, pp. 21–29. Phillip Klein, "The Social Theory of Professional Social Work," in H. E. Barnes, H. Becker and F. B. Becker, *Contemporary Social Theory*. New York: Appleton, 1950, esp. pp. 761–772. W. A. Friedlander, *et al., Concepts and Methods of Social Work*. Englewood Cliffs, N.J.: Prentice-Hall, 1958, Chap. II.

are observed and a technology that is within the general social work methodology, but the formalized procedure is not nearly so well developed. It is recognized that the best values of group life and the desired therapeutic results of group participation are not achieved automatically.

Group work is carried on in settlement houses and community centers, mainly in underprivileged neighborhoods, where joint activities for all ages are provided in game rooms, in arts and crafts rooms, on playgrounds and in gymnasiums, in summer camps, in special classes, in social clubs (such as dramatic and hobby clubs), and various other interest groups. The so-called youth-serving agencies, sometimes also referred to as character-building organizations, such as the Y.M.C.A., Y.W.C.A., Catholic Youth Organization, Boy Scouts, Girl Scouts, Camp Fire Girls, and the 4-H Clubs, are concerned mainly with group work activities. There is also group work specially designed for therapeutic purposes carried on in schools for the retarded and handicapped, in hospitals and convalescent homes, in children's homes, in homes for the aged, and in churches.

The most common activities conducted by group work agencies are outdoor and indoor athletics, education classes of a scholastic nature, music and dramatics, drawing, painting and sculpture, library and debating clubs, sedentary recreation such as reading and games, lectures and speeches by prominent people, mothers' clubs, health education classes, neighborhood improvement organizations, domestic science classes in cooking, sewing, household decoration, and clothing designing, and camping and country vacations.[4]

COMMUNITY ORGANIZATION. This third major social work methodology is concerned mainly with organizing the various social work agencies and welfare interests for the better supplying of social welfare services in the community. However, in social scientific terminology the term community organization has two slightly different connotations: the one is that of the sociological analysts of the community, the other that of the professional social workers. The two connotations are interrelated; both are concerned with continually maintaining the community at an acceptable level of efficiency; both, in the end, involve what amounts to the institutionalization of an essential welfare activity, namely, the continuous development of the community. In-

[4] Klein, op. cit., p. 776. On social group work in general, see: Witmer, op. cit., pp. 29–34. Gertrude Wilson and Gladys Ryland, Social Group Work Practice: The Creative Use of the Social Process. Boston: Houghton Mifflin, 1949. H. B. Trecker, Social Group Work: Principles and Practices (rev. ed.). New York: Whiteside, Inc., 1955. Helen V. Phillips, Essentials of Social Group Work Skill. New York: Association Press, 1957. Friedlander, op. cit., Ch. III.

cidentally, in this particular instance we also have a notable example of the institutionalization of reorganizational activity in the community.

The first connotation is related to the sociological approach which conceives of the community as a highly organized structural-functional system made up of a complex of social institutions that must be kept operationally equilibrated so that all of the community's various sectors of needs are adequately satisfied. Community organization in the second sense is that of the social work profession and particularly involves the use of established social work techniques and agencies to bring about the same ends as that of the sociological approach. Community organization in either or both senses is of obvious importance in systemic analysis, since it involves the health and welfare of the community and most of the institutions in most of the major institutional sectors; it has itself developed certain institutional features. Hence somewhat more attention will be paid to it than to some of the other, by no means unimportant, categories of contemporary institutionalized welfare activities.

Community organization in the sociological sense. In this interpretation, attention is focused upon the deliberately devised, organized procedures and agencies that seek to keep the community as functionally fit as possible. This means that efforts are made to halt disorganization, to reorganize various functional agencies, and to produce essential new agencies and functions to meet the needs wrought by social change. A community is always in a state of becoming, and when its inhabitants act as if it were static or automatically correcting, problems of all kinds will bedevil it.

Although the definitions of community organization in the sociological sense vary with respect to certain details, they have a fairly consistent general connotation. Blackwell points out that community organization consists of "a rationally directed effort to modify the social organization of a particular locality to achieve rationally designed coordination." He adds, "It is utilitarian, purposive, so that the needs of individuals may be more satisfactorily met." He points out also that "the process of community organization may be initiated within a selected segment of the social organization of the locality, or it may be comprehensive in its coverage."[5] Sanderson defines community organization as "a continuous process for obtaining the best integrated social interaction of individuals, groups and institutions within a community so as to enable it to act collectively and advance the common

[5] Gordon W. Blackwell, "A Theoretical Framework for Sociological Research in Community Organization," *Soc. Forces,* 33 (Oct., 1954): 57–64. Blackwell, "A Sociologist on School-Community Relationships," *Annals Am. Acad. Pol. & Soc. Science,* 302 (Nov., 1955): 128–135.

welfare." The nature of community organization is further clarified in his statement of its aims: "to develop relationships between groups and individuals that will enable them to act together in creating and maintaining facilities and agencies through which they may realize their highest values in the common welfare of all members of the community."[6]

Thus community organization is concerned with the correction of existing community problems, the anticipation of future needs before they become acute, and the timely preparation for them. Although the great bulk of community reorganizational activity is still devoted to the first task, the more alert the community the more is its attention and action directed to the second objective, for in the end this is the most economical way in almost every respect. Without any attempt at categorization as to objectives or at offering a complete inventory, the following are the types of projects toward which community organization efforts are directed.

Housing, redevelopment, property improvement, and zoned use of property.

Better highways, extension of parking facilities, traffic facilitation and control.

Control, possibly the elimination of, moral hazards such as red light districts or spot prostitution, road houses, gambling houses, narcotics traffic.

Health improvement, such as extension and improvement of clinical and hospital services, public nursing services, safeguarding of food dispensing services and of eating establishments, mental health, tuberculosis and venereal disease detection and control, rat and noxious insect and weed elimination.

Sanitary sewer improvement, especially sewage disposal plants, instead of dumping.

Clean-up and anti-litter campaigns.

Better fire protection.

Improvement of education facilities and services: increase and improvement of plant, salaries, curriculum, adult and other special education, consolidation, and so on.

Creation, expansion, and improvement of recreational means (play areas, parks, etc.) and services including recreational programs.

Water supply: extension, safeguarding against contamination, anticipation of future needs.

Delinquency, especially juvenile, and criminality.

Race and majority-minority group relations.

[6] Dwight Sanderson, *Rural Sociology and Rural Organization*. New York: Wiley, 1942, pp. 686, 687. See also Jessie Bernard, *American Community Behavior*. New York: Dryden, 1949, p. 43.

Every community, of course, will also have its own special problems and unmet needs that demand attention and treatment in the interests of well-being.

Community organization as social work methodology, with special reference to agencies. Community organization as a basic social work process or methodology does not concentrate attention upon the individual, as in case work, nor it is concerned with satisfying therapeutic and fulfilling activities carried on by and for persons in different kinds of groups. It is rather concerned with intergroup work; that is, the aggregation of interest groups and social work agencies of the community that maintain and develop interest in social work, that conduct the various kinds of social work activities, and that jointly integrate, plan, and organize and reorganize for the community's future social welfare.

The main agency for providing these intergroup relationships and for conducting the intergroup processes is known as the Council of Social Agencies, the Community Council, or some similar title. It is a cooperative organization, consisting of representatives of all kinds of organizations, increasingly both private and public, in the community which promote and conduct programs of social work, health, recreation, and education. Such diverse welfare interests and organizations as the family service agencies, the different kinds of child welfare agencies, the public health department, the public recreation department, the character-building agencies, including parent-teacher associations, the local mental health agencies, the social hygiene society, the school system, the chamber of commerce, the community centers, increasingly the churches and the ministerial association, the medical association, the bar association, the police department, the city federation of labor, civic and fraternal organizations, veterans' organizations, the city planning board, the county commissioners, and even farmers' organizations, may be represented. As a rule the representatives are more or less equally divided between lay board members (in the case of private voluntary organizations with boards of directors) and professional paid workers from the agencies. Some community welfare councils also have delegates-at-large supposedly representing the interests of the entire community.

The functions of the council are varied but interrelated. It is not a direct action agency; rather, it functions as a studying, counseling, coordinating and planning medium.[7] The council seeks to maintain an over-all view of the purposes and achievements of member agencies.

---

[7] For a comprehensive treatment of the nature, functions, and composition of community councils, see A. Hillman, *Community Organization and Planning.* New York: Macmillan, 1950, pp. 157–179.

This it does mainly in the discussions during meetings and through its various committees. It serves as a stimulus to the observance of scientific facts and principles and sound practices in the various welfare fields; usually there are standing committees for such problem areas as health, housing, deliquency, family welfare, child welfare, and recreation. It seeks to coordinate and dovetail the activities of the different agencies. In this same connection, the council tries to avoid duplication of services or activities on the part of the agencies. Most councils, for example, conduct a Social Service Exchange, which is a clearing house for cases to prevent several agencies from rendering similar services to a given case, but which at the same time serves as a means of assuring appropriate and adequate service. The council also seeks to improve both standards and services.

Paralleling the council in most urban communities is the Community Chest. Its first function is to raise funds which support, in whole or in part, the agencies affiliated with the council. This it does by means of the single annual drive that seeks to collect the funds as cheaply as possible, without annoying the citizenry at large and without resorting to "payroll looting" or any other high-handed methods. The Chest also allocates the funds among the several agencies, usually in consultation with the council. Most Chests require all member agencies to submit annual budgets which are checked and usually revised before they are approved. Business management practices, including uniform accounting standards, are usually established, and periodic audits of the books of the agencies are conducted.

The institutionalization of community organization. From both the sociological and the social work points of view, community organization is a more or less institutionalized, reorganizational undertaking and involves certain principles, procedures, techniques, and mechanisms.

Identification of the important community needs along efficiency and welfare lines, on the basis of the common values of the community, rests on the initial assumption that a fairly deep and widely shared discontent exists in the community with respect to certain conditions. But, to become dynamic and lead to community motivation, the discontent must be focused. The problem or problems must be specifically and clearly identified as to nature, if possible; as to some of the more important and generally comprehensible reasons why they exist; and as to their particular gravity or disorganizing effects. The problem needs to be the concern of many, even though the likely action of a corrective or therapeutic nature may be in behalf of segmental or minority elements of the community. Next, it is necessary to examine, as to both variety and functional efficiency, the adequacy of the existent service-rendering means of the community. This consists of identifying, inventorying, and analyzing the community resources and facilities—

natural, human, organizational, and institutional—that are available, or can be made available, for meeting the determined needs. It also involves estimating the cost of these needed services. Sometimes these activities involve fact-finding studies and surveys. Then objectives are set up, responsibilities are assigned to particular agencies, the proposed modification of possibly both the structure and function of certain applicable existing agencies is presented; new agencies to meet new needs may be suggested, the means of marshalling and utilizing the other pertinent resources and facilities are proposed.

When the planning and setting up of a program of action, or alternate proposals, to effect the solution is complete, different kinds of social action, often of a sequential nature, are involved next. A campaign educates the public to the needs, gaps, resources, and objectives, and the desirability and feasibility of the proposed solution or alternative solutions, by means of the press, radio, television, conferences and panel discussions, special bulletins, demonstrations, and exhibitions. Decisions are made through the approval of a solution or a choice among alternatives. In the case of action involving public bodies, this usually means arranging for the submission of the issues to the citizenry during an election. The reorganizing or creative action itself may mean turning the task over to the appropriate agency (health department, police department, engineering department, or, where the action is of a semi-public nature, the effecting of a special community organization, such as a housing commission, a bridge-building and operating authority, or a zoning board.

All of the preceding rests upon the functioning personnel and certain purposive organizations. Participation by as many interested and informed people of the community as possible should be encouraged, but especially essential is the involvement of leaders, both informal and formal, identified with and accepted by the various elements and groups in the community. It is the business of certain kinds of associations— committees, councils, commissions, corporations, authorities, or other forms of organization—to obtain the clarification and focusing of the discontent, to enlist the interest and good will of all the members of the community, to channel the aims and efforts of the concerned community members, and especially to serve as the actual procedural instruments in initiating and conducting the constructive activities.[8]

[8] Among the almost universal associations utilized in American cities for some of these services are the community councils and Community Chests, just noted above. More specialized, particularly focused and organized, and usually somewhat temporary associations are often also needed in carrying out particular reorganizational tasks; e.g., slum clearance, downtown renewal and redevelopment, traffic reorganization.

PUBLIC WELFARE ADMINISTRATION. A fourth area of social work methodology might be mentioned, although it is a complex of the basic services just discussed, plus certain others peculiar to the types of functions carried on by public agencies. Involved are a variety of standardized practices as employed by the public agencies dealing with delinquency and crime (the procedures of a correctional and rehabilitative nature in the jails, reformatories, penitentiaries, and prison farms, and in conducting probation, parole, and clinical services); the special procedures employed by the public assistance agencies and those used in the institutional care of the mentally ill and incompetent, of children and of the aged; the operation of physical health agencies (clinical, educational, investigative) and the nursing services they render.[9]

SOCIAL WORK AS AN INSTITUTION

The crucial nature of social work in a society like ours has required that it be more and more institutionalized. Increasingly, it shows all of the major components of a typical institution—a substantial body of values, a normative structure of codes and charters, physical equipment, and so on. It also has its methods of examination and its treatment procedures based on modern scientific knowledge.[10] But its special social organizational distinctiveness can be emphasized by an examination of two of its systematic characteristics; namely, the professionalization of its functional personnel and its agency or associational aspects.

As a profession, social work is comparatively new. Until quite recently most of its functional personnel were amateurs, volunteers, or persons rendering welfare services as a tangential aspect of their major occupation (as priest, minister, or public official). Some of its paid workers still do not meet what are deemed essential professional requirements in all respects.[11] But increasingly there is a realization that social work activity is so specialized as well as crucial that it cannot be conducted satisfactorily by untutored and untrained persons, however well-meaning and devoted they may be. Today more and more agencies, both private and public, depend on full-time professional workers to carry on all technical operations. Social work is developing a body of

[9] Cf. *Methods of Public Welfare Administration*. New York: United Nations, Dept. of Social Affairs, 1950.

[10] For a most skillful and comprehensive treatment of social work as an institution, see Helen L. Witmer, *Social Work: An Analysis of a Social Institution*. New York: Farrar & Rinehart, 1942, esp. the treatment according to Malinowski's conceptualization of institutions, pp. 18–66.

[11] Note the following: "Of the estimated 75,000 social workers in 1950 in the country, approximately only 16 per cent have had the full two-year graduate curriculum. Approximately another 11 per cent have had one to two years. Of the 73 per cent with less than a year of training, approximately 60 per cent have had no study at all in a graduate school of social work." Nathan E. Cohen, *Social Work: In the American Tradition*. New York: Dryden, 1958, p. 337.

specialized, exclusive, and distinctive knowledge derived in consider-able part from the social sciences, particularly sociology, psychology, social psychology, psychiatry, social economics, and political science, as well as from biology and medicine. It has a considerable body of principles and techniques of professional practice applicable in analysis, diagnosis, and treatment, based on carefully analyzed experience and increasingly on research and experiment. These social work practices, whether focused upon individual problems or upon group relationships, are not yet as highly developed as, for example, those in teaching, law, or medicine, but there is a development of patterns of performance based on theoretical knowledge, practical experience, discipline, and skill. It has its codes of professional practice, mainly set by its profes-sional organizations, but in the case of some types of activity also based upon specifications set by the legislation covering the type of welfare service.

Social work has developed standard educational and formal training minima which are required or recommended for the professional social worker. At present these consist of two years of graduate study in a professional school of social work beyond four years of college-level preparatory work. As of 1956 there were 49 such professional schools of social work in the United States (including Puerto Rico and Hawaii) and 7 in Canada. Most of these schools were members of the American Association of Schools of Professional Social Work, which, among various obvious concerns, is interested not only in training programs but also in the essentials in the certification of professional social workers. There is also a Council on Social Work Education con-cerned with content and standards in social work training. It should be pointed out, however, that despite these formal provisions for standard professional training, there is still considerable variation among the different states in the training actually required for social work positions. Some, for example, more lenient than others, will employ people of less than college-level training and with only a smattering of technical course work, or even none at all.

A final aspect of professionalization is the formal national associa-tion of social workers, known as the American Association of Social Workers. It consists of experienced social workers who have formal training, and it attempts to raise standards for training and practice in the profession. Nation-wide organizations of social work specialties also exist, such as the American Association of Medical Social Workers. There is also the National Conference of Social Work, the membership of which consists of social workers and representatives, both profes-sional and lay, of all manner of social work agencies, private and public. It holds annual meetings and provides a means of examination and dis-cussion of pertinent matters—conditions requiring social work, education and training for social work, new developments in social work practice, professional standards, and promotional activities—as well as being a medium for cohesion among its members. There are also state conferences in most states which carry on similar activities for social workers of the particular state.

A second notable institutional aspect of social work is that it is in large measure conducted by various kinds of so-called agencies. As an indispensable, established, community-wide and community-supported social activity utilizing specialized practitioners functioning with somewhat esoteric knowledge and technical expertise, and involving some degree of community division of labor, the social work services cannot be adequately rendered by individuals as private individuals or by informal, spontaneous groups. The agency is a definite, known organization where clients realize they can get help or where the public is aware that help is available. The agency is bureaucratically organized, providing adequate management, effective allocation and use of personnel, responsible expenditure of funds, and especially assuring continuity of activity.

Agencies conducting social work activities may be public agencies created by combinations of federal and state laws, and county and city ordinances, conducting various social work services already noted; they may be private agencies, local to national in extent, conducting various kinds of case work, group work, or community organizational functions; they may be agencies devoted primarily to giving social work services directly to clients (a family or child welfare agency) or offering both social work and other services (settlement houses, Scouts, the Y's, the Red Cross); or they may be organizations where the social work is auxiliary to the main activity, such as schools (visiting teacher service), hospitals (medical social work service), public health services (visiting nurses), courts, camps, vocational guidance bureaus, or organizations giving service to other social agencies, such as Community Chests and Councils of Social Agencies. In all cases the fundamental constituent elements of a functional organization exist: the administrative board which carries part of the community expectation of the agency, some sort of board of directors, or county commissioners, or other combination of persons representing the public; the administrative or executive and supervisory staff; the staff workers or work operatives; the office workers.

II: Recreational Institutions

Recreational institutions constitute another system of social welfare institutions contributing directly to individual and societal maintenance.

History shows that all human societies have devoted considerable time, effort, organization, and expense to such activities. Today, such activities reflect not only one of the basic sets of interests and preoccupations of the people in our society,[12] but also a widespread recognition of the absolute need for recreation as an aid to the physical and mental health and efficiency of individuals, as a means of social adjustment, and as an assurance of high productivity in the community.

The recreational activity of man, generally, is what he does with and in his leisure time, the time when he is not working or sleeping. Leisure is related inextricably to two other time-consuming functions, sleep and work. Sleep is a physiological absolute, and work is a necessity if the things that must be done for man's maintenance are accomplished. But work varies in time-consumption with the degree of technological development. In general, the higher the degree of technological development, the less the amount of time devoted to work by most people; hence, the more leisure time.

Leisure thus is all of man's waking time free from the world of work. In a large portion of it, he engages in recreational activity—activity which *re-creates* him physically, mentally, emotionally, spiritually, by doing pleasant, satisfying, non-profit, non-work, and often non-utilitarian things, however much energy these may require. Relaxation is best secured by engaging in some type of activity—usually more carefree—*other* than that ordinarily pursued. It provides antidotes to specialization and redeems man from the drab and ugly, the pressing and required, the stuffy, routine, and monotonous. It enables recovery from fatigue and from wear on muscles and nerves, from social strains,

[12] The following quantitative facts regarding American attention to recreation are noteworthy. In 1952 it was estimated that the American people spent around 10,000,000,000 constant dollars on recreation. J. F. Dewhurst and associates, *America's Needs and Resources.* New York: Twentieth Century Fund, 1955, p. 347. Furthermore, as of 1956 there were 17,000 organized camps in the United States serving 6,000,000 children; in 1956 there were 5,260 golf courses in the United States spread over a half million acres; men, women, and children golfers, numbering a total of 3,600,000, played 65,700,000 rounds of golf on these courses; the value of the land, courses, clubhouses, equipment and furnishings was $1,308,000,000; and the clubs spent $100,000,000 during the year on the maintenance of the courses and grounds. In 1956 the Society for the Preservation and Encouragement of Barber Shop Quartet Singing in America (S.P.E.B.S.Q.S.A.) had 26,000 adult male members in 650 local chapters. In 1955 more than 50,000,000 people visited the National Park Service areas, and in 1956 some 52,-556,084 used the recreational resources of the National Forests, and in 1955 more than 180,000,000 people visited state parks. Gleaned from "Recreation in the Age of Automation," entire number of the *Annals Am. Acad. Pol. & Soc. Science,* Vol. 313, September, 1957. In 1958 Americans spent 2,100,000,000 dollars on boating and owned 7,330,000 recreational boats, one for every seven families. *Time,* Jan. 26, 1959. It is also reported that expenditures for bowling during the last years of 1950–60 have been over $1,000,000,000 annually and that bowling is now the country's top participant sport, with 23,000,000 people bowling on 96,000 lanes. A. W. Baum, in *Sat. Eve. Post,* Jan. 16, 1960, p. 21.

from that which is painful or dangerous. It provides emotional and instinctive outlets that the daily tasks and routines do not furnish; it gives man an opportunity to freshen and develop his faculties and interests, to enrich his personality, and to express himself creatively. As far as the focusing of attention and the expenditure of time and energy is concerned, recreation is not vastly different from work, but it is different from the individual's major activity for economic adequacy; he does it for its own sake; he is usually not coerced into doing it, but does it on his own initiative because he wishes to and derives pleasure from it. Recreation is often determined by social class, age, sex, or education. Of course what some people do as recreation others do as work. What is a pleasurable and instructive hobby for some is boredom for others. It is equally obvious that recreation for some is much like their work; for example, the scholar who engages in reading and intellectual pursuits in his leisure time or the precision machinist who tries to play precision golf.

As to the nature of the participation, recreation may be isolative or a matter of individual activity, as in reading or in enjoying some hobby; it may be cooperative, as in dancing or playing together; it may be competitive, as in most games and contests. From the point of view of effect, recreation may be of a vicarious nature, sedentary and passive, such as engaging in purely substitutive romance, adventure, achievement, or heroism by watching a motion picture or a wrestling match or prize fight; it may produce sublimation, a refinement or exaltation of experience, as in listening to some poetry and music or reading some literature; it may have a creative or constructive effect, as in aesthetic or much of the do-it-yourself activity; it may be actually deteriorative as to health or morals, as in overexertion in games or interest in pornography.

Finally, it should be noted that recreation in its very nature is a useful adjunct to, and sometimes a necessity in, the conduct of other social welfare activities. For example, it is important in the prevention of juvenile delinquency, in the therapeutic programs of reformatories and penitentiaries, in treatment for the hospitalized generally, especially as a means of rehabilitation of the mentally retarded, mentally ill, and the physically handicapped, as a means of relieving tensions in factories and in military establishments, and as an outlet for aesthetic expression.

HISTORICAL AND MODERN RECREATION

History shows that recreation has varied greatly in its relation to work, to other institutional areas of life, and in the degree of its organization.[13] In the primitive condition of life, the line between labor and leisure

[13] Cf. Thomas Woody, "Leisure in the Light of History," *Annals Am. Acad. Pol. & Soc. Science*, 313 (Sept., 1957): 4–10.

was tenuous and shifting. Even the collective activities, usually involving considerable ceremony, that we think of as being of a recreational nature, such as the folk dances, the festivals, and the dramatic performances, were almost indistinguishably interrelated with all the rest of life. The great ancient civilizations directly involved in our cultural traditions and institutional forms, especially the Greeks and Romans, raised recreation to a major collective activity with their athletic games and contests, spectacles, and dramatic performances. But they were only occasional events for the masses of the population, not a part of the daily or weekly flow of life. The upper classes, free from grinding work, had much leisure to devote to reading, music, poetry, the theater, and dalliance. For the bulk of the population, recreation was only an occasional, almost incidental, part of a hard life. In the Middle Ages, on the whole, recreation was less specifically organized; aside from tournaments, which were essentially by and for the elite, joint recreational activity was part of religious events. Those relatively few at the top who had wealth and power had the leisure; poverty and labor were the lot of the great majority.

During our own American pre-urban period, our recreation activities were carried on mainly in the family and the small local community groups, and were shared by all the appropriate members of the family or the community. Until the last century, social life was sufficiently simple and uncrowded to permit most of the recreational needs of the population to be satisfied through the activities of other institutions. The less specialized nature of economic life permitted much restful and satisfying diversion simply in the change from task to task, each with its special challenge to skill and ingenuity. The rural village home made possible active games and dances and sizable gatherings of relatives and friends. The church had its festivals and ceremonials, and church and school together served as community centers. Modern American recreation still shows some of the characteristics of recreation in the primitive folk and ancient societies, and also some of its own former rural-village forms. For the most part, however, industrialization and urbanization have produced conditions that give modern recreation a significance heretofore lacking, with new and unique institutionalized forms.

People today are recreation-conscious as never before. Recreation is viewed as a regular and indispensable part of the total way of life, both individual and collective. Mechanized industry has produced the division of labor, the minute specialization, and the production-line type of work activity which has increased routinization and repetitiveness. Work at all levels—machine-tending, skilled work, professional activity—has become more concentrated, causing greater strain. Much work has become greatly depersonalized, with a consequent lack of mingling of work and play.

At the same time, various conditions produce more leisure and make possible more recreation. With the great efficiency of productive effort in general, workers in commerce and industry now have a 7- or 8-hour workday and a 35- or 40-hour week as against a 10-hour day and 60-hour week at the turn of the century. In fact, today the waking hours spent *away* from work are for many people more than those spent *at* work, even on work days. Even housewives with all sorts of gadgets at their command and smaller household units to care for, have much free time on their hands. Long week ends and vacations are standard for almost everyone. The greater use of mechanical physical energy has also resulted in a greatly reduced drain upon human physical energies.

The increase of per capita wealth and income has freed more earnings and savings for leisure-time pursuits, and modern technology has placed such recreation facilities as radio, television, and motion pictures within the financial reach of the whole population. The mass-produced automobiles should not be overlooked as an important factor in vacations and travel. Rapid transportation in general makes it possible to sandwich leisure time and recreation among other activities. Finally, the prolongation of life, the increase of per capita wealth, combined with more and more federal and state attention to the security of the aged, has given more people a longer period of leisure after retirement with vast recreational possibilities as well as essentials. What is especially significant in our society is that leisure and its related recreation has become the property of almost every person in it, and social and economic factors indicate that there will be more and more leisure in the near future. Although individuals and families still show considerable capability in providing for some of their recreational needs, they are incapable of providing a sufficient amount and variety of it. The great volume of modern recreation must be provided and it must be institutionally organized. The urban home plant—and the great bulk of American home plants are urban or urban-like—has shrunk to the point where it permits only sedentary activity. The modern nuclear, isolated family is relatively small and offers too few members for many stimulating recreations. Other institutions, such as the school and the church, even industry, are making efforts to provide certain recreational activities; but these efforts are partial at best. The very size and crowded conditions of city life mean that recreational space, facilities, and leadership must be planned and systematically provided. In brief, in our present American society, recreation, adequate in kind and amount, cannot be depended upon to emanate spontaneously from the community; it is not self-initiating or self-maintaining.

It must now be comprehensively organized, with fairly clear philosophy, objectives, programs, specialized agencies, and something in the way of a professionalized personnel. This means institutionalization.

Organized Recreation as an Institution

Although there is a growing recognition for the need of a large volume and variety of recreation and although there has been a tremendous extension of recreation programs and facilities all over the United States, especially during the last two decades, recreation still is not fully institutionalized in the way the economic, governmental, educational, and religious systems are. Recreation does show certain definite institutional features. Most forms have their folkways that determine for whom, by sex, age, ethnic group, or class, particular forms are proper. Mores are evident in phrases like "winner-loser," "good sportsmanship," "not cheating at cards." Clear-cut ideology, involving relevant values and supporting justifications, is pretty well established; it is, in fact, the basis of the moral and financial support and the organizational activities of lay community members, and it defines the objectives of the professional functionaries. Most forms of recreation—most obviously, games—have their definite rules. A more or less professionalized personnel exists, as managers and leaders, especially with respect to the more highly organized forms. It is particularly noteworthy that a sizable portion of the social workers engaged in group work are concerned with the formulation of programs and the actual conduct of recreational activities. Finally, and this is the most conspicuous and the most highly developed feature, recreation is characterized by a variety of organizational forms, each with their appropriate facilities, whereby the activities are actually conducted.

From the point of view of areal extent and interest there are numerous local, regional, national, even international, organizations for the promotion and protection of recreation. There is, for example, the National Recreational Association for recreation in general, and organizations for particular areas, such as the U.S. Golf Association, U.S. Lawn Tennis Association, the National Ski Association, the American Bowling Congress, the National Council of State Garden Clubs, the S.P.E.B.S.Q.S.A. (the barbershop singing organization noted previously), and dozens of others. Rivers lists nearly a hundred international organizations.[14]

A more revealing way of understanding recreational organizations is to examine them as to their conduct under either private (or semiprivate) or public (governmental) auspices. The private (and semi-

[14] T. E. Rivers, "International Relationships," *Annals Am. Acad. Pol. & Soc. Sciences,* 313 (Sept., 1957): 105–108.

private or semi-public) forms consist of the non-commercial or non-profit and the commercial organizations. The non-commercial private forms are conducted strictly for recreation as an end in itself. Their activities and facilities are usually limited to the membership of the organizations themselves, a membership determined by age, sex, religion, or other affiliation with the particular organization offering the recreation, or by race and, in some cases, by the specific recreational interest, such as dancing, bridge, or gardening. These organizations provide recreation that appeals to special groups; for example, card clubs, dramatic clubs, skiing clubs, bowling clubs, summer camps, country clubs offering golf, tennis, swimming, and other games, as well as the "nineteenth hole," organized forms for children and young people, usually with other than recreational functions added, such as the "Y" organizations or lecture courses, and the recreational efforts of churches, labor unions, and industrial and commercial organizations. The financial support, depending upon the range of their functions, is derived from membership fees, donations, funds from drives such as Community Chest drives, endowments, and other private and semi-public sources.

Private commercial recreation, to be discussed at greater length later, is conducted purely as a business proposition. It provides programs or activities, usually under competitive conditions, which appeal to people as paying customers. The basic consideration is obtaining the largest profit that the traffic will bear from the largest number of customers that can be attracted. Such activities are carried on by private ownership, but especially by corporations and syndicates which in some instances are very highly developed organizations. As examples there may be mentioned motion pictures, theaters (legitimate, variety, burlesque), resorts, amusement parks, boxing and wrestling matches, bowling alleys and pool halls, radio and television broadcasting systems, taverns, nightclubs, roadhouses, dance halls, roller skating rinks, gambling places, tracks for dog, horse, automobile, and motorcycle racing, and professional athletics.

Public recreation, provided by the local, state, and federal governmental agencies, takes various forms. It provides recreational opportunities for all the people who wish to avail themselves of them, regardless of age, sex, race, creed, or social or economic status. At the local level there are the municipal parks with their picnicking facilities, public golf courses and tennis courts, bridle paths, swimming pools, bathing beaches, pleasure piers, and zoos. There are the playgrounds, art galleries, museums, and municipal orchestra concerts, operas, and festivals. School plants are offered for athletic activities, lectures and forums, applied arts, literary, dramatic, and musical activities. State recreation agencies consist of state park systems, state forests, land and water areas, game refuges administered by a state game and park commission, reading opportunities provided by state library commissions and other agencies. At the federal level we have in the United States some 180 national, military, and historical parks, comprising nearly 24 million acres, and governed by the National Park Service; the United States Forest Service guards 180 million acres of national forests, portions of which are available for recreational activities; the Fish and Wildlife Service administers 17.5 million acres of wildlife refuges. These areas provide opportunities for camping, hiking, nature study, fishing, and in some instances for hunting. There are also fishing, hunting, boating, picnicking and camping facilities in connection with the conservation-power projects such as the T.V.A. and those in the Missouri Valley areas. These government agencies are managed by commissions, boards, bureaus, services and departments. They are supported mainly by taxation, but in various instances are supplemented by special grants, gifts, rentals, and admission and license fees.[15]

SPECIAL CHARACTERISTICS OF CONTEMPORARY AMERICAN RECREATION

Modern recreation is definitely, completely, and inexorably separated from work conditions for the great bulk of the population. The standardized, routinized, even mechanized working day permits little occasion for relaxation on the job and no free opportunity to take time out; the coffee break is itself a concession to this situation. Also, the pressure of modern work creates a daily need for something different.

An increasing number of industrial and commercial establishments are providing means of counteracting the effects of mechanization, and some of these are of a recreational nature: rest periods, paid vacations, showers, gymnasiums, club rooms, athletic fields, and the financing of teams in sport (softball, bowling, basketball) leagues. These, however, are largely surface remedies.

The forms of recreation engaged in are in part dependent upon the particular ecological setting of the individuals and groups involved. For example, in the city the recreation of most adults is of a sedentary nature—attending theaters, sitting in taverns, playing cards, watching athletic contests. In suburbia people engage in gardening, play golf, have barbecues. In the open country there will still be occasional neighborly gatherings, attendance at country fairs, and "visiting." More and more, however, all people engage in mass recreations.

[15] Cf. G. D. Butler, "The Structure of Public Leisure Agencies," *Annals*, 313 (Dec., 1957): 119–125. For concise treatment of these different private and public forms, see: H. D. Meyer and C. K. Brightbill, *Community Recreation: A Guide to Its Organization*. Englewood Cliffs, N.J.: Prentice-Hall, 1956, pp. 308–310. I. T. Sanders, *The Community*. New York: Ronald, 1958, pp. 323–326.

A third tendency is the decline of family recreation and the tendency for recreation to be specialized by sex and especially by age groups. Recreations, such as reading aloud, visiting, attending family reunions, church sociables, barn dances, in which the whole family participated, have in large measure disappeared. Most of the recreation of the members of the modern family is engaged in with persons outside the immediate family as they go to movies, attend sports or dramatic events, play golf or bridge, belong to clubs or formal recreational groups; and these activities are more and more by sex and age groups. There are the *Girl* Scouts and the *Boy* Scouts, the informal and formal *women's* clubs and *men's* clubs, and the Young Married People's clubs.

It is obvious, even to the casual observer, that not all is well with modern recreation; some of it is actually defeating fundamental recreational objectives, and some of it is morally and culturally questionable.

Modern recreation tends more and more to be of a massive nature. Mention need only be made of the huge amusement industries, the professional athletic leagues, and such huge over-all organizations as the American Bowling Congress. Despite the inadequate institutionalization of recreation, it is overstandardized in some of its forms, particularly the motion pictures, the radio and television programs, the popular journals and magazines. In some respects one sort of stuffy routine is simply substituted for another.

Also, much of the recreation is ready-made, and the participation is merely passive. They can "take 'em or leave 'em," to be sure, but if they "take 'em," they have to take what they get. Also, those partaking of it are spectators, threatened with the disease of "spectatoritis." Such recreation provides no creative opportunities. The reaction to this recreational situation is evidenced in the increasing interest in such challenge-producing activities as gardening, do-it-yourself, camping, hunting, and fishing. Quite a bit of recreation is of a faddist nature or determined by socio-economic pressures; for example, the winter vacation at Miami Beach, golf at the country club, prestige magazines, literary cults.

Finally, the most abundant, popular, and widely patronized forms of organized recreation are the commercialized forms. Commercialized recreation, like any other business venture, is conducted for profit; it has to make money. The main concern is the profit of the purveyor, not primarily the recreational welfare of the customers, or the physical, moral, aesthetic, or educational quality of the performance or service. It caters supposedly to "what the public wants," which means that it gauges its appeals by the greatest common denominator. All commercial recreation may not be below par aesthetically or morally or in its physical and psychological effects, but much of it is standardized on an appallingly low, even moronic, plane; much of it inflames or enervates, but does not produce catharsis; much of it is morally questionable, even hazardous; some of it ceases to be recreation and becomes dissipation and degradation. Various forms of it are subjected to governmental supervision and control, exercised under the police power and established by law, such as special taxing and licensing, censorship and review, and control over sales.

III: Health Institutions

Health is essential to the preservation of the species and the maintenance of life. Groups and cultures have been preoccupied with it as a continuous problem and have had various beliefs, largely superstitions, about it. In modern societies, the preservation, improvement, and control of health have come to be a major, institutionally organized maintenance task dovetailing with the reproductive and economic maintenance of the population. On his health depends in large measure a person's physical or physiological efficiency and his personality. The economic aspects of poor health are of particular significance, for illness not only makes him less productive, but also deprives him of his income as a worker and costs him medical expenses.

From the point of view of societal maintenance, the society's well-being depends upon a healthy labor force and on physical and mental fitness to meet international challenges of a technological, economic, and military nature. If there is much illness and physical unfitness among a population (for example, widespread malaria or tuberculosis in underdeveloped countries), there is lethargy, low vitality, low productivity, and poverty. Furthermore, in such a community personnel, resources, facilities, and funds must be withdrawn from positive, progressive, or constructive functions in order to care for the non-producing sick. Also, illness and physical and mental disability can be casual or correlative factors in other social problems, such as unemployability of persons, broken homes, delinquency, and crime.

During the last century there has been a combination of developments that has focused attention upon general health as a vital social concern and upon good health as a fundamental objective. First, there have been the appearance and the awareness of social conditions producing or contributing to ill-health. With the increasing physical mobility of an increasing population, there is an absolute need not only to protect against contagious and epidemic diseases, but also to eliminate them entirely, if possible. People are also aware of the effects upon health and fitness of bad housing, water supplies polluted by sewage and industrial wastes, unsanitary streets and garbage-ridden alleys, impure food and drugs, malnutrition, occupational diseases, accidents of all kinds, the diseases and organic weaknesses of different age groups, especially the degenerative diseases. The very inconvenience, suffering, and expense that accompany poor health and disability create a constant imperative desire for the improvement of the causal and contributory conditions.

Second, the remarkable advances of medical science and medical technology, including the public health technologies, have made us conscious not only of the possibility but of the social necessity of sickness eradication and death control. Important have been the knowledge regarding the place of microorganisms (bacteria) and parasitic plants and animals (hookworms, mosquitoes, flies, fleas, lice, rats) in the cause and spread of contagious and infectious diseases; prevention of infection by antiseptics, sterilization, and isolation of suspects and those already ill; the development of immunizing vaccines, serums, recently the antibiotics, and other biologicals for the treatment, and in some instances almost the elimination of such diseases as smallpox, diphtheria, scarlet fever, pneoumonia, hydrophobia, tetanus, typhoid, and recently poliomyelitis; the development of X-ray in diagnosis; anesthetics for surgery; the phenomenal advance of surgery, now extended to every organ and every part of the human body; the knowledge of the care and treatment of infants; the virtual elimination of children's diseases; the improvements in working conditions and the developments in industrial health and safety; and, by no means least, the advances in public health, including housing requirements, abolition of unsanitary tenements, pest eradication, quarantine and other control of endemic and epidemic diseases, inspection and protection of food and water, safe and rapid disposal of garbage and sewage, catastrophe control, the provision of medical, nursing, and hospital services.

At the moment, the health control and treatment involve four different task levels: (1) to treat adequately existing ill-health and disability; (2) to restore the afflicted to normal life as much and as soon as possible; (3) to discover and control conditions making for ill-health and disability; (4) to prevent to the fullest extent possible the deleterious conditions. The present situation with respect to health control implies several other things. First, there is the patent fact that good health is a purchasable commodity which a community can possess, within broad limits, to the extent it is willing to pay for it. Second, so extensively developed is this artificial bulwark against sickness, disease, and disability in our massive, complex, infinitely interrelated society, we cannot for a moment relax our efforts to maintain and advance health efforts. Third, the individual or the family can do little about ill-health; the conditions that produce it or contribute to it are in the community, and, under modern conditions, all treatment, control, and prevention are a responsibility of the community. Fourth, the maintenance and advance of health require a general and highly organized social attack; any approach which ignores this fact will be inadequate.

THE INSTITUTIONAL ASPECTS OF HEALTH

The maintenance and promotion of health, like recreation, in the United States, are a movement showing extensive organization and a considerable degree of institutionalization. The social organization for health shows a vast and diversely specialized personnel, the top levels of which are fully professionalized—are, in fact, in many respects models of professionalization. At the peak of the personnel pyramid are the highly professionalized physicians or doctors of medicine. Between one half and two-thirds of them the country over are still engaged in general practice. But the specializations are proliferating, and the specialized practitioners are mainly assembled in the larger towns and the cities where the people find the specialized services severally and jointly available. Among the better known medical specializations are internal medicine (with its subspecializations by organs and bodily areas), eye, ear, nose, and throat (increasingly separately specialized), surgery, further specialized for every organ and part of the body, dermatology (skin diseases), neoplastic diseases (tumors, cancers), obstetrics and gynecology, genito-urinary diseases, orthopedics (bones and joints), pediatrics (children's diseases), Roentgenology and radiology (X-ray), psychiatry and neurology (mental and nervous diseases), and geriatrics (diseases of the aged), a further specialization developing within internal medicine. Ranking next to the physicians and surgeons are the dentists, who are also showing some tendency to specialization among urban practitioners. As indispensable aids to physicians and, increasingly, to dentists are the rapidly professionalizing registered nurses, also developing further specialization correlated with that of the medical specialties. The medical profession has established for its candidates an extensive educational and training program consisting of two to four years of premedical work at the college level, followed by three or four years of special medical instruction in a professional medical college, usually followed by two years of internship in a hospital or clinic. To engage in medical practice a doctor must pass a strict examination by the state in which he intends to practice, and be properly licensed. The profession as a whole has a code of practice maintained and enforced by the local, state, and national medical societies. The dentists are similarly, though not quite so extensively, professionalized. To qualify as registered nurse, the candidate must now undergo a rather rigorous educational and training program and in some states pass a state examination preparatory to licensing.

Functionally related to the physicians and nurses are a whole complex of more or less professionalized specialists, such as biochemists, bacteriologists, and epidemiologists, clinical and laboratory technologists and technicians, nurse anesthetists, dieticians and nutritionists, clinical psychologists, hospital administrators and operators of clinics, physical and occupational therapists, optometrists and opticians, health educators, sanitary engineers and sanitarians, medical and psychiatric social workers, vital statisticians, veterinarians, practical nurses, and (the declining number of) midwives. Of more than passing significance as health personnel are the specially educated, technically trained, and governmentally registered pharmacists who prepare the prescriptions of physicians and dispense the drugs used in healing. Most of these occupations and callings have their basic ideologies and involve some set of professional roles requiring more or less complex and subtle knowledge and a special degree of technical competence and skill. In addition, there are such paramedical workers as osteopaths, chiropractors, chiropodists, and health cultists, and religious healers. It is conservatively estimated that the personnel directly connected with health in the United States today exceeds one million in number.

The health system includes a large number of highly and specially organized facilities and services in the form of hospitals, health centers, and clinics. Hospitals have come to have a central and indispensable place in the maintenance of health. Medical treatment today is complicated, elaborate, technically specialized, and at the same time all of its separate diagnostic, therapeutic, and other procedures must be functionally interrelated. To be effective, medical treatment requires special and expensive plants, machines, laboratories, and other equipment and facilities, a variety of special but interlocking procedures and therapies, and a specialized personnel of cooperating physicians and surgeons, nurses, anesthetists, technicians, pharmacologists, therapists, and dieticians. The hospital or the corporate medical organization for diagnosis and treatment provides these adequately and in all of the essential combinations. The place of these highly organized agencies in our health system is indicated by the fact that today about one out of eight persons is admitted to a hospital each year, and perhaps every third family has some member hospitalized during a year.[16] In 1956 there were over 6000 hospitals in the United States containing more than 1,500,000 beds; the total gross value of hospital assets was about $13 billion (of this about $10 billion, or 80 per cent, represented physical plant—land,

[16] Health Information Foundation, *Progress in Health Services*, March, 1958, and May, 1958.

buildings, and equipment). Some of these were conducted as private business undertakings for the profit of the operators, but as of 1956 about 90 per cent of the hospitals were non-profit agencies—a few as cooperative organizations including the membership and professional staff, and a few by fraternal orders, but the great bulk consisting of those provided and operated by religious organizations, especially the Catholic healing orders and the Protestant denominations, and by governmental units, local, state, and national. The larger proportion of these hospitals, both private and public, provide general treatment; for example, the community hospitals and those conducted by the Veterans' Administration. A considerable number, however, are specialized; for example, most American states provide special hospitals for the tubercular, the blind, the deaf and mute, the mentally and neurologically ill, and for orthopedic treatment and care. There are also such specialized private hospitals and sanitoriums.

In addition to the health services provided in hospitals, there are those provided in health centers, sanatoriums, and clinics maintained by private health agencies (for example, those conducted by a number of medical specialists), community organizations (for example, child welfare agencies), commercial and industrial establishments, unions, schools and colleges for the students, prison and charitable agencies.

A further fundamental organizational aspect is the manufacturers and distributors of drugs and health appliances. Most of the pharmaceutical compounds and vaccines, serums, antibiotics, and other biologicals, the anesthetics and antiseptics, the almost infinite array of medical and surgical tools and appliances used in the treatment and prevention of sickness, disease, and disability are manufactured by a relatively small number of corporations. Most of these have their own extensive research laboratories with a highly specialized personnel engaged in study and experimentation. These drugs and appliances are distributed through a huge system of wholesale and retail establishments. The retailing is not only by locally owned drug stores but, as in other retailing areas, increasingly by great chain store organizations.

A variety of voluntary health agencies are engaged in health education, in the raising of funds for research and for the treatment and prevention of disease and disability, and in the promotion of health in general. At the local level we find not only special voluntary groups concerned with particular local health problems and the local chapters of nation-wide health organizations but also so-called health councils in some communities. These community health councils are composed of physicians, nurses, teachers, public officials, parents, social workers, and public spirited citizens. They devote themselves to such tasks as promoting programs for immunization and vaccination, improving standards in the water and milk supply, promoting more vigorous standards for, and inspection of, foods and eating places, checking on vermin and pest control, improving garbage collection and sewage disposal, clearing local slums and improving housing conditions, bettering the community's maternal and child health services and especially its various kinds of hospital services.

At the national level large associations with local chapters carry on educational and fund-raising activities in particular health areas. Outstanding examples are the National Tuberculosis Association, the American Cancer Society, the Society for Crippled Children and Adults, the National Foundation for Infantile Paralysis, the American Heart Association, the National Committee for Mental Hygiene, and the American Social Hygiene Association. Some of the great life insurance companies, such as the Metropolitan Life Insurance Company and the Northwestern National Life Insurance Company, conduct systematic health education by means of paid advertisements in some of our widely circulating journals, thus reaching millions of citizens. The Milbank Memorial Fund functions as a study group. The Rockefeller Foundation since shortly after its establishment has been devoted to the study of health and the promotion, financing, and organization of health activities both within our country and abroad. The more recent Ford Foundation promotes and subsidizes health work on a national scale, including aid to hospitals.

As in the case of recreation, one of the most signal features of health organization is the activity of the governmental agencies at the local, state, and federal level. This is because of the recognition that, under modern conditions, health is much more than an individual, a family, or even a voluntary group responsibility. All sorts of public programs and agencies rendering many different types of services are essential to attain and maintain adequate health standards and conditions. The governmental health agencies alone can operate under the police power of the state to force and enforce absolutely essential health measures; they alone have the range of action and the exercise of authority over all the people and over wide areas; and for certain kinds of health activities, they alone have the financial resources and the organizational capacities and forms to carry them on.

We have already noted the fact that the states set minimum standards for the practice of the medical professions and require formal certification of proficiency. An increasing proportion of the future members of the medical profession are trained in medical schools and hospitals connected with state universities. To encourage an adequate number of physicians and nurses and to ensure adequate educational and training facilities, medical schools, which meet certain requirements, receive certain financial subsidies from the federal government.

Organized public (governmental) health services, of particular concern in this study, take two main and closely related forms: the prevention of the conditions that make for ill-health and disability and the assurance of minimal health conditions, in the way of both protection and treatment, for all categories of people but particularly for the more disadvantaged persons (indigent, handicapped). Among the important public health services conducted in varying combination of local, state, and federal agencies are the specifically preventive activities, such as the control of communicable diseases (typhoid, tuberculosis, the venereal diseases, diphtheria); the protection against the importation of contagious, especially epidemic, diseases from without the area or nation by scrutiny at sea and airports; the maintenance of quarantine regulations for persons with contagious diseases; the enforcement of the protective food and drug ordinances and laws, including the inspection of the manufacture of food and drugs, the regulation of the labelling and handling of milk, the inspection and licensing of eating establishments and food handlers; the conducting of immunization programs; the supervision of water supply and disposal of sewage and industrial wastes; the regulation of the work day, the prohibition of unsafe and unsanitary working conditions, and the control of industrial diseases; the enforcement of minimum housing standards; the application of safety practices; the restriction of child and woman labor under certain conditions, some of which directly affect health.

By way of minimal health conditions for the differentiated population, we note the special provisions for medical care for the indigent, such as visiting nursing services, free clinics and dispensaries, and public or publicly paid for hospital care. There are also the aforementioned special hospitals provided by most states, admission to which is on the basis of need, such as hospitals for tuberculosis, the mentally and neurologically ill, and those requiring orthopedic services.

There are also such important government health services as the maintenance of diagnostic laboratories; the maintenance of bureaus for the collection of vital statistics, particularly in this connection the statistics regarding communicable diseases and the causes of death; the conducting of regional and national health surveys; and, especially at the state level and federal level, research in the causes and prevention of disease and planning of health activities for the future.

Most local governments (towns, cities, counties) have their boards of health and, in the case of larger governmental units, a varied personnel complement of physicians, nurses, inspectors, quarantine officers, and so on. Many of them have laboratory, clinical, hospital, and other facilities for widespread treatment and care. Often also, health work is conducted by local public school systems and by the local public welfare agencies for their clients.

Most states have health departments providing certain sorts of laboratory testing, diagnostic facilities, and agencies for maintaining quarantines, inspecting water and food supplies, and collecting vital statistics. State departments of labor usually enforce the health requirements with respect to work places and work conditions; departments of agriculture inspect livestock and attempt to control animal diseases such as bovine tuberculosis; boards of control operate state hospitals.

Health at the federal level is now an activity of major governmental importance, having recently been placed under the jurisdiction of a department, the secretary of which has cabinet rank; namely, the Department of Health, Education, and Welfare. The chief health agency within the Department is the United States Public Health Service which provides a wide variety of agencies, such as hospitals, and services and which also cooperates with state health services and some private health agencies in the provision of funds and services. Under the 1954 revision of the Social Security Act, provisions were made for federal grants for general public health, tuberculosis control, venereal disease control, mental health, and heart disease programs. Maternal and child health and aid for crippled children is administered through the Children's Bureau in the Department of Labor. Almost every other federal department carries on some amount of activity in promoting or safeguarding human health, such as avoiding accidents and disability, providing inspection of livestock, immigrants, mines, or transportation facilities, providing various kinds of hospital services for certain segments of the population. The Veterans' Administration conducts a large number of hospitals for veterans, providing almost every kind of medical service required by adults, throughout the country, and most of the larger military installations provide medical and hospital services for the personnel, often including their families.

SPECIAL CHARACTERISTICS OF AMERICAN MEDICAL ORGANIZATIONS

There are certain other conditions in addition to those referred to in connection with the preceding discussion of the institutionalized health in our country, most also having organizational connotations, that should be noted. Although the organized health movement has reached significant proportions, the bulk of the actual treatment is still carried on by the private physician. Private medicine itself represents a degree of institutionalization; there is intensive training, careful selection, increasing specialization, a high degree of competence, and a high development of the professional spirit. But the position of the doctor in the health program of today, particularly with reference to the achievement of wider health objectives, is somewhat circumscribed. Fundamentally, he is a practitioner in a private doctor-client relationship.

Usually the patient does not consult the doctor until disease or organic disturbance or physical ailment is well advanced. Therefore, though the given doctor may be willing and capable of doing so, his significance in disseminating health information or of attempting prevention of disease or disability is slight; he confines his activity primarily to treatment. Furthermore, the nature of the doctor-patient relationship offers little inducement to preventive efforts; the services of the practitioner are paid for by the patient on a fee-for-service basis; if people are not ill, the physician has no income. He thus has a vested interest in the ill-health of the population, being paid not for keeping people well but for caring for them after they get sick. Even semi-public organizations of doctors —the local, state, and national organizations—are not in a position to carry on much prevention or engage in activities making for general health assurance, except through their journals, which have very limited lay circulation, or as agents of public bodies, or in rendering services in the private relationships that have community effects, such as in the poliomyelitis vaccination campaign.

In addition, the medical practitioner is almost entirely a middleman or distributor of medical knowledge and medical services and has little time or occasion to engage in medical research. The laboratory work that he does, or has done for him, is largely of a routine nature and is carried on primarily in conjunction with diagnosis and treatment. Some medical research is carried on by doctors with medical degrees, but they are connected with research organizations; most of it is conducted by Ph.D's in the biological, physical, and chemical sciences, the various combinations of these, and the psychological sciences, principally under university auspices.

There have been marked differentials in the medical services enjoyed by, or available to, people on the basis of rural or urban location, socio-economic class, involving especially the ability to pay, educational level, and race. Although such variations still exist to some extent, they are generally disappearing. In the first place, a greater health consciousness exists on the part of our population as a whole. Not only are people availing themselves, as individuals and families, of the health facilities that are offered and demanding more services,[17] but there is also a growing awareness that the health of the community as a whole is endangered if some of its people are not having health parity. The health chain is only as strong as its weakest links.

Various factors enter into the decrease of differentials. Improvements

[17] For example, in 1928–31 a survey by the Committee on the Costs of Medical Care reported an average of 2.6 annual out-of-hospital doctor visits for white persons in this country. The current National Health Survey by the Public Health Service reported 4.8 visits per person in 1957. Health Information Service, *Progress in Health Services*, Oct., 1958, p. 1.

in transportation, especially the extension of good roads into back country and the universal use of the automobile, have given the people in rural communities, mountainous districts, and small towns readier access to the more abundant and specialized services and the clinical and hospital facilities of the urban centers, although there still exist marked disparities in different parts of our country. The Hill-Burton Act of 1946 authorized, for the first time, federal financial assistance for a country-wide hospital construction program based on community need. This made possible the construction and improvement of hospitals in neglected rural areas and small towns. The Federal Hospital Survey and Construction Act of 1949 provided $150 million annually for five years to subsidize the construction of additional hospitals. In 1955 the Ford Foundation granted $200 million to non-profit hospitals. As the result of such assistance, there has been a considerable equalizing of hospital facilities. There has also been a considerable equalizing of medical services for low-income and indigent groups, whether white or colored, through the medical services provided by local and state public welfare organizations and especially those provided by public (city, county, or city-county) medical clinics and dispensaries, and public visiting-nurse services. Also, the relatively high recent income levels among the people generally have permitted them to enjoy more private medical services, and enabled them to prepare themselves financially through private voluntary prepayment health insurance arrangements covering medical and hospital expenses, and induced them to have such services when they seem to be needed.[18]

The great spread of prepaid voluntary insurance covering medical and hospital expenses is in itself a health phenomenon of note. To a considerable extent, this movement has followed the principle of group insurance; that is, large organizations, such as industrial and commercial establishments, colleges and universities, church organizations, labor unions, and so on, have provided blanket coverage for their employees and their families, the actual insurance procedure being conducted in most cases by commercial insurance companies. There is also the health insurance that may be purchased by the individual as an individual from insurance companies. Occasional group schemes have also been developed by physicians, hospital administrators, or other agencies within local communities. The National Consumer Survey of Medical Costs and Voluntary Health Insurance reports that 87 million people in the United States, or 57 per cent of the population, had some hospital insurance, and 74 million people, or 48 per cent of the population, had some surgical and other medical insurance as of July, 1953. The same

[18] On "Consumer Spending for Medical Care," see Health Information Foundation, *Progress in Health Services,* Dec., 1958, entire issue.

study also shows that of the $10.2 billion charged families for personal-health services annually approximately $1.5 billion, or 15 per cent, is paid by insurance benefits.[19] More recently—as of 1958—it is reported that hospital prepayment plans now cover 123,000,000 Americans.[20] Noteworthy also has been the proliferating of health and accident insurance companies and the expansion of life insurance companies into this field, especially during the last decade.

This program of private voluntary health insurance still shows some inadequacies. In most instances it does not provide for such preventive measures as regular physical checkups and immunizations even though these, quite obviously, could be both money and health savers even in the short run. Furthermore, these schemes cover only certain segments of the population, whereas the risks are universal. Most existing schemes pay only part of certain kinds of expenses for the insured. Some segments of the population needing such protection most—small farmers, certain racial and ethnic groups, indigent aged—do not come under group plans and cannot afford private arrangements.

There is occasional mention of the inclusion of a universally applicable medical and hospital insurance organization in the United States Social Security Program through a revision of the act establishing and maintaining this program. Great Britain, Norway, and Sweden have such national protective schemes operating quite successfully. This action has been vigorously opposed by the American Medical Association and some of the private insurance companies. However, almost everyone concedes that such national health insurance would make possible minimal services for the entire population, would distribute costs more equitably, and would provide supplementary funds for those already covered to some extent by private or group voluntary schemes.

It is surprising that, in spite of the spread of scientific knowledge in the United States and the increasing appreciation of science-founded technology, so many people should depend upon paramedical or even pseudomedical practitioners for health treatment—osteopaths who have limited training even for what they are legally permitted to do, chiropractors who are even less prepared, neuropathists and other drugless healers, and religious and other faith healers. There is also the wide resort to the so-called patent medicines, which to be sure are less harmful or possibly even harmless under the Pure Food and Drug Act but are of limited or questionable therapeutic value.

[19] O. W. Anderson, *National Consumer Survey of Medical Costs and Voluntary Health Insurance,* Summary Reports No. 2, pp. ii–3, No. 1, Health Information Foundation, 1954.
[20] Health Information Foundation, *Progress in Health Services,* March, 1958.

IV: Government in Welfare

A dominating feature of institutionalized welfare activity, obvious from all the preceding discussion, is that our governments—local, state and federal—have been assuming responsibility for welfare over and beyond the efforts of individuals, special interest groups, and voluntary private and semi-public welfare organizations. Our examination of organized social work, recreation, and health services as now provided shows a vast amount of regulation, expenditure of funds, use of resources, and provision of facilities by governments. It would seem to indicate that we as an organized people think the rendition of these services—ensuring the safety of the public, providing for recuperation and health, and protecting the morals of the people—the responsibility of the government in order to "insure domestic Tranquility" and "promote the general Welfare." Our governments have always assumed some of these welfare responsibilities, but their activities along these lines have expanded and been intensified since the 1930's. Of special significance at the federal level has been the creation during the 60's of the Department of Health, Education, and Welfare as a single federal department bringing together a variety of old and new federal agencies devoted to social welfare.

Many of these welfare activities are absolutely essential to individual and collective well-being in a society like ours, and are provided for by social legislation. In carrying the legislation into effect, the designated governmental agencies use the police power, a power which only governments have. Increasingly, also, there is the necessity of widespread standardization and equalization of requirements and of facilities and services; again, only governments can do these things adequately. All of the developments that have made for such extension of governmental welfare activity are likely to continue, and new ones are likely to appear; we can expect an increase in the amount, range, and intensity of such activity.

Finally, it should be noted that the concern for, and interest in, social welfare is now world-wide. There are not only great international semi-public organizations devoting attention to the various aspects of it, but some of the most widely approved and effective agencies of the United Nations, and in some instances of the League of Nations before it, are in considerable or large part providing welfare services of all kinds for the people of the world. Among the continuously operative agencies conducting different degrees and levels of such activities are the World Health Organization (W.H.O.), the Food and Agricultural Organization (F.A.O.), the International Labour Office (I.L.O.), and the United Nations Educational and Scientific Organization (U.N.E.S.C.O.). After both World Wars, the International Refugee Organization was active, and in connection with the effects of World War II, the United Nations Relief and Rehabilitation Administration (U.N.R.R.A.) and the United Nations International Children's Emergency Fund (U.N.I.C.E.F.) conducted crucial welfare functions.

BIBLIOGRAPHY

RECREATIONAL INSTITUTIONS

Anderson, N., "Leisure: By-product of Urbanism," in Anderson, N. (ed.), *The Urban Community: A World Perspective.* New York: Holt, 1959, pp. 347–474.

Annals Am. Acad. Pol. & Soc. Science, "Recreation in an Age of Automation," 313 (Sept., 1957): entire issue. Specialized articles in different aspects of recreation.

Clarke, A. C., "The Use of Leisure and Its Relation to Levels of Occupational Prestige," *Am. Soc. Rev.,* 21 (June, 1956): 301–307.

Cole, W. E., *Urban Society.* Boston: Houghton Mifflin, 1958, pp. 333–351.

Graham, Saxon, *American Culture.* New York: Harper, 1957, pp. 431–449.

Havighurst, R. J., and Feigenbaum, K., "Leisure and Life-Style," *Am. Jour. Soc.,* 64 (Jan., 1959): 396–404.

Larrabee, E., and Meyersohn, R. (eds.), *Mass Leisure.* Glencoe, Ill.: Free Press, 1958.

Martindale, D., *American Society.* Princeton, N.J.: Van Nostrand, 1960, pp. 430–485.

Meyer, H. D., and Brightball, C. K., *Community Recreation: A Guide to Its Organization.* Englewood Cliffs, N.J.: Prentice-Hall, 1956.

Panunzio, C., *Major Social Institutions.* New York: Macmillan, 1939, pp. 265–285.

Riesman, D., "Leisure and Work in Post-Industrial Society," in Larrabee and Meyersohn, *op. cit.,* pp. 363–385.

Sanders, I. T., *The Community.* New York: Ronald, 1958, pp. 322–341.

White, C. R., "Social Class Differences in the Uses of Leisure," *Am. Jour. Soc.,* 61 (Sept., 1955): 145–150.

Zelomek, A. W., *A Changing America at Work and Play.* New York: Wiley, 1959. Especially Part III on "Leisure, Mass Culture, and Man's Use of Them."

COMMUNITY ORGANIZATION

Beers, H. W., "Social Components of Community Development," *Rural Soc.,* 23 (Mar., 1958): 13–24.

Blackwell, Gordon W., "A Theoretical Framework for Sociological Research in Community Organization," *Soc. Forces,* 33 (Oct., 1954): 57–64.

Blackwell, Gordon W., "A Sociologist on School-Community Relationships," *Annals Am. Acad. Pol. & Soc. Science,* 302 (Nov., 1955): 128–135.

Friedlander, W. A., *et al., Concepts and Methods of Social Work*. Englewood Cliffs, N.J.: Prentice-Hall, 1958, Chap. IV.

Harper, E. B., and Dunham, A. (eds.), *Community Organization in Action: Basic Literature and Critical Comments*. New York: Association Press, 1959.

Hillman, A., *Community Organization and Planning*. New York: Macmillan, 1950.

Hoffer, C. R., "Social Action in Community Development," *Rural Soc.*, 23 (Mar., 1958): 43–51.

Hunter, Floyd, Schaffer, Ruth C., and Shepps, Cecil G., *Community Organization: Action and Inaction*. Chapel Hill: Univ. of North Carolina Press, 1957.

Murphy, C. G., *Community Organization Practice*. Boston: Houghton Mifflin, 1954.

Polson, R. A., "Theory and Methods of Training for Community Development," *Rural Soc.*, 23 (Mar., 1958): 34–42.

Ross, M. G., *Community Organization: Theory and Principles*. New York: Harper, 1955.

Ross, M. G., "Conceptual Problems in Community Organization," *Soc. Service Rev.*, 30 (June, 1956): 174–187.

Sanders, I. T., "Theories of Community Development," *Rural Soc.*, 23 (Mar., 1958): 1–12.

Sanderson, Dwight, *Rural Sociology and Rural Organization*. New York: Wiley, 1942, pp. 685–709.

Sower, C., and Freeman, C., "Community Involvement in Community Development Programs," *Rural Soc.*, 23 (Mar., 1958): 25–33.

SOCIAL WORK SYSTEM

Bondy, R. E., "Community Organization in Time of Crisis," *Proc. Nat'l Conf. of Soc. Work*. New York: Columbia Univ. Press, 1941, pp. 547–555.

Burns, Eveline M., *The American Social Security System*. Boston: Houghton Mifflin, 1951.

Clarke, Helen J,. *Social Legislation*. New York: Appleton, 1957, pp. 280–307, 437–464, 486–523.

Cohen, N. E., *Social Work: In the American Tradition*. New York: Dryden, 1958.

Council on Social Work Education of Am. Assn. of Soc. Workers, *Social Work as a Profession*. New York: 1953.

Friedlander, W. A., *Introduction to Social Welfare*. Englewood Cliffs, N.J.: Prentice-Hall, 1955.

Friedlander, W. A., *et. al., Concepts and Methods of Social Work*. Englewood Cliffs, N.J.: Prentice-Hall, 1958.

Kinneman, J. A., *The Community in American Society*. New York: Appleton, 1947, pp. 227–243.

Klein, Philip, "The Social Theory of Professional Social Work," in Barnes, H. E., Becker, H., and Becker, F. B. (eds.), *Contemporary Social Theory*. New York: Appleton, 1940, pp. 754–792.

Linford, A. A. (ed.), *Social Security in 1953*. Columbus, Ohio: National Conference of Social Work, 1953.

Stroup, Herbert H., *Social Work: An Introduction to the Field*. New York: Am. Book, 1948.

Wilensky, H. L., and Lebeaux, C. N., *Industrial Society and Social Welfare*. New York: Russell Sage Foundation, 1958.

Witmer, Helen L., *Social Work: An Analysis of a Social Institution*. New York: Farrar & Rinehart, 1942, Pt. III.

HEALTH INSTITUTIONS

Blackwell, Gordon W., "Behavioral Sciences and Health," *Soc. Forces*, 32 (Dec., 1953): 211–215.

Loftin, M. T., "Problems in Health and Medical Services," in Smith, T. Lynn, and associates, *Social Problems*. New York: Crowell, 1955, pp. 387–417.

Parsons, T., *The Social System*. Glencoe, Ill.: Free Press, 1951, pp. 428–479.

President's Commission on the Health of the Nation, *Building America's Health*. Washington, D.C.: U.S. Govt. Printing Office, 1953, 5 volumes.

Sanders, I. T., *The Community*. New York: Ronald, 1958, pp. 296–306.

Stern, Bernard J., *American Medical Practice*. New York: Commonwealth Fund, 1945.

SOCIALIZATION AND CULTURAL TRANSMISSION

Educational Institutions

The designation of educational institutions as the major media of cultural transmission to, and for the general socialization of, the young and other newcomers of a society stresses their main historical and contemporary functions. However, by the very nature of the processes of socialization, the educational institutions also carry on functions that have fundamental societal maintenance and regulative effects. They may, in a real sense, be referred to as supplemental maintenance and regulatory institutions.

There has always been some education; that is, some deliberate and more or less systematic imparting of social lore and experience. The human young have a greater helplessness at birth and during childhood at comparable steps in the life span than do any of the other mammals, and they have only the most rudimentary automatic proficiencies for life in human society. Nature has not equipped men genetically for human social life. All that men have ever had to live by in human groups has been acquired by learning. All children born into a human community have everything to learn, even how to live socioculturally with their own biogenic and psychogenic givens. At the same time, the human young are highly plastic and have greater potentiality for learning than any other mammal. Furthermore, the prolongation of infancy among human kind provides a long period of opportunity for comprehensively instructing and training the young before they are expected to assume the responsibilities of adulthood. In fact, this relatively long period of immaturity must be filled with socially positive preoccupations, interests, and activities if disorganization of the young and social mischief is to be avoided.

In human societies there is a sizable minimal body of cultural materials—common language, factual knowledge, ideas, beliefs, standards, techniques and skills, patterns of behavior for the various types of social relationships, and a vast body of institutional lore and institutionally systematized action—that the members must have and exemplify individually and collectively, if the individuals and the society are to survive. These materials—the essential cultural heritage—must be effectively transmitted to the young (and to all in-migrants) so that they perform as adequately socialized, that is, fully and competently participant or role-playing, members of the society. If the society (and its culture) is to carry on into the future, its present members, as its elemental components, must each make their contribution. This they cannot do without being given the necessary cultural materials to work with, without having their reproductive abilities "drawn out" (the real meaning of *educo*), without, at the same time, being motivated and disciplined to render their contributions in an honest and orderly manner. This socialization, including the preparation for contribution, must be carried beyond that provided in the family because of the limited perspective and eccentricities of the particular family and the limited knowledges and instructional skills and facilities of the parents. Even in simple societies, something in the way of a community educational system is deemed necessary if the essential quantity, quality, and scope of such materials are to be certainly and adequately imparted to each new generation.

All experience educates, but education itself ranges from mere random experiencing to the most highly organized procedures. As a process it involves various degrees of intention, purposiveness, informality and formality, quantity and complexity of materials imparted, and types of materials imparted; and, when more or less organized, there is a wide range of types of personnel and of social organizations and other facilities utilized for instructional, training, and disciplining purposes. In brief, the educational process, historically and contemporaneously, shows various degrees of institutionalization, which (1) range between simple or primitive and complex or industrialized-urbanized-statized societies, (2) are more predominant in the same society in different eras and at different stages of development, but also (3) are all operative in a given advanced society at a given time, since different aspects of experiencing range from the simple to the complex, and have various levels, degrees, and kinds of social or group objectives, purposiveness, and organization. At this point, it would be instructive to examine the more automatic and informal processes and also to note the different educational processes and agencies among the simpler, especially primitive, societies, leaving the major part of this chapter for discussion of the functions, instructural forms, and certain special and crucial features of the educational institutions of a complex modern society like our own.

Education through most of history has not been highly institutionalized; much of it has been—and still is—quite informal, even almost incidental; and much of it has been provided by other institutions as a sort of by-product.

Informal education is that learning and tutoring which the individual receives as a result of his interaction with his fellows in the daily, ordinary, life-situation routines of his community or society. In general, it consists of those processes, largely spontaneous, whereby the various stimuli and pressures of the sociocultural environment bear upon the more or less plastic, suggestible, inquisitive, acquisitive, and imitative human beings and thereby condition and shape their mental and overt behavior patterns. That these processes are tremendously effective in providing the individual with a great share of the conditioning necessary for group living, including the institutional ways, is unquestioned. The human young are everywhere born into families and communities having a culture. From birth to death this culture is a continual pressure upon the individual; it surrounds him like an atmosphere; from it or through it come the great proportion of the stimuli and the instructing and reshaping influences he receives throughout his life. These sociocultural influences bombard the individual during childhood, the years of highest receptivity and plasticity. We know that the deposits in the childhood mind persist throughout life, often with but slight modification.

The family has always performed highly significant educational functions, both among primitive and civilized societies. It is literally a psycho-social bridge between the generations whereby many values, ideas, attitudes, customs, codes, social habits, patterns for interpersonal and wider social relationships, and other valuable and essential cultural and behavioral elements are transmitted. The family not only transmits materials, but it provides opportunities for the practice, the observation of, and participation in many important activities necessary to satisfy life's needs, and serves to mould many habits essential for right social living. It is from some points of view a typical but miniature society in which the individual receives preparation for many of the standard roles of social life.

The incidental and informal educational processes, however, do not by themselves adequately transmit the cultural materials or prepare the individuals for competent social participation. The materials received are heterogeneous and divergent, not selective from the point of view of what is most needed in the changing society. The processes of transmission are, in the main, unplanned, unsystematic, and unintegrated, largely unconscious and haphazard, with the result that the materials received are almost a matter of chance. There are gaps, distortions, even downright contradictions among the materials, and no assurance regarding the necessary quantity, quality, variety, or range of the materials imparted to the next generation. It is especially unlikely that the common knowledge, the abstractions, or the rather specialized techniques can be thus properly transmitted. Also, in so far as the family is depended upon as an instructional medium, it should be noted that many parents are indifferent tutors and almost all are amateurs, regardless of their degree of devotion to their educational tasks.

For such reasons as these, all known societies, even the most primitive, have some consciously and specifically devised and formalized educational agencies. The informal means of transmission are supplemented by organized (institutionalized) devices for systematically and compulsively making the young acquire the essential elements of the social heritage. Only thus can they be given a properly extensive and sufficiently intensive instruction; only thus can a proper selection of necessary elements be made; and only thus can they be presented with sufficient emphasis and requisite skill to assure a margin of social safety.

Although the educational processes among the primitive or preliterate societies are themselves rather simple on the whole, at the same time, they combine the more or less informal transmission and socialization with formal procedures and agencies. In such societies the communities are relatively small and isolated, life is relatively unchanging, technology is simple, there is relatively little specialization, the means of communication are crude and slow, the language is not written; the people are relatively homogeneous genetically, ethnically, and ideologically; their over-all social organization is not very extensive or complicated. Although much, perhaps most, of the education in such a society is of an informal nature, there are also very definite efforts to instruct the young in a more or less positive, deliberate, aggressive, and systematized way. The young, in the relatively simple environment, learn much by imitation, observing, and participating with their parents, other elders, and their peers. But as soon as the tribe develops a stock of ideas, folkways, customs, beliefs, and skills that the members are conscious of as basically essential to existence, there begins to be some formalization of instruction. Important among these essential elements that need to be imparted with certainty are correct language, use of fire, hunting skills, planting lore and techniques, building principles and skills, marriage customs, child-caring, weaving, the making of pottery and other utensils, tool and weapon-making, magical lore, religious beliefs, incantations, rituals and other practices. The groups cannot afford to lose these precious acquisitions. Using the imitative bent of children, many of the preliterate people utilize the very games which the children play as tutoring devices. Proverbs, riddles, parables, myths, legends, fables, and other folklore—all almost universal and most appropriate media for oral transmission in societies without writing—are used as means of presenting and transmitting important sociocultural materials, especially the history and traditions, the values, and the ethical principles and requirements. There are also the institutional practices which it is the particular responsibility of parents to give their children. The father is expected to instruct his apprentice sons in how to make and set traps, how to chip flints and work metals, how to hunt, make fire, various tools and weapons. The mother teaches her daughters how to plant, gather food, dress skins, weave, care for babies, and make clothing. Most of the domestic and economic duties and skills and the etiquette and common folkways are thus imparted.

The initiation rites and the secret societies are the chief forms of formal primitive educative agencies, though they are not used for educational purposes by all preliterate groups having them. In most primitive societies, at puberty the boys, and among many, the girls, are obliged to go through a rather lengthy and complicated initiation ceremony before they are recognized as being fit to assume the dignities and duties and responsibilities of men and women. The old men and women, being the repositories of knowledge relating to the origin, growth, and function of the various cultural elements, especially the institutions, whether mundane or spiritual, and being versed in their practices, are the logical instructors and do take the most prominent part, although the whole group participates. These rites consist of instruction in tribal history and the legends; sex knowledge and the rules regarding sex relations; moral precepts; the rules of the family and its respective responsibilities; methods of fishing, hunting, fighting, and house-building; the rules and practices regarding the in- and the out-group; the laws relating to the class system; various religious and magical observances, rites, and myths; food restrictions; the relations to neighboring tribes; the content of property law; how to sing the songs and chants of the tribe; how to perform the dances; innumerable taboos covering every feature of life; in fact, all essential tribal lore and usage. By means of secrecy and mystery and the appeal to curiosity and wonder, by seclusion and the fear of the unknown, by hardships and tests of physical endurance, by the suppression of emotion and the insistence upon self-control, by the introduction of competition and rivalry to arouse pride and the desire to excel, the primitive instructors indelibly impress the tribal way of life upon the initiates and make them enthusiastic conformists. But always behind the instruction there is more than a hint of the power that can break those who fail or refuse to fall in line.

As the initiate advances to associations of deeper secrecy, he acquires more and more group lore, obtains enlarged tribal experience along with increasing maturity until he may in time become a member of the elders and perhaps a leader and instructor himself. It would be difficult to devise for preliterate men more adequate instructional agencies than the initiatory procedures and the accompanying secret societies. They represent the beginning of schooling in the strict sense of the term. The various ceremonies and practices constitute a cumulative course of instruction established by the group, chiefly for educational and regulative purposes. As a result the individual is not only able to take care of himself successfully, but is a cooperative participant in the affairs of the group and a depository of the group's agencies of perpetuation and well-being, capable in turn of becoming himself a transmitter.

Among some of the more advanced primitive societies, notably the Aztecs and Incas, there were schools of a sort.[1] Actually, in these particular primitive societies, education was conducted by a fairly well-organized and self-consistent system of procedures and agencies. It must also be noted, however, that although a considerable degree of institutionalization was reached, primitive education was accomplished primarily in the family and through other primary group associations; it was not conducted by large-scale formal organizations.[2]

The range of education in a given society among different eras and stages of development is well exemplified in the case of the United States, as the histories of American education so voluminously point out. There is a great difference in the education of today from that which existed in the early days of our history. In early, rural-agrarian America, much of the general education was conducted by the family. Boys learned much in doing the chores around the home and on the farm; and adult kinsmen and neighbors supervised the mastery of the relatively few and simple techniques that an adult male needed to know. Girls learned the arts of home-making from their mothers. Such common schools as there were, were elementary schools, largely devoted to the instruction which did not go much beyond "readin', writin', and 'rithmetic." The churches, especially through the parochial schools and other deliberate instructional efforts on the part of the priests and clergymen, supplemented the family and common school efforts. Occupational lore and skills, other than those imparted in the family, were transmitted by means of the apprentice system. Until well after the Civil War, education at the secondary level was mainly provided by private "Latin schools" and academies. College education was usually of a sectarian nature and was enjoyed mainly by a selected, fortunate group of young people from the middle and upper classes, and was largely confined to classical learning and literature. This "higher" aristocratic education was, in fact, a befitting mark of higher social-class position. For the most part, it has only been during the past century that education in our country has become "free," secular, univer-

[1] Cf. G. P. Murdock, *Our Primitive Contemporaries.* New York: Macmillan, 1934, pp. 384, 435.

[2] On primitive education, see: W. D. Hambly, *Origins of Education among Primitive Peoples.* London: Macmillan, 1926. H. Webster, *Primitive Secret Societies.* New York: Macmillan, 1932, pp. 49–73. R. Redfield, "Culture and Education in the Midwestern Highlands of Guatemala," *Am. Jour. Soc.,* 48 (May, 1943): 640–648. M. H. Watkins, "The West African Bush School," *Am. Jour. Soc.,* 48 (May, 1943): 676–681.

sal, "popular," more or less equalized for all, especially at the higher
levels, and generally graduated, standardized, and integrated through
a systematized and principally public educational system.

I: The Functions of Education in a Complex Modern Society

Education in a modern, complicated, rapidly changing industrialized-
urbanized society has to be a very different affair from that provided
spontaneously by kinship or religious groups or that of preliterate and
rural-agrarian societies. The minimal knowledge required by its members becomes daily more complicated and extensive. The inadequacy
of the older and simpler education is brought out when the functions
that modern education must carry out are noted. The ancient and universal ones are, of course, still essential, but a number of additional
and crucial ones are also imperative in a modern society.

Socialization of the members of the society, especially the young,
is the first and most fundamental function. In fact, most of the other
functions, as usually presented, are subfunctions of socialization. As
noted, all human experience socializes in some degree. Much of it occurs more pointedly in the home, and also through unavoidable participation in primary groups, all manner of special-interest organizations,
and activities of other institutions, but every society has tried to assure
an adequate amount, variety, and quality of socialization by means of
specifically established and competently conducted educational procedures.

As the institutionalized agency with the major responsibility for
socialization, it is the business of education to (1) inculcate social
values, norms, and directives; (2) develop right attitudes and habits,
and furnish most of the basic patterns of social behavior; (3) provide
the facts, principles, insights, and reasons upon which human beings
as more or less rational creatures can base their social behavior; (4)
cultivate, supervise, and manipulate ways of thinking and acting in the
interests of general social welfare and group prosperity; (5) provide
instruction, practice, training, and discipline in the appropriate forms
of social behavior, that is, learning to play the standard roles of age
and sex groups and all the other community participation roles; and
(6), at least in some measure, counteract, correct, or block anti-social
conditioning influences and agencies.[3]

[3] J. O. Hertzler, *Society in Action*. New York: Dryden, 1954, pp. 67–68, 95–
98, 322–324. M. W. Rodehaver, W. B. Axtell, and R. E. Gross, *The Sociology
of the School*. New York: Crowell, 1957, pp. 125–134.

A second major universal function of education, resting upon its socialization function and its related significance as the major systematized process of cultural transmission, is its function as a procedure whereby a society perpetuates itself, maintains itself, and continually renews itself as a society. This function lies behind most of the other institutionalized maintenance processes of any society. Education conserves, extends, renews, and transmits all of the culturally accepted values and ideals and the essential institutional ways so as to assure their continuity in time.

Certain specific gains accrue from culture transmission from generation to generation by means of education. First, the culture carefully built by man remains relatively intact; the processes of culture acquisition need not be repeated each generation. But what is even more important is the fact that the culture as thus maintained permits each new generation to spring from the achievement-shoulders of the preceding one. A second important gain accrues to man as the time-binding animal. By means of cultural transmission, he can live simultaneously in the past, the present, and the future. The massive cultural heritage from the past enables him to live wisely in the present on the basis of the informally and formally recorded experience of the past. At the same time, through his planning, goals, aspirations, and expectations, and the fact that all continuance and construction is sequential and projects itself into the future, each man of the present lives in the future; in fact, because of the transmission processes, the present is inseparable from the life of the future, and the men of the present are in some measure responsible for the future.

To assure societal continuity, education has a further function which relates it directly to scientific institutions; namely, the function not only of transmitting the cultural heritage, but also through some of its functional personnel, especially at the higher levels, to acquire, develop, diffuse, and apply *new* desirable knowledges and techniques and continually improve existing ones. In rapidly changing and expanding societies, this is absolutely essential if retrogression is to be avoided.

In carrying on these major universal functions of cultural transmission, socialization, and provision of the essentials for sociocultural contributions, education conducts several subfunctions, which may actually be deemed as further inplementations of the main functions.

It may be noted parenthetically that no society, including our own, may conduct these functions in anything near ideal or even hoped-for fashion, and the effectiveness will vary in different societies and with respect to particular functions. The fact remains, however, that none of the quasi or incidental educational agencies are doing them in more than sporadic or fortuitous fashion. They are ultimately the functions of the educational system.

A vital coordinate function is to sound out or discover and develop the capacities and potentialities of its children and young people. Every society needs to have its members self-fulfilled to the fullest extent possible; this is essential to their mental and spiritual health. But from the point of view of social organization, every society needs the fullest contribution to it by its members. In a society of great division of labor and specialization of function, there are an infinite number and variety of tasks to be conducted and roles to be filled; these require an almost infinite range—in diversity, complexity, and value rank—of human qualities and capacities. At the same time, there is vast variation in human endowment and developmental possibilities. The individual member of the society is unavoidably, by his very presence, a contributor for good or ill. When a society fails through its educational system to invest in the potentialities of its members, it is failing in the utilization of its most fundamental resource, its manpower. Insufficient education, unequal education, and miseducation—each is a great waste that modern societies cannot afford. Creative talent especially needs to be uncovered and developed. It should be specifically noted that illiterates, because of their unemployability in a society like ours, are a major national deficiency and burden.[4] At the same time the fact must be accepted that not all human qualities are good for the individual or for the society; some need to be sublimated or corrected; powers of self-discipline need to be developed to enable the individual to control them.

Closely related to the developmental function is that of selection and social placement of individuals. Not only does the educational system of a society need to sound out and develop the capacities of its oncoming citizenry; it needs also to test the young folks and sort them out on the basis of their respective qualities and direct them toward those positions in society where the performance requirements are compatible or more or less equated with their developed capacities. In the case of the individual, it means freedom from the strain of being expected to do more than he can readily perform and from the frustration of not having the chance to do what his abilities permit. When the formal schools of the society are efficiently performing their selective function, it also means that individuals are spared much wear and tear in the "school of hard knocks." For the society, it means relatively few misplaced individuals and less discontent; there is much greater likelihood of appropriately and more efficiently invested human potentialities;

[4] Cf. Eli Ginzberg, *Human Resources: The Wealth of a Nation.* New York: Simon & Schuster, 1958, pp. 53–58. See also H. E. Freeman and G. G. Kasselbaum, "The Illiterate in American Society: Some General Hypotheses," *Soc. Forces,* 34 (May, 1956): 371–375.

with the competent assignment to social stratum, the society readily maintains balance within the class structure.

An educational system like ours with its primary, secondary, and college levels of instruction and testing serves roughly to perform this function.[5]

The social control function of education is in part and in some of its aspects a distinct and additional function and, at the same time, a general summarizing function. The education of the people is a form of positive control. There is still much point to the contention of Socrates that if you make men wise, you make them good; at any rate, by educational procedures you can give men the facts and principles whereby they can act right. In general, what is taught and not taught is an important determinative factor in the values and attitudes held, the goals pursued, and the behavior practiced by the next generation. From the practical angle, the community must protect itself against all sorts of baleful influences by having adequately socialized individuals. It must develop individuals who are orderly and helpful members, who have pro-social instead of anti-social behavior. The systematic educational process does this in some part by the inward moulding and remoulding of the attitudes and the habits and thus the character of the young. The principle underlying this is: the better the inward formation of the individual, the less need for emphasis on the law and the activity of the police.

It should also be noted that a social system such as ours provides considerable practice in acquiring social control experience. As Queen points out,[6] children in school are required to do all sorts of things, are restricted in various ways, are subjected to various prohibitions, are supervised, disciplined, and policed, put through various drills, operate within a reward and penalty system, and must fit into a regimen that is bigger and more powerful than any individual in it. The informal relations among peers in school life also provide much training in social control, since the youngster not only learns various behavioral principles, but in order to maintain face among his associates must abide by them.

In every community or society, there is a basic moral code based on long social experience. This code indicates what is generally wrong and hence must be forbidden, and what is right and must be followed in the standard situations and relations. The people must feel a respon-

[5] Cf. T. Parsons, "The Role of General Theory in Sociological Analysis," *Alpha Kappa Deltan,* 29 (Winter, 1959): 12–38, esp. 32–37. For a critical discussion of the selective function, see W. L. Warner, R. J. Havighurst, and M. B. Loeb, *Who Shall Be Educated?* New York: Harper, 1944, pp. 141–148.

[6] S. A. Queen, W. N. Chambers, and C. M. Winston, *The American Social System.* Boston: Houghton Mifflin, 1956, pp. 71–72.

sibility to act according to the code. This awareness must start with the children in the school. However, because of the variations—sometimes actually contradictions—in the interpretations and emphases by the various other influencing and indoctrinating groups (family, religious organizations, government, class groups) and the counter influence of morally subversive groups and interests, these moral essentials must be inculcated in some minimal degree by the society's over-all instructional agency, the educational system. This system alone potentially assures general coverage, without gaps and partial or special-interest emphasis. It is obvious that there still is considerable uncertainty as to what is to be included in this instruction and how it is to be achieved.

A final function is to provide the society with a sense of unity and to enhance solidarity. This might be referred to as a non-academic function. In a complex, heterogeneous, stratified society, it is a function of formal education to teach children about the diverse racial, ethnic, cultural, and social class groups with which they unavoidably come into contact, and especially how to live decently and cooperatively with the members of these various other groups. It also serves as the community's educational and cultural center and seeks to integrate all of the members of the community. It enhances solidarity in that it does, in considerable measure, establish a foundation of common agreement as to positive general social objectives, common interests, and common objects of allegiance. It also seeks to motivate widespread response to community objectives. No other societal agency is in a position to do these things on a sufficiently broad basis.

In general, education, as a societal functional agency, does in a matter of days, months, or years what by the processes of slow, spontaneous, fumbling, trial-and-error acquisition or inexpert inculcation of social attitudes, rules, and ways would take several generations, and then, because of their unsystematic nature, would leave vast gaps. It also serves as a powerful means which society places in the hands of each of its members for achieving social control through self-control.

II: The Institutional Organization of Education

In order to carry on the functions just noted in a comprehensive manner for all of the pertinent portions of the population in a society, education must be highly organized; it must be extensive in coverage and elaborately institutionalized over the entire societal area.

The school in all of its forms and ramifications is the chief, the central, and the purposively specialized educational instrument—the very epitome of formal education. Ancient Egypt, Babylonia, and

China, the Hebrews, the Greeks, and the Romans had their schools; and medieval Europe developed them to a high level of proficiency. Schools have been conducted under various auspices during their long career, such as by and for particular social classes, especially upper classes in closed-class systems, by religious orders and sects, and by semi-public corporations, such as the medieval European universities and the guilds. They have presented various curricula, but mostly for special purposes; their teachers have been persons with differing kinds of professional specialties, such as the priests and public administrators.

Ancient Egypt had its palace schools for the sons of the Pharaohs, courtiers, future administrators, and other privileged persons; and the instruction was by "wise men" of the ruling classes. The schools of ancient Babylonia were connected with the temples; the instruction was by the priests and for the upper classes only. The ancient Hebrews had some extension of school services to the middle classes, but the instruction was by the priests and was mainly of a religious nature. The Romans provided education mainly for the upper levels of the population, but it was also somewhat stratified, that is, of differentiated type and content for each rank. Even in medieval Europe the various types of schools—monastery schools, episcopal or cathedral schools, and palace schools—were principally for upper-class boys; the instruction was by clerics and primarily to prepare the students for service in the Church.

Schools in our society are both public and private or semi-private. The very great proportion of the students, however, attend public schools, ranging from kindergarten to graduate school and conducted by the state through its local and larger political subdivisions—schools to which the students have access regardless of class, religion, or ethnicity, and increasingly irrespective of individual or family financial ability. The existence of the school, as a universal institution in our society instead of a class or other special-interest agency, depends on several conditions: first, recognition of the necessity of universal education for all categories of the population; second, sufficient wealth to support a considerable number of persons specially trained for and engaged in teaching and to afford extracting or withholding from the labor force most of its immature members and subjecting them to systematic instruction during this period of life.

The objective of the school is formal, systematic, professionally skilled, and selective instruction of the young. The experiences and the knowledge and techniques to be imparted are selected, graded, and organized. The teaching and administration is carried on by a particular personnel—a body of functionaries especially trained in educational procedures of management, supervision, teaching, and, in the higher schools, in research, with specialized knowledge and skills. The teaching techniques employed are selected because of their demonstrated efficacy in imparting the right experience at the right time and under appropriate conditions. Special plant and equipment are provided to expedite the whole process.

The school system of the United States is extensively organized and has a wide range. It penetrates the most remote and sparsely settled rural areas, as well as the towns and cities, and is accessible to every segment of the population, though not with uniform or equal provision. It provides an educational ladder consisting, in general, of the three levels, elementary, secondary, and higher, with the standardized steps of the present ladder being nursery school, kindergarten, six or eight years of elementary school, four or six years of high school (in the latter case, three years respectively of junior and senior high school), two years of junior college or four years of college, and the advanced specialized and professional and graduate schools. In addition to these there are various other types of schools of a public and semi-public nature, such as residential schools for the blind, deaf, mentally deficient, and the incorrigible; public evening schools offering a wide range and level of instruction; continuation schools; correspondence schools providing instruction in various areas and at differentiated levels; university-extension schools; vocational and technical schools, with the greatest number concentrating on agriculture, the trades, home economics, and business.

The importance of schools and schooling in our social system is indicated by the great number of schools, by the vast enrollment, and by the high level of schooling completed by the population. As far back as 1950, there were around 152,000 public elementary and secondary schools, 13,000 privately supported schools, and over 1800 institutions of higher education.[7] There were 21,000 public high schools in the United States in 1957. With respect to enrollment, Census Bureau figures show as of October, 1955, about 37.2 million persons 5 to 29 years of age were enrolled in school or college; this was 7 million more than in October, 1950. And of this date, 65 per cent of the total *male* population 5 to 29 years of age were in school, and 56 per cent of the female population were enrolled. A further breakdown by age groups shows that 94 per cent of males 5 to 13 years and 93.9 per cent of females 5 to 13 years were in school, while 38.1 per cent of males 14 to 29 years and 26.7 per cent of females 14 to 29 were in school. The level of schooling completed further indicates the importance of the school system. As of March, 1957, of the total population 14 years

[7] *Statistical Abstract of the U.S., 1954,* pp. 125, 127, 134.

of age and over, amounting to 119,333,000 (54,470,000 males and 61,863,000 females), among the males 76.2 per cent had completed at least 8 years of elementary school, 37.5 per cent had completed at least 4 years of high school, and 8 per cent had completed at least four years of college. Among the females, 80.2 per cent had completed 8 years of elementary school, 41.6 per cent had completed at least 4 years of high school, and 5 per cent had completed at least 4 years of college. Of the total population of 119,333,000, 14 years old and over, 93,410,000 had completed at least 8 years of elementary school, 71,-141,000 had completed at least 4 years of high school, and 7,637,000 had completed at least 4 years of college.

Not only is the total school population growing rapidly, especially with the increased birth rate of the last decade and a half, but the proportion of the population enrolled in schools has been increasing tremendously. Almost all children of elementary school age are in school; the great majority of those of high school age are in school; and an ever greater proportion of the population beyond high school age are seeking college or graduate degrees or are availing themselves of various kinds of adult education. We very definitely have mass education. Although the military system receives the greatest financial support (approximating half of the total annual federal budget), the school system of the United States is the largest public enterprise from the point of view of the number of people involved, both as functional personnel and as clients-recipients; all but a very small fraction of the population come under the direct influence of the American educational system for a period of time; all are utterly dependent upon it all of their lives in a hundred ways.

The school system shows all of the essential features of an institutionally organized area of life, although, as in all other major institutionalized areas of social life, some are stressed and elaborated more than others, and a few are unique.

The school system has a substantial foundation of conceptual, ideological, and other cultural elements. It has its basic underlying concepts and philosophy which take specific form in the declared objectives of the educational system and are in some measure actualized. It also has its basic values, especially those relating to the place, nature, and kinds of education in a democracy, involving both ideal and utilitarian societal and cultural considerations. These concepts and values combine in the ideology; that is, the body of consistent rationalizations and justifications on the basis of which we support, promote, and defend the system. Important also is the body of folklore, myth, and tradition which undergirds it and which does so much in determining the attitudes and the behavior, not only of the functional school personnel and the students, but also the citizenry at large. The school system even has its own peculiar language.

The school system has its own institutionally standardized behaviors and its own required routines. These rest upon a variety of codal elements ranging from its own peculiar folkways, mores, taboos, customs, rituals and ceremonies, and other informal behavorial expectations to the ever increasing body of formal rules established by the educational organization itself and the laws of the state bearing on education. These govern almost every typical relationship and operative requirement. It might be mentioned parenthetically that the students build up a body of rules for their relations with each other and with the official and teaching personnel which often has high regulative power and which often may be quite contrary to that of the system.

Related to the codal elements as concrete expressions and to the essential functions that have to be conducted are the rather well-standardized roles which administrators, teachers, students at all levels, members of the governing boards, and all other personnel and interested elements of the population at large perform.

A third institutional aspect—one of which the public is more widely conscious than the two just mentioned—is the essential operational personnel, especially in its associational forms. A given school system is a network of categories and groups of persons functionally interrelated in order to accomplish the educational objectives. Some of these interrelations, though taking relatively standard form, are largely of an informal nature; for example, the relations within student cliques and within teacher cliques and some of the relations between teachers and students. However, the relationships and operations that are functionally imperative are bureaucratically organized in all but the smallest school systems, in order to assure the adequacy and timeliness of their performance. There must be division of labor and forms of specialization among the functionaries; but these divided and specialized elements must be operationally integrated; hence, there must be line and staff organization. Authority must be exercised, both in the way of downward flow through the levels of the organizational hierarchy (from superintendent or president, to principal or dean, to teachers and clerks) and in the relationships of staff and students. The instruction itself, the ultimate objective, because of the very nature of growth and of the learning process, must be carried on by grades or successive levels, and these grades and the content at each level must be carefully established and sequences properly organized.

The typical categories of functionaries are (1) the school board members, boards of trustees or regents, or other governing boards which in a sense represent the constituency and which determine, or at any rate approve, the official policies of the schools;[8] (2) the administrators at several levels (superintendents, presidents, chancellors, deans, principals, chairmen of departments), most of whom have risen from the teaching ranks, who are responsible for the actual operation of the school as an organization; and (3) the teachers, who carry out the main objective of education—instruction and research.

Of these three categories, the teachers are the key personnel; the others exist mainly to enable the teachers to carry on their functions in the most efficacious manner. The teachers are the specialists in the educational system. Like the specialized functionaries in several other institutional areas, they are professionalized. Although they are not as highly professionalized as the medical and legal groups, they are certainly so at a higher level than the clergy, and at least equally as much as the specialists in business and government. There is increased stress in the teaching profession upon the special knowledges needed and upon rather definitely prescribed training in instructional and investigative techniques. Publicly set certification requirements must be met at the elementary and secondary levels, and increasingly rigorous advanced degree requirements must be fulfilled at the higher levels.

This professional personnel is organized into associations, some of which are quite broadly inclusive in their membership, others more specialized. The purposes of the organizations have a wide range, including at one extreme the promotion and improvement of education in general, and at the other, obtaining recognition, promotion, and security for the members as professionals. There are local and state associations of teachers and administrators and the National Educational Association, the largest professional organization in the world. These include all personnel and attempt to serve as unifying organizations, support programs of educational expansion, seek larger appropriations for the support of schools, aim at promoting the professional status of teachers, and carry out programs of interpretation of the schools to the public. There are several federations and labor unions of teachers affiliated with the A.F.L. and the C.I.O. Colored teachers are organized in the American Teachers Association. There are subdivisions in the more general associations and also special organizations for kindergarten teachers, school adminstrators, school board mem-

---

[8] The following are the major functions of boards of education in our American educational system: (1) determine over-all educational policies for local use; (2) set local tax levies for the financial support of the schools; (3) appoint, assign, and dismiss superintendents, principals, and other school employees; (4) decide curricular and extra-curricular programs; (5) determine type of organization of schools; (6) secure school sites and approve construction of buildings; (7) determine special services—kindergarten, vocational training, health services, guidance services, etc.; (8) approve budgets for all aspects of operation.

bers, deans of women, registrars, and audio-visual instructors. The welfare of those engaged in higher and professional education is promoted by the American Association of University Professors, which is especially concerned with such matters as academic freedom and tenure, pensions, salary schedules, and the encouragement of favorable legislation for education. Special organizations exist to promote vocational, adult, classic, civic, scientific, and other educational interests. There are a multitude of associations for accrediting schools and colleges. The professional teacher-patron combination of people concerned with education is exemplified in the Parent-Teacher Association which has chapters in almost every school. Some of our American educational organizations also have world affiliation in such organizations as the World Federation of Educational Associations and the World Organization of the Teaching Profession.

A fourth institutional aspect, and the other phase of the personnel structuring, is the students. These are not only the most important human element, since it is for them and them alone that the system exists, but all of the other institutionalized agencies and procedures revolve around them. With free and compulsory education up to 14 or 16 years of age, depending upon the particular states, the students make up the greater proportion of the population of elementary and secondary age groups; they are drawn from a growing proportion of the population of college age, and increasingly with the development of adult education involve in some measure people of all age groups beyond the college age. They come from both sexes, from all social classes, from various ethnic groups, and from the various religious groups of the population in all sections of the country.

In the system they are formally organized by grades. They participate in the learning-training process as enrollees in specialized subject-matter classes or courses. They are also organized as clubs (for example, for debating or the pursuit of other academic interests and as athletic teams). At the college level, and occasionally at high school level, there are fraternities and sororities with their main emphasis upon such extra-curricular but college-related interests and activities, including mutual admiration, as exclusives, matrimony, and vertical social mobility. They are informally organized, or perhaps it would be more accurate to say that they tend to coalesce informally as cliques, on the basis of the social strata, the ethnic, and the religious groups from which they come.

There are several peculiar characteristics of the school system which have a direct relationship to the personnel. The students have had nothing to say about the policies, the structure, or the program of which they are the beneficiaries, nor are they expected to have. They have to accept the school as given, principally, of course, because they are the learners, with limited life experience, and hardly in a position to determine what they should learn or by means of what facilities and procedures.

A closely related feature concerns the teacher-pupil relationship. The relationship is fundamentally one of leader and follower. It is better if the teacher is both an intellectual and a natural leader, but by virtue of the fact that the teacher has been appointed by some authoritative board, the students have to take what they get. Furthermore, the authority in the relationship is exercised in one-way fashion; it originates in the governing board and is exercised by the teachers as they transmit the special knowledges and skills that the students need; the students, unavoidably, are subordinate.

A fifth, and unique, institutional feature of the school system is the curriculum and the standardized instructional procedures. The school cannot teach everything or give every sort of training. It always has to be selective. It has to select from the infinite variety and forms of culture certain knowledge, techniques, arts, and ideals that the community, or society, or nation-state considers to be most important for its survival and stability. The central concern is the preparation of the young people as fully as possible for their many-faceted obligations in tomorrow's world. The items selected, reflecting in some measure those advanced by special-interest groups, but mainly and finally selected jointly by the governing boards and the upper administrative and scholarly levels of the professionals operating under public mandate, constitute the curriculum. At the elementary level, it includes as far as possible those things that every citizen must know—the society's language, reading, writing, arithmetic, some history, and elementary ethical principles and moral disciplines. From there on up, it becomes more and more diverse and specialized as to kinds and combinations of subjects presented, depending upon the different educational objectives of the different categories of students at the different educational levels. A major consideration in constructing the curricula of schools is to get into them those essential forms and qualities of knowledge and those types of training and skill development that are least likely to be acquired through general life experience or by means of the informal and non-school educational influences and procedures. The instructional techniques employed will also differ in the different areas and at the different levels. In general, the teaching techniques are selected because of their demonstrated efficacy in imparting the right experience at the right time and under appropriate conditions.

A final institutional feature—most obvious of all to the observer—is the physical plant. The school system must have the grounds or campuses and the buildings with classrooms, offices, laboratories, assembly-rooms and gymnasiums, to house its staff and students and in which to carry on its procedures. In the buildings it must have equipment, such as furniture, books and journals, laboratory and other experimental materials, maps, audio-visual machines, calculating machines, athletic equipment, musical instruments, and so on.

III: The School System and the Community

The school system as a vast, mainly public, institution has a peculiarly integral and reciprocal relation to the community and society. Not only is it an organic part of the modern community, but as an organization it is exceeded only by the state itself in universality, massiveness, in unified influence, in portion of the population covered by its activities, and in public concern about it as a crucial, community-wide agency. The other institutions, other than the state, consist of a multiplicity of organizations (for example, separate families and kin-groups, separate and private industrial and commercial concerns, separate religious sects and denominations), and are the special expressions of diverse interest groups, and exercise limited controls over limited numbers and categories of persons. This relationship of school system and community has several significant organizational ramifications.

The school system does not exist in a vacuum; it is a creature of the community. Next to the state, it comes nearest to being the main common expression of the community's activities, ideals, goals, and expectations; and, also next to the state, it is the most important functional agency, including especially its significance as chief effecter of the ideals, goals, and expectations as well as of the more utilitarian functions already noted. Also, as a community system, it reflects the general cultural and social milieu of the community: its technological level, its demographic composition, its other major institutions in their locally or regionally peculiar forms and functions, the stratification system, the social organization, including especially the ethnic, economic, and political organization, the general educational level of the people and their *Weltanschauung*.

At the same time, the school system, as a generally recognized, highly influential creature of the community, is not entirely a free agent. What is taught is, of course, always selected and selective; the school system is subjected to all manner of efforts to control it by numerous special-interest groups in order to in some way advance their interests. These efforts take such forms as trying to control the type of persons elected to the governing boards; influencing legislation governing education; trying to influence the granting of educational funds according to "or else" principles; seeking favorable elements or slants in the curriculums;

seeking to prescribe right textbooks; trying to influence the selection and tenure of teachers on the basis of their suitability, with respect to their economic, political, ethnic, or religious points of view. Among the groups exercising such pressures are Chambers of Commerce and other business groups, labor organizations, mothers' clubs, farm organizations, religious groups, veterans' organizations (the American Legion and the Veterans of Foreign Wars), other patriotic organizations, such as the Daughters of the American Revolution, the bar associations, fraternal organizations, civic clubs, political parties, and military groups.[9]

The relationship between the community and its school system is an ambivalent one. Not only is the school system controlled by the community and reflects its structure, interest, and objectives, but it in turn influences and controls the community as it shapes the students in its charge; and the community otherwise reacts to the influences exercised by the school, especially its unavoidable moulding effects. This, of course, is another way of saying that the school system is performing its essential and typical functions. But there is a certain circularity in the situation with somewhat disturbing implications. The school is an expression of the community, but it is difficult for the stream to rise higher than its source, or for the education to rise above the community's existent educational level. The very people that the school system has shaped are the influential public which at any given time exercise control over the system, indirectly as the general population, and directly through the representative governing boards; it is always the past generations and the present adult generation that, through the schools, exercise the control, especially over the new, oncoming generation. To avoid the obvious rut, a special obligation is put upon the cultural, especially the educational, elite in every community to point out educational shortcomings to the public, to provide new educational perspectives, and continuously to stimulate reorganization. For the existing generation must always first be improved in order to improve the generation that follows.

A fourth important aspect of the school in the community is its relationship to all of the other institutions of the community as well as to all of the other agencies that do some educating. Although the school is the specific, purposive, and formally established instructional agency in complex societies, it functions jointly with all of the other institutions of the community in the educational process. For, not only

[9] On these influences and controls, see: Queen, Chambers, and Winston, *op. cit.*, pp. 74–76. B. N. Meltzer, H. R. Doby, and P. M. Smith, *Education in Society.* New York: Crowell, 1958, pp. 171–172. W. O. Stanley, B. O. Smith, H. D. Benne, and A. W. Anderson, *Social Foundations of Education.* New York: Dryden, 1956, pp. 497–537.

does each social institution, or more correctly each cluster of social institutions, constitute an area to be learned, but each institution itself educates. Each institution specifically educates those participating directly as functionaries and beneficiaries; in general, though, the whole citizenry is in some degree conditioned and otherwise influenced by it (for example, by aesthetic institutions, even though not directly involved either as creators or interested enjoyers). As Bottrell puts the situation:

"Each social institution has its built-in guidance system, its tools and techniques, its patterns of relationships, its expectations to be internalized in the behavior of those directly involved, those served by it, and the community generally.

The learning related to social institutions is taught through the "textbook of first-hand experience." The induction is gradual; the teachers are many; the learning situations are numerous; the practice is continuous; the reinforcement is constant; the evaluation is vigorous; the rewards are observable."[10]

It should also be noted that as the school tries to epitomize the fundamental experiences of social living, all of the other institutions—family, church, industry and business, recreation, government—in a real sense converge in it.

The community provides a great array of agencies and influences that have educative effects. There are, first, those which have specified educational functions, such as the family and home, the church, especially Sunday Schools, libraries, extension services, lecture courses, museums, art galleries, pamphleteers, labor unions, 4-H clubs, settlement houses, welfare organizations, health information agencies, recreational centers, and governmental agencies at all levels. Second, there are those with incidental educative influence, such as gangs, playgroups, cliques; office, shop, and factory; business, professional, and social organizations; motion pictures, radio, and television; newspapers, books, journals, magazines, the omnipresent flood of comic books and tabloids; and commercialized recreation.[11]

All of these non-school agencies combined have a potent educative effect. Children spend a relatively small part of their waking time in school or under direct school influence; the rest of the time other agen-

---

[10] H. R. Bottrell, "Educative Processes in Their Community Setting," in H. R. Bottrell (ed.), *Applied Principles of Educational Sociology*. Harrisburg, Pa.: Stackpole, 1954, pp. 22–38, specifically, p. 25.

[11] For an excellent and still timely discussion of how the community educates, see: J. K. Hart, *A Social Interpretation of Education*. New York: Holt, 1929, pp. 247–254. See also the articles in the special issue, "The Public School and Other Community Services," *Annals Am. Acad. Pol. & Soc. Science*, 302 (Nov., 1955): pp. 1–73, especially those dealing with the United States.

cies are impinging upon them. However, some of them are not as influential as they once were. For example, as noted in the chapter on familial institutions, the family has steadily forsaken some of its traditional educational functions, and the church seems to be having less and less significance in moulding even the ideals, not to mention the moral behavior, of the young people. Other agencies, along with the general extension of experience that they provide, also do much educating, both good and bad; for example, the motion pictures, commercialized recreation, radio, television, the press, tabloids, and comics.

In general, the other educative agencies of the community are by no means substitutes for the school; at best they are correlates. The school system still has the major responsibility for education in the community; it must still provide the floor of subject-matter essentials, the positive social values, moral principles, and ideals, and the minimal social discipline and training.

In spite of the educative functions of most of the other institutions of the community, most of the responsible personnel of these and the public at large seem to operate on the principle that the schools should assume the sole instructional, training, and disciplinary responsibility. However, it should be stressed as a fifth aspect that formalized education is not a cure-all for all social problems; the school cannot do everything. It cannot teach all manner of subjects or train in every marketable skill; it cannot provide an infinite number of services; it cannot prevent juvenile delinquency or bad marital relations; it cannot itself educate all and each toward sound health, physical and mental; it cannot substitute for other agencies in instructing in ethics and providing all discipline. It is a finite system, operated by human beings, with an elaborate set of minimal core functions which it must perform in the total division of labor. It exercises its influence during only a limited portion of the day, week, and year. Parents, church, and other community agencies need to shoulder many of such duties instead of ignoring them or resigning from them. Now that most adults enjoy a thirty-five or forty-hour week and labor-saving devices have shortened the hours devoted to home chores, perhaps parents might resume some of their traditional educational tasks.

IV: Special American Educational Requirements

Although our American educational system must conduct all of the standard educational functions, it also has certain tasks to perform for us as a total society, because of such factors as democratic ideological orientation, our vast areal extent, with, however, an ever greater mobility between and interdependence of regions, our increasing technological advance, the increasing tempo of our rate of social change, and the inescapable necessity of living in a shrinking, interlocking world.

A high level of education for the people at large is indispensable to our democracy; education is, in fact, a condition of its survival and of its ever becoming that which it undertakes to be. In a democracy, all agreement and decision regarding the kind and quality of social action and all social convictions and goals emerge ultimately from the individual citizen. The very social system of the society as organized is the continuous creation of the men who man the positions and perform its roles. Public opinion, the ultimate determinant of all that goes on in a democracy, is after all the collective expression of the larger portion of the interested citizenry; and political decision is expressed through universal suffrage. Therefore, to be an adequate participant, the individual needs to (1) have his intelligence developed as fully as possible; (2) be well-informed; (3) have the capacity of personal self-determination developed; (4) have his moral qualities developed and exemplify a high level of social consciousness; and (5), especially, be developed and trained to make his fullest economic, political, and other institutional contributions. Such educational development is necessary in order to make democratic institutions function as well as, or preferably better than, those of societies directed by more or less absolute individual or special-group rule. Democracy demands of every citizen what in other forms of social organization is demanded of only a segment of society. In a democracy, semi-literacy, ignorance, indifference, purposelessness, ineptness of some portion of the population impair the opportunities and the social efficacy of all in the end, and constitute a standing invitation to disaster. Furthermore, every nation today, whether democratic or totalitarian, both as a competitor and as a cooperator with other nations, needs to have its every human resource developed and utilized. Only the best general education on a nation-wide scale will make this possible, and to do so, it must have certain essential features.

The basic education must be free, that is, publicly provided without special tuition charges to the parents; it must be generally available throughout the area of the society; and it must be compulsory for all children and youths up to an agreed-upon age. There can be no uneducated segments of the population.[12] Closely related to this point is the fact that there also must be equal opportunity for all to acquire this education and it should be of equal quality. A democracy cannot afford

12 This is another way of saying that it must be universal and cover every individual. The point of this is brought out in connection with the universal franchise. Each individual counts for one, and no one for more than one. Votes are counted, not weighed.

to have the equality of educational opportunity impaired because of present social standing, wealth and income, cultural traditions, race, nationality, religion, or social class. Nor should it be impaired because of regional differences in the provision of such opportunity. Ability and potentiality in a free and mobile society are not graded or distributed on the basis of such differentials; they are found everywhere. Also, it now seems essential that equal educational opportunity be available throughout adult life as well.

The curricular content of this education should fully and clearly envisage the more universal (or perhaps the average) needs in the way of subject-matter and training to enable the students to meet the average requirements of effective societal participation. The content should be more extensive and offer opportunity for specialization according to capacity at each educational level. There should be a continual levelling-up, not levelling-down, of the educational opportunity; that is, higher and higher levels should be available to more and more people. A static democracy is a deteriorating one; to progress, a democracy must have ever higher education of its citizenry.[13]

Great regional inequalities in educational opportunity exist in our country. The education available in rural areas is usually inferior to that of the cities. There is a great variation among states and regions; for example, as of 1954, we find a difference in median years of formal schooling completed by persons 25 years of age and older ranging from 12.0 years in Utah down to 7.6 years in South Carolina; persons 25 years or older with less than 5 years of formal schooling range from 3.9 per cent in Iowa to 28.7 per cent in Louisiana; the adult population that has 4 or more years of college education ranges from 8.1 per cent in California to 3.1 per cent in Arkansas.[14] More or less closely correlated with these differences are the great variations among states with respect to (1) the ethnic, especially racial, composition of the population with related differential educational facilities; (2) tax ability and financial support of education; (3) physical facilities, such as buildings, laboratories, libraries, and other equipment; (4) professional requirements for teachers, for example the amount of college preparation re-

[13] The U.S. Census Bureau in a report issued in January, 1960, based on a survey made in March, 1959, indicates marked advances in formal education in our country. The illiteracy rate has fallen to the lowest level on record; only 2.2 per cent of all Americans 14 or older are now unable to read and write as compared with 2.9 per cent in 1940. The level of schooling among U.S. adults is also higher than ever. Now half the adult population has had at least 11 years of schooling as against 9.3 years in 1950 and 8.4 years in 1940. About 43 per cent of the adult population have finished high school—about double the 1940 proportion. In 1959, 8 per cent of adults had completed college, in comparison with 6 per cent in 1950, and 4.6 per cent in 1940.

[14] National Educational Association, Research Division, *Educational Differences among the States.* Washington: N.E.A., 1954, pp. 4–5.

quired; (5) both the range and quality of the curriculum; and (6) such matters as proportion of drop-outs at different educational levels.

These areal differentials create a grave situation in a country like ours. General education cannot be thought of any more as a matter of purely local or even only regional concern. People no longer tend to live their lives in the same community in which they received their basic education. Both individuals and families have great physical mobility. The change of residence is particularly from rural to urban areas, and from the more economically and culturally backward states and regions to the more advanced. There are also other regional interdependencies —political, economic, and cultural in the narrow sense—that involve the quality of the educational institutions of the different regions. The upshot of this mobility and exchange of people and this interregional interdependence is that the young need to be educationally prepared to live anywhere in the United States. The citizens of every local community, every state, and every region have a direct stake in the educational services which are provided in every other area. The most up-to-date communities may find themselves flooded with immigrants with fourth-rate basic education. Every school today is educating a future citizen of the national community.

This situation implies the desirability of a nation-wide equalization of financial support, a nation-wide uniformation of basic curriculum, and a nation-wide equalization of facilities and professional requirements. The peculiar combination of local, state, and federal action by which this is to be achieved is still being heatedly debated.

As science and technology advance, we are confronted with new discoveries and inventions, new mechanisms and techniques in every department of our individual and collective physical, intellectual, and social life. Invention and misadventure are continually changing our physical environment and our physical means and modes of existence. We have to be able to use the inventions and know-how to live with them safely and profitably in the ever new physical setting. Our social environment is being transformed and retransformed; the local community is declining; the family pattern is changing; the class system is in continual flux; some occupations are disappearing, and new ones are arising; automation is having profound effects upon both the personnel and the organization of industry and commerce; the interdependencies of individuals and groups are becoming ever more extended and intricate. An extending science and technology challenge the validity or relevance of much of our thinking along political, economic, religious, and ethical lines. Science and technology have enormously enlarged the size of the individual's world; whether he likes it or not, he is a denizen, if not a citizen, of the entire world; and accordingly, as never before, needs a knowledge of geography, economics, history, sociology, demography, ethnology, reigning ideologies, languages, literatures, comparative religion, international politics, and, of course, science itself.[15]

But the situation requires even more than flexibility and readiness for adjustment. Every change requires more change. Our very discoveries and inventions present the necessity of other discoveries and inventions both within the particular phenomenal area and in correlated areas. In order to cope with this situation, the citizenry must be encouraged to participate in the accelerated production of new, and often strategically essential, knowledge. It is necessary to cultivate new interests, arouse curiosity, develop a spirit of inquiry, stir the imagination, and—the eventual objective—stimulate discovery and invention, even teach the principles and techniques of these.

The educational system, informally and formally, needs to educate all people for some degree of participation, depending upon individual capacity and position, in continuous social reconstruction. The system has the obligation to develop theoretically and technically proficient special personnel (1) to make the competent analyses and assessments of conditions and (2) to plan and execute the necessary modifications. Such preparation for change is a large order, but the need must be faced—and soon.

The increase of time available for leisure activities focuses attention upon utilization of that time. The increasing labor-saving combined with the increasing wealth of the country, from the standpoint of economic manpower and of family finances, make it possible to lengthen compulsory basic schooling beyond the general 14-year and even the 16-year period. It is less and less necessary for youths to enter the labor force at 14 or even at 16. As rich a nation as ours not only can afford to extend basic education at least into the early twenties, but, in view of the multiplying needs for knowledges and proficiencies, can hardly afford not to do so. Beyond this is the fact that the situation opens the possibility of continuing education as an important life preoccupation to almost every adult who wants it.[16]

Some amount of adult education is essential for several reasons. First, it is necessary to supplement and bring up to date the formal schooling received during childhood and youth, to supplement in a more

[15] Ruth Benedict states, with special reference to children, "Education in our world today must prepare our children to adapt themselves to unforeseeable conditions. It must give them a basis on which they can make their own decisions in situations not yet on the horizon." "Transmitting Our Democratic Heritage in the Schools," *Am. Jour. Soc.*, 48 (May, 1943): 722–727 (724). It is clear, however, that citizens of all ages need such orientation and proficiency.

[16] I am indebted for some of these viewpoints to M. J. Adler and M. Mayer, *The Revolution in Education.* Chicago: Univ. of Chicago Press, pp. 28–29, 43–44.

systematic way the incidental educational influences, and to supplement and correct the partial education and mis-education provided by the mass-information agencies. Second, it is desirable that adults keep up with the times somewhat systematically in the way of acquiring appropriate contemporary knowledge, acquiring new perspectives, and retooling conceptually and even vocationally for the new age.

It is necessary for a society to give the young marketable skill in the crafts and techniques that will enable them to earn a livelihood; every society needs a great array of technically competent persons. The progress of technology in a complex society, and the consequent intensification of the division of labor has multiplied the vocations requiring specialized training. Until recently only the preparation for the traditional higher professions and the higher levels of engineering practice was formally provided for by special schools. The bulk of the work disciplines and skills were acquired in the home or as apprentices to master craftsmen. Today town and city young folks, especially, acquire almost no such proficiencies in the home; and labor unions, as part of their protective efforts, have forced business and industry practically to abandon apprentice training. Some big corporations have so-called apprentice schools, but these are mainly for the training of higher level technical and administrative specialists beyond the reach of unions.

Hence, increasing attention is being paid to trade and industrial education, which includes training for employment in manufacturing, commercial, construction, technical, and service occupations, and also training in home-making and agriculture. Increasingly, the schools as primary educational agencies, particularly the public high school, the so-called trade schools, and the schools in agriculture and engineering at the college level, have had to assume the responsibility for providing such training.[17]

In a free, competitive, open-class society, vertical social mobility is not only a precious opportunity and a motivation to achievement, but it also functions as a means of selecting and appropriately locating individuals in the stratification system. Our educational system, by its very nature and by conducting its essential functions, has a direct relationship both to social mobility as a process and to differential social status. In the first place, the educational system has a primary function of sounding out abilities and selecting and further developing individuals for life positions which are compatible with their abilities. This it does, after a fashion, grade by grade.

Second, it makes it possible for them, according to their talents and developing proficiencies, to move to higher educational levels, which in turn are more or less correlated with social status levels. The educa-

[17] Cf. W. P. Loomis and Louise Moore, "Occupational Education in the Schools," *Annals Am. Acad. Pol. & Soc. Science,* 302 (Nov., 1955): 68–73.

tional ladder is thus one of the fairly effective means of ascending the social ladder. In fact, we are given to the notion that the elevation of a person's climb on the educational ladder is one of the best indices of his preparation for a position in the economic and honorific structure of our open-class system. In this connection, the youngsters in the educational system of a socially mobile, open-class society also learn what is essential to higher status or what is essential to prevent loss of status. Third, in a • general way, the level of formal education accomplished is one of the telling badges of level of social standing; the higher the educational level, the higher the social standing.

Much of our upward mobility in the United States has undoubtedly been made possible by our educational system. However, there are some grounds for believing that our school system is not facilitating social mobility as well as is fondly supposed. The very nature of our class system, even though an open-class system, holds individuals to their given class at a given time by inevitably determining their social values, perspectives, objectives, and financial standing, thus determining their ability to incur expenditures for educational and other socially advancing opportunities. The result is a blocking effect upon the operation of the educational conveyor belt. A rather high correlationship exists between the social class of students and their participation in, or the degree to which they avail themselves of, the school's activities, level by level. For example, some studies show that whereas a very large proportion of upper- and upper-middle-class young folks go to college, where the basic knowledge, training, and social sophistication essential to upper-class position is achieved, a very small proportion of the lower-middle- and lower-class children go on to college. Also, lower-class children start dropping out as soon as compulsory legislation permits, and drop out at an increasing rate above this age. It is likewise pointed out that teachers, themselves largely middle-class, represent a middle-class point of view and, more or less unconsciously, favor middle- and upper-class-children in various ways. This is also in large part true of the members of boards of education. Industry and business are depending upon college-trained persons for even the lower supervisory jobs, not to mention the higher technical and administrative positions.

Although the agencies of mass communication do much educating, much of it works at cross purposes with the essential objectives of institutionalized education. These agencies exist mainly for the commercial purposes of the private corporations that operate them. They produce or provide what the public demands, or will submit to and pay for, in the way of entertainment or information. They are not primarily concerned with educational objectives, and they do not operate under educational controls. Much mis-education occurs along social lines. For example, radio, television, the pulp press devote much time to gangsterism, crime, dope, vice, marital triangles, and gossip regarding social parasites, thus countering the influence of school and church. What to do about this situation poses an increasingly pressing problem and points to an urgent task.[18]

BIBLIOGRAPHY

GENERAL

Adler, M. J., and Mayer, M., *The Revolution in Education.* Chicago: Univ. of Chicago Press, 1958.

American Journal of Sociology. Symposium on "Education and the Cultural Process," 48 (May, 1943): entire issue.

Annals Am. Acad. Pol. & Soc. Science, "The Public School and the Community Services," 302 (Nov., 1955): entire issue.

Beals, R. L., and Hoijer, H., *An Introduction to Anthropology.* New York: Macmillan, 1953, pp. 570–599.

Brookover, W. B., *A Sociology of Education.* New York: Am. Book, 1955.

Clark, B. R., "The 'Cooling-out' Function in Higher Education," *Am. Jour. Soc.,* 65 (May, 1960): 569–576.

Davis, K., *Human Society.* New York: Macmillan, 1949, pp. 195–233.

Ebersole, Luke, *American Society: An Introductory Analysis.* New York: McGraw-Hill, 1955, pp. 412–441.

Giddings, F. H., *Civilization and Society: An Account of the Development of Behavior in Human Society.* New York: Holt, 1932, pp. 263–324.

Gerth, H., and Mills, C. W., *Character and Social Structure: The Psychology of Institutions.* New York: Harcourt, Brace, 1953, pp. 251–256.

Graham, Saxon, *American Culture.* New York: Harper, 1957, pp. 406–430.

Gross, Neal, "The Sociology of Education," in Merton, R. K., *et al.* (eds.), *Sociology Today.* New York: Basic Books, 1959, pp. 128–152.

Martindale, D., *American Society.* Princeton, N.J.: Van Nostrand, 1960, pp. 289–297.

Mead, Margaret, *The School in American Culture.* Cambridge: Harvard Univ. Press, 1951.

Mercer, B. E., and Carr, E. R. (eds.), *Education and the Social Order.* New York: Rinehart, 1957, esp. pp. 227–259, 459–487, 565–570.

Parsons, T., "The School Class as a Social System: Some of Its Functions in American Society," *Harvard Educ. Rev.,* 29 (Fall, 1959): 297–318.

Perry, R. B., *Realms of Value: A Critique of Civilization.* Cambridge: Harvard Univ. Press, 1954, pp. 411–439.

Queen, S. A., Chambers, W. N., and Winston, C. M. (eds.), *The American Social System.* Boston: Houghton Mifflin, 1956, pp. 60–86.

Rodehaver, M. W., Axtell, W. B., and Gross, R. E., *The Sociology of the School.* New York: Crowell, 1957.

---

[18] On three possibilities, see R. B. Perry, *Realms of Value: A Critique of Civilization.* Cambridge: Harvard Univ. Press, 1954, pp. 419–420. See also R. M. Hutchins, "Is Democracy Possible?" *Sat. Rev.,* 42 (Feb., 1959): 15–17, 58.

Stanley, W. O., Smith, B. O., Benne, H. D., and Anderson, A. W., *Social Foundations of Education*. New York: Dryden, 1956.

Waller, W., *The Sociology of Teaching*. New York: Wiley, 1932, pp. 6–13, 103–119.

Warner, W. L., Havighurst, R. J., and Loeb, M. B., *Who Shall Be Educated?* New York: Harper, 1944.

Williams, R. M., Jr., *American Society: A Sociological Interpretation*. New York: Knopf, 1960, pp. 282–322.

MOBILITY

Brookover, W. B., "The Implications of Social Class Analysis for a Social Theory of Education," *Educational Theory*, 1 (Aug., 1951): 97–105.

Caplow, T., *The Sociology of Work*. Minneapolis: Univ. of Minnesota Press, 1954, pp. 216–221.

Floud, J. E., Halsey, A. H., and Martin, F. M., *Social Class and Educational Opportunity*. London: Wm. Heinemann, Ltd., 1956.

Hertzler, J. O., "Some Tendencies toward a Closed Class System," *Soc. Forces,* 30 (Mar., 1952): 313–323, esp. 318–319.

Hollingshead, A. B., *Elmtown's Youth*. New York: Wiley, 1949, pp. 192–200.

Kahl, J. A., "Educational and Occupational Aspirations of 'Common Man' Boys," *Harvard Educ. Rev.*, 23 (Summer, 1953): 186–203.

Mercer, B. E., and Carr, E. R. (eds.), *Education and the Social Order*. New York: Rinehart, 1957, pp. 260–262.

Neugarten, Bernice L., "Social Class and Friendship among School Children," *Am. Jour. Soc.*, 51 (Jan., 1946): 305–313.

Sewell, W. H., Haller, A. O., and Straus, M. A., "Social Status and Educational and Occupational Aspiration," *Am. Soc. Rev.*, 22 (Feb., 1957): 67–73.

Sibley, Elbridge, "Some Demographic Clues to Stratification," *Am. Soc. Rev.*, 7 (June, 1942): 322–330.

Warner, W. L., Havighurst, R. J., and Loeb, M. B., *Who Shall Be Educated?* New York: Harper, 1944.

Warner, W. L., Meeker, M., and Eells, K., *Social Class in America*. Chicago: Univ. of Chicago Press, 1949, pp. 24–29.

Wilson, Alan B., "Residential Segregation of Social Classes and Aspirations of High School Boys," *Am. Soc. Rev.*, 24 (Dec., 1959): 836–845.

OVER-ALL REGULATION AND ORDERING

Governmental Institutions

The regulation of the action of the individuals and groups in almost all relationships, whether of a continuous or recurrent nature, is imperative in any society, since a society must have established order, peace, internal cohesion, and effective operation. The continuous dissension, conflict, and other separative tendencies among the individuals and groups of the society must be kept in hand. Regulation is the means of achieving these ends. Furthermore, without order and peace none of the society's essential communicative, perpetuative, maintenance, or expressive functions can be conducted. No society can long endure individual or group irresponsibility in matters deemed essential to its welfare; no society can permit depredations within it by its members or outsiders; no society can allow violations of its rules and requirements to go unpunished.

The governmental institutions are the means of specifically establishing and formally maintaining order, method, coordination, and security among human groups through a system of standardized restraints and compulsions enforced by appropriate public organizations. To insure and implement government the society must have rules, regulations, laws, and ordinances; it must have the agencies to enforce that conformity with them that enables the society to operate; it must have agencies to decide the degree of non-conformity involved in alleged transgressions and to fix penalties; and it must have agencies for punishing the violators.

Since this order, coordination, and security must prevail within the entire area of joint participation, the cluster of governmental institutions are found among all groupings larger than the kinship group; that is, in all more or less complexly organized societies, which in their nature are *politically* organized societies. The governmental institutions are thus the epitome of societal regulation; they constitute societal regulation in its most universal and highly organized forms, and control, functionally assist or supplement, promote, and provide ultimate enforcement and sanction for almost all other social institutions. The permissiveness, as well as the final effectiveness, of almost all other institutions rests upon the support given them by the governmental institutions. Even poor government is better than none.

The governmental system is the largest and most inclusive of all the systems. It is the system of public institutions. Its interests—not necessarily opposed to, and often complementary to, those of the other systems—have a wider range and scope than the others. In fact, it has, and must have, all other interests and institutions under its over-all and ultimate supervisory and regulative scope in so far as these other interests and institutions affect public order and well-being. Governmental agencies and procedures are applicable to everyone alike within the government's jurisdiction, and its requirements are binding upon all. This fact does not hold true of any other institution unless it has some direct relationship to government or authorization from government. Participation in religion, in a particular industry, commercial organization, or occupation, in education beyond a certain point, or in recreation is a voluntary matter.

As the final regulative and authorizing agencies, governmental agencies must have the power to perform their functions—final power to prohibit, suppress, require, encourage, tolerate, and permit different kinds of social activity. Governmental agencies, as against any of the other institutional systems, possess a monopoly of force, a monopoly of the right to use ultimate, comprehensive, and legitimate physical coercion, even to the extremity of administering death as punishment. Without force as an ultimate sanction, violators, whether individuals or groups, could not finally be suppressed, and their anti-social actions would threaten the existence of the entire society. When government loses its supreme power to force compliance with its requirements, it loses its ability to govern. There can be no equality of power with other institutions, or threat to the government's exclusive use of power by other institutions. This does not mean that other groups and associations do not use force on their members, but the type and degree, especially that of a physical nature, is usually authorized or permitted by government. Only government legally exercises, or threatens to exercise, or permits to exercise force within prescribed areas and limits. This legitimate use of power is referred to as authority; without this legitimation governmental power would be merely naked force. Governmental force, as authorized, is not force indiscriminate. Every government has means for establishing the justification for the different uses of force, and instruments for determining that force is applied in different types of situations, where it is applied, and how it is to be applied. The force that modern governments command overshadows the power of all other organizations in modern society. In the wielding of this force, governments use police forces, armies, navies, investigative committees, courts, information and propaganda bureaus, administrative agencies, and corrective and penal agencies.

The coercive powers of government are reflected in various powers. Notable are (1) the police power, or the power of government to regulate without taking possession of property, a power deemed necessary to protect the safety, health, morals, and possessions of persons; (2) the right of eminent domain, or the power to appropriate property for public uses; (3) the taxing power, or the power to levy compulsory contributions for government maintenance and other public purposes; (4) the judicial power, or the power of the courts to interpret law, settle disputes, and fix penalties for violation of the law; (5) the penal power, or the power to correct and punish violators of the law; and (6) military power, the power to raise and maintain military forces, and conduct armed warfare against external enemies.

Because of their all-inclusiveness, their ultimate supremacy over all other institutions, and the fact that they direct and authorize all legitimate use of force and punishment in societal regulation and maintenance, the governmental institutions may be said to constitute a super-social system.

The people may be ruled, sometimes for a long while, by conquerors, by kings ruling presumably by divine right, by representatives of a special class, or by dictators, but ultimately, as history attests, even in preliterate and illiterate societies, the political organization can function only if it is permitted to do so by the majority of persons in the society. Government rests upon the consent of the governed; what is done governmentally is determined by some sort of agreement as to what is correct action for the whole; the authority as expressed reflects the will of the people. Sooner or later the rule of the conqueror is broken, as witness Africa today. Kings ruling by divine right, or their descendants, discover that they have their positions only at the sufferance of the people; the rule of dictators is short and many of them have not died in bed; the power of political machines is temporary. In the end, the governed govern.

Careful observation shows that though the forms are not very precise, there undoubtedly exist, even among the most simply organized preliterate societies, the rudiments of a regular government over and above the mere authority belonging to the head of each family or clan. The notion of a state of anarchism or of absence of political organization among preliterates is sheer fiction. Government of some sort and degree has been necessary almost from the outset; and the peace and order and efficient functioning achieved by even the simplest government have rested on a cornerstone of force. The necessity of government seems to arise from the fact that as soon as any group of more than one family exists, need for order and regulation arises which requires some extra-family authority as an umpire and perhaps also some civil organization for its satisfaction. The interest of the community or society must be felt over and above that of the individuals and families and other lesser groups composing it.

Available evidence seems to indicate that the range and degree of organization of government vary directly with the degree of development and complexity of the society. Government is rudimentary in the small, simple societies. The individuals and families are known to all. Any breach of the rules is immediately known, and the violators may expect commensurate punishment. Informal methods of control— habit, tradition, customs, mores, criticism, ridicule, gossip, pressure of community opinion, withdrawal of reciprocity, ostracism—suffice for the most part. Authority is administered by hereditary governors (fathers, patriarchs, chiefs, in some instances) or, in some relationships or activities, by natural leaders; it is not vested in organizational officials. Furthermore, there is homogeneity of population and culture, considerable similarity of interests and objectives, relatively simple technology and limited division of labor, limited wealth and simple property forms and arrangements, relative isolation from other communities, and so on. This general situation prevailed for 99 per cent of the approximately one million years that man has inhabited this earth, in the opinion of Murdock.[1]

More formal government is a quite recent development in human history, and the result of more or less determinable sociocultural developments and conditions. Sheer number of members (of course, dependent upon technology and other conditions) is an important factor. Murdock's study showed primitive communities seldom have more than 300 inhabitants. When physical, technological, and industrial conditions (beginning in Neolithic times, around ten thousand years ago) permitted communities of as many as 1000 or 1200 members, we find the appearance of some formal governmental controls. Face-to-face relationships can no longer be maintained; social conditions, activities, and relationships become increasingly complex; informal and limited controls no longer suffice.

With the development of societies into those of modern structure and functions, the number of factors requiring highly institutionalized government themselves multiply. The main, recurrently appearing factors in the emergence of formal governmental institutions, according to rather definite consensus, can be enumerated as follows:

(1) Population growth, increase in aggregation and density of population over a wider territory.

---

[1] G. P. Murdock, "Feasibility and Implementation of Comparative Community Research," *Am. Soc. Rev.,* 15 (Dec., 1950): 713–720.

(2) Increasing demographic heterogeneity.

(3) Increasing cultural heterogeneity.

(4) Increase in the number and diversification—ethnic, regional, occupational, religious—of interest-groups.

(5) Often the development of an intensive, especially irrigated, agriculture.

(6) A complex industrial division of labor and multiplication and specialization of functions.

(7) Increase in wealth, and variation in economic conditions (wealth, property) among the different segments of the population.

(8) Increasing status differences and sharpening of class distinctions.

(9) Increasing individualism.

(10) Multiplication and increasing diversification, anonymity, impersonality, and contractual nature of relationships among people.

(11) Increase in contact and interdependence of groups.

(12) Commerce or trade on a substantial scale, and an impersonal market economy.

(13) The conduct of extensive public enterprises—irrigation, wall-building, highway construction.

(14) Urbanization, especially the appearance of the city-state.

(15) Defense against similar complex powerful systems.

When these and other conditions begin to appear, the regulation and coordination of the people and their activities must be formally organized and conducted by an adequately empowered, structurally and functionally specialized, territory-wide super-agency.

I: The Features and Functions of the State

In more or less complex societies the state in some form—tribe-state, city-state, nation-state—is the essence and epitome of the governmental institutions, the operating embodiment of government. It is the frame-group,[2] that over-all system of governmental institutions that unites under a single scheme of political control the inhabitants of a given, exclusive, and separate political community.

The state, like other institutions, arises from many sources under varying conditions among preliterate peoples, and comes into being gradually and almost imperceptibly. It may develop from a war-group confronted with the necessity of suppressing local and private antagonisms among its members and of disciplining and organizing them in

[2] K. Mannheim, *Systematic Sociology: An Introduction to the Study of Society* (J. S. Erös and W. A. C. Stewart, eds.). New York: Phil. Lib., 1957, p. 118.

order to give them unity and strength against other hostile groups. In many cases it grows out of conquest by a tribal group and the necessity of maintaining a military hold upon the members and the land of the conquered tribe. Again it may grow out of hereditary classes or castes assuming supreme authority and having devolve upon them the responsibility for order. Among others, it may result from such economic factors as the accumulation of wealth, especially in the form of physical property, which requires cooperation for its protection and transmission. Again, the state may be a spontaneous organization or configuration of contiguous clans and other areal groups for mutual protection and strength, and for other forms of cooperation.

The state has special characteristics in different kinds of societies, for example in totalitarian as opposed to democratic societies, and it will vary greatly in certain structural and functional respects at different periods of the life of a given society. However, there are certain essential features as a basic social organizational agency common in any society.

The state includes within its purview all of the people occupying the governmentally demarcated territory. Its membership is compulsory, not voluntary. All individuals and associations owe it allegiance. It is also the final and all-embracing agent whereby the solidarity of these people is developed and maintained.

Its governmental jurisdiction is confined to the specifically designated territory, and a signal feature is the control and protection of this territory.

It is the agency that has vested and centralized in it the complete and unquestioned monopoly of force on the basis of which it exercises supreme governmental authority over these people.

This power and authority, as exercised, whether in totalitarian or democratic governments, rests ultimately upon the sovereignty of the citizens of the state. This means that the source of power is in the people; they formulate and eventually express the societal will; they have the power in the end to extend or withhold the right to coerce and rule by the particular agents and agencies of the state, which are the implementers of sovereignty.

The state as the governmentally empowered agency is the omniscient and omnipotent regulatory, directive, and ultimate compulsive agent in carrying out the rules of the society. It is, and must be, the super-authority. Through its power to limit individual and group action and property rights, and to force action, it can penalize its constituents and carry out enforcement of its decrees. It is also the final arbiter, advisor, moderator, and coordinator among societal elements, and has the ultimate creative role. It also exercises legitimate violence against external enemies as defined by the state leaders.

The action of the state takes place according to law.

Its essential functions are conducted by an array of implementing subinstitutions, such as the legislatures, the judiciary, executive, and administrative agencies, the police and military, each with its accepted, established, and standardized procedures for carrying out its various governmental purposes.

Finally, the state represents the common governmental will, and is endowed with the united power of the entire community.

The state, as the over-all operative agent of government, conducts a number of functions which, although they cannot be sharply categorized, since they occasionally overlap and tend to sustain each other, do indicate the extent and the range of the activities of the state.

The state's primary function, of course, is to make all of the regulative requirements of government effective within the given political domain. The state, as the carrier of supreme authority and as the agency ultimately responsible for all essential functioning, is charged with the task of establishing and maintaining universal order, and this is effected by means of regulatory activity. Specifically it is its business to prevent and arbitrate disruptive antagonisms, dissensions, and conflicts, to prevent all sorts of predatoriness and destructiveness, to prevent crime and delinquency, to punish all malefactors, and, conversely, to encourage the hundreds of essential cooperative tasks and forms of united behavior. The state through its regulatory power is the ultimate formally organized way in which necessary discipline is imposed upon the people. It alone can make the rules of universal application which state the proscriptions and requirements of order that are binding upon all who live within the entire geographical area; it is also the sole agent for the securing and administration of justice; and, finally, it is the all-powerful enforcing agent with the authorization, the capacity, and the means to compel and to punish. This it does because it represents the common will which insists, though not always in clear terms, upon common, united, orderly, secure, and reasonable living together. The state thus functions as the primary coercive apparatus of the society, and as the guarantor and the guardian of public order.

The state is also the over-all internal protective agency for its citizens. It protects against both physical and social, or rather anti-social, hazards. The following protective functions are standard in our state.

(1) At all levels, from local to national, through its police and military forces, it protects the citizenry against such hazards as physical harm by others, human depredations and criminality, accident, disorder and rebellion.

(2) It provides fire protection at local levels and also state and even national standards for fire protection equipment for all manner of

inflammable structures, and through some of its federal agencies protects against and fights forest and prairie fires.

(3) It provides means of advanced detection of, and protection against, other physical catastrophes such as floods, snowstorms, and hurricanes.

(4) It protects health through efforts at detection and prevention of both endemic and epidemic diseases, including occupational diseases, through quarantine and other medical requirements, through sanitary measures and building codes, through the Food and Drug Act, milk ordinances, and other provisions to safeguard the quality (prevent the adulteration or reduction of quality) of food supplies.

(5) It provides such protection against missile and atomic attack as the public defense agencies may be able to devise and carry into effect.

(6) It provides protection against fraud; for example, against misrepresentation of qualities of goods and services, the sale of property that does not exist, and misrepresentation of identity.

(7) It provides protection of the individual's finances through usury laws, government insurance of bank deposits, the examination of stocks and bonds (by the Security and Exchange Commission), and through credit and interest controls.

(8) It seeks to protect minorities against discrimination in industry, education, housing, the exercise of the franchise.

Related to this is the function of the state as enforcer of the indispensable and irreducible social-action requirements of all other institutions and organizations.

The state has always served the function of protecting the group against aggression from without by other groups, and of carrying on what has been deemed by the group's rulers to be necessary acts of aggression against other groups. Both of these functions require total coordination of effort by the society through one central agency, and the state, by means of its specialized military institutions, is the only agency capable of doing this. Closely related to the military functions of the state are the diplomatic functions, or the conducting of all sorts of other relations with other states in the interests of the particular state and of reciprocity and harmony, as well as the conducting of negotiations for the prevention or forestalling of war and for adjudicating conditions and relations after war. In general, it is a function of the state to uphold the prestige, honor, security, and integrity of its people against those of other countries.

The state has always functioned as the guarantor and protector of certain freedoms and rights, at least for certain elements of the population. By freedoms is meant the different exemptions or liberations from restraint, from submission to power or exploitation or control. However, there cannot be freedom unlimited; hence, the provision of rights, or the specific freedoms claimed, permitted, guaranteed, and enforced by a politically organized society for its people; in brief, the socially guaranteed and socially limited freedoms. The modern state, and especially though not exclusively the democratic state, in the interests of its preservation and efficacy, which in the end rest upon the fulness of life of its citizenry, legitimately utilizes its coercive apparatus for the guarantee and protection of a sizable list of rights which social-political experience has demonstrated to be essential. The state is the only agency that can continually emancipate its inhabitants from excessive authority, monopoly, special privilege, and discrimination, as exercised by some elements within its domain against other elements. Always there is the danger that special interest groups—social classes, organizations, cliques, blocs, majorities or powerful minorities—try to usurp certain freedoms and rights of other categories and groups. There are always also neglected or weak elements in the population that do not or cannot make their human and social needs known or recognized. In every society there are also exclusions of certain portions of the population from free and full participation in its activities; such exclusions are a not-so-subtle form of suppression. Finally, most of the freedoms and their rights are essential in a complex society as a partial compensation for the large amount of standardization, uniformation, regimentation, and ordination to which the citizenry must be subjected for regulatory and maintenance reasons.

We Americans have a long list of rights that we insist, by common consensus, our state should preserve, protect, and advance. They include those emphasized through the ages and those of recent derivation —life and safety of one's person, especially including freedom from seizure and illegal arrest and imprisonment; liberty of action and disposal of one's person; maintenance of innocence until formal proof of guilt; equal and impartial justice in the courts; trial by a jury of equals; free and equal suffrage; freely elect public officials and, by direct ballot or through freely chosen representatives, a continuous voice in the making of laws and in the determination of public issues; eligibility for public office if certain qualifications are met; redress for grievances; formation, expression, and communication of opinions in speech or writing to one's fellows; freedom of the press; freedom of religious beliefs, and enjoyment of one's particular mode of worship without interference; association and assembly with and to hear one's fellow-men, and organization for a wide range of activities; educational, cultural, and expressional opportunities; exploration by the individual mind, and experimention and invention; residence in places of one's choice and change of residence; the holding and exchange of property; the making of contracts; marriage to whom and when one chooses, within certain defined limits, or option not to marry; conduct of one's occupation and choice among a wide range of occupations; a great variety of economic opportunities and conduct of legitimate business; the holding of property, its administration within a range of permitted uses and abuses, and its transmittal; and, as important as any, the right to be considered as persons regardless of age, sex, class, educational level, occupation, race, and other characteristics. This is by no means a complete inventory, but it does represent the limitation by the state, in behalf of the entire citizenry, of many historical, governmental, ecclesiastical, class, caste, and special individual prerogatives.[3]

The state has the task of regulating a variety of other than purely governmental activities in the public interest. Notable are:

(1) The regulation of marriage, parent-child relations, and divorce.

(2) The regulation of conditions affecting public health, including efforts to control endemic and epidemic disease, the maintenance of quarantine, the health inspection of immigrants and imports at ports of entry, the regulation of the quality, and the safeguarding of the production and sale of foods and drugs, the examination of food handlers, and the inspection of eating places.

(3) The regulation of education at the elementary and secondary level for both public and private schools.

(4) The regulation of various occupations affected with public interest, including most of the professions.

(5) The regulation of business, industry, agriculture, and labor.

(6) The regulation of non-governmentally provided public utilities supplying power, transportation, and communication.

(7) The regulation of credit, interest rates, and prices, and the determination of tariffs.

(8) Control of the issue and supply of fiduciary money.

(9) The assurance of the universal validity of units and standards of measurement, weight, quantity, and value; supervision of the maintenance of these standards; punishment for their violation.

(10) The setting of standards for, and regulation of, building construction and housing.

(11) The regulations for the use of water and prevention of contamination of water supplies.

(12) The supervision and the conservation of resources.

(13) The regulation of labor-management relations with respect to tactics, strikes, boycotting, picketing, and so on.

(14) The supervision of the standards and practices of vocational

---

[3] See especially two excellent recent works on rights and freedoms: R. F. Cushman, *Civil Liberties in the United States.* Ithaca: Cornell Univ. Press, 1956. M. R. Konvitz, *Fundamental Liberties of a Free People: Religion, Speech, Press, Assembly.* Ithaca: Cornell Univ. Press, 1957.

groups affected with great public interest (for example, electricians, plumbers) and of most professional groups, and regulation through examinations and licensing.

(15) The safeguard of the moral quality of printed matter, pictures, theatrical productions, motion pictures, and radio and television broadcasts.

(16) The regulation of gambling in its various forms.

The designation of the modern state as the service state or welfare state is justified for it promotes and provides for the general welfare in a variety of ways. It has come to be the institution bearing the ultimate responsibility for general well-being. As such it has had to take on many functions once left to individual or private initiative, or conducted by other institutionalized organizations but lost by them in the transition from primary to secondary group life. The state also has to develop many systematic functions heretofore carried on partially, sporadically, or not at all. In general, today, we have our over-all institution, the state, furnish the necessary services not achievable in other ways and do for us what we cannot conveniently, profitably, or adequately carry on as individuals or private groups, or what we do not care to turn over to private or semi-private organizations. In essence, the state has been called upon to render a great variety of services that cannot be conducted by other institutional organizations in sufficient extent, universality of applicability, and with sufficient certainty. Thus, in the modern state, government has actually come to be considered not only as an agency exercising ordering, regulatory, and protective functions, but also as a great constructive agency, a means of enabling the mass of men to realize social good on the largest possible scale. The state—with the approval of various effective minorities, if not always clear-cut majority—is continually invading new social service provinces and administering them for the people; there seem to be no limits to its range. It is becoming the general agent for providing all public and also many private needs.

The following are among the more prominent social welfare functions conducted by the modern state at the local, state, regional, or national level, although by no means a complete inventory of the services.

(1) To provide the public educational system and to assume the responsibility for the provision and the supervision of those educational services deemed minimal for all; increasingly to provide all levels of educational opportunity.

(2) To teach trades and vocations and make provision for rehabilitation along these lines.

(3) To assume responsibility for much moral and social training and protection of the young.

(4) To assume responsibility for the care of the aged, the depend-

ent, the delinquent, the mentally and physically defective and handicapped, and persons otherwise underprivileged.

(5) To promote and provide public employment service.

(6) To provide employment, sickness, old age, and survivor's assistance and insurance.

(7) To provide schemes of hospitalization and compensation for workmen suffering illness or accident incurred in the course of employment.

(8) To provide child welfare and maternal health and maintenance services.

(9) To provide for public sanitation (for example, street cleaning, garbage collection, insect and rodent elimination); provide public medical aid and nursing services; promote public health and provide all kinds of hospitals.

(10) To conduct necessary public utilities—power, light, heat, water supply, (local) street transportation systems, sewage treatment or disposal (and sometimes, utilization of sewage as fertilizer), and waste, garbage, and rubbish disposal.

(11) To promote internal and foreign commerce and trade.

(12) To provide for the construction, maintenance, and patrol of highways and waterways.

(13) To take the initiative in the development, the careful utilization and conservation of resources.

(14) To carry on or subsidize projects in irrigation, drainage, land utilization, and the development of water power, electrical power, and atomic power.

(15) To own public lands for protective and preservative purposes, and provide public playgrounds.

(16) To provide facilities for public recreation (playgrounds, swimming pools, skating rinks) and for aesthetic and cultural satisfaction and achievement (art galleries, museums, libraries, opera, orchestras and bands).

(17) To conduct the postal system.

(18) To provide a system of weather reporting and forecasting.

(19) To own and operate public airports.

(20) To develop industrial and housing sites; provide low-rent housing; provide financial assistance for home construction (housing loans).

(21) To provide the means and opportunities for the study of the greater and more urgent questions of social policy. This involves many kinds of research and the collection of statistical and other information bearing on the welfare of the people, and is done, for example, by the Departments of Agriculture, Commerce, Health, Education and Public Welfare, and by the Bureau of the Census.

(22) To produce some redistribution of income through the tax system, with emphasis on corporation taxes and graduated personal income taxes (though some would question this as a service).

There is one other function of marked importance in the operation of the state. This function is not concerned with the performance of various protective, regulative, and service tasks, but with the actual making of decisions regarding the performance of these other functions. Decision-making is necessary to get the right things done at the right time, and to prevent erroneous action. Two very general categories of decisions need to be distinguished: general and specific.

General decisions involve the processes by which the general will is arrived at. The entire qualified electorate participates by means of general voting procedures. Thus, as an entire electorate, we make decisions regarding the party in control, the incumbents for elective offices, constitutional amendments, general policies, bond issues, broad moral issues, such as permission of certain kinds of gambling (for example, bingo).

But the great volume of governmental decisions are specialized decisions, since many decisions are too complicated or involve matters too technical for adequate handling by the entire electorate. A vast number of specific and highly specialized decisions, therefore, must be made by specifically assigned and more or less specialized bodies among the various branches of government. Two special principles involving a more special and expert focusing of decision are resorted to; first, the principle of representation, whereby the problem of great numbers is managed through the election of representatives (for example, the national Congress, the state legislatures, the county commissioners, and city councils) who are supposed to have or acquire the special information and make the special decisions for the group as a whole; and, second, the principle of delegation of power to experts and specialists with the technical knowledge, training, and fixed sphere of authority, or to committees, commissions, boards, and authorities which by special study acquire expertise or know-how to make the decisions. The state, like most other large organizations, depends upon such experts to make decisions regarding specific aims, which are a part of the general aims; technical matters (engineering decisions, legal decisions and interpretations, financial decisions); means and procedure (establishment of standards and specifications, rules, letting contracts); external affairs (foreign relations, foreign aid, military policies and plans); long-time matters (organizational or social planning).

The success in making these more complicated decisions for the whole depends in part upon the efficacy of the processes used to select the decision-making representatives or experts. There are mainly three such processes: (1) election by the constituency; (2) appointment by administrative officials; or (3) special testing as conducted by civil service or merit system boards and other forms of examinations. Each procedure has its merits and demerits with respect to the selection of any given type of expert.

II: The Structuring of the State

The state is structurally composed of a number of subsystems, some consisting of categories of people, some ideational-ideological, some legal, and some associational in nature.

THE CITIZENRY AND ESPECIALLY THE ELECTORATE

Fundamentally, the state consists of all the people occupying its territory who are citizens. All those born within this general area of political jurisdiction are automatically citizens; foreign-born inhabitants achieve citizenship through a process known as naturalization which consists of formally conferring by a federal court the rights and privileges of a native citizen upon the foreign-born when they have met certain legally established requirements.[4]

The electorate consists of that portion of the citizenry who are qualified to vote; in brief, the franchise wielders. The franchise is limited by voting qualifications which in various jurisdictions include age (in U.S., 21 or over), residence requirements (with respect to sufficient period of residence in the state, county, and local ward or precinct), citizenship, literacy (in some states), tax payments (for example, head tax in some states), registration, and various special provisions, such as the disfranchisement of certain kinds of offenders against the law, and those declared mentally incompetent. All of the structures to be noted below emerge from the will of the electorate, represent or reflect the electorate in one way or another, and function for the electorate. Not only are the citizenry, especially the electorate, the ultimate beneficiaries of all government, but they are also the holders of sovereignty, the source of all opinion and the cooperators

---

[4] "A candidate for American citizenship must: be a member of either the white or the African race and twenty-one years of age; have resided in the United States continuously for five years; be able to speak English; be devoted to the principles of the Constitution; be of good moral character; have entered the country legally; renounce his former allegiance and take the oath of allegiance to the United States; prove that he is neither an anarchist nor a polygamist; pay the required fees . . . ; and follow the prescribed procedure." D. R. Taft, *Human Migration.* New York: Ronald, 1936, p. 314.

in public decisions, the determinants of public consensus, the source of all political functionaries, the payers of all taxes, the sharers in military service, and the population from which all political factions, parties, and organizations are constructed.

There are two especially important types of subsystems within the electorate of a nation-state like ours; namely, political parties and the various forms of political-interest groups, including the so-called pressure groups.

Political parties are associations of citizens organized around certain more or less distinctive beliefs and principles, regarding the objectives, functions, and policies of government; and they are more or less united in political action. They are the way the diverse political attitudes, beliefs, opinions, and purposes are expressed, and then, through elected officials, converted into action. They vary greatly in different nations in number, durability, openness, and importance. In our governmental system, they have a secure and indispensable place, and have pretty consistently exemplified the two-party system—two major parties contending for the control of government upon fairly equal terms. Although less variety of viewpoint is displayed with the two-party system as against a system of five or six (or even on occasion of several dozen) parties, the decisions come nearer to being majority decisions of the electorate. Also, the party in power conducts the government, and the party out of power furnishes fairly unified, clear-cut, and forceful criticism of the party in power—something non-existent with a multiplicity of out-of-power parties.

The importance of parties in the political process is attested to by the functions they perform.

(1) They frame a party platform which is their body of statements regarding the controversial issues at stake.

(2) They thus dichotomize issues, declare their stand regarding them, and take sides, thus articulating the issues.

(3) They propagandize and engage in partisan political campaigns, thus bringing the issues before the electorate.

(4) They select and groom candidates for public office who stand on the party's side of the issues, present and promote these candidates, try to organize opinion behind them, and mobilize voting majorities for the determination of the issues and the election of their candidates.

(5) Through the elections, policies and legislation are determined, public officials selected, and an identifiable and responsible control over the government established for the designated period. Parties thus furnish an organization facilitating the operation of government. At the same time, if the organization is to maintain its control, it must be responsive to the general will.

(6) Parties also serve as effective lines of communication between the citizens and their state.

Our two parties show certain differences in traditional strength in various regions and in the economic, religious, ethnic, educational, and class composition. However, the degree to which these diversities are maintained fluctuates as does the position of the parties with respect to the issues relating to the situations involving the diversities. Each party, for that matter, is never pure or perfectly united on beliefs and objectives; rather, it is a hodgepodge of people with diverse economic interests, religious convictions and membership, ethnicity, diverse educational backgrounds, and so on. Thus it must compromise and integrate numerous conflicts in order to gain and hold power. Furthermore, in a nation with such blended population and such widespread, even universal, common values and interests as ours, the issues often are not of a nature to adapt themselves to sharply contrasting party stand; hence, the not uncommon resolving of party platforms and political campaigns virtually into tweedledum and tweedledee.

Another highly significant set of citizen subsystems within the electorate consists of the political special-interest groups. There are a considerable variety of these ranging from informal but sometimes highly effective ones, at least regarding certain kinds of issues, such as a group of aroused neighbors, to tightly and formally organized ones such as the National Association of Manufacturers or the United Automobile Workers. These special-interest, or, as they are increasingly referred to, pressure groups, seek to exert influence or power over the agencies of government in order to realize their own objectives. These groupings have various values, beliefs, interests, norms, and interpretations that they wish to advance. They are effective as they gain access to, and influence over, the men who decide policy in government. But they have more specific techniques that contribute to this end.

They seek to influence political parties and elections.

They appeal to the public through propaganda of all sorts, thus attempting to shape public opinion. This they do informally, for example, by doorbell-ringing, but mainly through time purchased from the agencies of mass communication and through their own publications and other means of broadcasting.

They seek to make direct, personal contacts with legislators and public administrators. This they do by means of what is known as lobbying. The lobbyists who do the lobbying are interest-group leaders or, increasingly, highly trained and highly paid professional influencing specialists, who, by personal agency, seek out legislators and administrative officials, and in the case of legislators seek by various means to persuade them to pass bills favorable to their interest-groups or to vote against unfavorable bills, and with respect to other officials seek to get them to act pro or con, as the case may be.[5]

The great range of interests promoted by these political interest-groups is indicated in the following classification of well-known, highly organized ones. There are, of course, thousands of informal and formal groups, local, state, and national in coverage and influence.

Business: for example, National Association of Manufacturers; Association of American Railroads; American Bankers Association; Edison Electric Institute; Chamber of Commerce of the United States; the various trade associations, such as automobile manufacturers and steel manufacturers.

Agriculture: for example, American Farm Bureau Federation; National Grange; National Farmers Union; California Fruit Growers Exchange; National Cooperative Milk Producers Federation; the organizations of wheat growers, cotton growers, rice growers, and so on.

Labor: for example, American Federation of Labor–Congress of Industrial Organization; United Mine Workers of America; United Automobile Workers.

Patriotic and Veteran: for example, Daughters of the American Revolution; American Legion; Veterans of Foreign Wars; American Veterans Committee.

Professional: for example, American Bar Association; National Education Association; American Medical Association.

Reform and General Policy: for example, Americans for Democratic Action; National Committee to Uphold Constitutional Government; League of Women Voters; For America.

Race, Religion, and Nationality: for example, National Association for the Advancement of Colored People; National Conference of Christians and Jews; Klu Klux Klan; Indian Rights Association.

Welfare and Civil Liberties: for example, American Public Welfare Association; American Civil Liberties Union.

Peace and International Policy: for example, American First Committee; American Association for the United Nations; United World Federalists.[6]

To this classificatory list should be added organizations promoting different kinds of sectional or regional as well as national interests (conservation of resources, water control); educational organizations (the Parent-Teachers Associations at the local, state, and national level); most of the great industrial and commercial corporations (General Motors, U.S. Steel, American Telephone and Telegraph Company,

---

[5] These techniques suggested by W. N. Chambers, in S. A. Queen, W. N. Chambers, and C. M. Winston, *The American Social System.* Boston: Houghton Mifflin, 1956, pp. 356–357.

[6] This list is a slight revision and adumbration of the classification of Chambers, *ibid.,* p. 355.

the oil companies); the women's organizations (Business and Professional Women's Clubs, American Association of University Women); and so on.

Political interest-groups are not all pernicious as is so widely believed by the man in the street. Almost all are one-track, to be sure; that is, they promote a single or a few related types of interests, often greatly at variance or conflicting with other interests. All are also more or less selfish in the sense that they want their own interests advanced regardless of others. Some, however, are what might be called personally disinterested interest-groups. The participants in these do not press their own immediate self-interests, but rather represent or work for other elements of the population unable to represent themselves or for causes that cut across various groups and areas. The interest-groups of a humanitarian nature, for example those working for underprivileged groups, for child welfare, or for disease prevention, are cases in point.

What should be particularly emphasized is the fact that these groups have a legitimate and essential function in the political process. Representing as they do many community or national interests deemed highly important by their proponents, they are a way of supplementing the expression of interests and objectives of the political parties. What is more, they usually present their views with precision and directness, as against the not infrequent circumlocution of political parties. In general, they inform legislators and administrators in detail as to the interests and wishes of different segments of the electorate. Their lobbyists are often specialists in their respective lines; as such, they provide the officials with much special information of value. These organized interests operating either under their own name or through political parties propose much of the legislation passed by the state legislatures, and originate much legislation in Congress, as well as provide much of the content of this legislation. They also provide administrative agencies with much data, much knowledge of techniques and procedures, and are the stimulus for much administrative action.

The Constitution

Most states have a general enabling scheme or device known as the Constitution. As McBain has pointed out ". . . every country is and has been historically, except in time of revolution or other serious upheaval, governed under something that may be called a constitution." The historical and contemporary constitutions "vary greatly in form and content, source and tangibility, stability and permanence."[7] Some are

---

[7] H. L. McBain, "Constitutions," *Ency. Soc. Sciences.* New York: Macmillan, 1931, Vol. 4, pp. 259–262.

unwritten, as in Great Britain, but in the United States and in most other countries they are written. Despite these variations, a constitution is the basic charter or set of formulae for the state, providing for the essential structurings, arranging for the conduct of the essential regulative and service functions of the government, and, in general, stating what the government shall and cannot do. More particularly, and with particular reference to our American Constitution, a constitution systematically and specifically does the following things:

(1) It sets forth the powers of government and states the fundamental governmental principles and objectives.

(2) It provides the fundamental and paramount law which has primacy and supremacy over all momentary legislative and administrative law and executive order, to the intent of which all later law must conform. The constitution has final legal validity and authority; and the validity of all other law is determined by its constitutionality.

(3) It provides for the fundamental operational agencies whereby the legislative, executive-administrative, and judicial functions of the state shall be performed. It grants the special and appropriate powers to these basic organs, and specifies their jurisdictions. It states the specifications for the selection of official personnel, their rights, responsibilities, and duties, and the practices to be followed by them.

(4) It prescribes the rules for the people (the governed) in their relationships with the government agencies, including their duties and responsibilities (to obey the law, to be taxed, to render military service).

(5) It states and guarantees the perquisites, liberties, and rights of the citizens, as well as the deprivations to be endured.

THE THREE MAJOR FUNCTIONAL SUBDIVISIONS OF THE STATE

Every state has the task of carrying into effect the basic principles and functions of government, often more or less precisely set forth in its constitution. These purposes are effected by means of the three major functional branches of government: the legislative, the executive-administrative, and the judicial. In general, the function of the legislative branch is to formulate the will of the citizenry in the form of laws; the function of the executive-administrative branch is to govern, that is, to carry on all of the essential regulative, protective, and service operations assigned to the government; and the function of the judiciary branch is to determine the guilt of those accused of violating the law, to fix penalties for the guilty, to settle controversies among individuals and groups of the citizenry, and to interpret the meaning and intent of the law when questioned. In Western societies these structures are formed at three levels, levels of power distribution and areal and jurisdictional extent: local, state or provincial, and national. In the United States the local units consist of counties (over 3000), towns and townships, and municipalities; there are now 50 states; and above these is the ever more powerful and pervasive federal government. The local and state governments carry on functions not assigned to the federal government.

Each of the three branches at each level is bureaucratically organized; each of the bureaucracies, small or extensive, has its subsystem of offices; that is, its corps of officials, elected or appointed, who conduct the governmental operations.

The legislative branch is the particular instrument of the state that formulates and enunciates the current authentic rules or laws of the state, the laws that are binding upon all residing within the territory of the state. Historically, the laws have been made by conquerors, by kings, by dictators, by oligarchies, or by the elegible citizenry, when they exist, acting *en masse,* or when they become more numerous and areally diffused, through their chosen representatives. Among most primitive peoples the legislative function of government is not very important since the law in effect is not enacted but largely customary in nature. In dictatorial states, legislatures are largely rubber-stamp agencies, since the law is mainly dictated by the dictator or the dictatorial clique or inner circle. In modern democratic states, the law is presumed to be the expressed will of the free citizenry and is enacted by legislatures or assemblies consisting of the chosen representatives of the sovereign people. The constituent representative members, the legislators, are mainly non-professionals regarding the law, though in our system, especially at the state and federal level, the largest single occupational category among the members is usually lawyers. Their selection is ordinarily based on party affiliation or allegiance, and they are often pledged in advance to support certain measures. Usually, in their non-committed action, they reflect public opinion as far as they can sense it.

In the United States the legislative organizations, at the local level, take such forms as town meetings, boards of county commissioners or supervisors, and the councils of municipalities; at the state level, there are legislatures or assemblies; and at the federal level is found the National Congress composed of the Senate and the House of Representatives. Among these, every higher level legislative body makes some laws that have primacy over those of the lower legislatures.

Modern legislatures at the state and national level, with very few exceptions, are bicameral in nature, two houses presumably representing different cross sections of the general interest. The members of our American Senate, for example, represent their state as a whole, while the members of the House of Representatives represent districts of approximately equal population within the state, thus supposedly reflecting more intimately and directly the interests of this more limited number of people and more specific communities. Each also has certain distinctive characteristics as to performance and some differentiation of performance; only the Senate, for example, approves treaties with other nations or approves presidential appointments; all bills for raising revenue can originate only in the House of Representatives. The internal organization of modern legislative assemblies is based primarily on the committee system. There are nearly as many committees as there are types of legislative problems. The committees carry on the special investigations involved, including public hearings, examine policy involved, try to anticipate the reception and effectiveness of the proposed legislation, and draft, or have drafted for them, the tentative statement of the law.

The modern legislative assembly is much more than a mere law-making body. It exercises other functions not always directly related to law-making, notably the following.

Since national finances embody broad legislative policies, legislatures directly control such finances through the tax measures and appropriations which they must approve. Through committee investigations and reports, debate upon the budget, final control over legislation proposed by the administration, and so on, they exercise much administrative control. Other well-known functions of American assemblies are participation in the revision or amendment of the Constitution; ventilating public policy through their debates, and thereby serving as an organ of public opinion; acting as an executive council to assist the executive; sitting as a high court in impeachment cases; and canvassing the results of elections of their own membership and, in some instances, elections to other offices.[8]

The executive-administrative branch of government is concerned with the actual management of the offices of state. Its business is to carry out all of the manifold operations of the actual process of government; conduct the essential regulatory, protective, supervisory, conserving, and constructive operations of the state; carry on policing and military preparedness; conduct international relations; draw up operating budgets and supervise taxation and public financing; administer and supervise all sorts of internal affairs such as health, education, the provision of money, the regulation of credit, banking and exchange, mining and manufacturing, agriculture, interstate trade, communication and transport; detect and treat law violators, and enforce law generally; plus most of the other general functions of government men-

---

[8] This list of additional functions of legislatures, almost literally stated, is presented by W. P. Shepard, "Legislative Assemblies," *Ency. Soc. Sciences.* New York: Macmillan, 1933, p. 360.

tioned above. Among primitives, the administrative organization is simple; the administrative tasks are relatively few and uncomplicated since most of the corresponding functions are conducted by and for primary groups, and authority is not clearly defined or sharply differentiated with respect to the performance of particular functions. But in the modern state, administration has not only come to be enormously complex, differentiated, and massive, but has also come to be the most ubiquitous governmental system as the state has been compelled to take on more and more regulative and service functions.

Administration is the complex of functions, organizations, and apparatus utilized in the processes of detecting public needs, formulating purposes, and securing the money-power, the essential man-power properly organized to conduct the numerous and diverse functions, and all of the technological aids essential in realizing the purposes. From one point of view, administration is a hierarchy of officials and related staffs rendering public services and thus positively carrying into effect the will of the state. More concretely, it is a vast number of interrelated bureaucracies operating at all three levels of government. At the federal level there is the chief executive—the President—operating now by means of the ten major administrative departments—State, Interior, Treasury, Commerce, Agriculture, Labor, Defense (subdivided into Army, Navy, and Air Force), Health, Education, and Welfare (since 1953), Post Office, and Justice. The heads of the first eight constitute the President's Cabinet, and the heads of the last two (the Postmaster General and the Attorney General) along with the Vice President sit with the Cabinet. The Cabinet thus functions as a general advisory body for the President and as the major agency for coordinating federal governmental operations. Each department consists of a large number of subagencies. Also directly under the President, and rendering special services to him, are the Bureau of the Budget, the Council of Economic Advisors, the National Security Council, and the Office of Defense Mobilization. There are also numerous other administrative agencies variously known as commissions, systems, administrations, boards, corporations, and authorities, organized mainly on the basis of the functions to be performed, such as the Tennessee Valley Authority, Veterans Administration, Civil Service Commission.

In most American states there are four levels of administration: the central state government, consisting of the governor and his departments and other bureaus; the counties, operating through the boards of commissioners or supervisors and such officers as treasurer, auditor, sheriff, assessor, and recorder; the greatly varying set-up of cities (municipalities), villages, towns, boroughs, and townships; and finally, various types of districts and precincts, usually organized for specific purposes—schools, road maintenance, police patrol, and so on.

Several developments in public administration are particularly noteworthy. First, the tasks before the various administrative bodies are coming to be more and more technically complex and specialized, thus requiring increasingly a specialized-professionalized personnel. This means a greater tendency toward appointment by the executives of higher bracket positions and greater resort to Civil Service selection of many other levels and varieties of personnel. This trend and necessity could also be stated as the decline of the amateur and the increasing dominance of the expert in the conduct of governmental operations. A second trend is toward more centralization of functions, a trend due in part to the increasing interdependence of governmental agencies at all levels and between all levels. Somewhat related to this is a third trend in administration, namely, the problem of increasing duplication, overlapping, and indefinite delineation of duties both within and among the major agency divisions at each level, and among different levels.

The third major operative branch of the state differs from the legislative in that its task is not to make law (though in effect it does so to some extent) and from the administrative in that its function is not to carry into effect the mandates of the Constitution and the statutes in rendering governmental services. The judiciary is a separate body of officials—judges—who through the judicial organizations, the courts, independently assess presumed violations of the law, and, especially, in all cases of disagreement or uncertainty, authoritatively interpret the law, ascertain its relevancy to the facts of particular cases, and by review and reinterpretation keep the law as applied abreast of social change and changing human behavior.

The judicial function involves the courts of trial and the courts of appeal and review, though there cannot be a sharp dichotomy between the two. The main function of the courts of trial, often referred to as the lower courts, is to determine whether or not those accused did violate the law, civil or criminal. The machinery of trial consists of (1) the judge who interprets the pertinent law, umpires the actual trial proceedings, summarizes the facts revealed in the trial, and upon determination of guilt imposes the punishment or damages; (2) the attorneys representing both the accuser and the accused; and (3) in our system, the jury, composed of randomly selected qualified members of the electorate who, on the basis of the evidence as presented to them, determine the guilt or innocence of the accused. In general, the accused must be given a fair trial according to the prevailing principles of justice. The guilty must be impersonally and augustly penalized or treated in such a manner that the principles of the state are upheld.

Equally important are the courts of review, or perhaps the reviewing functions of the courts. Decisions of the trial courts—local, state, and federal district courts—often are appealed and must be reviewed by the higher courts, particularly the supreme courts of the respective states, and the circuit courts of appeal and the Supreme Court of the United States. The action of these courts involves the power of judicial review. The exercise of this power requires these courts to state what the Constitution means with respect to the case at hand. It also involves the power to review the validity, according to the Constitution, of the acts of all other organs of government, legislative and administrative, national, state, and local, and thus to promulgate authoritative interpretation which shall be binding on these organs. Thus the action of the lower courts, the statutes and administrative rulings, state and national, and all action of governmental units are reviewed and declared in conformity with, or contrary to, the Constitution. Actually, of course, the judges of the courts apply old rules, but these old rules are adjusted or stretched to cover new situations, often undreamed of by the makers of the rules. Thus these courts not only make the Constitution in effect what they interpret it to be but, as they render decisions regarding the intent and applicability of laws and rulings, help to make new law.[9]

In determining the violation of the law, in interpreting the law, and in supporting the enforcement of the law, the judiciary is "nothing less than the law in action."

The division of labor is not nearly as clear-cut as may be implied from the preceding discussion. Actually, there is much interdependence, reciprocity in sustaining each other's functions, and some overlapping and duplication of functions. All three branches, for example, contribute to the determination of what is law. This interdependence is also brought out in the relationship between the executive-administrative branch on the one hand and the legislature and the courts on the other. Administration looks to the legislature for its organization and structure, its appropriations, its tasks, often its methods; and it accounts to the legislature for its acts and expenditures. It carries out legal requirements and has to operate within the limits of general legislative policy. The legislature also checks on the efficiency of the operation of the administrative agencies. The administration and the courts are also in constant contact with each other. The judicial system stands as the ultimate controlling system. It holds the entire administrative system within the bounds of law, and offers redress to those whose rights have been infringed upon by official action.[10]

Conversely, the national executive, the President, has various constitutional controls over Congress—the veto power, for example—

[9] There is the recent development of certain special kinds of local courts for authoritative review and legal disposition of particular kinds of situations; e.g., juvenile courts, family (or domestic relations) courts, and traffic courts.

[10] Cf. L. D. White, "Administration, Public," *Ency. Soc. Sciences.* New York: Macmillan, 1930, Vol. 1, pp. 440–450, esp. p. 447.

and appoints, with the approval of the Senate, the members of the Federal Courts, including the Supreme Court, thus in some measure at least affecting the ethos of the courts. The governors of the states also have various controls over their legislatures. The administrative departments, commissions, and bureaus are also actually engaged in much *de facto* legislation in the form of administrative orders, regulations, and rulings. These administrative rulings are continually and, in many instances, permanently modifying, extending, contracting, and reinterpreting the intent of legislation. Thus the executive-administrative branch in performing the various functions is actually engaged in law-making as well as law enforcement—law which is the product of doing things. It may be pointed out parenthetically that the problems with which legislation has to deal are becoming more and more difficult and complicated, requiring a degree of specialized knowledge and expertness possessed only by permanent, specially selected administrative officials. With the extension of the scope of government to the wide array of public services, government is becoming more and more administrative and relatively less legislative in character. There is a distinct probability that more and more legislative authority will have to be delegated to administrative bodies of specialists in the near future.

Finally, it should be noted that, although the judiciary is the most nearly autonomous of the three major branches of state, its jurisdiction is limited by the action of the various legislative bodies, and the pronouncements of the courts are ineffectual except as they are supported and enforced by the executive-administrative agencies.

THE LAW

The legal system, or complex of institutions, constitutes a fourth basic structural-functional aspect of the state in operation. It is intertwined with the other operative systems of the government; in fact, it combines or synthesizes them. The law is for the citizenry and ultimately by them; its enactment by legislative, but also to some extent by administrative bodies and the judges, occurs according to constitutionally established procedures, and its intents and enforcement must be compatible with the tenets of the Constitution; through the judiciary the state interprets and applies the law and determines the guilt or innocence of those accused of violating it; and through its innumerable departmentalized policing, administrative, and service organizations, the state assumes the responsibility for carrying out the ever changing regulations and provisions of the law.

Nevertheless, the law in modern states has a systematic nature of its own that justifies thinking of it and treating it as a distinct body of governmental institutions. Like most institutions, it has its own specialized professional personnel, as well as its comprehensive, valuational, conceptual, and organizational structuring. The lawyers are the counsellors of the citizenry in all legal matters, and the prosecutors and defenders of the accused; they are numerous among lawmakers and administrators, and compose the entire judicial personnel. So prominent are they in our American government that it has jocosely been remarked that it is "a government of the lawyers, by the lawyers, and for the lawyers."

The interpretation or the maintenance of the various kinds of order and regularity that man is concerned about involves different kinds of laws. One finds frequent mention, for example, of natural law, the law prior to any institutional law and involving the principles of regularity supposedly governing the constitution and operation of the universe and all that it contains; the Divine law, or the commandments of Deity; the moral law, the rules of right and wrong crystallized in the mores and customs; canon law, the rules established by the ecclesiastical authorities of the Church; scientific laws, the systematized and verified general truths regarding empirical phenomena discovered by scientists; martial law, the law administered by the military power of a government when it has superseded the civil authority in time of rebellion or war; and military law, the rules by the legislature of the state for the government of the military forces in peace and war. All institutionalized organizations have their laws.

In this examination of governmental institutions we are concerned mainly with jural law. It is fundamentally a further development of the moral law of the given society. But it is the rules of a society as a political organization; that is, it is the code consciously created and formally established, usually stated in written form, and maintained, interpreted, and applied by the appropriate executive-administrative and judicial agencies of the state. It consists of the ever changing body of those rules expressly enacted by the various levels of legislative bodies of the state, plus the principles that are derived from the experience of the judges in the administration of justice and expressed in their decisions, and the growing body of rules and directives contrived by the administrative bodies. All of these rules are construed in the interest of the internal order, peace, and efficient operation of the entire society. These rules of the organized societal game are at any time a sort of a concrete, formalized summation of the various principles of social conduct as found in the norms of the society, but they have been made definite, standard, and officially punishable within the entire area of jurisdiction. They supplement and predominate over all the informal controls and the rules of lesser organizations. They withdraw a large number of acts from individual or group direction. The rules are imposed by, backed by, enforced by, and their violators punished by the full coercive power of the state.

Even the most simple societies have more or less explicitly understood rules that serve as social restraints and guides to conduct. These
rules among preliterate people are unwritten because writing is unknown, or, if known, not in common use. They are usually rather
simple because social life is simple; and the rules, although governing
all significant departments of life, are not very numerous. They are
largely informal in nature and are enforced by the social pressures
usually emerging from, and expressed by, the primary group. The
primitive social rules are found, concretely, in the customs and traditions, and in the folkways and the mores of the tribe. In the more advanced preliterate societies or those in a state of transition to more
complex forms, the most basic rules may come to be more precisely
stated, and in order to remember them and transmit them more readily,
they are grouped by fives so that they can be indicated and memorized
by finger- and toe-counting, as in the case of the Ten Commandments
of the ancient Hebrews, the ten commandments of ancient Buddhism,
or the Negative Confessions of ancient Egypt.

Although the social rules of the simpler societies were rather few,
simple, and informal, they were adequate in giving group life coherence
and stability; they were felt to be binding and were generally obeyed;
they were respected or even feared because of threatened punishment,
not only by community obloquy but also in more specific ways by certain authorities, such as chiefs or even supernatural agents.

This primitive law was based upon many generations of trial and
error, and though it had its fictions and superstitions, it had in it those
elements of group wisdom in the conduct of social life that had preserved and prospered the group. Modern common law, which is the
lineal descendant of primitive custom law, brings down to later stages
of sociocultural life the body of experience that no individual could
secure within the period of a single lifetime.

But such a rule system is quite inadequate in a complex, secondary-
group society. There is almost no natural social solidarity or group
cohesiveness. There are usually many social groups with different customs and traditions, different folkways and mores, different convictions
as to right and wrong. Because of wide interdependence, every individual and group have to be ruled by the rules. With the rapid social
change, the society needs sharp revisions of its culturally inherited
rules, and especially does it need many new rules that have no antiquity
or ancestral authority behind them. The rules must be impersonal and
impersonally administered. In order to apply adequately to the current
situation, they need to be specifically enacted and precisely stated so
that their intent and behavioral requirements—acts imposed or forbidden—are fairly clear to everyone, and they need to be hard and
fast. Inner coercion, moral sense, or more or less informal agency is

inadequate for conformity or for enforcement. Thus complex societies have had and do have institutionalized law—the formalized law of the state. This law consists of the almost infinitely diversified body of rules that are seriously and specifically formulated and enacted by political authority. It is continuously revised, reinterpreted, and supplemented. It expresses and makes social policy, is, in fact, a creative as well as a created agency of the state. It is widely publicized and universally applied and is enforced by the impersonal and formal coercive apparatus of the all-powerful and all-pervasive Leviathan, utilizing the staffs of agents especially empowered and selected to carry out these functions —police, prosecutors, judges, penal institutions.

The general function of the legal system is to provide the positive and negative rules and directives for internal peace, order, security, and welfare. In order to do this, one of its selective functions is to make public policy, lay down moral imperatives, decide social, especially moral, issues, provide the vehicles for carrying out government policy, and thus assure social solidarity and societal operation. The legal system, however, has certain specific functions.

The laws define certain acts required of the citizenry as individuals and as members of different kinds of groups; they also specify the essential actions of their various categories of governmental officials. They also specify, or indicate, acts permissive under given conditions.

They define the acts prohibited; that is, misdemeanors and criminal acts that are offenses against the law and hence punishable.

They prescribe the penalties both for the failure to act in the prescribed ways and for violations of prohibitions, and prescribe definite procedures by which the penalties are to be applied.

The laws expedite the constitutional allocation of public authority.

They define, endorse, and guarantee the civil rights and liberties (privileges) of individuals and groups in the society, especially rights over property, public, joint, and private.

Consequently, the law in effect structures the power (superordinate-subordinate) relationships of the society; it maintains the status system and protects the various strata against each other, both in governmental and non-governmental organizations and relationships.

It regulates contracts and provides the bases for the adjudication of disputes regarding contractual relations between individuals and groups.

In its definition, guarantee, and regulation of the liberties among men, it tends to prevent abuses of power and to maintain equality of opportunity among unequals.[11]

---

[11] Cf.: E. Durkheim, *The Division of Labor* (G. Simpson, transl.). Glencoe, Ill.: Free Press, 1933, p. 3. E. Litwak, "Three Ways in Which Law Acts as a Means of Social Control: Punishment, Therapy, and Education," *Soc. Forces,* 34 (Mar., 1956): 217–223.

The diversity as well as the crucial nature of law is brought out by the more common classifications of laws from the point of view of origins, public or private jurisdiction, and types of action regulated. In modern, advanced civil societies like our own, as many as five different kinds of law may be distinguished from the point of view of origin. There is, first, the common law, the residues of centuries of experience crystallized into customs and sanctioned practices. Much of it may still be unwritten, but the essential rights and obligations are set out in clear formulae as political laws reflecting the common will and enforced by central authority. Second, there is the constitutional law. This is the fundamental body of law, unwritten or written, dispersed or codified, stating more or less explicitly, and often somewhat inflexibly, the basic principles and organization of the government of a particular state or combination of states, the distribution of powers among, and the functions of, the agents and agencies of government, the rights and duties of these agents, and the relations of government and citizens, including the rights of citizens. Third, there is enacted or statutory law, the result of continuous effort by legislative bodies to keep the working rules for every relation and function of group life up to date, permitting no new problem of order or well-being to go unregulated or unprovided for. Similarly, it seeks by repeal or revision to discard or improve rules that are antiquated, ineffective, unduly harsh, or that are not approved or sustained by a majority or an effective minority of the citizenry. Enacted law is thus a means of continually readjusting and re-establishing the principles of order. Fourth, there is what might be called judicial law. The judges and courts in applying and interpreting the law and in rendering decisions regarding particular cases in dispute establish precedents which in effect are new law. Fifth, in modern states operating by means of many bureaucracies, there is what might be called administrative law, which consists of the rules established by executives and the various administrative agencies in carrying out their functions. At the federal level, for example, there are the rules of the Federal Reserve System or of the Internal Revenue Service. Administrative law recently, especially in the United States, has assumed great significance. Administrative and regulative bodies, with general powers and duties given them by the Constitution and by act of legislature, have been under the necessity of devising specific rules to enable them to carry on their assigned tasks. Some of these rules, supported by the courts, have almost achieved the authority and effectiveness of formal legislative law. A possible sixth source at the local and state levels are the rules that emerge from popular initiative and referendum decisions.

Another categorization involving most of the kinds of law just discussed is that which distinguishes between public and private law.

Actually these two types of laws constitute a fundamental dualism in the legal system of highly organized states. Public law is the total body of rules which regulate the activities of the state as such; that is, law governing the officials and the administrative agencies of all kinds as they conduct their legally empowered and legally fixed functions in fulfilling the objectives of the state. Included here is the constitutional law governing all administrative agencies, criminal law, and international law. Private law, not related to the operation of the state as such but issuing from the state, regulates all activity other than state activity. All civil law (that relating to the whole panoply of rights of all citizens) and all commercial law are private law.

A third classification, also involving kinds of law already noted, relates to types of behavior involved. Civil law consists of those rules governing the ordinary relations of private individuals with each other in politically organized society. It has both common law and statutory law elements. It is the codification of the rights of individuals, including property rights, and includes the law regarding private agreements and contracts and the law of torts. Criminal law is the law relating to criminal offenses. It is the body of rules whereby a community protects itself against acts that endanger or impair its internal peace and the security and well-being of its citizens. It defines and classifies crimes and prescribes penalties for violation. Commercial law is that part of the law which is applicable to business transactions. It includes the law regarding contracts (as in the buying and selling of real estate, goods and merchandise, and intangibles); the formation and conduct of business organizations (partnerships, corporations); credit instruments and transactions; and commercial services (insurance, banking, and public utility services). It involves criminal law, for example as it relates to restraint of trade, fraud, unfair competition, maladministration of estates.[12]

Some law is morally neutral; for example, the law that merely provides rules of thumb for the rendering of certain acts, such as making contracts effective. But the great body of the law is concerned with right and wrong, required or prohibited, acceptable or non-acceptable behavior as determined by the cultural experience of the community or society and as expressed in the common values. The rightness and wrongness is embodied in the complex of moral norms of the community, in what Angell refers to as the "moral web."[13] One of the chief objectives of the great body of the law is to express positively, give

[12] For more extensive treatment of the different kinds of law here mentioned, see the corresponding articles in the *Encyclopaedia of the Social Sciences*.

[13] R. C. Angell, *Free Society and Moral Crisis*. Ann Arbor: Univ. of Michigan Press, 1958, p. 41.

social authority to, and supplement these norms so that they can be enforced. Especially in a democracy, the effective law at any given time is the fairly direct expression of the moral convictions of the majority or the effective minority of the citizenry. It must be acceptable to them and enforceable among them.[14] If the community morality does not penetrate and back the law, or if the underlying moral principles change and the law does not adjust correspondingly, the law becomes a dead letter. In either case it is not enforceable. Furthermore, because of the close tie between the laws laid down by public authority and the moral norms, no authority in any kind of government can stay in power long where laws flout these norms.[15]

THE MILITARY SYSTEM

Although the military system in our nation is a subdivision of the executive-administrative branch of government, it is so massive in terms of personnel involved, so ubiquitous, and expends such a large portion of public funds that there is much justification for focusing special attention upon it as a vast governmental structural-functional agency by itself.[16] Military institutions, however, have their *raison d'être* in war. The military system is concerned with the legitimate and institutionalized waging of war and the defense of the group against war. War is conducted by governments and is, in fact, one of the oldest, most universal, most absorbing, most highly organized, and most consistently glorified of the activities of government. Furthermore, through the centuries, it has been the most highly institutionalized use of force—physical, psychological, social—that mankind has been able to muster.[17]

Although warfare itself is often ignoble, always disastrous, and usually feared, it has been an integral institution of every organized group. It is an extension into intergroup or international relations of the prin-

[14] The changing social conscience is demonstrated in such recent, socially approved rules as those relating to the regulation of traffic, noise, and "nuisances," and the desegregation legislation and court decisions. Reckless driving on crowded modern highways is both immoral and illegal.

[15] *Ibid.,* p. 30.

[16] "In many respects, the military establishment has now become the largest business, industrial, and administrative organization in the country." C. H. Coates, "The Role of the Military Sociologist in Operations Research," *Soc. & Soc. Res.,* 42 (May–June, 1958): 327–331.

[17] Note the following in connection with war as a major preoccupation of peoples. Out of 950 years of French history, the French were at war over 80 per cent of these years, and only one quarter-century was free of an important war. Out of 875 years of English history, 72 per cent were war years, and only one quarter-century was free from war. Of 275 years of German history, 29 per cent were war years, but no quarter-century was free from war. P. A. Sorokin, *Social and Cultural Dynamics.* New York: Am. Book, 1937, Vol. III, Pt. II.

ciple of force. Government, we have noted, has the sole, legitimate monopoly of force, and the exercise of force in behalf of the politically organized group is its special prerogative. However, force is used internally to preserve order and welfare. When used in international relations, that is, against external groups or other nations, it is still used presumably to protect internal order and well-being against disturbances from without, but externally its function is to intimidate, repel, weaken, even destroy other nations, and its invariable effect has been to create international chaos and anarchy. Thus we have the paradoxical situation noted by MacIver and Page to the effect that nationally and internally the state is the great instrument of social security, while internationally, under modern world conditions, it is the greatest menace to that security.[18]

The war situation involves a peculiar set of circumstances. Politically, the world is composed of nation-states and their dependencies. However, the nation-state is the largest inclusive social system in the world today. It regulates all subsystems within it; these are subservient to the extent necessary to assure order and cooperation; it is the protector and promoter of all beneficent subsystems within it. But, historically, there has not been an effective super-state or super-national system to regulate the relations among states. The best efforts to date— the League of Nations and the United Nations—to develop something in the way of an international regulative and adjudicative agency still leave very much to be desired. The relations among states are not ordered by any widely effective rule of law; and the police power that states use for internal order is effectively lacking at the international level. Thus, when the interests of one national society conflict with those of another, one of the main functions of the individual state is to try to settle the conflict, amicably by diplomacy if possible; if not, by war. Therefore, in terms of organizational principles, war is a state institution that seems to be necessitated by the lack or the ineffectiveness of appropriate interstate institutions.

There may be serious intergroup conflict within a nation. This civil war or rebellion is between two or more portions of the nation and is usually owing to a sectional, racial, nationality, religious, or socioeconomic class group, or some combination of these, seeking redress of grievances and aspiring to greater political recognition and power. It is directed against the larger body of the nation which considers itself the main guardian of the national sovereignty. Rebellion may also be the revolt of a dependency against the controlling power.

Our main concern is with the international war; that is, war among

[18] R. M. MacIver and C. H. Page, *Sociology*. New York: Rinehart, 1949, p. 463.

two or more sovereign nation states or between two opposed coalitions of such states. Usually, it is an effort to resolve or liquidate a crisis situation that involves friction, tension, sharp disagreement as to objectives, maladjustment, and profound suspicion, fear, and hostility; in terms of actions, it is an attempt to destroy the opposing nation or allies or remove them from the international scene.

War is due to many infinitely complex factors. Some are incidental and others purposive, some unpremeditated and others premeditated, some transitory and others more or less continuous. It is the function of the sociology of war to determine and analyze these causal factors.[19] Suffice it to say that offensive warfare has been conducted to acquire territory in order to improve the man to land ratio and acquire manpower or labor supply, physical resources, and markets, in the form usually of colonies or protectorates; to acquire strategic economic or military sites (for example, the Dardanelles and Straits of Singapore); to extend dynasties; to extend or advance a religion (Christianity, Muslimism); to extend a socio-economic or political ideology (democracy, free-enterprise capitalism, communism, or some form of fascist totalitarianism); to liberate oppressed peoples or protect small countries against tyranny and oppression; to humiliate, dominate, or exterminate a social, religious, nationality, or other ethnic stock; to weaken or conquer a rival state. Defensively, nations protect their territories, their resources, their people, their standards of living, their liberties, their institutions—all that they look upon as good and indispensable.[20]

War has been definitely institutionalized in almost all cultures. At its base we find the underlying concept of group preservation and welfare. Although conceded to be costly, it is looked upon as a species of insurance, or perhaps a form of maintenance, which is necessary as long as predatory activities on the part of others are possible. Related to this attitude are ideologies and values approaching religious creeds

[19] Cf.: L. L. Bernard, *War and Its Causes*. New York: Holt, 1944. J. D. Clarkson and T. C. Cochran (eds.), *War as a Social Institution*. New York: Columbia Univ. Press, 1941. L. Montross, *War through the Ages*. New York: Harper, 1944. J. U. Nef, *War and Human Progress*. Cambridge: Harvard Univ. Press, 1950. Sir Arthur Salter, *et al.*, *The Causes of War: Economic, Industrial, Racial, Religious, Scientific and Political*. New York: Macmillan, 1932. A. J. Toynbee, *War and Civilization*. New York: Oxford Univ. Press, 1950. Q. Wright, *The Causes of War and the Conditions of Peace*. New York: Longmans, Green, 1920. Q. Wright, *A Study of War*. Chicago: Univ. of Chicago Press, 1942, 2 Vols.

[20] The actual waging of modern war is a process that reveals a fairly definite pattern. It is a matter of stages, not necessarily sequential and usually with considerable overlapping. For concise presentation of the signal features of this process, see: J. O. Hertzler, *Society in Action*. New York: Dryden, 1954, pp. 288–289. W. Waller, *War in the Twentieth Century*. New York: Dryden, 1940, pp. 22–29.

or cults in their nature. There is an organization of established and almost universal sentiments, attitudes, myths, legends, and ceremonials which makes the precipitation and perpetuation of a war a fairly easy matter. Included are highly standardized and universally recognized procedures and techniques in conducting warfare—incidentally, the subject-matter of a very sizable and impressive literature. There is the organized and specially trained personnel—armies, navies, air forces—and trained and honored functionaries with specialized duties and special privileges, such as military officers, ministers of state, and diplomats, often a dominant caste in a society. There is the stupendous array of equipment used in the destruction of the physical and social resources, as well as the people, of the enemy. Finally, though warfare is lawless in the sense of being a procedure of force, it has its rules and codes, which seek to regularize the procedures, limit its ruthlessness, fix responsibilities and duties for combatants and noncombatants, give title to conquest, and otherwise attempt to introduce order and fairness into a process that can never be anything of the kind.[21]

To carry on this institutionalized war activity, or to be prepared to do so, requires an extensive and efficient organization. The military systems of the nations have been the indispensable mechanism whereby this has been done throughout history. In the United States, the military system is a separate department of the executive-administrative branch of our federal government, the Department of Defense, under the Secretary of Defense who is a member of the President's Cabinet. It consists of three subordinate departments, the Army, the Navy, and the Air Force, each governed by its secretary. The vast impact which this system makes upon our society can be demonstrated with respect to expenditures. In the United States Federal Budget for 1955, the expenditures for Direct Military Services were 44.9 billion out of a total of 65.6 billion, and Veterans' Benefits and Interest amounted to another 4.2 billion.

The military organization has probably been the archetype of bureaucratic structure, and its operation the epitome of bureaucratic organization. It consists of millions of men, all acting with a single purpose and will and with the almost automatic precision of a complicated machine, a machine designed to cope with crisis situations and not to disintegrate in such a situation. All the multiple functions must fit

---

[21] In addition to the previous references to war as a social institution, see: M. J. Adler, *How to Think about War and Peace.* New York: Simon & Schuster, 1944. S. Andrzejewski, *Military Organization and Society.* New York: Grove Press, 1954. B. Malinowski, "An Anthropological Analysis of War," *Am. Jour. Soc.,* 46 (Jan., 1941): 521–550. *Am. Jour. Soc.,* 48 (Nov., 1942): most of issue. R. E. Park, "The Social Function of War," *Am. Jour. Soc.,* 46 (Jan., 1941): 551–570. W. F. Ogburn (ed.), *American Society in Wartime.* Chicago: Univ. of Chicago Press, 1943.

together perfectly. It has its hierarchical structuring with rigidly maintained levels from commander-in-chief down through successive commissioned and non-commissioned officer and technical ranks to the men in the ranks. The flow of commands is in one direction only; orders come from the top and carry rank by rank to the bottom; everybody obeys, and is responsible to, someone above him. Duties are assigned, and penalties for violation or failure to perform are stressed, generally known, and enforced. Obedience and cooperation are absolutely essential, as is also both horizontal and vertical coordination. Rigorously maintained discipline overrides all individual wills. Proficiency and precision in all essential operations is developed by drill. Succession to authority is arranged for, since it must be clear, undisputed, and immediate, to take care of the emergency situation. Most of the tasks are routinized, and many different types of roles are highly standardized. Although, in our case, the President, a civilian, is commander-in-chief of the armed services in both war and peace, and although the secretaries of defense and of the three major military arms of the system are also civilians, and although all commissioned officers are nominally commissioned by the President, the entire officer group—those actually in charge of the many organization subdivisions and of all military operations—are selected, trained, and specialized professionals.[22]

The military machine must be interested in science, physical, psychological, and social, and a utilizer of every applicable correlated technology. In an age of ever greater scientific and technological advance, the ultimate protective agent of the nation in a world of equally advanced potential enemy nations must not only be prepared but, if possible, better prepared at any given time than the potential enemies. Consequently, the achievements of the scientists present arms for the military organization.

Notable in recent times are gun (sic!) powder, artillery, gasoline engines, heavier-than-air planes, biological and chemical warfare, electronic devices such as radar, atomic fission, jet propelled planes, and social psychological intelligence, administration, and mass communication information. Historically, every scientific discovery or invention that has been at all applicable to military ends has been appro-

22 On military organization, see: S. Andrzejewski, *op cit.;* H. Brotz and E. Wilson, "Characteristics of Military Society," *Am. Jour. Soc.,* 51 (Mar., 1946): 371–375. F. D. Freeman, "The Army as a Social Structure," *Soc. Forces,* 27 (Oct., 1948): 78–83. S. P. Huntington, *The Soldier and the State.* Cambridge: Harvard Univ. Press, 1957. S. A. Stouffer, *et al., The American Soldier.* Princeton: Princeton Univ. Press, 1949, 2 Vols. A. M. Rose, "The Social Structure of the Army," *Am. Jour. Soc.,* 51 (Mar., 1946): 361–364. G. D. Spindler, "The Military—A Systematic Analysis," *Soc. Forces,* 27 (Oct., 1948): 83–88. A. Vagts, *A History of Militarism.* New York: Norton, 1937.

priated technologically by the military organization. Some, in fact, were first used for military ends.[23]

A related crucial technological task is to keep the military organization or establishment and the military equipment up to date, for in an age of great and rapid technological development, much of it has become archaic by the time it has been produced. A further significant aspect of this situation is that so-called military science today is made up of an enormous amount of immensely complicated scientific knowledge and technical know-how, and its use requires specialized knowledge and skills among all levels of the personnel. Even the private is a specialist of some kind.

Modern technology as utilized in the military establishment of modern nations has brought certain outstanding changes in the objectives of the establishment and in its structure and operation. These changes have been analyzed by Janowitz. He points to the following, among other modifications, which are especially significant from the social organizational point of view.[24]

(1) The modern revolution in military technology has greatly increased the destructiveness of warfare. Hence, the military establishment is more and more concerned with "deterring violence" than with "preparing to apply violence" (p. 16). This also tends to "civilianize" military thought and organization as military leaders concern themselves with broad ranges of political, social, and economic policies" (p. 16).

(2) The new military technology has greatly widened the scope of automation in new weapons—weapons, it should be noted, which in the main are highly complicated machines, used in highly complicated procedures. This complex military machinery and the requirements of research, continual development, and technical maintenance add a considerable array of technical (civilian) role-players; that is, persons who carry on highly technical functions involving roles that are not all military in the traditional sense. In brief, the military establishment is made up more and more of technically specialized persons.

(3) This technical specialization has greatly increased the complexity of the "skill-structure" of the modern military establishment. Moreover, the ever more complex division of labor and detailed specialization of function are tending to change the professional requirements. In the selection of officers, technical competence is supplanting

[23] Cf.: J. F. C. Fuller, *Armament and History*. New York: Scribner's, 1945. F. R. Allen, *et al.*, *Technology and Social Change*. New York: Appleton, 1957, pp. 352–387. W. Kaempffert, "War and Technology," *Am. Jour. Soc.*, 46 (Jan., 1941): 441–444.

[24] M. Janowitz, *Sociology and the Military Establishment*. New York: Russell Sage Foundation, 1959. The selection of items and the phrasing, except for direct quotations, are those of the present writer.

"birth, social connections, and inherited social status" (p. 27). The military professional now needs "expertise, responsibility, and corporateness" (p. 27). Even in combat, greater and greater importance attaches to the technically specialized. The "military type" of enlisted personnel is also diminishing. Janowitz in a table (p. 32) shows that the traditional military type of personnel has decreased from 93.2 per cent of the total in the Civil War to 28.8 per cent in 1954, with a corresponding increase in scientific-technical, administrative-clerical, and skilled maintenance, service, and operative personnel (in 1954, 71.2 per cent of total). Another aspect of this is the great specialization of the enlisted personnel (private first-class, second-class, master sergeant, technical sergeant, staff-sergeant; airman first-class, second-class, and third-class).

(4) Although the military organization continues "to emphasize authoritarian, stratified-hierarchical, and traditional dimensions" (p. 17), and, in order to fulfill "combat goals" will, of necessity, continue to have its own special kind of bureaucratic organization, it nevertheless is undergoing reorganization as it adapts itself to the new kind of warfare that it must be prepared to wage. Not only does modern mechanized warfare require new skill structures, but it also modifies authority and discipline. With the old close-order formation based on relatively low fire power, the discipline needed to be direct and rigid. But now as the soldier is part of a crew operating a high-powered weapon or machine requiring split-second decisions and tactics in his specialized part of the total operation, he cannot be routinized. His role is one of constant improvization regardless of his service or weapon, whether on the ground, the seas or undersea, or in the air.[25] "Improvization is the keynote of the individual fighter or combat group" (p. 37). Thus technical proficiency of the team members is coming to be more important than formal authority. Consequently, "military authority must shift from reliance on practices based on *domination* to a wider utilization of *manipulation*" (p. 38). The officer thus has to rely less for his authority on traditional rank and grant of bureaucratic power and more upon his demonstrated managerial skills, operational proficiencies, and his ability to develop positive organizational loyalties.

War, like any other form of conflict, cannot go on forever; it is much too expensive. Some form of accommodation always must take place. Means must be sought to prevent it. Hence, peace-making and peace-maintaining procedures are really a part of the war complex. In fact, for centuries nations have been gradually establishing customs and agencies making for peace among nations, most of which have

[25] It can be added that in modern machine warfare, the action has to be that of a close-knit team. There can be no prima donnas or lone heroes in the operation of a jet bomber, submarine, or intercontinental missile.

become highly institutionalized. First must be mentioned peace conferences and treaties for the settlement of disputes, especially with respect to the division of territories, the disposition of displaced peoples, and the rights and responsibilities of the parties to the dispute, both conquerors and conquered. Treaty-making is a highly formalized procedure. Some measure of security or at least temporary order has been brought about by treaties, but in the end, nothing but the honor of the parties and the unimplemented and often indecisive world opinion assures conformity and enforcement. Second, there is the whole complex of alliances, understandings, and diplomatic procedures connected with the maintenance of a balance of power among potentially hostile powers. Third, there are the practices and institutions calculated to forestall or prevent hostilities, such as trade agreements, concessions, financial aid, economic conferences, regional organization of states, such as the Organization of American States, the services rendered by the ministers or secretariats of state, the diplomatic staffs of the embassies, the consular service agents, and other agencies that promote peaceful international political and economic arrangements and cooperation. Finally, there are the international organizations for international peace, administration, and adjudication, such as the League of Nations and its successor, the United Nations Organization, and the World Court.

Thus far, however, these various devices and agencies have not provided any high degree of assurance of world peace. Even the United Nations, although it renders many valuable services through its various subdivisions, which make for improved social conditions, and contribute to better understanding among peoples, can only contribute directly to world peace through the world forum that it provides. It has no *power* to enforce peace. This situation involves certain fundamental organizational principles, which point to the fact that peace among nations can be secured only through the same means by which it has been secured among the various elements within nations. The principles can be set forth in terms of three propositions. (1) Peace in an area, whatever its size, is a matter of order and security. (2) Order and security rest upon some final authority armed with coercive power. (3) This empowered authority functions through essential social machinery, through a framework of special organizations and institutions implementing police power. In brief, there must be a Levianthan, not a debating club, representative *of* all parts, but also with delegated coercive and punitive power *over* all of the constituent parts. This international mechanism must serve as a disciplinary agent and be able to compel obedience and punish disobedience. It is obvious that the existent institutional machinery working for world order must be reconstructed, and additional new machinery must be devised and constructed in line with these principles.

Finally, there is the problem of a world-wide public opinion, unified enough and strong enough to support such exercise of authorized power. The world-community does not exist to any notable degree as a psychological and spiritual reality with a high degree of unity in its determinative values, beliefs, conceptions of ends, will, and spirit.[26]

III: Some Characteristics of the American Governmental System

There are several outstanding characteristics of the American governmental system. In most instances they are not exclusively confined to the United States, but they are interrelated, apparently part of a trend, and a matter of considerable moment to the student of American social organization.

Governmental agencies are an increasingly ubiquitous and important factor in our lives. Odegard has called attention to several aspects of this burgeoning that are of marked significance.[27] Recent estimates indicate a total of some 110,000 different governmental units in this country. Of these, the national government in Washington is one massive organization. But prior to the admission of Alaska and Hawaii as states, there were in addition to this one major unit, 48 state governments, 3000 counties, 17,000 incorporated municipalities, around 17,000 towns and townships, over 60,000 school districts, and nearly 12,000 other special districts. An obvious problem is that of organizing this complex political mechanism so that it best serves the American people. Some re-organization would seem to be desirable, especially in the way of the reduction of the number of units. Various suggestions have been made, such as the consolidation of school districts, the consolidation or even the abandonment of towns and townships (in the states that have them), and the establishment of consolidated city-county units wherever possible to administer city, county, and school district functions. This latter consolidation would be quite in line with the trend toward the extended community. Such changes alone, it is estimated, would reduce the number of independent governmental units to about one-fifth of the present number, and there is a strong likelihood that in many instances services could be provided at lower

26 Cf. J. O. Hertzler, "Some Basic Sociological Postulates Underlying World Organization and Peace," Soc. Forces, 22 (Dec., 1943): 125–130.

27 P. H. Odegard, "Politics: A New Look at Leviathan," in L. White (ed), Frontiers of Knowledge. New York: Harper, 1956, pp. 94–115.

cost to the taxpayer. It is also worth noting that the number of workers employed by the state, local, and federal governments, not including the armed forces, was estimated at around 6,356,000 in July, 1951. This represented a gain of more than 100 per cent since 1930, or four times the rate of growth of the United States population during the same period.[28]

Related to this extent of government in general are the complexity of the federal government and the proliferation of governmental agencies. The federal government is made up of more than 1800 departments, bureaus, divisions, and authorities. Moreover, they are continuously increasing, it has been said, by both spontaneous generation and nuclear fission. As Odegard points out, divisions grow into bureaus, and bureaus into departments, and departments in turn spawn bureaus and divisions. Once established, few federal agencies ever die; each develops its vested interests. As Jimmy Byrnes put it: "The nearest approach to immortality on earth is a government bureau."[29] It would seem that some of the functions assigned to these agencies are often as much the result of accident and pressure as of administrative logic. Ex-President Hoover once noted that brown bears come under the Department of Agriculture, grizzly bears under the Treasury, and polar bears under the Department of Commerce. The federal government also receives an increasing proportion of funds raised for governmental support. Odegard notes that, until rather recent times, from two-thirds to three-fourths of all taxes collected went into state and local treasuries, and only one-fourth to one-third to the federal government. Now, however, the situation is reversed, and Washington receives from two-thirds to three-fourths of the total tax-take. Federal expenditures themselves increased from less than $457 million in 1900 to $66.5 billion in 1956. Thus, while our population increased from slightly under 76,000,000 in 1900 to about 168,000,000 in 1956, that is, somewhat more than doubled, our federal expenditures increased more than 140 times.

The expansion of government in terms of common indices has been almost breathtaking. For example, while the national population has multiplied by some 30 times since 1790, the number of civilian employees of the United States government has multiplied over 1500 times, and the debt by over 3000 times; and the end is not in sight. Although the rate of expansion of state and local government has not been as spectacular as that of the federal government, it has greatly exceeded the rate of population growth. The government would seem to increase in geometric ratio in relation to the arithmetic rate of increase of population and of the extent of the political area.

[28] *Business Bulletin,* Cleveland Trust Co., July 16, 1952.
[29] Quoted, Odegard, *op cit.,* p. 110.

Related to the quantitative increase in federal agencies is the quite apparent tendency toward increasing federal assumption of regulative and service tasks formally conducted by state and local governments. In fact, there seems to be an increasingly unavoidable development of federalism. The basic reason probably is that we are less and less a collection of physically separated and somewhat culturally distinctive states and regions and more and more a continent-wide nation-state of interrelated and interdependent people with more and more wants and needs that can only be fully satisfied by an over-all and territory-wide agency. Many of the major functions of government must be conducted on a nation-wide scale if they are to be conducted adequately, fairly, equally, and without partiality. The protective and regulative functions demonstrate this rather forcibly: protection against both endemic and epidemic and contagious diseases; establishment of safe minimal quality and regulation of nationally or widely distributed foods and drugs; regulation of public utilities, especially power and transportation, almost all of which operate on an interstate basis; regulation of agriculture, labor, shipping, certain businesses such as chain stores; regulation of banking and insurance and of credit and interest rates; regulation of water supply and its quality (river basins are interregional); attempts to control racketeering and gambling; and the regulation of mass communications.

The political freedoms and rights, as established under the Constitution, are for all people, regardless of race, class, or creed, everywhere within the boundaries of the United States. Needless to say, these have been very unevenly maintained in different states and sections. It has been increasingly necessary for the federal administrative agencies and courts to intervene in order to guarantee uniformly and universally these freedoms and rights.

The host of services provided by the welfare state has to be available to all everywhere without state or regional variation or discrimination. This holds true for such services provided by the federal government as the provision of funds for housing construction, aid to hospitals, the social insurance and assistance program, in fact, all of the services provided by the Department of Health, Education, and Welfare, created in 1953, the protection of savings deposits, the provision of interstate highways, the weather reporting and forecasting service, the provision of public pleasure grounds on national lands.

In order to conduct properly this burgeoning array of protective, regulative, and service activities, without unevenness and neglect of some, not only must they be available to all parts of the country, but they must be provided on a national scale, their over-all administration universalized, and this, paradoxical as it may seem, means the administration must also be nucleated and centralized; and the federal government is the ultimate centralizing agent.

We have a maze of overlapping and apparently duplicating governmental units. As the federal agencies have assumed functions or supplemented functions once managed by the state and local governments, the state and local units have not always given up these functions, or a clear-cut division of labor and specialization in rendering the different types of services have not been worked out. The confusion in rendering social assistance services, in housing development, and in urban development are cases in point. In so many instances, there is also little coordination between jurisdictional boundaries and functional boundaries. This situation is especially apparent in connection with the suburban development of our cities. As suburbs develop and penetrate the rural hinterland of the central cities, innumerable problems regarding the respective responsibilities of the city, the suburban community, whether unincorporated or corporated, and the contiguous rural governmental units sometimes become quite complicated. This is particularly significant with respect to the rendering of such services as police and fire protection, water, sewage and garbage disposal systems, and often also the provision and management of streets, schools, and recreational facilities. Needless to say, the allocation of costs and the problem of raising taxes among the different units are not simple.

Along with the sheer expansion of government, there has been an enormous increase in the amount and scope of administration action, especially during the last half century. The multiplying of governmental tasks requires more and more administrative agencies—departments, bureaus, commissions, authorities, boards—to carry them out. In connection with their assigned administrative tasks, the agencies also exercise powers partly legislative or sublegislative, and partly judicial in nature. These boards have the power to make rules and regulations closely akin to laws. We find this to be the case especially in the fields of health, public utilities, revenue (the Internal Revenue Service, for example), and in industrial relations. The citizenry must conform to these rules in meeting the requirements of the agencies or if they wish to enjoy their services.

Efficient administration and execution of tasks of modern governments require a great specialization of knowledge and a high degree of technological competence. More and more our biggest business—government—rests upon expertise and the expert. There is, for example, increasing need for skilled scientists and technicians in those departments and bureaus concerned with agriculture, commerce, taxation, diplomacy, crime detection, forests and forestry, health, food, drugs, conservation, social work, population, education, weather, soil, water, and, of course, all of the military services, to mention only a few of the obvious ones.[30] State governments especially have arranged for appointment of many officials rather than trust to election. Almost all elected officials today have technically trained assistants. Sometimes their selection rests upon the judgment of the elected officials, but increasingly standardized informational and technical requirements are established for the many jobs, and the specialized personnel is then selected by means of special examination procedures—Civil Service or Merit System examinations—on the basis of which they are certified as competent. There is also a definite tendency toward professionalization of public service positions. Professional lawyers have always constituted the higher personnel of the judiciary branch as judges, prosecutors, investigators, and so on. But we find, increasingly, professional accountants in the tax departments, people with earned advanced degrees in the diplomatic service, trained engineers in all of the services involving physical construction, registered physicians and nurses and professional chemists and biologists in the health services, certified social workers in the welfare services, city managers in municipal government, and so on.

Incidentally, as government becomes more extensive and more technically specialized, the average citizen has more and more complicated choices and decisions to make, and he feels himself quite lacking in many instances in the knowledge to make these decisions.

Although most of these trends in our government have been unavoidable, and even desirable from the point of view of the citizenry, since all, regardless of class, occupation, state of wealth, or party persuasion are beneficiaries, and although most of these trends have been quite in line with the primary maintenance duties of a modern democratic government particularly with respect to the general welfare of individuals and society as a whole, still some of these trends pose certain problems. How much farther can these processes go? How much of a good thing becomes too much? How much more government can we stand? How much more in the way of aids and services can we afford to give? For they are not created out of nothing; all citizens in some way and in some degree pay for them. How much more of universal providing can we allow ourselves to take without personal and group deterioration?

The situation provides the threat of a disease called statism, a form of overinstitutionalization, and statism can mean overorganization, regimentation, compulsion, and stifling conformity rather than freedom of choice and action. It may result in the impairment, even the destruction, of individual initiative and planning, individual responsibility,

[30] Cf. T. Swann Harding, "The Place of Science in Democratic Government," *Am. Soc. Rev.*, 6 (Dec., 1947): 621–627.

and self-reliant and creative individualism. In our case, the warning is against the development of "Uncle-ism"; that is, a dependency upon Uncle Sam, bordering upon parasitism, for many things or services that individuals and groups should be obtaining and doing for themselves.

B I B L I O G R A P H Y

GENERAL

Arnold, T. W., *The Symbols of Government*. New Haven: Yale Univ. Press, 1941.

Beals, R. L., and Haiger, H., *An Introduction to Anthropology*. New York: Macmillan, 1953, pp. 443–468.

Brewster, R. W., *Government in Modern Society: With Emphasis on American Institutions*. Boston: Houghton Mifflin, 1958.

Brinkley, W. E., *American Political Parties*. New York: Knopf, 1945.

Bryce, J., *The American Commonwealth* (abridged ed.). New York: Macmillan, 1908.

Burnham, J., *The Managerial Revolution*. New York: John Day, 1941.

Chambers, W. N., in Queen, S. A., Chambers, W. N., and Winston, C. M. (eds.), *The American Social System*. Boston: Houghton Mifflin, 1956, pp. 265–397.

Corry, J. A., *Elements of American Democratic Government*. New York: Oxford Univ. Press, 1947.

Cowen, E. S., *The Constitution and What It Means Today*. Princeton: Princeton Univ. Press, 1954.

Corwin, E. S. (ed.), *The Constitution of the United States: Analysis and Interpretation*. Washington, D.C.: U.S. Govt. Printing Office, 1953.

Cousens, T. W., *Politics and Political Organizations in America*. New York: Macmillan, 1942.

Davis, K., *Human Society*. New York: Macmillan, 1949, pp. 478–508.

De Grazia, A., *The Elements of Political Science*. New York: Knopf, 1952.

Drucker, P., *The New Society*. New York: Harper, 1956.

Hoebel, E. A., *The Law of Primitive Man: A Study in Comparative Dynamics*. Cambridge: Harvard Univ. Press, 1954.

Hogan, J. D., and Ianni, I. A. J., *American Social Legislation*. New York: Harper, 1956, pp. 102–137.

Janowitz, M. (ed.), *Community Political Systems*. Glencoe: Free Press, 1960.

Key, V. O., Jr., *Politics, Parties, and Pressure Groups*. New York: Crowell, 1953.

Kornhauser, W., *The Politics of Mass Society*. Glencoe: Free Press, 1960.

Lipset, S. M., *Political Man: The Social Basis of Politics*. Garden City, N.Y.: Doubleday, 1960.

Lowie, R. H., *The Origin of the State*. New York: Macmillan, 1927.

MacIver, R. M., *The Modern State*. Oxford: Clarendon Press, 1926.

MacIver, R. M., *The Web of Government*. New York: Macmillan, 1947.

MacIver, R. M., and Page, C. H., *Society*. New York: Rinehart, 1949, pp. 453–467.

438The Major Systems of Institutions

Martindale, D., *American Society*. Princeton, N.J.: Van Nostrand, 1960, pp. 357–380, 404–428.
Michels, R., *Political Parties* (Eden and Cedar Paul, transl.). Glencoe: Free Press, 1949.
Odegard, P. H., "Politics: A New Look at Leviathan," in White, L. (ed.), *Frontiers of Knowledge*. New York: 1956, pp. 94–115.
Peel, R. V., and Roucek, J. S. (eds.), *Introduction to Politics*. New York: Crowell, 1946.
Rheinstein, Max, *Max Weber on Law in Economy and Society*. Cambridge: Harvard Univ. Press, 1954, pp. 13–41, 338–348.
Schneider, E. V., *Industrial Sociology*. New York: McGraw-Hill, 1957, pp. 457–484.
Schreftgiesser, Karl, *The Lobbyist: The Art and Business of Influencing Lawmakers*. Boston: Little, Brown, 1951.
Schulz, E. B., *Essentials of Government*. Englewood Cliffs, N.J.: Prentice-Hall, 1958.
Swisher, C. B., *The Theory and Practice of American National Government*. Boston: Houghton Mifflin, 1951.
Truman, D. B., *The Governmental Powers*. New York: Knopf, 1951.
Williams, R. M., Jr., *American Society*. New York: Knopf, 1960, pp. 215–281.
Young, K., "Society and the State," *Am. Soc. Rev.*, 11 (Apr., 1946): 137–146.

FUNCTIONS OF THE STATE

Barker, E., *Principles of Social and Political Theory*. Oxford: Clarendon Press, 1951.
Cole, W. E., *Urban Society*. Boston: Houghton Mifflin, 1959, pp. 295–298.
Heald, M. M., *A Free Society*. New York: Phil. Lib., 1953, pp. 100–107.
MacIver, R. M., *Society*. New York: Long & Smith, 1931, pp. 195–202.
Schneider, E. V., *Industrial Sociology*. New York: McGraw-Hill, 1951, pp. 466–479.
Queen, S. A., Chambers, W. N., and Winston, C. M., *The American Social System*. Boston: Houghton Mifflin, 1956, pp. 271–277.

LEGAL SYSTEMS

Allen, C. K., *Law in the Making* (6th ed.). Oxford: Clarendon Press, 1958.
Davis, K., *Human Society*. New York: Macmillan, 1949, pp. 61–70.
Gurvitch, G., *The Sociology of Law*. New York: Phil. Lib., 1942.
Hoebel, E. A., *The Law of Primitive Man*. Cambridge: Harvard Univ. Press, 1951.
MacIver, R. M., and Page, C. H., *Sociology*. New York: Rinehart, 1949, pp. 175–181.
Pound, Roscoe, *Social Control Through Law*. New Haven: Yale Univ. Press, 1942.
Radin, Max, *The Law and Mr. Smith*. Indianapolis: Bobbs-Merrill, 1938.
Seagle, W., *The Quest for Law*. New York: Knopf, 1941.
Timasheff, N. S., *An Introduction to the Sociology of Law*. Cambridge: Harvard Res. Comm. in Soc. Science, 1939.

MILITARY INSTITUTIONS

Andrzejewski, S., *Military Organization and Society*. New York: Grove Press, 1954.

Clarkson, J. D., and Cochran, T. C. (eds.), *War as a Social Institution*. New York: Columbia Univ. Press, 1941.

Day, G. M., "The Sociology of War," *Soc. & Soc. Res.*, 25 (Nov.–Dec., 1940): 103–114.

Freeman, F. D., "The Army as a Social Structure," *Soc. Forces*, 27 (Oct., 1948): 78–83.

Janowitz, M., *Sociology and the Military Establishment*. New York: Russell Sage Foundation, 1959.

Park, R. E., "The Social Function of War," *Am. Jour. Soc.*, 46 (Jan., 1941): 551–570.

Spindler, G. D., "The Military: A Systematic Analysis," *Soc. Forces*, 27 (Oct., 1948): 83–88.

Stouffer, S. A., *et al.*, *The American Soldier*. Princeton: Princeton Univ. Press, 1950, 2 vols.

Waller, W. (ed.), *War in the Twentieth Century*. New York: Dryden, 1940.

Walter, Paul Jr., "Military Sociology," in Roucek, J. S. (ed.), *Contemporary Sociology*. New York: Phil. Lib., 1958, pp. 655–672.

Wright, Quincy, *A Study of War*. Chicago: Univ. of Chicago Press, 1942, 2 vols.

The Stratification System: A Quasi-Institution

The stratification system, sometimes referred to as an institution and certainly showing some institutional features, is a universal, organized feature of every known society, although it is much more structurally and functionally significant, and also more obvious, in a large and complex society than in a small and simple one. The elemental situation leading to a stratification system is that of social differentiation. Members of a society are alike in that they belong to the human race and share a more or less common cultural heritage. Beyond this, great, almost unlimited, diversity exists as to the qualities of individuals, the characteristics of different segments and categories of the population, and sociocultural conditions, especially the life situations of the diverse portions of the population. There are, for example, the two sexes, the differentiated age grades, the groupings, the different kinds and levels of vocations and occupations, the different social levels, the urban and rural population, and the holders of the different combinations or bundles of institutional statuses and roles. Furthermore, a society performs multiple functions which require performers with varying kinds and qualities of ability, training, and social attitudes, and who, for certain kinds and levels of tasks, are scarce. Therefore, the categories of persons performing tasks are differently evaluated by the society and consequently vary as to the prestige and deference accorded them.

Thus, a society is divided into various contributory subgroups, each with somewhat distinct capacities and resources, physical and social location, social function, and evaluations of them, although congruence of these tasks, roles, and valuations is far from perfect. Each differentiated element not only has certain special characteristics but also assumes certain norm-directed and usage-prescribed obligations and activities.

This societal differentiation is both vertical and horizontal. Vertical differentiation means that the dividers can be conceived of as in a vertical plane; for example, the sexes or occupations of a given grade are divided from each other by vertical lines. Horizontal differentiation, with the dividers running horizontally, is the major or master form of differentiation, including in each of its various ranks most of the vertical forms of differentiation, and it is summarized and organized by the stratification system.

By stratification is meant that the population of any community or society falls roughly into graded horizontal layers or ranks or strata, with penumbral areas of transition between the layers; the total strata constitute a sort of hierarchy. The essence of a stratification system *is* this hierarchic division of society. The strata are mainly generalized, loosely articulated aggregates, even categories, of people, rather than crystallized social groups; they exist quite apart from the particular individuals who fall within the different layers. The people within each stratum have approximately the same social rank, or as both Davis and Bierstedt have put it, each stratum consists of a cluster of somewhat similarly evaluated statuses. Each stratum includes both sexes, all age groups, and persons with varying other physical, psychic, and social characteristics; and they can be conceived of as being somewhat socially and culturally separated from each other.

A stratification system has certain typical characteristics. The ranks are differently evaluated. This scaling rests upon a commonly accepted set of valuations regarding the typical and expected social actions, contributions, and other socially important aspects of the members of each stratum, which, in turn, derive from the general value system of the society. The highest layers are most highly evaluated, and the successively lower layers have proportionately lesser value attached to them. It is obvious that any sort of ranking of individuals is possible only within a given scale of valuation. The general value orientation also operates to determine the major criteria of rank.

This differential evaluation means that the individuals of the community or society, on the basis of their respective incumbencies in given layers or strata, regard each other as superior, equal, or inferior; that is, those of higher layers are regarded as superior by those of lower layers, though this may be done grudgingly, while those of approximately the same stratum look upon each other as more or less equal. Thus, although there is relative equality within the given layers, there are distinctions of higher and lower, superior or inferior, among strata. The lower ranks usually accord some deference to the higher ranks.

Social prestige, esteem, honor, privileges, and rights, and to some extent responsibilities (varying with the different systems) are unequally assigned to the persons and families in the different strata, and exist in ascending degrees among the successively higher layers. These differences in prestige and esteem are usually accompanied by differences in opportunity and rights along almost all socially significant lines, especially economic, educational, recreational, cultural, and leisure. Position and rating are important determinants of opportunity. The different ranks also vary in the rewards, material and social, which they receive. In general, each rank carries with it a more or less distinguishable and inimitable array of permitted, forbidden, and enjoined behaviors.

The stratification system includes a power, authority, and control organization. The higher ranks have more power; that is, the social ability or position enabling them to exercise dominating influence and to command services and compliance to demands. The higher ranks also, informally or formally, exercise more authority; that is, the right to set values, determine policies, pronounce judgments, and act as social leaders.

Almost invariably, therefore, the strata in their relationships with each other receive differential treatment, and a considerable degree of accepted superordination and subordination prevails among them. The members of the upper strata with their prestige and power carry, assume, or are granted the right of directing the activities of the large number of persons lower in the hierarchy. There are gradients of dominance and subordination among the strata. It is quite accurate to state that these inherent precedences and degrees of subordination among the members of the different strata constitute a sort of pecking order.

The members of each stratum tend to have certain similarities, uniformities, and modalities, not only of prestige and esteem, of privileges and rights, of duties and obligations, of power and authority, but also of values, of attitudes and psyche, of ethics and ethos, of beliefs, of life perspectives and objectives, of ideologies, of acts, and ways and style of life. Each stratum has common meanings and norms that prescribe what behavior may be, should be, and must be. Thus, each stratum thinks and feels and performs socially in a more or less distinctive and distinguishable manner. Each is a sort of subculture with its own complex pattern or network of characteristics as well as a category of persons. The community or society, in general, has certain expectations regarding the behavior of the different strata.

Finally, the people in the given stratum tend to identify themselves with that stratum. Their consciousness of place in the societal hierarchy produces among them a class consciousness and a consciousness of difference with respect to the other strata, which are reflected in their stratum ideologies, interests, and activities. Various studies show a considerable amount of self-placement as to status.[1]

---

[1] Cf. Bernard Barber, *Social Stratification: A Comparative Analysis of Structure and Process.* New York: Harcourt, Brace, 1957, pp. 208–212, 228.

I: The Social Functions of the Stratification System

A stratification system rests upon the elemental and universal fact of social inequality among the differentiated elements of any society, even the most humane and democratic. The inequality is social, not necessarily as to biological endowment, mental capacity, or spirituality. There are especially inequalities in the ability to perform socially in a given society, or socioculturally defined and designated inequalities among individuals and categories of persons. There are also other socially significant inequalities, such as the variations in volitional capacity and the infinitely wide range of human energy, tastes, qualities, perspectives, objectives, and aspirations. The major functions of the stratification system stem from the fact that it is a somewhat standard combination of devices and processes not only for coping effectively with social inequality through the adjustment of unequal elements with each other, but also for advantageously utilizing inequality.

The stratification system functions, first, as a means of placing, locating, and arranging individuals, families, certain groups and categories in the over-all social system; that is, a way of locating unequals in some kind of rank order, so that they know where they belong in the storied structure. This assignment and identification is roughly proportional, though with glaring exceptions at any given time, to social qualities, interests, cultural characteristics and proficiencies, and social achievements, as these are evaluated at the given time. Ideally the stratification system provides for all individuals a nearly appropriate niche. Here they find their best chance to live and work among their fellows with what they have to offer. Thus the stratification structure provides a graded series of asylums.[2]

Second, it is the way of providing for social integration and solidarity among the unequals. By means of it the various categories of unequals of the community or society are socially organized for internal order, reciprocity, cohesion, and peace, especially by equilibrating and coordinating inequalities of status and by regularizing the gradations of vertical social space. The members in all their diversities and combinations, in all their own peculiar interests and ends, must be knit together. By means of a stratification system, hostility among the diverse elements is kept down and solidarity is effected. Stratification thus

---

[2] The social pocesses involved in the assignment and location of human beings in the stratification system are referred to as the processes of ordination. For an analysis of them, see J. O. Hertzler, *Society in Action*. New York: Dryden, 1954, pp. 343–346, 348–349.

makes for a certain amount of unity in diversity, complementary diversity, and a relative equilibrium among unequals. It provides an orderly framework of mutual service and cooperation among the various social strata.

A third major function relates to the division of labor of a society. The stratification system is a way of cooperatively (though not always with the approval of particular persons affected) distributing unlike and unequal functions among unlike and unequal persons and groups. It more or less effectively utilizes the differential contributory social proficiencies and potentialities for social performance. Hence, it makes possible a functional articulation and utilization of the varied elements. The stratification system is thus a systematized division of labor, a division of varied personnel into complementary societal functions.

Finally, and directly related to the preceding function, the stratification system provides a hierarchy and a channelling of authority and control. All cannot have equal authority in any group or society. There need to be a hierarchy and flow of authority. If these did not exist, the interacting individuals, groups, and categories would be in a state of incessant confusion, misunderstanding, even conflict. The authority and control must move downward, and the decision of each superior authority or stratum must be mandatory upon the respective inferior or subordinate ranks or authorities. A stratification system, whether that of a community or a large-scale formal organization, alone provides the mechanism and the relations for this flow of authority to the successive levels of the particular social system. In the main, the major control positions go to the upper strata, and the non-control positions to the lower strata.

In general, it can be said that a functional hierarchy is an indispensable ingredient in the establishment, maintenance, and regulation of a society. A healthy society must possess a stratum composition determined by the social importance of various functions, services, and authority and control requirements. Even a classless society would have a pyramidal structure reflecting differences of functions and of abilities and would be operating as a vehicle for equilibrating its different and unequal elements.[3]

[3] Cf. Eva Rosenfeld, "Social Stratification in a 'Classless Society,'" *Am. Soc. Rev.*, 16 (Dec., 1951): 766–774. On the functions of the system, see: C. A. Anderson, "The Need for a Functional Theory of Social Class," *Rural Soc.*, 19 (June, 1954): 152–160. K. Davis, *Human Society*. New York: Macmillan, 1949, pp. 91–94, 366–368. K. Davis and W. E. Moore, "Some Principles of Stratification," *Am. Soc. Rev.*, 10 (Apr., 1945): 242–249. J. O. Hertzler, *Society in Action*. New York: Dryden, 1954, pp. 343–346. R. L. Simpson, "A Modification of the Functional Theory of Social Stratification," *Soc. Forces*, 35 (Dec., 1956): 132–137.

II: The Institutional and Quasi-Institutional Aspects of the Stratification System

The strategic nature of social functions performed by the stratification system brings out its systematic nature. Closely related to this is the fact that the stratification system is occasionally referred to as being "institutionalized." There is also the tendency now and then to think of any social system by virtue of its established and systematized character as having all of the organizational features involved in institutionalization. But social system and social institution are not identical organizational entities. A social institution is a social system, but a social system does not necessarily have the full panoply of institutional features. The concept institutional is not a catch-all for systematization of action, and the term should not be loosely used. There also seems to be an assumption on the part of some that stratification systems are institutionalized because they are so universal; but universality of a sociocultural form does not necessarily imply or involve institutionalization.

That the stratification system is institution-like in certain significant ways is unquestioned. But it also has features which distinguish it from the standard and accepted sets of institutions. A close and critical look may require one to say that the stratification system is a *quasi-institution*; that is, it is like full-fledged institutions in some respects, but also different in certain crucial aspects.

Both the stratification systems and the definitely institutional systems, such as the familial, economic, political, and educational, are major structural-functional features of all societies. All of these systems have strategic and apparently related significance in the societal scheme of things, in the opinion of the theoretical and empirical partners in societal analysis. But are the stratification systems also institutional in character? Do social stratification and the other social institutions involve similar or different structural characteristics? Do they have similar, related, overlapping, or definitely diverse areas and types of functioning? What is the nature of, and what are the objectives in, the processes and procedures of each?

Both quasi-institutions and standard institutions have as characteristics definite social establishment, patterned relationships, an effective normative system, special and essential functions, and special, appropriate, and effective operational procedures and instruments.

Both the stratification system and the standard institutional systems have a high degree of organization; they have highly systematized structural forms; there is recurrence, continuity, and standardization of pattern in the interactions of the individuals as they behave in the respective systems. Both are means of ordering, regulating, and establishing common or recurrent social relationships in the interests of social efficiency and peace. The contacts and actions of people as they are involved in both systems do not occur randomly, but are controlled and channellized by numerous factors in the sociocultural environment. The stratification system, like particular institutional systems, operates with the assistance of the other institutional systems. Also, the local and regional forms of stratification, within the larger society, vary like the institutional systems.

The ordination processes whereby stratification systems are maintained are similar in some respects to institutionalization processes. By virtue of these processes, the norms of the stratification system define, and its values underscore, the arrangements and placements characteristic of the system. The sentiments, folkways, customs, traditions, and mores are also adjusted to these arrangements and support them. The expectations and arrangements are fixed in the attitudes and habits of all concerned.

However, when we examine the stratification system and the other institutional systems from the standpoint of their dominant functions and major societal effects, we note certain marked differences. The full-fledged institutional systems exist in order to satisfy the various standard and newly arising individual, social, and societal needs, needs in the way of orderly reproduction and recruitment of population, of physical maintenance, of internal order and protection against external aggression, needs in the way of all manner of innovation, acquisition, organization, preservation, technological application, transmission of cultural elements, and induction into the cultural ways, needs with respect to satisfactory beliefs regarding forms and procedures of relationship to the supernatural, needs of orderly aesthetic expression and enjoyment, needs for recreation, for social welfare, social security, and for health. The institutional system is a complex of many institutions operating in the major sectors of need-satisfaction in any community or society. The separate institutional systems, by sectors, can be said to be a differentiation on a vertical plane. Each institutional system is an overlapping part of a division of function on the basis of sectors or categories of parallel need-satisfaction.

On the other hand, the stratification system is not an organization of a special service, or functional, area of societal life; it is mainly a system of instrumental orientation.[4] Its outstanding characteristic is the arrangement of the socioculturally unequal population in the variously valued and hierarchized layers or strata. The primary concern or interest of all involved seems to be the existent location of persons, families,

---

[4] T. Parsons, *The Social System*. Glencoe, Ill.: Free Press, 1951, p. 158.

and categories in the respective strata. The main objectives—with the functions as actional expressions of objectives—seem to be accommodating the strata of unequal elements with each other, providing mediating linkages, and regulating their participation in the hierarchies of the larger community. Even in an open stratification system in which presumably the processes of selection, assignment, and re-assignment of persons to the different strata operate with a fair degree of efficiency, the basic interest is still structural; that is, getting into a stratum as such. Furthermore, the very selecting and assigning are not done by the stratification system but by institutional organizations, such as the educational, economic, even political. The stratification system, as such, has no functional agencies.

Conversely, almost every functional type of institution is an organized system of differential positions built around a major function, which is its *raison d'être*. Each institution has its unique system of stratification. In addition, the stratification system as a whole is mainly actually operative in certain of the major institutional systems, particularly the economic, the political, the educational, and the religious.

The social mobility processes, although they do function roughly as means of expediting selection, placement, and replacement of persons and families in the systems of strata, are thought of and utilized by the socially mobile as ways of achieving or gaining stratum position, of climbing the social ladder.[5] After all, what social mobility boils down to in a system like our own, is catching up with or, if possible, passing the Joneses. the *position,* with its rewards, is the foremost consideration; the differential qualitative or quantitative social contribution, approximate or proportional to ability, is rarely thought of. In brief, the main function of the stratification system seems to be hierarchical status structuring, and this consists specifically of the maintenance and legitimation of stratum positions. In rigid systems, supernatural sanctions and social force may be used to maintain the system. This organization of strata, however, is practically the end of stratification—an end in itself.

It should also be noted in connection with vertical mobility in the stratum structure that when persons achieve a different stratum or niche, they perform somewhat different institutional—political, economic, ecclesiastical—roles.

Furthermore, the stratification system, with its stress upon superordinate-subordinate relations, and by the fact that it involves social space and produces and maintains social distance, has a "tendency to-

---

[5] It should be pointed out by way of qualification, however, that by social mobility the upwardly mobile are trying to satisfy prestige needs, which are perhaps a psychic necessity, especially in a competitive society.

ward closure."[6] As noted before, even in the most democratic social systems, there is something in the way of consciousness of place or class consciousness, which is essentially a consciousness of difference with respect to the valued prestige, privilege, power, and various immunities and amenities, or lack of these. In general, a stratification system has the effect of maintaining certain separations, avoidances, and proscriptions among the people of a society. This is manifested in the restrictions on interclass marriage and family relations, in ethnic group relations, in class-uniform neighborhoods, class-uniform religious groups and other associations, and in other forms of social participation. Thus, as Tumin has pointed out, the stratification system may have *dysfunctional* features which outweigh the general arranging functions.[7]

The specific pertinent common and distinctive characteristics that follow are not meant to contrast all of the comparable structural-functional features of institutional systems with the stratification system, but are presented as comparisons and contrasts most pertinent from the standpoint of stratification systems having the characteristics and functions of institutional systems.

Every stratification system has its set of values, which, in turn, reflects the common and established values of the community or society as these relate to prestige and rank. There can be no ranking without a scale of valuation. The stratification system's values are the bases by means of which the different degrees of prestige of the strata are determined as well as the basis of the criteria for eligibility for positions in the different strata. In an open system the values lie behind the efforts to move up and avoid moving down the social ladder. What the people do in their respective strata or levels—how they play their roles as members of a given stratum, and what they are expected to do and not do—is a matter of the common value-orientation. But these values and evaluations are of a *scalar* nature and are attached to invidiously ranked positions.

On the other hand, the values of institutional systems have to do with need-ends. They set up ends, both individual and group, in the way of social good things for the population as a whole, solving problems of functioning together in fundamental need-satisfaction. They provide concepts of quality of performance for the individuals as they play their roles in the functioning of the institution.

The main feature of the normative system of a stratification system, as of any institutional system, is its regulative function. Each stratum

---

[6] Kurt Mayer, "The Theory of Social Classes," *Harvard Educ. Rev.* (Summer, 1953): 149–167.

[7] M. M. Tumin, "Some Principles of Stratification: A Critical Analysis," *Am. Soc. Rev.*, 18 (Aug., 1953): 387–394.

has a more or less distinguishable and inimitable array of norms with respect to permitted, forbidden, and enjoined behavior. However, the behavior prescriptions and proscriptions are relevant to each stratum as stratum; they are concerned with how the members of the stratum behave toward and with each other, and how they behave toward members of other strata. As far as the community or society is concerned, stratum behavior norms seem to exist primarily for their differentiating effects.

The norms of institutional systems, by contrast, are mainly concerned with need-satisfying performance, regardless of the stratum of the performer; the behavior effects sought are those of adequate reciprocal or cooperative effort in a functional division of labor.

It is also significant to note that the stratification system has no organizational facilities of its own for carrying out the expectations with respect to the duties, obligations, and responsibilities of the rank or stratum status-role combination; these are actually performed in the various standard institutional sectors; for example, in family, economic, political, or religious activity.

The norms of a stratification system are demonstrated in its symbols, both in characteristic activities or ways and objects or possessions. Among the significant symbols of stratum are the language and speech patterns, the conventions, in some systems the style and quality of clothing, the types of recreational activities, the sex relations, the church affiliation, and, in general, the style of life of the respective strata. These are "indicators" and "indices"[8] of stratum. Their major function seems to be to identify the members as stratum members.

In institutions, as we have noted, the symbols exist as means of aiding the institution to carry on its particular functions; they are mainly cuing, motivating, and regularizing devices regarding institutional effort.

There are certain marked differences among the aggregates or even the groupings of people in the stratification as compared with institutional systems. The very strata of a stratification system, as we have noted, are in large measure statistical aggregates rather than crystallized social groups; each stratum is a rather generalized, loosely articulated combination of individuals, families and categories of persons in the hierarchical series of ranks.[9] The strata themselves are not necessarily concrete entities of which the participants in the society are fully aware.[10] Furthermore, classes are not as internally cohesive and specific as institutional groups.[11] In most cases also the strata exist quite apart

[8] The apt terms of Barber, *op cit.*, pp. 135–185.

[9] R. M. Williams, Jr., *American Society: A Sociological Interpretation.* New York: Knopf, 1960, pp. 110–124.

[10] Barber, *op. cit.*, p. 77.

[11] A. M. Rose, *Sociology: The Study of Human Relations.* New York: Knopf, 1956, p. 222.

from the particular individuals who occupy the positions in them.

It has also been noted that the strata are not strictly functional agents.[12] They are too diffuse to be said to have specific functions as institutional groups do.[13] There is some basis for the contention that persons as members of a stratum have mainly only a level of functioning among the hierarchically differentiated strata.

The psycho-social groupings that we do have—those that come about as the result of class consciousness or a sense of class-belonging—are more inclined to be mutual-admiration or mutual-commiseration collectivities, or groupings of people who are more comfortable with each other. We refer to such class groups as those informal ones that consist of people of similar rank visiting or eating or playing together and other class cliques, and as the more formally organized ones, such as country clubs, dinner-discussion clubs, dancing clubs, the strata-distinguished religious denominations, the more or less class-distinguished occupational groups, such as professional organizations and labor unions, and in some societies, political parties. These are pursuing rank interests, or types of rank-determined interests, or conducting other than rank functions with the cooperation of fellow stratum members. When these so-called class groups do become formally and societally functional, they usually carry on their functions in various institutional sectors; that is, when they have essential and specific functions, these functions are connected with traditional institutions. For example, the functions of labor parties are essentially of a political nature; Business Men's Organizations, Chambers of Commerce, the National Association of Manufacturers, workingmen's organizations have economic functions as their primary justification in the social order. Actually, they do not to any great extent carry on stratification functions in so far as such exist, such as stratum selection and stratum assignment, but are institutional organizations used by social classes or strata for stratum ends.[14] Furthermore, the most important and effective elevators used in social mobility in a system like ours are institutional organizations, such as economic institutions, the army, the church, political institutions, and the educational system.

By contrast, as we have noted, institutional systems have distinct and standard functions to perform in the satisfaction of individual and social needs; when the functions are no longer needed the institutional ways of conducting them cease to be. Similarly, the institutional groupings and organizations exist in order to carry on the satisfaction of the

[12] Williams, *op. cit.*, p. 124.

[13] Rose, *loc. cit.*

[14] Cf. Barber: "No particular group is ever *either* a social class organization *or* not; it is always organized *more or less* along class lines." *Op. cit.*, p. 231.

particular categories of needs by established informal or formal team-work.

Finally, it should be noted that new institutions come into being when new categories of needs appear in the community that can be best satisfied by institutionalized instruments. New hierarchical layers or sublayers, on the other hand, appear mainly as the result of changes in institutional arrangements or structures—technological, economic, ideological, or political changes.

III: The American Stratification System

Despite their pretensions of equality and fraternity, Americans are very much preoccupied with, and involved in, social stratification. The subject, with special reference to the American scene, has been receiving extensive descriptive and analytical attention among the social scientists, especially the sociologists. In fact, the social scientific literature on social stratification bulks larger than that about any other aspect of our society or any other area of sociological analysis.[15] This stream of social scientific literature has continued without abatement. It has concerned itself with theoretical analysis and interpretations, with methodological procedures, and with a sizable body of empirically oriented studies. Although the general population is not doing much thinking about stratification in the sense of reasoning about, explaining, and justifying or denouncing differentially evaluated and empowered strata, very many are exceedingly conscious of the American stratification system; they act in relation to it, and much of their working—and possibly their dreaming—time is related to it. The ones on top are concerned about staying up and hanging on to their stage of the pyramid; many of the rest are concerned about ascent. There is much point to the contention that social stratification is a major preoccupation of the American people. This preoccupation is reflected in almost every aspect of their lives—their values, objectives, and perspectives, their occupations and changes of occupations, their purchasing and consumption, their residence, their family and sex life, their religious affiliation, education, and recreation and leisure. Among some also there seems to be a feeling that stratification is un-American—a violation of our frequently stated ideals of equality. Some, though deeply involved as social beneficiaries of its esteem and privileges structure and as ma-

[15] For example, H. W. Pfautz, "The Current Literature on Stratification: Critique and Bibliography," *Am. Jour. Soc.,* 58 (Jan., 1953): 391–418, listed 333 references on social stratification, and the present writer presented a bibliography of 192 items in *Society in Action,* 1954, pp. 418–423.

nipulators of its power features, contend that there is no stratification. A psychologist might conclude that some at least among us have an anxiety, if not a guilt, complex about our stratification system.

To understand the American stratification system, we need to know where it lies among the major types of such systems. They can be arrayed and roughly classified from the point of view of the relative rigidity of the strata, particularly the rigidity of the dividers between the strata, and the fixity of position, both contemporaneously and over the generations. Most stratification systems can be located along a continuum with a pure caste system with complete rigidity and fixity at one pole and a completely open and fluid class system at the other, with now increasingly scarce estate systems between the two.[16]

In a pure and ideal caste system the stratum position of an individual, and his ancestors and descendants, is inherited and fixed, ascribed, and mandatory for all time, under the customs, mores, and even the law; it usually is supported by religion as well. Each stratum is a closed system with its very definite location on the superiority-inferiority and dominance-subservience scale. The stratum positions of the individuals of the society are not changeable by any option or action of individuals; they cannot rise or fall, irrespective of personal abilities, attributes, desires, or efforts. Marriage is completely endogamous. In general, stratum location is sharply determined and permanent.

At the opposite pole is the class system. The American stratification system is a class system; in fact, our class system epitomizes this form of stratification. Our brief discussion of the American system will bring out the more important aspects of this type. Nevertheless, class in America is not too precise; our classes are somewhat nebulous; there are great variations from community to community. Also, different studies making an effort to determine criteria of class, that is, measures for identifying class members and for determining gradations of social appraisal, show that considerable variation exists with respect to what is found and used in different communities. The separate testing items also appear in different combinations in different communities. The number of classes into which communities seem to be divided, either on the basis of studies by social scientific investigators or in the opinion of the more thoughtful and better informed inhabitants, vary considerably also.

The traditional American class division is into upper, middle, and lower classes. But Warner and associates have fixed upon a refinement of this three-part division and use six: upper-upper, lower-upper,

16 For concise analysis of the estate system, see: Hertzler, *op. cit.*, pp. 231–232. Kurt Mayer, *Class and Society*. New York: Random House, 1955, pp. 7, 16–21.

upper-middle, lower-middle, upper-lower, and lower-lower. Hollings-head found five, and Centers posits four main classes.[17] The number of classes yielded by any method of demarcation will vary, not only with the firmness of the distinctions, but also with the points of comparison. Most differentiations into social classes are more or less arbitrary and often of the moment. The class situation in each community is also always somewhat peculiar and almost unique. The class structure of a community may vary according to the age of the community, its size, its complexity, the ethnic composition of its population, its historical and cultural background, its economy, its urban or rural nature, even its regional location.

Nevertheless, the objectively discernible reality of social classes in American life is unquestioned. A class in America is a horizontal category of persons set off from the rest by more or less institutionalized social status. Each class has a place in the rank hierarchy of the community. At any given time any person in our society is an occupant of some general class, and can be more or less readily identified as such. The individual member is accorded community status based on his class affiliation. This gives him at any given time, and depending on his class, a fairly distinctive set of privileges and disprivileges, esteems and disesteems, freedoms and restrictions, opportunities and limitations.

The nature of our class system is best brought out by indicating its typical general characteristics, characteristics that it shows in almost all of its manifestations, even though there may be the particular variations from community to community noted above.

Classes have no formal establishment or fixity in our system. They have no legal description or standing, as in most caste and estate systems, and no religious rationalization and support as in some more (former India) or less (pre-twentieth century England) closed systems. Empirical studies show that they are largely a matter of the consensus of the particular community.

Although all persons are born into a class by virtue of the membership of their parents, and although this locates them in an unequally evaluated stratum of a hierarchy of strata, they are all free and equal in principle. We maintain the thesis of equality of opportunity and of freedom of achievement. Not only the extensive array of rights provided by our Constitution, but the everyday working mores assures this. Although this equality and freedom are never perfectly enjoyed, each does exist in actual fact in large measure. We do have a consider-

[17] W. L. Warner and P. S. Lunt, *The Social Life of a Modern Community,* Yankee City Series, Vol. II. New Haven: Yale Univ. Press, 1942. A. B. Hollingshead, *Elmtown's Youth.* New York: Wiley, 1948. R. Centers, *The Psychology of Social Classes.* Princeton: Princeton Univ. Press, 1949.

able number of intellectual, political, and economic freedoms that relate directly to performance and position in our class system. We have the freedom to be educated, to change occupations, to utilize economic opportunities, to engage in physical and social mobility, and especially the freedom to compete with our fellows. Neither the principle nor the reality of these freedoms and equalities exists in any of the more closed and rigid types of stratification systems.

A correlate of the principles of equality and freedom is the principle that higher or lower position in the class system is available to everyone, if they have the essential characteristics and meet the requirements for role performance in the given class. The freedoms and equalities make possible for everyone the acquisition of the prerequisites for higher class membership. Our system thus does not place any categorical limitations on the person with respect to his class position.

In turn, and related to the preceding characteristic, is the fact that vertical social mobility, that is, the movement of individuals and families up and down the social ladder through the storied structure, is permissive and commonplace. But even more in our case, it is a right. Furthermore, something is deemed to be wrong with people who do not aspire to ascend the social ladder. We have a mobility orientation; that is, mobility attitudes, objectives, and patterns of behavior operating as persevering, motivating, guiding aspects of the individual personality. Vertical social mobility is a fundamental aspect of our American social system; upward vertical mobility is part of our American dream.

In our open-class system, rules govern accessibility to the higher valued positions, conditions, things, and symbols. The important fact in connection with this social mobility which is built into our class system is that class position in our dynamic society is achieved for a considerable portion of the population. Although the movement that is aspired to is upward, all have to contend with a social gravity that holds down and, in time, brings down the less efficient competitors.

As a result of this social accessibility and social mobility, the social classes in our system are quite fluid and continually changing as to membership. Persons and groups are ceaselessly being distributed and redistributed up and down among the strata. There are continual additions to, and departures from, any given class. Actually, given individuals and families may have location in several different classes in the course of their lifetimes.

However, each class in any community at any given time has a fairly distinctive pattern of traits, a set of more or less exclusive and restricted participations within the limited layer, a stratum solidarity, and more or less formalized out-group relations with all other classes.

At the same time, the different classes are not demarcated from each other by sharp, tangible boundaries. Rather, they are separated by penumbral or shaded areas of transition of class-characteristic traits and perquisites. The distinguishing characteristics of a given class are probably of a modal nature, and can be thought of as existing midway between its penumbral boundaries.

A final characteristic that has been getting recent attention is the differential power dimension of our class system. The higher classes hold and exercise the most social power, particularly strategic economic and political power. This power diminishes class by class as we move down through the layers. The economic power possessed by the upper ranks is exercised in the form of control over others through the use of wealth, the expenditure of income, the control over employment and its conditions, the control over prices and credit, the control that is exercised by sponsors or advertisers over the mass media of communication, the control—subtle and by no means always intentional—through gifts to various agencies in the community, the control similarly exercised through membership on the boards of directors and as officials, not only of the massive industrial, commercial, and financial organizations of the community, but also of fraternal orders, welfare, and recreational organizations. The political power is exercised through economic inducement and aids and various other pressures over political parties, candidates, officials, legislators, public bureaus and agencies.[18]

In addition to noting the salient characteristics of our American class system as a system, an equally revealing approach is to indicate the more common characteristics of American classes as classes. Such characteristics in their differential appearance among the different classes actually amount to criteria or tests of class—high, middle, or low. Although the criteria to be noted are numerous, the list is by no means a complete inventory; rather it includes only the most frequently appearing ones the country over. Most of the criteria are not exclusively American, but are found among most modern democratic-capitalistic societies that have open-class systems. Furthermore, no single criterion has an absolutely standardized weight as applied in the testing of membership for any given class. For example, with respect to the upper classes, power may compensate in part for wealth, income, or inherited family position. The number and combination of criteria as applied also differ from community to community, and in a given community at different times. The different classes, however, have directly ob-

[18] Cf. Floyd Hunter, *Community Power Structure: A Study of Decision Makers.* Chapel Hill: Univ. of North Carolina Press, 1953. C. Wright Mills, *The Power Elite.* New York: Oxford Univ. Press, 1956.

servable external or objective characteristics which take several forms. Only the commonly current will be examined.

The socio-economic criteria are primary determinants of class.

There are variations in wealth or property or property ownership: the well-to-do, those of moderate means, those of limited means. Long-standing individual or family wealth is usually more honorific than recently acquired wealth. Closely related to wealth is income. Finer gradations of income involve its amount, nature, and source; that is, whether it comes from interest and profits, rent, salary, or mere wages. Also closely related is occupation. The innumerable occupations found in our society not only are very differently remunerated, but they carry different degrees of honor and prestige, depending upon their complexity, the requisite mental and social qualities required, the level of skill demanded, the attractiveness or freedom from repugnant qualities, routine or manual nature, and degree of domination or subordination which the occupation carries with it. The honored occupations elevate those engaged in them, whereas lower occupations degrade their workers.

Wealth, income, and occupation provide differential purchasing power and social power; they imply direct or indirect administration of economic enterprise; they make possible very different levels of economic and social amenities. They make possible also the occasionally somewhat conspicuous indulgence in philanthropy as a demonstration of wealth and an evidence of superiority.

The standard and plane of living and consumption always constitute an important set of criteria. Wealth, income, and occupation provide means for living conspicuously and in approved fashion. They are translated into symbols of status rank; that is, prestigeful ecological area of residence, cost or rental, physical condition, furnishings, and operating of the home, the price and vintage of the automobile, personal services of others enjoyed, commanded, and displayed, food and clothing, health and recreational facilities enjoyed, and so on.

A second important category of criteria are those of a cultural nature. Important are the amount and kind of formal education. Those who have attended and graduated from college or professional school rate higher than those who have had only some amount of high school or trade school education, and these, in turn, rate higher than those who have attended only elementary schools. There are also obvious gradations among the colleges and schools attended. Moreover, there is a rough correlation between level of education and life income.

Skill in the fine arts or at least some patronage of them is important, as is also the devotion of leisure time to intellectual and cultural achievement. The types of recreational activities of the individuals or families are determinants of prestige, as are the political and social views that are held. Additional distinguishing criteria of quality are a cultivated demeanor, polite speech patterns, good manners, conformity to the requirements of etiquette, and participation in certain symbolic social rituals, such as teas, cocktail parties, debuts, and the like. The family patterns, including child-rearing, husband-wife relations, and fertility, differ among the classes. The Kinsey and other reports have shown a considerable variation among the classes in sexual behavior.

Family, family reputation, and kinship affiliation are important determinants. Whether an individual comes from a prominent family or an inconspicuous one, of a good family or one of no account, is a rating factor that often operates to his advantage quite apart from personal characteristics and economic or other achievement. The length and eminence of recorded lineage are also factors; prestige inheres, for example, in being the descendant of an "old" family or being a Mayflower descendant.

The affiliation with, and participation in different kinds of, associations and organizations comprise another important class-determining factor. In the main, the members of different classes belong to differently ranked formal and informal organizations. For example, with respect to religious affiliation, there is an important difference between belonging to the Episcopal or Congregational church and to the Holy Rollers. The upper classes belong to the prestige-carrying, leisure-time organizations, such as country clubs, athletic clubs, and study and discussion clubs (often mainly mutual admiration organizations). Even the fraternal organizations and service clubs have differential ranking and give graded status and prestige.

Race and nativity are significant determinants of class standing. Ethnicity, in fact, is such a weighty divider and ranking factor that it produces its own special kind of stratification; for example, the caste-like system prevailing in white-nonwhite relations. Negroes, Indians, Mexicans, and Orientals are practically excluded from white class consideration in different parts of the country. European nativity and nationality have been and still are to some extent important in class determination. In many communities, upper-class rating requires Anglo-Saxon or northwestern European origin. Length of sojourn in the United States is also a factor; old American stocks are rated higher than recent arrivals and their descendants.[19]

In general, each class tends to have not only a somewhat distinctive and distinguishable generalized pattern of daily living, but it also has a life style, including the presence or absence of a certain flair, spirit, and

[19] Cf. M. Harris, "Caste, Class, and Minority," *Soc. Forces,* 37 (Mar., 1959): 248–254.

cultural sophistication in its living. The American Way of Life has its levels.[20]

One of the most important functional features of an open-class system like our own is its permissive mobility from class to class. Our society provides an array of social institutions that enable individuals to move up and down the social ladder. These institutions operate as channels or routes of vertical circulation. These institutions also serve as sifters, testing and selecting, sorting and grading the persons of the population, and distributing and locating them in the strata where their functions, obligations, and rights are commensurate with their tested abilities. These selective and placement agencies never operate perfectly, however, and some persons are always over- or underplaced.

Economic institutions are of first importance in this connection. In our country the vast material resources available for exploitation, the ever advancing technology producing all sorts of new possibilities in almost all aspects of production, and in servicing and marketing, the infinite division of labor, and graded occupational specialization offer almost unbelievable advantages and opportunities for social ascent through the acquisition of wealth. Most of the leaders, or the recent ancestors of the leaders, in American industry, finance, transportation, and trade rose from obscurity. Graded occupations, each with specific requirements for satisfactory performance, generally function as means of testing, selecting, and distributing individuals along the occupational ladder. The way up is through a hierarchy of increasing knowledge and skill. Position on this ladder, from common labor to executive and professional man, is roughly commensurate with class standing; climbing the economic ladder is climbing the social ladder.

In time of war, the army provides opportunity for rapid advancement of the strategist, the leader, or specialist, regardless of original position. In peacetime, promotion is largely based on seniority, and higher social status may be almost automatically achieved. Through successive promotion to higher military ranks men mount to higher social position.

When religious organizations are growing in social standing, they serve as both elevators and selectors. Both the Catholic Church and

---

[20] On characteristics and criteria of class in America, see: R. Bierstedt, *The Social Order*. New York: McGraw-Hill, 1957, pp. 420–425. W. Goldschmidt, "Social Classes in America: A Critical Review," *Amer. Anth.*, 52 (Oct.–Dec., 1950): 483–498. J. O. Hertzler, *Society in Action*. New York: Dryden, 1954, pp. 224–231. A. B. Hollingshead, "Selected Characteristics of Classes in a Middlewestern Community," *Am. Soc. Rev.*, 12 (Aug., 1947): 385–395. J. A. Kahl, *The American Class Structure*. New York: Rinehart, 1957, pp. 8–10, 19–220. M. L. Kahn, "Social Classes and the Exercise of Parental Authority," *Am. Soc. Rev.*, 24 (June, 1959): 352–366. Kurt Mayer, *Class and Society*. New York: Random House, 1955, pp. 22–54. R. M. Williams, Jr., *American Society*. New York: Knopf, 1960, pp. 88–106.

the Protestant denominations in the United States offer innumerable examples among their clergy of men of very humble origin who reached positions of great social prominence through the high positions they achieved in their churches. They also are a frequent factor in the social position of laymen. The different Protestant denominations and sects are roughly correlated with certain social classes. Shifting to, or affiliating with, a socially more prestigeful denomination may be an expression of a higher rank on the ladder already achieved, but it may also be a way of achieving higher social rating.

Service of the state has always been a ladder. In a democracy, active membership in political parties and the holding of office, whether local, state, or national, provide opportunity for ascent for many. Humble folk and immigrants' sons have become mayors and governors; and a frontiersman, a rail-splitter, an Ohio canal boy, a Vermont farm boy and one from Iowa, a boy from a small town in Missouri, and another from Kansas have all become President.

Marriage has often led one of the two parties into either a higher or lower social stratum, although a step up is hoped for. The poor but aggressive or deserving bridegroom marries the rich and sometimes homely heiress and thereby achieves working capital or a job and higher social position. The ambitious mother of the poor but beautiful girl marries her, if possible, to the rich or socially prominent man.

An educational system that provides training and specialized knowledge from the nursery school up to the highest technical and professional levels, and that is theoretically accessible to all members of the society, is a widely utilized and most effective means for social elevation, equal to, or even more efficient than, our economic system. Probably the bulk of students attending state universities have social elevation in mind as one of their primary objectives. Furthermore, schools are testing, selecting, and distributing agencies par excellence for nearly everyone who comes under their influence. In fact, an efficient and just selection and placing of persons are among the major functions of an educational system in a democracy.[21]

---

[21] On social elevators, see: P. K. Holt, "Occupation and Social Stratification," *Am. Jour. Soc.,* 55 (May, 1950): 533–543. E. C. Hughes, "Institutional Office and the Person," *Am. Jour. Soc.,* 43 (Nov., 1937): 404–413. G. Kolks, "Economic Mobility and Social Stratification," *Am. Jour. Soc.,* 62 (July, 1957): 30–38. E. A. Ross, *Principles of Sociology.* New York: Appleton, 1938, pp. 457–468. J. Roth and R. F. Peck, "Social Class and Social Mobility Factors Related to Marital Adjustment," *Am. Soc. Rev.,* 16 (Aug., 1951): 478–487. P. A. Sorokin, *Social Mobility.* New York: Harper, 1927, pp. 164–211. W. L. Warner, *Democracy in Jonesville.* New York: Harper, 1949, pp. 144–148. For some evidences of a tendency toward closure of our class system, see: G. Sjoberg, "Are Social Classes in America Becoming More Rigid?" *Am. Soc. Rev.,* 16 (Dec., 1951): 775–783. J. O. Hertzler, "Some Tendencies toward a Closed Class System in the United States," *Soc. Forces,* 30 (Mar., 1952): 314–323.

B I B L I O G R A P H Y

Barber, Bernard, *Social Stratification: A Comparative Analysis of Structure and Process.* New York: Harcourt, Brace, 1957.

Bendix, R., and Lipset, S. M. (eds.), *Class, Status, and Power: A Reader in Social Stratification.* Glencoe, Ill.: Free Press, 1953.

Bierstedt, R., *The Social Order.* New York: McGraw-Hill, 1957, pp. 40–432.

Buckley, Walter, "Social Stratification and the Functional Theory of Social Differentiation," *Am. Soc. Rev.,* 23 (Aug., 1958): 369–375.

Cuber, J. F., and Kenkel, W. F., *Social Stratification in the United States.* New York: Appleton, 1954.

Davis, K., "A Conceptual Analysis of Stratification," *Am. Soc. Rev.,* 7 (June, 1942): 309–321.

Davis, K., and Moore, W. E., "Some Principles of Stratification," *Am. Soc. Rev.,* 10 (Apr., 1945): 242–249.

Gerth, H., and Mills, C. W., *Character and Social Structure: The Psychology Social Institutions.* New York: Harcourt, Brace, 1953, pp. 306–341.

Goldschmidt, W., "Social Classes in America: A Critical Review," *Am. Anth.,* 52 (Oct.–Dec., 1950): 483–498.

Hertzler, J. O., *Society in Action.* New York: Dryden, 1954, pp. 206–244, 343–346, 348–349, 418–423.

Janowitz, M., "Social Stratification and the Comparative Analysis of Elites," *Soc. Forces,* 35 (Oct., 1956): 81–85.

Kahl, J. A., *The American Class Structure.* New York: Rinehart, 1957.

Kornhauser, A., "Public Opinion and Social Class," *Am. Jour. Soc.,* 55 (Jan., 1950): 333–345.

Loomis, C. P., and Beegle, J. A., *Rural Sociology: The Strategy of Change.* Englewood Cliffs, N.J.: Prentice-Hall, 1957, pp. 167–201.

Mayer, Kurt, *Class and Society.* New York: Random House, 1955.

Nam, C. B., "Nationality Groups and Social Stratification in America," *Soc. Forces,* 37 (May, 1959): 323–333.

Reissman, Leonard, *Class in American Society.* Glencoe, Ill.: Free Press, 1960, pp. 169–290.

Schwartz, R. D., "Functional Alternatives to Inequality," *Am. Soc. Rev.,* 20 (Aug., 1955): 424–430.

Simpson, R. L., "A Modification of the Functional Theory of Social Stratification," *Soc. Forces,* 35 (Dec., 1956): 132–137.

Rose, A. M., *Sociology: The Study of Human Relations.* New York: Knopf, 1956, pp. 222–266.

Warner, W. L., *American Life: Dream and Reality.* Chicago: Univ. of Chicago Press, 1953, pp. 52–72, 191–209.

Warner, W. L., "The Study of Social Stratification," in Gittler, J. B. (ed.), *Review of Sociology.* New York: Wiley, 1957, pp. 221–258.

Warner, W. L., Meeker, M., and Eells, K., *Social Class in America.* Chicago: Science Research Associates, 1949.

EXPRESSION

Religious Institutions

Religious institutions have been and can be variously categorized from the point of view of the functions they fulfill for mankind. They have been extensively presented as major societal maintenance institutions by Sumner and Keller.[1] There is every evidence also that most of mankind from the dawn of history has rigidly regulated itself socially by means of religious institutions. In much of what follows we will note the pertinence of religious institutions in these respects: their significance in sustaining and maintaining communities through their cohesive and integrative effects; their vast influence in regulating conduct through their values, rules, sanctions, and frequently in history through their powerful functionaries and organizations.

Most of those who are informed about religion and religions would concede that religion is the most fundamental and absorbing expression of human consciousness. Religious institutions in all societies, whether consisting of preliterate or civilized men, are a more or less organized and institutionalized way whereby individuals and groups express their awe of the unknown, the uncertain, the inexplicable, and the uncontrollable of which they are conscious in their physical and sociocultural environment, and whereby they satisfy their sharply felt needs for adjustment to, and communion with, this extra- or supernatural realm. The primary function of religious institutions is to canalize the emotions, beliefs, and practices related to these expressional needs. They differ from all other institutions, therefore, in that they are not primarily concerned with behavioral adjustment to the tangible, observable, and comprehensible aspects of the physical and social environments. Their main province is the human emotional, mental, and spiritual adjustment to the vast realm beyond the empirical, the known, and the controllable; and their formulation is in expressed faith. But since this reaching out with and among man's fellows to satisfy these expressional needs has had to be done in a regularized, hence institutionally organ-

---

[1] W. G. Sumner and A. G. Keller, *The Science of Society*. New Haven: Yale Univ. Press, 1927, Vol. II, pp. 737–1481.

ized, manner, it has unavoidably produced both individual and group regulative and maintaining effects. Thus, the regulative and maintaining functions of religious institutions follow as valuable secondary boons.

Religion itself is a spontaneously appearing, inimitable, perennial, and universal attribute of man. Its beginning is unknown. Almost among all known peoples and in all times and places there are aspects of individual consciousness, poignant human experiences, and absorbing individual and social quests that are denominated as specifically religious. Yet, it is something difficult to catch and define, for the perceptible aspects of religious experience are exceedingly varied and multiform in their significance, intensity, degree of differentiation from other individual and social activities, cultural associations and manifestations, geographical and chronological bearings, and levels of meaning, value, and spirituality. Religion has meant many different things in many cultures and societies; it means many different things to different people in the same society even at a given time. One can ask Buddhists what Buddhism is, and Mohammedans what Mohammedanism is, and Christians what Christianity is, and find that none can explain in a way so definite or so reassuring that every other Buddhist or Mohammedan or Christian would accept the definition and agree to what must be included as essential or what must be rejected as contrary or unimportant. Nor is it easy to contrive a definition that will cover all forms of what has been known as religion from the lowest to the highest and yet describe to the satisfaction of the devotees the characteristics of the most evolved forms.

Religion as a perennial and universal attribute of man and as an element of cultures is paralleled by the universality and persistence of religious institutions in some degree and form. Religious institutions have always been major institutions everywhere. Everywhere they have had the expressional, regulatory, and maintenance features noted above. But, as with respect to religious expression itself, so the institutional forms and practices varied widely. A given form or practice may be sacred in one society and profane or secular in another. Some institutional set-ups have elaborate and even bureaucratically organized forms and others very little hierarchical and operational organization; some erect great physical structures for administration, assembly, and worship, while others have simple ones. Some have elaborate creeds and ideologies, and others very simple ones or none at all; some have sacred books, and others are without written principles and records; some have personalized supernatural beings or powers, and some do not; some have a conception of an eternal afterlife with future rewards and punishments, and some do not; some have highly professionalized functionaries, and some do not.

Yet, when one examines the expressions of religion as a whole and penetrates beneath the medley of social customs and practices, the bewildering array of cult forms and ceremonials, the maze of divinities and revelations, the confusion of creeds and dogmas, one finds certain common essences of need, attitude, thought, belief, viewpoint, and interpretation that enable one to define generally the phenomenon religion. One also finds certain recurrent, almost universal, types of institutional features—values, norms, practices and rituals, associational forms, disciplinary agents, and so on—the modal aspects of which may be presented.

Religion as a profound human experience is something quite apart from its organizational and theological forms. Furthermore, it is such a protean experience that one cannot, even with elaborate qualification, make a definition of religion that covers all forms from the lowest to the highest and from the ancient to the most modern. The analyst must largely confine himself to indicating the *kind* of experience that is involved, and the general ways in which it is assessed, interpreted, and expressed.

Religion and religious systems are not an expression of man's biological nature, such as his sex drives and reproduction, his need of nutrition, health and shelter, nor of purely sociocultural needs, such as the transmission of knowledge, socialization, and socially-devised protection against community chaos. Religion is an aspect of man's psychic and spiritual tendencies and potentialities. Man perceives and experiences more than comes to him through the five senses; he thinks and wonders and imagines; he wants to know and have reasons for what he knows; and he needs explanations for what he cannot comprehensively and objectively understand; he evaluates and he establishes values and is concerned about their quality and their ultimate significance.

Man lives in an atmosphere of uncertainty, insecurity, and incompletion. As he faces the more or less recurrent crises and certain haunting perplexities—the holocausts of nature, flood, epidemic and plague, drought, famine, war, accident, sickness and disease, vast and sudden change, personal defeat and humiliation, conflict and dissension, injustices, the nature and meaning of life, the unpredictability of the future, the mystery of death, the enigma of the hereafter—he wonders about the security of himself and his group, about his continuity. There are the disillusionments, the humiliations, and tribulations as he associates with his fellow men, as well as the urgent social needs that seem to be beyond his satisfaction and control. There is often a sense of personal inadequacy and a feeling of not having a sufficiently good and full life. There is often the concern about the nature of transcendental values and the uneasiness about what he should prize most highly in the way of ends and conduct. Man is so perplexed, so helpless in such an inscrutable, frustrating world, the uncertainties, obscurities, and solicitudes of which are for him very real, that he feels the necessity of some sort of explanation, some sort of security and certainty[2] against mischance and the unknown in all its innumerable forms; he wants cosmic peace, positive affirmations of stability and continuity, spiritual serenity, some assurance of a mode of reconciliation as a policy of welfare, some adjustment to, and identity with, the ultimates and absolutes.

Religion thus develops out of man's experience with the *mysterium tremendum et fascinosum* (the tremendous, fascinating mystery). He has the conception of an all-pervasive, invisible, irresistible, omnipotent, wonder-working, supernatural, superempirical, certainly extraordinary and extrahuman power or essence which is the cause and manipulator of the forces and processes at work in the universe, the controller of the uncontrollables and the mysteries. Man feels that he is crucially dependent upon this mysterious essence or this power or those powers, and that they mightily affect his present well-being, often also his ultimate destiny. This essence or power of energy is symbolically designated by such terms as God or gods, mana, Spirit of the Universe, Tao, Brahman Atman, Oversoul, the Uncaused Cause of Causes, the Cosmic Mind, and the Supraessence. Its realm is that of the holy, the sacred, the divine, and not the profane, secular, and human. In some religions this power or powers are personalized and vested with anthropomorphic characteristics and attributes. Sometimes they are given abodes on earth (Olympus, Sinai) or in an imagined place (Heaven) which still has very earthy structure and equipment. The basic attitudes of men toward the supernatural are fear, awe, trust, love, dependence, reverence, devotion, allegiance, as well as the fundamental and strictly religious attitudes of belief and faith.

Especially significant in religion, however, is the strongly felt need of getting into helpful relationship with this power or essence or spirit, of communing with it, of conforming with its principles and will, of acquiring help, inspiration, and strength from it, of becoming identified with it through eternity, and even of utilizing it in mundane affairs. Various types of behavior patterns are resorted to in the different religions to establish and maintain this relationship.

Thus, in general, religion is several things. It is, first, a deliberate attempt to get into helpful relationship with powers, personalized or impersonal, that are believed to control the unknowns. In this respect, it is an effort to reach out beyond the material, the social, the readily knowable, observable, and foreseeable, the relative, the temporary, the things and affairs more or less within man's natural means of con-

[2] An "Insurance Principle," as Sumner put it.

trol, and to achieve a harmonious relationship with this power. Most men personify that unseen power or powers, since they cannot communicate with an abstraction, or conceive of an abstraction as an agency.

Second, religion consists of a set of hypotheses and postulates which we know as beliefs. These are the products of the consciousness and the imagination of individuals and groups. They include dogmatic affirmations regarding the nature of the universe; the nature of the supernatural power or powers, including their sacredness or sanctity, their benevolence or hostility, and their ability to affect both the present individual and social welfare as well as the eternal destiny of mankind; the ultimate meaning of life; the nature of the afterlife and eternity; the nature of the rewards and penalties for conformity or non-conformity with the beliefs and prescribed and proscribed actions. These combine into a faith. Faith rests not upon logic or demonstrated fact, but upon the need that it fills. Faith involves not only meanings and ideas, but also ideals, objectives, and aspirations. It is "the substance of things hoped for, the evidence of things not seen" (Heb. 11:1). It has a dynamic quality; it gives men strength to move mountains. To have faith is to be faithful; that is, to hold fast to values and to their implications, to cherish the object or objects of valuation as something good, to translate the values and ideals into thought and action, and often to propagate them.

Third, religion is always more than a system of beliefs; it is for each body of adherents a system of techniques—of activities, of rituals and routines—whereby men, individually and collectively, do try to get themselves into harmony with the supernatural realm, propitiate the power or powers believed to be immanent in the universe, and attempt to control or utilize them.

Everyone has religion in some measure, whether the most confirmed atheist or the most devout believer, for, as Sumner put it, no intellect, however emancipated, can get away from the conception of the enveloping mystery of the unknown and the unknowable. In fact, he points out, it is precisely the mind which is best stocked and most scientifically trained that senses the mystery most poignantly.[3] Furthermore, both philosophic and scientific study lead to the conclusion that religion is a permanent, necessary, and inevitable part of individual and societal human life. Religion will persist as long as the experiences of men carry their thoughts to the mysteries of life that are beyond their immediate abilities in factually explaining causes and relations. Perry has noted, quite appropriately, that if all historic and positive religions were to be eradicated and man were to begin over again without a fairly

[3] Sumner and Keller, *op. cit.,* p. 1467.

systematic set of religious beliefs and patterns, the situations that prompt him to be religious would motivate him to invent religion anew.[4]

In spite of its preoccupation with the supra-mundane, religion, in all its observable forms and expressions, is very much a matter of mental processes, human cultural construction, social processes, and past and current social conditions, as are also science, philosophy, language, art, and ethics of mankind. This conditioning of religion is revealed in its different elements. The attitudes, ideas, interpretations, and explanations regarding the unknown and supernatural and omnipotent, of necessity, are in the form of beliefs, not objectively and empirically determined facts; and beliefs are more or less satisfying imaginative constructs. As has often been pointed out, the quality of sacredness attributed to the superempirical and supernatural, and to the forces, objects, events, and entities in which the supernatural inheres, is not intrinsic to these, but is superimposed by men. Two pieces of wood fastened at right angles to each other may be merely part of a chicken coop, or, if men think of it as such, they may be a sacred cross. Sacredness is not directly observable; it is believed to inhere in things. Furthermore, any belief that has currency and yields satisfaction is satisfactory to a collectivity of persons; it has been necessarily collective as a culture emergent, and is collective in its maintenance; its validity and importance rest in considerable part upon the fact that it is held by others. A belief held solely by a lone individual is suspect to others, and a precarious thing for the holder.

The world of religion generally reflects social structures, processes, values, and concepts. The beliefs, just mentioned, are the result of reflective thinking, and reflective thinking is a social emergent. Any object or activity is religious if it has some functional connection with these processes of interaction defined as religious by the adherents of the religious group. "Hymn-books, organs, stained-glass windows, preaching, baptizing, and even playing basketball in the inter-church league may all be religious if implicated in a process that is mainfestly so."[5] Many of the conceptualizations of religion are reflections of life as it is lived on earth, a reflection of cultural themes and emphases. The conceptions of the nature of the afterlife are usually in terms of quite earthy human needs; the conceptions of heaven with respect to physical conditions and equipment, organizational structure, the stratification system, the authority system, and so on, reflect the organization and the values and interests of the society and age of those who are to populate heaven. The Happy Hunting Grounds of the Plains Indians,

---

[4] R. B. Perry, *Realms of Value: A Critique of Civilization.* Cambridge: Harvard Univ. Press, 1954, p. 463.

[5] T. H. Grafton, "Religious Origins and Sociological Theory," *Am. Soc. Rev.,* 10 (Dec., 1945): 726–739.

the Valhalla of the ancient Teutons, the heaven of the Book of Revelations are cases in point.

The god or gods are not only cast in man's image and personalized, but, depending upon the organizational and authority patterns, the major cultural themes of the society, and the wishes and interests of the people living in that society, the gods may be ascetic or they may easily, even joyfully, submit to the temptations of the flesh; they may be prudent or profligate; they may be friendly, tolerant, and humane, or wrathful, revengeful, and cruel; they may be peace-loving or warlike; authoritarian or democratic. In a society at a low intellectual and cultural level, living in a circumscribed environment, the gods are crude, local, and often malevolent ghosts or spirits. As conceptions of human personality, the dignity of man, and man's ethical views have been elevated, the gods improve in moral qualities.

The jurisdiction and sphere of the gods reflect man's grasp of community and his systems of physical science. A universal religion rests upon a conception of universal cultural diffusion. When, finally, the conception is reached that all nature is governed by natural law, the theistic view assumes that the deity works through scientifically established natural means. The methods of establishing friendly relations with supernatural powers have been the same as those employed to approach human rulers, namely, by gifts, petitions, messengers or intermediaries, and tributes.[6]

Invariably the rules, regulations, and principles of general social conduct of the members of the religious group reflect the past and present ethical values and moral needs of the community. Furthermore, when religion becomes a part of a culture, it takes on a collective character. The beliefs are jointly held; the ends to be obtained concern the entire group; the ritual behavior in its very nature is interactional; the moral behavior required is for the adherents as group members.

The diversity of religions is as great as the diversity of the societies in which the religions originate or function, because religious phenomena are unavoidably interacting with other social phenomena already diverse. Related to this is the fact that the constituent elements of a given religion vary according to the character and stage of development of the culture of which it is a part. When the sentimental and intellectual reactions are in a low or rudimentary culture, religion is crude; when culture is chaotic, the religion will be so also; the more extensive the cutural horizons, the higher the plane of thought, the more expansive the religious ideas and viewpoints.

Finally, when the social and, *pari passu,* the intellectual conditions

[6] Cf. C. H. Toy, *An Introduction to the History of Religion.* Cambridge: Harvard Univ. Press, 1924, pp. 8–9, 265–266, 307–309, 450–465, 478–479, 484.

and climate of a society change, the religion also changes in parallel manner, though usually somewhat belatedly. Historically, new conditions, new social forces, and new ideas, whether from outside or generated within the society, have been likely to produce new or greatly revised religious beliefs, to lead to new rules and rites, and often to produce new sects. Social conditions in the late Roman Empire facilitated the initial spread of Christianity and at the same time did much to determine the character of the church as it evolved, particularly with respect to organization, policy, ritual, and even dogma. Protestantism was the result of social, scientific, technical, economic, and political developments in Europe in the sixteenth century as much as it was a reformation development in Christianity itself. The rise of Methodism in eighteenth-century England relates closely to the Industrial Revolution and parallel changes in political philosophy. The multiplicity of highly cohesive "holiness" sects in the United States in the present century seems to relate to the separative and impersonalizing effects of industrialization-urbanization.[7] It should also be noted that if a new religion or religious sect did arise, it could not gain a following except for social conditions favoring its acceptance.

The accommodative tendency of religion has been demonstrated among us during the last century. As physical and biological science has advanced, man's conception and grasp of the natural have greatly modified his interpretation of, and dependence upon, the supernatural; and as social science and his social consciousness have developed, the relative emphasis upon God and man has been modified. As men have gained confidence in their accumulated knowledge and their demonstrated ability to manipulate nature and themselves, they have felt more secure; they have worried less both about this world and about the next. Religion has become less God-centered, more man-centered; less passive, more creative; but at the same time less sacred, more secular.[8]

I: The Institutionalization and Institutional Content of Religion

The converse aspect of religion as a sociocultural product is the fact that it ". . . is a necessary corollary of man's existence,"[9] and conse-

---

[7] Cf. J. B. Holt, "Holiness Religion, Cultural Shock and Social Reorganization," *Am. Soc. Rev.*, 5 (Oct., 1940): 740–747.

[8] On the theme of this section, see also T. F. Hoult, *The Sociology of Religion*. New York: Dryden, 1958, pp. 20–27.

[9] Raymond Firth, *Elements of Social Organization*. New York: Phil. Lib., 1951, p. 216.

quently is an integral and highly influential factor in the social organization of any society. Radcliffe-Brown has pointed out that ". . . any religion is an important or even essential part of the social machinery . . . part of the complex system by which human beings are enabled to live together in an orderly arrangement of social relations."[10] Religion is almost everywhere and all times massively institutionalized; in fact, in some cultures, especially those of primitives, it has been the dominant institution and has always been a major institution making a definite and profound impress upon the entire society. Everywhere the religious system has performed highly important, even crucial, social and societal, as well as individual, functions—functions quite apart from those purely religious. It has assumed peculiar group, especially associational, forms, varying according to the social conditions of the society and the religious attitudes, especially the degree of accommodation to the secular world of the members of the particular types of religious groupings. Furthermore, because of the functions they perform, religious institutions are closely interrelated with most other institutions.

From earliest times, religion has assumed institutionalized forms, at least partly because it does certain important things of a generally significant nature for individuals and communities, and it does not and cannot exist without social expression. Such activities, as we have repeatedly noted, must be and everywhere are institutionalized. Even in the most highly personalized religion, in the fleeting cults, and in the modern secularized forms, there is noticeable, however veiled, the influence of institutionalization. Newly organized religions cannot outlast a single generation without taking on institutional forms. Different religious systems the world over, though varying greatly as to specific factors, functions, and features, will almost all conform to the general pattern of institutions.

Although the values undergirding the different religious systems vary greatly in explicitness and scope, most of them have certain common categories of values. Most religions place values on man with respect to his place and function in the universe and in relation to the supernatural entities; he is insignificant in some, and of infinite worth in others. Most religions have values regarding the supernatural entities themselves; regarding the kind and quality of individual and group behavior that conforms to the will of the god or gods; regarding life and death; regarding here and now as against the hereafter and eternity.

The beliefs of a religion in most instances are couched in the form of a body of ideas, doctrines, dogmas, articles of faith, ideals, and

[10] A. R. Radcliffe-Brown, *Structure and Function in Primitive Society.* London: Cohen & West, 1952, p. 154.

ideologies rationalized and systematized in the form of theologies and creeds, and occasionally also in legends and mythologies. These are the more or less reasoned interpretations of the religious experience of the particular group; they give the religious views stability, consistency, and order; invariably they are authoritatively established. Some are much more elaborate, systematic, and well-rationalized than others.

The theologies, and for that matter the whole body of beliefs, of different religious groups differ and conflict because of the diverse interpretations of their religious experiences and their diverse world views. For the individual believer of the particular religious group, however, the theology brings clarity, order, and durability into his religious experience; it spares him the pangs of indecision; with it he has assurance regarding the nature of the unknown. For the group, it makes possible unity of belief and the social transmission of the religious conceptions.

The conduct supposedly required by the supernatural power both among men and toward him, if rapport with him and his followers is to be had, is stated rather specifically in commandments, lists of taboos, bodies of ecclesiastical or church law, moral codes, books of discipline, and so on. These define religiously satisfactory or essential behavior, and they prohibit undesirable or dangerous behavior. In some instances they also include more or less explicit statements of the penalties here, but especially hereafter, for their violation.

Most religions have their individually and collectively performed rituals; that is, complexes of standardized practices and techniques which have numerous functions—such as serving as a means of communicating with the supernatural; of expressing awe and obedience, love, reverence and homage; of making appeals to the deity or deities; of appeasing and propitiating; of securing emotional unity among their own members; of increasing the intensity of their religious feeling; of hallowing other events to which religious significance attaches; and frequently of propagating their faith. As Wach points out, these are practical expressions of religious experience, as distinct from the intellectual; they are religiously inspired acts.[11] Almost universal forms are sacrifices and offerings; sacred music and drama; dances or other rhythmic or united responses or performances; feasts and fasts; processions and processionals; masses and sermons; hymns and chants; invocations and benedictions; the birth, baptismal, communion, marriage, and death rites; liturgies and ceremonials; bowing, kneeling, prostrating, prostituting, and making obeisance; immersing; making pilgrimages; giving alms; tithing; obeying commandments and other

[11] J. Wach, *Sociology of Religion*. Chicago: Univ. of Chicago Press, 1944, p. 26.

moral codes; observing Sabbaths and other holy days; such other negative or tabooed acts as refraining from certain foods and wearing certain kinds of garments; abstaining from sex acts at certain times, denying certain pleasures, avoiding certain places and associations, and abstaining from using certain words; and above all, insistence on prayer, both private and group. Related practices include the more gross actions in the form of incantations and other magic-working routines, used in an effort to manipulate the wonder-working spirits for mundane utilitarian purposes, and certain propitiatory performances that may amount to efforts at bribery, flattery, even coercion of the spirits.

In each religion, these actions and words tend to be set in form and sequence. They codify and organize the important religious actions. When performed as prescribed, they have great "virtue." They give reinforcement to the common religious values, beliefs, and ends. They help to remind the devotees of the holy realm, and to revivify and strengthen their faith in this realm.

Among almost all religious groups, whether large or small, whether hierarchically organized or taking the form of a local congregation, the greater proportion of these techniques, in one form or other, constitute a set of established patterns usually referred to as worship. The widespread practices of instructing, indoctrinating, and proselyting or missionizing, with various degrees of pressure, may also be placed in this general category of institutional elements.

Almost all religions have sacred objects which function as emotion-charged and emotion-eliciting symbols of different aspects of the supernatural world, such as the cross or crescent, wine, fire, the sun, flags, statuary, images. These represent in tangible form the intangible realm of gods, and relationships with the gods. They are means in which the unseen world is made real to men. All religions have special material equipment and paraphernalia for conducting their worship and for carrying on their multiple organizational activities. Notable are (1) physical edifices, such as shrines, temples, tabernacles, church buildings, abbeys, cathedrals, equipped with altars, baptismal founts, organs, pulpits, parish halls, office equipment, not to mention such special and increasingly common additions today in the United States as steam tables, gymnasiums, bowling alleys, and nurseries; (2) costumes and vestments for the specialized functionaries, and for the laity on certain occasions; and (3) such written aids as sacred books (Bibles), prayer books, and hymn books.

Among the most obvious features of religious institutions are the associations or organizations of religious human beings. These consist of persons with similar religious attitudes and interests, holding to a common body of beliefs, values, and objectives. As a group they feel that their massed agreement regarding their beliefs and practices makes these not only the most efficacious but often the sole means of salvation. Religious bodies are face to face only in their local manifestations; mainly, they consist of persons and groups scattered over wide areas, even globally, and bound together by an effective system of communication.

Religious organizations can be instructively examined from two different points of view: first, as to the functional differentiation of their personnel and, second, as to the different types of organizational systems into which they resolve themselves.

The personnel of most religious associations can be divided into the laity and the various kinds of sacerdotal specialists. The laity are the great mass of cooperating, rank-and-file devotees of a common faith— the element for which all aspects of religion exist in the last analysis. The specialists are of various kinds. Among the originators of religious ideas and movements are prophets, messiahs, and founders. Many religions have had specialists in the occult, such as seers, magicians, and diviners. From the point of view of the religious system as an operating entity among men, the most important category consists of the specialized organizational functionaries, the priesthood or clergy, usually with some degree of hierarchical organization among them. They are specially fitted, and in many religions specially selected, to carry on various functions. They, along with some of the other special functionaries just noted, are presumed to have exceptional insight into, and influence with, the unseen power because of their charisma or sanctity, and hence serve as intermediaries between the laity and this power. Their functions are numerous and varied. They are the expert class that is versed and certificated in doctrine, and they provide and teach the special knowledge and interpret the lore and myth; they preach, exhort, and admonish; they perform acts of intercession, mediation, and conciliation between the human beings and the supernatural; they preside at the assemblies, at the rites of passage, conduct most of the other rituals, particularly the formal collective worship of the group; they are empowered to receive confession, arrange forgiveness, and fix penance; they usually advise on numerous matters, serve as counsellors, sometimes function as healers, and provide various other social, psychological, and spiritual services. In some instances, they proselyte and missionize and organize new groups for their faith; in some instances, they too envision new religious forms and inspire and lead new movements; and in most religious organizations, they perform a host of administrative or supervisory functions, relating to the more mundane operation of the institutional machinery. The separateness and authority of these sacerdotal specialists is often enhanced by special attire and livery, and by special social privileges and rewards.[12]

Almost all religions have actual organizations—their forms of covenanting—actual formal, purposive machinery, through which they are maintained and promoted. Their numbers usually include members of both sexes and of all ages, and are differentiated as just noted. The functions of these organizations include the nurturing of the sacred and keeping the profane in its place; assisting the individuals and groups through crises; expediting the codes of behavior; providing a common sustaining spiritual and social fellowship; functioning as a channel of communication among the members; and in general, maintaining and sustaining the effectiveness of the beliefs and the solidarity of the individuals collectively holding them, and functioning as an effective going concern for the body of the faithful.

The particular organizations by means of which religious action is conducted differ from age to age and society to society. They reflect the social organizational principles and forms of the particular society. In the primitive kinship or tribal society, the social group will itself be the religious organization; the tribal god will be a sort of chieftain. A society with a high degree of social and political solidarity will have a tightly knit over-all ecclesia as its religious organizational form. An authoritarian society is likely to have a monolithic religious organization and an authoritarian god. A heterogeneous society like the United States is likely to have infinite diversity, and an individualistic society with religious freedom will have much personal or private religion.

The actual forms, at least as they have developed in Western civilization, fall into more or less distinguishable types, on the basis of such criteria as extent, degree of religiosity-secularity, exclusiveness or generality of creed and membership, and stability. The classification scheme that has emerged, and is pretty generally adhered to, had its inception in the writings of Ernest Troeltsch, especially in his *Social Teachings of the Christian Churches*.[13] The chief forms as now distinguished follow.

The ecclesia, or church-type of organization, variously subdivided as to subtypes, has dominance over a wide territory, national or even international in extent. It strives to be co-extensive with the society; and although it is not the only religious organization, it usually is the official religious body of the country—the state church. All members born within its territory are considered to be members by virtue of their residence. It is well-adjusted in beliefs, ideology, and practices with the

---

[12] Wach has distinguished nine types of religious specialists. *Ibid.,* pp. 331–383. On religious specialists, see also Hoult, *op. cit.,* pp. 122–136.

[13] O. Wyon, transl., 2 Vols. New York: Macmillan, 1931.

dominant ideological and authoritative elements of the society; in the main, it lends itself to the support of the prevailing social order. It functions best in an authoritarian order. Its own authority is usually centralized and hierarchical, and its organization is bureaucratic. It is not reformative in its objectives; it does not directly contradict or oppose the secular powers or trends; it accepts the world as it is, and tries to control it in the interest of itself as an organization. Mental and administrative routineers are more prized among its specialized functionaries than prophets and reformers. The Catholic Church of the thirteenth century came close to being a universal church. The Anglican Church of England, the Greek Orthodox Church in Greece, and, until recently, the Lutheran Church in Germany are instances of national churches.[14]

The sect is usually a rather small, closely knit, exclusive in-group, whose members join voluntarily and under strong conviction of the high value of the faith. The members are usually from the lower classes, usually somewhat embattled dissidents or protestants from the more formal and established religious organizations of the society. Often their dissent is owing to dissatisfaction with the leadership, or with compromises of doctrines and ethics of the church or denominations from which they have broken off. Their leadership is charismatic rather than administrative-dogmatic. The whole personnel is characterized by religious and ethical fervor, fundamentalist beliefs, and great devotion and loyalty; the stress is on live, not somnolent, religious principles, and on perfection of conformity to these. The members look upon themselves as somewhat withdrawn from the world in religious belief and activity. All out-group persons are looked upon as lost souls. Members of such groups are usually engaged in active proselyting; for example, early Christianity, the Mennonite groups extending over several centuries, though not active proselyters, and in the United States, the Christian Scientists and Mormons until recently, and such groups as the Jehovah's Witnesses, Nazarenes, and Churches of Christ. In time, as a sect loses its pristine fervor and eccentricity and settles, it tends to become a denomination.

The denomination is especially characteristic of the United States, with its cultural heterogeneity, its individualism, its freedom of religious thought and action. Within the United States, there are literally hundreds of more or less distinct denominational organizations. Most de-

---

[14] The term church actually cannot be very precisely defined; it has various meanings and implications. In American usage, it seems to be almost synonymous with religious organization, and may mean an ecclesia, a denomination, a sect, or even a local congregation. The particular meaning must usually be judged from the context.

nominations have developed from sects; they may, in fact, be said to be sects in an advanced state of development, sects that have come to a compromise with the existing social order, sects grown large, tame, and tolerant. They are stable and settled organizations, usually of considerable size, complexity, and territorial extent. Like the ecclesia, most of the members are recruited by birthright, though there are occasional efforts at proselyting. The beliefs of denominations are rather simply dogmatized and tempered for easy acceptance by large numbers of people; the religious discipline and required action are also rather formalized and conventional. They have lost their sect-like fervor and exactitude. They represent infinite variations of a body of common, respectable religious beliefs and practices of the society. To be sure, each denomination's combination has to be better than the others, or it loses its justification for existence; but all are tolerant—at least not condemnatory—of the others, and see merit in the others. There can be, and is, interchangeability of membership within the class level without great violence to beliefs or practices. In the United States, we have as examples various branches of Methodists, Lutherans, and Baptists, and dozens upon dozens of more unitary groupings. Although accommodated to the world in general, they tend to reflect different levels of temperament, rationality, spirituality, religious conservatism-liberalism, aesthetic sense, educational development, and world view; and they are limited by class, by race, still to some extent by nationality, and by regional boundaries.

The cult is at the farthest extreme from the ecclesia. The cult is a small religious group characteristic of an atomized society. Its potential and actual members actually are largely confined to dwellers in metropolitan areas; they often consist of social flotsam and jetsam. They flourished in ancient Alexandria and Rome, as they do today in cities such as New York, Chicago, or Los Angeles. The members hold to extremist and exotic beliefs and doctrines. The cult is not exclusive as is a sect; it is usually small, short-lived, and often local. It is usually loosely organized and often built around a single dominant leader—an Aimee Semple McPherson or a "Father Divine."

Another aspect of religious organization, especially in the United States, has to do with the different types of government, including operational policy, prevailing among the religious bodies, especially among the denominations. These take three main forms in our country.

Under the congregational form of government, the control is vested independently in the local congregation; it chooses and controls its minister, decides upon its own budget and its disbursal, and generally makes all other decisions respecting the operation of the local congregation. Local authority is delegated to an elected board which acts for the congregation in administrative matters. The local bodies unite on state, regional, and national levels, but their purpose is to discuss common interests affecting the denomination as a whole, and not to carry on governmental matters. As examples of this pattern of organization, there are the Congregational and Christian Churches, the Baptists, Disciples of Christ, and Unitarians.

The episcopal pattern consists of a church-wide or denomination-wide centralized ecclesiastical hierarchy. The hierarchical officialdom controls local congregations and local appointments of priests or clergy; organizational authority flows from the highest office down to the members. In the United States, the Roman Catholic Church represents this hierarchical ecclesiastical control in its most extreme form, with authority in matters of faith and conduct of the affairs of the church vested supremely in the Pope, and then relayed downward through the cardinals, archbishops, bishops, monsignors, and finally parish priests. Most moderate, that is, providing local congregations with some autonomy and permitting some lay representation in developing church polity, is the Methodist Church. Between these two—the Catholic and the Methodist—is the Protestant Episcopal Church

In the presbyterian form of government, the main control of the total organization is in the hands of the presbytery, or body of preachers. However, the hierarchy is modified by lay representation in governing bodies. Ministerial rank is not strictly graded; local congregations are managed in considerable part by the elders, who, among other things, have the right to choose among the candidates who present themselves for ministerial appointment. The various Presbyterian and Lutheran bodies are the best examples of this form of church management in the United States.

Note should be taken of various kinds of cross-denominational organizations in the United States. At the local community level, there are ministerial associations, local organizations of members of the clergy, usually limited to the Protestant denominations, who meet periodically to consider common religious and moral problems; and local church councils, ordinarily consisting of both clergymen and laymen from the different congregations, in which they consider interchurch welfare, activities, and cooperation, as well as often give attention to community welfare, for example with respect to school improvement, health, interracial understanding, control and treatment of delinquents, family problems, industrial relations, or Sunday observance. At the national level, there are such organizations as the Federal Council of Churches of Christ in America, the American Council of Christian Churches (confined to fundamentalist groups), and the interfaith organization, the National Conference of Christians and Jews.

II: Some of the Major Functions of Religion

The place of religion in the simple, preliterate societies is quite definite; as a complex it fits into the whole social organization and functions dominantly in every part of it. In societies like ours, however, its place is less clear and more complex. With the diversity of religious viewpoints, there are differences of opinion as to the essential features of religion; and there are different opinions as to the essential functions of religion. Nevertheless, for most of the population of heterogeneous advanced societies, though less for the less religious portion, religion does perform certain modal individual and social functions.

Although the inner functions of religion are not of direct significance in social organization, they have important indirect consequences. If the inner functions of religion are performed, the individual is a composed, ordered, motivated, and emotionally secure associate; he is not greatly frustrated, and he is not anomic; he is better fitted to perform his social life among his fellows. There are several closely related inner functions.

In the last analysis, religion is the means of inducing, formulating, expressing, enhancing, implementing, and perpetuating man's deepest experience—the religious. Man is first religious; the instrumentalities follow. Religion seeks to satisfy human needs of great pertinence. The significant things in it, at the higher religious levels, are the inner emotional, mental, and spiritual occurrences that fill the pressing human needs of self-preservation, self-pacification, and self-completion. The chief experience is the sensing of communion, and in the higher religions, of a harmonious relationship with the supernatural power. Related to this is the fact that most of the higher religions define for the individual his place in the universe and give him a feeling that he is relatively secure in an ordered, dependable universe. Man has the experience of being helpfully allied with what he cannot fully understand; he is a coordinate part of all of the mysterious energy and being and movement. The universe is a safe and permanent home.

A number of religions also satisfy for many the need of being linked with the ultimate and eternal. Death is not permanent defeat and disappearance; man has a second chance. He is not lost in the abyss of endless time; he has endless being. Religion at its best also offers the experience of spiritual fulfillment by inviting man into the highest realm of the spirit. Religion can summate, epitomize, relate, and conserve all the highest ideals and values—ethical, aesthetic, and religious —of man formed in his culture.

There is also the possibility, among higher religions, of experiencing consistent meaning in life and enjoying guidance and expansiveness. The kind of religious experience that most moderns seek not only provides, clarifies, and relates human yearnings, values, ideals, and purposes; it also provides facilities and incitements for the development of personality, sociality, and creativeness. Under the religious impulse, whether theistic or humanistic, men have joy in living; life leads somewhere. Religion at its best is out in front, ever beckoning and leading on, and, as Lippman put it, "mobilizing all man's scattered energies in one triumphant sense of his own infinite importance."[15]

At the same time that religion binds the individual helpfully to the supernatural and gives him cosmic peace and a sense of supreme fulfillment, it also has great therapeutic value for him. It gives him aid, comfort, even solace, in meeting mundane life situations where his own unassisted practical knowledge and skill are felt by him to be inadequate. He is confronted with the recurrent crises, such as great natural catastrophes and the great transitions of life—marriage, incurable disease, widowhood, old age, the certainty of death. He has to cope with frustration and other emotional disturbance and anomie. His religious beliefs provide him with plausible explanations for many conditions which cause him great concern, and his religious faith makes possible fortitude, equanimity, and consolation, enabling him to endure colossal misfortune, fear, frustration, uncertainty, suffering, evil, and danger. Religion usually also includes a principle of compensation, mainly in a promised perfect future state.

The belief in immortality, where held, functions as a redress for the ills and disappointments of the here and now. The tensions accompanying a repressive consciousness of wrongdoing or sinning or some tormenting secret are relieved for the less self-contained or self-sufficient by confession, repentance, and penance. The feeling of individual inferiority, defeat, or humiliation growing out of various social situations or individual deficiencies or failures is compensated for by communion in worship or prayer with a friendly, but all-victorious Father-God, as well as by sympathetic fellowship with others who share this faith, and by opportunities in religious acts for giving vent to emotions and energies.

In providing for these inner individual functions, religion undertakes in behalf of individual peace of mind and well-being services for which there is no other institution.

In addition to the functions of religion within man, there have always been the outer social functions for the community and society. The two have never been separable. Religion is vitally necessary in both societal maintenance and regulation.

The value-system of a community or society is always correlated with, and to a degree dependent upon, a more or less shared system

[15] W. Lippman, *A Preface to Morals*. New York: Macmillan, 1929, p. 50.

of religious beliefs and convictions. The religion supports, re-enforces, reaffirms, and maintains the fundamental values. Even in the United States, with its freedom of religious belief and worship and its vast denominational differentiation, there is a general consensus regarding the basic Christian values. This is demonstrated especially when there is awareness of radically different value orientation elsewhere; for example, Americans rally to Christian values vis-à-vis those of atheistic communism. In America also all of our major religious bodies officially sanction a universalistic ethic which is reflective of our common religion. Even the non-church members—the freewheelers, marginal religionists, and so on—have the values of Christian civilization internalized in them. Furthermore, religion tends to integrate the whole range of values from the highest or ultimate values of God to the intermediary and subordinate values; for example, those regarding material objects and pragmatic ends. Finally, it gives sanctity, more than human legitimacy, and even, through super-empirical reference, transcendent and supernatural importance to some values; for example, marriage as a sacrament, much law-breaking as sinful, occasionally the state as a divine instrument. It places certain values at least beyond questioning and tampering.

Closely related to this function is the fact that the religious system provides a body of ultimate ends for the society, which are compatible with the supreme eternal ends. This something leads to a conception of an over-all Social Plan with a meaning interpretable in terms of ultimate ends; for example, a plan that fulfills the will of God, which advances the Kingdom of God, which involves social life as part of the Grand Design.[16] This explains some group ends and provides a justification of their primacy. It gives social guidance and direction and makes for programs of social action. Finally, it gives meaning to much social endeavor, and logic, consistency, and meaning to life. In general, there is no society so secularized as to be completely without religiously inspired transcendental ends.[17]

Religion integrates and unifies. Some of the oldest, most persistent, and most cohesive forms of social groupings have grown out of religion. These groups have varied widely from mere families, primitive, totemic groups, and small modern cults and sects, to the memberships of great denominations, and great, widely dispersed world religions. Religion fosters group life in various ways. The common ultimate values, ends, and goals fostered by religion are a most important factor. Without a system of values there can be no society. Where such a value system

[16] Cf. Firth, op. cit., p. 241.
[17] Cf. W. L. Kolb, "Values, Positivism, and Functional Theory of Religion," Soc. Forces, 31 (May, 1953): 305–331.

prevails, it always unifies all who possess it; it enables members of the society to operate as a system. The beliefs of a religion also reflecting the values are expressed in creeds, dogmas, and doctrines, and form what Durkheim calls a credo. As he points out, a religious group cannot exist without a collective credo, and the more extensive the credo, the more unified and strong is the group. The credo unifies and socializes men by attaching them completely to an identical body of doctrine; the more extensive and firm the body of doctrine, the firmer the group.[18]

The religious symbolism, and especially the closely related rites and worship forms, constitute a powerful bond for the members of the particular faith. The religion, in fact, is an expression of the unity of the group, small or large. The common codes, for religious action as such and in their ethical aspects for everyday moral behavior, bind the devotees together. These are ways of jointly participating in significantly symbolized, standardized, and ordered religiously sanctified behavior. The codes are mechanism for training in, and directing and enforcing, uniform social interaction, and for continually and publicly reasserting the solidarity of the group.

Durkheim noted long ago that religion as ". . . a unified system of beliefs and practices relative to sacred things . . . unite[s] into one single moral community . . . all those who adhere to them."[19] His view is that every religion pertains to a community, and, conversely, every community is in one aspect a religious unit.[20] This is brought out in the common religious ethos that prevails even in the denominationally diverse audiences at many secular semi-public and public occasions in the United States; and it is evidenced in the prayers offered, in the frequent religious allusions, and in the confirmation of points on religious grounds.

The unifying effect of religion is also brought out in the fact that historically peoples have clung together as more or less cohesive cultural units, with religion as the dominant bond, even though spatially dispersed and not politically organized. The Jews for 2500 years have been a prime example, though the adherents of any world or interpeople religion are cases in point. It might be pointed out that the integrating function of religion, for good or ill, has often supported or been identified with other groupings—political, nationality, language, class, racial, sociability, even economic.

Religion usually exercises a stabilizing-conserving function. As such

[18] E. Durkheim, *Suicide* (G. Simpson, transl.). Glencoe, Ill.: Free Press, 1951, p. 159.

[19] E. Durkheim, *Elementary Forms of Religious Life* (J. W. Swain, transl.). New York: Macmillan, 1915, p. 47.

[20] Cf. especially T. Parsons, *Structure of Social Action*. New York: McGraw-Hill, 1937, Chap. XI.

it acts as an anchor for the people. There is a marked tendency for religions, once firmly established, to resist change, not only in their own doctrines and policies and practices, but also in secular affairs having religious relevance. It has thus been a significant factor in the conservation of social values, though also in some measure, an obstacle to the creation or diffusion of new ones. It tends to support the long-standing precious sentiments, the traditional ways of thinking, and the customary ways of living. As Yinger has pointed out, the ". . . reliance on symbols, on tradition, on sacred writings, on the cultivation of emotional feelings of identity and harmony with sacred values, turns one to the past far more than to the future."[21] Historically, religion has also functioned as a tremendous engine of vindication, enforcement, sanction, and perpetuation of various other institutions.

At the same time that religion exercises a conserving influence, it also energizes and motivates both individuals and groups. Much of the important individual and social action has been owing to religious incentives. The great ultimate ends of religion have served as magnificent beacon lights that lured people toward them with an almost irresistible force, mobilizing energies and inducing sacrifices; for example, the Crusades, mission efforts, just wars. Much effort has been expended in the sincere effort to apply the teaching and admonitions of religion. The insuperable reward systems that most religions embody have great motivating effects. Religion provides the most attractive rewards, either in this world or the next, for those who not merely abide by its norms, but who engage in good works.

Religion usually acts as a powerful aid in social control, enforcing what men should or should not do. Among primitive peoples the sanctions and dictates of religion were more binding than any of the other controls exercised by the group; and in modern societies such influence is still great. Religion has its own supernatural prescriptions that are at the same time codes of behavior for the here and now. It provides enforcement for these prescribed behavioral essentials through its emotional appeals, its use of great ideals and goals, its leaders, but especially all-seeing and all-powerful supernatural agents and its system of future and eternal rewards and punishments. Particular organized religions have also exercised vast social control, not only through their own, often very extensive, secular activities only, but also through supporting and augmenting the social power of the ruling socio-economic and political group of the society.

Thus far the great positive functions of religion have been discussed. However, the social scientific examination of religion in society must

21 J. M. Yinger, *Religion, Society, and the Individual*. New York: Macmillan, 1957, p. 301.

also point to several negative—disorganizational or retarding—socio-cultural effects that religion has demonstrated again and again.

The conserving function of religion can easily slip into the rigidify-ing or ossification of both beliefs and action, and thus make for archa-ism. To be sure, all institutions tend to develop inflexibility in their functioning and fail to keep abreast of the needs of the times. However, these tendencies seem to be greater in organized religion than in most other institutional fields. There is so much of the "dead hand" in theology, ritual, and the forms of organization.

This is doubtless owing to the facts that the major preoccupation of religious institutions is with the unknown and mysterious and that, since they rest upon faith and belief, they cannot be checked so readily by normal procedures of perception, understanding, and investigation. The doctrine is derived from revelation and authority, and hence is strongly authoritarian, even infallible, in character. After the doctrine has been systematized, the rules of faith established, and the forms of worship fixed, then any deviations and opinions at variance with the officially accepted teachings are classed as heresy. Not only is experi-mentalism not encouraged, but it is looked upon with suspicion. Reli-gious organizations, as organizations, are likely to develop precedents, to routinize activities, and to acquire a momentum that gives them a holdover power in many of their operations after these have ceased to have pertinence and timeliness. More than any other institutional sys-tem, religious institutions have a protected position and claim to have a unique finality. The matter is summarized in a phrase by MacIver: "Revelation stands in the way of revaluation."[22]

Another major disorganizational aspect has to do with the fact that religion, by its very nature, has produced cleavages and divisions re-sulting in alienation, intolerance, bigotry, bickering, sharp disapproval of other men's consciences and convictions, and eventually confusion, bewilderment, and sometimes vicious antagonisms, including large-scale, bloody warfare. This divisiveness has demonstrated itself both between proponents and followers of some of the major world religions (for example, between Christianity and Mohammedanism) and be-tween separate segments within a major religion on occasions and under circumstances where religious belief or practices are involved. Because of variations of beliefs, there is always the schismatic tendency. Each religious organization tends to have its special set of God's Commands, and many of these affect social action.

In the United States, the major cleavages are (1) between the Catholic Church and the Protestant churches as groups, especially with respect to a considerable number of pertinent social issues, and (2)

[22] R. M. MacIver, *Society*. New York: Farrar & Rinehart, 1937, p. 319.

between the smaller, newer fundamentalist sects and the older, larger Protestant denominations, though there are also still cleavages within the great denominations. These Protestant cleavages rest not only upon doctrinal differences, but relate also to such factors as class differences, racial and nationality differentiation, and regional divergences in viewpoints on crucial social issues.

Religious division and conflict grow out of the fact that religion is fundamentally a matter of beliefs about the extrahuman and the supernatural which have been rationalized and systematized in the form of theologies, creeds, and usually mythologies. Each religious group is convinced that it has the only true faith and the only method of salvation. Since the efficacy of these beliefs, articles of faith, and sanctified practice, because of their very nature, cannot be proved by any mundane means, every divergent set of beliefs is a standing criticism, challenge, even a nullification of every other. The followers of any given belief can feel secure in their faith only when all contending or contrary faiths have been eliminated.

Every religious group is always, by its very nature, a highly ethnocentric group. It is not only superior; it is always right. In fact, it cannot continue to exist if there is doubt as to its sole and fundamental rightness and truth. Other religious groups are always benighted heathen or non-believers. Hence there is always some degree of at least quiet intolerance, always some latent—and often active—prejudice and antagonism. There is also a suspicion as to how these beliefs of others, and the influence of the organizations that promote the beliefs and organize and administer the action correlated with the beliefs, will affect the religion-related social action of the respective adherents.[23]

III: The Relation of Religious Institutions to All Other Institutions

Although religions are probably not as well integrated with other institutions or as dominant in a society like ours, as was the case in primitive and ancient societies, they nevertheless are a prominent part of the total institutional system. First, this is evident in the fact that there tends to be a congruence among all institutions wherever studied; the principle of sociocultural compatibility applies; the religious institutions must

[23] On religious conflict, see J. O. Hertzler, *Society in Action.* New York: Dryden, 1954, pp. 284–286. A. M. Rose, *Sociology: The Study of Human Relations.* New York: Knopf, 1956, pp. 498–500.

fit with the total way of life, be in accord with the other highly important and influential institutions of the community or society. Secondly, religious institutions are in a continuous state of functional interdependence and reciprocity with other institutions. Not only are the religious institutions affected by other institutions, but they also have much direct influential effect on conscience and ethics, on public policy, on government and law, on the economy, education, art, and science. The religious institutions lend these others their sanctions, their symbols, and their patterns of thought. Religious institutions are dominant over all others in a theocratic society, and still exercise much influence even in a secularized society like our own.

GENERAL INTERRELATIONSHIPS

In the case of the family, religion affects the choice of marriage partners, the structure of the family (for example, through its insistence upon monogamy or its permissiveness of polygamous unions), the relations among family members (the support of patriarchal control), the ethics of sexual behavior (virtue before and after marriage), the attitudes toward divorce, and the attitudes and practices regarding procreation (the use of contraceptives). In the United States, even though civil marriages are everywhere legal, the greater proportion of marriages are performed by religious officials; most of the important family ceremonials must still have religious sanction in many of the more secularized families.

Religious institutions show a close relationship with political institutions. This is even the case in the United States where we have complete separation of church and state, and sectarian or denominational neutrality in political affairs. Among us, a general Christian atmosphere influences the tone and limits of government; the blessings of religion are sought upon and for formal political occasions. In general, religious ethics are important in political action (for example, reformist activities), and in the formulation and administration of the law. Neither political parties nor factions can long withstand the opposition of religious groups to their practices and objectives if deemed questionable from the religious point of view. Historically, the organizational structure of religion has been a reflection of governmental structure.[24] Historically also, the massive legal codes of most of the civilizations of history have been attributed to divine, or at least have been supported by the belief of divine, authority for them. The close ties between

[24] "In France, for instance, there is still a bishop, as a rule, wherever there was a Roman Municipality, and an archbishop wherever there was a provincial capital." J. M. Robertson, *A Short History of Christianity*. London: Watts, 1902, p. 209.

religion and government are further revealed in the frequent conflict over hegemony between political and religious organizations, and the fact that totalitarian governments, fascist or communist, seek completely to control religion or to destroy it, so that they do not have to compete with it as a controlling agent or accommodate to it.

Military institutions have also been connected with religious institutions. Warfare has frequently been used to advance religions. Religion, in its conformity to the world, in wartime has usually blessed the military efforts of the state and joined in condemning those of the enemy. At the same time, some of the more humanitarian elements in religious organizations have condemned war as an institution.

There is much reciprocity between religious and economic institutions. The relationship between the Protestant ethic and the spirit of capitalism as developed by Max Weber has been widely discussed. The Protestant ethic, with its stress upon individualism, upon a life of action (work) as a prime means of advancing the Kingdom of God here and now, upon the avoidance of self-indulgence and weakness, upon self-discipline, honesty, thrift, and capital accumulation, on good works, and upon worldly individual success as a special sign of grace or heavenly favors, according to Weber, has created a psychological and ethical climate, favorable to the development of capitalist ideology and practices—and though this is definitely post-Weber—to the development of "Norman Vincent Peale-ism." Troeltsch and Tawney have also discussed the close relationship between Protestantism and Western capitalism, though differing in some respects from Weber's main points.[25]

Religious ethics also have an influence upon business and industrial practices, especially as to personnel relations and obligations and relations of producers, distributors, and consumers. Small factions within the larger religious organizations have, from time to time, challenged the going economic order and suggested reforms, for example, in working conditions (long hours, unhealthful conditions, morally hazardous conditions, and worker-employer relations). Religion in the main, however, has and does support the economic order. The free American denominations in all their activities are dependent upon their members for financial support, and the members are economic men in the present order.

Religious organizations have always had a direct concern with edu-

---

25 Cf.: Max Weber, *The Protestant Ethic and the Spirit of Capitalism* (T. Parsons, transl.). New York: Scribner's, 1930. R. Tawney, *Religion and the Rise of Capitalism*. New York: Harcourt, Brace, 1926. E. Troeltsch, *Social Teachings of the Christian Churches* (O. Wyon, transl.). New York: Macmillan, 1931.

cational institutions, because of the fact that education is the basic controlled socialization procedure. Education has been looked upon as an essential means of developing early religious values, attitudes, and loyalties. A completely secular educational system is quite recent in Western culture; in fact, until the nineteenth century, most secular education at all levels was provided under the auspices of religious organizations. In the United States very few sects and denominations attempt to provide elementary or secondary education for their members, though most put much effort into providing college education. The Catholics and some of the Lutheran denominations, of course, are the notable exceptions in that they provide both elementary and secondary parochial schools, though not all of their members avail themselves of these opportunities. A converse aspect of the situation is the fact that the multiplicity of American sects and denominations with their vast diversity of beliefs are greatly concerned about keeping public education free from particular religious influences.

Christianity, especially in the ancient and medieval eras, was much concerned with social welfare. From the outset it stressed alms and aid to the unfortunate. The hospices, as they developed, provided institutional care for the sick, orphans, the widowed and deserted, the feeble-minded and insane, unmarried mothers, the aged, and the unemployed, as well as shelter for travellers. In spite of the assumption of responsibility for much welfare work by the welfare state, the various churches and denominations operate hospitals, orphanages, and other child-care agencies, homes for the aged, social settlement and neighborhood houses. They also provide, in some instances, services to transients, aid to the handicapped, services to displaced and refugee persons and families, casework and family counseling, and psychiatric counseling services. They also frequently carry on or provide personnel for various other charitable enterprises, more or less informally, by means of their men's clubs, women's aid societies, and young people's organizations.

In simpler societies, the religious rites, rituals, ceremonies, and holy days were closely associated with what we call recreation. Today religious organizations conduct or foster various kinds of recreation as part of their own activity programs and in their own plants, such as bowling, dances, bridge, bingo, parties, suppers, all sorts of gymnasium sports, and interchurch bowling, baseball, and basketball leagues.

There has always been a close interdependence between religious and aesthetic institutions. Much of art, especially in the form of painting, statuary, the dance, music, drama, and literature has been religiously inspired. Such art forms have been used as media of religious expression, in general, as well as for particular organizational purposes; for example, in the symbolization of deities, sacred persons, sacred places, and sacred states, in the sacred books, in the sacred structures, in the hymnology, as media of instruction and indoctrination.[26]

Special Relationships

A somewhat different aspect of the interrelationships of religion with other areas of life is the relation of religious and scientific institutions, and the relationship between religion and morals.

Religion and science are frequently presented as in conflict, and they are made to be so by some of their respective devotees. Actually though, they are intimately related, both historically and with respect to their functional jurisdictions. Man's original religion, in considerable part, grew out of his desire to understand, interpret, and, if possible, to control nature. At the beginning there was no distinction between religion and science. Primitive man's religion was also his science, and vice versa. Science as a method of investigation, discovery, interpretation, and invention developed slowly. In fact, the actual separation of science from religion is a relatively recent matter. In the medieval and early modern Western world, the scientific services were still largely rendered by Christian monks.

At the present time, they are functionally correlated institutions. Both are concerned with the explanation of the universe and an interpretation of its constituent structures, forces, and processes. But religion is concerned with providing explanations and interpretations of the vast unknowns, the illimitable supernatural realm beyond the grasp of the senses, the realm of beliefs regarding the nature of things. Science is concerned with the known or what is potentially knowable. By means of its methods of exploration and investigation, it is continually extracting knowns from the heretofore unknown, and accumulating new facts and principles. Thus science continually takes over explanatory and control tasks from religion. The vaunted differences between religion and science do not present a situation that requires reconciliation, as some put it, but simply a recognition of division of interpretative labor in accommodating to the phenomena of the universe. Religion is not unscientific, and science is not irreligious; strictly speaking, however, neither can be the other.

Science, of course, has done much changing of the views of men regarding the cosmos; many causes, processes, and essences, once unknown or attributed to the supernatural, have been securely placed in the realm of the real and the usable. As science penetrates new areas of the unknown and presents definite new facts and principles regarding

26 For further treatment of some of the institutional interdependencies just mentioned, see: Wach, *Sociology of Religion*, pp. 205–330. Hoult, *op. cit.*, pp. 175–380.

these areas, religion is, or should be, continually modified; for example, with respect to its ethics, its conceptions and interpretations of space and time, and of human welfare and ends. But there will always be much that we are more or less conscious of or concerned about that we do not comprehend or understand at any given time; and this world beyond science and revealed by faith only will always be very important. Religion and science thus will continue to be cooperators in making man feel at home in the universe.

Of special significance also is the close tie-up in practice everywhere and at all times between religious institutions and the ethical systems of peoples. The ethical system is so important in the order and operation of a society that there is some justification for considering it a separate block of institutions. However, it does not have a separate and distinct set of needs which it must satisfy, as do the major institutional orders. Rather, the ethical system operates through all the other institutional systems, and stands behind all other institutions. The ethical principles and requirements, because of their very nature, come into play in all of the various obligations of life—professional, civic, domestic, philanthropic, recreational, social. They express themselves entirely in other institutional relationships—sexual relations, domestic relations, economic relations, play relations, and health relations. In general, the ethical system of a people is a universal regulative agency which, of necessity, must permeate every area of social life.

There is a tendency among many to make religion and ethics practically identical with respect to their influence on conduct. They both do have regulative effects; but their ultimate objectives differ. Fundamentally, ethics is concerned with the relationships of men here and now on earth; religion is concerned with the relationship of man to some higher power, or powers, or idea. Ethical systems consist of the standardized or systematized and more or less durable ideas of right and wrong, or good and bad, in the daily conduct among a people, along with the accompanying principles, mores, customs, and the definite codes. They set up ways of acting that are approved of and required, and designate others that are definitely forbidden and punished. They exist because men must act in certain ways while among their fellows. Their objectives are, therefore, purely temporal and social; certain conduct is necessary in social groups here and now.

The interdependence of religion and ethics is reciprocal. Each sustains the other and is used by the other. First, religion has been almost everywhere appropriated to support the ethical codes. People have been clever enough to see that if they put these purely social requirements under the irrefutable and inexorable jurisdiction of the omnipresent, omniscient, and omnipotent gods, and if they utilized the scheme of supernatural rewards and punishments to support their purely mundane codes, these codes would have an efficacy that no mere social imagination or desire for group welfare would provide. It would give them at least the appearance of inviolability and of transcendental importance. There is no doubt that religion has given morality an auxiliary motivation and support.

On the other hand, religion has frequently appropriated at least portions of the ethical codes. This is in part owing to the fact that in the last analysis the ultimate check upon a man's religion is his conduct, and the conduct we can know about consists essentially of his performance among his fellows. Hence we find a blending of religious and moral requirements. Ethical rightness is supposed to reflect religious beliefs; religious correctness is reflected in moral behavior. Religion is supposed to supply the source, nature, and sanctions of moral goodness; at the same time it is usually a supporter of the social order as ethically envisaged.

This reciprocity is evidenced in the intermingling of the duties to gods and men, in the conduct codes of the world religions, both local and universal. Notable as ethical requirements having central religious significance are the great moral triad of Zoroaster with its life pattern woven out of good thoughts, good words, and good deeds; the Noble Eightfold Path of Gautama consisting of right views, right aims, right speech, right conduct, right livelihood, right effort, rightmindfulness, and right contemplation; the innumerable Confucian principles of behavior for the superior man. There are also vast bodies of precepts, admonitions, proverbs, parables, and myths interwoven in the religions of all people—primitive, ancient, modern. Both religious and moral requirements are stated in the bodies of commandments, as in the Negative Confessions of the ancient Egyptians, the ten commandments of Gautama, and the decalogues of the Hebrews. The enunciation of the law of love is surprisingly frequent, appearing in the proverbs of many primitives, in the thought of Laotze, Gautama, Mencius, and of course in the Hebrew and Christian thought. Especially significant is the frequent and widespread appearance of the Golden Rule, or the Silver Rule, as its negative expression is sometimes called, in both the religious and secular literature of many cultures.[27] The great legal codes of antiquity continually intermingle the duties to the gods and to men. Almost all of the religions emphasize, at least in certain areas of life, service, kindness, justice, charity, and righteousness.

It should be noted that although religion has tended to elevate the moral standards of most societies in most instances, primarily it has given its sanction to the current codes and standards, which means that

27 Cf. J. O. Hertzler, "On Golden Rules," *Int. Jour. Ethics*, 44 (July, 1934): 418–436.

it has sanctioned a great variety of conduct.[28] It should also be noted that the social demands of religion sometimes lag behind the moral standard; they sanction the mores of some previous time. The moral standards, relating directly and absolutely to essential action, must meet immediate behavioral needs. Religion, being in the main conservative, catches up later.[29]

IV: Some Special Characteristics of American Religion

Certain special characteristics and trends of American religion relate directly to special characteristics of American social philosophy and societal makeup and to certain changes that have been taking place in American life. Although startling in some instances, they are nevertheless quite understandable. Many factors are involved: among the more important are the increasing urbanization of the population with all that it implies in the way of effects upon the individual, family, and community life; the increasing development of science and technology and the effects, not only on the daily physical life, but also in the thinking of the people; our social-political philosophy of complete religious freedom; our class system and "success" philosophy; and certain highly influential changes in other closely related institutional areas.

One of the marked features of American religious life during the last three decades has been the soaring membership in almost all faiths. The National Council of Churches reports that in the last 30 years United States church membership has doubled while the population increased by 40 per cent. If we go back to 1880 we find that only 20 per cent of the American people were members of American churches. As of 1956 some 60 per cent were stated to be church members. Membership in American churches is now growing at a rate of approximately 3 per cent per year, while the population is growing at a

[28] "It [religion] has supported the use of the old, in the matter of foods, instruments, processes, and products, has favored both war and peace, wealth and poverty, diligence and idleness, virginity and prostitution, humility and ostentation, indulgence and austerity. It has prescribed game-laws, cannibalism, human sacrifice, the killing of the aged, suicide, incest, polyandry, polygyny, slavery, and the levirate, has guaranteed all forms of property-holding, of inheritance, and of government, has both favored and proscribed commerce and the taking of interest; it has been forced to bend to new vices." W. E. H. Lecky, *History of European Morals.* New York: Appleton, 1869, Vol. II, p. 294.

[29] On the relation of religion and ethics, see: Sumner and Keller, *op. cit.,* pp. 1463–1464. Wach, *Sociology of Religion,* pp. 49–53. Firth, *op. cit.,* pp. 225–226. Yinger, *Religion, Society and the Individual,* pp. 28–30. R. M. MacIver and C. H. Page, *Society.* New York: Rinehart, 1949, pp. 168–174.

rate of one and one-half per cent per year. According to the 1956 *Yearbook* of the Council of Churches, there were 60,148,980 Protestants in the nation, 1,700,000 more than in 1955. Roman Catholics numbered 34,563,851, up 1,167,204 from 1955. Jews numbered 5½ million, the same as reported for the previous year; and Eastern Orthodox communicants, 2,598,055, up 212,000.[30] There are other evidences of an apparent increase of interest in religion, such as the very considerable increase in the number of religious books published, the rise of many religious books to best-seller lists, the popularity of syndicated religious columns in some newspapers, the numerous articles on religion in mass-circulation magazines, and the popularity of motion pictures involving religious themes.

In spite of these surprising figures on the increase of church membership and these other apparent evidences of religiosity, no responsible person maintains that the American people are three times as religious today as they were in 1880. Certainly, there is not much evidence of a more rigorous conformity to the fundamental principles of Christianity, nor do the social ethics show any notable improvement.

A number of causal or contributory factors of varying and still undetermined weight and validity have been advanced to explain this increase in organizational membership and apparent concern for things religious. Some credit it to a more and more concerted quest for security in our present kind of world; for example, a groping for supernatural protection against annihilation by A- or H-bombs or engulfment by the expanding Communist world. Herberg finds the increased interest in religion arises out of a personal need that modern man has to preserve some remnant of personality and inwardness against the massive erosions effected by a mass culture.[31] There is also the possibility that with increasing rationality, scientism, stress on technology, the often disillusioning pursuit of happiness, gain, and success, people need the comfort and assurance that firmly established religious goals sometimes give. Niebuhr notes that our "gadget-filled paradise" does not necessarily prepare men to attain to the final goals of life or "fulfill the meaning of human existence."[32]

There also seem to be more specifically sociological and social psychological factors. With the marked increase in marriage and birth rates, there has been a corresponding increase in young families with young children. Many of these depend not only on the schools but also

---

[30] *Yearbook of American Churches for 1956.* New York: National Council of Churches of Christ in U.S.A., 1956.

[31] Will Herberg, *Protestant, Catholic, Jew: An Essay on American Religious Sociology.* Garden City, N.Y.: Doubleday, 1956, p. 61.

[32] Reinhold Niebuhr, *Pious and Secular America.* New York: Scribner's, 1958, p. 13.

on various church organizations and influences for a considerable amount of ethical instruction and social disciplining. Also, with the shrinking in size of home plants, the churches with their Sunday Schools, parties, athletics, and recreational activities provide various activities for the children that relieve the pressure at home. The very fact of increasing memberships provides certain utilitarian and egotic advantages, such as the opportunity for making valuable economic, especially professional, contacts, with an implied commitment by the contactee because of a joint, even selected, membership; the opportunity to meet right and respectable people; and enjoyment of the prestige, or at least the comforting thought, of doing the right thing. The churches provide the opportunity of belonging to a respectable club. There is also the fact that the old people are an ever larger proportion of the population. They are closer to the end and want some sort of insurance against the uncertainties of eternity.

Perhaps the most important factor of all grows out of the anonymity and loneliness of individuals and families under the conditions of modern urbanized, crowded, culturally massed, secularized, secondary-group life. Most of the churches have succeeded in establishing themselves locally as integral communities, as welcoming associations of friendly cooperative people. It is questionable whether many of the adherents are very clear about the nature of the beliefs they nominally support, or care very much what they are; the belonging is more important for them.

Also causally or correlatively related as factors in the increasing church membership is the secularization of religion, and the development of the so-called institutional church.[33]

THE GREAT DIVERSITY OF RELIGIOUS ORGANIZATIONS

It is virtually impossible to describe the system of religion of contemporary American society according to any standard characteristics. It is made up of a great diversity of denominations and sects, each with its somewhat distinctive beliefs and organizational forms. Many of the organizations vary with respect to the stratum level of the bulk of their respective members.

One of the most conspicuous features of religion in our society is its great heterogeneity. We even find among us followers of Buddhism, Mohammedanism, and Hinduism. However, the great bulk of affiliates with religious organizations falls within three major rubrics. On the

[33] Needless to say, this vast increase in church membership has created considerable concern about over-taxed church plants, bulging Sunday Schools, church additions, new buildings, and shortage of ministers and other professional personnel.

basis of a survey conducted by the U.S. Census Bureau in March, 1957, these estimates of the religious leanings of Americans, ages fourteen years and over, are available.[34]

Protestant	79 million	or	61.2 per cent of total
Roman Catholic	30.7 million	or	30.7 per cent of total
Jewish	3.9 million	or	3.2 per cent of total
Other religion	1.5 million	or	1.3 per cent of total
No religion	3.2 million	or	2.7 per cent of total
Not reported	1.1 million	or	0.9 per cent of total

These general figures tell us only part of the story with respect to diversity. Although Roman Catholicism presents a united front, it has had to contend with nationality diversities and disagreements, though these have been kept down. Judaism is divided into three different groups on the basis of degrees of orthodoxy-liberalism. Protestantism is infinitely splintered. Most of the 258 different religious groups most recently reported are Protestant sects or denominations. More than 90 per cent of all Protestants in the United States, to be sure, are members of 10 denominational families: Baptist (with 23.5 million according to the Census report indicated above), Methodist (16.7 million), Lutheran (8.4 million), Presbyterian (6.7 million), and with lesser numbers in order of membership, Episcopal, Disciples, Congregational Christian, Churches of Christ, Evangelical and Reformed, and Evangelical United Brethren.[35] The remainder of Protestants are distributed among many smaller denominations and sects, some with memberships of only a few thousand. Many of the Protestant denominations themselves are further diversified. For example, the *Yearbook of American Churches for 1957,* based on the 1955 situation, reports 27 different subdenominations or sects among the Baptists, 22 among the Methodists, 19 among the Lutherans, 14 among the Mennonites (with a total membership of 168,624), 10 among the Presbyterians, and lesser subdivisions among others. Not only are there these multiple separations and variations among and within the denominational families, but it is also significant to note that many new sects are continually being formed, though most of them are small and short-lived.

[34] Reported in *U.S. News and World Report,* Feb. 7, 1958. In view of the discrepancy between the figures quoted from the *Yearbook of American Churches* and the present ones, it should be noted that the National Council of Churches, the U.S. Census, and the separate religious bodies themselves, use different methods and criteria of reckoning, and also that the respective estimates were made at different times.

[35] The Church of Christ Scientist releases no figures, and Jehovah's Witnesses keep no membership roll.

There are certain more or less obvious factors responsible for this situation. We have complete separation of church and state and no established or state church. This means that under our Constitution there is no partiality by the government toward any one group, nor may government finance religious groups, undertake religious instruction, blend secular and sectarian education, or use secular institutions to force any religion on any person. The government must be neutral when it comes to competition between sects. It may not make a religious observance compulsory, nor may it coerce anyone to attend church, observe a religious holiday, or take religious instruction.[36] There are thus no official beliefs or requirements.

A related factor is the complete religious freedom, as guaranteed by the Constitution, and a widespread religious tolerance with respect to both belief and worship. The freedom of religion permits any variety of belief among or within denominations or sects. Thus we can have theological variation with a range including Unitarians-Universalists and other humanists at one extreme, through the great number of middle-of-the-roaders, though even these have their Fundamentalist-Modernist and Conservative-Liberal wings, to the Penitential Holiness Church at the other extreme. There may be wide differences in given denominations; for example, those of High, Low, and Broad Churchmen among the Episcopalians. In general, religious freedom encourages both the refinement and the splintering of beliefs, and invites corresponding suborganizations built around the beliefs. At the same time, tolerance relieves the likelihood of any serious restraints upon diverse or even eccentric beliefs, and of discrimination against, or persecution of, those holding them.

Of central importance is the great cultural and ethnic heterogeneity of the American people. Because of our immigrant origin, we are of different races and of many different nationalities. Many of our population, or their ancestors, were dissenters in Europe and came to the United States as a haven of religious freedom. The immigrant nationalities often settled in considerable isolation by nationality or religious grouping. With the differential cultural assimilation and with the succeeding more Americanized generations came splits of various kinds. Some of these earlier organizational cleavages still persist; for example, several of the separate Lutheran synods still rest upon original nationality-language differences. Several of our larger denominational families have not yet fully emerged from the regional-racial slavery (now White-Negro) issue. There is also the great diversity of value-systems, of

[36] These and other points were brought out by Mr. Justice W. O. Douglas in *Zorach v. Clauson* (U.S. Supreme Court, 1952).

moral norms and behavior, of levels of intellectual sophistication and education, of social participation and power, of socio-economic status and ideology among the population—all of which tend to bring with them compliant kinds and interpretations of beliefs and different kinds of religious activities.

Such diversity is bound to bring some divisiveness and lack of religious unity either in belief or in religiously inspired effort. Of course, a sort of general Christian commonality prevails, and there is no utter or even serious separation, but in spite of tolerance, there is still considerable sectarian bigotry. Also the sects frequently seek social dominance over each other, try to convert the members of rival sects, and feel sorry for the unregenerate others. Also there is significant theological diversity and a frequent inability of the members or representatives of the different religious bodies to get together on important ethical-humanitarian issues. One notes the occasional lack of rapport or community among the large denominations, and especially the divisiveness between the larger and old denominations and the newer sects and cults, such as the Mormons, the Christian Scientists, the Nazarenes, and Jehovah's Witnesses. There are the marked differences with regard to the ethics of certain population issues, minority group problems, war, and democracy. It is at least amusing to note that bingo (or the profits made from it) is blessed for some religionists and sinful for others. All this means compartmentalization of religious beliefs and norms, and fragmentation of religious efforts.

At the same time, it should be pointed out that there are coordinative efforts among America's diverse religious groups. There is less and less controversy among denominations regarding doctrinal issues which once so divided them. Ministers, especially the younger ones, trained in given denominations' seminaries, are more and more interchangeable. There is wider interdenominational cooperation among certain lines made possible by means of the Federal Council of Churches of Christ in America (founded in 1908), and the interreligion cooperation through the National Conference of Jews and Christians, as well as by means of similar local and regional organizations. There is also a slight tendency toward church mergers. Since 1906 there have been at least 14 specific mergers affecting 32 separate religious bodies; notable fairly recently is the amalgamation of the Congregational and the Christian denominations, and the unification of several branches of Methodism.

American religion shows another special feature, closely related to the heterogeneity of the American population and American religious freedom and religious diversity. Religious organizations, especially the Protestant ones, have shown a close relationship to the system of strati-

fication almost from the beginning.[37] As early as the 1730's this alignment of members of given classes with particular types of religious
groups was evident. The older, more formal religions continued among
the dominant groups. The newer sects and denominations formed on
the frontier, and members were often recruited from dissenting and
sometimes refugee followers of various European ideological, reformative, or revolutionary movements. These people were more likely to
be mainly of the middle and lower classes. In the contemporary United
States, social class accompanies religion within the local community
and over the nation. When the national scene is viewed in its totality,
each major faith has its peculiar stratification features. The Roman
Catholics have a great class spread, and all classes are bound together
in the one great fellowship. However, because of historical selective
factors, especially the fact that such a large portion of the American
Catholic population is so largely recruited from lower-class Europeans
that have migrated to this country during the last century, a much greater
proportion of Catholics are lower and middle classes. This is in contrast
to the fact that the great proportion of the American upper classes are
Protestants, quite out of proportion to the ratio of Protestants to Roman
Catholics, Jews, and other general religions in the United States. The
Jews show some tendency to be socially stratified somewhat in correlation with their three major subdivisions on the basis of variations in
orthodoxy-liberalism, the most liberal being the most likely to be upper
class. Increasingly, however, a greater and greater proportion of the
Jews of the United States fall alongside the upper level Protestant
denominations in terms of income, education, and occupation. Yet,
relatively few Jews are accorded upper-class status outside their own
ethnic groups.

The Protestant denominations and sects, however, reflect the whole
range of American social strata, and different ones can be roughly correlated with given general class level. Since two-thirds of American
church members are Protestant, attention can be given mainly to the
relation between Protestant religious organizations and American social
classes. Attention has been given to this phenomenon by social scientific

[37] Religious values and organization have often influenced and have apparently always been involved with stratification systems. Furthermore, religion has usually supported existing stratification systems. Notable instances are
the 4000-year-old caste system of India, the older more rigid class system of
England (The Anglican Book of Prayer: "Lord, make me satisfied with my
station!"), and the support of the ethnic, especially racial, stratification in the
United States by certain denominations. It is also interesting to note that
Christianity itself in its early centuries was mainly a lower-class religious movement. Its members were scoffed at by the Roman and Eastern upper classes as a
collection of slaves, paupers, and riff-raff. Jerome, himself one of the great
Church Fathers, said that "the community of Christ" was recruited from *de
vili plebecula*."

investigators since the 1920's. The Lynds and Douglass[38] found significant positive correlations between Protestant church members and socio-economic status. Successive studies have made possible certain rather substantial generalizations. It should be understood that there is no precise and complete correlation. All denominations have members from all social classes, but particular denominations and even local congregations of these denominations and sects tend to draw their members from one class or immediately contiguous classes of the social strata. However, as Liston Pope has pointed out, although the membership of a church may cut across class lines, "control of the church and its policies is generally in the hands of officials drawn from one class."[39]

In general, the middle and upper classes are represented principally among the Episcopal, Congregational, and Presbyterian Protestant denominations; the middle predominantly and, to a small extent, the upper classes among the Methodists, Baptists, Lutherans, and Disciples of Christ; the lower classes by such organizations as the Holy Rollers, Jehovah's Witnesses, Seventh Day Adventists, Nazarenes, Church of God, the Four Square Gospel, and the Church of Divine Science.

In general, the upper- and middle-class denominations are characterized by a membership composed mostly of professional, business, managerial, upper white-collar, and upper-level service vocations, and have a higher income level, higher educational and cultural attainment. Their religious organizations are the older established denominations with a more formal and secularized religion which is likely to stress religious and ethical properties and aesthetic elements. The lower-class denominations, and especially sects, consist largely of industrial, craft, semi-skilled, and lower white-collar workers, with, on the whole, lower incomes and more limited education. Their religion is the emotional sort, characteristic of people suffering exclusion and culture shock; it is mainly fundamentalist and evangelical; for example, the holiness and Pentacostal sects.

In spite of the increase in membership and what might be interpreted as an increase in religious interest, there is much point to the contention that American religion is becoming more and more secularized. This secularization is also related to religious diversity; for with many contending religious groups, none are dominant, and there is a lack of specific unification on religious issues. As early as the 1920's the Lynds noted that the churches in Middletown seemed to be consciously en-

---

[38] R. S. and H. M. Lynd, *Middletown*. New York: Harcourt, Brace, 1929, pp. 530–531. H. P. Douglass, *The Springfield Church Survey*. New York: Harper, 1926, pp. 41–42.

[39] Liston Pope, "Religion and the Class Structure," *Annals Am. Acad. Pol. & Soc. Science*, 256 (Mar., 1948): 84–90.

gaged in secularizing their programs in order to retain the interest and
support of their members as they attached more and more significance
to getting along in the world.[40] Various factors are involved in this
weakening of the line between the sacred and the secular. Because of
the impact of the development of science and the dissemination of
scientific knowledge among the population, many of the precious mysteries of the past once explained on supernatural grounds are not
supernatural any more from the point of view of many church members. Also important is the fact that as a society becomes more culturally
complex and its population becomes more and more heterogeneous, the
religious backgrounds, interests, and aspirations of the people come to
differ widely, and economic, artistic, intellectual, or other interests become substitutes for the strictly religious pattern. Also as religious consensus becomes more diffuse and weak, dominant secular value-themes,
such as success and social service come to be more and more important.
It is possible also that the very tolerance of Americans in religious matters makes agreement regarding religious fundamentals less certain.
At any rate, there is less attention to sacred tradition and supernatural-
ism, less stress on doctrinal matters, creedal demands, and what was
once called religious observances, in fact, a considerable liquidation
of belief in transcendental ends and supernatural entities. Religious
beliefs and activities, as rigorously defined, seem to occupy a relatively
small share of the satisfactions that people expect to enjoy in life.[41]
There is also a definite decline in revivalism, especially among the
comfortable upper- and middle-class denominations, such as the Episcopalians, Presbyterians, Congregationalists, Methodists, and Baptists.

What are some of the substitutes and effects of this secularization
of religion? It is coming to be dominated by utilitarian standards and
success values. If you "think positively," you will be successful in your
business or profession, be promoted, get rich, be asked to join the best
clubs, and so on. The congregation is a sort of Kiwanis chapter or even
country club for the right people—both sexes and all ages. In fact, there
seems to be evidence of a complete reversion of values. "What is good
for the bitch-goddess Success is good for God." It would seem that for
many people success has become the modern equivalent of salvation.

The present church seems to exercise relatively little moral authority,
in spite of the fact that its membership is such a large part of the population, in itself possibly an evidence of secularization. Church membership is so easy. The church no longer provides a challenging and
demanding reformative code of its own; it depends on the value themes

---

[40] *Op. cit.,* Ch. XXII.
[41] W. S. Salisbury, "Religion and Secularization," *Soc. Forces,* 36 (Mar.,
1958): 197–205.

and the ethics of the environing social order. The church membership seems to have no pronounced moral consensus; for example, with respect to business ethics, polite gambling, population ethics, war, and divorce. It should be said, however, that the churches are probably closer together on the so-called social creeds than they are on theology.

A secular society is also distrustful of ecclesiastical authority. When religion becomes secularized, the religious professionals—clergymen and priests—are relatively less influential than political, economic, educational, and scientific leaders. An increasingly stressed development in the secularization of our religion is its alliance with psychotherapy— psychotherapy clothed in religious terms; individuals find easy salvation on the couch for the sorts of problems that were met in much more rigorous fashion under a sterner religious regimen. One other evidence of secularization, among many possible ones, is the conversion of holy days into commercialized, vulgarized holidays; Easter, for example, is an orgy of Fifth Avenue fashion and Christmas, a studiously fostered orgy of merchandise bartering involving informal, but nevertheless somewhat strict accounting methods.

The development of the so-called institutional church during the present century has been another significant religious and social organizational phenomenon. Confronted with the competition with other community agencies for attention, with new interests (some closely related to secularization), with the very real problems of an increasingly urban membership, with constituents having more free time and leisure, and with the necessity of competing with other churches, there has been a tendency for modern town and city churches to develop and conduct a considerable number of service programs and projects, and also to develop the physical facilities and sometimes provide additional specialized personnel to conduct these programs. Most of this resolves itself into an additional and extended non-religious "busyness."

Among the services provided are the conducting of various kinds of recreational and entertainment activities, sometimes for all ages, such as basketball, baseball, billiards, pool, bowling, card games, suppers, dinners, parties, dramatic clubs, dancing clubs, senior citizen clubs, photography clubs, and movies. Many of these recreational services, in addition to being a means of retaining and developing a hold on members of all ages, also, by providing recreation under safe supervision and auspices, are creating a defense against the more gross, commercialized forms of recreation. Many of the institutionalized churches also have Wolf Packs, Brownies, and Boy and Girl Scout troops, and conduct summer camps. A recent "must," coming with the burgeoning of the birth rate, has been the installation of nursery schools and kindergarten facilities, particularly for the Sunday care of the young, while their parents attend to other church activities. Some provide facilities for adult education. Some, especially those with a humanistic emphasis—and these have been increasing with secularization—carry on social problems discussion clubs concerned with such items as labor problems, the Negro problem (often somewhere else), housing, marriage and family problems, civic problems, and international affairs; some also maintain forums and lecture programs. Musical opportunities are offered by choirs for all ages, orchestras, and bands. Some conduct various social welfare activities, such as providing employment services, deaconess or even visiting nurse service, health classes and clinics (especially baby clinics), day nurseries, aid to the handicapped. Another recent "must" is the provision of marriage and family counselling and psychiatric counselling services.

This vast extension and diversification of church functions have added demands made upon the clergyman or priest and his associated aids. In addition to the professional's traditional functions as preacher, teacher, leader of rituals and worships, and confessor, he now is expected to conduct or be responsible for one or more of such additional functions as budget-maker and financier, public relations man, administrator and promoter, civic leader, mental counsellor, arbitrator and conciliator, educational director, psychiatrist, social worker, athletic coach, and recreational director.

Not everyone is pleased with this whirl of activities of the modern institutionalized church. In a survey conducted by the Associated Press in June 1956 and released July 29, 1956, a considerable number of the pastors felt that they were "swamped." One spoke of the "day-to-day triviality" of the church, its round of fund drives, bazaars, luncheons, dinners, and bake sales. All this, he said, is "admirable, but it is not religion." Another stated that the churches have kept adding "odds and ends of new responsibilities until they resemble a modern drugstore or shopping center." A noted European churchman, after a visit here, suggested that American churches in a way resemble "people's clubs." A mother wrote that "our church is destroying our home" by its constant, week-long rush of meetings, recreation, fellowships, and other activities.

In connection with both the increase of church membership and the development of the institutional church, four special necessities stand out for the modern American congregation: the increase in size and in complexity of equipment of the church plant; the diversification of skills and services to be provided by its professional personnel; the increase of the church budget; and last, and not without significance, with widely scattered members coming to church by auto and the problems of parking on contiguous streets, the absolute essential that all church plants also include a parking lot involving space in the ratio of one auto parking space for every 2 to 3 people attending peak-attendance events.

All of the characteristics of American religion here examined cause some concern to those who are concerned with the reign of religion at its best, and give considerable significance to a statement made by Walter Lippman more than 40 years ago:

"When churches cease to paint the background of our lives, to nourish a *Weltanschauung,* strengthen man's ultimate purposes and reaffirm the deepest values of life, then the churches have ceased to meet the needs for which they exist."[42]

BIBLIOGRAPHY

GENERAL

Annals Am. Acad. Pol. & Soc. Science, "Religion in American Society," 332 (Nov., 1960): entire issue.

Argyle, M., *Religious Behavior.* London: Routledge & Kegan Paul, 1959.

Davis, K., *Human Society.* New York: Macmillan, 1949, pp. 509–548.

Douglas, H. P., and Brunner, E. de S., *The Protestant Church as a Social Institution.* New York: Harper, 1935.

Dunlap, K., *Religion, Its Functions in Human Life.* New York: McGraw-Hill, 1946.

Durkheim, E., *The Elementary Forms of the Religious Life* (S. W. Swain, transl.). Glencoe, Ill.: Free Press, 1947 (orig. 1915).

Eister, A. W., "Religious Institutions in Complex Societies," *Am. Soc. Rev.* 22 (Aug., 1957): 387–391.

Firth, Raymond, *Elements of Social Organization.* New York: Phil. Lib., 1951, pp. 215–250.

Good, Alvin, "Religion," in Roucek, J. S. (ed.), *Social Control* (rev. ed.), Princeton, N.J.: Van Nostrand, 1956, pp. 107–117.

Goode, W. J., *Religion among the Primitives.* Glencoe, Ill.: Free Press, 1951.

Green, A. W., *Sociology.* New York: McGraw-Hill, 1952, pp. 414–452.

Grafton, T. H., "Religious Origins and Sociological Theory," *Am. Soc. Rev.,* 10 (Dec., 1945): 726–739.

Hertzler, J. O., "Religious Institutions," *Annals Am. Acad. Pol. & Soc. Science,* 256 (Mar., 1948): 1–13.

Hoult, T. F., *The Sociology of Religion.* New York: Dryden, 1958.

Kirkpatrick, C., *Religion in Human Affairs.* New York: Wiley, 1929.

Malinowski, B., *Magic, Science and Religion.* Boston: Beacon Press, 1948.

Niebuhr, H. R., *Social Sources of Denominationalism.* New York: Holt, 1929.

Niebuhr, H. R., *Pious and Secular America.* New York: Scribner's, 1958.

Nottingham, Elizabeth K., *Religion and Society.* Garden City, N.Y.: Doubleday, 1954.

Martindale, D., *American Society.* Princeton, N.J.: Van Nostrand, 1960, pp. 277–289.

Mumford, L., *The Conduct of Life.* New York: Harcourt, Brace, 1951, pp. 58–76; 86–91.

---

[42] W. Lippman, *A Preface to Politics.* New York: Holt, 1917, pp. 181–182.

Parsons, T., *The Social System*. Glencoe, Ill.: Free Press, 1951, pp. 367–379.

Perry, R. B., *Realms of Value: A Critique of Civilization*. Cambridge: Harvard Univ. Press, 1954, pp. 463–492.

Pfautz, H. W., "The Sociology of Secularization: Religious Groups," *Am. Jour. Soc.*, 61 (Sept., 1955): 121–128.

Radcliffe-Brown, A. R., *Structure and Function in Primitive Society*. London: Cohen & West, Ltd., 1952, pp. 153–177.

Wach, J., *Sociology of Religion*. Chicago: Univ. of Chicago Press, 1944.

Wach, J., *The Comparative Study of Religion*. New York: Columbia Univ. Press, 1958.

Weber, Max, *The Protestant Ethic and the Spirit of Capitalism* (T. Parsons, transl.). London: Allen & Unwin, 1930.

White, L. A., *The Evolution of Culture*. New York: McGraw-Hill, 1959, pp. 354–362.

Yinger, J. M., *Religion in the Struggle for Power*. Durham, N.C.: Duke Univ. Press, 1946.

Yinger, J. M., *Religion, Society and the Individual*. New York: Macmillan, 1957.

DIFFERENT TYPES OF RELIGIOUS ORGANIZATIONS

Francis, E. K., "Toward a Typology of Religious Order," *Am. Jour. Soc.*, 44 (Mar., 1939): 649–682.

Hoult, T. F., *Sociology of Religion*. New York: Dryden, 1958, pp. 77–82.

Nottingham, E. K., *Religion and Society*. Garden City, N.Y.: Doubleday, 1954, pp. 62–64, 67–69.

Pfautz, H. W., "The Sociology of Secularization: Religious Groups," *Am. Jour. Soc.*, 61 (Sept., 1955): 121–128.

Troeltsch, E., *Social Teachings of the Christian Churches* (O. Wyon, transl.). New York: Macmillan, 1931, pp. 333–343.

Wach, J., *Sociology of Religion*. Chicago: Chicago Univ. Press, 1944, pp. 109–205, 370–374.

Wach, J., *Church, Denomination and Sect*. Evanston, Ill.; Seabury Western Theological Seminary, 1946.

Wiese, L., and Becker, H., *Systematic Sociology*. New York: Wiley, 1932, pp. 624–642.

Yinger, J. M., *Religion, Society and the Individual*. New York: Macmillan, 1957, pp. 142–155.

FUNCTIONS OF RELIGION

Dunlap, K., *Religion, Its Functions in Human Life*. New York: McGraw-Hill, 1946.

Hunt, C. L., "Religious Ideology as a Means of Social Control," *Soc. & Soc. Res.*, 33 (Jan., 1949): 180–187.

Loomis, C. P., and Beegle, J. A., *Rural Sociology: The Strategy of Change*. Englewood Cliffs, N.J.: Prentice-Hall, 1957, pp. 203–210.

Nottingham, E. K., *Religion and Society*. Garden City, N.Y.: Doubleday, 1954, pp. 12–18.

Yinger, J. M., *Religion, Society and the Individual*. New York: Macmillan, 1957, pp. 49–72.

STRATIFICATION AND RELIGIOUS ORGANIZATIONS

Dynes, R. R., "Church-Sect Typology and Socio-Economic Status," *Am. Soc. Rev.,* 20 (Oct., 1955): 555–560.

Goldschmidt, W. R., "Class Denominationalism in Rural California Churches," *Am. Jour. Soc.,* 49 (Jan., 1944): 348–355.

Holt, J. B., "Holiness Religion: Cultural Shock and Social Reorganization," *Am. Soc. Rev.,* 5 (Oct., 1940): 740–747.

Hoult, T. F., "Economic Class Consciousness in American Protestantism," I, II, *Am. Soc. Rev.,* 15 (Feb., 1950): 97–100; 17 (June, 1952): 349–350.

Hoult, T. F., *The Sociology of Religion.* New York: Dryden, 1958, pp. 278–319 (includes extensive bibliography).

Obenhaus, V., Schroeder, W. W., and England, C. O., "Church Participation Related to Social Class and Type of Center," *Rural Soc.,* 23 (Sept., 1958): 298–308.

Phelps, H. A., and Henderson, D., *Population in Its Human Aspects.* New York: Appleton, 1959, pp. 310–314.

Pope, Liston, *Millhands and Preachers.* New Haven: Yale Univ. Press, 1942.

Pope, Liston, "Religion and the Class Structure," *Annals Am. Acad. Pol. & Soc. Science.,* 256 (Mar., 1948): 84–91.

Warner, W. L., Meeker, Marcia, and Eells, K., *Social Class in America.* Chicago: Science Research Associates, 1949.

Yinger, J. M., *Religion, Society and the Individual.* New York: Macmillan, 1957, pp. 131–133; 156–194.

AMERICAN RELIGIOUS TRENDS AND CONDITIONS

Braden, C. S., *These Also Believe: A Study of Modern American Cults and Minority Religious Movements.* New York: Macmillan, 1949.

Clark, E. T., *The Small Sects in America.* New York: Abingdon Press, 1949.

Cogley, J. (ed.), *Religion in America: Original Essays on Religion in a Free Society.* New York: Meridian Books, 1958.

Dynes, R. R., "The Relation of Community Characteristics to Religious Organization and Behavior," Sussman, M. B. (ed.), *Community Structure and Analysis.* New York: Crowell, 1959, pp. 254–268.

Hoult, T. F., *Sociology of Religion.* New York: Dryden, 1958, pp. 82–90, 94–113.

Niebuhr, H. R., *Pious and Secular America.* New York: Scribner's, 1958, esp. pp. 1–13.

Nottingham, E. K., *Religion and Society.* Garden City, N.Y.: Doubleday, 1954, pp. 72–81.

Salisbury, W. S., "Religion and Secularization," *Soc. Forces,* 36 (Mar., 1958): 197–205.

Schneider, H. W., *Religion in the Twentieth Century.* Cambridge: Harvard Univ. Press, 1952.

Sullenger, T. E., "The Church in an Urban Society," *Soc. & Soc. Res.,* 41 (May–June, 1957): 361–366.

Yinger, J. M., *Religion, Society, and the Individual.* New York: Macmillan, 1957, pp. 265–294.

Art Institutions

Though the aesthetic urge and the art forms through which it is expressed, as well as the aesthetic interests of people generally, would seem to be part of the more luxurious, dilettante, or even effete aspects of life, art has been universal in man's social life, as common as his economic and religious interest and activity. Quite apart from its significance in itself, it has been universal in almost every phase of man's individual and social life in every known society and epoch, as archaeology, ethnology, and both art history and social history record. Even among the crudest of primitive men of which we know, living in the hardest natural environments, the theme of subsistence or mere physical existence never dominated their life to the exclusion of the arts.[1] Art is neither an incidental, isolated, nor accidental phenomenon among men. The aesthetic need is another one of those universal needs that must be satisfied in some adequate and more or less standard manner for everyone. Giving reality to artistic impulses and interests is not a mere idle pastime, not a mere submission to something fugitive and superficial in the life of man. It is a stern necessity of life, a form of individual and social catharsis whereby emotional and spiritual tensions are released, and a means of satisfying the unfulfilled yearnings of men as they are psychically constituted. Furthermore, the aesthetic life cannot be divorced from the rest of life; it is an integral part of the totality.

Art is important in social organization, for it has profound effects upon individuals in many of their interactions with each other and also upon groups. Not only does it have its own related and relevant social organizations, but everywhere it has pronounced institutional features.[2] Every one of us is confronted with art in its informal and formal, its

[1] Raymond Firth, *Elements of Social Organization.* New York: Phil. Lib., 1956, p. 155.

[2] Many social scientists, especially some sociologists, are becoming aware of the vast social significance of art in general, of art as social cause and effect, and of art in its various institutional forms. In fact, a "special" sociology, the sociology of art, is in process of rapid development, as attested by the burgeoning literature on the subject.

spontaneous and deliberately devised and manipulated manifestations. We are involved with art when we attend concerts, symphonies, operas, ballets, art galleries or dramatic performances, as we read about them in the newspapers and weekly and monthly journals, as we listen to or read poetry or other literature, as we view the magazine covers and advertisements, as we turn on our radio or television, as we attend a motion picture, as we behold buildings, or as we walk or ride through the business district of our town.

Art institutions are a special type of institution, however. They operate in an area of human individual and social life concerned with the sense-perceptions, the emotions, the expressional urges, the imagination, the sensory and spiritual satisfactions of men. The institutions are the means whereby these sensuous and spiritual needs and expectations are satisfied. By virtue of the more personalized, abstract, and, in the case of much art, the more transcendent, nature of both artistic expression and reception, and the variable nature of the media through which expression is sought, the institutional features are less precise and more difficult to get at than they are, for example, in the case of economic, political, and educational institutions; they are more like those of religious institutions, in this respect.

By art is meant, in general, the conscious and more or less articulate expression of aesthetic experience in some form perceptible through the human senses, mainly visual or auditory. Art takes common media or materials—stone, cement, paints, fabrics, sounds, metals, lines and other marks, words, bodily movements—and does something to them. By means of procedures, more or less formalized in all societies, it uses these materials; it shapes and arranges and combines them as symbols of sensed values and signal experiences, as special artifacts suffused with aesthetic meaning and charm. They then speak a widely understood language.

The essence of art is in aesthetic experience and aesthetic expression. Aesthetic experience has to do with the perceiving of something or the registering of consciousness regarding something that has being and value in the environment, something that arouses aesthetic interest. This something may be a combination of sounds, or colors, or shapes, or movements—some aesthetic element—which gives, to those persons involved, full and pure feeling and sensation, and possibly also intellectual satisfaction. It is something in nature or something that man has created that is good to behold, something to enjoy, something that pleases in terms of unity, proportion, diversity, balance, harmony, or unbalance; in terms of its total qualities, contrasts, blends, similarities, repetitions, gradations, intervals, rhythms; in terms of signal meanings or reactions suggested, as in the case, for example, of a symphony, a painting, a piece of sculpture, a sunset, a landscape, a human face. The experience with the interest-arousing object, or sound, or movement focuses and absorbs attention; it engages the resources of body and mind; it provides charm of sound or line or form or color or motion, and thus gives sensuous joy; it arouses imagination and provides spiritual stirring and fervor; it inspires contemplation, and produces trains of expectation and response.

The art product—the painting, the symphony, the sonnet, the piece of sculpture or architecture, the dance—is a distillation of the artist's aesthetic interest and experience. It reproduces or represents and interprets significant aspects of life and reality as he experiences them. Usually also, since in the expressional process there is always selection, choice, discrimination, and rejection of some aspects of things, art constitutes an appraisement or judgment, or even criticism of life. Thus it both questions and underscores the values of men as it depicts living realities.

But art goes beyond this. It takes the limitless, unorganized experience of men and the sensed characteristics of nature, and composes them; that is, it expresses them as complete, understandable units. Even more, it can be said that the essence of art is its expression of the wholeness of things—"the quality of the universe as felt by the artist." As the Wilsons put it, "Art is the expression of the intrinsic qualities men find in reality—in things, persons, events, or life as such. To use the phraseology of culinary art, the artist is concerned to bring out the flavour of the universe."[3] In brief, if the work of art is truly art, it expresses various phases of even the infinite in finite form; the form is finite, the content is infinite. Thus art enables us not merely to conceptualize and utilize our experience with ourselves and the universe, but it also visualizes both current realities and ultimates. It potentially expands the life of the spirit far beyond its normal limits.

Art is a process—the making and the enjoying-utilizing of art—and it involves what Gotshalk aptly refers to as "the artistic transaction."[4] The constituent elements of this transaction include the creative process as conducted by the artist, the work of art created, and the art public or the society for which the art product is usually intended and which appreciates and variously utilizes it. Both the artist as creator and the public as appreciator are involved in the aesthetic experience that is embodied in the work of art.

The work of art is created by the artist. It is he who has the ineffable experience, the expressional urge, to represent in the most attractive,

[3] Godfrey and Monica Wilson, *The Analysis of Social Change*. Cambridge: The Univ. Press, 1945, p. 79. See also the analysis of E. Cassirer, *An Essay on Man*. New Haven: Yale Univ. Press, 1944, pp. 137–170.

[4] D. W. Gotshalk, *Art and the Social Order*. Chicago: Univ. of Chicago Press, 1947, p. xiii.

revealing, and meaningful form the sensations, the emotions, the imaginings, the ideas, the spiritual surges that have powerfully stirred his own nature in his relationship with the object or situation of interest. He is driven to creation by the intensity of the pleasure, or interest, or even the tension he feels, by the luminosity of his contemplation, and the craving to bring some sort of order out of chaos. There is something which attracts him, compels him to grasp it as it passes, and then through himself as the inspired agent, to project it creatively into the sense world. As Rodin put it, "In representing the universe as he imagines it, the artist formulates his own dreams. It is his own soul that he celebrates."[5] The artist externalizes aesthetic experience and makes it available and communicable for all who can understand its language.

The artist, like all others, lives his own life under its peculiar combination of conditions and experiences. He is always an individual; his perception, evaluation, and vision of what he beholds is thus always somewhat unique, a reflection of his own inimitable coloring and genius; and his creation, the art product, is an immediate and more or less vivid expression of his personality elements. At the same time he is unavoidably a product of his total milieu, and this in its various manifestations not only suggests themes but it also conditions, regularizes, and even restricts him. Although there is always a give-and-take between the artist and milieu, it is also probably a fact that every work of art represents, in some measure at least, a struggle between the originality of the artist, on the one hand, and the general conditions of the culture and society, as well as the institutions and conventions of the particular art itself, on the other.

The work of art is the form, the object, in which the aesthetic expression is couched in a more or less permanent form—the proportioned physical shape, the melodious sounds, the connected words, the rhythmic motions, or combined masses, lines, and colors. It is a resultant independent of the materials or methods used in its production and of the person who used them; it is a new and special creation. Yet, the art object, like its creator, embodies the more or less generalized interests and wishes of some considerable segment of expressive mankind. It cannot fail to reflect the impulses and yearnings, the emotional and intellectual movements, the imaginative and spiritual resources and achievements of its time. The work of art in itself is a sort of window upon the world, a view or interpretation of some aspect of the physical or sociocultural arena. It may have value in itself. But its chief significance in the artistic process is its function as the medium or vehicle

[5] Quoted from *L'Art* by D. H. Parker, *The Analysis of Art*. New Haven: Yale Univ. Press, 1926, p. 11.

of communication of aesthetic experience to all beholders of it. The art product, to carry a communicable and transmissable aesthetic message, must have certain standard and established features; or it will not be a language, but only a hodgepodge of incomprehensible elements. The window must be clear so it can be looked through.

The public or audience consists of the great body of non-creative or inadequately creative beneficiaries of the work of art. They are the appreciators, the people who get enjoyment from their experience with it, from their identification with it as a thing of value. They also set the standards for its production, distribution, and consumption; they function as the jury that criticizes it, judges its worth, accepts or rejects it, and thus determines its durability; they provide the rewards for the artist. In the last analysis, the artistic creation exists for the public. Its ultimate function is to enable those without the creative proficiencies or opportunities to enjoy vicariously the aesthetic rapture through the artist's inspiration and creation. If it is not too far removed from common experience, it, in some measure, arouses, duplicates or recreates among the appreciators the psychical and spiritual experiences of the author.[6] Many of the public, of course, are unaffected except by the most tawdry art; others are only momentarily and superficially influenced. But for some, the fine, pure art object achieves its supreme mission; it provides its appreciators not only with sensuous rapture, but it may lead them to meditate and contemplate; to dream dreams, to achieve sublime exaltation and purification of spirit, and to feel that unity and harmony of experience that is akin to union with the infinite.

Although all art production in some measure involves all three phases of the artistic transaction just discussed, the productions differ in the quality and purity of the aesthetic experience, in the objectives or purposes of the creators, and in the degree to which the parties to the transaction are directly or indirectly involved. The arts thus are sometimes divided into four categories: the fine arts, the practical or applied arts, the popular arts, and the commercial arts.

In fine art, the primary objective is to present the aesthetic interest and impulse in its purest expressional form, as in the concerto, the poem, the painting, or the piece of sculpture. The centrality or eminence of the intrinsic perceptual entreaty, the sufficiency of the imaginative appeal, the satisfaction of the aesthetic need, quite apart from other considerations, are essential features. Fine art at its best provides a selected, refined, and vivified revelation of the perceptual properties of things and situations. Fine art objects are created for the satisfaction

---

[6] As John Dewey put it long ago, "A work of art . . . is recreated every time it is esthetically experienced." *Art as Experience.* New York: Minton, Balch & Co., 1934, p. 108.

to be derived from them in themselves. Fine art in a very real sense is art for its own sake, for what it alone can do for man as an aesthetic creature; it alone transmits a pure aesthetic experience.

The practical or applied arts, such as textile-designing, ceramics, basket-making, dress-making and tailoring, landscape gardening, and the culinary arts are concerned with products with practical usefulness, but not without considerable attention also to their aesthetic characteristics. The products present a combination of utilitarian and aesthetic appeal. The piece of pottery or the woven article is first of all useful; but its maker or designer also intended it to have appealing design, coloring, and texture; and it was planned to provide aesthetic satisfaction to its user or beholder.

The term popular arts is used in two senses. Folk art, or the art of the entire people of a non-educated, non-urbanized, non-industrialized folk society, relates to their poetical, story-telling, musical, dancing, and pictorial activities. The people of this type of society are not only the active participants in these artistic activities and the enjoyment of them, but they serve also as the active contributors, generation after generation, to their creation and modification. Mass art, the popular art of industrialized, urbanized, massed society of today, is represented by the motion picture, jazz, the magazine story, the serial novel, and radio and television plays—all made available to a mass public by means of mass media. There may be considerable aesthetic appeal, for not all popular art is poor, impure, or puerile. Its main function, however, is to entertain. It is devised for all sections of an enormous population; it consists of uniform or machine-made products turned out on an enormous scale.

The commercial and propagandist arts, such as advertising in all its forms and the use of art forms for special and usually selfish purposes, have persuasion of the spectators as their primary purpose. The art appeal—the pictorial advertisement, the singing commercial, the carefully devised sob-story or patriotic poem, the appealing ceremonial—is devised to get people to purchase a product, accept a viewpoint, support an ideology, or fall in line in some other sort of procession.

The art of a people and an epoch is not an eccentric and exceptional feature of life. Nor is it a private matter, but rather an inherently universal and representative, social and public one. Consequently, it is intimately and integrally related and relevant to every aspect of social life. It is a social product, an institutionalized aspect of the total social organization, and a dynamic factor performing several fundamental social functions quite apart from its aesthetic functions.

Art, like every other manifestation and expression of human need and activity, unavoidably reflects—even more, is conditioned and determined by—most of the dominant phases of the whole environment, physical and sociocultural, from which the needs derive and in which the satisfying activity occurs. Minimally, the environment is the frame in which the whole artistic transaction occurs; it provides all the conditions permitting its start, all the materials out of which the art object is made, all of the inducements, most of the attention-focusing themes, most of the pressing expressional problems, the appreciators or targets, and the locale for the transmission and retention of the art product.

The significance of the environment, especially the cultural and social environment, as it affects art production is brought out in the effects of the environment on the artist. As Gotshalk has pointed out in his synthesis of effects, the environment furnishes him with the diversity of things by which his sensitivity is awakened and stimulated, and also from which all his symbols are drawn. This sociocultural milieu supplies the artist with joyous and tragic or otherwise poignant and determinative occasions that have affected his personality and especially his sense of values. It provides him with the traditions that operate as premises of his creative work and with the techniques and the conditions making possible the development of his abilities into technical skills. It constitutes for him a contemporary climate of opinion—values, crucial interests, aspects of the run of attention—which modify the quantity and quality of his imaginative thinking and provide him with themes and with the influences and pressures that serve as "catalytic agents of inspiration." It also provides the physical materials of his art, the market for his wares, including commissions and patrons, the social complex in which his productions will be accepted, enjoyed, and for certain types, utilized, and in which they may possibly have physical and cultural survival.[7]

In addition to this general social framework within which the artist lives and reacts, there is the influence of the specific subcultural groupings to which he belongs because of his position in the social hierarchy. The influence of such relevant facts as his social position, his racial background, his religious affiliation, and his nationality status will usually considerably influence his perception of things social and cultural, and affect his attitudes, interests, and objectives.

From the broader cultural perspective, disregarding for the moment the specific, human instrument involved in its creation and presentation in concrete forms, art is a product of, and reflects the context of, the time and place in which it receives its form. It is an integral part of the total culture. It expresses in many of its products the social and eco-

[7] *Op. cit.,* pp. 78–82.

nomic forces of the time and the area, the cultural level in general and the technological and metacultural level in particular, the national characteristics of the society, such as its freedoms, its predominant ideologies and preoccupations, its political organization and philosophy, whether democratic or totalitarian, its stratification system, its dominant institutions, its social psychological and psychopathic states, the impersonal style and fashion of the epoch, the whole ethos, spirit, and tone of the civilization, its trivialities as well as its grandeurs. The total art symbolizes and epitomizes almost all of the currently outstanding features and trends of the particular culture and social milieu.

The fact that art is a product, hence in some measure a reflector, and always an integral part of its culture is borne out by the fact that it rises, flourishes, declines, and falls together with this culture.[8] In general, art is a "record and celebration of the life of a civilization."[9]

I: The Institutionalization of Art

Art is not only a social product. Its production is also institutionalized in some degree in all societies where there has been a differentiation of the arts. The graphic and plastic arts, the musical arts, the oral and dramatic arts, the dance, and the combination of these—each has its characteristic fixed and standardized features.

Non-institutional factors account for some of this. These forms of expression are more or less regular because they must be done through certain media—substances and materials of various kinds, certain colors and combination of colors, and different kinds of sounds. Physical laws governing some of these must be observed. Limitations of the human body of an anatomical and physiological nature set certain uniformities for the artistic product, as in the dance or ballet and in the skilled manual manipulations of materials. Also the uniformities and limits of human nature, particularly with respect to psychological endowment and the acquisition of attitudes, levels of imagination, and technical proficiencies are also standardizing factors of some significance.

There is also the deliberate regularizing of, and even restraint upon,

[8] Cf. J. K. Feibleman, *Aesthetics: A Study of the Fine Arts.* New York: Duell, Sloan & Pearce, 1849, p. 164. For a most exhaustive treatment of the correlation of art and the important societies and cultures and epochs of history, see P. A. Sorokin, *Social and Cultural Dynamics.* New York: Am. Book, 1937, Vol. I on "Fluctuations of Forms of Art."

[9] Dewey, *op. cit.,* p. 326.

certain kinds and degrees of artistic expression for social ethical reasons. The aesthetic and other expressional impulses are bound up with the feelings and emotions; thus, by themselves they may easily be excessive. Also, because of the emotional potential that they carry and their high power of suggestion, they have a strong formative influence on personality. Therefore, almost all civilizations have subjected art forms to rather close scrutiny, and have sought to safeguard the general public against art or expressional performances that would degrade or weaken morally, incite to anti-social behavior, or needlessly or dangerously inflame the passions. Today both church and state exercise such safeguards to some degree.

The uniformity and standardization of aesthetic expression of especial concern here, however, are those due to its universal institutionalization. Certain ways and forms have been discovered and developed that produce results satisfactory to large numbers of producers and consumers of art. Each art has more or less standard form or structure for its productions, standardized techniques of creation and performance, established values and criteria of quality, and a style or styles for itself in a particular epoch. Musicians have scales and the rigid disciplines of counterpoint and harmony that operate with almost mathematical exactitude. Painters, etchers, sculptors, and architects have rules and principles as to symmetries and other features that are generally followed. The oral arts must conform to principles of meter and rhythm and certain aspects of the physics of sound. Literature has its standards as to line and form and treatment of content. In all arts the basic forms and techniques are well standardized within broad limits; and a large body of knowledge about these standards exists. Productive excellence requires conformity with them, and refined taste and appreciation require a knowledge of them.

It should also be noted that art as an institution has its special schools in which skills for making art and capacities for sensing and appreciating the aesthetic are developed; it has its organizations of artists in the form of more informal schools—cliques holding similar values of styles; and more formal academies of art. It has its organizations of consumers, associations for the study, promotion, wider provision or more general availability, endowment, and wider enjoyment of art for themselves and for the public (the Lincoln Art Association, the Civic Music Association). It has also its utilitarian equipment, such as concert halls, theatres, opera houses, galleries, museums, studios, and instruments and tools.

The institutionalization of art grows out of the fact that it is a form of communication. Although in most cases it is an individual creation, its significance, its justification, rests upon the message it transmits to the audience or public. The artistic genius, left to himself without rules and somewhat standard procedures, would have only a very remote likelihood of revealing to others in any comprehensible and communicable form the values and the great moments which he felt.[10] Even the highly individualistic artist—the deliberate rebel or the escapist beatnik—merely departs from the standard in some minor degree, though he may do it in a flamboyant manner; he does not realize to what extent he has himself been conditioned by the institutional atmosphere of his epoch and his art.

In general, if art departs too widely from its long-established canons, it becomes or is deemed to be aberrant, grotesque, fugitive, pathological; few understand it, enjoy it, or support it. It suffers the penalty of obscurity, temporary vogue, and even rejection. This type of art will not endure because it does not serve its aesthetic functions for the great number of appreciators of art. Hence, the chief institutionalization of art comes in order to conserve and perpetuate the hard-won expressional forms and techniques. It is not imposed by the state or other major controlling systems but by the artists themselves and their public. These canons, too, are the fruits of long experience, the results of trial and selection through the ages.

One other institutional feature of art, more or less peculiar to it, is its style. The particular artist usually has a style; that is, unique use of the more standard forms of art expression, reflecting his own particular personality and artistic genius. However, it is the style of a group or school of artists, or especially that of an entire culture or epoch, that is a sort of special feature of the general institutionalization of art. It consists of a set of artistically significant traits among the works of a certain limited cultural area and period; it is a kind of addendum to, or modification of, the general institutionalized requirements in delineation, even a sort of peculiar institutional overtone of, or a special and distinctive configuration for, the given time and place.

A change of style implies some modification of techniques and forms, even subjects, in response to changing cultural emphases, especially dominant values, interests, and ideologies (the whole temper of the society), and also in the technology and the material media used in artistic production (plastics, new paints, new tools and instruments).

The artist of an epoch conforms in a general way more or less unconsciously. But under the influence of style, the endeavors of most of the artists, working separately and often independently, are found to

[10] "We have no idea how an artist might portray reality in the absence of any previous attempts to portray it. . . . Man's first attempt at a work of art, were we to come upon it, we should not recognize as such. . . ." A. Hauser, *The Philosophy of Art History*. New York: Knopf, 1959, p. 370.

show common tendencies. Their individual aims are subordinated to an impersonal, superindividual trend.[11]

II: The Individual and Social Functions of Art

The examination of functions is particularly important in a study of society as a going concern. In what ways does art enter into the organization and operation of a society? Human and social expressions have human and social effects; and between the expression and effect are process and function. What do art institutions do? They perform certain functions both for individuals and for the group as a whole.

The functions for the individual are of two general sorts, both of which have been touched upon. The first is to take the expressional impulse, the creative state of the artist—usually an exceptional individual, at least with respect to aesthetic sensitivity and creative ability—and enable him to present it in the most attractive and permanent forms, making it understandable and accessible so that it can be transmitted. The second function of art institutions for individuals rests upon the fact that although the rank and file of men have artistic impulses, they do not have them to a sufficient degree for adequate expression or lack the ability or opportunity to express them. By means of sufficiently institutionalized art, the average man is enabled to share with the artists and the performers much of the intense experience that great art offers. Through art, the average person may achieve detachment from the prosaic and the routine, the frustrating and the chaotic, the ugly and repugnant. Through it, he may gain at least momentary or occasional absorption of self and the buoyancy of spirit.

The social functions of art are varied. Some, especially those conducted with utilitarian objectives, are studied and intentional. But the great and enduring social functions, like the individual ones, are largely unintentional; they are functions that inhere in the very nature of art and art institutions as they operate in a society; yet, they have potent social and societal significance. Some of those to be discussed have been at least mentioned before, though in other analytical contexts.

Art serves as a common language of communication. Although much

[11] For further discussion of some of the institutional features of art, see Hauser, *op. cit.*, pp. 207–236; 369–377. For some aspects of a particular art, music, see M. F. Bukofzer, "Musicology: The Anatomy of Contemporary Art," in L. White, Jr. (ed.), *Frontiers of Knowledge in the Study of Man*. New York: Harper, 1956, pp. 166–177.

of it is special and representative of particular segments of the population, and all of it is reflective of its particular culture, at the same time, it is an expressional aspect of the common human in mankind. Its finer nuances may be missed by some who come into contact with it elsewhere and in other eras, yet it speaks a more universal language with more common symbols than any other medium of communication. Cro-Magnon Magdalenian art, primitive African art, ancient Egyptian, Babylonian, Hindu, or Greek art, pre-Columbian American Indian art, recent or contemporary French, German, Russian, Chinese, or Japanese art, in most of their forms, convey messages that we contemporary Americans or any other people of any other place and era can understand. We need no Rosetta Stone of art to assist us in the translation.

Works of art, because of their ready communicability, are among the best instruments of cultural diffusion and the development of understanding; in fact, they are about the only media of complete and unhindered communication among men in a world of barriers that limit community of experience.

Art tends to unify collective life. Works of art that are not too esoteric or eccentric, that are fairly close to common life, tend to form social bonds, not only between the artists and their beneficiaries, but also among the co-appreciators of the common interest and joy; for example, a *Saturday Evening Post* cover by Norman Rockwell. In general, the very aesthetic feeling induced, whether by a piece of fine or popular art, is overindividual; the persons affected, as they are lifted out of their narrow selfhood, become kindred selfless enjoyers.

Art is a potent teacher, not by rules or by pedagogical techniques, but by symbols, and by means of them, presenting imaginative transfigurations of human relations, values, experiences, ideals, and goals. Plato, in his *Republic,* stressed the value of right art, especially poetry, music, and myth, in subtly conditioning the people, particularly the young, and inculcating in them the fundamentals for wise living. He would have recognized a deep truth in the saying, "Let me write the ballads of the country, and I care not who writes its laws." Aristotle in the *Politics* also noted that character can be moulded insensibly by the fascination of noble music or by the attraction of great literature. The fine arts, particularly, through their symmetry and orderliness and the grandeur of the emotions and ideas that they can inspire, can be means of reaching the moral sense, can even serve as means for moral discipline.

Some art forms, through holding up fictional characters as models, help to create and maintain social roles. Art has practical teaching aspects also. By means of works of art, we can and do effectively teach much history, biography, psychology, political science, and sociology,

giving endless information about human beings past and present. States-
men have used art to teach peoples about their past, to present their
ideologies, and to focus interest on future objectives. Priests have used
the arts, particularly sculpture, painting, poetry, and music, to present
in vivid form the chief beliefs of their religion.

The function of art as an agent of social control is closely related to
the didactic function. Art has been and is a subtle, attractive, and
powerful tool in the hands of society for guiding and regulating, as well
as shaping, human social behavior. This guidance and control is enforced by the appeal to sensation, emotion, and imagination expressed
in sensuous forms, patterns, and symbols.[12] It is frequently a more
pervasive and effective agent of control than industry, custom, law, or
government. Its effectiveness inheres in part in the fact that, unlike these
other agents which control from without, it controls from within through
aroused imagination and illuminated values and meanings. Art has been
widely used by society's general controllers; but through the adroit
manipulation of its symbols, it also has been and is being utilized by
all sorts of special-interest groups seeking some sort of control over
other people, particularly races, social classes, political factions, advertisers and sellers of all sorts, propagandists, the great misleaders, and
the converters, in order to mould attitudes and opinions. Art has also
served to make rule and authority tolerable, sometimes even attractive.

As social objects, works of art function as specific records of the
cultures and societies in which they are produced, for, as noted before,
they are not only reflectors but also in themselves products of many
social influences. They record the dominant themes and portray the
dominant institutions (the religious institutions of the Middle Ages, the
commercial institutions of the United States today); they record public
events and illustrious personages of the past; they have functioned as
eloquent indexes of the modes of feeling, the inner aspirations, and the
spirit of peoples long vanished. The art reflects the conditions of science,
the technology, religion, philosophy, social structure, and class cleav-
age, even the society's state of mental health. Many societies are dead,
but we know much about them—their economics, laws, government,
their attitudes and values—because these live on in their sculpture,
their mosaics, their dramas, their ornaments, their utensils, their literature, their architecture; for example, the growing knowledge we have
regarding ancient Egypt, Babylonia, Assyria, the Hittites.

The art of a culture or society functions well as a gauge of its civiliza-
tional qualities. The stature of a society can be measured by the stature
of its arts. The art is a mark of the major interests, of the internal

---

[12] For the classical discussion of art as an agent of social control, see E. A.
Ross, *Social Control*. New York: Macmillan, 1901, pp. 257–274.

power, of what is deemed desirable or worthwhile to do, of the psychic state of the people. A decadent people are likely to have a decadent art, a materialistic people a materialistic art, a psychotic people a psychotic art. As a sensuous expression, it is a sensitive indicator, and thus passes the ultimate judgment upon the quality of a group or a civilization.

Art has been and is used to commemorate the distinguished past and present. Odes, elegies, statues, portraits, paintings, buildings, overtures, and pageants have been produced to honor some great event or hero, and serve to revivify their significance for us of the present. Art products are also used to enhance commemorative events, such as centennials, important holidays, and rites of passage, and to impress with emotional and spiritual underscoring such occasions as dedications and inaugurations.

Even limited exposure to fine or true art can tend to remould the prevailing thought processes, values, and ideals of a community or society. Through its presentation of the more distinctive, the more beautiful, the near-ideal, the finer possibility, it suggests corrective, even newly and positively constructive action for the community—a central mall, some regulation of building construction in the interest of harmony, the provision of parks preserving natural beauties, the outlawing of excessive noise, the removal of ugly buildings, the disguising of junkyards and auto graveyards. Art has related to social movements; for example, in the glorification of the workers by Orozco and Rivera in Mexico. It has suggested the reorganization of social relations; for example, *Uncle Tom's Cabin* by Harriet Beecher Stowe. Although the actual discussion of some social problems may be difficult or forbidden in some political climates, these same problems can be brought before the public in art forms in a subtle and effective way.

The arts, especially the fine arts, can provide a tonic, a bolstering, or restoration of spirit, especially in times of anxiety, irritation, restlessness, and profound dislocation. They help individuals and groups to reestablish balance, repose, rhythm, and order in their lives. Art may provide catharsis for certain segments of the community as well as for the artists and the skilled performers; it can give a certain sense of mastery or achievement in time of uncertainty or frustration; it can provide something in the way of group wish-fulfillment. The arts can be used as morale builders; for example, in the use of national commemorations and national anthems in inspiring a sense of unity and giving strength, courage, and hope.

Finally, although this by no means exhausts the list of functions, art may have a recreational function. Both the making and the enjoyment of art, whether fine or popular, can be play, pastime, relaxation, entertainment. Quite apart from its aesthetic qualities, it can be attention-occupying and pleasure-giving through the excitement which it creates, the reminiscence which it inspires, or the information it provides.

III: The Interrelation of Art with Other Institutions

This discussion is in one respect an extension of the preceding section. Art reaches functionally into almost all major extra-artistic channels of social living. It both uses, and is used by, most other institutions; it serves almost all of the other institutions in various ways. The reciprocity is greater, however, with some institutions than with others. The relations are not only of a cooperative or mutually beneficial nature, but other institutions—church, state, business, school—criticize art in terms of their own needs, and art passes judgment upon them.

There has been a close relation between art and religion. In simple societies, most art seems to be of religious origin and related to religion.[13] Historically, also, religious organizations have had much control over art. But even in complex, more or less secularized societies, art is utilized by the church for its purposes. Art enters into its iconography, its symbolism, its literature, its ritual and ceremonial. Religion uses painting (for example, of significant personages, scenes, events), sculpture (for example, to symbolize deities or founders, evidenced by the statuary of Buddha all over southeast Asia), the drama and pageantry, the dance, poetry. Architecture is massively involved in its edifices—shrines, temples, cathedrals; in fact, the religious architecture has been so dominant at times that the architecture of the general epoch has taken its characterization from the church architecture (Gothic, Romanesque, Byzantine). Religion often has had much influence upon aesthetic ideals, as well as created a demand for different kinds of art. So influential is religion in art, and so important is art in religion even in a society like our own, that there can be said to be religious art with a style of its own. This art aids in creating the essential emotional and intellectual atmosphere for the religion among its devotees; it serves as a constant reminder of aspects of belief and as an agent in worship, praise, and piety. Finally, there is the influence exerted over art by religious organizations to insure its moral acceptability—the opposition to obscene, salacious, immoral art.

Although there has not been as consistent or frequent influence of the state upon art as in the case of religion, nevertheless it has been felt. Under some kinds of government, the influence is deliberate and

[13] A. S. Tomars, *Introduction to the Sociology of Art.* Mexico City, 1940, p. 292.

far-reaching. The influence that the state or government has exercised has usually not been of a political character as such, but rather it has been the influence of the class or other type of group or organization exercising major power in the state—the Church in medieval times, the aristocracy in feudal society, the dictatorial clique in a totalitarian society. Art forms have been and are utilized as means of glorifying the state, for propaganda purposes, and as ornamentation of public buildings.

Government in general creates a condition of order which makes artistic production possible. In effect, however, the type of government also affects the production of art. Under a democratic government there is a considerable freedom of artistic expression; under absolutist governments art is usually "goose-stepped" or must follow the "party line."[14] Governments, past and present, have subsidized art and art organizations (the music, theater, and writers' projects of the Works Progress Administration in the 1930's) and promoted art by means of prizes (Prix National in France), grants, stipends, or pensions for artists; they have provided opportunities for the enjoyment of art (the Freer Art Gallery and the Mellon Art Collection in Washington, D.C., and the art museums, symphony orchestras, choruses, opera, and drama provided by, or partially subsidized by, the governments of various cities). In some instances they exercise censorship, preventive and even punitive, especially over graphic art, the theatre, and literature if it is deemed to be morally (in Boston, for example) or ideologically (the U.S.S.R.) out of line.

Closely related to art is also one of the major activities of government; namely, war. War has provided many themes for art. Art has been consistently used to glorify war and to commemorate military events. War may divert men and their attentions and energies and also materials from art. In a military society, art will bear a military character; in a society stressing things economic above all others, art shows very little military influence. Modern impersonal, long-range mechanized warfare, as compared with the former valorous, hand-to-hand combat conducted with weapons requiring personal skill, has lost much of the glamour that once inspired art.

The relation of art to education has already been touched upon in the discussion of the didactic function of art. In addition, it might be said that art forms can function as media of instruction with respect to the portrayal of human types, of social conditions and social events, of the characteristics of an epoch, as exemplified in some of contemporary audio-visual instruction. In turn, education can be used as a means of

14 Cf. E. J. Simmons, "Controls in Soviet Literature," *Pol. Quart.,* 23 (Jan.–Mar., 1952): 15–31.

tapping and developing artistic potentials in would-be artists. It also can do this for many of the rank and file of the population, not to make them artists but rather to make them more capable of enjoying aesthetic expressions. Education can also aid in developing taste in the consumption of things and services; it can develop awareness of ugliness, discord, confusion, and gaucherie, and, conversely, it can assist in developing a liking, a preference for the ordered, the harmonious, the composed.

Some art bears a close relationship to the stratification system, especially in a complex society. Popular art, whether the folk art of simpler societies or the mass art or commercially persuasive art of societies like our own, does not show so much stratum correlation. But fine art in complex societies is usually associated with the upper classes, not because they create the art or because artistic creators stem from them primarily, but rather because of such facts as their patronage, since the upper classes in considerable part provide the means of livelihood for the artists. They also support the fine arts because of their higher degree of education and cultural sophistication. They understand art better and have the leisure to enjoy it. Furthermore, they tend to use fine art productions, especially graphics, paintings, and architecture as badges of rank and prestige. The middle and lower classes merely enjoy the copies. There is considerable evidence, however, in established stratification systems that each stratum has somewhat distinctive levels of artistic interest and understanding and that class enters into the selection of subject matter and its stylistic treatment. Class consciousness may also be reflected in art; for example, in the stress upon proletarian themes in a society in transition to industrialism, or social-climbing themes in an upwardly mobile society like ours.

Art is closely intermingled with technology. Men have expressed art in their productive techniques and in their useful products. Among primitives, the artist was the craftsman, and vice versa. Most people embellish the things they make and live with—textiles, clothes, implements, buildings, ornaments—with art. Conversely, technology aids art in various ways. In our time it has greatly enhanced the communicability of art, through new forms of printing and lithography, and the development of mass communication generally, including particularly radio, motion picture, and television. It has provided new tools and techniques for artists; for example, the pneumatic chisel for sculptors. It has provided new materials for artistic production and reproduction, such as new pigments in painting, new plastics, concrete, photographic film, especially color film.[15]

---

[15] For extended examination of the relationship between art and the stratification system, religion, and government, see Tomars, *op. cit.*, pp. 141–379.

IV: Some Special Characteristics of American Art Institutions

There is a vast and increasing preoccupation with art in our United States. At the same time, our art world is one of strange, paradoxical, and almost incomprehensible contrasts. It has its positive and negative, desirable and undesirable aspects when considered from the point of view of the ultimate and non-transferable (to other institutions) functions of art in a society. We have had, and now have, our gimcracks, our poor imitations and adaptations of foreign art, our peaks of frivolity, prudery, and bad taste, our shortlived (often justifiably so) fads; but we also have our moments of stark beauty, of artistic originality and greatness. Furthermore, every expressional feature of human life can be and is displayed in variant ways; and among a people as demographically, ethnically, and culturally diverse as we are, different segments of the population, as appreciators and utilizers, react to and assess these expressions differently.

It is essential that we know what the important attitudes toward art are, what is happening in the way of emphases and trends among the different forms and levels, and what some of the more evident effects of these trends are.

The attitudes toward art, both of producers and consumers among us, are often presented on a sort of vertical, even hierarchical, scale— a stratification of the members of our art world according to interest, taste, and to some extent social class; namely, the highbrows, the middlebrows, and the lowbrows.[16] As in all hierarchical arrangements of people, no hard and fast lines can be drawn between the levels. However, the highbrow artists think they produce only "fine" art, and the highbrow appreciators, in the main, are disturbed by interests in art below the fine level, for example the devotion to art by the popular press, the radio, and television. They approve the viewpoint of Ortega y Gassett that "the average citizen [is] a creature incapable of receiving the sacrament of art, blind and deaf to pure beauty." The middlebrows and lowbrows make up the great bulk of the art world, and the distinctions between them cannot be sharply drawn. Among the middlebrow producers are the large groups of successful artists who work for industry, advertising, and mass media, and the artists of greater pretensions who nevertheless exercise their craft for the millions, such as writers of popular fiction or of the best sellers in any field.[17] Among the

16 These views are developed at some length by Russell Lynes, *The Taste-makers*. New York: Harper, 1954, pp. 310–333.

17 Jacques Barzun, "Artist against Society," *Partisan Rev.*, 19 (Jan., 1952): 60–77, esp. 70.

middlebrows, as Lynes identifies them, we also find many educators, museum directors, movie producers, art dealers, lecturers, magazine editors, and dispersers of advertising art. Prominent among the middlebrows are the cultural do-gooders and those who pursue what is represented as art. Much of the lowbrow art is that of the folk and the art involved in the functional artifacts of daily use, the art of the average man. The lowbrow "goes in" for what he likes—sunsets, landscapes, beautiful women, comics, B-grade sentimental or Western movies, and so on, whether the intellectuals have approved of them or not. Highbrow, middlebrow, and lowbrow art lovers are all on the increase, and as appreciators they are leaving their diverse kinds of impress upon our art.

Another categorization of art, briefly discussed earlier, although having general applicability, is especially significant in America. It distinguishes among the forms of art at the different evaluational and functional levels. Here, to call attention to the forms of direct pertinence in contemporary America, we have first the fine arts. Fine art is freely created art, produced without pragmatic or utilitarian objectives, as a masterly, imaginative, unique, and voluntary, individual expression of the aesthetic urge. Among the popular arts, the folk art is the traditional art which emerges from the simple, rural, non-industrialized society. Practical or applied popular art, as the name implies, is mainly exemplified in such aspects of our life as home architecture, home furnishings, automobiles, almost all of our gadgets and appliances, our clothing, and the widely enjoyed music, photography, and painting. The mass art is the syndicated, mechanically produced art put out by corporations according to well-established and tested patterns and formulae, and intended primarily as a salable commodity yielding a financial profit.

The fine arts are flourishing; there is a distinct acceleration in both the volume and variety of their creation. Although the interest in them is still more noticeable among the intellectuals and upper classes, attention to them is percolating down to all levels of the population. Folk art is increasingly rare among us. There are a few surviving or carefully fostered remnants of it in certain more culturally isolated areas (for example, the Ozarks, the Tennessee hill country, or among the Cajuns of Louisiana), among certain racial (for example, American Indian tribes) or nationality elements (for example, Americans of Czech, Danish, or Mexican descent), or in the form of certain studiously and nostalgically fashionable resurrections (for example, hand weaving, square and other folk dances, folk songs and ballads). On the other hand, the practical arts and the mass arts affect every last one of us during every moment of our lives. The production of mass art has grown into a major industry. Because of its volume, its overshadowing presence, and the fact that it is so actively promoted by its dispensers, it cannot be disregarded in any consideration of American art. It is not only one of the outstanding features, but also a major determinative force in our mass culture. Much of it has usurped the functions of fine and traditional art in setting the styles, the manners, the images, the standards, and the goals of life for millions, almost as though some forms of it (especially the comic strips, pulp fiction, radio and television serials, and commercial jazz) "were the organ of an unofficial state religion."[18] It almost amounts to a subculture among us.

An appraisal of mass art brings out both positive and negative features. Positively, some of it does have a coarse, though healthy, grassroots vigor, without which a culture becomes either arid or effete. Also, there is a continual seeping-down into, and an appropriation by, mass art (for example, in advertising) of elements from the fine arts which give the higher and more formal art features a wider audience and influence, unconsciously advancing public taste. Mass art has produced paperback reprints of literary masterpieces and low-priced long-playing records of great music. Furthermore, some of the movies, some of the popular music, some of the best-seller novels and long-run plays, some of the materials presented by radio and television, though produced for mass consumption, are often fine art creations.

But the more obvious, negative aspects are a matter of weighty concern. First, mass art is highly standardized or conventionalized; it is, in fact, stereotyped as to form, design, and subject. It is deliberately constructed according to strict, rigid, and inexorable rules for each type of art for the moment. These are rules which the producers have found by experience to be determinative if the novel, the film, the television play, the magazine cover, the dance-song, the advertisement is to reach the mass market. It represents almost as much rigidity and uniformity of patterning as if it were subjected to party-line formulae of production. All artistic production, as we have noted, requires a certain amount of institutionalization; but in modern mass art it has been carried to the point where it has become stultifying.

This points to a second characteristic of mass art; namely, that it is least common denominator art. To reach the mass market, it must be geared down or averaged to the point where it makes some kind of appeal to the greatest number of people. Thus, it cannot be intended for specially perceptive levels or segments of the population, but must be accommodated to the most common capacities for awareness, comprehension, and appreciation. It must reflect everybody's experiences; there can be few subtleties, little reference to the esoteric, the rare, or

---

[18] Milton Klonsky, "Along the Midway of Mass Culture," *Partisan Rev.,* 16 (Apr., 1949): 348–365 (349).

refined. Because it not only reflects but also perpetuates mass values, it misses much of its mission as art; it only exceptionally uplifts or provides new experiences; it mainly entertains.

A third point has to do with the quality of the influence which some of it exercises. In general, only a minority tends to enjoy works of art from the viewpoint of the artist; that is, judges it according to aesthetic criteria. The majority of appreciators or those exposed to works of art identify themselves, not with the creator of the art product, but with the content of the work. They are emotionally and mentally affected by its message. Thus, some mass art, with its marital triangles, sentiment, brutality, gun play, and vulgar comedy, although perhaps serving as a healthy outlet for anti-social behavior, on the one hand, may prove an unethical, dangerous influence, on the other.

Fourth, some mass art, particularly in advertising, is used primarily for social control purposes. Such art is a studiously, and frequently a decidedly cleverly, devised and manipulated means to non-aesthetic ends. As such, it is pseudo-art in that it depicts the character of things as some person or some group would have them represented in order to influence us, and not as freely created pieces of expression. Thus we receive deliberately loaded interpretations.

Finally, it should be noted that our American mass culture is an imperial culture; that is, it is widely exported and widely copied. Some of our mass art, as a sizable portion of our mass culture, has an authority as great abroad as at home. American jazz, comics, movies, and so on are found in Europe, Latin America, Japan, some of Southeast Asia, and even in the Soviet Union. The influence thus exercised by it may convey impressions about us that are not entirely fair.

There are negative aspects that relate to the fine arts in America also. The creator of fine art is still a somewhat forgotten or ignored person so far as the general public is concerned, in spite of the great boons that he provides. Relatively few artists can wrench a decent living from our society. In so many cases, they must have some other remunerative employment, such as teaching or commercial art, with the result that their artistic creativeness is in effect a spare-time avocation. In this same connection, there is still a tendency on the part of much of the population to look upon the artist as a sort of freak, or dilettante, or even a parasite.

There is a tendency for some of our fine art to be extremist. In our American art world, as in any other, consideration must always be given to the avant-garde, on the one hand, and the exponents of the grass roots, on the other. Furthermore, an art work should not sacrifice novelty and individuality of insight. But art which is highly subjectivist, or abstract, or complex, or divergent from established patterns does not reach into the accumulated experience of most of us; it does not convey a determinable message to the potential appreciators, and hence fails in some of its mission; it takes on the characteristics of a distinctly private enterprise.

There are certain disturbing evidences of lack of aesthetic appreciation in our community life, which cause some uneasiness among a growing number of people. In some states there are still billboards outraging our countryside, and still litter from passing automobiles along the highways. The extension of cities and highway systems devours the ever scarcer natural beauty spots. In the center of our cities, fine, often historic, old buildings are torn down to make way for parking lofts and lots. Our advertising is not only omnipresent, but some of it is blatant, moronic, and sometimes questionable as to the veracity of its claims. No society can dispense with the grandeur of spirit, the tidiness, the gaity, the serenity for the individual and the community that comes with beauty.

The positive aspects of our American art institutions and our artistic life more than counterbalance the negative. Americans, especially since World War II, have recovered from their adolescent embarrassment about the crudeness of their frontier culture, so notable in the nineteenth and early part of the twentieth century. Not only the intellectuals and the artists, but all of the appreciators of fine art have overcome that feeling of provincialism and refuse to acknowledge a continuing submission to the influence of Europe. They insist, and rightly so, not only on our emancipation, but also on our autonomy. We have a substantial and growing American literature, painting and sculpture, and music. What is more, *our* art is now copied and imitated, even in the U.S.S.R.

Several related features of our artistic creativity are noteworthy. There is first of all the freedom of our artists both in the use of design and themes.[19] Among us there is "an absence of official standards [which] must in the long run prove inherently superior to the system of centralization and monopoly which older cultures have usually developed."[20] Unlike the situation in much of the contemporary world, the American artist does not have to follow the party line. Partly because of this freedom much of our art is independent, experimental, highly original, and has freshness and verve. Our experimental artists are getting away from the traditional ways and means; they are trying out new materials and techniques, discovering and inventing new symbolic ways of expressing, interpreting, and internalizing human experience. Thus in our painting, music, and poetry especially, there is an explora-

---

[19] This creative freedom is not to be confused with, nor is it entirely inconsistent with, the occasional efforts at censorship of some art works in some few American communities.

[20] Jacques Barzun, *op cit.*, pp. 60–77 (68).

tion of new areas of the spirit, a probing of new forms of human experience, and a presentation of new perceptions and new perspectives in somewhat new forms of creativeness. There also seems to be among us, increasingly, a spirit of open-mindedness, a love of diversity and of new talents unknown to the Old World. To be sure, some of the new art—now, as always—is faddist, too extreme, or otherwise inadequate and unaccountable in its forms and interpretation, and hence ephemeral; but momentarily it challenges us both as creators and appreciators.

Although artistic creativity is not directly correlated with economic life, a substantial economic surplus among a people does create favorable conditions both for art production and art appreciation. We are most fortunate in this respect. Our wealth and its related high standard of living enable us to support artists as non-material producers, making possible a good market for artistic products and services, and enabling us to provide for all sorts of artistic activities—exhibits, the maintenance of collections of art, the provision of all sorts of instruction in art and of prizes and awards. Also, a highly developed industrial democracy like ours provides unlimited opportunities for the use of art in daily life.

There is a notable dynamism about our American artistic consciousness. The facilities for artistic creation, education, and general enjoyment are increasing at an accelerated rate, and evidence of this utilization is abundant. Moreover, the current interest in art is by no means entirely owing to active promotion by intellectuals, philanthropists, museum and gallery directors, or art dealers; nor is it mainly the effete preoccupation of the aristocratic and leisured. It has grass-roots currency, stability, and vitality. Furthermore, the former enemies of fine art—many men in industry, business, and the professions—are taking up art as an important phase of "culture," and are becoming not only patrons but aficionados of art. Also, some knowledge of art and devotion to it are a current badge of social class and a means of acquiring class distinction. Notable also is the interest in art on the part of students in American colleges and universities, as evidenced in their enrollment in courses in the history and appreciation of art, in courses providing technical preparation and practice in the fine arts, and in applied art courses. Another encouraging fact is the enormous number of people who paint, write, and compose with professional skill, even though they do not do these as a means of livelihood.

Today everyone has access to art. There are more than two thousand art museums and galleries in America in which are housed not only our own creations, but also a fair share of the artistic treasures that once belonged to the great collections and the patrons of art of Asia and Europe. There is a growing attendance of Americans at the art museums and exhibits. As of 1952 there were 659 symphony orchestra societies in the United States. We have an increasing number of journals, many of them with expanding circulation, devoting themselves to the fine arts, the beauty of home and grounds, and the fine art of living in general. Some of our mass magazines, such as *Life* and *Time* have devoted page after page, not only to reproductions of the old masters, but also to the very latest works of the avant-garde. The summer art festivals, such as Aspen, the summer barn theatres, and the community playhouses provide opportunities for enjoyment of art and practice in its reproduction. Nor must we forget the considerable variety and number of book clubs with their huge memberships.

American art enjoys increasing financial and organizational support. There is the financial support and patronage of the wealthy members of our society. The enormous wealthy organizations, such as the Ford and Guggenheim Foundations, provide funds for a variety of instructional and promotional purposes. Civic organizations are lending varied support. Many of our municipalities provide outdoor theatres and stadiums as well as indoor facilities for dramatic, orchestral, and operatic performances, and maintain art galleries and museums. From these and other sources, money is available for prizes, travel funds, and training scholarships. It is just possible that no other people since the Renaissance have provided such extensive subsidies for so many kinds of artistic activities.

There has been a wave of art teaching at all instructional levels. The public primary and secondary schools are teaching art in order to give children a chance to express themselves; there is even some encouragement of bold original production by children. More specifically, at the public school level there is instruction in literature, the graphic arts, and music. High school bands and orchestras are found almost everywhere, and are among the most important and prized organizations in smaller communities. As already noted, our colleges and universities have a variety of art courses in their curricula. Nor must we ignore the instruction, both for laymen and professionals, given at the various art centers and such activities as the growing membership of creative writing courses, institutes, and conferences held in every part of the country during the summer.

Finally, there are the evidences of a rise in general aesthetic appreciation: the development of architecture for homes, for industrial, commercial and governmental buildings, and for bridges and other engineered structures, which is aesthetically satisfying as well as functional; the conscious efforts to beautify factory grounds and plants, commercial buildings, and public places; the new attention paid to river valleys, water fronts, and the approaches to our cities; the anti-billboard and anti-litter campaigns; the movement to preserve and increase the national and state parks and monuments with their natural beauties.

The major subject matter and concern of the present chapter were aptly summarized by Todd four decades ago:

"That age which skimps its art atrophies a very large part of its creative energies. That society which consciously cultivates its art impulses lives broadly and stamps its name upon an epoch in human history."[21]

B I B L I O G R A P H Y

GENERAL

Albrecht, M. C., "The Relationship of Literature and Society," *Am. Jour. Soc.,* 59 (Mar., 1954): 425–436.

Barnett, J. H., "The Sociology of Art," in Merton, R. K., *et al.* (eds.), *Sociology Today.* New York: Basic Books, 1959, pp. 197–214.

Cassirer, E., *An Essay on Man.* New Haven: Yale Univ. Press, 1944, pp. 137–170.

Dewey, John, *Art as Experience.* New York: Minton, Balch & Co., 1934.

Duncan, H. D., "Sociology of Art, Literature, and Music," in Becker, H., and Boskoff, A. (eds.), *Modern Sociological Theory.* New York: Dryden, 1957, pp. 482–497.

Feibleman, J. K., *Aesthetics: A Study of the Fine Arts in Theory and Practice.* New York: Duell, Sloan & Pearce, 1949.

Firth, Raymond, *Elements of Social Organization.* New York: Phil. Lib., 1951, pp. 155–182.

Gotshalk, D. W., *Art and the Social Order.* Chicago: Univ. of Chicago Press, 1947.

Hauser, A., *The Social History of Art.* New York: Knopf, 1951, 2 vols.

Hauser, A., *The Philosophy of Art History.* New York: Knopf, 1958.

Hirn, Y., *The Origins of Art.* New York: Macmillan, 1900.

Maritain, Jacques, *The Responsibility of the Artist.* New York: Scribner's, 1960.

Martindale, D., *American Society.* Princeton, N.J.: Van Nostrand, 1960, pp. 486–549.

Meadows, P., and M., "The Social Determination of Art," *Soc. & Soc. Res.,* 26 (Mar.–Apr., 1942): 310–313.

Mueller, J. H., *The American Symphony Orchestra: A Social History of Musical Taste.* Bloomington, Ind.: Ind. Univ. Press, 1951.

Mukerjee, R., "The Meaning and Evaluation of Art in Society," *Am. Soc. Rev.,* 10 (Aug., 1945): 496–503.

Mukerjee, R., "Sociological Approach to Art," *Soc. & Soc. Res.,* 30 (Jan.–Feb., 1946): 177–184.

Mukerjee, R., *The Social Function of Art.* New York: Macmillan, 1950.

Perry, A. B., *Realms of Value: A Critique of Civilization.* Cambridge: Harvard Univ. Press, 1954, pp. 323–353.

[21] A. J. Todd, *Theories of Social Progress.* New York: Macmillan, 1922, p. 500.

Read, Herbert, *Art and Society*. New York: Macmillan, 1937.

Read, Herbert, *The Grass Roots of Art*. New York: George Wittenborn, Inc., 1955.

Ross, E. A., *Social Control*. New York: Macmillan, 1901, pp. 257–274.

Schuessler, K. F., "Social Background and Musical Taste," *Am. Soc. Rev.*, 13 (June, 1948): 330–335.

Tomars, A. S., *Introduction to the Sociology of Art*. Mexico City, 1940.

AMERICAN ART INSTITUTIONS

Barzun, Jacques, "Artist against Society," *Partisan Rev.*, 19 (Jan., 1952): 60–77.

Barzun, Jacques, "Our Country and Our Culture," *Partisan Rev.*, 19 (Sept., 1952): 424–431.

Berger, J., "Artist and Modern Society," *Twentieth Century*, 158 (Aug., 1955): 148–154.

Jenkins, Iredell, *Art and the Human Enterprise*. Cambridge: Harvard Univ. Press, 1958.

Klonsky, Milton, "Along the Midway of Mass Culture," *Partisan Rev.*, 16 (Apr., 1949): 348–365.

Lynes, Russell, *The Taste-Makers*. New York: Harper, 1954.

Meier, N. C., *Art in Human Affairs*. New York: McGraw-Hill, 1942.

"Our Country and Our Culture," *Partisan Rev.*, 19 (May, June, Sept., 1952): 282–326, 420–450, 562–597.

Index